My Political Struggle

My Political Struggle

M. Asghar Khan

OXFORD

UNIVERSITY PRESS

Great Clarendon Street, Oxford OX2 6DP

Oxford University Press is a department of the University of Oxford.
It furthers the University's objective of excellence in research, scholarship,
and education by publishing worldwide in

Oxford New York

Auckland Cape Town Dar es Salaam Hong Kong Karachi
Kuala Lumpur Madrid Melbourne Mexico City Nairobi
New Delhi Shanghai Taipei Toronto

with offices in

Argentina Austria Brazil Chile Czech Republic France Greece
Guatemala Hungary Italy Japan Poland Portugal Singapore
South Korea Switzerland Turkey Ukraine Vietnam

ISBN 978-0-19-547620-0

Typeset in Times
Printed in Pakistan by
Namaa Lica Printers, Karachi.
Published by
Ameena Saiyid, Oxford University Press
No. 38, Sector 15, Korangi Industrial Area, PO Box 8214
Karachi-74900, Pakistan.

Dedication

My political journey was possible because of the cheerful companionship of my wife, Amina, without whose encouragement and resolve this would not have been possible. This book is dedicated to my son, Omar, who believed in my values and struggled to help in trying to achieve them.

CONTENTS

PREFACE

In my earlier book, *We've Learnt Nothing from History*, I have written about the major political events in Pakistan since its creation and the failure of army generals and politicians to learn from their past errors. There is however much more to this story and I thought that I should write about my experiences in politics to complete the picture as I saw it over three decades. This book is based on Tehrik-i-Istiqlal's record of events (19 December 1971–12 January 1975), and a diary that I kept of events thereafter. But rather than reproduce the diary in full, I thought it would be more appropriate to give a general overview of events as I saw them and reproduce only those entries of the diary that are likely to interest the reader.

This book does not, therefore, contain much of the story that has been covered in *We've Learnt Nothing from History*, particularly the disastrous policies of General Yahya Khan that led to the dismemberment of Pakistan. It, however, contains much that should complete the picture that has brought the country to its present state.

In the difficult task of sifting the material that my diary contains, my brother-in-law, Aleem Afridi, has been a great help. He has made valuable suggestions that should make the book more readable.

Any diary of daily events, if reproduced as it was written, would inevitably reflect the writer's thoughts on and reaction to events as he saw them when they occurred. With the passage of time, his assessment of people and events may not necessarily remain the same and could have been revised. Rather than make any changes, I thought it would be better to leave the contents of my diary as they were originally written, often under immense stress and without the benefit of hindsight. I have, however, deleted material that, in my opinion was unlikely to interest the reader and was not important enough for inclusion in this book.

I feel that an apology is due to those who may be offended by any remarks that I have recorded with which they may not agree or which they feel do not do them justice.

Grandfather—Sardar Samad Khan.

Father—Brigadier Rehmatullah Khan.

The author (seated first from left) with Father and brothers, 1949.

The author with a F-104 'Starfighter', the first supersonic aircraft in the
Pakistan Air Force, 1965.

The author and Mrs Asghar Khan with Miss Fatima Jinnah, Peshawar, 1964. The lady on the right is Mrs Rehman.

President Ayub Khan, Zulfikar Ali Bhutto and Ghulam Farooq Khan at Tashkent, 1966. Marshal Zhukov is on the left.

Meeting Ayub Khan at the Round Table
Conference, Rawalpindi, March 1969.

With Abdul Wali Khan at the Round Table
Conference, Rawalpindi, March 1969.

Round Table Conference, Rawalpindi, March 1969, Justice Murshad and the Author are seated at
the far end.

Public meeting, Lal Diggi Maidan, Chittagong, 1970.

Col. Pasha (Col. Aslam Khan).

Reception on arrival in Karachi, 20 February 1977. The BBC reported the crowd as 1.6 million.

Public meeting in Abbottabad, 1977.

Tehrik-i-Istiqlal delegation in Kabul with Dr Najib (fifth from left), September 1987.

The author with Ms Benazir Bhutto.

With granddaughter Yasmeen during house arrest in Abbottabad.

The author with his family, 1990.

Omar Asghar Khan, Peshawar, 1964.

SECTION ONE

༄༅

The Beginning

The Early Years

I was born in Jammu on 17 January 1921. My grandfather, a Malik Din Khel Afridi, had moved to Kashmir c.1855 from Tirah, in the tribal territory of the North West Frontier. He had four sons of whom my father was the youngest. My grandfather, who died c.1903, had settled in Buttal Balian, near Udhampur in Jammu province of Kashmir State. His sons joined the state armed forces and my uncle, Summander Khan, in whose house I was born, was living a quiet life, having retired from service as a major general. He had more leisure than my father and gave us all his attention. A kinder man would be difficult to imagine. No trouble was too much for him. He had no children of his own and treated us with unimaginable love and affection.

I was the second of eleven children born to my mother—eight sons and three daughters. My father had another son from an earlier marriage, who was about 20 years old when I was born. My uncle, aunt, my parents and my siblings and I lived, as was the custom in those days, as one family. My father joined the Jammu and Kashmir army, took part in the Second World War in East Africa and was a major when I was born. He retired as a brigadier in 1944. My father was a strict disciplinarian and professionally very competent. He could not tolerate incompetence or laziness and set a high standard of morality and character in his personal life. As children, my brothers and I saw very little of him, dreaded his strict nature and spent most of our time in our uncle's care. Our aunt was also like a mother to us; our uncle and aunt gave us so much love and affection that had it not been for the balancing factor of the terror that our father inspired in our minds, we might have been thoroughly spoilt. As it turned out, the balance was perfect and I do not think that I suffered as a result. As I grew up, I began to feel closer to my father than I had as a youngster and this relationship continued to grow until his death in 1966. My mother, with a new child every year-and-a-half to two years, was kept so busy that she could give us very little individual attention.

The early years passed very quickly and at the age of 12, I came across an advertisement in a newspaper which invited applications for interview for admission to the Prince of Wales's Royal Indian Military College (RIMC) in Dehra Dun. The age of entry was 11–12 years and after successful completion of six years at this college, one could appear for an examination for entry into the Indian Military Academy (IMA) for service as a commissioned officer in the Indian Army. I immediately made up my mind to try to get into this college and began to pester my father about it. Since the tuition fee was about Rs125 per month which was about one-fifth of my father's total salary, he was reluctant at first but finally agreed to allow me to try. I was selected in the interview and went to Dehra Dun in March 1933. The six years that followed were very interesting and rewarding. RIMC, as it was called, was probably the best school of its kind in India at that time. Run on the lines of the English public school, it combined liberal education with a military environment, only sufficient to induce us to lead a regular disciplined life, new to most Indian children. The emphasis was very well defined and the products of this college did well in comparison with those of other schools in India at that time. The principal and all the staff were British, except the Urdu and Hindi language teachers. The college had a mosque, a temple and a *gurdawara* and we were marched daily in time for evening prayers to our respective places of worship. Facilities for all kinds of sports were ample and the surroundings and the environment clean and healthy. I was an average student in class and had nothing to show in the way of brilliance in any particular field.

A convention that caused me considerable annoyance was that of children entering school in India with wrong birth records. Since there were no birth certificates, it was normal for parents to show the child's age a year or two less than their actual age. This put those children at a disadvantage whose date of birth had been recorded correctly. So at the age of 12, I was in a class whose average age was 13 or 14. I would have much preferred to have dropped a class but had to struggle throughout my educational career with some children my seniors in age. Some thirty years later when I put my own children in school, I remembered my experience and when my son Omar was experiencing a little difficulty in class, I asked the principal, much to his surprise, to put him back in a lower class. I wanted him to feel comfortable in class and not undergo the experience I had in school. I think Omar benefited from this decision.

In 1939 I took the entrance examination held in Delhi for the Indian Military Academy (IMA) at Dehra Dun. In those days, only fifteen boys were selected for the Indian Army every six months for officers' training. Twelve were selected through an open examination and three were taken from the ranks of the Indian Army. I was one of the twelve who passed the open examination. Another, also from the RIMC, was Sahibzada Yaqub Khan (later lieutenant general in the Pakistan Army). The examination at Delhi was an interesting affair. There were almost equal marks for the written examination and the interview. The members of the interview board were five or six senior British military or civilian officers and Sir Hissamuddin Khan of Peshawar. Sir Hissamuddin Khan knew my father and the interview was a pleasant affair. A few general questions were asked by the panel and Sir Hissamuddin Khan asked me to do a cartwheel. This I did and so ended the interview. I am sure that my cartwheel, though not perfect, got me good marks and I had no difficulty in being one of the twelve selected for the IMA. Yaqub Khan was also selected. One of the other three selected from the ranks of the Indian Army was Tikka Khan, who also rose to be a general in the Pakistan Army.

Yaqub and I lived in Srinagar and were required to be medically examined at the Combined Military Hospital (CMH) at Sialkot before joining the IMA. When we reported to the CMH at Sialkot, we were given laboratory tests and examined by Major Puri of the Indian Medical Services (IMS). Yaqub was declared fit but I was told that I was suffering from a serious disease and did not have long to live. I was admitted into the hospital and told to limit my movements as any exertion on my part was likely to reduce my lifespan further. Major Puri made a rough guess of how long I would survive and said it was not likely to be more than two to three months. I was told that my laboratory test had shown that I had albumin in my urine which was at a dangerous level. Yaqub bade me farewell and I asked him to inform my father in Srinagar about the state of my health. I felt perfectly well but spent an anxious two days in the hospital until my father arrived with a doctor from Srinagar with a few medical books. These showed that albumin had been considered a dangerous thing in the past but recent tests had shown that some of the Cambridge University rowing crew had albumin in their urine and research on the subject had revealed that albumin was of two kinds—caustic and functional. The caustic variety was considered dangerous but functional albumin was quite harmless. In my case, the albumin turned out to be functional. Major Puri was sufficiently convinced and I was declared fit for joining the IMA.

The two-and-a-half years' course at the IMA was reduced to one-and-a-half years because of the war. Yaqub and I graduated from the IMA at the end of 1940 and I was commissioned in the 9 Royal Deccan Horse. Immediately afterwards, however, the Indian Air Force asked for volunteers from the army for the Indian Air Force. I was one of those who volunteered, was interviewed and selected without having to do a cartwheel! Wing Commander Shubrato Mukerjee, the senior-most Indian Air Force officer at the time, was one of the members of the interview board.

The Indian Air Force (IAF)

The air force training started with a short period at the Initial Training School at Walton, in Lahore, followed by three months at the Elementary Flying Training School at Begumpet in Hyderabad Deccan, where I learnt to fly the Tiger Moth, a small bi-plane trainer. After Begumpet I went to Ambala to fly the Hawker Audax, also a bi-plane, which was the aircraft used in the Royal Indian Air Force at the time. On completion of the training at Ambala, I was posted to No. 3 Squadron Royal Indian Air Force at Peshawar in 1942. The Squadron was commanded by Squadron Leader N.A.N. Bray, an RAF officer, and was equipped with Hawker Audax and Westland Wapiti aircraft. The Wapiti was of an even older vintage than the Audax. After some time in Peshawar, the squadron moved to Kohat. Our stay in Peshawar and Kohat included short periods at Miramshah in Waziristan, where the air force was required to support the army in operations against the tribesmen in North and South Waziristan.

After two years at Peshawar, Kohat and Miramshah I was posted to No. 9 Squadron Indian Air Force, at the time in the Arakan, Burma. The war had entered its final phase, the Japanese Army's thrust towards India had been checked but it was still active in Burma. The Japanese Air Force had ceased to be a threat in this theatre though its army still posed a problem. No. 9 Squadron was commanded by Squadron Leader Adams of the RAF and was divided into two flights. One was an Indian flight under my command and the other was Canadian, commanded by Flight Lieutenant Gerry Marr of the Royal Canadian Air Force. The squadron was based at various airfields south of Chittagong on the Arakan coast and later at Akyab and we were employed in bombing and strafing Japanese ground positions. No. 9 Squadron continued its role in support of the army till the end of the war in 1945. I then took over command of No. 9 Squadron and we were moved to Ranchi. Here we were equipped with Spitfire aircraft, a more modern fighter at the time, and from Ranchi we moved to Gurgaon near Delhi. After a few months there, I was posted as the chief flying instructor at the Advance Flying Training School at Ambala where I remained till Partition, except for a short interlude in Delhi. Whilst in Delhi, Air Commodore Janjua and I were members of the Armed Force Reconstitution Committee, which was responsible for dividing the assets of the Indian Armed Forces. This did not take much time, and it was in Delhi, that I had my first meeting with Quaid-i-Azam Mohammad Ali Jinnah in November 1946 about which I have written in my book *We've Learnt Nothing from History*. It was also from here that I went to Karachi on 14 August 1947. I returned to Delhi the next day. A few days later I was in Ambala and was scheduled to leave by train for Lahore on 23 August 1947.

My wife, Amina, and I lived in an air force house in Ambala and on my posting to Pakistan, the house was allotted to Wing Commander Nair, a South Indian officer of the technical branch of the IAF. Nair and his wife had arrived in Ambala a few days before our scheduled move and lived as our guests in our house until our departure. The killing of Muslims in India, particularly in East Punjab, had started but there was complete censorship on the news and we knew very little of what was happening. Nair, who appeared to know more, told me a few days before our date of departure not to travel by rail and to ask the Royal Pakistan Air Force (RPAF) commander-in-chief designate, Air Vice Marshal Perry Keen, to send an aircraft for me and my wife to travel to Pakistan. I thought it absurd that I, a squadron leader, should ask for a special aircraft for myself. Nair, however, was insistent and said that even if I did not agree, he would send a message to Air Vice Marshal Perry Keen for an aircraft to be sent for us. So, without my approval and entirely on his own initiative, he sent a message to the commander-in-chief designate of the RPAF, at the time in Delhi. I was therefore surprised, when two days later, I was informed that a DC 3 (Dakota) aircraft had arrived to take us to Pakistan. Air Vice Marshal Perry Keen's luggage was being transported to Peshawar and he had directed that the aircraft should land *en route* at Ambala and pick us up.

As the aircraft took off from Ambala for Peshawar, I saw that some houses were on fire in almost every village till the Pakistan border near Lahore. These were obviously houses of Muslims. The eastern border of Pakistan was clearly demarcated by burning houses on the east of the border. It was an unforgettable sight. We learnt later that all the Muslims who were being evacuated by train on 23 August, by which we were to travel to Pakistan, were massacred. Wing Commander Nair had done us a good turn and saved our lives.

The Pakistan Air Force (PAF)

In 1957 at the age of 36, I was appointed the commander-in-chief of the Pakistan Air Force, probably the youngest commander-in-chief of any air force. I always believed that one must not hang on to a job. I had seen servility in service officers and a hankering for extension of service and believed that such an attitude proves ruinous for a fighting service. I was, therefore, fully prepared to retire at the age of 40, on completing my four-year tenure as commander-in-chief. However when in 1961, Field Marshal Ayub Khan, the president of Pakistan, asked me to continue for another four years I was so involved in the modernisation and development of the PAF that I accepted the offer with enthusiasm but with the resolve not to accept a third term. I believe that this decision was an important factor in the air force achieving a high professional standard. I could advise the government without fear of not being given another extension. I could run the air force with only one consideration, to prepare it as a sharp and deadly weapon without the fear of upsetting people who might be powerful in the higher echelons of government.

When Ayub Khan asked me in March 1965, whether I would like to continue for another term, my reply was therefore an emphatic no. The eight years in command of the PAF and the earlier years before I assumed this responsibility were an important part of my life and my attachment with the service was more than that of a profession. It had been a privilege to be associated with such a fine body of men and we had striven together to make it an effective fighting machine. I had lost two of my brothers, Asaf and Khalid, in air crashes in the PAF and severing my bonds with it was therefore, to say the least, an emotional experience.

My departure from the PAF, however, involved an important principle and I did not think twice about calling it a day. The president agreed but insisted that I should go to PIA (Pakistan International Airlines) as its chief executive and as head of civil aviation and tourism. I had no desire to take up this or any other job and I argued against it but in vain. Ayub Khan was insistent. After a lengthy argument, in which I tried to explain that I had been looking forward to some rest and did not wish to take up any job, I agreed to the president's suggestion that I should go to PIA until he could find someone else to relieve me. With the appointment of Nur Khan as my successor I was happy in the knowledge that the PAF was in safe hands. I continued to shoulder my responsibilities in the PAF with full enthusiasm until the last day and left Peshawar on 23 July 1965 to take up my responsibilities in PIA and civil aviation. Although I was not enthusiastic about this job, I put in my best in the three years that I was with the PIA.

Adventure in Kashmir

During the formative period of Pakistan, whilst I was commanding the PAF Flying Training School at Risalpur, I had been involved in supporting the operations in Kashmir. In October 1947, my brother Major Aslam Khan, was actively involved in the fighting in the Muzaffarabad sector of Kashmir where he led a group of Pakistan Army volunteers and tribesmen. After the capture of Muzaffarabad he led the assault on Baramula and moved on to a spot just a few miles from Srinagar. Indian Army reinforcements had by that time begun to arrive and Brigadier Sher Khan, director of military operations at GHQ, decided to move Major Aslam Khan to Gilgit to organise and lead the operations in the northern areas of Kashmir. Major Aslam Khan handed over command of the operations in the Muzaffarabad/ Srinagar sector to Lieutenant Colonel Akbar Khan and moved to Gilgit.

As commander of the air force at Risalpur, I assisted these operations by transporting individuals and supplies to Gilgit in Harvard trainer aircraft and later in DC 3 (Dakotas). My younger brother Anwar Khan, also of the Pakistan Army, was operating in Gilgit and continued to do so for some time.

The story of Major Aslam Khan, known as 'Colonel Pasha', has been described by Dr A.H. Dani in his admirable book *History of Northern Areas of Pakistan* (see Annexure 1.1).[1]

PIA and Civil Aviation

PIA was an interesting experience. I never grew fond of this life but did all I could to improve the quality of service of the airline and its technical and professional competence. During these three years, the airline achieved the lowest accident rate and the highest net profit (Rs55,000,000) achieved till then. Many new routes were opened and an all jet fleet introduced. A new uniform was given to the airhostesses and the quality of service improved. Whereas the first two, accident rates and the net profit, can be measured, the latter, that is, the quality of service, is always a matter of judgement.

The first few weeks of my tenure were taken up with the September 1965 war and its aftermath. These experiences have been recorded in some detail in my book *The First Round*, published soon after the war. The September 1965 war followed so soon after my retirement from the air force and I was so involved with it that it was more or less a continuation of my air force service. It was only when I had left it all behind in January 1966 that I really settled down to my PIA responsibilities. I learned to fly a Boeing aircraft and got a pilot's commercial license. The ground school was a tough course and it was a job to find the time from my executive functions to devote to classroom work. I got myself examined by a Federal Aviation Agency examiner from the US and during my travels on PIA usually flew in command of the aircraft.

It was in PIA that I got my first experience of the paralysing effect of bureaucratic control. It appeared that the whole system was designed to stop one from working. I wrote a lot of rude letters to the government and often had to disregard official instructions to keep the airline and civil aviation moving forward. Ghiasuddin Ahmed, the defence secretary, with whom I had to deal quite a lot, appeared incapable of taking a decision which blocked all progress. President Ayub Khan's illness during the latter part of 1967 further slowed down the bureaucratic machinery.

Civil Aviation was headed by Air Commodore B.K. Dass, a person of sterling qualities, extremely industrious and honest. But he had two faults. He was loyal to an unreasonable degree and in order to prove his impartiality was often hard on Christians. Dass also had a problem coming to work on time. It was nice having him with me. Masud Mahmud, a policeman, was incharge of tourism. A thoroughly obnoxious character and a bully to the core, he was a pain in the neck, both to me and to his subordinates. Pompous and full of himself, Masud Mahmud symbolised in his person, the image of a police officer in a South American dictatorship. Others too must have spotted these qualities in him, as after leaving tourism and after trying his hand at various appointments, he landed up as the head of the Federal Security Force (FSF), the Gestapo created by Zulfikar Ali Bhutto. He was also later involved in the murder of Nawab Ahmed Khan case, in which Zulfikar Ali Bhutto was pronounced guilty by the Supreme Court, and was hanged by Ziaul Haq. The FSF was used to terrorise the public and Masud Mahmud at last found a job commensurate with his qualities.

The Start

My political journey started with a press conference that I addressed in Lahore on 17 November 1968. Zulfikar Ali Bhutto, who had left Ayub Khan's government a few months earlier, had come to see me at Abbottabad where I was settling down to a quiet life. Bhutto had by then begun to speak out against Ayub Khan's policies which he had so staunchly supported for almost a decade. As he had started to voice his views in public, he feared arrest. The Nawab of Kalabagh, the governor of Punjab, was close to Ayub Khan, and Bhutto feared that Kalabagh would have him 'eliminated'. Bhutto had launched his Pakistan People's Party (PPP) and asked me to join him and help him in his political struggle. I had no intention of coming into politics and told him so. We had a lengthy discussion on the prevailing political situation and on his pleading, I promised that should he be arrested I would speak up in support of his right of expressing his views and criticising the government. I felt that this was the right of every citizen and Zulfikar Ali Bhutto had every right to do so. A few days later, Bhutto was arrested and to keep my promise, I travelled to Lahore and addressed a press conference there.

My statement was blacked out in the press except that it appeared in the late edition of the *Nawa-i-Waqt* of Lahore. The next day I was asked by Javed Iqbal, the president of the Lahore High Court Bar Association to address the Lahore High Court lawyers. I accepted his invitation and addressed a large gathering of lawyers at the Lahore High Court Bar Association This event was widely reported in the press and I received numerous invitations from district bar associations throughout the country to address them. I started to accept these invitations and these journeys, without any planning or preparation, become large processions. I was not prepared for this spontaneous response but thought that an effort for the restoration of people's rights should be made. Having made a statement for the right of the people to speak, I could not go back on the struggle that I had launched. It appeared that a lid had been taken off a boiling pot of people's suppressed emotions. The tempo of the public expression and of defiance built up to a very high pitch and I was careful to restrain the people from indulging in lawlessness and succeeded in keeping the demonstrations peaceful. Z.A. Suleri the editor of *The Pakistan Times*, known to be a supporter of the government, in his foreword to my book, *Pakistan at the Cross Roads*, wrote a year later:

Air Marshal Asghar Khan's advent in politics, only a year ago, proved epoch-making. Never before in the history of Pakistan had a stranger made such a deep personal impact on the national scene. The phenomenon was partly due to the fact that no one before had given a clearer articulation to the people's rebellious feelings against Ayub's autocratic regime. The statement of November, 17, 1968 had the effect of a clarion call. It must however be said that the nation had a pre-vision of his stature through the series of articles which he wrote for the press. They contained his political philosophy and made a wide appeal. The simplicity of diction reflected the sincerity of purpose. When therefore he declared his intent to enter the political arena, he was at once recognised as a leader capable of leading his people to democracy and freedom. The enthusiastic crowds of hundreds of thousand, which attended his meetings and listened to these historical utterances, were proof positive of the fact that he was the man of the hour.

The second reason for the acclaim was that his emergence took place in the context of the failure of the professional politicians. Undoubtedly Ayub had failed the people but it was the politicians' collective failure which paved the way for his upsurge. Air Marshal Asghar Khan represented a refreshing change. He was a man with a difference in another respect. In the corrosive climate of multi-dimensional corruption, he was known for unimpeachable integrity. As the builder of the Air Force, which made a telling contribution during the 1965 War, his prestige was great both generally and among the Armed Forces. As such he was a power to reckon with; he could not easily be pounced upon by the government. His unassailability gave an irresistible strength and momentum to the democratic movement.

What made him above all a national figure was the fact that he took his stand on a national rather than a parochial plank. He became equally popular both in the East and the West. That he did not join politics to grab power is evidenced by his quittal at the moment the goal of the restoration of democracy had become visible through President Yahya's clear-cut schedule for the transfer of power. Not many will agree with his prognosis of the situation and the decision for retirement he had taken on that account. The road to national destiny is beset with pitfalls and the people would have liked the assurance of his selfless leadership. The last word on the Air Marshal's political career—fond as he is of the simple life of retirement—is however not yet said.

Change of Dictators

The movement continued at a hectic pace until Zulfikar Ali Bhutto was released and thus there was no reason for me to remain in this field. In this process, however, I had had close association with a large number of political activists and workers who had voluntarily joined me in our struggle for a common cause, without any guidance or help. Ayub Khan was still in the saddle and apart from Bhutto's release, nothing else had changed. Mujibur Rehman of the Awami League had been arrested in East Pakistan on charges of conspiring against the state. There was resentment in East Pakistan against the government's policy of discrimination against the Bengalis. Ayub Khan ignored public sentiments and continued his policy of suppressing the dissidents.

As a measure of protest against the repressive policies of the government, I renounced my awards of Hilal-i-Pakistan and Hilal-i-Quaid-i-Azam. In March 1969 Ayub Khan called a round table conference (RTC) of political leaders in Rawalpindi. Mujibur Rehman who was in jail was not invited. Since he represented the viewpoint of the people of East Pakistan, there was little point in holding a conference without him and the political leaders of West Pakistan insisted on his presence. This demand was eventually conceded and Mujibur Rehman was released and invited. Zulfikar Ali Bhutto and Maulana Bhashani of East Pakistan who had been invited refused to attend. Bhutto told me that Bhashani had advised him not to attend as they would in any case benefit from any concessions that the conference may be able to extract from Ayub Khan. I was invited to attend and did so.

At the opening day of the conference Vice Admiral A.R. Khan, Ayub Khan's defence minister, issued a statement to the press accusing me of working for foreign powers and against the interests of Pakistan. I objected to this and withdrew from the conference. The minister of information, Khwaja Shahabuddin, apologised on behalf of the government, and the conference proceeded. The RTC lasted three days and Ayub Khan agreed to hold general elections on the basis of 'one man one vote'. On Mujib's six points, he said that he would leave it to the newly elected assembly to decide. The newly elected National Assembly was also to take a decision on the future of 'one unit'. Ayub Khan announced his decision to hand over to anyone the National Assembly elected to replace him. The conference proceeded smoothly and Ayub Khan conceded all the demands of the opposition. A way had been found to end the deadlock and to make a new beginning on the road to democracy. All this time, General Yahya Khan, the commander-in-chief of the army, who had been close to Ayub Khan since he was a brigadier and was also the one who had done all the planning for Ayub Khan's takeover in 1958, was waiting for an opportunity to replace his benefactor. When there were some demonstrations against the government in Punjab, engineered by the military and civil intelligence, the latter being controlled by Yahya Khan, through his brother who was the head of the civil intelligence, Ayub Khan held a conference and decided to impose martial law in certain cities. Altaf Gauhar, information secretary at the time, in his book, *Ayub Khan: Pakistan's First Military Ruler* gives an authentic account of how Ayub Khan was replaced by Yahya Khan (see Annexure 1.2).[2] This was a betrayal of the nation after the successful round table conference, but mine was the only voice against this treacherous act. In a press statement, Zulfikar Ali Bhutto on the other hand welcomed Yahya Khan's martial law. It was clear that the struggle for democracy had not ended. Yahya Khan who was close to the centre of power all this time was not unaware of the role of Zulfikar Ali Bhutto and the foreign office in creating a situation which resulted in the 1965 war and of its political consequences. He maintained close contact with Zulfikar Ali Bhutto throughout 1970 but maintained an impartial stand prior to and during the country's general elections at the end of the year. He had been advised that no political party would emerge with a clear majority and felt that he would be able to preside over a coalition at the centre.

Immediately after Ayub Khan's exit and Yahya Khan's takeover, a number of political leaders amongst them, Nurul Amin, Chaudhri Mohammad Ali, Nawabzada Nasrullah Khan, Wali Khan and myself met in Lahore and decided to merge our parties into one political party. We felt that only a party with roots in both wings of the country could help to keep the country together. Wali Khan left for the UK after agreeing in principle to the merger of his National Awami Party (NAP) into this party and said that Mian Mahmud Ali Kasuri, the secretary general of NAP, would call a meeting of the national council of his party and get their approval. The day after he left, I contacted Mian Mahmud Ali Kasuri who said that Wali Khan had not left any instructions with him and said that in the circumstances, he could not call a meeting and that in any case he was certain that the national council of his party would not agree to any such suggestion. The remaining parties decided to merge and the Pakistan Democratic Party (PDP) was formed. A meeting of all these parties was held in Dhaka and Nurul Amin was unanimously elected its president. I did not seek any office. The PDP was a good start to give the country a national party representing experienced political leaders from both the wings. However the narrow mindedness of some of the West Pakistan politicians and their attitude towards their East Pakistan colleagues made it difficult to function. I found working with them a frustrating experience and eventually decided to quit the newly formed PDP and to leave politics altogether. I felt that the purpose of my entering politics had to an extent been achieved. However, I soon discovered that this was easier said than done. My short stay in politics and the tempo of political life that it had generated made it very difficult for me to quit this life. Under pressure from the many people who had joined me in my political struggle, I returned to continue my efforts to ensure that the new military dictator steps down after his promised elections and the country is launched on a democratic path.

The Tehrik-i-Istiqlal (or Gonno Oiko Andolan as it was called in Bengali) was thus launched and we began our preparation for the 1970 elections. Time however was too short to field party candidates by awarding them tickets in the different national and provincial constituencies. Hence we decided to allow our members to contest as independent candidates.

I contested from the Rawalpindi National Assembly constituency and failed to get elected. Most of the others met a similar fate. Zulfikar Ali Bhutto had launched a powerful election campaign in West Pakistan, particularly in Punjab and Sindh and he managed to win a sizable number of seats in both these provinces. He had made wild promises which he had no intention of fulfilling. Similarly Mujibur Rehman had mobilised East Pakistan behind his six-point programme that promised to free the Bengalis from the 'exploitation' of the West Pakistan political establishment. The hysteria that this campaign generated made it virtually impossible for any sane voice to be heard. Yahya Khan undid 'One Unit' which had eliminated the political advantage East Pakistan had enjoyed by virtue of the edge it got in the National Assembly. He announced that general elections were to be held on the basis of adult franchise. This was accepted in East Pakistan but Mujibur Rehman's six-points had by then captured the imagination of the Bengalis. The largest election campaign in Pakistan's history started with Yahya Khan's accession to power and as Mujibur Rehman mustered support in East Pakistan, Zulfikar Ali

Bhutto launched a powerful campaign in West Pakistan. Neither thought it necessary to woo the other half of the country. Although he never toured West Pakistan, Mujibur Rehman had a party there whereas Zulfikar Ali Bhutto made no effort to form his party in the east wing, the more populous part of the country. Without some support in East Pakistan, he could not have hoped to form a government in the centre. It would therefore appear that Zulfikar Ali Bhutto who aspired for national leadership intended to lead the country without any presence in the east wing. He maintained close liaison with Yahya Khan and his political staff officer, Lieutenant General S.G.M.M. Peerzada.

In 1965 Zulfikar Ali Bhutto, at the time Ayub Khan's foreign minister, had advised the president to embark on a military adventure by launching an armed attack in the Indian held part of Jammu in the Akhnur sector. This he said was based on the foreign office assessment that India would not react by attacking Pakistan. Ayub Khan had accepted this assessment and the attack was launched on 1 September. He was therefore totally unprepared for the Indian attack that took place on the early morning of 6 September in the Lahore sector of Punjab. Bhutto's logic, with which Ayub Khan agreed, was that Pakistan would thus cut off India's road link with Srinagar and be in a position to capture most of Jammu and Kashmir without having to resort to an all out war with India. Although I had by then relinquished command of the PAF, I asked to see President Ayub Khan on the morning of 3 September and expressed my opinion that India would react by launching an attack in Punjab, if we continued in our action in the Akhnur sector of Indian-held territory of Jammu and Kashmir. I was amazed when the president expressed his conviction that India would not do this and said that Zulfikar Ali Bhutto had assured him that there was no such possibility. Bhutto was too shrewd a person to really believe that India would not react and one is therefore left with the inevitable conclusion that he thought that India would react in an all out offensive and thought that a military defeat would result. He thought that he could then make some arrangement with the Indian leadership and take over from Ayub Khan. In a conversation that I had after the 1970 elections with Abdul Hamid Khan Jatoi, an eminent PPP leader of Sindh, I was told that after the success of the PPP in the 1970 elections, he had asked Bhutto what he proposed to do to curb the power of the armed forces in national affairs. He told me that Bhutto had replied, 'Don't worry about that. By the time I have finished with them they will be fit only for Guards of Honour.' Earlier in 1969 after being released from prison when he had asked me to join PPP, I had wanted to know what his programme was. He had replied in all seriousness that the people are fools and his programme is to make a fool of them. He had said, 'Come join with me and we will rule together for at least twenty years. No one will be able to remove us.' Zulfikar Ali Bhutto had many qualities but he was an odd mixture of good and evil, a rare genius who had an unlimited capacity for mischief. His many qualities and failings have been admirably summed up by Sir Morrice James, a former British high commissioner in Pakistan in his book *Pakistan Chronicle*:

Bhutto certainly had the right qualities for reaching the heights—drive, charm, imagination, a quick and penetrating mind, zest for life, eloquence, energy, a strong constitution, a sense of humour and a thick skin. Such a blend is rare anywhere, and Bhutto deserved his swift rise to power. From the end of 1962 onwards, I worked closely with him and it was a pleasure to deal with someone so quick-witted and articulate. We got on remarkably well; I never thought of him as a friend, but his attitude towards the British High Commission and myself was often approving and appreciative.

But there was—how shall I put it?—the rank odour of hellfire about him. It was a case of *corruptio optimi pessima*. He was a Lucifer, a flawed angel. I believe that at heart he lacked a sense of the dignity and value of other people; his own self was what counted. I sensed in him ruthlessness and a capacity for ill-doing which went far beyond what is natural. Except at university abroad, he was mostly surrounded by mediocrities, and all his life, for want of competition, his triumphs came to him too easily for his own good. Lacking humility he thus came to believe himself infallible, even when yawning gaps in his own experience (e.g. of military matters) laid him—as over the 1965 war—wide open to disastrous error.

Despite his gifts I judged that one day Bhutto would destroy himself— when and how I could not tell. In 1965, I so reported in one of my last dispatches from Pakistan as British High Commissioner. I wrote by way of clinching the point that Bhutto was born to be hanged. I did not intend this comment as a precise prophecy of what was going to happen to him, but fourteen years later that was what it turned out to be.[3]

It is sad that the leadership of the PPP even today is not prepared to accept these facts and defends Bhutto's role in Ayub Khan's and Yahya Khan's time and later when he himself wielded power. When martial law was imposed in 1958, he wrote to President Iskander Mirza expressing 'his imperishable and devoted loyalty' and had added, 'When the history of our country is written by objective historians your name will be placed even before that of Mr Jinnah. Sir, I say this because I mean it and not because you are the president of my country.'[4]

Later he had advised Ayub Khan to make the district commissioners the presidents of the Muslim League and the superintendents of police the general secretaries. His advice to launch an offensive in the Akhnur sector of Jammu and Kashmir and his refusal to allow the National Assembly to meet after the 1970 elections were not the acts of a patriot. It would be a tragedy if a political party, that refuses to own its mistakes and has learnt nothing from the past, is entrusted once again with the power of controlling the destiny of the nation. It is equally tragic that the Muslim League, that has supported every dictator since the creation of Pakistan and whose leadership led its workers to attack the Supreme Court when it was to hear arguments in a case against its prime minister, should be equally unrepentant. It would be sad if the people of Pakistan should place their destiny again in the hands of people who are not prepared to learn from the past. It could only be because they believe, as Zulfikar Ali Bhutto did, that the people of Pakistan are so foolish or so simple that they can be easily fooled. Something that he managed to prove right and did it so successfully.

Military Power and Politics

South America used to be regarded as a region of political instability where governments were frequently toppled by the intervention of the armed forces. Pakistan however has not been far behind—a country where for half a century now, the army has either ruled directly or has been controlling the politics of the country. During this period the military governments have enjoyed the support of western democracies, particularly the United States and it is likely that they will continue to do so until the people's will is asserted through united and powerful political thought. Unfortunately most political parties have either by aligning themselves with military rulers, or by corruption, discredited themselves to an extent that they are not likely to inspire confidence and will not therefore be able to lead the nation. This is likely to take time. This view was also expressed by Huseyn Shaheed Suhrawardy in his memoirs written shortly before his death in 1963:

The course of politics in Pakistan, ever since its creation on 14 August 1947, leads one irresistibly to the conclusion that it has been conditioned by the desire of those in real authority, the forces that actually determined the government policies and actions, to delay the introduction of democracy as long as possible, and, just when it was on the verge of fruition and all steps had been taken to enable it to function, to suppress it altogether.

...This phase of military dictatorships and military saviours is in apparent conformity with the general world movement for supplanting and suppressing democracies (as democracies in their turn have supplanted oligarchies and kingships); and even where democracies have theoretically been restored in their ding-dong battle against such dictatorships, they have in fact never been free but have always been directed and controlled by the military, who, having once tasted blood, find it advantageous and necessary in their vested, as well as newly-acquired, interests to keep civilian power in subordination.

Military officers, high and low, were put in charge of important administrative civilian posts for which they were untrained and unfit and were even given judicial powers to try offences and pass severe sentences which were successively reviewed by several grades of the military hierarchy to the progressive disadvantage of the convicted. Not only retired but also active military personnel, high and low, and members of their families were rewarded with posts, lands, licences, permits and pecuniary advantages commensurate with their ranks, their influence or their family connections.

The military, therefore, are a class interested in the continuance of a system so beneficial to them, and a body of disciplined personnel is thus ready and prepared to exert itself to the full to maintain its gains and privileges and to prevent a reversion to those bad old days when for a mere pittance its members could be called upon to endanger their lives to safeguard the independence and security of their motherland. Hence, experience shows, and illustrations are not wanting, that military dictatorships tend to perpetuate themselves, overtly or covertly.

> It would be incorrect to state that in the short history of Pakistan attempts have not been made from time to time to give to the country a democratic government; but they have ended in frustration and failure.[5]

It is sad that in spite of half the country having been lost, we have learnt nothing. Suhrawardy's fears have proved right and what remains of Pakistan will not be stable politically until we learn the lessons of history.

Yahya Khan began his almost three years in power with some important political initiatives. He abolished 'One Unit' and recreated the four provinces of West Pakistan. The 'One Unit' had done away with the majority of East Pakistan in the National Assembly and had reduced its parliamentary strength to bring it at par with West Pakistan. The abolition of 'One Unit' was a popular move in East Pakistan as well as in the NWFP, Sindh and Balochistan. These three provinces of West Pakistan did not relish the majority of Punjab in the West Pakistan legislature. The re-assertion of the position of East Pakistan in national politics and the six points of Mujibur Rehman found powerful support amongst the people in the eastern half of the country. Yahya Khan announced that elections would be held in October 1970. This was a very long period of campaigning and gave Sheikh Mujibur Rehman and Zulfikar Ali Bhutto almost a year to reach the people— Mujibur Rehman for his six points and Bhutto for his social revolution which he had no intention of implementing. Yahya Khan's administration remained neutral and allowed political parties to campaign without any hindrance.

Yahya Khan had thought that no party would emerge with a clear majority in the National Assembly and that a coalition of parties would have to form the central government. He did not believe that Mujibur Rehman or Bhutto would be able to get a clear majority in the centre and doubted that Zulfikar Ali Bhutto's PPP would get a majority even in Punjab.

A massive cyclone devastated large areas of East Pakistan in August and elections had therefore to be postponed to December. The government did little or nothing for the aid of the victims of the cyclone and this gave Mujibur Rehman the opportunity to whip up public sentiments against what was in fact a West Pakistan government.

Bhutto too used the extra time to make wild promises and to build up his position in West Pakistan.

The election of December 1970 organised by Yahya Khan produced results that he had not expected: the Awami League of Sheikh Mujibur Rehman won all the National Assembly seats in East Pakistan except two—those of Nurul Amin and Raja Tridiv Roy. In West Pakistan, Zulfikar Ali Bhutto's PPP emerged as the largest party with comfortable majorities in the two larger provinces of Punjab and Sindh. The only proper thing to do was to call a meeting of the National Assembly and ask it to form a government. If this had been done, Mujibur Rehman's Awami League would have formed a government in the centre with the support of some smaller parties from West Pakistan, particularly in the NWFP and Balochistan. Mujibur Rehman would have, as he told me in one of my meetings with him, modified his six points to rule the whole country. 'I am not a fool to give up half of Pakistan when I can rule the whole country,' he had said. But this was not to be. With Zulfikar Ali Bhutto's collaboration and advice, Yahya Khan launched a massive military operation in East Pakistan. Thousands were killed, Mujibur Rehman and the workers of the Awami League were arrested and an attempt was made to deny by force the people of East Pakistan their legitimate rights. A debauch general and a power hungry politician brought disgrace and suffering to the country and the largest Muslim nation was torn asunder. The military debacle caused great resentment in the armed forces and some army officers were arrested for planning a coup to oust Yahya Khan, and amongst them was my brother-in-law, Colonel Aleem Afridi. A meeting of the UN Security Council was called in New York to consider a Polish resolution for a ceasefire in East Pakistan and Zulfikar Ali Bhutto, who by then had been made Pakistan's foreign minister by Yahya Khan, was sent to New York to represent Pakistan. He did not attend the UN Security Council meeting for three days because of indisposition and when he did, on 15 December, he rejected the Polish resolution and staged a walk out from the Security Council. The next day Dacca (now Dhaka) fell and Lieutenant General A.A.K. Niazi, commander of the Pakistan Army in East Pakistan, surrendered. Nearly 93,000 servicemen were taken prisoner and were later transferred to Indian jails.

In this state of turmoil and uncertainty, resentment in the Pakistan armed forces grew and the chief of the general staff of the Pakistan Army, Lieutenant General Gul Hassan Khan and the commander-in-chief of the PAF, Air Marshal Rahim Khan, got in touch with Zulfikar Ali Bhutto in New York and asked him to return to Pakistan to take over from Yahya Khan. Arrangements were made to have him flown to Islamabad. Having satisfied himself that conditions were safe for his return he flew back to Islamabad. Yahya Khan did not need much persuasion to step down and Zulfikar Ali Bhutto was sworn in as the president and martial law administrator.

With the unfettered power that he now enjoyed, Bhutto began to behave more like a *wadera* [feudal lord] than a popularly elected leader in a democratic country. Criticism of the government was not tolerated and severe measures were adopted to curb public dissent. Having opposed Ayub Khan's authoritarian rule and having witnessed the disastrous consequences of Yahya Khan's stupidities, I could not sit back and accept a continuation of dictatorial rule. I therefore embarked on a campaign to criticize Zulfikar Ali Bhutto and his authoritarian policies.

NOTES

1. Ahmad Hasan Dani, *History of Northern Areas of Pakistan* (Islamabad: National Institute of Historical and Cultural Research), 1989, pp. 364–371.
2. Altaf Gauhar, *Ayub Khan: Pakistan's First Military Ruler* (Lahore: Sang-e-Meel), 1993, pp. 474–483.
3. Sir Morrice James, *Pakistan Chronicle* (London: C. Hurst & Co. Ltd.), 1993, pp. 74–75.
4. Sherbaz Khan Mazari, *A Journey to Disillusionment* (Karachi: Oxford University Press), 1999, p. 77.
5. Mohammad H.R. Talukdar (ed.), *Memoirs of Huseyn Shaheed Suhrawardy* (Dhaka: The University Press Limited), 1987, pp. 7–8.

Annexure 1.1
Excerpt from *History of Northern Areas of Pakistan*

Colonel Pasha—The Victor

The achievement of a country's freedom is as important as its further defence and consolidation of military strength. While freedom fighters are responsible for the first, for the second task we have to look to another soldierly personality who was inducted by force of circumstances into this area, perhaps aside his own choice by sheer luck, to liberate as much territory of the Northern Areas from the control of the Maharaja of Jammu and Kashmir and to defend that territory against any future invasion. ... That undaunted man, throughout this brief period of struggle, remained widely known as Colonel Pasha—stoutly built, short figure of indomitable courage and strength, inherited from his ancestral Afridi stock of Tirah in North-West Frontier Province but in whose veins also ran the blood of the land—a cast that smacks of mountain daring and wild hunting, a whimsical sport that instilled into him the love of the hills and a geographic acquaintance with the region that is rarely combined with military command. It is this nature together with the military tradition inherited from the father, Brigadier Rahmatullah, again of the Kashmir State force, that qualified the colonel to wield an authority over mountain-dashing soldiers, still waiting to be organised and trained for hide-and-seek fight against veteran soldiers of the enemy— a series of dashing attacks to seize food, clothings and weapons from the enemy, with which to smash the opponents' strength. That dare devil commandant bears the real name of Major Mohammad Aslam Khan (retired as brigadier in 1963), one of the nine brothers, born at Jammu on 27 August 1918, Commissioned in 1939, posted at Rattu for nearly two years in 1941, one of the heroes of attack on Kennedy Peak against the Japanese in the Burma front during the Second World War, winning Military Cross, but later after the war resigned from Kashmir State army and posted as G-II in the Indian army 5th Division at Ranchi and finally opting for Pakistan, saw adventurous service in Jhelum valley.

With the liberation of Gilgit and its provisional government wishing to join with Pakistan and seeking protection, the choice for accepting this offer was not so simple one as the responsibility was great. ...The only other officer, who combined confidence in Pakistan High Command with rich experience of local geography and men, was Major Mohammad Aslam Khan who was then fighting in Uri sector. He was flown away from that sector, stripped of the then position in Pakistan Army with a promise that he would get back his position if he returned alive, and straight [a]way thrown onto Gilgit with total military powers and no further assurance of men or weapon to expect from Pakistan. His mission was to defend the country so far acquired and liberate as much territory as possible on his own responsibility with whatever men and material available here. It was an order to achieve impossibility but only dare-devil person, such as Colonel Pasha, could accept just to wield a dictatorial command over men of unbreakable determination like the lofty mountains of the region. As an example of his unique position, he cited to the author an instance of extreme exasperation even on the point of arresting the Political Agent Sardar Mohammad Alam Khan when he opposed his move to send the Gilgit Scouts outside his Agency to Skardu and that could be averted only by the mediation of high

Pakistani officials. A second instance relates to the authority delegated to him to confer commissioned ranks to those brave officers of the Scouts who had rendered meritorious service during freedom struggle. Among them were Babar Khan, Shah Khan and Ghulam Murtaza who were made Lieutenants.

Colonel Pasha's first arrival in Gilgit on 30 November 1947 by plane was to assess the local situation and to provide first of all a military base for the execution of authority by the Political Agent. ...When Colonel Pasha arrived, he had the immediate object of raising an Azad force from Gilgit. With this end in view he met all the JCOs of the Scouts, Colonel Hasan Khan, Major Ehsan Ali and Lieutenant Colonel Abdul Majeed Khan. Various reasons are given to explain why Majeed withheld his hand of cooperation but Major Ehsan quickly came forward to lend all his support. Colonel Pasha was determined to mobilise all available personnel in Gilgit, discuss plans with them and push forward his scheme of launching an offensive. One proposal was to send Major Ehsan to Ladakh. He then suggested advancing towards Gurez for raids on Bandipur. But before any action of advance could be undertaken, firm preparation was necessary. With these ideas Colonel Pasha returned to General Headquarters in Rawalpindi on 3 December 1947. ...As he recounts, he asked for material help at the General Headquarters. He could get only a sum of rupees four thousand from Major General Sher Khan. Half of this sum he spent in purchasing blankets and old clothes at Raja Bazar, Rawalpindi, which were dropped by plane in Bunji. With him came his younger brother Major Anwar, who was made Brigade Major here, and Captain Azmat Ali appointed as DQ for general administration. Another brother Wing Commander (later air marshal), Asghar Khan, then incharge of Risalpur Training School, started surveying Chilas and other areas as far back as 9 December 1947. It is this survey which led to droppings of material by using Dakota, Halifax and finally Harvard planes.

Back in Gilgit, where Colonel Pasha established his headquarter, he raised the strength of the combined force to about 2,000 men, equipped them with whatever arms that were captured from the Kashmir State force and trained the rest with dummy wooden rifles. ... The plan that Colonel Pasha made, covered the immediate objective—to advance into the blank area and occupy as much territory as possible during the winter before the enemy had chance to re-enter; to hold the enemy at the two passes at the south-east and south-west and stop their passage with strong force so that in the next summer season there was no possibility of the enemy to retake possession of the ground so conquered; and finally to neutralize enemy's strength in Skardu and conquer the whole of Baltistan and integrate it into Northern Areas. The entire plan, as it appears, covered those 'frontier' areas which fell outside the main valley of Kashmir and Jammu. Colonel Pasha could hardly hope to invade Kashmir from this northerly direction as he had no means to do so. If he could hold Zojila pass, the only other direction where he could advance was Ladakh and cut it away from Jammu and Kashmir. This aim of conquering Baltistan and pushing the border to the very gates of Kashmir was a scheme of no mean order and this perhaps was the mission for which he was sent to Gilgit. Colonel Pasha was a man of steel frame to achieve his objective in the most unfavourable season of the year.

In accordance with the original scheme discussed in Gilgit, Colonel Pasha gave a new shape to two forces, the first he significantly named Tiger Force to be commanded by Colonel Hasan Khan, and the second was called Ibex Force to be commanded by

Major Ehsan Ali. The task of the Tiger Force was to advance to Tragbal and Gurez and continue striking at Bandipur with a growling noise of a tiger to keep the Indian Force away from approaching the bounds of Northern Areas. The task of the Ibex Force was to hop, like an ibex of this area, over high ranges along the Indus river, first meet with the Indian detachment at Rondu, occupy Skardu and advance onward towards Kargil and Ladakh so as to stop Indian army advancing from the valley of Kashmir into this direction. The greatest hurdle was the most unfavourable winter season with deep snow obstructing the path of advance which could only be braved by the hardy soldiers of this region. But there was the hard task-master, the commandant, who directed every step of the move and was ready to change plan in response to the changing circumstances. When the Ibex Force was stuck at Skardu and there was hardly any chance of that force advancing towards Kargil in winter, Colonel Pasha moved his headquarter to Chilam and began to train another force there in the snow fields around Burzil. Even when the training was on, these snow-fed soldiers from Hunza and Yasin were asked to wrap their feet and legs with rags and were ordered to march across the Deosai plain wading through fifteen feet thick snow and reach Kargil, Dras and Zojila in three days. Commanded by another icy cold-proof soldier, Lieutenant Shah Khan of Hunza, the force was literally and operationally called Eskimo Force as they had to challenge the ice-sheets of 12,000 foot high plateau of Deosai, sit and sleep on snow-capped high peaks and hammer surprise attacks on the enemy to snatch food, clothing and weapons from them. It is in this scheme of offensive action during the worst season of the year with weather-worn soldiers of steel physique and inexhaustible energy, driven by Colonel Pasha, to achieve the objective without fail, that lay the real defence of the Northern Areas.

Within the scheme outlined Colonel Pasha gave enough freedom to his commanders to use their intelligence and initiative to go ahead with their force, create confusion in the enemy ranks by their surprise move and destroy the possibility of any advance by Maharaja's soldiers. The tactic that he adopted suited the genius of the local soldiers who were proficient in holding their own on hill tops and ambushing the enemy in the valleys by a volley of concentrated fire that would surely lead to either utter destruction of the enemy or their confused escape for life. Such moves were possible because the commandant knew the land inch by inch and he could issue instruction and send supplies of men and material and even divert platoons and companies from one sector to another. The best example of such a diversion was the dispatch of a batch of 60 men to Thurgo Pari under the command of Subedar Mohammad Ali to ambush the advance of an Indian battalion along the Indus under Colonel Kirpal Singh. The subedar divided his platoon in two sections, one posted on the northerly hill and another on the southern but men were disposed in such a fashion that in groups of three they hid behind separate boulders. When the enemy was down in the valley shots were fired from north and south and it appeared as if all the boulders on the top were angrily falling on the heads of the enemy. There could hardly be any protection from the volley of fire. The whole battalion was routed. The scheme was well designed and the command was well executed to its successful end.

After Colonel Hasan Khan had achieved in winning control over Gurez–Astor route and was well placed on Tragbal pass, the other most important objective was to push ahead towards Kargil, Dras and Zojila because it was along this direction that the enemy had been trying to break through and send reinforcements for the relief of the besieged men in Skardu. With that aim in view Colonel Pasha had instructed Major Ehsan Ali to occupy Skardu as quickly as possible and advance ahead along the Indus valley route towards Parkuta, Kharmong and Ladakh. When Major Ehsan was stuck up in Skardu, Colonel Pasha despatched the reserve force under the name of Eskimo Force towards Kargil and Zojila to do the job earlier entrusted to Major Ehsan Ali. And for that objective he mobilised all the soldiers that he could lay hold on, in any sector where fighting was going on. Even from Skardu some platoons were sent to this direction for finishing the job as quickly as possible. Some of the most important battles were fought later in this sector and it goes to the credit of Colonel Pasha that he evolved a plan not only to close this route for the Indians but also to deploy his soldiers according to his policy of offensive action throughout the area of Ladakh. Although the main headquarter was not occupied because of Indian superiority of air supplies, yet his men surrounded the capital and they moved forward far ahead in the south upto Padam towards Jammu. In fact he was on the point of crossing the boundary of the State of Jammu and Kashmir and enter Indian territory in Himachal Pradesh when he sent a wireless message to the General Headquarters in Rawalpindi consisting of three words 'Attacking Himachal Pradesh'. This position of Colonel Pasha, achieved in six months by the end of June 1948, was much more than what was expected of him. The General Headquarters, then under a British c-in-c, was not interested in snatching any Indian territory. They were more than satisfied with the splendid work so far done by Colonel Pasha. In early July 1948 Colonel Pasha was recalled to Rawalpindi and posted as private secretary to the commander-in-chief of the Pakistan Army. Colonel Pasha had the satisfaction of extending the boundary of Gilgit to the very gates of Kashmir and for this achievement he was awarded Hilal-i-Jurrat by government of Pakistan and later promoted to the rank of brigadier. After retirement Brigadier Aslam Khan has chosen to remain in this area away from politics quietly remembering his older days of gallantry but at the same time adding to develop tourist industry in the form of Shangrila hotels in this isolated trans-Himalayan zone.

ANNEXURE 1.2
Excerpt from *Ayub Khan: Pakistan's First Military Ruler*

Ayub Khan asked the information secretary to prepare his farewell speech and the letter he should write to Yahya. It would not be a letter of resignation because he would only step aside and proceed on three months leave. He gave no indication of the arrangements he had made with Yahya about his own future.

Ayub studied with great care his abdication speech and letter to Yahya. He made a few changes and added one or two new points. He then took up a file which was lying beside him and pulling out a paper said to the information secretary, 'Here are the guidelines I have given to Yahya.' According to the guidelines Yahya, after taking over, would arrest all the agitators and some of the more irresponsible political leaders and restore law and order and take steps to revive the economic life. Ayub put down the file and said, 'He will carry out my orders. He has promised to sort out Bhutto, though I think Asghar Khan is more dangerous than him.' It was clear that Yahya had led Ayub to believe that the army would put down the agitation and eliminate his political opponents and put him back in power after three months. ... He was still ruminating when the ADC announced the arrival of Yahya Khan. They remained together for sometime and after Yahya left, Ayub said, 'The poor man was crying at the thought of his supreme commander leaving in such painful circumstances.' Actually, Yahya had come to see the text of Ayub's broadcast before it was recorded and the letter before it was signed and despatched. ...

Ayub recorded his abdication speech in his study. Yahya sat on the sofa on one side wearing a gloomy expression. ... Ayub finished his speech and walked over to shake hands with Yahya whose eyes were glistening with tears. The moment Ayub and Yahya left the room a colonel in dark glasses walked in and told the members of the broadcasting unit to stay where they were. He then seized the tape recording and the rest of the equipment. All this was done quite brusquely. The instrument of power was now in Yahya's hands!

...The information secretary was told to be at GHQ where Yahya was going to record his speech. An officer met him at the gate and conducted him to the office of the military secretary to Yahya. There he found Yahya, and three of his generals, Hameed, Peerzada and Gul Hassan, huddled around the radio set listening to Ayub's broadcast. They looked like a bunch of thieves bending over the booty and were a little startled as if caught red-handed. A little later Yahya came into his office and settled down with his script in front of him. His co-conspirators all stood pasted along the wall in front of him. ... After the recording Yahya leaned back in his chair and said, 'I don't know about you fellows but I definitely deserve a drink.' The wall in front of him seemed to crumble in embarrassment. The bearers arrived with the drinks but the civilians took their leave to allow the ruling junta to booze itself without any bind....

Ayub expected to stay in the President House for three months and to retain his personal staff. The house was adjacent to the president's secretariat and every morning Yahya and his staff officers would pass by the house and find the old man sitting on the lawn. His presence was a constant reminder of their crime. The day after he seized power Yahya issued a notification appointing three of Ayub's men, A.R. Khan, Mian Arshad Hussain and Fida Hassan, as his advisers. But the notification was immediately withdrawn because GHQ did not like carrying the dead wood of the old regime. The next day General Peerzada, who had become Yahya's principal staff officer, complained that sitting in the President House Ayub was issuing orders and signing papers. The last straw was the resignation of S.M. Zafar, the former law minister which, Peerzada claimed, Ayub had accepted after handing over power but had antedated his signature. Peerzada conveyed it to Ayub that his presence was causing annoyance to the people and it was in his interest to leave the city. Ayub was visibly distressed: 'So Peerzada has become the prime minister. He is a devious rascal. I never trusted him.'

1 April was a hazy morning when Ayub left for Swat. ... Just before getting into the car he remembered something and went back to the House where he had lived for twenty years, first as commander-in-chief and then as president. He returned with some magazines and files which he handed over to his ADC and got into his car.

As the car moved out of the porch Ayub leaned out of the window to wave the final goodbye. The car turned left and went past the gate as the sentries stood to attention. Spotted shadows of trees were falling on the narrow road stretching into a wasteland of 'bitter and ungrateful sands'.

SECTION TWO

❧

Tehrik-i-Istiqlal's Record of Events
19 Dec 1971–12 Jan 1975

In this section I have reproduced key events from the archives of the Tehrik-i-Istiqlal. These events are a prologue to my own diary entries in Section 3 of this book.

19 Dec 1971, Rawalpindi
While Air Marshal Asghar Khan was addressing a public meeting, he was attacked with stones by a mob of Pakistan People's Party (PPP) workers led by local MNAs of the party. Air Marshal Asghar Khan had been demanding that Yahya Khan should resign and power should be transferred to the National Assembly.

16 Jan 1972, Karachi
Air Marshal Asghar Khan's public meeting in Nishtar Park was disturbed and subjected to brickbatting. A number of people sitting on the stage were injured.

4 Feb 1972, Bahawalnagar
Air Marshal Asghar Khan's public meeting was disturbed and the stage was attacked by members of the PPP.

8 Feb 1972, Lahore
A reception at the Hotel International in honour of Air Marshal Asghar Khan arranged by lawyers, trade union and student leaders, was attacked by people armed with lethal weapons and steel bars. A large number of those present, including Ahmad Saeed Kirmani, were injured. The attack was led by the *salar* [commander] of the PPP Guards Lahore, and PPP members of the national and provincial assemblies. The governor of Punjab, Ghulam Mustafa Khar, visited

the scene of disturbance twice. The next day, when he was asked by the press about this incident, he promised to conduct an enquiry and take appropriate action. Nothing is known about it so far.

20 Feb 1972, Peshawar

Air Marshal Asghar Khan's public meeting at Chowk Yadgar was attacked by armed hooligans and PPP workers. Explosions occurred near the stage. The attackers resorted to brickbatting and stoning, which led to an ugly situation. The police were also attacked by the PPP workers. This sparked off a police strike throughout the North West Frontier Province (NWFP).

27 June 1972, Rahimyar Khan

While addressing a public meeting at Rahimyar Khan, Air Marshal Asghar Khan was subjected to repeated attacks by PPP workers led by their local office bearers. The police who were present did nothing to stop them. On the contrary, the police provided protection to the attackers. A number of people were injured.

10 July 1972, Sukkur

Air Marshal Asghar Khan's farm in Sukkur district was taken over by an armed gang led by Ghulam Qadir Bhutto, a prominent member of the PPP of Sukkur. The farm house was looted, the tractor taken away and five hundred maunds of wheat and other property removed.

1 Aug 1972, Abbottabad

Air Marshal Asghar Khan's house was totally burnt down under extremely suspicious circumstances. Most of his belongings were also destroyed in the fire. A police enquiry was ordered. However, nothing is known of its findings.

6 Sept 1972, Sahiwal

Air Marshal Asghar Khan's public meeting at Sahiwal was attacked by PPP workers and hooligans who were armed with sten guns and revolvers. These people forced their way to the stage and beat up the leaders of the Tehrik-i-Istiqlal. Mr Moinuddin Shah (information secretary, Tehrik-i-Istiqlal) received head injuries. Reports were lodged with the police but rather than take action against the miscreants, cases were registered against the Tehrik-i-Istiqlal workers who had been the victims of the attack.

9 Sept 1972, Sargodha

A public meeting addressed by Air Marshal Asghar Khan was attacked by PPP workers and hooligans.

24 Nov 1972, Rawalpindi

Air Marshal Asghar Khan's meeting at Liaquat Garden was subjected to a well organised attack at which continuous firing took place for over forty minutes. Known hooligans from Lahore in the company of PPP MPAs and MNAs made repeated efforts to attack the leaders of Tehrik-i-Istiqlal. One person armed with a knife was disarmed after he had succeeded in reaching the stage and was approaching Air Marshal Asghar Khan from the rear.

20 Dec 1972, Lahore, Multan

A Tehrik-i-Istiqlal procession in Lahore, which was led by Air Marshal Asghar Khan was repeatedly attacked by armed hooligans and PPP workers. These people brickbatted and stoned the silent and peaceful procession which was observing the restrictions imposed by section 144 and was strictly within the limits of the law. The police and the administration provided protection to these people and allowed them to harass and attack the processionists throughout its march. At the termination of the procession, hooligans attacked and murdered Khawaja Rafiq in the presence of the district magistrate and the police.

A Tehrik-i-Istiqlal procession in Multan was attacked by armed hooligans and PPP workers who had been brought from all over the Punjab. Tehrik-i-Istiqlal workers, who had been the victims of this attack, were arrested, including Babu Ferozuddin Ansari (chairman, Tehrik-i-Istiqlal, Punjab) and Mehr Mohammad Rafiq (president, Tehrik-i-Istiqlal, Multan). Mukhtar Awan, minister for law of Punjab, had for a number of days prior to the date of the procession stated publicly that he would 'wipe out' Tehrik-i-Istiqlal's workers, if they dared to take out a procession and that 'rivers of blood would flow'.

25 Dec 1972, Karachi

Whilst coming out of the Quaid-i-Azam'a mausoleum after offering *fateha*, Air Marshal Asghar Khan was attacked by workers of the PPP shouting pro-PPP slogans and stoning and brickbatting took place in the presence of the district magistrate. A number of Tehrik-i-Istiqlal workers were injured.

28 Dec 1972, Karachi

While he was returning from University of Karachi after addressing a gathering of students, Air Marshal Asghar Khan's car was chased by a jeep with armed men who tried to block the way and tried to ram their vehicle into his car. A serious accident was narrowly averted and in spite of the fact that a report was lodged with the police and details of the vehicle given, nothing has been heard about the investigation.

7 Jan 1973, Karachi

PPP workers attacked Air Marshal Asghar Khan's public meeting at Nishtar Park and fired with revolvers and pistols.

21 Jan 1973, Karachi

While addressing a meeting of the PPP workers, the central minister for law, threatened that Air Marshal Asghar Khan's eyes would be gouged and his hands chopped off.

26 Feb 1973, Karachi

Air Marshal Asghar Khan's daughter, Mrs Shirin Awan, was prevented from boarding a PIA plane for London where she was proceeding to join her husband who is posted there in a Pakistani bank. All travel formalities in connection with her journey had been completed by her and permission obtained from the State Bank of Pakistan and other authorities concerned, for her departure. Later, on a writ being filed in the High Court, she was allowed to proceed abroad.

9–18 March 1973, Liaquatpur (Rahimyar Khan distt)

During Air Marshal Asghar Khan's tour of Bahawalpur division between 9–18 March 1973, PPP workers and hooligans carried out numerous attacks on him at a number of places. It was only the alertness of the workers of Tehrik-i-Istiqlal and the sympathy and support of the audiences that prevented them from physically harming him. At Liaquatpur on 5 March 1973, a person, Hazoor Bakhsh, son of Khair Mohammad, disclosed that he had been hired to attempt to assassinate Air Marshal Asghar Khan. The details of this were given by Air Marshal Asghar Khan at a well represented press conference at Rahimyar Khan on 16 March 1973. However, nothing appeared in any newspaper the following day.

7 April 1973, Abbottabad

Tariq Khan, Air Marshal Asghar Khan's brother, was arrested under Defence of Pakistan Rules on a charge of attempting to overthrow the government. He was subjected to torture and efforts were made to get him to make a statement involving Air Marshal Asghar Khan in an alleged conspiracy. Having failed to cook up a case against Air Marshal Asghar Khan, the government released Tariq Khan after a detention of three months in a civil prison and in Attock Fort.

19 April 1973, Mianwali

While addressing a meeting at Mianwali, the central minister for information, stated that not only Tehrik-i-Istiqlal workers but also their families would be wiped out.

27 April 1973, Kamoke

Whilst Air Marshal Asghar Khan was proceeding to meet his workers, his party was attacked by PPP workers armed with sten guns and revolvers and a jeep belonging to Raja Mohammad Afzal Khan (MPA of Tehrik-i-Istiqlal) was burnt.

29 April 1973, Lahore

A procession was taken out in Lahore by the PPP workers against Air Marshal Asghar Khan. Abuses were hurled at him and his effigy burnt. This procession was led by four provincial ministers.

At the end of a PPP procession, members of the ruling party and hooligans known to have connections with the present regime attacked the house of Sheikh Hafiz (vice president, Tehrik-i-Istiqlal Lahore) and seriously injured his nephew, Sheikh Javed Nazir, who succumbed to his injuries two days later.

30 April 1973, Lahore

Colonel Aleem Afridi, Air Marshal Asghar Khan's brother-in-law, was arrested for alleged involvement in a conspiracy to overthrow the government. He was subjected to torture and was kept for seven days in an underground dungeon without windows, doors and without any toilet facilities. He was given inhuman treatment for a long period until a writ was filed and the authorities concerned were directed by the High Court of Lahore not to subject him to inhuman treatment.

The governor of Punjab publicly stated that he would not give protection to Air Marshal Asghar Khan in future and that he would not be allowed to address any public meeting in Punjab. A similar statement was made by the chief minister of Punjab, the minister for communication and the minister for law.

2 May 1973, Nathiagali

Colonel Aleem Afridi's house was broken into by a detachment of the police under the control of the SHO Nathiagali. The police broke the front door and two other doors and removed some items including the jewellery of Mrs Aleem Afridi (Air Marshal Asghar Khan's sister). She has since been informed that the police entered the house under government instructions but no prior information was conveyed to her nor any warrant of search produced.

18 May 1973, Quetta

At Air Marshal Asghar Khan's public meeting, members of the PPP fired pistol shots. A number of persons were injured, including the brother of the chairman, Tehrik-i-Istiqlal, Balochistan.

23 May 1973, Quetta

When Air Marshal Asghar Khan had boarded the PIA plane at Quetta for Karachi and after the engines had been started, all the passengers were told to disembark and identify their luggage once again. When this was done, one suitcase was found which was not claimed by any passenger. Air Marshal Asghar Khan was told that this action had been taken because information had been received that a suitcase had been loaded on the aircraft which contained a bomb. This suitcase was not opened or inspected in the presence of the passengers and although the incident was widely reported in the national press and was the subject of editorial comments in some, no explanation was given by the government.

26 May 1973, Multan

When Air Marshal Asghar Khan had left his hotel for dinner at a worker's house, his hotel was surrounded by nearly two hundred people. The police was present and in spite of section 144 being in force in the city prohibiting the assembly of more than four persons, they did nothing to disperse these people. The siege of the hotel continued throughout the night and Air Marshal Asghar Khan was forced to spend the night out of the hotel.

27 May 1973, Multan

When Air Marshal Asghar Khan was addressing a press conference at Multan city in a worker's house, the house was surrounded by a crowd of 150 to 200 armed people led by Mukhtar Awan (minister for law, Punjab) who had earlier addressed the crowd and publicly promised an award and complete protection to any person who would kill Air Marshal Asghar Khan. In spite of the fact that a magistrate and a large police force was present, the PPP workers and hooligans were allowed to brickbat the house. After a few minutes of brickbatting the crowd began firing at the house. One bullet was fired at the window of the room where Air Marshal Asghar Khan was addressing the press conference which missed him narrowly. The house remained under siege for over two-and-a-half hours. At about the same time a crowd attacked and ransacked the house of Babu Ferozuddin Ansari (chairman, Tehrik-i-Istiqlal, Punjab). They fired indiscriminately and destroyed all the furniture. Mehr Mohammad Rafiq (president, Tehrik-i-Istiqlal, Multan city) was manhandled and beaten by those hooligans and received head injuries. The car in which he was travelling was stoned and its wind-shield and window glasses shattered.

28 May 1973, Lahore

At 02:00 hours two shots were fired at the house in which Air Marshal Asghar Khan was staying at Shah Jamal Colony, Upper Mall, Lahore, from outside the boundary wall. The Tehrik-i-Istiqlal guard on duty returned the fire and the attackers escaped.

5 July 1973, Jaranwala (Lyallpur distt)

While proceeding to Lyallpur (now Faisalabad) where he was to address a public meeting the following day, Air Marshal Asghar Khan was stopped by the police and prevented from proceeding further.

26 July 1973

Air Marshal Asghar Khan's car was chased by armed men in a jeep and two trucks and he was fired upon by a man in the jeep. It was later discovered by the press that the jeep was registered in the name of IG Police, Sindh.

28 July 1973, Karachi

The Tehrik-i-Istiqlal office in Liaquatabad, which was to be inaugurated by Air Marshal Asghar Khan was attacked a short while before his scheduled arrival by armed men in the presence of the police who did nothing to stop them. Mr Rauf (secretary, Tehrik-i-Istiqlal, Liaquatabad) was shot and a number of other workers injured. The office was burnt and all furniture and records destroyed. A car belonging to Dr Rahimul Haq (secretary, Tehrik-i-Istiqlal, Sindh) was also burnt.

30 Nov 1973, Khanewal (Multan distt)

When Air Marshal Asghar Khan and his party had alighted from the railway train in Khanewal railway station and were getting into their cars to proceed to Multan, they were suddenly attacked by the police with batons. This was without provocation of any kind. Air Marshal Asghar Khan received injuries on his shoulder, chest and knee. When he reached Multan, the house where he was residing was surrounded by armed police who kept him confined to the house from the evening of 30 November 1973 to the early hours of 2 December 1973 when he left for Mirpur (Azad Kashmir). During this period he and about seventy other Tehrik workers, who were under siege along with him, were kept without food.

13 Jan 1974, Karachi

Air Marshal Asghar Khan's place of residence was cordoned off by the police who tried to stop him from leaving the house to address an indoor workers' meeting. When his car was effectively stopped, he began to walk to the place of meeting. The deputy superintendent of police (DSP) on duty asked the magistrate present for permission to arrest Air Marshal Asghar Khan. The magistrate refused this permission as Air Marshal Asghar Khan, he said, was not violating the law. In spite of this the DSP arrested Air Marshal Asghar Khan, used force to put him into a police van and took him from Nazimabad to Defence Society. On arrival at Defence Society the DSP denied having carried out any arrest and asked Air Marshal Asghar Khan to alight and refused to take him back to Nazimabad from where he had arrested him and kept him waiting in the police van from 16:00, when he was arrested, to 22:30 when he was eventually brought back to Nazimabad.

8 May 1974, Chashma (Mianwali distt), Khushab (Sargodha divn)

On arrival at Chashma Barrage from Dera Ismail Khan, Air Marshal Asghar Khan was stopped by a magistrate and a police force and informed that he could not enter Punjab. The magistrate refused to offer any explanation or produce a written order. The barrage was blocked with heavy machinery and Air Marshal Asghar Khan was forced to walk towards Mianwali nineteen miles away in scorching heat. For the two-mile distance that he covered on foot, abuses were hurled at him under the directions of the magistrate. He was then picked up by a bus and later travelled by car. On the way he was attacked by hooligans brought by the police to Khushab. He and a number of other people were injured and the windscreen of his car smashed.

28 Nov 1974, Daira Din Panah (Muzaffargarh distt)

While travelling from Leyyah in Muzaffargarh district to Dera Ghazi Khan, Air Marshal Asghar Khan was stopped at Daira Din Panah and taken away by the police to his home in Abbottabad. The police were able to show no written order or warrant of arrest.

11 Dec 1974, Sukkur

Air Marshal Asghar Khan's entry into Sukkur city was prevented by the police which had blocked all roads leading into the city. When he returned to his farm, it was surrounded. He remained in a state of siege until 13 December when he was allowed to travel to Hyderabad.

13 Dec 1974, Hyderabad

From 13 to 17 December, Air Marshal Asghar Khan was kept in a state of siege in the house in which he was staying in Latifabad. He was forced to stay with some forty other men in a confined space without adequate rations. When a writ was moved in the High Court and the court decided to send a person to see the state of affairs, the siege was lifted and Air Marshal Asghar Khan was allowed to travel to Karachi.

28 Dec 1974, Jhelum

Air Marshal Asghar Khan was stopped by the police at Jhelum Bridge and prevented from travelling towards Lahore. No written order was shown.

12 Jan 1975, Lahore

Air Marshal Asghar Khan, Mian Mahmud Ali Kasuri, M. Anwar, Miss Rabia Qari were stopped at Fane Road when travelling to address a public meeting at Mochi Gate. The police officer showed no written orders nor had any warrant of arrest. When Air Marshal Asghar Khan and his companions decided to resist their unlawful restrictions on their freedom, they were beaten by the police, thrown into a truck and driven out of Lahore. They were released six hours later.

SECTION THREE

❦

Diaries, 1975–2001

Diary 1975

Sunday, 9 Feb 1975, Lahore

A very successful public meeting at Mochi Gate. Six trucks loaded with PPP 'workers' arrived at the ground one hour before the scheduled start of the rally but were beaten away by our workers. I spoke for over an hour. Police baton charged and tear gassed the crowd repeatedly. Tried to drive them away. After the meeting the public accompanied my car in a procession to Bhati Gate. It was with great difficulty that I was able to get away. The crowd took out a procession up to Data Durbar where it was baton charged by the police. Malik Hamid Sarfaraz and Shakil Ahmed of Faisalabad were injured. About 25 workers were arrested and a few others hurt. They had come from far and wide (Mardan, Swat and Hyderabad). Their morale was very high and they were in great spirits.

Monday, 10 Feb 1975, Lahore, Serai Alamgir

Discussed party strategy with Moin Shah, Wazir Ali, Babu Ferozuddin Ansari, Zaman Jafri, and Ahmed Raza Kasuri. Left for Serai Alamgir and called on Rabia Qari before leaving. She was full of complaints about Wazir Ali. I reprimanded her for attending the public meeting on the 9th, contrary to my advice. She said that she was better than most men and would not listen to such advice. I agreed that she was more courageous than most men. A remarkable woman but quite impossible to control. An individualist—not amenable to any form of discipline.

No trace of Fateh Mohammad Khan of Uttam (Gujrat district) who had announced a donation of Rs100,000 on 6 February. Asked Raja Afzal to track him down and obtain the money from him. Was informed later that he had left for the UK.

Friday, 14 Feb 1975, Abbottabad

Managed to get the deputy commissioner's signature on Ali's domicile certificate with great difficulty and also on my 'financial status'. It is a herculean task to cut through the red tape. The DC wanted the AC's certificate before be would sign. The AC wanted the *tehsildar's* certificate who wanted the *patwari* and *girdawar* to sign before be could sign. Since it is virtually impossible to find and satisfy all of them, obtaining such a certificate is a virtual impossibility. These certificates are required for Ali's admission into the National College of Engineering at Karachi. Our whole system appears to be designed to stop everybody from working and moving ahead.

Friday, 28 Feb 1975, Lahore

Bhutto's gimmick, a strike on Kashmir today. No rail, air or road transport. All offices were closed and all activity suspended. Lights were put out for 15 minutes and Radio and TV observed a one-minute silence. Twenty-nine minutes out of thirty, were devoted to the strike in the 9 o'clock TV news. The whole thing was a complete farce designed to fool the public and impress the people with Bhutto's concern over Sheikh Abdullah's agreement with Indira Gandhi. The advocate of a thousand year's war is now trying to bury the Kashmir issue with fanfare with a one day strike.

Monday, 3 March 1975, Rahimyar Khan, Bahawalpur

Received reports that the government had arranged an attack on us at Rahimyar Khan railway station at the time of our departure (by Khyber Mail). So I decided to leave by road for Bahawalpur. Met Mukhdoom Ruknuddin at Mianwali Qureshian. Police followed us all the way. Another police force with a magistrate had blocked the road, 15 miles short of Bahawalpur. They wanted to search and disarm us. After one hour of argument we were allowed to proceed. Ten miles from Bahawalpur we again found the road blocked and our cars were stoned. My car, driven by Chaudhri Anwar's (chairman Tehrik-i-Istiqlal, Rahimyar Khan) brother, broke through the barricade. The second car followed and in the process, one of the PPP hooligans was injured. On arrival at Bahawalpur, Manzoor Ahmad Mohal, MPA, who had been travelling in my car, was arrested for injuring the man.

Wednesday, 5 March 1975, Bahawalpur, Lahore

Left Bahawalpur by Khyber Mail at 12:30. Was given a very good send off by workers and students. We were met by workers at all stations up to Lahore and they travelled with us up to the next station, when a new batch of workers joined us. Police and FSF were present at every station in large numbers. They had sealed all approaches to the station and tried to prevent people from reaching us. Workers however managed to break the cordon. Multan and Chichawatni were particularly tightly guarded. The road to Faisalabad is connected with Chichawatni. It appeared that the government did not want us to get off at these two places and enter Multan or Faisalabad.

Thursday, 6 March 1975, Lahore, Serai Alamgir

Addressed a press conference at Mian Mahmud Ali Kasuri's residence, on our experiences of the Bahawalpur trip and government atrocities against students. Mufti Mahmud (president, Jamiatul Ulema-i-Islam, Pakistan) has said that the United Democratic Front (UDF) would try to reform the government and would cooperate with them in the present difficult situation!

The UDF appears quite incapable of facing the situation created by the government. Arrived at Serai Alamgir in the late afternoon. Called earlier on Abdul Hamid (chairman, Ferozson's) who informed me that he could not publish my book for fear of government's anger.

Saturday, 15 March 1975, Abbottabad

The Ides of March. Police arrived to serve summons to appear before a Gujrat magistrate for a speech made somewhere in Gujrat district. Probably at Durria on 6 February 1975. Since I was not in the office at the time, Ziae sent them away. There are now 30 cases registered against me and if they intend to summon me for each of these, the police will have a busy time calling on me. If this represents a change in government policy, it is an interesting development.

Sunday, 23 March 1975, Serai Alamgir, Lahore

Decided that 23 March would be a good day for confrontation with the government. Boarded Tezgam at Jhelum. Was met by workers at Lala Musa, Gujrat, Wazirabad and Gujranwala. Police presence was prominent at the last two stations. Large crowds received us at Lahore railway station. Police cordoned off the platform and baton charged the crowd. Rabia Qari was injured and broke her hipbone. Wajid Razvi, Manzoor Mohal, Zaman Jafri and many others were injured. My sons Omar and Ali had their baptism of Pakistani politics. They had come to pick me up, received minor injuries and were arrested. Ali was arrested first and Omar seeing him in the police truck thought that he should not be left behind. Sent a blanket for each of them for the night. Thirty-seven of our workers were in the civil lines police station and were in high spirits. Among others arrested, were Moinuddin Shah, Hamid Sarfaraz and Ziae. Had dinner at Mian Mahmud Ali Kasuri's. Because of the stench in the lockup, Ali sent for an incense stick! Could not find one!!

Monday, 24 March 1975, Lahore
Addressed a press conference. Omar and Ali were released this afternoon. Addressed those released briefly at Mian Mahmud Ali Kasuri's, and later entertained them to tea at Lords. Mian Mahmud Ali Kasuri dropped in after dinner to discuss shifting of Rabia Qari from Ganga Ram Hospital, where she is very unhappy. Dr Khalida Usmani is very keen that Miss Qari should stay there but I do not think that Miss Qari will agree.

Tuesday, 25 March 1975, Lahore, Abbottabad
Called on Rabia Qari in the hospital on our way out of Lahore. She was in great pain but in high spirits. A truly brave woman. Saw in the papers (*Pakistan Times*) that a bomb had been thrown into a compartment of the train in which I arrived at Lahore on 23rd. The ignition cord was disconnected and an explosion averted. The explosive weighing six pounds was in a tin.

Shah Faisal of Saudi Arabia was assassinated by his nephew today. His death will be felt throughout the Muslim world.

Thursday, 10 April 1975, Abbottabad
Met J.A. Rahim, ex-secretary general of PPP. Left for Serai with Raja Afzal. I was stopped by the police opposite Rawat police station and was told that we could not proceed towards Lahore. On return to Rawalpindi was told that I could not even go to Islamabad, Came to Izzat Hayat's house in University Town. Mian Mahmud Ali Kasuri,

M. Anwar and Chaudhri Zahur Elahi called after dinner and decided to file a writ in the Supreme Court tomorrow. The police who had surrounded the house kept a close watch all night.

Friday, 11 April 1975, Rawalpindi

ASP Lodhi and others kept pestering me until 02:00 in their effort to take me away to Abbottabad. I refused. Press conference at 11:00. Left for Maulana Ghulamullah's mosque in Raja Bazaar at 12:45. The police blocked our way on Murree road. Traffic was held up. Minister of state Major General Jamaldar's car happened to come along. People tore up its flag. ASP Lodhi tried to remove me forcibly into a police car but failed. Addressed the prayer congregation after Friday prayers. In the meantime the Supreme Court had issued an injunction to the police not to remove me from Rawalpindi for another two days. The Supreme Court will decide about admissibility of writ filed by Chaudhri Zahur Elahi on my behalf.

Friday, 13 June 1975, Serai Alamgir (Jhelum)

Osman's court martial. Charge? His reasons for leaving the army were 'prejudicial to good order and military discipline'. He had cited the East Pakistan debacle, military action in Balochistan, low professional standard of the army, involvement of the army in politics, torture of his father and his own victimisation' as reasons for his resignation. Mian Mahmud Ali Kasuri and Mushir Pesh Imam appeared for the defence. Prosecution requested time to engage a civil counsel and the court martial was postponed to 28 June.

Saturday, 6 Sept 1975, Lahore

149 Shah Colony where we are staying was surrounded by nearly a hundred armed police at 8:00. Roads were blocked and I was prevented from leaving the house. Called M. Anwar. He saw the chief justice of Lahore High Court and then Justice Qureshi (vacation judge, High Court). Qureshi gave a written order to lift the restrictions. I was set free at 15:30. Hearing will take place in the High Court on 8 September.

Understand that a lot of people were present at Baghbanpura, Jallo Mor and at the unknown soldier's tomb where I was to go. Surprisingly or rather understandably, Jamaat-i-Islami was allowed to hold a meeting at Gol Bagh. Poor attendance: 200 people at the announced time of meeting and not more than 3,000 two hours later. This in spite of full loudspeaker publicity.

Saturday, 13 Sept 1975, Serai Alamgir (Jhelum)

Osman's court martial begins. The dullest and the most ridiculous court martial in my entire service experience. It is evident that the court has been told to convict Osman. A dummy court with a telephone on the table—a hotline with GHQ. Mushir did as well as could be expected.

Read in the *Pakistan Times* about Aleem's appeal in the Supreme Court. They confirmed the sentence of death passed by the GCM but recommended reduction.

Read of General Khatemi's (c-in-c, Iranian air force) death in a flying—probably gliding—accident. Sent a telegram of condolence to his wife, Princess Fatemah.

Dr Mazhar Ali Khan telephoned from New York again insisting that I come there to address a convocation.

Sunday, 14 Sept 1975, Serai Alamgir

Osman came in the morning and spent the day with Mushir preparing for the court martial tomorrow. Mushir is working very hard on the case but the court appears to have been told to convict Osman. Mushir feels that a person cannot be convicted on his own evidence and since the only evidence being produced is Osman's letter of resignation there is a good case to go to the High Court (after the conviction).

Monday, 15 Sept 1975, Serai Alamgir, Abbottabad

Second day of the ridiculous court martial which had started with one telephone on the court's table, today there were two telephones and sometimes both would ring simultaneously and the president of the court, Lieutenant Colonel Yaqoob Malik, would get instructions from GHQ. It is evident that it is a dummy court. The president is the court and the prosecutor all in one. A thoroughly unpleasant affair. The army is obviously in bad shape. Mushir is doing his best under the circumstances. I had to come away as Omar is leaving for London on the 18th morning. Mushir will attend court tomorrow and then seek an adjournment. Mian Mahmud Ali telephoned from Serai Alamgir to pass a message from Maulana Noorani about Lahore elections. He wanted our cooperation. Told him that Mushir would convey my views to Maulana Noorani on his return to Karachi. Reached Abbottabad at 20:30.

Tuesday, 16 Sept 1975, Abbottabad

A policeman arrived with summons for Omar, Ali and Ziae. Ali's name was incorrectly listed (Muhammad Asghar, son of Air Marshal Asghar Khan). Razvi sent him away and told him that Omar and Ziae were not there. Summons were for 23 March occurrence at Lahore railway station when the police had baton charged our workers without provocation. They have been charged under section 307 of CPC (attempt at murder). How extraordinary!

Omar is to leave early on the morning of the 18th. Not sure whether he will be allowed to board the plane.

Gohar Ayub came and suggested that the selection of Tehrik candidates should be postponed until the new party programme reaches the people. Decided to call a meeting of the central parliamentary board.

Called on Begum Mahmuda Saleem. She feels that NAP will not be banned but decision will go against Wali Khan and certain other individuals.

Thursday, 18 Sept 1975, Abbottabad

Missed Omar, but just as well that he is away from the general air of persecution here. He has grown up to be a responsible and studious young man ever since he left the army and is taking life seriously. Will, I am sure, make good use of his three years at Essex. Have arranged to send him the *Nawa-i-Waqt* and the weekly *Al Balagh* so that he is kept abreast of news from home.

Saturday, 15 Nov 1975, Lahore

The fourth amendment to the constitution taking away the power of the High Court to grant bail before arrest was passed in the National Assembly amongst rowdy scenes late last night. Three members, including Mian Mahmud Ali Kasuri, were thrown out of the chamber under orders of the speaker for obstructing the passing of the bill. Mufti Mahmud and Chaudhri Zahur Elahi were injured.

Tuesday, 25 Nov 1975, Rawalpindi

Maulana Shah Ahmed Noorani of the JUP, Maulana Mustafa Al Azhari, Maulana Abdus Sattar Niazi came to lunch. Mushir was the host. Later attended meeting of heads of opposition parties in Islamabad. Mufti Mahmud, Maulana Noorani, Nawabzada Nasrullah Khan, Prof. Ghafoor Ahmed, Pir Pagara, Sherbaz Mazari, Mushir Pesh Imam, Maulana Ali Azhari and Mian Mahmud Ali Kasuri attended. Agreed on: (1) no talks with government in future; (2) resignation from assemblies if necessary at a later date; (3) convention of opposition MNAs and MPAs and heads of political parties on 3 December at Lahore and; (4) convention of lawyers before 15 December.

Friday, 19 Dec 1975, Karachi

Prayers at Maulana Shah Ahmed Noorani's mosque in Saddar. Went to Katrak Hall for a meeting (Black Day) to mark the completion of four years of Bhutto's misrule. Were stopped by the police, *lathi* charged, arrested and then released. Went on foot in a procession, were stopped by the police and the public was baton charged. After two hours of blockage by police and attempts to persuade us to leave, we (Shah Ahmed Noorani, Sherbaz Mazari, Obaid-ur-Rehman and myself) were arrested, lifted bodily and put in a police truck and taken to Soldier Bazaar police station. Were released after two hours.

Jamaat-i-Islami and Muslim League were not present at today's incident.

Thursday, 25 Dec 1975, Peshawar

Stayed in Jan's Hotel all day. Tight police surveillance outside. Had talks with Inamullah Khan, Mufti Samiuddin and Fani. Major Sardar Khan Orakzai came from Kohat in the evening. Shifted to Inamullah Khan's office in Khyber Bazaar at 22:30. Police on duty outside was taken by surprise and lost us in pursuit—they were late in starting. Inamullah's office was not very comfortable but spent a tolerable night. Inamullah's office is near Mahabat Khan mosque and we felt that police could not easily prevent me from going to the mosque and then to Chowk Yadgar.

Friday, 26 Dec 1975, Peshawar, Abbottabad
Police arrived outside at about 11:00. Got my van over from Jan's Hotel and drove to Mahabat Khan mosque at about 12:15. Learnt there that Maulana Shah Ahmed Noorani has been arrested on arrival at Peshawar airport. Walked out after prayers to Chowk Yadgar. Usual drama. Baton charge, tear gas and arrests. After some resistance I was taken away by the police to Tehkal police station. I learnt later that Gohar Ayub and about 90 others were taken to Gor Ghatri police station. At about 16:30 Gohar Ayub and I were driven to Abbottabad.

Saturday, 27 Dec 1975, Abbottabad, Fateh Jang, Khushalgarh, Bannu
Left Abbottabad at 10:15. Was stopped at Haripur by police and was told that I could not proceed further. After arguing for an hour, and telephone conversation with SSP Hazara, Masud Shah I left for Bannu. Stopped at Fateh Jang and met Maulvi Mohammad Hussain. Was met by Kohat police at Khushalgarh Bridge. Arrived in Bannu at 17:15 and was received by Khaliq Dad (chairman, Tehrik-i-Istiqlal, Bannu district) ten miles outside Bannu.

Wednesday, 31 Dec 1975, Bannu, Kohat, Rawalpindi
Was stopped ten miles from Kohat by Arbab Mohammad Akbar Khan s/o Arbab Ahmed Ali Jan (retired commissioner). Akbar Khan, (AC Kohat), and by Sher Taj (SP Kohat). They had blocked the road with trucks, jeeps and about 30 armed police. Was informed that my entry into Kohat where I was to address a workers convention was banned. Moved on. Was met by workers three miles from Kohat at Jermyn bridge. Was stopped again near the gate of Pakistan Air Force base and diverted on Khushalgarh road to Rawalpindi. Decided to address a press conference tomorrow. Gohar Ayub telephoned to say that Sardar Bahadur Khan had died at 8:30. A bleak ending to 1975.

Diary 1976

Tuesday, 9 Jan 1976, Abbottabad

Heard of the death of Zhou Enlai, the Chinese leader, on the morning radio news. Had met him during the 1965 war, when I went to China to seek military aid and to brief him on the military situation. Had met him again in October 1965, when I went to Beijing to take part in the October Day celebrations and in January 1966, when I accompanied Ayub Khan to the Chinese capital on a secret visit. He was a truly remarkable man. Had amazing mastery over detail. Knew the rate of fire of different guns, performance of aircraft and tanks and was as familiar with matters connected with aviation and military equipment as he was with political or economic matters. He was skilful in negotiations and had a deep knowledge of world affairs. His loss will be keenly felt in China.

Sent letters to Bandyal (chief secretary, NWFP) and Orakzai (IG police, NWFP) about the incidents of 26 December and 31 December when the administration and the police had held me in unlawful custody for two hours and had stopped me unlawfully from entering Kohat.

Tuesday, 27 Feb 1976, Lahore, Sheikhupura, Lahore

Learnt the details of Babu Ferozuddin Ansari's pathetic role from Azim Butt and Moin Shah. Apparently a lady had called at Azim Butt's office, looking for wallpaper. On seeing my photograph, had volunteered the information that her brother-in-law, Captain Amanullah, is in the Tehrik-i-Istiqlal but was about to join the PPP. Azim Butt conveyed this information to Moinuddin Shah, the party's provincial chairman, who along with Shakil Ahmed went to see Captain Amanullah, on 17 February. There they saw Zaman Jafri, Tanveer Tabish, Babu Ferozuddin and his two sons engaged in a discussion. Babu Ferozuddin and Captain Amanullah were unnerved on seeing Moin Shah and Shakil Ahmed. Assuming that they knew about these changes Amanullah told Shakil Ahmed that they had been negotiating with Khalid Malik, (press secretary to Bhutto) to join the PPP and that he, Captain Amanullah, had had two interviews with

Bhutto in this connection. According to him, Bhutto had assured him that they would be rewarded 'beyond their expectation'.

The following morning Bhutto flew specially from Rawalpindi, on his way to Sweden, to be present at a brief ceremony which had been arranged at the Government House, Lahore, at which Babu Ferozuddin Ansari was to announce his resignation from Tehrik-i-Istiqlal and join the PPP. Press and TV were present in large numbers. At 10:00 a staff car with Khalid Malik went to pick up Babu Ferozuddin from Amanullah's house. In the meantime Babu Ferozuddin, encouraged by Captain Amanullah's information that Bhutto was willing to reward them 'beyond their expectations', decided to lay down certain terms. He presented these terms in writing (written by Captain Amanullah) to Khalid Malik. These were that Mr Bhutto must announce first to the press that: (1) Babu Ferozuddin would be the PPP chairman, Punjab. (2) One son of Babu Ferozuddin would be appointed a session judge and the other an assistant secretary in a Pakistani mission abroad. (3) Babu Ferozuddin would have at his disposal ten other civil service appointments to which he could appoint people of his choice. (4) Zaman Jafri would be given license for a textile mill and loans for this purpose. (5) Tanveer Abbas Tabish would be made the manager of a UBL branch.

When this announcement had been made, Babu Ferozuddin would arrive and announce his decision to join the PPP. Khalid Malik begged Babu to be reasonable but to no avail. Khalid Malik, accompanied by Zaman Jafri, Captain Amanullah and Tanveer Tabish, went to Government House to see Bhutto who was waiting for him. When Bhutto learnt of Babu's terms, he abused him and asked for Ferozuddin to be produced before him, when the PPP chief returned from abroad, for this 'dirty blighter to be taught a lesson of his life'. Bhutto ordered the other three to be thrown out of the Government House. On hearing this, Babu Ferozuddin nearly passed out and had to be revived. A befitting finale to a drama of an unscrupulous politician.

Monday, 8 March 1976, Peshawar, Abbottabad
Met a retired subedar who had been in charge of the army supply corp detachment located at Risalpur under my command in 1947/48 for supply dropping in Gilgit-Skardu area. Revived old memories. This gallant body of men had been used by us in the PAF on Dakotas and

Halifaxes. The Halifax had panniers (tanks) fitted under the wings. These panniers had supplies loaded in them and tied with a rope. At the front end of the open panniers one or two of these men would be tied with a 'monkey chain' of sorts. When the aircraft reached the zone where the supplies had to be dropped, a light inside the panniers was switched on from the cockpit. That was a signal for the jawan (soldier) to untie the rope and kick out the supplies.

Monday, 15 March 1976, Serai Alamgir, Abbottabad
Julius Caesar was murdered 2,416 years ago today for being overambitious and for trying to impose a hereditary rule over the Romans. It appears that some people have not learnt any lesson from Caesar's fall and other similar incidents in history.

Went to Islamabad and saw Mian Mahmud Ali Kasuri and had useful talks with Maulana Noorani. He agreed to give a statement in favour of Shias who are protesting at Sargodha against the court's attitude in not allowing them to take out a *Zuljanah* procession. Discussed possibility of joint candidates for next general election that Bhutto is likely to announce.

Saturday, 20 March 1976, Lahore
Party election for Punjab were held. Mian Mahmud Ali Kasuri was elected chairman. He polled 79 votes against 64 for Moinuddin Shah. Mumtaz Tarar was elected general secretary, defeating Hamid Sarfaraz. Moinuddin Shah did not take his defeat very well and was sulking. Meeting of the national working committee held. Later in the evening had dinner at Mian Mahmud Ali Kasuri's house. Moinuddin Shah was absent from both.

Sunday, 21 March 1976, Lahore
Meeting of the national council for the party elections was held. I was elected president the third time for a two-year term. Pesh Imam was elected secretary general and Malik Wazir Ali senior vice president.

Monday, 22 March 1976, Lahore
Hanif Ramay called in the morning and discussed possibilities of the Tehrik-i-Istiqlal's cooperation with the Muslim League. Mushir and Allama Ehsan Elahi Zaheer addressed a press conference. Lunched

with Akbar Khan Bugti. Moinuddin Shah, who had been sulking, called. Spent some time cooling him down. Dinner with Mian Mahmud Ali Kasuri; took Moinuddin Shah along. The usual political embrace (between Mian Sahib and Moinuddin Shah).

Sunday, 25 April 1976, Abbottabad (Tarbela Township)
Addressed a well attended meeting at Tarbela Township (Haripur) this evening on our way back, Gohar Ayub Khan was arrested under DPR 49 and PPC 124-A. Came back to Abbottabad and saw off Gohar Ayub at 22:30. He and his wife took it very well. This is the first arrest of a Tehrik leader (except for short term detentions for minor offences) and indicates a change in government policy towards Tehrik-i-Istiqlal. I welcome this new development, as it will give a new dimension to the struggle.

My telephone has been cut for the second night between 22:00 and 08:30. Probably the monitoring intelligence staff are not available for night duty.

Monday, 26 April 1976, Abbottabad
Talked with Raja Afzal on the telephone and asked him to take care of Gohar Ayub who will probably be in Gujrat jail. Tassaddaq telephoned to say that Mushir is arriving in Rawalpindi from Lahore tonight. Telephone is now normal. Went to see Zeb (Mrs Gohar Ayub). She was in high spirits. Met Begum Ayub Khan there after a long time. Her youngest daughter Shakila was also present. It appears that she has forgiven me for being the cause of ousting her husband. Begum Ayub Khan is a very intelligent person and very charming.

Tuesday, 27 April 1976, Abbottabad, Rawalpindi, Abbottabad
Discussed the draft of the agreement between Muslim League and Wazir Ali. Did not like it at all. It was a crude effort to get us into another kind of UDF. No mention of ratio of seats between parties for the election, which is the crux of any such alliance. The draft stipulates that I will be the future prime minister. The head of the alliance will be the future president—presumably the Pir of Pagara. That I will be the chairman of the central parliamentary board and that these nominations will be for five years. This I thought was ridiculous and I told Maulana Noorani so. He agreed with me. The selection of any

future prime minister will be made by the parliamentary group, which is returned to the National Assembly and will obviously depend on the relative strength of the parties in the alliance. Moreover, leadership is earned and not conferred. I found the whole idea rather repulsive. Any such announcement would also be ridiculed—and rightly so by all right thinking people. Suggested changes in the draft and the ratio of seats for the various parties. Maulana Noorani agreed. Mushir will stay on tonight in Rawalpindi, will meet Mufti Mahmud and will try to arrange a meeting of leaders of parties to try to sort this out.

Returned to Abbottabad at 19:00. Raja Afzal telephoned. He had been to see Gohar Ayub in Gujrat jail. Gohar was in high spirits. M. Anwar telephoned to say that he is trying to withdraw the papers from Mian Faqir Mohammad and will handle Gohar Ayub's case himself. Wazir Ali telephoned to say that Gohar has been given class 'A' in jail. Talked with Zeb who was quite cheerful.

Shavi, Osman, Alia and Tina came down from Nathiagali to visit Aleem at Haripur jail and later spent the night with us.

Monday, 3 May 1976, Rawalpindi
Met Maulana Noorani. Raja Munawwar MPA, Muslim League came from Lahore. Later Mufti Mahmud, Maulana Noorani, Sherbaz Mazari and Mian Kasuri came for dinner at Tassaddaq's. Raja Munawwar was also there. Decided that heads of parties should meet at Rawalpindi on the 13th to sign the agreement and should make up their minds by that date. Mufti Mahmud and Sherbaz Mazari are going to Hyderabad on the 10th where they will see Wali Khan in jail on the day of his trial and consult him about the agreement.

Thursday, 6 May 1976, Abbottabad, Rawalpindi
At a meeting of the national working committee. discussed the desirability and mode of cooperation with other opposition parties. Everyone expressed reservations about Pir of Pagara (president of Muslim League) who was so involved in horse racing that they thought that he had little time for politics. They were, therefore, not ready to accept him even as a titular head of the alliance. It was also decided that the ratio of the seats between parties should be agreed upon beforehand. Decided to send Mumtaz Tarar to Lahore to convey this to the Muslim League working committee, which is in session

there. Had dinner with Mian Kasuri at Islamabad. Met Sherbaz Mazari, Mufti Mahmud and Maulana Noorani there. Sherbaz informed me that NDP would not join the alliance, as they, along with JUI and Jamaat-i-Islami, were likely to form another alliance. He thought that cooperation between the two groups could be worked out later. Told Mushir to inform the Muslim League and rehash the agreement dropping references to the future president and prime minister of the country and the duration of the alliance being five years.

Thursday, 13 May 1976, Abbottabad, Rawalpindi, Abbottabad

Allama Mustafa Ali Azhari, the JUP MNA, also came along with Noorani. Discussed the course of action after the UDF's stand following the *amir* Jamaat-i-Islami's suggestion that there was nothing much wrong with Bhutto. Jamaat-i-Islami, Nasrullah Khan of PDP and Mufti Mahmud of the JUI had opposed any prominence being given to Tehrik-i-Istiqlal. Muslim League working committee had agreed to the draft agreement provided the other constituents of the UDF also agreed. I think they did this knowing very well that there would be no agreement. Khar and his group have expressed their disenchantment with the UDF and the Muslim League, since they feel that most of their people are in league with Bhutto. They had also noted that Mufti Mahmud had met Bhutto on 7 May and Malik Qasim had spent three hours with the head of the FSF on 5 May in his office. I feel that the sooner we come out openly against such elements, which are a bogus opposition, the better.

Agreed to call a meeting of the national working committee at Lahore on 5 and 6 June and hold a joint meeting of the central parliamentary board of the JUP and Tehrik-i-Istiqlal on Sunday, 13 June in Lahore.

Friday, 14 May 1976, Abbottabad

Talked with Allama Zaheer in Lahore. Allama confirmed that he would attend the student's seminar at the Punjab University on 17 May. Gohar Ayub, who had been released on 4 May, called. I emphasized the need to spend some money on the NWFP organisation. He said that he was not in a position to do so. Said he would try to collect some funds but was not very hopeful. Party councillors, who elected him chairman NWFP, in the hopes that he would bring in funds, are in for an unpleasant surprise. I will have to meet their financial requirements and have decided to sell some of my land in Haripur which should meet the party's needs for a few months.

My brother, Tariq showed me a letter he had received from Farooq Adam in Haripur jail today saying that his brother Iftikhar Adam, also in Haripur jail, had learnt that a murderer, who had about forty murders to his credit, had been released unexpectedly on bail from Mardan jail and it is believed that he has been commissioned by the government to assassinate me. Decided to send Ziae to Mardan to make enquiries and Tariq to Haripur to get some more details about this man.

Thursday, 27 May 1976, Abbottabad

Read in today's *Nawa-i-Waqt* that warrants of arrest had been issued for me for a speech at Ghazi on 16 May. Some of our workers, including Tahirkheli (chairman Ghazi) had been arrested on similar charges.

Inamullah Khan (general secretary of the NWFP Tehrik), Younas (treasurer), Yaqub, (chairman Peshawar city Tehrik), and Abdullah Sani came to finalise financial arrangements for running the party in NWFP. Drew up a list of contributors. I said I would give Rs500 a month and suggested Razvi should also give Rs500. These gentlemen went to see Gohar who expressed his inability to help as he was spending already on his tours. Anyway, Younas appears to be a livewire and is making all out efforts to make the party financially solvent. They hope to collect about Rs3,750 per month from party members.

Received a telegram from Khaliq Dad of Bannu saying that he is leaving politics. He is a PWD contractor and I think he has found the going rather tough.

Saturday, 29 May 1976, Rawalpindi, Jhelum, Gujranwala

Addressed the district bar. Nearly 75 per cent of the members were PPP including the bar president and general secretary. But in spite of their leanings, their response was excellent. Left Jhelum for Gujranwala at 15:30 and attended district and city workers' convention. About 600 workers attended. Very lively and enthusiastic. Very well organised.

Tuesday, 22 June 1976, Abbottabad (Balakot)
While Gohar Ayub was speaking, DSP and ACP brought an order showing that Section 144 was in force. I tore up the order and threw it away. A baton charge followed. We then walked in procession to Naseem Bangash's house. Addressed a meeting, had lunch and then participated in the convention of Kaghan party workers. Left Balakot at 16:30. At Mansehra the police was waiting for us and arrested two of our workers. Altogether a very good day. Good political work.

Wednesday, 23 June 1976, Abbottabad
Gohar Ayub Khan was arrested at 03:00 this morning under Section 188 CPC for the Balakot incident. Learnt later that he had also been charged under MPO 16 and DPR 42 and 49.

Thursday, 24 June 1976, Abbottabad
Gohar Ayub Khan was shifted to Peshawar central jail early this morning.

Captain Mahmood of Muslim League (Qayyum) called to make a fantastic suggestion. He said that Qayyum Khan would leave the government and join the opposition provided he was acknowledged as the leader. Told him that Qayyum Khan could not come out of the government unless he is sacked and could not oppose the government unless Bhutto wished him to do so. I had to listen to his nonsense for two hours.

Sunday, 18 July 1976, Muzzaffargarh, Multan, Rawalpindi, Abbottabad
Was woken up at 05:15 and informed that Haider Osman and Zawar Shah had come from Multan to tell me that the government had arranged for hooligans to stop me on my way to Multan. They suggested that I should leave earlier than the scheduled time of 07:00. Left at 06:15 and arrived at Multan at 07:15. Addressed the convention of party workers Multan district.

Friday, 30 July 1976, Abbottabad, Peshawar
Reached Attock bridge at 16:00 where I was told by the police on duty not to go further but to await the arrival of a DSP from Peshawar, who was on his way. I forced my way over the bridge. Addressed workers

at the provincial office in Peshawar. Excellent function. Good response. Many new faces. Some people announced joining the party.

Wednesday, 11 Aug 1976, Quetta

Anwar Durrani's house was surrounded by the police at 23:30 last night and I was informed in the morning that I would not be allowed to leave the premises during my stay in Quetta. Ziae managed to come in at about 10:00 but Khudai Noor and others were not allowed to enter. An ASP, a DSP and about a dozen other police officers and a large armed police force remained on duty. Khudai Noor addressed the meeting at Kutchlak which was very successful. He and Colonel Tassaddaq addressed another meeting at Ziae's house. This meeting was also very well attended.

Thursday, 12 Aug 1976, Quetta, Karachi

The siege continued until the departure time of the aircraft for Karachi. Left at 17:00 and arrived at Karachi an hour later. Was given an excellent welcome at Karachi. Finalised my programme of a tour of Sindh and my stay in Karachi. Spoke with Amina on the telephone as she had been calling to enquire about my detention in Quetta.

Saturday, 14 Aug 1976, Karachi

Meeting of the national working committee at Pesh Imam's house. Only eight members attended because of floods and the interruption of train services from the north. So no formal meeting was held as the quorum was not complete. Discussed cooperation with the JUP and the division of seats between parties. Went to the Quaid's mausoleum. Big public response. Police could not control the crowd. Zahoor ul Hassan Bhopali (MPA, JUP) joined our working committee meeting at 17:00.

Tuesday, 17 Aug 1976, Karachi, Hyderabad, Karachi

Left Karachi at 08:00 by road. Went straight to the central prison, Hyderabad to attend the trial of NAP prisoners. Met Wali Khan, Kaswar Gardezi, Attaullah Mengal, Senator Hashim Gilzai, Habib Jalib, Sher Mohammad (Sheroff), Afzal Khan, Arbab Sikander and others.

Went to Latifabad (followed by police in trucks) to Saeed's house. On arrival the police cordoned off the house and informed us that no one would be allowed to enter. They began sending away workers who tried to come. Talked with Inspector Allah Bux who was on duty and he made it plain that I would not be allowed to move around in Sindh. Decided to call off my tour and return to Karachi.

Wednesday, 18 Aug 1976, Karachi, Lahore
Left for Lahore at 08:30. Went straight to the special tribunal trying Raja Afzal, Hanif Ramay, Khakwani and Raja Munawwar's case. Altaf Hussain Qureshi and Ijaz Qureshi were also being tried.

The chairman of the tribunal, obviously because of my presence, said that he would not proceed with Raja Afzal's case today. Told the chairman that the tribunal was a 'fraud' and its members devoid of conscience and character. The chairman ordered that I should be arrested but the police present made no move to carry out his orders. A rumpus followed. (Malik Hamid Sarfaraz yelled at the chairman 'Shut up' and told him that he would be hanged). It was quite a scene. Raja Afzal, with whom I talked for a few minutes, had lost a lot of weight.

Lunched with Allama Zaheer, Malik Hamid Sarfaraz and Ziae. The row in the court today has probably ended all chances of Raja Afzal being released on bail by this tribunal.

Saturday, 21 August 1976, Abbottabad
Mian Mahmud Ali Kasuri telephoned from Islamabad to tell me that the UDF is not attending the leaders' conference convened by the JUP. Suggested that we should send someone. Told him that I had already told Allama Zaheer this morning that he and Wazir Ali should represent us at the meeting. Maulana Noorani informed me later that he had addressed a press conference and had postponed the proposed conference. Just as well.

Monday, 23 Aug 1976, Abbottabad
Afghan President Daud's third day in Pakistan. Having deliberately antagonised Afghanistan and after a continuous exchange of cheap political sabre-rattling, Bhutto has performed a volte-face under Soviet and Indian pressure. Only he is capable of this and is now all

sugar and honey to his one time adversary. Daud's visit follows Bhutto's to Kabul in June this year.

Iran's massive investment in India and both Iran's and Russia's desire to see an area of peace in the subcontinent is likely to prove decisive in shaping the course of Pakistan-Afghanistan relations, at least during Bhutto's tenure. Iran's keen desire to see uninterrupted and easy transit of its goods across Pakistan and Pakistan's increasing dependence on Iran's economic aid leaves Bhutto with little choice especially in view of the weak economic position his inept policies have landed Pakistan in.

The assessment that I had made over two months ago in the presence of Begum Wali Khan and Sherbaz Mazari during their visit to Abbottabad in June was: (a) Bhutto will release NAP leaders. (b) He will probably hand over the government of Balochistan and NWFP to them or hold elections in the two provinces. Elections appear to be necessary because NAP and JUI will find it impossible to run the provinces—the position in the provincial assemblies having changed in the intervening period in favour of the PPP. (c) He may even rename NWFP and call it Pakhtoonistan as a gesture to the Pakhtoons and thus try to pull the carpet from under Wali Khan's feet, who has not made this demand so far. I expect these developments to take place within the next two months.

Tuesday, 24 Aug 1976, Abbottabad, Haripur
Amina, Omar and I went to Haripur jail to see Aleem. Osman was also there. Aleem served us some custard. Very well made. He has the late Qurban Ali Khan's (one time AGG Balochistan) cook, who is serving a life sentence for murder, working for him. Aleem also has another cook for Pakistani food. I think Aleem is living and eating better in jail than Shavi and his children outside. He has a sitting-cum-dining room, a bedroom, a fan, radio and a TV. A pitch and put golf course, two cooks, a couple of *khidmatgars* (domestic servant). This is not bad for jail.

Friday, 10 Sept 1976, Abbottabad
The passing away of Mao Zedong yesterday at the age of 83 will probably result in a tussle for power in China which may last for quite some time. If this happens, China will have little time for others and

its influence in world affairs will, to that extent, be impaired. Mao was undoubtedly one of the greatest men of this century who shaped the China of today and who had a profound effect on the lives of millions outside his own country.

Friday, 17 Sept 1976, Abbottabad

I issued a press release about the situation in Dir yesterday which did not appear in the papers today. This is what I had expected. Osman has been sent off to Dir.

The TV and radio were full of Bhutto's speech at Muzzaffarabad which incidentally was a poor defence of his political inconsistencies— and I fear that we will be fed on this speech for the next ten days (until another equally painful performance replaces it). Khurshid's Liberation League's merger with the PPP highlights the erosion of political values that is taking place in our national life and the spread of political opportunism on a scale hitherto unknown even in our society.

Friday, 1 Oct 1976, Abbottabad

Altaf Hussain Qureshi and Ijaz Hussain Qureshi of *Urdu Digest* were sentenced to two years imprisonment by a special tribunal. 'Democracy is our politics' another promise fulfilled by Bhutto.

Newspapers reported yesterday's meeting of the Lahore High Court Bar Association in which the members passed a resolution—201 votes for and 24 against—in favour of the fifth amendment which restricted the powers of the judiciary. It must be the most shameful performance of the Lahore High Court Bar Association in its long history. It is the Punjabi intellectual's delayed response to Bhutto's slogan of *'Roti, Kapra aur Makan'*.

Wednesday, 6 Oct 1976, Abbottabad

'Labour week' is in full swing. Banners, dinners and variety shows for workers; a labour conference in Islamabad and TV and radio programmes would make it appear that this is a poor man's government, if it was not for the miserable plight of the people and the mounting corruption and utter waste of government resources by the ruling junta. Some 22 labour leaders have been released in Sindh—so the papers say—but thousands are rotting in jail. PT display in the Kim Il Sung Korean style is being organised at

Rawalpindi for the Saudi Arabian monarch King Khalid's visit; so it appears that we are in for a big dose of 'big brother' brainwashing. To top it all, another boat of Pakistanis fleeing the country was rounded up near Abu Dhabi and over a hundred people either thrown overboard or drowned. This is the second such incident in a month.

Sunday, 10 Oct 1976, Abbottabad
The king of Saudi Arabia arrived in Islamabad today and was given a North Korean style reception. It looked thoroughly stupid.

Mian Mahmud Ali Kasuri telephoned to ask whether he should attend a banquet being given by the government in honour of King Khalid. He said that Mufti Mahmud had said that opposition MNAs should not attend, as they had not done so for the Shah of Iran. I advised Mian Sahib that he should as it would be discourteous if he did not. He also said that Allama Zaheer had advised him to seek an interview for me with the king. I advised him against it, as the king would only meet those, who his hosts (our government) wished him to meet. Mian Sahib is coming here on Friday night.

Friday, 15 Oct 1976, Abbottabad
Mian Mahmud Ali Kasuri, Wazir Ali, Raja Afzal and Colonel Tassaddaq arrived from Rawalpindi. The first three appeared very dejected and demoralised about the political situation and felt that no political work was possible. Had no practical suggestion except that the fifth amendment, curtailing civil liberties and the powers of the high courts, should be challenged in the Supreme Court and an all-parties conference should be called. Tassaddaq was of the view that there was plenty of scope for work. The people, he said, were with us and the administration was sympathetic.

Sunday, 17 Oct 1976, Abbottabad
Women's week starts tomorrow, which will be followed by a *kissan's* week. Some other weeks will follow but the average Pakistani's 'week' is one of misery and suffering. Jails are overflowing with political prisoners. Complete suppression of basic human freedom and rank corruption and incompetence are the order of the day. Propaganda and the news media, however, are projecting a Pakistan that only exists in the imagination of our rulers.

Z.A. Bhutto is visiting the Pakistan Military Academy, Kakul and in preparation for his visit, we have been without water since yesterday.

Tuesday, 19 Oct 1976, Abbottabad
A ridiculously abbreviated version of my press statement appeared in the *Nawa-i-Waqt* of today. It is evident that the last newspaper of the so called 'free' press has finally succumbed to the pressure of the government and press statements are of little value.

Saturday, 23 Oct 1976, Abbottabad
Received a letter from Sherbaz Mazari suggesting an all-parties (opposition) meeting at the summit level. I am not in favour as without general agreement on the course of action to be adopted, for which informal prior discussions are necessary, such a get-together without any results is likely to create disappointment amongst the public.

Tuesday, 26 Oct 1976, Abbottabad
Talked with Mian Mahmud Ali Kasuri in Lahore. He wanted me to attend the conference hosted by Sherbaz Mazari in Lahore. Informed him that I had already written to Sherbaz.

Chaudhri Sher Ali Khan came from Rawalpindi with a message from Tassaddaq that difficulties were being created by the government in the way of our conference next month. Asked Tassaddaq to come over tomorrow for discussion.

Osman turned up later in the evening from Dir. His resignation has been accepted and he will be leaving the army in a fortnight or so. His account of events in Dir confirmed my worst fears. The army has been killing men, women and children indiscriminately. About 500 bodies of civilians have been counted. Many more have been killed (their bodies were taken away by their relatives). There have also been cases of rape and large scale looting. Initial military action started when a crowd (largely unarmed) had collected on a hillside to protest against the government's forest rules. Fearing trouble the army had taken positions next to them and had trained their guns (machine gun and artillery) on them. Every thing was quiet until one solitary shot was fired. On hearing this shot, the trigger-happy army opened up on the crowd with all they had—machine guns and artillery. About 250 people were killed.

The whole episode brings no credit to the army. It is, I feel, a disgrace that the armed forces should be used or allow themselves to be used against our own people. Senior officers have been corrupted and the army has lost its soul and character.

Officers are being paid Rs30 a day for killing our brethren in Dir; JCOs get Rs12, NOCs Rs10 and troops Rs8. Osman estimates that ten million rupees are being spent daily on allowances, rations and fuel by the army in Dir. Two army divisions are employed in Dir and with four in Balochistan, only eight divisions remain in Punjab.

Osman said that the people of Dir were showing their contempt for the army by adopting a dignified and hostile demeanour. The locals were not cooperating with the army and the administration—not surprising.

Thursday, 4 Nov 1976, Abbottabad

Left for Rawalpindi at 07:16. Attended the court of the assistant commissioner in the Rewat case—my criminal complaint against Habib Lodhi, the SP, and Sardar Naseem Akhtar, an ASI. The accused appeared in court and a new date was fixed for hearing for 7 December.

Saw the site for the camp on Chountra-Adiala Road. Police was on the site and was checking people going towards the site. It was obvious that the government intends stopping us from assembling. Gave necessary instructions for alternate arrangements.

Saturday, 6 Nov 1976, Abbottabad, Rawalpindi

Was informed at 01:30 by Zafar Ali Shah that police (about 1000 strong) attacked our former central office on Murree road which was the alternate site for the party conference and ransacked the place. Took away all tents, cut the telephone lines and removed everything. Decided to leave earlier than planned for Rawalpindi. Left at 06:00. Was stopped twice en route by the police. Refused to stop. Drove the van myself to avoid Khushaal Khan (the driver) being arrested and arrived at the Murree road office, which was completely surrounded by police. Found about three dozen workers, who had been there all night. Addressed them and later met the press. Decided to hold an emergency meeting of the national working committee tomorrow at 10:00 and a press conference at 15:00.

Met workers at Tassaddaq's house and Karachi workers in the hotel. Learnt that about 500 workers had been arrested during the day and the previous night in Rawalpindi alone. Amongst them are the chairmen NWFP and Balochistan Tehrik; Sardar Khan Orakzai (central vice president); district chairmen of Abbottabad, Mardan, Peshawar, Kohat; Kamaluddin Marri; Idrees Bajwa (VP Punjab) and numerous other office-bearers. Had asked workers to dinner at the Murree road office. Police did not allow anyone to enter but allowed the few who were already present to stay. So spent the night at Islamabad in Mian Mahmud Ali's room in the government hostel.

Sunday, 7 Nov 1976, Rawalpindi, Abbottabad

National working committee meeting in Islamabad. About eighteen members and seven others attended. Useful exchange of views. Agreed that the decision to hold the conference was correct and the government's action had gone in our favour. Addressed a press conference in the afternoon at Colonel Tassaddaq's. Reports indicated that 614 of our workers were in police lockup mostly in Rawalpindi, including the entire delegations from Balochistan and Chitral.

Monday, 8 Nov 1976, Abbottabad

Police and security staff surrounded my house because Bhutto is in town today.

Tuesday, 9 Nov 1976, Abbottabad

Bhutto addressed a meeting of a few carefully screened individuals at the army parade ground (Baloch Regimental Centre) after the venue was changed twice. The security arrangements in town yesterday and today have been so tight and his public contact so limited that it has created an unfavourable impression among the general public. Wajid Razvi was stopped from taking his morning walk on Shimla Hill (where Bhutto is staying in the Government House) and I had to chase an intelligence man out of my compound. It is evident that Bhutto and his security experts are worried about his safety. A bomb explosion near his dais in the Mohmand Agency—a few minutes before his arrival—had killed the assistant political agent a few days ago and he is, therefore, taking no chances. In spite of all these precautions, the likelihood, however, is that he will not die of old age.

Thursday, 11 Nov 1976, Abbottabad
Tassaddaq telephoned to say that 76 of our workers had been released and some more were expected to be released today or tomorrow. He also said that Maulana Shah Ahmed Noorani wished to meet me.

Friday, 12 Nov 1976, Abbottabad, Rawalpindi, Abbottabad
Went to Rawalpindi and met Khudai Noor, Anwar Durrani and the Balochistan workers who had been released yesterday. They were all staying at my brother Laji's [Brigadier Aslam Khan] place. Also met Idrees Bajwa, Khawaja Asim of Sialkot, Major Sardar Khan Orakzai, Qayyum Pahat, Mahmud Khan and some fifty other workers from different places who had been released on bail. Consensus was that in future on such occasions bail should not be sought.

Monday, 22 Nov 1976, Abbottabad
Maulana Shah Ahmed Noorani, Prof. Ghafoor Ahmed, Senator Khawaja Safdar and Sherbaz Khan Mazari came and stayed for lunch. Discussed possibilities of cooperation and putting up joint candidates for elections. Agreed to meet again at Karachi on 4 or 5 December when Prof. Ghafoor Ahmed will make a proposal for the basis of cooperation. Maulana Thanvi has sighted the moon. So Eid will be on 2 December.

Saturday, 27 Nov 1976, Rawalpindi, Jhelum, Mandi Bahauddin
Left Rawalpindi at 08:45. Had lunch with Raja Afzal at Serai Alamgir. He has been released on bail. He had been detained under the defence of Pakistan rules and had been tortured in police custody. He is with us but will not be active in politics for a while.

Friday, 3 Dec 1976, Karachi
Visited the Karachi party office on Jehangir road to meet workers. Met Maulana Noorani and Shah Farid ul Haq at Pesh Imam's. Agreed with Maulana Noorani on the following quota for National Assembly seats in the event of an all-parties election alliance between us:

PA	NA	JUP	TI	UDF	NDP
(100)	(43) Sindh Urban	9	3	6	–
	Rural	3	3	16	3
(240)	(116) Punjab	16	42	56	2
(80)	(26) NWFP	1	12	6	7
(40)	(7) Balochistan	1	1	2	3
(460)	192	30	61	86	15

Monday, 6 Dec 1976, Lahore, Shamsabad

Addressed a press conference at 4 Fane Road. On Mian Mahmud Ali's and Allama Zaheer's suggestion agreed not to criticise the UDF's conduct except in the mildest terms. Called on Arif Nizami of *Nawa-i-Waqt* to condole on his mother's death. Held discussions with Abu Saeed Enver, Mian Mahmud Ali, M. Anwer, Hamid Sarfaraz and Allama Zaheer. Left for Shamsabad after lunch at 4 Fane Road. Stayed with Raja Afzal for the night.

Wednesday, 8 Dec 1976, Abbottabad

Weight is creeping up again! Tours always act as weight raisers. Too much eating and plenty of chatter but unfortunately talking does not help to lose weight. Wrote to Prof. Ghafoor Ahmed MNA (secretary general of the UDF) about his absence from the Karachi talks and the general attitude of the UDF.

The local SHO brought the summons from DIK. Told him that I do not accept summons and that they would have to arrest me if they wanted to produce me in court. Learnt from Tassaddaq that hearing in the Rewat case had been fixed for 1 February 1977.

Saturday, 11 Dec 1976, Abbottabad

A letter was received yesterday asking me to appear in Lahore to explain why death duty should not be paid by me on Lalajan's death. My father, Lalajan, had given all his property to Tariq and Farooq during his lifetime—with my consent. I, therefore, gave the letter to Tariq and asked him to explain the situation to the office concerned in Lahore.

Wednesday, 15 Dec 1976, Abbottabad

Schedule for elections appeared in today's newspapers. Seven days will be allowed for nomination papers to be filed and the entire procedure of scrutiny of papers, rejection, appeals and final withdrawals will be completed within 19 days of the first announcement of the dissolution of the assembly. After that, thirty days will be allowed before polling day. This emphasizes the need to complete our selection of candidates well in advance. This is what I have been saying for over a year but the old guard in the party, thinking on traditional lines, have not been in favour. They prefer selection after the announcement.

Friday, 17 Dec 1976, Abbottabad, Rawalpindi, Abbottabad

Left for Rawalpindi at 12:30 and met Maulana Noorani. Gave him a draft agreement and suggested that we should finalise our arrangements about division of seats and the function of the central parliamentary boards. Agreed that a joint meeting of the central parliamentary boards of the two parties should be held at Lahore on 25 and 26 December. Mushir telephoned to say that he had it on good authority that parliament would be dissolved on 25 December and election announced on that day.

Sunday, 19 Dec 1976, Abbottabad

Mian Mahmud Ali Kasuri telephoned. The government announced its decision to give all government owned land to landless tillers. More reforms will be announced by provincial governments in the next five days. All indications suggest that elections will be announced very soon.

Saturday, 25 Dec 1976, Abbottabad, Lahore

Stayed at 4 Fane Road. Prof. Ghafoor Ahmed of Jamaat-i-Islami called to explain his absence at our meeting in Karachi on 4 December. He said he had not come because Maulana Noorani did not ask him to dinner (meeting was at 19:00) and because Pir of Pagara (President of the UDF) was also invited and that in his presence there was little point in Prof. Ghafoor being present too. (The professor is the secretary general of the UDF). Had a joint meeting of parliamentary boards of the JUP and Tehrik-i-Istiqlal. Decided to call for applications for the award of party tickets for a possible election.

Sunday, 26 Dec 1976, Lahore

The JUP delegation called at 17:00 and we continued our discussion about possibilities of cooperation with the UDF. Decided to meet Nawabzada Nasrullah Khan who is heading a committee of the UDF to explore possibilities of cooperation. Had a useful discussion and I made it clear that we would only associate formally after all the important matters, which could cause a rift later, had been sorted out and agreement reached. Explained that the basis of division of seats and ratios between parties must be settled first. Gave him our detailed proposals in this regard. He will try to work out a formula. The UDF has now decided to contest the elections and appeared inclined to fight the elections jointly with us but obstacles in the way of an alliance between eight or more parties are considerable.

Monday, 27 Dec 1976, Lahore, Abbottabad

Called on Maulana Noorani in Islamabad and briefed him on my meeting with Nasrullah Khan. Noorani had not attended the meeting, having returned to Islamabad earlier yesterday.

Friday, 31 Dec 1976, Abbottabad

Mian Sahib has not received his clearance to proceed for *Umrah* but still hopes to go. Learnt that the National Assembly is being summoned—probably on 6 January. Mian Sahib thought that another amendment to the constitution was in the offing.

So ended 1976 a year of trials and tribulations, of floods and earthquakes. Perhaps the most important happening was the passing away of Zhou Enlai and Mao Zedong. Events of great importance not only for China but for the whole world. The next decade or two could see China emerging as a world power. In the western world, Jimmy Carter's election as the new US president could bring a change in American policies and the beginning of new initiatives.

In Pakistan, Bhutto's fascism has been firmly established. The seeds of a police state that were sown in 1972 have now reached their logical fruition. Hatred against him has grown but so has a sense of helplessness. With political processes blocked, the emergence of a national alternative has been retarded. The image of a true opposition has dimmed and the nation is afflicted by a state of despair and confusion.

It now appears more likely that a change will not come by normal democratic processes and we may be in for a repetition of events that have led to political changes in Pakistan in the past.

Diary 1977

Sunday, 2 Jan 1977, Abbottabad, Rawalpindi
Zeb and Akhtar Ayub called in the morning. Akhtar does not wish to leave the Pagara Muslim League but will cooperate in the elections. His position is sound in the Haripur provincial constituency. Zeb informed me that Gohar will contest one National Assembly seat but does not wish to contest the provincial assembly seat.

Friday, 7 Jan 1977, Abbottabad, Lahore
Heard from Arif Nizami of *Nawa-i-Waqt*, who telephoned, that Bhutto had announced the general elections will be held on 7 March for the national and 10 March for provincial assemblies.

Saturday, 8 Jan 1977, Lahore
A busy day. Large number of workers called. Also had visits from Arif Nizami of *Nawa-i-Waqt*, a correspondent of Mazhar Ali Khan's *Viewpoint*, and Prof. Ghafoor Ahmed of Jamaat-i-Islami.

Held a joint meeting of the parliamentary boards of JUP and Tehrik at JUP office. Decided about division of seats between JUP and Tehrik and the quantum of seats for the UDF in Sindh, NWFP, and Balochistan.

Sunday, 9 Jan 1977, Lahore
Another meeting of joint parliamentary boards of the JUP and Tehrik-i-Istiqlal. Surveyed National Assembly seats of Punjab. A very busy day. Rush of party workers. Election tempo appears to be building-up.

Mukhtar Hassan and Mujeeb Shami of *Islami Jamhooria* called and said that Javed Hashmi wished to join Tehrik-i-Istiqlal. Agreed to be present at his press conference tomorrow.

Monday, 10 Jan 1977, Lahore
Attended a meeting of heads of political parties at Bajwa's residence which continued for six hours. Eventually after a lot of haggling on ratio of seats it was agreed to form a new organisation to be called the National Alliance with a common flag and if possible a common election symbol. It was agreed that Tehrik-i-Istiqlal and the JUP should have 36 per cent of the seats in Punjab and out of this Tehrik would have 23 seats. A press conference will be addressed jointly by the parties tomorrow. Decided to postpone my departure by a day.

Friday, 14 Jan 1977, Abbottabad, Peshawar
Called on Mufti Mahmud in Peshawar and met Inamullah Khan and other workers. Our talks with NDP and JUI are not progressing satisfactorily. They are adamant not to concede more than five national and ten provincial seats to us keeping 16 national and 40 provincial for themselves—the total seats being 26 national and 80 provincial seats. It appears that talks will break down here and the matter may be resolved in Lahore when the central parliamentary board of the alliance meets on the 16th.

Saturday, 15 Jan 1977, Peshawar, Lahore
Talks continued between parties for seats. Left for Lahore and went to Mian Mahmud Ali Kasuri's. Mian Sahib had returned from Murree today. Mushir has also arrived. Prof. Ghafoor called to discuss organisational structure of the alliance. Later went to Muslim League House at 19:00. Discussions started at 21:00 after dinner. Sherbaz Mazari and Begum Wali Khan of the NDP suggested that elections in Balochistan should be boycotted in the conditions prevailing there. Agreed to discuss this matter after consultation with representatives from Balochistan tomorrow.

Sunday, 16 Jan 1977, Lahore
Khudai Noor arrived to inform me that the heads of Baloch parties had met in Quetta and had unananimously recommended that elections should be boycotted in the province. Agreed with this recommendation. Mufti Mahmud addressed a press conference to that effect. Central parliamentary board met the whole day until 03:00 on 17 January Agreed on over 100 seats in Punjab and 26 seats in NWFP, others will

be decided tomorrow. Got a seat in Karachi for Mushir which was not being given earlier. Agreement over a seat between Malik Qasim and Mian Mahmud Ali Kasuri could not be reached. Central board agreed that the three provincial candidates in Peshawar NA-I constituency should be with my agreement.

Monday, 17 Jan 1977, Lahore

My 56th birthday. Time has passed swiftly. My school days, life in the army, 25 years in the Pakistan Air Force, and finally, the nine years of politics still appear to be a recent occurrence. The pace of the last five years especially has been hectic.

Decided to contest the election also from Lahore, if Mian Mahmud Ali Kasuri is not given the constituency of his choice and we are forced to take the Gulberg cantonment constituency.

Mian Mahmud Ali Kasuri, Khurshid Kasuri, Abu Saeed Enver and Wazir Ali came at midnight to consult about distribution of seats. Mian Sahib had not been given the constituency he had a right to as a sitting member, so we decided that Khurshid Kasuri would contest from that constituency.

Wednesday, 19 Jan 1977, Karachi

Filed my nomination papers today. Great deal of enthusiasm amongst workers. Papers have also been filed on my behalf in the Abbottabad, Peshawar and Rawalpindi constituencies. Prof. Ghafoor Ahmed of Jamaat-i-Islami, Professor Shah Farid ul Haq, Maulana Haqqani and Zahoor ul Hassan Bhopali called. Discussed distribution of seats in the Sindh provincial assembly.

Thursday, 20 Jan 1977, Karachi

Spent a busy day preparing for the election campaign which cannot start properly until provincial candidates are nominated which has not been done as yet.

Visited the JUP office in Jutland Lines and addressed a large crowd which had assembled there. Later discussed election arrangements with the two likely provincial candidates and my election agent Masud Naqvi. Shah Farid ul Haq and Maulana Haqqani called to discuss distribution of Karachi seats. Agreed on three provincial seats in

Karachi and to ask Jamaat-i-Islami for a Nazimabad seat for Dr Rahim
ul Haq.

Tuesday, 21 Jan 1977, Karachi

Scrutiny of nomination papers for National Assembly today. Was
informed that my papers had been accepted at Peshawar, Rawalpindi
and Karachi. No news from Abbottabad as yet. Disputes over
provincial seats continues. Disagreement in NWFP has not been
resolved.

Met some lady workers and formed half a dozen committees for
work. Addressed a meeting at Burns Road organised by Abdul Hamid
Chapra.

Saturday, 22 Jan 1977, Karachi

Prof. Ghafoor Ahmed called. Discussed distribution of seats in NWFP
and Dr Rahim ul Haq's seat in Nazimabad.

Heard the news that all the chief ministers had been returned
unopposed as they had not allowed anyone else to file his nomination
papers on these seats. Indicates the type of elections we are heading
for.

Sunday, 23 Jan 1977, Karachi

Addressed a public meeting at Nishtar Park of about 100,000 people.
Excellent response. It was the first meeting of the election campaign.
No interference by the police or the administration. Had dinner at
Mushir's. Maulana Noorani and Mian Tufail of Jamaat-i-Islami and
Sherbaz Mazari also spoke.

Monday, 24 Jan 1977, Karachi, Hyderabad, Karachi

Arrived at Hyderabad at 12:50 and led a procession. Very large crowd
about 100,000. It appeared that almost the whole town had turned out.
Wild enthusiasm. Reached the fort at 16:00. Took about three-and-a-
half hours to travel three miles. Gathering was 100,000 plus. Very
good response.

Federal Security Force with fixed bayonets and police were out in
full strength but people ignored them.

Tuesday, 25 Jan 1977, Karachi

Prof. Ghafoor Ahmed of Jamaat-i-Islami called. Later discussed NWFP seat allocation with Qazi Hussain Ahmad of Jamaat-i-Islami (Amir NWFP), Inamullah Khan and Mukhtiar Bacha.

Addressed large meetings at Mahmudabad, Burns Road and Akhtar Colony, all organised by Jamaat-i-Islami. Returned at 01:00. A very busy day.

Wednesday, 26 Jan 1977, Karachi, Sukkur

Large reception at Sukkur airport from where I went in a procession into the city followed by a large public meeting. Dr Anwar Piracha was being pressurised to withdraw in favour of the JUI candidate but advised him not to do so.

Public response in the public meeting was excellent and I made a strong attack on Bhutto. Mian Tufail and Maulana Noorani also spoke.

Friday, 28 Jan 1977, Rawalpindi, Abbottabad

Led a massive procession of cars, vans and buses from Khanpur to Abbottabad. Over 400 vehicles and 3,000 men participated. Addressed a large crowd, in Abbottabad city chowk, at the termination of the procession.

Saturday, 29 Jan 1977, Abbottabad, Peshawar

Spent a very busy morning meeting delegations of workers and prospective candidates. Amir Jamaat-i-Islami of Hazara called to discuss Tanawal seat. Left for Peshawar at 11:30 and arrived at Nowshera at 14:00. Was given a tremendous welcome on arrival and addressed a large crowd at the main square on the road. Spoke for about 15 minutes and went in a procession through Peshawar city.

Sunday, 30 Jan 1977, Peshawar

Addressed a very large public meeting at Jinnah Park. Other National Alliance leaders also spoke. Later had dinner, arranged by the NDP, hosted by Nasim Wali Khan. Met at Haji Bilore's residence with Mufti Mahmud, Nasim Wali Khan and Prof. Ghafoor Ahmed to discuss allocation of seats. Begum Nasim Wali Khan was adamant on keeping all the seats in Mardan and Peshawar district for her party. Very rigid and unbending in her attitude. So was Jamaat-i-Islami. Every one has a very exaggerated notion of their own importance. Tried my best to accommodate everyone and narrowed down differences with the NDP. Mufti's attitude relatively more accommodating. Will meet again tomorrow.

Monday, 31 Jan 1977, Peshawar
Finalised the distribution of seats in NWFP today. Agreed on 29 for the NDP, 16 for the JUI, 15 for Tehrik and 9 for Jamaat-i-Islami. Some seats could not be contested, total being 80. Jamaat was most unhappy with their quota and staged a walk-out. However, they will come round to accepting it in the end. Their tactics in negotiations were rather stupid. Held an election coordinating meeting.

Tuesday, 1 Feb 1977, Peshawar, Haripur, Havelian, Abbottabad
Addressed a very large meeting at Haripur and another at Havelian on my way to Abbottabad. Qayyum Khan was to come in a procession from Rawalpindi but abandoned the idea. His meeting at Abbottabad was disturbed and the gathering was small.

Wednesday, 2 Feb 1977, Abbottabad
It appears from newspaper editions of today—all obviously inspired from statements of the government ministers—that the government has had a bellyful of criticism and may either postpone the election or clamp down and impose restrictions on assembly, public meetings, etc.

Friday, 4 Feb 1977, Rawalpindi
Addressed a mammoth public meeting at Liaquat Bagh. Crowd was over 200,000. Excellent response. Made a strong attack on Bhutto and his government. Took me one hour to extricate myself from the crowd and reach the house, about three-quarter of a mile away.

Saturday, 5 Feb 1977, Rawalpindi, Gujranwala
Addressed meetings at Gujar Khan, Sohawa, Dina, Jhelum, Serai Alamgir, Kharian, Lala Musa, Gujrat, Wazirabad and Rahwali. Tremendous reception everywhere. People cheered wildly and we entered the city with a riotous cavalcade of over 300 cars and buses.

It is obvious that Bhutto's rejection is now complete.

Sunday, 6 Feb 1977, Gujranwala, Lahore

Arrived at Lahore railway station at midday by car from Gujranwala and led a very large procession—about 100,000 strong—through the city to Nasar Park. Later addressed a very large public meeting of about 300,000 people.

Wednesday, 9 Feb 1977, Peshawar

Addressed a women's meeting at Syed Tanvir-ul-Hassan Gilani's residence in the city. About 200 ladies attended. Amina was there and Zeb addressed them too. Later held two public meetings, the second a very large one at Chowk Fawwara in the cantonment area. Also took out processions after the meetings.

Learnt that my PPP opponent Gul Mohammad in the Peshawar NA constituency had been disqualified by the election commissioner because his name was not in the voters' list (on an appeal filed by Yusaf Khattak). The contest is now a straight fight with Yusaf Khattak.

Thursday, 10 Feb 1977, Lahore, Sahiwal

Addressed public meetings at about a dozen places *en route* to Sahiwal. Meetings at Bhai Pheru, Pattoki and Okara were large. Tremendous welcome by the people.

Friday, 11 Feb 1977, Sahiwal, Multan, Sahiwal

Malik Qasim telephoned from Lahore to say that Colonel Tassaddaq had telephoned from Rawalpindi to say that he had reliable information that government had sent 2,200 rifles to Lahore for use in our Multan public meeting today. Left for Multan via Vehari and addressed about 15 wayside meetings including those at Arifwala, Mandi Burewala and Vehari. Arrived at Multan at 19:30 and addressed a mammoth public meeting at the Qasim Bagh stadium.

Saturday, 19 Feb 1977, Faisalabad, Jhang, Sargodha, Lahore

Campaign is in full swing. Addressed a meeting at Jhang and Sahiwal *en route* Sargodha. Arrived in Sargodha at 19:00 and spoke first as the main procession had not arrived (via Chiniot). Excellent response. Left after dinner at Akram Hinjra's and arrived in Lahore at 1:00.

Bakhtiar (Mian Mahmud Ali Kasuri's son) had accompanied me on the tour with Mian Sahib's car. He was so excited that he kept talking, non-stop all the way from Sargodha. A real chip of the old block.

Sunday, 20 Feb 1977, Lahore, Karachi

Arrived at Karachi airport at 12:45. The airport was surrounded by a large crowd on the taxi apron. Got down with great difficulty and came in a mammoth procession to Burns Road.

Tremendous public response. This was undoubtedly the largest procession in Pakistan's history. It was remarkable that the procession should have been nearly its full size from the starting point—Karachi airport is 10 miles from the city. Addressed a fabulous public meeting at Burns Road. Wild cheering by the crowd. Arrived at Anwar's at 01:30. BBC reported the crowd to be 1.6 million.

Saturday, 5 March 1977, Rawalpindi

A week of meetings and processions. Addressed a very large public meeting at Shaheed Chowk on Murree road and led a procession through the city. Excellent public response and a record crowd. When the procession reached Jamia Masjid it was stoned from inside the compound and tear gassed. It was night and was not clear whether the tear gassing was by the police. The IG of police denied that it was the police but I feel that the police was hand in glove with PPP hooligans.

Diverted the procession and avoided a bigger clash which might have spread greater alarm and despondency and reduced the number of people coming out to vote on 7 March. About ten persons were injured but not very seriously—two received bullet wounds. Altogether a very successful day.

Monday, 7 March 1977, Abbottabad, Rawalpindi

Election day. Got up early. Hectic activity. Visited polling stations in Abbottabad, Havelian, Haripur, Wah, Tarnol and then in Rawalpindi. Tremendous enthusiasm among the public and a very large turn-out. It was evident that rigging was taking place on a large scale in women's stations.

Results started coming in after 17:00 and indicated that this election at the end of a massive people's movement had been a big fraud.

Sunday, 8 March 1977, Rawalpindi, Lahore

Addressed a crowded press conference at Colonel Tassaddaq's house. Election results and reports of yesterday's happenings confirmed that countrywide rigging of election had taken place. About 50 people had been shot in different places, mainly in Karachi and Hyderabad, and hundreds wounded by bullets. Armed gangs had raided polling stations. Polling boxes had been tampered with and extra ballot papers stuffed in the boxes by the police and presiding officers.

Told the press that I would ask the PNA to boycott 10 March elections of provincial assemblies and call on the chief election commissioner to resign. Arrived at Lahore at 21:00 for meeting of central council of PNA. Decided that members elected to National Assembly will not go to the Assembly and called a countrywide strike on 11 March.

Decided to meet again tomorrow. Results announced so far showed that I had won from Abbottabad-II and Karachi-VIII by comfortable margins. Lost in Rawalpindi and Peshawar and was running to a close finish in Abbottabad-I against Iqbal Khan Jadoon. Massive rigging had taken place in these three constituencies against me.

Wednesday, 9 March 1977, Lahore, Rawalpindi

The PNA council met again and agreed: (1) resign our National Assembly seats; (2) strike on 11 March; (3) demonstrations from 13 March onwards. Left Lahore at 14:30. Met Toyne Mason, Gavin Young of BBC, *Observer* correspondent and Baer of *Newsweek*.

Thursday, 10 March 1977, Rawalpindi, Abbottabad

Left Rawalpindi at 09:45 after seeing the polling for provincial assembly seats. There were hardly any people and it was therefore proved that the people had voted for the PNA on 7 March. Addressed workers at Haripur and then went on to Rajoya. A young man of this village had been shot and killed on 7 March in Karachi whilst trying to protect a ballot box in Maulana Haqqani's constituency. Maulana Noorani telephoned from Karachi asking me to come to Lahore for tomorrow's meeting of the PNA.

Tuesday, 11 March 1977, Abbottabad, Rawalpindi, Lahore
Left Abbottabad at 04:30 to avoid difficulties likely to be caused by traffic stoppage because of a 'strike'. Arrived in Lahore at 13:00. Strike was successful. Complete stoppage of work in Karachi, Hyderabad, Multan, Faisalabad, Gujranwala, Peshawar but some shops on The Mall and Saddar areas in Rawalpindi and Lahore were open.

Attended the PNA council meeting. Decided to start protest demonstrations from 14 March if: (1) elections are not annulled; (2) chief election commissioner is not removed and a new election commissioner, who inspires confidence, not appointed; (3) prime minister does not resign.

Saturday, 12 March 1977, Lahore
Mufti Mahmud addresses a press conference at PNA headquarters (Muslim League House) to announce decision taken yesterday.
Bhutto addressed the nation on TV and Radio. Not a bad performance considering the tight spot he is in.

Met at 4 Fane Road with other PNA leaders and agreed on a press release rejecting Bhutto's terms for an agreement.

Monday, 14 March 1977, Lahore
Went to Neela Gumbad Mosque at 16:00 and came out to violate Section 144 after *Asr* prayers. Tremendous public response. It was a job getting into the mosque and then coming out. Almost impossible to walk which I eventually managed to do for some 200 yards. It was very hot and humid and the rush of the people made it unbearably uncomfortable.

Peter Gill of *Daily Telegraph* (London) called. Dined with Allama Ehsan Elahi Zaheer. Incidentally police did not interfere with my procession at Lahore but public was baton charged at a number of other places and our workers were arrested. First day of the movement started with a bang.

Mufti Mahmud telephoned to say that he had received a letter from Bhutto to which he had replied seeking clarification of the subjects we wanted to discuss. Learnt later that Rafique Bajwa (secretary general of PNA) had met Bhutto secretly yesterday.

Tuesday, 15 March 1977, Lahore

Demonstrations continued today for the second day throughout the country. Some people were killed, three in Multan alone, where a police station was set on fire. The central council of the PNA met and accepted Rafique Bajwa's resignation from office of secretary general. He was also removed from membership of JUP. This was done for his secret meeting with Bhutto two days ago.

Wednesday, 16 March 1977, Lahore

Meeting of PNA council continued today. Discussed appointment of new secretary general. Maulana Noorani suggested Mian Mahmud Ali Kasuri's name, Nawabzada Nasrullah Khan proposed Malik Qasim and Sherbaz Mazari proposed Prof. Ghafoor Ahmed. Pir Pagara made some objection to the nomination of Mian Sahib. Finally Prof. Ghafoor was selected. The procession in Lahore was led by Maulana Obaidullah Anwar. Seven persons were injured by bullets. Called on them in Mayo Hospital. Heard that three people had been killed in Hyderabad and Khaliq Khan, our chairman Hyderabad, had suffered a bullet wound. PNA received another letter from Bhutto asking for negotiations. Decided to send him a reply similar to the previous one. Had dinner with Javed Hashmi. Decided to lead a procession in Lahore again on Friday, 18 March.

Thursday, 17 March 1977, Lahore

An eventful day. Osman and I went to a dinner at Mei Kong (a Chinese restaurant) hosted by Malik Hamid Sarfaraz and others. As we were leaving at about 23:00 a large police force led by DIG Asad Alvi, SP Mohammad Khan and DSP Niazi along with 14 truck loads of policemen took us into custody. Amongst those taken were Mujeebur Rehman Shami, editor of *Islami Jamhooria* weekly, Malik Mumtaz, correspondent of *Islami Jamhooria*, Malik Hamid Sarfaraz, Javed Hashmi, Bashir Zafar, Khurshid Kasuri, Osman and myself. We were taken to Chung police station on Ferozpur road. After an hour, Khurshid and I were taken to Manava police station near Batapur on the Wagah border where Mian Mahmud Ali Kasuri joined us and from there to Behni, a rest house about half a mile from the Indian border. The place was surrounded by about 500 reserve police under SP

Aurangzeb. We arrived there at about 01:30 and got our beddings (provided by the police) at 09:30.

Friday, 18 March 1977, Manava rest house, Kot Lakhpat jail, Lahore

Behni rest house is a quiet place, situated on the BRB syphon on the left bank of the river Ravi. It is about twenty miles by road, eight miles or so being on a *kutcha* road. We were heavily guarded the whole day and were told at about 23:00 that we were to move to Kot Lakhpat jail. We arrived there at about midnight. Malik Hamid Sarfaraz, Mujeebur Rehman Shami and Bashir Zafar were already there in the superintendent's office. We were lodged in a barrack with a compound about 25 feet by 20 feet. The barrack is about 25 feet long and 15 feet wide with verandahs on both sides. It has electricity and fans and a ramshackle bathroom.

The procession that I was to lead from Data Darbar today was led by Chaudhry Rehmat Elahi of Jamaat-i-Islami who was arrested.

Saturday, 19 March 1977, Kot Lakhpat jail, Lahore

Heard today that Maulana Noorani, Sherbaz Mazari, Begum Nasim Wali Khan and Mir Ali Ahmed Talpur were arrested yesterday.

M. Anwar came to see us along with Omar Kasuri.

Sunday, 20 March 1977, Kot Lakhpat jail, Lahore

Heard about riots in Karachi. About thirty persons were shot there according to BBC. Was told that Hanif Ramay, Khakwani and Raja Munawwar were being kept in isolation in this jail. Protested to the superintendent and asked that they should either be given the same treatment as us or that I should also be put in similar accommodation.

The superintendent informed us that Hamid Sarfaraz, Khurshid Kasuri and Mujeebur Rehman Shami were to move out from our barrack to another accommodation in this prison. We refused to comply and said that we would resist this. They were not moved.

In the evening the results of the Indian elections started coming in showing a close contest between the Congress and the Janata Party with the latter in the lead.

Monday, 21 March 1977, Kot Lakhpat jail, Lahore

I was woken up at 04:30 by the deputy superintendent who informed me that I had been released for a meeting which Mufti Mahmud had called in Lahore. I refused to leave the jail until: (a) the emergency is lifted; (b) all political prisoners and detenus are released.

M. Anwar and Omar Kasuri called and I informed them of my decision. Laji [my brother Aslam Khan] and Anwar called. I met them in the barrack instead of the office as I suspected my removal by force if I went out there. My fears proved correct as the jail superintendent informed me in the afternoon that I was to move to a separate accommodation. I refused and said that he would have to use force. We, therefore, prepared for 'battle' and bolted our barrack doors from inside before going to bed so that forcible ejection would be rendered difficult. A large police force remained outside the jail throughout the day.

Tuesday, 22 March 1977, Kot Lakhpat jail, Lahore

Wazir Ali, Mushir Pesh Imam, Malik Qasim and Ashraf Khan (a Khaksar) came to talk with me on behalf of Mufti Mahmud to persuade me to give up my stand and join them in their deliberations. Wazir Ali thought that my stand would weaken the movement. I explained that my terms to remove the emergency and release political prisoners were conditions to come out of jail and did not in any way detract from our main aim to secure Bhutto's exit. I advised him to go along with any decision of the temporary leadership of the National Alliance, provided it was not in conflict with the alliance's main demands. Their meeting was continuing today and they left disappointed. Mian Mahmud Ali Kasuri, Khurshid, Hamid Sarfaraz and Mujeebur Rehman Shami agreed fully with my stand.

Bolted ourselves in again for the night. However, I expect the other leaders to be locked up again by tomorrow and my concession of being allowed to leave jail withdrawn when that happens.

Wednesday, 23 March 1977, Kot Lakhpat jail, Lahore

Pakistan Day. Heard on BBC that National Alliance had rejected Bhutto's offer of negotiations and that a formal reply will be sent today.

Indira Gandhi resigned yesterday because of her crushing defeat in the Indian general elections. It goes to her credit and to that of the Indian people that they have held their elections in a relatively free atmosphere. We still have a long way to go to establish democratic traditions in Pakistan.

Some 60 PNA prisoners arrived in the jail today presumably on charges of violating Section 144.

Mian Mahmud Ali Kasuri was busy today getting improvements made in our lodgings: a wash basin, European type WC, fly proofing, pegs for hanging clothes, etc. Mujeebur Rehman Shami made some *halwa* in anticipation of the arrival of Maulana Mufti Mahmud and Maulana Noorani who were leading processions in Lahore. But they did not turn up.

Thursday, 24 March 1977, Kot Lakhpat jail, Lahore

Heard on BBC this morning that Mufti Mahmud, Maulana Noorani and Malik Qasim were arrested which resulted in violence and burning of a telegraph office in Lahore. They were later released. Laji came to enquire whether there was any message for Abbottabad as he was going there. Could not see him but sent him a note and asked for some clothes. Also asked Amina to come if she wished.

Friday, 25 March 1977, Kot Lakhpat jail, Lahore

Heard on BBC that a large number of PNA leaders had been arrested. Omar Kasuri came in the evening and told me that Tariq had been arrested at Abbottabad as also Wajid Razvi. He said that a telephone call had also been received at 4 Fane Road a short while ago to say that Amina had also been arrested but another call a few minutes later said that our house at Abbottabad had been surrounded by a large police force and that her arrest was expected. Zeb (Mrs Gohar Ayub) was also in the house at the time. I feel that they must be taking out a women's procession in Abbottabad and the police was probably taking preventive steps. Osman is in Lahore and was telephoning to check up. Amer Raza, president of Lahore High Court Bar Association and two other lawyers, one of them a member of the bar council, were brought to Kot Lakhpat jail, having been arrested earlier today.

Saturday, 26 March 1977, Kot Lakhpat jail, Lahore
Countrywide strike called by the PNA. Couple of explosions in Rawalpindi. The National Assembly met today and PPP members took their oath. No PNA member was present.

Sunday, 27 March 1977, Kot Lakhpat jail, Lahore
The strike yesterday was a success and it appears that resistance is widespread and that pressure is being maintained.

Monday, 28 March 1977, Kot Lakhpat jail, Lahore
Bhutto was sworn in as prime minister today at a ceremony in Islamabad. No opposition member attended. Omar Kasuri came to see us in the afternoon.

A magistrate arrived in the morning for remand. Since the requirement is that the accused are only remanded before a magistrate in court, we turned him out and refused to talk to him. Whilst leaving he said that we were to appear in court on 11 April. He almost ran for his life.

Tuesday, 29 March 1977, Kot Lakhpat jail, Lahore
Amina, Laji, Ali and Osman visited with eatables, foreign newspaper cuttings and clothes. Amina intends to take part in a women's procession in Lahore tomorrow.

Friday, 1 April 1977, Kot Lakhpat jail, Lahore
About 50 prisoners arrived today, many were injured. These were some of those imprisoned in yesterday's procession of ulema who were badly beaten up by the police. Over 30 ulema, including Allama Ehsan Elahi Zaheer, have been arrested but they were not amongst this batch.

Amina was to address a meeting of women at 4 Fane Road today. Mian Mahmud Ali, Shami and Hamid Sarfaraz recited the *azan* at night in response to a call for *azans* from rooftops all over Pakistan throughout the night to 'ward off evil'. There were *azans* from other parts of the prison as well.

Saturday, 2 April 1977, Kot Lakhpat jail, Lahore
Amina came to see me with court permission to finalise election accounts. Ali was not allowed to come. She is planning to stay here

for a few more days, probably until the 9th. Mian Sahib's assistant also called to inform him that Mian Sahib's stenographer, Ajmal, had been arrested on a trumped up charge in connection with explosives. Learnt that Allama Zaheer and others had been released soon after their arrest.

Monday, 4 April 1977, Kot Lakhpat jail, Lahore

Amina, Laji, Anwar, Ali and Saleem (Anwar's son) called. Saw a statement of Maulana Maudoodi in the daily *Wafaq* in which he had asked Bhutto to lift the emergency and release prisoners when he felt the opposition was willing to sit around a table to discuss all points of disagreement. I was disturbed with this statement since this was quite contrary to the uncompromising stand the PNA had adopted. Decided to write to Maulana Maudoodi.

Tuesday, 5 April 1977, Kot Lakhpat jail, Lahore

BBC reported that Mushtaq Ahmad Gurmani was negotiating between Maulana Maudoodi and Bhutto and that Nasrullah Khan and Pagara had met Maulana Maudoodi last night. BBC said that a move is afoot to reach a compromise with the government.

The High Court decided it had jurisdiction in our case and will start regular hearings from tomorrow. M. Anwar called in the evening. Told him to convey my views to Maulana Maudoodi.

Shakoor, a soldier from Swabi, Mardan, undergoing three months imprisonment, joined us as a *mushakatti* [prison aid]. Other three are Riaz, Maqsood and Saleh Mohammad who are all army *jawans* [soldiers] two are undergoing RI. The jail has about 700 army deserters out of a total of 1,100 prisoners. There are about 180 political prisoners connected with this movement.

Heard on BBC that a women's procession attacked a police station in Hyderabad and secured the release of 18 political prisoners.

Friday, 8 April 1977, Kot Lakhpat jail, Lahore

Amina came on her third visit in connection with election accounts. She is leading the women's procession tomorrow morning to protest against the meeting of the provincial assembly. Plans to leave for Abbottabad on Sunday.

Chaudhry Saeed and Wazir Ali came today. Mian Sahib, Khurshid and Hamid Sarfaraz are to appear in court on Monday. Shami and I will probably appear later or maybe the court will come to Kot Lakhpat. Have decided to defend myself.

Saturday, 9 April 1977, Kot Lakhpat jail, Lahore

BBC news said that a women's procession in Karachi yesterday had clashed with the police and snatched police rifles. Heard in the afternoon news that violent clashes have taken place in Lahore. About 30 persons were reported to have been killed and some 250 wounded. Amina, who was leading a women's procession, was arrested and later released. Ali was also arrested. Amina was injured, though not seriously. BBC said that this was the biggest demonstration of this movement. Probably the biggest in the 30 years of Pakistan.

Sunday, 10 April 1977, Kot Lakhpat jail, Lahore

Amina called this morning. She had bruises on her arms and shoulders and a lump on her head. Signs of the police beating. She was however in good spirits. She had been arrested at 09:30 yesterday, kept in a police station along with Sabiha Shakil and four other ladies and released at 18:00.

Ali is in Mughalpura police station with some others. We said *ghaibana namaz-i-janaza* for those killed yesterday—about 20 at least. About 200 were injured.

Amina said that the morale of the men and women was remarkable. They showed exemplary courage and determination.

Today's *Nawa-i-Waqt* said that Shirin, my daughter, was leading a women's procession in London today. It appears that the Asghar Khan family is fully involved.

Monday, 11 April 1977, Kot Lakhpat jail, Lahore

Mian Sahib, Khurshid and Hamid Sarfaraz went to the High Court. Mian Sahib told the judges that I want to explain my point of view personally as to whether or not I wish a lawyer to defend me. The court did not decide. Asked Mian Sahib to read out my statement in court tomorrow or alternatively hand it over to the court in which I have declined to defend myself. A magistrate came to inform us that 25 April had been fixed as the date for hearing of our case. Mujeebur

Rehman Shami shouted at him and told him to get out. Since we were locked in, the magistrate was not beaten up.

Tuesday, 12 April 1977, Kot Lakhpat jail, Lahore

Amina and Ali came. Ali had been released yesterday on bail. A policeman had aimed a rifle at him and was about to fire on 9 April when he was running away to avoid arrest. Fortunately he stood still and the policeman brought down his rifle. He refused to come out of the police station when he was being released but since his bail was granted he was told that he would be taken out if he did not leave. They are both going back to Abbottabad tomorrow.

In the High Court, Mian Sahib presented my statement in which I had declined to defend myself. Omar Kasuri came in the evening. Told him to inform BBC that 'Soft Nose' (Dum Dum) bullets had been used by the Rangers and the police in the demonstration on 9 April in Lahore. Nawabzada Nasrullah Khan left today to meet Mufti Mahmud in Haripur.

Wednesday, 13 April 1977, Kot Lakhpat jail, Lahore

BBC in its 06:10 broadcast said that the situation in Pakistan had deteriorated and the movement had spread widely. It said that there was a rift within the PPP and some of its members were likely to revolt. It said that Bhutto was likely to take some initiative within the next few days.

Dr Ijaz Qureshi decided to join Tehrik-i-Istiqlal today. He is in the next door cell in jail and will make an announcement when he is released, which could be tomorrow.

Thursday, 14 April 1977, Kot Lakhpat jail, Lahore

Dr Ijaz Hussain Qureshi, our jail mate, sent out his statement to join Tehrik-i-Istiqlal today. Court forbade publication of my statement made to the court day before yesterday. BBC broadcast Bhutto's interview. Khurshid feels that he is ready to quit. I did not agree. More sacrifices are necessary. BBC also broadcast Rahim Khan's resignation from ambassadorship in Spain. Sardar Ahmad Ali (PPP MNA from Kasur) resigned his seat in the National Assembly. More violence all over the country. Mubashir Hasan and Hafeez Kardar also announced their resignations from the PPP.

Friday, 15 April 1977, Kot Lakhpat jail, Lahore

Protest demonstrations on a large scale all over the country. PPP workers (or FSF in civilian clothes) attacked PNA demonstrators in Lahore and a few other places. At Lahore a cinema house belonging to a PPP man was burnt when the crowd was fired upon from the roof of the cinema. Later the crowd was fired upon from the top of a PPP office. People set the building on fire and one person climbed on to the roof from where the crowd was being fired upon. Bare-handed and with only a dagger, he stabbed the person using a sten gun and threw him on to the road below. The whole episode was a remarkable demonstration of courage of the highest order. The PNA crowd was completely unarmed and the PPP people armed with sten guns. In the face of heavy fire the public persisted in attacking the building. Over 100 were injured with bullet wounds and five were killed.

Lieutenant General Gul Hassan, our ambassador in Greece, resigned. Bhutto called on Maulana Maudoodi at the latter's residence today. Maulana issued a statement later that he had told Bhutto that he must go. The PNA council reiterated our demand for Bhutto's resignation.

Saturday, 16 April 1977, Kot Lakhpat jail, Lahore

Sardar Sikandar Hayat, Anwar Ali Noon, Zakir Quraishi and Balakh Sher Mazari and two other PPP MNAs called on Bhutto to resign.

Bhutto is addressing a press conference tomorrow. Omar Kasuri called. Voice of America and BBC reported Bhutto's position to be difficult.

Sunday, 17 April 1977, Kot Lakhpat jail, Lahore

Heard Bhutto's nauseating speech and saw him on TV. It appears that he has no desire to leave as yet. He announced banning of drinking, night clubs and invited the ulema of the PNA to join his advisory council for the implementation of the *shariat* in Pakistan. He wants to put all top PNA leaders into one jail, probably Kot Lakhpat, to 'facilitate discussions'.

Monday, 18 April 1977, Kot Lakhpat jail, Lahore

Heard that PNA leaders are probably being collected at Sihala near Rawalpindi. Shaukat Hayat, who had been expelled from PPP yesterday, Abdullah Rokri and Balakh Sher Mazari resigned their membership of the National Assembly.

Radio Pakistan reported that Amina led a procession in Peshawar and it ended peacefully.

Tuesday, 19 April 1977, Kot Lakhpat jail, Lahore

News of firing by PPP workers on PNA processions at Hyderabad and Faisalabad. Five killed in Hyderabad and three in Faisalabad. PPP took out a 10,000 strong procession in Lahore. Men were armed and fired at a bank. One boy was killed. The PNA also took out two processions, which were larger. Similar demonstrations in other cities. Two leftist labour unions (BBC described them as communist) took part in the PNA demonstration. Twenty-five unions including the Karachi shipyard and railway, have called for a nationwide strike starting tomorrow.

Wednesday, 20 April 1977, Kot Lakhpat jail, Lahore

Mujeeb Shami, Hamid Sarfaraz and Khurshid left. High Court ordered release of every one without asking for bail but a personal bond of Rs1000. Mian Mahmud Ali and I did not sign the bond and stayed on. Amina was to take out a procession in Rawalpindi today. The 20:00 Radio Pakistan news bulletin reported that the procession had been baton charged and tear gassed. A few shops had been burnt. Sent her a message through Khurshid Kasuri not to go to Karachi because of PIA strike and possibility of getting stuck there. Heard that a bomb had been thrown into the car of a Lahore PPP MPA. Large scale disturbances all over the country. Labour unions have called for countrywide strike of vital unions and have said that strike will continue until Bhutto resigns. PNA has called for complete strike on Friday, 22nd.

Thursday, 21 April 1977, Kot Lakhpat jail, Lahore

Allama Iqbal's 39th death anniversary. Little did he know that Lahore will be aflame within 40 years of his death. But if he stood for a revolution in people's thinking, that revolution appears to have occurred and decadent vested interests should disappear. The women's role in this movement will inevitably bring them forward as partners in our national life. The police should never again be the same offensive machine that it has been for over a hundred years and the poor man should get his rights more than ever before. The people's voice should in future be heard and rigging of elections should no more be easy. But more sacrifices are required. The goal is visible but we have not reached there as yet.

Voice of America and BBC announced the complete paralysis of communications in Pakistan. Karachi port, airport and railways are at a standstill. One train driver refused to stop the train when people had lain down on the track. Two men were run over and killed and many wounded. The angry crowd burnt the train. Looting and burning of buildings in Karachi. Thirteen people killed and hundreds wounded in Karachi. No traffic on roads. Not even cycles were allowed to move. Foreign airlines are bypassing Karachi. This is the beginning of the end for Bhutto. But he is so callous and so obsessed with his self-importance that he will try some more tricks before he leaves.

Tikka Khan is being brought into the Senate and will probably be sworn in as the senior minister. When pushed to the corner—which he will be in a few days—Bhutto may well hand over to Tikka in the hope that he is thus given the protection that he needs.

Curfew was ordered in Karachi early in the morning. Papers reported that Mufti Mahmud had been moved to Sihala against the protest of Haripur jail inmates.

Radio Pakistan announced later (at 20:00) that martial law has been declared in Karachi, Hyderabad and Lahore. It appears that Bhutto's PPP which had been armed and brought out a few days ago has failed to suppress the people. Bhutto had announced as recently as the 19th that he was lifting section 144 everywhere.

Saturday, 23 April 1977, Kot Lakhpat jail, Lahore
The Voice of America reported 25 killed yesterday. BBC expressed some doubt about Bhutto's ability to stay in power. Situation yesterday was bad and probably the worst since the beginning of the movement.

Sunday, 24 April 1977, Kot Lakhpat jail, Lahore
Nawabzada Nasrullah Khan, Wazir Ali, Jan Mohammad Abbasi, M. Anwar, Allama Zaheer and S.M. Zafar were arrested last night and brought to Kot Lakhpat. Earlier they (PNA) had made a statement

calling the imposition of martial law 'high treason' and had decided to send teams to call on Ziaul Haq (chief of army staff) and the martial law administrators at Karachi, Hyderabad, and Lahore. They had said that the PNA would not rest until the present illegal government is overthrown. It was a very well worded statement.

One boy, who was riding a scooter and showed the 'V' sign, was shot by the army in Lahore. Decided to write a letter to the armed forces. Curfew also imposed in Sialkot and Bahawalnagar (BBC). Begum Wali Khan and Bashir Bilore were arrested.

Censorship was imposed from today. Radio Pakistan had reverted to its old role (of lies and no news) and with press censorship in operation, the only source of news is the foreign radio. It appears that the army (at least its high command) is being used in full support of Bhutto. *Daily Telegraph* and *Guardian*, two English papers which had been supporting Bhutto, wrote in their editorials of yesterday that Bhutto's political career seemed to have ended and suggested that he should go.

Wednesday, 27 April 1977, Kot Lakhpat jail, Lahore, Sihala
Was woken up at 23:00 last night and was told that Pir of Pagara wanted to speak to me on the telephone from Islamabad. Went to the prison superintendent's office and spoke to Pir Pagara. He conveyed Mufti Mahmud's message asking me to come to Sihala where all other opposition party heads had been assembled. Left at 01:30 by car with police escort. Arrived at 05:30. Nasim Wali Khan, Sherbaz Mazari and Maulana Noorani are lodged in a hut along with me and the others are in another nearby hut. Pir Pagara came about midday and had a discussion which continued till the evening. A pleasant change after Kot Lakhpat. Decided to ask the government to send Sardar Abdul Qayyum Khan of Azad Kashmir as well as Mian Kasuri, M. Anwar, S.M. Zafar and Zahurul Haq—all barristers—here.

Thursday, 28 April 1977, Sihala
Saudi ambassador called with a message from King Khalid that efforts should be made for a settlement. Told him that we would do everything which is in the interest of the country and thanked him for the king's interest.

Sardar Qayyum arrived from Palandri. Large scale arrests of workers in and around Rawalpindi, to forestall the much publicised 'long march' on the 30th.

Bhutto addressed the joint session of parliament. Accused the United States of financing the PNA. Also made derogatory remarks about United Kingdom, West Germany and Egypt. He appears to be desperate.

Friday, 29 April 1977, Sihala
Foreign Minister of United Arab Emirates called with a similar message from the Sheikh of Abu Dhabi, head of the United Arab Emirates, as we had received from King Khalid.

Finalised a press statement in reply to Bhutto's speech of yesterday and gave it to Pir Pagara—who visits us daily—to read it out to the press. Also finalised our demands for Bhutto. However, I do not hold out much hope of a settlement.

Saturday, 30 April 1977, Sihala
The Pir of Pagara's much publicised 'long march' to Bhutto's residence in Rawalpindi did not materialise. Many people had reached Rawalpindi in spite of severe restrictions *en route*. Buses and cars were stopped and searched. Train services disrupted and Rawalpindi looked like an occupied city. Some clashes. Baton charge and tear gassing of processions. The Pir of Pagara was at the Intercontinental Hotel—hardly the place to launch his 'assault' on the prime minister's residence. He was confined to his room where Bhutto called on him. Amina addressed the women at Raja Mahboob's residence.

Altogether not a day of triumph. Mufti Mahmud who has gangrene in one leg was advised hospitalisation.

Sunday, 1 May 1977, Sihala
Mufti Mahmud went to CMH Rawalpindi. I do not think that he will be able to rejoin us. His condition is serious. A pity. He is a good old soul. Courageous and very useful to the alliance.

Pagara addressed a press conference and created considerable confusion by suggesting that we (the PNA) are willing to give up our demand for Bhutto's resignation. His being outside is proving quite an embarrassment. However, Amina and Ali repaired the damage a bit as their statement was broadcast by BBC and Voice of America quoting me as saying the we were still united in asking for Bhutto's resignation. Ashraf Khan, the Khaksar chief, was arrested yesterday. Begum Wali Khan was sick and a nurse had to be called in to look after her.

Monday, 2 May 1977, Sihala
Saudi ambassador called at our request. Bhutto's letter had arrived a few minutes earlier addressed to Mufti Mahmud asking that we should make some suggestions to break the deadlock. Briefed the Saudi ambassador on the general line of our approach.

Tuesday, 3 May 1977, Sihala
Mufti Mahmud called here from the CMH to inform us about Bhutto's visit. Bhutto had called on Mufti Mahmud at CMH and asked for our proposals to end the political deadlock. Mufti told him about our three main demands, that is, his resignation, renunciation/annulment of the results of the national and provincial elections and the appointment of an impartial election commission. He had also explained that the first was merely a formality as he would be called upon by the president to continue as a caretaker prime minister. Bhutto appeared unwilling to agree to the dissolution of the National Assembly but said that the matter could be discussed. He said that he would send four of his ministers to discuss the problems with us. After discussion with Mufti Mahmud we decided that dissolution of the National Assembly was a fundamental issue on which there could be no compromise. We also did not agree to meet his ministers. Gave Mufti Mahmud the typed copy of the proposals which he would hand over to Bhutto. Decided to wait for 48 hours for his reply before issuing a statement which Nawabzada Nasrullah undertook to prepare which would be issued as a kind of a White Paper on the talks.

Received letters from Mian Kasuri and Hamza expressing anxiety at the Pir of Pagara's role and his press statements which they feel have damaged the movement. Pir Pagara came in the afternoon. He had been under severe criticism by the council of the PNA. Nawabzada Nasrullah advised him to keep his mouth shut, which he and his mouthpiece, Hassan Mahmud, find very difficult to do. The PNA council has elected Sardar Sikandar Hayat Khan as acting vice president and Mian Mahmud Ali Kasuri as acting secretary general in place of Ashraf Khan and Choudhry Rehmat Elahi respectively. The council also decided to defy martial law and Section 144 by observing martyr's day on Friday, 6 May when processions and meetings will be held. Nasrullah Khan and others were very agitated about this and wanted to direct the council not to defy martial law. I opposed this and said that since we were in jail we were in no position to offer advice to the council and that they were fully competent to take such decisions. Mian Tufail and Nawabzada Nasrullah Khan, Prof. Ghafoor and Sardar Abdul Qayyum thought that Friday's demonstration would damage our cause.

Wednesday, 4 May 1977, Sihala

Newspapers reported the Pir of Pagara as having said that there were 50 per cent chances of our negotiations with the government succeeding. I told Prof. Ghafoor that the Pir of Pagara had been told yesterday that he must refrain from making any further press statements and that this statement of his has damaged the chances of success of the Friday demonstration. I said that if the Pir of Pagara cannot be controlled I would feel free to issue statements explaining the correct position and my point of view.

Mufti Mahmud called from CMH. He has given our demands to Bhutto's military secretary who had called on him at his request. Prepared a statement on foreign policy for Pagara to issue tomorrow on our behalf. Nasrullah Khan finalised another statement giving the history of our negotiations to be issued on Friday, 6 May.

Thursday, 5 May 1977, Sihala

Mufti Mahmud called. He told us of his meeting with Qaddafi's foreign minister who had pleaded with Mufti Mahmud as if he was Bhutto's ambassador. It is odd how Arab rulers who have no democracy in their own country are advising us to settle an issue which springs from the denial of democracy. The Libyan foreign minister's statement to the press today was highly objectionable in which he stated his view that an 'international conspiracy' existed, and said that the USA was collaborating with the PNA. My reaction was that we should take a clear and strong line against such agents of Bhutto who were being sent to us to influence public opinion against us. The papers today and our radio prominently repeated a ministry of defence statement attacking my letter to defence services officers. Just as well because it will now certainly reach every officer. Decided to wait till the evening and issue our White Paper on negotiations tomorrow. My statement on foreign relations (jointly agreed) is being issued by Pir of Pagara today.

Received some magazines and a note from Amina who is still in Rawalpindi and is taking part in a demonstration tomorrow. BBC announced the arrest of Mian Mahmud Ali Kasuri and 300 workers in the PNA office at Lahore. Curfew has been re-imposed in Karachi, Hyderabad, and Lahore to deal with the demonstration planned for tomorrow.

Friday, 6 May 1977, Sihala
Newspapers reported the PNAs proposals which had been sent to Bhutto. Demonstrations were held all over Pakistan. BBC announced in its evening bulletin that Amina had been arrested by the police at Rawalpindi whilst leading a women's demonstration. In Lahore three men were shot by the army whilst defying the curfew. Two were shot in Hyderabad. Many were injured.

Saturday, 7 May 1977, Sihala
No news of Amina all day but was told by Sardar Abdul Qayyum Khan's man (who brings his dinner every day) that she had been confined at Colonel Tassadaq's house for seven days.

Sunday, 8 May 1977, Sihala
Read in the newspapers that Amina has been externed from Rawalpindi—and interned in Abbottabad—for a month. She left for Abbottabad last night. Mufti Sahib and the Pir of Pagara called. Bhutto addressed a press conference in Lahore and complained that our list of demands was very lengthy. Earlier Saudi Arabian ambassador called. Did some plain speaking to him.

Large scale arrests of workers all over the country yesterday. Ziae has also been arrested.

Monday, 9 May 1977, Sihala
Ali came. Amina has been interned for a month in the house at Abbottabad. Mufti Mahmud and Pagara called. Maulana Maudoodi

addressed a press conference at Lahore and took a tough line. Bhutto returned to Rawalpindi after a tour of Lahore and Karachi. The PNA (Pagara being the spokesman) said that we would not meet Bhutto's ministers and there could be no negotiations until Bhutto accepted the main demands that is, his resignation and new elections.

Tuesday, 10 May 1977, Sihala
BBC reported firing by police in Mirpurkhas where one person was killed and some injured. Army firing in Lahore where five persons were injured. Pir Pagara arrived at 05:00. He had not been to bed and thought that he would drop in before going to sleep.

Mufti Mahmud returned from CMH (after completing his treatment). He said he had agreed to meet Bhutto at Sihala tomorrow. Held a stormy meeting. Sherbaz, Maulana Noorani, Ashraf Khan (the Khaksar leader) and I felt that Mufti should not meet Bhutto again (he has met him thrice since coming to Sihala) until he agrees to the holding of fresh elections. I also advised him not to hold discussions—which he has been doing—with his military secretary and private secretary. Failed to convince Mufti that it is highly improper that the head of the PNA should hold political negotiations with Bhutto's secretary. Mufti said he would resign if we had no confidence in him. Explained that it was not a question of confidence but the propriety of maintaining the right level. Eventually decided that Mufti would receive Bhutto at Sihala to tell him that our stand was unchanged and no further dialogue can take place until he first announces his willingness to hold fresh elections.

Wednesday, 11 May 1977, Sihala
Defiance of martial law at Lahore yesterday. Police was used for tear-gassing but army was kept back. Also in Hyderabad. Large procession at Sialkot. Army fired in the air. Processions also at Multan. Curfew extended in Karachi.

A woman was beaten to death with rifle butts in Mirpurkhas yesterday. Strike in Karachi and Hyderabad.

Bhutto called on Mufti Mahmud at 21:15 and stayed for an hour-and-a-quarter. All the others were asked to stay together in the yard of our cottage. He did not shift from his position. Still not willing to concede the necessity of holding National Assembly elections. Wanted to discuss all the issues and wanted a 'package' deal. Pir Pagara came earlier and said that Bhutto had met his National Assembly members and indicated that he would agree to re-elections.

Thursday, 12 May 1977, Sihala

Decided that Mufti Mahmud should not meet Bhutto until he agreed with our three demands, that is, resignation, elections, and election commission. I drafted a letter to Bhutto, which we agreed would be signed by Mufti Mahmud and sent today. In this we made it clear that Mufti would not meet him again until he announces agreement with our three demands. Letter was sent to Bhutto in the evening.

The National Assembly discussed an adjournment motion on my letter to chiefs of staff and officers of armed forces. Bhutto and Tikka Khan spoke and Bhutto repeated his statement that legal action was contemplated against me for 'high treason'. Tikka Khan said that a court martial could be held.

Friday, 13 May 1977, Sihala

We learnt early in the morning that no visitors were being allowed to see any one of us today. The PNA had called for the observance of black day all over the country today. Demonstrations, meetings, etc. Bhutto addressed the National Assembly, also on radio and TV. Read out Mufti's letter, which I had drafted (it sounded good). He then rejected our demands and announced that he would hold a referendum to ask whether people wanted him to stay as prime minister or not. Since he has no representative character and the National Assembly, whose parliamentary leader he is, is a rigged assembly he has no right to seek a vote by referendum. Bhutto did not deny the report in the Gujrati *Millat* of Karachi of 6 May in which the chief election commissioner had admitted that rigging had been on such a vast scale that looking into individual cases was not the remedy. He had said only holding general elections again would put things right.

Was woken up at 22:30 and told that the 'party was off', and we were being dispatched back to prison. Said our goodbyes. I was the first to leave in a police jeep at 11:35. Was told that I was being taken to Lahore but learnt on the way that our destination was Sahiwal. Maulana Noorani, Prof. Ghafoor and Mufti Mahmud were to leave in the morning. The first two probably by air to Karachi and Mufti

Mahmud probably via Bhutto's house to Haripur. Sherbaz complained of a backache—a chronic slipped disc—and did not relish a jeep ride to, he had no idea, where. Begum Nasim Wali Khan, we suggested, should leave in the morning with Mufti Mahmud as her chaperone. I slept for about two hours on the way.

Saturday, 14 May 1977, Sahiwal prison
Arrived at Sahiwal at 07:00. Ironically I was lodged where Bhutto had been in 1968. I had visited him here at his request. Malik Qasim and Zahid Sarfaraz of Muslim League are also here in a barrack. There were about 1,200 political prisoners in this jail but they have, I was told, since left on bail and only 12 remained.

Heard on BBC that demonstrations had been held in most cities. Three persons have been killed by army firing in Karachi and two by the police in Multan. Rumours have it, that three army brigadiers have resigned in Lahore and that a general in Lahore had also resigned. However, Bhutto has denied these rumours.

Sunday, 15 May 1977, Sahiwal
Sahiwal jail was built in 1873 and is spread over 332 acres. It is one of the oldest jails in the country. The room where I am lodged is a one room cottage with a verandah on all four sides. It has European type WC and wash basin in an adjoining bathroom. The compound is approximately 2,000 square yards. Prince Mamoon-ur-Rashid Abbasi of Bahawalpur who was a prisoner here a few years ago has planted a number of trees and flowering bushes in the compound. Some of the political prisoners who have lived in the room, I am in, have been Khan Abdul Ghaffar Khan, Bizenjo, Ataullah Mengal, Khan Bakhsh Marri, Mujibur Rehman and Zulfikar Ali Bhutto. I am trying to find out about others, particularly during the British days. The roof of the cottage is sloping and is made of old Bangalore tiles. Old large red bricks have been used on the verandah floor. There are three small cells in the compound for convicts or *mushakkatis* who stay the night here. I have only one person working for me, Rafi Rafique, an ex-army *jawan* undergoing a one year sentence for absence without leave. Mercifully he can cook quite well. I am trying to get another man—a Pushtun—to keep up my Pushto.

There was trouble in Multan again yesterday and four more persons have been killed. The city has been handed over to the army and a curfew imposed.

Monday, 16 May 1977, Sahiwal

Heard on BBC's 05:00 international service that Amina had been moved from our house to some other place. Could have been taken to stay with Begum Wali Khan at Khanpur. The Pir of Pagara has been placed under house arrest at Islamabad but Mufti Sahib is still at Sihala. Yesterday's *Nawa-i-Waqt* reported my shifting to Sahiwal, Mian Tufail to Bahawalpur, Nasrullah Khan to Mianwali, Ashraf Khan to Rawalpindi jail, Maulana Abbasi to Kot Lakhpat, Maulana Noorani and Prof. Ghafoor initially to Karachi and Begum Wali Khan to Hazara. Sherbaz was not mentioned. Also said that Sardar Abdul Qayyum Khan had been shifted to Rawalpindi but they probably meant Pulandri in Azad Kashmir.

Read in the *Nawa-i-Waqt* in the evening that Amina had been moved to Dadar rest house. No further details. Superintendent jail, Khawaja Nazir Ahmed, who had been away at Lahore, called. Told him that I wanted to see my lawyers. Wrote a letter to M. Anwar and to Farooq to be sent through the jail authorities early tomorrow after clearance by censor. These letters are on a government form and the space given only allows half a dozen lines. I am being kept strictly in isolation and not even the normal jail staff is allowed to meet me. Chaudhry Munir Ahmad, an assistant superintendent, is the only person who normally sees me. Rafi Rafique is my only companion but the jail superintendent said he will give me another person, as the work—cooking, washing of clothes, scrubbing of floors and dusting— is too much for one man. Rafi Rafique is from Abdul Hakim near Talamba in Multan district and appears a good type.

Tuesday, 17 May 1977, Sahiwal

Dispatched the letters to M. Anwar and Farooq. BBC reported three persons killed in Alipur (Multan district) and baton charge on a procession in Peshawar. Disturbances in Sindh in protest against the Pir of Pagara's arrest.

National Assembly passed a bill yesterday for the proposed referendums. National Assembly also passed a bill regularising the imposition of martial law, thus rendering infructurous cases pending in the high courts of Sindh and Lahore against imposition of martial law. Decision and punishments awarded by martial law authorities cannot now be challenged in any court of law.

Wednesday, 18 May 1977, Sahiwal

BBC's early morning news mentioned disturbances in Sahiwal and my being in jail here. Also mentioned that Bhutto had been in this jail too in 1968. BBC also said that Justice Sajjad Ahmad Jan had confirmed his statement which appeared in *Millat* of 6 May that rigging had been so extensive—he cited the case of half of the National Assembly seats—that another general election was the only remedy.

Martial law continues in Karachi, Hyderabad, and Lahore but curfew has been relaxed in Karachi and Hyderabad and lifted in Lahore. Some more trouble in Multan where curfew is still in force. Trouble also in Khanpur. *Nawa-i-Waqt* of today reported that Nawabzada Nasrullah Khan had been brought back to Sihala where Mufti Mahmud is still lodged and that the Pir of Pagara and Mufti Mahmud had had a meeting with the Kuwaiti foreign minister who had come to help resolve the differences. It appears that negotiations are again to be resumed. Could mean a return to Sihala but let us wait and see.

Sent another communication to the High Court asking for my lawyers to visit me. Was told by the assistant superintendent that the two letters I had written yesterday to M. Anwar and Farooq have been sent by Sahiwal CID to AIG, CID at Lahore for clearance and censoring. These will then be returned to Sahiwal jail for posting to Lahore. Remarkable red tape. No wonder people try to smuggle their letters instead of adopting the correct channels.

Thursday, 19 May 1977, Sahiwal

BBC news suggested that talks were being resumed at Sihala with Mufti Mahmud. Newspapers reported that Prof. Ghafoor was also being brought there. The Pir of Pagara had been released and had issued a strong statement against Bhutto calling for the observance of a 'black day', tomorrow, which is a Friday, throughout the country. Martial law authorities also announced re-imposition of curfew in cities under martial law as a counter move. Newspapers also reported that Sherbaz Khan Mazari is continuing his hunger strike at Mianwali jail for the fifth day.

Superintendent jail called. Told me that I could sleep out in the yard if I wished but could not meet any one in jail nor could any one else be allowed to stay with me. The only person who visits me for taking of orders for rations is Chaudhry Munir, the assistant superintendent. He said that Amina was alone at Dadar with some women police in addition to the normal police force.

I completed two months in jail yesterday (Kot Lakhpat, Sihala, and Sahiwal).

Saturday, 21 May 1977, Sahiwal
Sardar Abdul Qayyum Khan came about midday, loaded with fruits, biscuits, etc. A very welcome visit as I had not seen any outsider since the 14th. Told me about Bhutto's meeting with Mufti Mahmud, Nasrullah Khan, and himself. Bhutto has given an assurance—for whatever it is worth—that he will agree to re-elections for the National Assembly but we must first sit round a table for discussions. Said that he wanted to make a 'package deal' and sort everything out in three or four days. Gave him my reactions. He left for Lahore from where he will go on to Rawalpindi. Sardar Abdul Qayyum told me of the disgraceful manner in which Maulana Noorani was being kept in a police lock-up at Garhi Khairu near the Sindh-Balochistan border. He had met him at Jacobabad, where he had been brought, and Prof. Ghafoor at Dadu. He had flown in a special government plane from Karachi to Jacobabad and Larkana. Today he had flown from Lahore.

Monday, 23 May 1977, Sahiwal
BBC and VOA reported two 'bombs' having been thrown at Ghulam Hussain of PPP when he was leading a procession yesterday at Mandi Bahahuddin. One is said to have hit his arm. Both did not explode. Twenty people have been arrested. General Sher Ali has been arrested and taken to Sheikhupura. Senator Zahur ul Haq, along with a number of others, has also been detained. Police was also looking for Abu Saeed Enver. It appears that Bhutto is preparing for a second round

of 'talks' with us. This is a *wadera's* (feudal lord) style of negotiations. I am expecting to move tonight or tomorrow.

Tuesday, 24 May 1977, Sahiwal
Pagara has asked for the release of all political prisoners before negotiations are held. Sardar Qayyum is on the second leg of his 'meet the leaders' journey. Will probably complete his travels by tomorrow. BBC said that a reply was expected to be sent to Bhutto by Thursday.

Wednesday, 25 May 1977, Sahiwal
A very hot night. Could not sleep indoors and took my bed out at 02:30. (The jail superintendent has allowed me to sleep outside). Although it was a little cooler outside, the mosquitoes kept me awake.

Thursday, 26 May 1977, Sahiwal
BBC news this morning said that Sardar Qayyum had finished his 'meet the leaders' tour and talks were expected to be started very soon. Bhutto, BBC said, has agreed to holding of elections to National Assembly, but PNA sources are doubtful about the outcome. So am I. No appeal has been issued by PNA central leadership for demonstrations tomorrow.

Saturday, 28 May 1977, Sahiwal
Radio and newspapers suggest that talks are about to start. It appears that I and others, who feel similarly, such as Noorani, Sherbaz, Nasim Wali Khan and Ashraf Khan, are being kept away so that talks can be better 'managed'. It also appears that some of our friends are extra keen to start a dialogue. Interesting though not unexpected.

If we are not moved within the next 24 hours and talks are started without us, the motive would be obvious.

Sunday, 29 May 1977, Sahiwal
Third day without power. No lights, no fans. It is quite hot in this place. Newspapers reported that Sherbaz Mazari was shifted to Faisalabad and is now in Jinnah hospital, Karachi. Shaukat Syed, the physician, should take good care of him.

Power supply was resumed at about 14:00 but went off again at 22:00. Uncomfortable with heat and mosquitoes inside, so took out my bed at about midnight and managed to get some sleep.

Monday, 30 May 1977, Sahiwal
BBC reported that the Pir of Pagara had said in Rawalpindi that I was being ill-treated. I had 'become pale and that my throat was infected'. He said that I was probably being given medicines by the jail doctor which had aggravated my ill health.

Prof. Ghafoor Ahmed is reported by the newspapers to have reached Sihala. Mushir is reported to have had a heart attack and has been moved to Jinnah hospital. Talks are being held on Friday, 3 June at Rawalpindi. Each side is being represented by three persons.

Tuesday, 31 May 1977, Sahiwal
More newspapers report of my 'illness'. Dr Akhtar and Dr Iftikhar, both professors of medicine, were asked by the High Court to medically examine me. They came about 11:30. Stayed for about half-an-hour. Power supply was resumed before the doctors arrived and put off after they left.

Electricity again remained off most of the day from 08:00-11:00 and 14:00-18:00. It appears that this is being done to harass me as a matter of policy. Slept outside. Electricity in the rest of the jail is functioning.

Wednesday, 1 June 1977, Sahiwal
BBC reported that Amina had been released yesterday and that Dr Akhtar had visited me here. Today's papers make it clear that electricity is being cut off in other jails also to harass political prisoners. Prisoners in Faisalabad jail are on hunger strike—Bhutto's way of creating the climate for negotiations which are starting on Friday, 3 June.

Electricity remained off the whole day. Heard on the radio in the evening that Mian Tufail Mohammad and Jan Mohammad Abbasi of Jamaat-i-Islami had been released though the three musketeers (Maulana Mufti Mahmud, Nawabzada Nasrullah and Prof. Ghafoor Ahmed) are still in detention in Sihala. PNA has decided to observe protest day tomorrow and a day of 'prayer' on Friday, 3 June. Electricity remained off the whole day.

Thursday, 2 June 1977, Sahiwal

The BBC's morning news said that the government had accused Jamaat-i-Islami of terrorist activities. Farooq Maudoodi, Maulana's son, is accused of organising these activities.

Mufti Mahmud, Nasrullah Khan and Prof. Ghafoor Ahmed were released today. Lahore High Court in its judgment today declared martial law in Lahore—unconstitutional—and the seventh amendment to the constitution ultra vires. Government is appealing to the Supreme Court.

Friday, 3 June 1977, Sahiwal

Malik Qasim was released from Sahiwal jail early this morning. The High Court sent M. Anwar, the assistant advocate general and a bailiff of the court, to see me. The High Court was not satisfied with the report of the doctors and felt that they had not examined me satisfactorily. They asked me whether I wished to go to a hospital and saw my living conditions. I told them that I did not wish to go to a hospital but would prefer to be transferred to Kot Lakhpat jail.

Saturday, 4 June 1977, Sahiwal, Rawalpindi

Heard on BBC at 22:00 last night that I had been released. Was also told this by the jail superintendent, a short while later. He also said that the police had come to take me to Rawalpindi. I told him that since I had been released I would not go with the police. Assistant superintendent jail came three or four times between 23:00 and 01:00 to try to get me to leave. Police force of about 40 men under Sub Inspector Sher Mohammad came into my compound at about 01:15 and tried to force me to leave. I refused and told them to 'get out'. They came again at 02:30 when I had just gone to sleep and threw me out by upturning the bed. I was forced to leave at 04:00 and driven in a car direct to Rawalpindi. Arrived at 11:30 in my night pyjamas, at the party office.

Sunday, 5 June 1977, Rawalpindi

A large number of our workers called. PNA leaders had a meeting at Islamabad. Sherbaz and Noorani had not arrived from Karachi so decided to meet again tomorrow.

Monday, 6 June 1977, Rawalpindi

A large number of persons called including Ahmad Jan, MNA elect from Lakki (Bannu), Ghulam Dastgir of Gujranwala and our workers from Sargodha and other places. Addressed women workers at Chaudhry Siddiq's. Attended a reception by Sardar Abdul Qayyum Khan. PNA leaders had a meeting and we were told about discussions of our team with Bhutto. Considered his two proposals and decided to ask for 're-election' rather than 're-polling'.

Thursday, 9 June 1977, Rawalpindi

Sardar Ali called with a message from Abu Saeed Enver to tell me that he had been informed by a reliable person in government intelligence service that I had been administered two drops of mercury and Sherbaz Mazari, Malik Qasim and Mian Tufail Mohammad one drop each, whilst in prison presumably between 14 May and 4 June (when I was in Sahiwal). He said that this was a slow poison which acted in about six months by attacking the bones. He said that he had contacted the Hamdard Dawakhana which had advised sugar cane juice and milk 'lassi' as an antidote. I asked Syed Inayat Ali Shah to consult some good doctors in Lahore and let me know. If this has been done—and I would not put it beyond Bhutto, it could have been done through the milk which I was supplied—then the other two persons, the *mushakkatis*, would also be affected. One was Abdur Rehman an ex-serviceman from Lachi in Kohat district and the other Rafi Rafique, also an ex-serviceman from Abdul Hakim near Talamba in Multan district. I am sure both had some milk though not in the quantity that I took every day, about two full glasses.

Had lunch with Prince Aurangzeb at Islamabad. Aurangzeb had joined us recently and as a consequence spent two months in Peshawar jail.

Saturday, 11 June 1977, Rawalpindi

Called on the parents of two boys who had been killed during the movement. Shaukat came from Lahore and informed me that if mercury has been taken in any form, side effects would appear within seven days. The bowels are affected and gripping pain and convulsions occur. He had consulted some eminent doctors.

Monday, 13 June 1977, Abbottabad, Rawalpindi
Left Abbottabad at 07:45. Dropped Amina at Rawalpindi and attended PNA meeting at Islamabad. Mufti informed us of his discussions with Bhutto. He was not willing to agree to our share in government in the case of elections or to holding elections on 14 August.

Tuesday, 14 June 1977, Rawalpindi
PNA meeting at Islamabad, at 09:00. Decided to maintain our stand of elections on 14 August with all necessary safeguards. Mufti told us about his evening talks with Bhutto and we agreed to meet in the morning. He did not agree to August elections. Bhutto has called a meeting of chiefs of staff tomorrow.

Wednesday, 15 June 1977, Rawalpindi
PNA meeting at Islamabad considered Bhutto's proposal for a council of implementation to supervise the implementation of the accord with elections in October. Decided to insist on August elections.

Government announced that accord had been reached. Met after dinner and I expressed surprise that this announcement should have been made when we had agreed in the morning that announcement would only be made when the details have been worked out and the document signed. I addressed a press conference and explained that only a verbal agreement on broad points had been reached and many hazards lay ahead in the interpretation of the understanding on various important issues. I was not very hopeful of an agreement being reached because of the evidence of foul play on the part of the government even during the period of negotiations, of large scale issue of arms licenses and arrests of our workers.

Friday, 17 June 1977, Rawalpindi
Another meeting—a stormy session of PNA at Islamabad. Mian Mahmud Ali Kasuri said that the PNA negotiations team had been formed by Bhutto and this upset Nawabzada Nasrullah, Prof. Ghafoor and Sardar Qayyum. Smoothed the situation with difficulty.

Wednesday, 22 June 1977, Rawalpindi
Amina left for Karachi with Ali. She was given a very good reception at the airport. PNA meeting at Islamabad. Finalised the draft for submission to the six men committee.

Osman, who had gone to Abbottabad yesterday, returned late at night. Spoke to Amina in the morning. She is quite excited about her reception in Karachi and is busy addressing meetings there. Met in the evening and finalised the draft. Nasrullah Khan did his best to soften it down. I feel that if left alone he would agree with Bhutto's conditions for the agreement. All, except Maulana Noorani and I, appear to be agreeable to any kind of settlement. Jamaat-i-Islami is moderate in its approach and the Muslim League is following a hard line for public consumption but adopts a soft line in our discussions. Ashraf Khan of the Khaksars appears now to be in agreement with Nasrullah Khan. Sardar Abdul Qayyum Khan is also soft in his approach. Mufti Mahmud's thinking is close to Nasrullah Khan's.

Thursday, 23 June 1977, Rawalpindi

Bhutto returned from his six-day tour of Libya, Saudi Arabia, Kuwait, Abu Dhabi, Iran and Afghanistan. Appears that he had undertaken the tour in order to: (a) Impress public opinion in Pakistan with a warm reception by Arab countries. (b) To mend his fences with the Shah of Iran who is annoyed with him for having talked of a threat to Pakistan from Iran and his leaning towards the Soviet Union. (c) To collect some funds from his 'bankers'.

I am sick of receptions and dinners and am longing to get away from this life of chatter and entertainment but that appears impossible. Only Bhutto can help by putting me back in jail.

Nasrullah Khan told us of his meeting with Bhutto earlier in the evening. Nothing much had transpired except that the draft had been handed over to him.

Saturday, 25 June 1977, Nathiagali

Osman telephoned Prof. Ghafoor and was told that they are meeting Bhutto at 10:30 this morning. Called on M. Anwar and also met Mian Arshad, one time foreign secretary. Received a telephonic message from Mufti Mahmud that I should come down for a meeting to consider the government's draft. Could not reach in time so decided to go tomorrow.

Khurshid, Chandi Begum (Abida Hussain) and Khurshid's wife along with Chandi Begum's husband, Fakhr lmam, called.

Sunday, 26 June 1977, Nathiagali, Rawalpindi

Attended a PNA meeting. All, except Sherbaz and Begum Nasim Wali Khan, were present. Decided to stick to our draft and finalised it with a few minor changes. Agreed to make this our last position.

Monday, 27 June 1977, Rawalpindi

PNA meeting at Chaudhry Zahur Elahi's house at 11:00. Had another look at the draft. Maulana Noorani had a major row with Prof. Ghafoor, whose nerves are on edge. It appears that the pressure of work is too much for him. Decided to send a covering letter with the draft tomorrow.

Dinner by Jamiat Ahle-Hadith at the Press Club. Went over to brief Begum Wali Khan, who had arrived late from Lahore, about our morning discussions.

Z.U. Khan of daily *Jang* telephoned to say that Hafeez Pirzada had issued a statement to say that the government would not receive our draft if we insisted that this was not negotiable.

Tuesday, 28 June 1977, Rawalpindi

Party heads discussed Bhutto's press conference and decided, at Prof. Ghafoor's insistence and Nasrullah Khan's advocacy, to drop the idea of sending the letter that Wazir Ali had drafted yesterday and which had been approved by the council.

Bhutto had spoken to Mufti Mahmud today and had agreed that our latest draft should be handed over by Prof. Ghafoor to Hafeez Pirzada tomorrow.

Wednesday, 29 June 1977, Rawalpindi

PNA meeting at Islamabad. Prof. Ghafoor handed over the final draft to Pirzada. Lunched with Wazir Ali and Maulana Noorani at Wazir Ali's. Bhutto asked to meet Mufti Mahmud and they met alone for an hour. He asked for one more day to consider our draft. Mufti agreed and it was decided that final meeting of the two teams would take place on Friday, 1 July. Prof. Ghafoor is meeting Pirzada again tomorrow morning to clarify points in the draft.

Friday, 1 July 1977, Abbottabad, Rawalpindi

Left for Rawalpindi at 16:00 pm. Mufti Mahmud informed us that he was having another meeting with Bhutto at 20:00 and had, therefore, postponed our meeting scheduled for 18:00. In his meeting with Bhutto earlier in the day the services chiefs had briefed Mufti Mahmud on Balochistan and also Azad Kashmir. The talk was mainly political. Surprising that Mufti should have listened to this after a clear agreement in our council that no briefings by Services chiefs or their representatives would be received. Bhutto had probably arranged this to impress PNA that Bhutto had the support of service chiefs.

Saturday, 2 July 1977, Rawalpindi

Mufti's meeting with Bhutto ended at 06:30 when both sides announced having reached an accord. This is the second such announcement.

Called on Prof. Ghafoor to find out details of agreement reached between our team and Bhutto. Mazari and Nasim Wali Khan also came there.

PNA council met at Choudhry Arshad's at Islamabad where Nawabzada Nasrullah Khan hosted a dinner. Mian Mahmud Ali Kasuri and Khalid Ishaque expressed their views on the changes proposed by Bhutto in the draft and agreed that the proposals could not be accepted without considerably weakening our position and enhancing Bhutto's capacity to create mischief and again rig the election. The main point being that the accord should be given constitutional status. Agreed to meet again next day. Maulana Noorani arrived from Karachi and joined us in the deliberations at 22:00.

Saturday, 3 July 1977, Rawalpindi

Met in the morning at Choudhry Arshad's at Islamabad and resumed discussion of Bhutto's proposals. Lawyers had studied the proposals overnight and gave their considered views on the same lines as yesterday. Decided to continue our discussions until we agreed on a line to be adopted. Broke for lunch and met again at 18:00. Decided that Bhutto's proposals could not be accepted and I was asked to address the press which had assembled. This briefing was in place of Prof. Ghafoor, the secretary general, who usually briefs the press.

This created the erroneous impression that a rift had occurred in the PNA and that Prof. Ghafoor had resigned. After our meeting and before others left, Sardar Abdul Qayyum Khan had to leave for another engagement as also Sherbaz Mazari and Begum Wali Khan giving strength to the impression that there had been a major row in the meeting. Understood later that this incorrect report was conveyed to Bhutto within a few minutes by intelligence and this conditioned his reaction and led to his addressing a press conference shortly after midnight in which he announced that the talks had virtually broken down and that he could offer no more conditions to the PNA. Before this press conference at about 21:30 Mufti Mahmud, Nawabzada Nasrullah Khan and Prof. Ghafoor went to see Bhutto to convey to him the rejection by the PNA council of his proposals. Prof. Ghafoor had to be pushed to go. He was refusing to go as he felt that our stand was a volte-face from the commitment the team had already made. Mufti Mahmud stayed with Bhutto for an hour.

Sunday, 4 July 1977, Rawalpindi

Met at Colonel Tassaddaq's in the morning to consider Bhutto's proposals. Since Bhutto had said that he would give his reactions to the PNA council's decision, we decided to meet again after Sardar Abdul Qayyum Khan's dinner.

Bhutto had addressed a press conference at 13:30 today after his meeting with our team followed by a cabinet meeting.

Had dinner at Sardar Abdul Qayyum's and met after dinner. Since no reply had been received from Bhutto, opinion was sharply divided on our course of action. Maulana Noorani and I felt that we should now break off talks and re-launch our movement. Sherbaz Mazari agreed with us and Pir Pagara gave us qualified support. Others felt that we should take advantage of whatever concessions Bhutto was willing to give and sign the accord. Mian Tufail Mohammad and Prof. Ghafoor represented the extreme position that the Jamaat-i-Islami could not take part in any movement. I informed the council that I would not attend their deliberations when they decided to meet again tomorrow by when they hoped they would have received Bhutto's reply. Learnt at midnight that Bhutto had addressed a press conference at 23:30, his second that day, in which he had resiled from his earlier stand not to negotiate with us. He had now said that he was willing to meet our team tomorrow, 5 July.

Monday, 5 July 1977, Rawalpindi, Murree

Went to bed at 01:30 and was woken up by Osman at 02:00 and informed that the army had surrounded the house and an army officer had come to take me away. Saw the army captain, Kafait, the son of Haji Yousaf Khan of Mardan, an NDP elected MNA. A polite young man, he took me, luggage and all, to the Corp HQs officers mess at Chaklala. Found Prof. Ghafoor already there as also Rao Rashid, an IG of police, who is the head of DIB or in charge of the prime minister's security. Mufti Mahmud, Nasrullah Khan, Maulana Noorani and Vaqar Ahmed, cabinet secretary, arrived shortly later. Were billetted in single officers' quarters with Maulana Kausar Niazi, Hafeez Pirzada, Tikka Khan, Masud Mahmud of FSF and half a dozen other federal ministers lodged in rooms opposite us. Was told that army had taken over and Bhutto had been removed. An inevitable end to an inglorious five-and-a-half years of a power-hungry, mad man in office.

Left the corp officers' mess for Punjab House Murree at 21:00. Were received on arrival by army station commander and AC Murree. Punjab House, where the Punjab governor and chief minister usually live when they visit Murree, is a pleasant change after Sahiwal and Kot Lakhpat. Earlier General Ziaul Haq announced his programme after the imposition of martial law. Constitution will not be abrogated though some of its clauses will not be operative for the duration of martial law; Fazl Elahi Chaudhry will stay as president; chairman of joint chiefs of staff and the three Services chiefs will assist the president in running the country; national and provincial assemblies have been dissolved; central and provincial governments and governors dismissed; high court chief justices have been appointed governors; election will be in October; political activities will be suspended until further notice; postings made by the previous government will be reviewed; FSF will be re-organised.

Wednesday, 6 July 1977, Murree

Relaxed and chatted all day. Asked Brigadier Dogar (army station commander, Murree) to ask General Ziaul Haq to either come here or send some one to see us as we wished to talk with him about two points: (a) Immediate release of all political prisoners. (b) 'Protective custody' which we were supposed to be in.

Was allowed to use the telephone. Spoke with Amina.

Saturday, 9 July 1977, Murree

Spoke with Amina at Nathiagali on the telephone. She told me that Ali and Osman had gone to Rawalpindi yesterday and would come to Murree in the evening. Ali telephoned later to say that he had completed his formalities and was awaiting his visa which he would try to get today.

Discussed the agenda for our meeting with Ziaul Haq. I managed to get Ali smuggled into my room for half an hour at night to see him before he went off to UK to try to get admission in a polytechnic for architecture. There is virtually no education in architecture in his college in Karachi.

Sunday, 10 July 1977, Murree

General Ziaul Haq was to visit us today but we heard on the radio that he had gone to Karachi for a two day visit.

Heard on the TV of the introduction of stringent martial law orders. Death sentence for resisting police or damage to government property and cutting of hands for theft. BBC commentary by Mark Tully suggested that Ziaul Haq may be having second thoughts about October elections.

Monday, 11 July 1977, Murree

General opinion amongst us, the detenus, was that the martial law orders announced yesterday were far too severe and not consistent with the declared object of allowing normal political activities prior to the elections.

Mufti Mahmud told me yesterday that I could perform a great service to Islam. When I asked him how I could do this, he said that I had very good relations with Maulana Shah Ahmed Noorani and I could help to remove the differences between the Brelvi and Deobandi schools of thought that have divided the Muslims of Pakistan. I told him that I did not know what these differences were and did not feel qualified to undertake this task. He said that the only difference is that the Brelvis believe that the Prophet (PBUH) was 'Noor' (a spirit) whilst the Deobandi maintain that he was human. He said that he would suggest that I should sit down with both of them and listen to their arguments and then give a decision. They both should agree to abide by my judgment, whatever it is. He said that so far as he was concerned, he would agree with my decision and since Maulana Noorani held me in high esteem, he should also do the same. He suggested that I should speak to Maulana Noorani about this and assured me that the Deobandi school of thought would agree to any ruling given by me. He felt that because of the position that Maulana Noorani held amongst his followers, the Brelvis would accept Maulana Noorani's decision and the differences between these two schools of thought would end. This, he said, would be a great service to Islam. I promised to discuss this suggestion with Maulana Noorani. On our daily stroll I told Maulana Noorani of my talk with Mufti Mahmud and about his suggestion. Maulana Noorani was very interested in what Mufti Mahmud had said, but felt that the matter was not that simple. He asked me to wait until our evening tea the next day.

When we all got together at tea and Mufti Mahmud, Nawabzada Nasrullah Khan, Prof. Ghafoor Ahmed and Maulana Shah Ahmed Noorani were present, Maulana Noorani asked Nawabzada Nasrullah Khan what sort of a person Gandhi was. Nasrullah Khan said, 'Do you mean "Gandhiji"?' 'You are calling him Gandhiji? He was a rogue,' said Noorani. This upset Nawabzada Nasrullah Khan who said, 'You may not agree with the political views that he held, but no one can deny that he was a great man and deserves everyone's respect.' Maulana Noorani reacted with further derogatory remarks about Mahatma Gandhi which upset Prof. Ghafoor Ahmed and Mufti Mahmud, who also joined in the brawl in support of Nawabzada Nasrullah Khan.

The tea over, when Maulana Noorani and I were alone, he asked me, whether I had noticed the reaction of Nawabzada Nasrullah Khan, Prof, Ghafoor Ahmed and Mufti Mahmud about a simple question about Gandhi. The differences between us, he said, are far deeper than Mufti Mahmud would have us believe and cannot be resolved in the manner that he has suggested.

Tuesday, 12 July 1977, Murree
Heard that Gohar Ayub had been released and spoke with him on the telephone. Ali left for London last night. Amina saw him off at the airport.

Amina telephoned in the evening and read out a letter received from Omar. He has stood third in a class of 90 and is thrilled with his success in the annual examinations. I am very glad that he has settled down so well in the university.

Wednesday, 13 July 1977, Murree
General Ziaul Haq telephoned Mufti Mahmud late last night apologising for not being able to visit us on the 10th as promised and said that he would come on Friday or Saturday. Nur Khan came to tell us on behalf of Ziaul Haq that he was determined to hold elections in October. I asked Nur Khan why Ziaul Haq thought that we needed reassurance. Nur Khan stayed for lunch and then went to see Bhutto. Spoke with Amina. She is leaving for Abbottabad tomorrow.

Thursday, 14 July 1977, Murree
GOC Murree telephoned Mufti Mahmud to say that Ziaul Haq will be visiting Murree tomorrow and that he wished to see Mufti Mahmud in the Divisonal HQ. Saw Ziaul Haq's press conference on TV. Decided to ask to be sent to jail if we were not released immediately.

Friday, 15 July 1977, Murree
General Ziaul Haq accompanied by Lieutenant General Chishti (corp commander), Major General Arif (staff officer) Major General Akram (divisional commander) and Ghulam Ishaq Khan (secretary general-in-chief) came to Murree and held two-hour talks with Mufti Mahmud, Nasrullah Khan and Prof. Ghafoor Ahmed. Later came for lunch to Punjab House. Talked about (1) our release, (2) release of political prisoners, (3) election time table, (4) Balochistan and a few other points. Said he would put our views before the council at their meeting tomorrow and let us have their decision. They are likely to agree to allow us visitors from tomorrow, release us on the 19th, allow committee meetings during the remaining part of July, worker's meetings in August and full campaigning during September (except

processions). It was our unanimous impression that Ziaul Haq was likely to hold elections. He has fixed 6 October as the date.

Anwar telephoned from London. Said, Ali had had his interview and was likely to get admission to Thames Polytechnic. Omar was returning to Pakistan for his summer holidays at the end of the month.

Saturday, 16 July 1977, Murree

Visitors were allowed today so I had a busy day. PPP former ministers were moved to Murree from Abbottabad. Begum Wali Khan came. She told us of her conversation with Ziaul Haq. Said that she had told him that if any one left the PNA he would be finished politically. Her remark was meant for Maulana Noorani and myself since we had told them that in the event of PPP boycotting the October elections there would be no justification for the continuance of PNA.

Tuesday, 19 July 1977, Murree

Was told that Ziaul Haq had telephoned Mufti Mohaud last night that we would be kept here until 25 or 26 July and that they had agreed to most of our other suggestions about election schedule.

A large number of people came to see us again today but we were told at about 11:30 that all visits were banned except from the family. Asked that Osman also be included in place of Omar and Ali. This was agreed. Raja Afzal of Shamsabad and Shaukat Hussain called. The pressure of visitors had been so much during the last few days that we welcomed the restrictions placed earlier. Although we have resented being kept here for another week we are thankful that we will live in peace for a few more days.

Spoke to Ghulam Ishaq Khan on the telephone and told him that cases were being brought up in court against PNA workers for political speeches made in the few years during the movement. He promised to look into this. Also told him that we wished to see the Pir of Pagara, Mian Tufail, Ashraf Khan, Sardar Abdul Qayyum Khan and Begum Wali Khan for consultations.

Thursday, 21 July 1977, Murree

Discussed the agenda for the PNA's central executive meeting which we wished to hold here on 23 July. Prof. Ghafoor spoke to the Pir of

Pagara who suggested that we should discuss the points without him. He would agree with us. So decided to constitute committees for (1) framing PNA's constitution, (2) revising the PNA's manifesto, (3) collecting data of PPP's corruption and excesses. Decided to hold the PNA's council meeting in Lahore on 5 August.

Saturday, 23 July 1977, Murree
Discussed future of PNA in the event of Bhutto's PPP boycotting the election. Nasrullah Khan and the others are in favour of keeping the PNA intact whereas Maulana Noorani regards this as a negation of democracy and the imposition of one party state—just what we had fought against under Bhutto. Moreover in the event of the failure of PNA, Bhutto would re-emerge as the alternative. No opposition in the election would result in a low poll and give credence to Bhutto's claim that the people had boycotted the election. However, the decision is vital for the future of Pakistan and we (Tehrik-i-Istiqlal and JUP) will discuss this in our national working committees before taking a decision.

Mir Khalil-ur-Rahman of *Jang* telephoned. Also spoke with Wazir Ali, Mushir and Khurshid Kasuri in the Tehrik's new central office which has opened yesterday in Lahore.

Sunday, 24 July 1977, Murree
Chaudhry Zahur Elahi, J.A. Rahim, Salahuddin of *Jasarat*, Saeed Hassan and some others were released from Karachi jail yesterday. Chaudhry Zahur Elahi has a great deal of influence in the Muslim League and may determine their policy in the next few weeks before the election.

We were expecting to hear about our release but did not.

Monday, 25 July 1977, Murree
General Ziaul Haq telephoned Mufti Mahmud to say that we would be released on 28 July and that his representative would see us tomorrow or the day after to discuss the election programme, election rules and to enquire where we wished to be taken. He also asked whether we wanted any protective arrangements after release. He will be making a similar enquiry from Bhutto. Mufti Mahmud replied that we did not require any security arrangements.

Tuesday, 26 July 1977, Murree
Local GOC, Major General Akhtar, called to enquire where we wished to go when released and whether we wanted protection at our places of residence. Every one gave their requirements of transport. I said that I will make my own arrangements. Told him that we did not need any protection.

Thursday, 28 July 1977, Murree, Rawalpindi
General Ziaul Haq called in the afternoon after his lunch with Bhutto. Told us that we were being released. Mufti Mahmud and the others left under escort by government cars. I left with Colonal Tassaddaq and Osman, and had tea with Begum Abida Hussain.

Monday, 1 Aug 1977, Abbottabad, Rawalpindi, Serai Alamgir
Talked with Gohar Ayub about survey of provincial assembly seats in NWFP and left for Rawalpindi at 09:30. Met Major General Ehsan-ul-Haq (chairman defence production) who thought that he was being appointed political adviser to the chief martial law administrator. Major General Rao Farman Ali Khan, who is also acting as a political adviser to Ziaul Haq, called. Mian Mahmud Ali Kasuri and Anwar Ali Noon came from Lahore. They are negotiating with Qayyum League to explore the possibility of cooperation. Fakhr Imam, Abida Hussain's husband came and joined me upto Serai Alamgir, which we reached at 19:30. Raja Afzal was having a meeting of his workers in preparation for the elections.

While in Rawalpindi, also called on the chief election commissioner who had announced the election schedule earlier in a press conference. Nomination papers are to be filed between 8 and 18 August. Withdrawals on 1 September and election on 18 October.

Thursday, 4 Aug 1977, Lahore, Karachi
Second day of national working committee meeting decided that Tehrik should stay on in PNA though I was given the power to leave it if at any time I thought this to be in the interest of the country. Met the press. Met a large number of people at the new central office.

PPP announced its decision yesterday to take part in the elections.

Saturday, 6 Aug 1977, Karachi, Lahore
Haji Maula Bux Soomro and Abdul Hamid Khan Jatoi travelled by the same flight. They are planning on a group in Sindh, separate from the PNA. Appeared alright in the present circumstances. Akbar Khan Bugti has similar plans for Balochistan.

Sunday, 7 Aug 1977, Lahore
Meeting of the party leaders at Chaudhry Zahur Elahi's house. Saranjam Khan of Mardan joined us.

At the party leader's meeting it was decided that Haji Maula Bux Soomro, Abdul Hamid Khan Jatoi and Ali Ahmed Talpur would be allowed to join the PNA (but they did not wish to join any particular party). Ahmed Mian Soomro and Rahim Bux Soomro met me and will be joining us probably tomorrow along with Arz Khan Jhakrani of Jacobabad. More are expected to follow suit.

Monday, 8 Aug 1977, Lahore
Abdul Hamid Khan Jatoi called. Saw M. Anwar and told him that I would like him to stand for the National Assembly from Rawalpindi.

Ahmed Mian Soomro, Rahim Bux Soomro and Arz Khan Jhakrani announced their decision to join Tehrik-i-Istiqlal. Saranjam Khan of Mardan also joined yesterday.
Bhutto arrived in Lahore in the afternoon. Approach roads to the airport had been blocked by the administration causing congestion. PPP workers stoned motor cars and burnt two petrol pumps. Maulana Shah Ahmed Noorani and Javed Hashmi were injured when the car they were travelling in was attacked by PPP hooligans.

Wednesday, 10 Aug 1977, Lahore
Met Maulana Noorani, Prof. Shah Farid ul Haq, Wazir Ali, Pesh Imam and Zahoor ul Hassan Bhopali at Mian Mahmud Ali Kasuri's residence. Discussed PNA's attitude regarding 36 per cent quota of seats in Punjab for JUP and TI. Wrote a letter to Mufti Mahmud, which was given to Wazir Ali to hand over. In it we said that if our quota was not given we would put up our own candidates against PNA candidates on the seventeen provincial and five national seats in

Punjab. A committee with Pir Pagara was set up to decide which additional seats could be given.

Thursday, 11 Aug 1977, Lahore

Begum Dost Mohammad Khan Khakwani, sister of late Nawab Iftikhar Mamdot, called. Iqbal Burney and Mian Zahid Sarfaraz called in the evening. Correspondent of *Keyhan International* interviewed me. Dinner with Mushir and Iqbal Burney. Saranjam Khan who is standing for NA-I Peshawar also joined us. Iqbal Burney and Zafar Iqbal (a friend of Altaf Gauhar) thought that Bhutto had captured the political initiative and that elections might be postponed. Did not agree with him about the political initiative except that he had temporarily gained a political advantage. Both of us agreed that martial law authorities were handling the situation badly. Public whipping of a police constable yesterday and its wide publicity had created considerable sympathy with the victim. This is indicative of the public's attitude towards martial law.

Friday, 12 Aug 1977, Lahore, Rawalpindi

Lieutenant General Gul Hassan Khan, our former ambassador who had resigned recently, and others called. He had been released after arrest on arrival from abroad a few days ago. Explained the circumstances of his arrest—writing a letter to the armed forces during the movement. He has been asked to leave the country, which he is doing. Wants to be our ambassador in Switzerland when PNA government is formed.

Tuesday, 16 Aug 1977, Lahore

Bhutto announced his intention yesterday to contest from NA-83 Lahore-III national seat. Khurshid Kasuri is our candidate. Chaudhry Zahur Elahi called in the office; suggested that I should contest this seat against Bhutto. I did not agree to fight him on the ground of his choosing.

Held a meeting with Wazir Ali, Dr Ijaz Hussain Qureshi and Khurshid Kasuri to discuss desirability of starting a party newspaper. Decided that time was too short and the requirement of funds too large to start such a venture at this stage. Decided to establish contact with certain newspapers and felt that this should suffice. Met the press at

Omar Kasuri's in the afternoon. Saw M. Anwar in the evening. He is not willing to contest the Rawalpindi national seat as he is busy preparing a case against Bhutto. Maqbool Sharif of *Pakistan Times* started work with me as public relations adviser.

Thursday, 18 Aug 1977, Shamsabad, Abbottabad
Chaudhry Zahur Elahi arrived at Shamsabad at 06:00. Discussed Gujrat seats with him and advised him not to stand for NA-83 Lahore-III against Bhutto as Mian Mahmud Ali Kasuri is determined not to give up the seat. Chaudhry Zahur Elahi has also filed his paper and wants Mian Sahib to withdraw.

Friday, 19 Aug 1977, Lahore
Discussed allotment of party tickets in NWFP with Gohar Ayub and Fakhruz Zaman Khan. Did not like allotments made by Gohar and decided to change these in certain cases. He is too anxious to bring in newcomers even though they may abandon us after the elections. This system of award of party tickets is rotten. Completely centralised in which the local workers have no say. Intend to pattern it on the system in vogue in UK where the constituency party invites applications, interviews candidates and 'adopts' the most suitable person.

Omar Kasuri and his brother Bakhtiar arrived from Lahore. They were disturbed by Chaudhry Zahur Elahi, Hanif Ramay and Ashraf Khan (of Khaksar) filing nomination papers in Khurshid's constituency in NA-83, Lahore-III. Spoke to Mian Sahib on the telephone.

Tuesday, 23 Aug 1977, Abbottabad, Lahore
Pir Pagara has played havoc with allocation of seats in Sindh allotting almost all to the Muslim League.

Wednesday, 24 August 1977, Lahore
Haji Maula Bux Soomro and Mir Ali Ahmed Talpur called. Spent the day in the office finalising allocation of seats for NWFP, Punjab, and Sindh. Chaudhry Zahur Elahi organised small demonstrations in his compound against me and the Tehrik-i-Istiqlal for saying that a merger of PNA parties was not possible and for nominating Mian Kasuri for NA Lahore-III constituency in which Chaudhry Zahur Elahi is interested.

Thursday, 25 Aug 1977, Lahore
Spent the morning in the central office, finalising the list of Tehrik candidates for NWFP, Punjab, and Sindh. Balochistan list was also finalised by the PNA under Mufti Mahmud giving us only two out of forty provincial seats.

Maulana Shah Ahmed Noorani called and we discussed differences developing within PNA.

Attended meeting of PNA heads of parties at Rana Khuda Dad's house. Gave them a bit of my mind and tried to iron out differences. An entirely unworkable team, incapable of tackling the country's problems. Meeting lasted from 21:30 to 03:00 on Friday.

Saturday, 27 Aug 1977, Lahore
Yusuf Khan Khattak called. Was very concerned with the manner in which the NWFP was being handed over 'on a platter' to NDP and JUI He is addressing a press conference on the subject.

Attended a meeting of PNA central parliamentary board at Chaudhry Zahur Elahi's house. Finalised the Punjab list and agreed that Mian Mahmud Ali Kasuri will withdraw from the contest in favour of Chaudhry Zahur Elahi, since this was the wish of the other parties.

Sunday, 28 Aug 1977, Lahore
Addressed the press after Mufti Mahmud's press conference and announced Mian Mahmud Ali Kasuri's withdrawal from NA-83, Lahore-III. Attended a brief session of PNA's meeting at 17:00 at Chaudhry Zahur Elahi's house. Made final adjustments in seats. Met Hafeez Kardar, the cricketer and one time PPP MPA. He is now in Tehrik-i-Istiqlal.

Monday, 29 Aug 1977, Lahore
Held a meeting with Mian Kasuri, Khurshid Kasuri, Maqbool Sharif and Wazir Ali and decided to go ahead with a party newspaper. Appointed a committee with Khurshid as the convener and asked them to get the newspaper out by the end of September 1977.

Wednesday, 31 Aug 1977, Lahore, Abbottabad

Left Lahore at 05:30 for Rawalpindi. Met Chaudhry Zahur Elahi and Maulana Kausar Niazi and was told that they were trying for Ali Asghar Shah's withdrawal from the election contest on the Rawalpindi seat against me.

Left Rawalpindi at 19:30 and arrived in Abbottabad at 21:15 where a letter of resignation was awaiting me from Gohar Ayub Khan who had expressed his dissatisfaction with the distribution of seats by the Tehrik's central parliamentary board for the NWFP. The parliamentary board had changed the allocation recommended by Gohar, who himself had not turned up in spite of my having told him to attend. Although he has written that he is resigning from the chairmanship of the NWFP, I feel that he will leave after the election and probably go to the Muslim League. He has not forgiven me for having contributed to his father's exit.

Saturday, 3 Sept 1977, Abbottabad, Peshawar

Heard that Zulfikar Ali Bhutto had been arrested early today on a charge of involvement in the murder of Nawab Ahmed Khan.

Tuesday, 13 Sept 1977, Abbottabad, Khanpur, Abbottabad

Bhutto was released on bail in Nawab Ahmed Khan murder case. CMLA held a meeting with political leader today for setting rules of conduct.

Thursday, 22 Sept 1977, Rawalpindi, Abbottabad

General Ziaul Haq annulled those clauses of the constitution, which interfered with the functioning of the courts, and had been brought in by Bhutto as amendments to the constitution. As a result Justice Yakub Ali ceased to be the chief justice and Justice Anwar ul Haq has been appointed to replace him.

Saturday, 1 Oct 1977, Rawalpindi

Ziaul Haq announced indefinite postponement of elections and curtailment of all political activity. A poor speech. Reasons were not convincing—need to complete legal proceedings against Bhutto and deteriorating law and order situation. The first was a plausible excuse but the second was not justified. Law and order situation is perfectly normal. People are now convinced that Ziaul Haq intends to stay.

Sunday, 2 Oct 1977, Rawalpindi, Abbottabad
Simon Henderson of BBC called earlier at Rawalpindi. He was of the view that Ziaul Haq would not hold elections.

Thursday, 6 Oct 1977, Lahore
Discussion on PNA continued and deliberations of the national working committee were concluded today. Forty members (including twelve special invitees) took part in the discussions. Seven were in favour of staying in PNA at all costs (prominent amongst them being Gohar Ayub, Fakhruz Zaman Khan, and Anwar Durrani).

Thirty-three favoured leaving PNA and out of them seventeen favoured leaving only when a suitable opportunity arose. Decided to hold a meeting of the party council on 8 and 9 December and of the national working committee on 9 and 10 December in Lahore. Also decided to hold party election after six weeks of membership drive.

Addressed a press conference and asked for announcement of a fresh election date. Met Akbar Khan Bugti and discussed the general political situation.

Friday, 7 Oct 1977, Lahore
Decided that we will take a stand against the repeal of the 1961 family law ordinance and if other PNA parties did not agree, make this the reason for leaving PNA.

Saturday, 8 Oct 1977, Lahore
Nawaz Sharif of Ittefaq Foundries called with Wazir Ali. Had a get-together with JUP (Noorani, Abdul Sattar Niazi, Shah Farid ul Haq and Bhopali) before the PNA council meeting. JUP was averse to our leaving the PNA on what they called a religious issue. They themselves had not decided to leave as yet.

The PNA session was a very stormy one with JUP accusing the PNA's leadership of grave acts of omission and commission. Discussed the agenda for talks with General Ziaul Haq on 13 October. The general had invited ten leaders of PNA to talk with him on the 13th and it was decided that the nine party leaders and the secretary general should go and that we should ask for early election and for a definite date of elections to be announced.

Thursday, 13 Oct 1977, Rawalpindi
Met Ziaul Haq in GHQ lecture hall along with other PNA leaders. Stayed for three-and-a-half hours and discussed date of election, Hyderabad case, Attock case and other matters. He was not willing to give a date for the election but said that the two or three cases now pending against Zulfikar Ali Bhutto would take four or five months to be decided and that elections would be held within 60 days after that. However, he also said that if the cases are decided by December, elections could be held in March. My impression is that elections are not likely before October 1978.

Held another meeting of PNA central council at Mufti Mahmud's lodging at the Saddar mosque at 18:00. It was decided to defer the question of leadership of future PNA government.

Attended a dinner hosted by Ziaul Haq. All nine PNA leaders, Prof. Ghafoor Ahmed and four leaders of Pukhtoon Khwa were also there. At this meeting Ziaul Haq told us that some PNA leaders had begged him to postpone the election.

Saturday, 22 Oct 1977, Quetta, Karachi
Nawab Akbar Khan Bugti and his group announced their decision to join the Tehrik-i-Istiqlal. Left by PIA at 15:00. Received at the airport by Nurud Din Jatoi, Admiral Muzaffar Hassan (the new Tehrik chairman, Karachi) and workers.

Monday, 24 Oct 1977, Karachi, Lahore
Called on Maulana Shah Ahmed Noorani and discussed PNA. It appears that JUP will leave PNA but not as yet.

Wednesday, 26 Oct 1977, Lahore
Called on Maulana Maudoodi (at his invitation) and discussed the future of PNA. He was concerned at the possibility of its breaking up. Explained our assessment and the unlikelihood of the PNA being able to run a government in the future.

Called on Mian Mahmud Ali Kasuri and continued discussion with him, Wazir Ali, and Khurshid about leaving PNA.

Thursday, 27 Oct 1977, Lahore, Rawalpindi, Abbottabad
Was told last night on the telephone by W.D. Khan (political officer
in the Foreign Office) that Shah of Iran would see me on 30 October
and I should arrive in Tehran on the 29th. Left Lahore in the morning,
Sorted out foreign exchange, visa, etc. It was a job cutting through
the endless red tape. Left for Abbottabad at 17:00 and stopped on the
way at Rehana to condole with Begum Ayub Khan on Shaukat Ayub's
death.

Friday, 28 Oct 1977, Abbottabad, Rawalpindi
Gohar Ayub called. It is obvious that he has decided to leave us. Left
for Tehran by PIA at midnight.

Saturday, 29 Oct 1977, Rawalpindi, Tehran
Arrived in Tehran at 02:50. While at lunch, received a call that the
Shah would see us at 15:30. Mushir and Khurshid were with me. A
very pleasant meeting.

Monday, 31 Oct 1977, Tehran
Amir Taheri of *Keyhan International* had breakfast with me. Mahmud
Taheri, his brother, called to interview me later on behalf of the
Tehran Journal. Called on Prime Minister Amouzgar.

Tuesday, 1 Nov 1977, Tehran
Laid a wreath at Reza Shah Pahlavi's mausoleum. Also offered *fateha*
at General Khatemi and Iskander Mirza's tombs. The former is buried
in the grounds of Reza Shah's mausoleum and the latter in the Zahedi
graveyard very close to Reza Shah's.

Andrew Whitley of BBC called. He was covering the movement
during its peak in April and we used to hear his dispatches when we
were in Kot Lakhpat jail in Lahore.

Thursday, 3 Nov 1977, Jeddah, Makkah, Jeddah
Dr Meenai, a vice president of the World Islamic Bank and a friend
of Mushir, called. He lives in Jeddah.

Mushir, Khurshid and I performed the *Umrah* with a Pakistani
guide provided by the embassy. He is the official translator in the
embassy and a graduate of the Madina University. He explained every

thing to us and made the *Umrah* very interesting. The *Umrah* (time at Haram Sharif) takes three hours if performed properly, including *maghrib* prayers. This does not include the travelling time.

We said *isha* prayers at Makkah and returned to Jeddah for dinner with Dr Meenai.

Saturday, 5 Nov 1977, Abu Dhabi
Pakistan ambassador in the United Arab Emirates, Brigadier Anwar-ul-Haq, and our counsel in Dubai, Murad Khairi, called. The ambassador explained that Sheikh Zaid was very friendly with Bhutto and may not therefore be very happy to meet me, his main political opponent. I explained that my visit was entirely private to see my daughter and no interview need be arranged.

Monday, 7 Nov 1977, Abu Dhabi
The ambassador called to say that Shaikh Zaid had a cold but he had arranged meetings with Sheikh Suroor bin Mohammad, the chamberlain to the court, and Ahmed Khalifa al Suweidi, the foreign minister. The latter had called on us when we were in captivity at Sihala. Called on both these gentlemen. Was told by Suweidi that the Sheikh would also wish to see me. So called on Sheikh bin Sultan al Nahyan, the president of the United Arab Emirates. Meeting was of about an hour duration (after dinner). He appeared anxious to explain that although he considered Bhutto to be a friend of his, his real friendship was with Pakistan. A pleasant meeting.

Thursday, 10 Nov 1977, Rawalpindi
Spent the day finalising the draft letter to Mufti Mahmud about our decision to leave the PNA and also a statement for the press. Sent the letter along with Omar Kasuri to deliver to Prof. Ghafoor Ahmed, the secretary general of PNA at Karachi. Asked Obaid-ur-Rehman and Dr Rahim-ul-Haq to accompany Omar Kasuri. The letter is to be delivered at 11:00 tomorrow when I make the announcement at Rawalpindi. Akbar Khan Bugti arrived from Karachi and Khudai Noor from Quetta. Addressed a press conference on my visit abroad.

Friday, 11 Nov 1977, Rawalpindi
Armistice day. Addressed a press conference at Tassaddaq's house. Had asked many of our top leaders to be present. Some twenty of them came. They included. Dr Ishtiaq Qureshi, Mian Mahmud Ali Kasuri, Pesh Imam, Akbar Khan Bugti, Khudai Noor, Nuruddin Jatoi, Munir Shah, Prince Aurangzeb, Abu Saeed Enver and Allama Zaheer. Chaudhry Zahur Elahi of Muslim League turned up about half an hour before the press conference to try to stop us leaving the PNA. Told him that we had made up our minds and would go through with it.

I am sure that the decision to leave the PNA is the right one. It is impossible to work with them. Leaving the PNA would not affect the programme of the army which will in any case try to hang on as long as possible. The army is likely to keep the PPP alive as a threat and will use it for delaying its programme of holding elections but these will have to be held sooner or later and then the decision taken today will have been fully vindicated.

Sunday, 13 Nov 1977, Abbottabad
Khan Abdul Qayyum Khan called and assured us of his cooperation. He said that he would address a press conference on the 15th. He said his cooperation was unconditional and he would be satisfied with any number of seats he and his party are given in the next election. He wants the Peshawar National Assembly seat for himself.

Monday, 14 Nov 1977, Abbottabad, Lahore, Abbottabad
M. Anwar died last night in Lahore. His death is a great loss to Tehrik-i-Istiqlal and the country. A fighter for human freedom and democracy he was also the prosecutor in Bhutto's trial in the Lahore High Court. Flew to Lahore to attend *janaza* prayers.

Friday, 25 Nov 1977, Abbottabad (Mansehra)
Attended a meeting of NWFP working committee at Wajid Razvi's for a short while. The meeting decided in my absence that Gohar Ayub should be expelled from the party for continuous breach of party discipline. Decision was unanimous.

Monday, 28 Nov 1977, Lahore

Went to Wazir Ali's where I had dinner. Aitzaz Ahsan talked non-stop for two hours. Kardar, a much quieter man, and other Tehrik lawyers were present, Dr Ijaz Qureshi and Mujeeb Shami were also there. A magistrate called at the party office earlier to convey a warning from martial law authorities that I should not meet workers except three or four at a time.

Wednesday, 30 Nov 1977, Karachi

Nafis Siddiqui and his wife came and wanted to join Tehrik-i-Istiqlal. He will announce his decision in Lahore on 11 December. Agha Shahi telephoned from Islamabad to say that Ziaul Haq wanted to know about my conversation with the Shah of Iran. Told him that I will brief him on my return to Rawalpindi about the middle of December.

Friday, 2 Dec 1977, Karachi, Thatta, Hyderabad, Tando Allahyar, Mirpurkhas

Met workers and citizens at Dr Yusafzai's. Had lunch there and arrived at Hyderabad at 15:30. Met workers in the old city. Left for Mirpurkhas and was stopped by people at Tando Allahyar where I addressed workers. Arrived at Mirpurkhas late in the evening. Addressed the press, as I had done at Hyderabad. Addressed workers at Mirpurkhas.

Salim Bugti, Zia Ispahani, Ashraf Liaquat Ali Khan, Fakhruddin Lotia, Major Nizam, Anis Ahmed Khan, Ahmed Mian Soomro and Qazi Hafiz are with me on the tour. Mushir and Nuruddin Jatoi returned to Karachi. Response everywhere was excellent. Was mobbed by the people. It appears that the decision to quit the PNA has been well received.

Saturday, 3 Dec 1977, Mirpurkhas, Shahdadpur, Nawabshah, Sakrand, Moro, Khairpur, Sukkur

Addressed meeting at five places *en route*. Tremendous response, especially at Nawabshah. It appeared that the decision to leave the PNA has been hailed by the people. All those who had accompanied me from Karachi, except Mushir and Nuruddin Jatoi, were with me in a procession. In Sukkur, Dr Piracha had asked some 300 persons to dinner. A very good gathering.

Sunday, 4 Dec 1977, Sukkur, Shikarpur, Jacobabad, Sukkur
Called on Haji Maula Bux Soomro at Shikarpur. Invited him to join Tehrik-i-Istiqlal. He was evasive as expected and wanted to see Bhutto buried before he would take an initiative.

Addressed the press at Ahmed Mian Soomro's place at Jacobabad. Lunch at Mir Arz Mohammad Khan Jhakrani. Very large gathering. Many notables announced their decision to join Tehrik. Attended a reception by Hindu Panchayat. More people joined Tehrik. Attended a reception by Akbar Khan Bugti at his Jacobabad house where a large number of people from Nasirabad and Kachi districts belonging to various tribes joined the Tehrik. Returned to Sukkur and Rohri in the evening.

Monday, 5 Dec 1977, Sukkur
Taj Mohammad Jamali (ex federal minister in Bhutto's government) came to lunch. Agha Hilaly also came, and stayed for lunch. Taj Jamali appeared keen on a rapprochement with Akbar Khan Bugti and would then join Tehrik-i-Istiqlal. The problem is the distribution of seats in the Nasirabad and Kachi districts.

Thursday, 8 Dec 1977, Sukkur, Lahore
Laji [my brother] telephoned from Rawalpindi to say that he had received a message from GHQ (Major General Arif) that Ziaul Haq wanted to see me on 11 December. Told Laji to tell him that it was not convenient for me to go there on the 11th and that I could come on the 13th.

Sunday, 25 Dec 1977, Abbottabad, Rawalpindi
Called on Ziaul Haq and discussed rationing scale in rural areas, relaxing of the ban on political activities, release of Attock conspiracy case prisoners and other matters.

Saturday, 31 Dec 1977, Vehari, Makhdum Rashid, Multan
General Ziaul Haq telephoned from Rawalpindi to say that I should not make any political speeches at gatherings. He complained that I was contravening martial law orders.

Diary 1978

Sunday, 9 April 1978, Quetta, Karachi

Lieutenant General Chishti telephoned to say that General Ziaul Haq would be contacting me to ask me to see him, on 15 April. Presumably about a national government. I explained that I could not return to Rawalpindi before the 19th and would be available after that date.

Monday, 10 April 1978, Karachi

Met Dr Ishtiaq Hussain Qureshi at his residence along with Mushir Pesh Imam, Dr Rahimul Haq, Obaid-ur-Rehman, Nafis Siddiqui, A.B. Awan and Malik Anwar Ali Noon. Briefed them on my talks with Lieutenant General Chishti. General opinion was not in favour of joining the national government. All, except A.B. Awan, were strongly opposed to the idea.

Tuesday, 11 April 1978, Karachi

Prof. Shah Farid ul Haq and Zahur ul Hassan Bhopali met me. Discussed general political situation. JUP wished to keep in step with us and would stay out of national government if we stayed out.

Wednesday, 12 April 1978, Karachi

Mushir received a telephone call from CMLA's headquarters at Rawalpindi inviting him to a meeting with General Ziaul Haq on the 15th.

Saturday, 15 April 1978, Sukkur

Mushir telephoned from Rawalpindi to say that Ziaul Haq had declined to meet him and our delegation (Mian Mahmud Ali Kasuri and Mushir Pesh Imam) without me. This was in spite of the fact that Major General Arif had confirmed on the telephone that Mushir would be welcome.

Thursday, 20 April 1978, Abbottabad

Ziaul Haq addressed a press conference on his return from Saudi Arabia. Confirmed my view that he has no intention of parting with power if he can help it.

Monday, 24 April 1978, Abbottabad

Telephoned the station commander (army) Abbottabad and told him that on my morning walk, I had noticed that the sentries on duty outside the Army Medical Centre gates are wrapped up in blankets. I told him that I did not wish to interfere in the administration of the army but since seeing a soldier on duty wrapped up in a blanket spoils my walk, I would be grateful if he would give them over coats instead, unless of course there was a new army instruction permitting them to wear blankets.

Sunday, 30 April 1978, Lahore

Dr Ijaz Qureshi, Mian Mahmud Ali Kasuri and Wazir Ali called in the evening and discussed the general situation. Dr Ijaz advocated joining hands with the army rulers to guide them and to transfer power to civilian hands. I explained that so far as I could see, they have no intention of handing over power, looked down on politicians and did not want any genuine sharing of power.

Monday, 1 May 1978, Lahore

Had lunch with Akbar Khan Bugti. Exchanged views on the general situation. I asked him to exercise moderation in his statements, which often have an alarming effect on our workers. He is prone to come out with what is in his subconscious, which often, would be better left unsaid.

Wednesday, 3 May 1978, Rawalpindi, Abbottabad

Shortly after arrival in Abbottabad Azizul Hassan, the new commissioner Hazara division, called. He came again at 13:00 and accompanied me to the 'Baloch' rest house where I met Ziaul Haq and stayed with him for an hour. Ziaul Haq talked about the situation in Afghanistan, need for a national government and tried to reassure me that he would announce the date of elections after Bhutto's case was finally decided, which he expected would be some time in July. I told him that the general impression was that he had no intention of parting with power and expressed my view that the process of accountability had been reduced to a farce. He was emphatic that he would hold elections and would allow political activities to be resumed as soon as Bhutto's case was decided. He said that if the

Supreme Court confirmed the sentence awarded by the High Court, he (Ziaul Haq) would have him hanged. I told him that this would be wrong and unwise.

It was altogether an interesting meeting. I declined his invitation to the Tehrik-i-Istiqlal to join the national government.

Ziaul Haq told me that the dentist, Zafar Niazi, was 'deeply' involved in a conspiracy. Difficult to believe. He and his wife are supporters of Bhutto and he has been meeting him frequently in jail on a professional basis.

Thursday, 11 May 1978, Rawalpindi
Osman telephoned to say that his father, Aleem Afridi, had been released. The jail superintendent had informed Aleem's daughter Alia, on the telephone at 14:30 and she wept as she heard the news. Aleem has been in custody since March 1973 for conspiracy to stage a coup to oust Bhutto.

With his release and that of Brigadier F.B. Ali and Major Farooq Adam, all those detained in the Attock conspiracy case are now free.

Saturday, 13 May 1978, Abbottabad
Telephoned Khudai Noor and asked him to send details of the charge-sheet against Akbar Khan Bugti, his son, Chakar Khan, and Hazur Bukhsh Domki. I intend writing to Ziaul Haq about this and also about the charges against Sardar Khan Bahadur of Azad Kashmir who saw me yesterday. He was convinced that he was being persecuted intentionally.

Sunday, 14 May 1978, Abbottabad
Gave a statement about press freedom. About fifty pressmen have been arrested so far and five have been awarded 'stripes'. Their agitation is mounting. Most of those arrested have been sentenced to up to one year's imprisonment including Nisar Osmani of *Dawn* (Lahore) to 12 months RI and Abdul Hamid Chhapra of *Jang* (Karachi) to six months RI.

Tuesday, 16 May 1978, Abbottabad
Lieutenant General Fazle Haq, Corp Commander Peshawar and a 'Rimcollian' from RIMC (my old school), telephoned to ask me to dinner on 21 May. Agreed. Wazir Ali telephoned from Lahore to say that he had been to see Abdul Hamid Chhapra in Kot Lakhpat Jail. He was in good spirits.

BBC's 20:15 news said that Mairaj Mohammad Khan had been arrested in Rawalpindi this morning. ostensibly for saying that Ziaul Haq had no intention of holding elections. The total number of persons arrested so far in the last few days is now over 80.

In a letter addressed to Chief Justice Anwar ul Haq, Bhutto has asked that he (Anwar ul Haq) should not sit on the bench to hear his appeal on 20 May. He has said that by accepting the temporary responsibility of acting president of Pakistan (for about ten days during President Fazle Elahi Choudhry's absence abroad) Anwar ul Haq had seriously undermined the sanctity of his office as chief justice. Moreover, he had not been appointed to this post by him (Bhutto) and could not, therefore, be expected to be impartial. Bhutto has suggested that all the other judges of the Supreme Court should constitute the bench to hear his appeal.

Chief Justice Anwar ul Haq is expected to give his decision on this request within the next few days.

Wednesday, 17 May 1978, Abbottabad, Haripur
Went to the Civil Hospital for my medical board required under the rules for commutation of pension. The medical board was Pakistani style. No checks. A cup of tea and plenty of talk—politics. A member of my medical board was the eye specialist, a young man from Miramshah, North Waziristan, whom I had met along with his brother Faqir Khan (also a doctor) when I visited Cardiff, Wales, whilst on a tour of Great Britain in 1973. He was surprised that I remembered him. I was declared fit.

Mark Tully of BBC, who is in Rawalpindi for a few days from Delhi, telephoned.

Thursday, 18 May 1978, Abbottabad, Mardan, Sakhakot, Saidu
Habibullah Khan Daulat Khel, our former chairman of Swat district, is now ready to rejoin us. Said he will do so tomorrow at lunch to

which he has invited us. Is thoroughly disenchanted with Jamaat-i-Islami and says that if there is a single Jamaat-i-Islami man anywhere, you do not need Satan there.

Sunday, 21 May 1978, Kalam, Chakdara, Peshawar

Maulana Qazi Abdul Hannan of Chakdarra who has spent 40 years in Deoband joined us today. Mufti Mahmud was his pupil at Deoband and he does not have a very high opinion of Mufti Mahmud's religious knowledge. Qazi Abdul Hassan is about 90 years old. He had joined Deoband in 1902 at the age of 12.

Chief Justice Anwar ul Haq rejected Bhutto's plea that he (Anwar ul Haq) should not sit on the bench which is to hear his appeal against the death sentence by the Lahore High Court. He ruled that all the judges of the Supreme Court—nine, including him—will hear the appeal. Daily hearings have started with effect from yesterday.

Dined with Lieutenant General Fazle Haq, corp commander and martial law administrator NWFP. Ijlal Hyder Zaidi, the chief secretary NWFP, was also there. Fazle Haq said that elections would be held in March-April 1979, that Bhutto would be hanged if the Supreme Court upholds the decision of the High Court and that political activities would be allowed after a decision about Bhutto was taken, which he expected in July or August 1978. He is anti-NAP politically and says he is a Muslim Leaguer by conviction. However, he is impartial in his duties as martial law administrator.

Monday, 22 May 1978, Peshawar, Abbottabad

Maulana Noorani arrived in Karachi today after a three-month tour of East Africa and the Middle East. CMLA's secretariat (General Ziaul Haq's office) was burnt by what radio reported was an accidental fire in an air conditioner. Prime minister of Iran was reported by Andrew Whitley, BBC's Tehran correspondent, to have said that Iran would stop all aid to Pakistan if Bhutto is hanged. Later (today) our newspapers reported that the Iranian ambassador in Islamabad had said that the Iranian prime minister had not been reported correctly.

Friday, 26 May 1978, Rawalpindi

Javed Hashmi, Ehsan Bari and Sheikh Rasheed called in the evening and suggested that they should have some responsibility in the party which would facilitate their work amongst the youth. Agreed in principle.

Sunday, 28 May 1978, Rawalpindi, Abbottabad

Amina and I attended the Supreme Court hearing in the Bhutto case. We stayed there for a couple of hours. The counsel for defence, Yahya Bakhtiar, was reading the defence and the progress appeared very slow. However, Mian Mahmud Ali Kasuri who was also there said that the case should finish by the end of July.

Thursday, 1 June 1978, Karachi

Had dinner with Nazir Ahmed. Mushir was also there and Admiral and Begum Ahsan joined us after dinner. Nazir was very critical of the martial law regime. He felt that the martial law had achieved what G.M. Syed had not been able to achieve in Sindh for the last 30 years. That separation was much more talked about now and hatred for the Punjabi army was stronger. He felt that if these people stayed on much longer the country would face a real threat of disintegration.

Saturday, 3 June 1978, Karachi

Nuruddin Jatoi called. He has stopped sulking. Is very sensitive about his position and complained that Mushir has been neglecting him on every occasion. Asked him not to be so sensitive about every thing.

Monday, 5 June 1978, Karachi

J.A. Rahim, former secretary general of PPP, called. He wants to join Tehrik-i-Istiqlal but decided to think it over as he has a reputation of being a diehard socialist.

Wednesday, 7 June 1978, Abbottabad

Incidently there have been rumours about Ziaul Haq who has been out of circulation for nearly three weeks now. These rumours range from house arrest, pleurisy, slipped disc and flu to heart attack. As if to prove these rumours wrong he appeared on TV last night presiding over a conference. I am sure there is nothing seriously wrong but his absence from public view since 19 May is rather unusual.

Ahmed Mian Soomro telephoned to say that his father, Haji Maula Bux Soomro, was upset because some Urdu newspaper had reported me as having said that he (Haji Maula Bux) was advising General Ziaul Haq to stay on in power. I denied having done so.

Sunday, 11 June 1978, Rawalpindi, Gujrat, Abbottabad
General Ziaul Haq telephoned about 23:30 to ask me to a dinner meeting with him at Rawalpindi on 15 June. He asked me to bring two or three persons with me. He suggested Mian Mahmud Ali Kasuri and Pesh Imam. I agreed to meet him. He explained that the purpose was to chat about the general situation, budget, etc. He also wanted to consult us on calling a larger meeting a week or so later. He said that the reported rumour about the political parties being banned under martial law was wrong.

Tuesday, 13 June 1978, Abbottabad
Mushir telephoned in the morning. Told him to come to Rawalpindi on 15th evening for the meeting and dinner with Ziaul Haq. Mushir telephoned again to say that Altaf Gauhar had sent a telex to ask me to come to London even if for a few days. He said that arrangements have been made for me to meet a number of leading British newspaper journalists. A postponement of the visit now would be embarrassing. Omar and Ali are coming from London and the earliest I can leave conveniently is 25 June. Moreover a visit abroad at this time would pose a public relations problem. Told Mushir that I will decide when we meet on 15 June in Rawalpindi.

Thursday, 15 June 1978, Abbottabad, Rawalpindi
Dinner with General Ziaul Haq. His advisers were also there and Mushir and Wazir Ali accompanied me. He invited the Tehrik to give him people of his choice for the interim government. I declined this offer. He also said that he would hold elections in 1979, possibly in March or April and that the work on the voters' lists would be completed well before that date. He said that he would be announcing relaxation of restrictions on political activities and that a military tribunal would be set up to speed up the process of accountability.

We got the impression that the martial law authorities do not wish to hold elections until they can ensure that the result will be exactly as they would like it to be—which is always difficult to achieve.

Friday, 16 June 1978, Rawalpindi
Amina and I, Mushir and Wazir Ali attended a dinner in honour of the visiting Chinese vice prime minister, Keng Piao. PNA heads of parties, except Sherbaz who is not in the country, were there as also Kausar Niazi and Ghaus Bux Bizenjo. The dinner was a dull affair, bagpipes and all. Mr Keng Piao made a good speech in support of Pakistan.

Ziaul Haq asked me to accompany him in a helicopter for the opening of the Thakot Bridge on the Silk Road tomorrow.

At dinner on 16 June, Ziaul Haq had told me that he had tried to stop Omar from resigning from the army and said that if he had stayed on he could have been a lieutenant colonel by now. Omar was bent on leaving and is happier out of the army. He would in any case have resigned during last year's movement and the military action against the people.

Sunday, 18 June 1978, Rawalpindi, Thakot, Abbottabad
At Ziaul Haq's invitation, flew along with some other guests (General Chishti, Ghulam Ishaq Khan, Agha Shahi, Ehsan ul Haq) to Thakot for the opening of the bridge and the Karakoram highway by the Chinese vice prime minister, Keng Piao. It was I think my first flight ever in an army craft. Returned to Abbottabad where we had lunch at the Frontier Force Regiment officers mess. After lunch Ehsan ul Haq came over to the house and talked about the general situation. He left for Rawalpindi at 18:00.

Monday, 19 June 1978, Rawalpindi, Abbottabad
General and Begum Abid Bilgrami called. Gave him the manuscript of my book *The First Round* to read, particularly the chapter entitled 'Brigadiers in Command' in which I have written about him and Gul Hassan.

Left for Islamabad at 17:00 and attended a dinner given by the visiting Chinese vice premier. Amina also came with me and Wazir Ali and Mian Mahmud Ali Kasuri came from Lahore. A typical Chinese dinner. About 120 guests.

Tuesday, 27 June 1978, Abbottabad
A Pakistani correspondent of Daily *Keyhan International* called to interview me and told me that General Chishti had met Bhutto in jail yesterday. Zia had agreed to spare his life if two heads of state gave

a guarantee for his good conduct. In that event Bhutto would be externed.

Saturday, 1 July 1978, Abbottabad

Naseerullah Khan Babar, former governor NWFP in PPP's government, called to discuss the general situation. He is a Rimcollian (RIMC) which he joined after my departure in 1939.

Omar telephoned from Shirin's (London). He has done very well in his exams and has got a first division BA (Hons). His economics paper is being published. Ali has also done well and has passed his first year exam in architecture.

Monday, 3 July 1978, Abbottabad

Ghani Khan, Abdul Ghaffar Khan's eldest son, came for dinner. He is an interesting person. Poet and a Pushto scholar, he is not in active politics but is actively interested in politics. He disagrees with Wali Khan on many issues.

He is a 'Pakistani' at heart and does not believe in any extra-national stunt such as the 'Pakhtoonistan' slogan. However he is a good Pakhtoon and wants the development of Pakhtoon culture within Pakistan. Aleem was also at the dinner.

Tuesday, 4 July 1978, Abbottabad

Mian Mahmud Ali Kasuri telephoned to suggest that Anwar Ali Noon and Aitzaz Ahsan be invited to the national working committee meeting on 6 and 7 July at Rawalpindi. Agreed to Anwar Ali Noon.

Newspapers reported that Muslim League has agreed to join the martial law government. Mian Tufail (Amir Jamaat-i-Islami) has met Ziaul Haq who has decided to resume negotiations with the PNA for the formation of a civilian-military government. Mufti Mahmud is against the Muslim League joining the government if PNA cannot reach an agreement with Zia. Malik Qasim is opposing joining the government and has asked for a meeting of the Muslim League Council (if granted permission). So the situation is thoroughly confusing and Ziaul Haq will take these people for a ride for some more time. Maulana Abdus Sattar Niazi, who regards himself as the founder of the PNA, has given a statement that the Jamiat-ul-Ulema-i-Pakistan will not leave the PNA. Maulana Noorani has said at

Nawabshah that the JUP will decide on 6 July whether it should stay in the PNA or leave it.

The daily *Dawn* of today reported that Mairaj Mohammad Khan had been brought from Attock jail to see Ziaul Haq before being released. Mairaj said that Ziaul Haq expressed his neutrality between the parties of the 'right' and 'left' and promised early elections and early resumption of political activity. General Ziaul Haq has however acquired a reputation for inconsistency and has repeatedly gone back on his assurances.

Wednesday, 5 July 1978, Abbottabad, Rawalpindi

The first anniversary of Pakistan's third martial law. Ziaul Haq celebrated it by inducting a cabinet of ministers. Muslim League and a few independents in addition to some generals. Khawaja Safdar, Zahid Sarfaraz, Chaudhry Zahur Elahi, Fida Mohammad Khan and Mohammad Ali Hoti as well as Mahmud Haroon and Jogezai, all from the Muslim League of varying vintage, were named ministers. Some more will be named later—negotiations will be resumed and I think that Jamaat-i-Islami will find it difficult to stay out. Javed Hashmi resigned his membership of Tehrik-i-Istiqlal and was named a minister of state for students and youth. I am not surprised.

Thursday, 6 July 1978, Rawalpindi

Informal meeting of national working committee at 60 Harley Street, Safdar Ali Shah's residence. Forty-two members attended. It was decided that henceforth Tehrik-i-Istiqlal would adopt the role of an effective opposition to government. This had become necessary after induction of a martial law-Muslim League government. We would also insist that national elections should be held first and provincial elections should be held either simultaneously or immediately afterwards. It was also decided that the civilian members of the government should resign at least 90 days prior to the holding of elections.

The national working committee felt that Ziaul Haq did not intend to hold elections in the foreseeable future.

Friday, 7 July 1978, Rawalpindi, Abbottabad
Addressed a press conference. Announced national working committee's decision that henceforth Tehrik will function in opposition to government. Also criticised Muslim League, which it is reported, has been paid Rs20 million by Ziaul Haq. With interest this amount should have become Rs50 million by now. Called for early elections and lifting of ban on political activities. Also asked that politicians who have joined the martial law government should be made to quit government 90 days before the elections and should not be allowed to contest elections.

Saturday, 8 July 1978, Abbottabad
Lieutenant General Fazle Haq, corp commander Peshawar and martial law administer Zone B (NWFP) is in Abbottabad. I was invited to attend a meeting with him in the Town Hall tomorrow which I declined.

Tuesday, 11 July 1978, Abbottabad, Rawalpindi
Two office bearers of the Punjab Teachers Association called to complain about the attitude of the martial law administration. They said that at the prompting of Jamaat-i-Islami the office bearers of their association have been posted to remote places in Punjab in order to make their working difficult.

Thursday, 13 July 1978, Rawalakot
Today's daily *Jang* reported that PNA (or what is left of it) is again considering joining the martial law government and that Jamaat-i-Islami is strongly of the view that they should do so. Apparently they do not want to leave the field for the Muslim League alone.

Wednesday, 19 July 1978, Abbottabad
Wrote to General Ziaul Haq about Dr M.Z.K. Niazi, the dentist, who is under detention in Jhelum jail. Bhutto's appeal before the Supreme Court is in its last lap. Yahya Bakhtiar, the counsel for Bhutto, has finished reading the evidence and is half way through his arguments.

Thursday, 20 July 1978, Abbottabad
Foreign Secretary Shah Nawaz Khan telephoned to say that the Chinese ambassador had informed him that they would like me to visit China for two weeks from the first week of August. They have suggested that the party should comprise between three to five persons. I propose to take Wazir Ali and Wajid Razvi with me and possibly Dr Rahim ul Haq. Omar will also accompany us.

Friday, 21 July 1978, Abbottabad
Nawa-i-Waqt reported today that the Pir of Pagara was likely to be the next president of Pakistan after Fazl Elahi Chaudhri retires in August.

Heard on 21:00 news that Haji Murad Khan Jamali had been shot dead in Quetta today. He was the president of the Balochistan Muslim League.

Saturday, 22 July 1978, Abbottabad
Yesterday being Shab-i-Barat, there were no newspapers today. We were, therefore, spared the ordeal of looking at some more photographs of Ziaul Haq. The speed with which our newspapers change their tune and find hidden qualities in our rulers is sickening.

Tuesday, 25 July 1978, Abbottabad
The government issued a White Paper on the rigging of the March 1977 election by Zulfikar Ali Bhutto. It appears to be a good effort and gave the details of the extent to which the PPP government went.

Admiral Muzzaffar Hassan (chairman, Tehrik-i-Istiqlal, Karachi) telephoned to say that Nuruddin Jatoi had given notice to Jamil (Tambakoowala) to terminate his party membership. Nuruddin Jatoi's interest in the party and his political work is confined to getting rid of people from the party.

Received a letter from Begum Niazi, wife of Dr M.Z.K. Niazi who is in Jhelum district jail, to thank me for my letter to General Ziaul Haq seeking his release. Apparently Dr Niazi has been locked up for having been found to be in possession of two cyclostyled pamphlets, which were found in his clinic. The pamphlets were anti-martial law.

Monday, 31 July 1978, Rawalpindi

Attended a reception in the Chinese embassy on the occasion of the Chinese armed forces day. Met Khan Qayyum Khan who told me that the government (martial law) was not taking action against Iqbal Khan Jadoon (for malpractices in the March 1977 election) because they want him to oppose me in Abbottabad in the next election.

Wednesday, 2 Aug 1978, Abbottabad, Muzaffarabad, Abbottabad

Left for Muzaffarabad. Addressed a reception at the press club there. Met delegations in the afternoon and opened the Azad Jammu and Kashmir Tehrik central office. Arrived at Abbottabad at 19:00.

Sunday, 6–21 Aug 1978, Rawalpindi, Beijing

Syed Wajid Razvi, Wazir Ali, Omar and I left by PIA for Beijing on 6 August at the invitation of the Chinese government and returned to Islamabad on 21 August.

Besides Beijing, we visited Sheng-yang, An-shan, Shanghai, Soochow and Soo Chan. It was a fascinating visit. The Chinese communist society is highly organised. It is obvious that the Chinese have worked very hard and made great progress. They are very self-critical and know that they have to work hard to catch up with advanced countries. The difference in the earnings of the highest and lowest is about one to eight. Only ministers are allowed cars and every one else either uses public transport or cycles. There are no motorcycles in China.

Beijing is an interesting city. During our stay there we visited the 'Evergreen Peoples Commune', 20 km from Beijing, the capital. It has a population of 42,000 and a worker's force of 20,000. The commune has fourteen brigades and four management stations, one each for fruit trees, animal husbandary, industries and farm machinery. Vegetables are its main produce. The commune has a total acreage of 2,670 hectares, — vegetables on 1,667 hectares and about 1,000 hectares for other crops (maize, wheat and rice). Last year the commune supplied to the state 135,000,000 km of vegetables. The gross value of industrial production for last year was ¥21 million (Rs126 million). Fifty per cent of income is spent on current production expenditure, 40 per cent as salaries, 3 per cent as tax to the state, 3 per cent for public welfare fund and 4 per cent for increasing production annually (investment). The commune has primary, middle, and high schools for children, fourteen dispensaries with 'bare foot' doctors and one 40-bed hospital. (A new 100-bed hospital is being built). The 'bare foot' doctors are high school graduates with five months medical training in elementary medicine.

We visited a typical family house. People on the commune work up to the age of 65 (60 for women). Women are given 45 days maternity leave. After retirement, workers are given a pension of ¥23 for life. (People with no one to look after them, such as a son or a wife, are sent to old age homes). The family we visited at the commune earned ¥1,700 and after meeting their expenditure save approximately half this amount. Savings are kept in the bank, which gives an interest of 3 per cent.

We discussed with the vice chairman of the revolutionary committee of Lei Ning province, the method adopted in China after liberation in taking over business and industry. This, we were told, was done over a seven-year period and the people were divided into three categories. The comprador bourgeoisie (the agents of outside powers), the bureaucrat bourgeoisie (the agents of the reactionary regime) and the nationalist bourgeoisie (who were amenable to advice and were nationalist and therefore sympathetic to the revolution). The property of the first was taken over, the property of the second was also nationalised, whereas the third, the nationalist bourgeoisie, were allowed to function with some adjustments. For example, they were allowed to run their business and get a percentage of the profit. Almost every Chinese city has such capitalists to this day. Many are managers of their business and some hold high offices in various tiers of the country's administration. The idea was to get the cooperation of the third category of bourgeoisie and to isolate the first two categories. Private properties, such as houses were allowed to be retained by the nationalist bourgeoisie.

They were also allowed to collect rent for their house—though rents were controlled. Party membership is said to be over 30 million. A party member has to study Marx and Lenin and Mao Zedong's thoughts. He has then to be prepared to work selflessly for the people, to indulge in self criticism and to work in harmony with others for the glory of the party and the people. He has to have two party members as sponsors and if the primary organisation of the party is satisfied he is accepted as a member. The period of initiation is one year. Later we saw a show by the Beijing opera of traditional dances and songs. Razvi was shocked by the performance of the ballerina because when she swung round, her skirt would lift up and once or twice the man performing with her, picked her up. I explained to him that the ballet was the ultimate in the art of dancing and this was a part of it. However he could not get over it and thought that the Chinese have deviated from the puritan line.

Workers are given one day off in the week plus seven national holidays. A worker is given twenty days leave to see his parents before he gets married and seven to ten days leave after marriage. If a husband and wife work in different places (that is if they live separately), they can get twenty days in the year to live together.

Two judges of the Shanghai High Court (Shanghai has provincial status) called on us at the Cheing Chan Hotel to explain the judicial system of China. There are no professional lawyers. However, an accused can ask the court to give him a lawyer. These are professionals or workers with knowledge of law and the court generally provides a person of the accused's choice. He is not paid for this work since he is already drawing a salary for his other job. Cases are normally decided in three months and appeals in a month. Cases at the commune level are generally settled by compromise. Those that cannot be settled go before the district court. The general approach is to reform the person. Since there is very little private property there are not many civil cases.

Saw the Futan University on the outskirts of Shanghai. The vice chancellor told us that the policy of the cultural revolution implemented by the 'Gang of Four' has done grave damage to the development of China and a whole generation has grown up in this chaotic atmosphere. He also said that the influence of the 'Gang of Four' still lingers on and has to be erased. Incidentally the 'Gang of Four' is the subject of criticism in almost every aspect of Chinese life—from a children's nursery, ballet, drama or a commune to a steel factory.

Those who comprised this gang were Wang Hung-wen (former vice chairman of the central committee), Chang Chun-chiao, (member of the standing committee of the political bureau), Chiang Ching (Chairman Mao's wife and member of the political bureau), and Yao

Wenyuan (member of the political bureau). They had tried to seize control of the state after Mao's death.

Later spent a delightful one hour at a nursery in the premises of the Tsaoyang neighbourhood committee office and a kindergarten nearby. The children were between 3½ to 6 years of age. They sang a number of songs for us and put on a dance show. A little girl led each one of us by the hand around the classes and put on a show for us. It was a very well run kindergarten.

We then visited some flats and chatted with the inmates. One family of two persons lived in a room 10 feet by 10 feet. They had two beds, an almirah, a sideboard, two chairs and a table 4 feet by 4 feet. They also had a radio. The husband was aged 70 and his wife was 58. The husband was receiving a pension of ¥65 and the wife ¥61 per month. Both had been working in a textile mill. They were able to save ¥40 a month. Life, they said, was very secure. Their only daughter and her husband were both working. The lady was saving for a TV set but she preferred to wait till she could buy a colour TV which cost ¥800. An ordinary TV with a 19 inch screen cost only ¥200. The room had its own electricity meter. Three families share a kitchen.

There used to be eight categories or grades for salaries, now there are more, probably sixteen. The highest grade 1 earns ¥460 and the lowest ¥40. When the grades were revised the salary for grade 1 was fixed at ¥560 but premier Zhou Enlai volunteered to take only ¥400. There are very few people in grade 1. The vice chancellor of Futan University gets ¥360 and ministers in the government who are in grade 4 or 5 get ¥300. Workers get between ¥40 and ¥150. Skilled workers may get as much as ¥180. Managers or directors of communes or factories generally get less—around ¥90. A worker, if he is assigned to another duty, continues to draw his original salary. The teaching staff is paid well. Assistant lecturers get ¥70 and the scale is ¥70-110. The lecturers' scale is ¥100-180, professors get ¥150-220. Similarly heads of department may get ¥180-300. Pensions are 70 per cent of salary drawn and are given for life. Retirement age is 60-65 for men and 50-55 for women. There is no unemployment in China.

There are five autonomous regions in China. Inner Mongolia, Xinjiang, Tibet, Guangxi and Wingar. The last is inhabited by the Khwai (or Muslims). There are approximately 10 million Khwai in Ninghsia Autonomous Region and some more Muslims in other parts of China. Ninety per cent of the people of China are of the Han race (not to be confused with Chingez Khan who was a 'Mon'—or Mongol). Han is pronounced as 'Khan' in Chinese.

There is very little difference between a province and an autonomous region. However, autonomous regions are allowed to teach their own language in schools—in the Chinese script—and use it in official business in addition to Mandarin Chinese. The autonomous regions are inhabited by people of a racial stock other than Han and are in a majority in their own province. In Xinjiang the main race is Kazaks and some of them are Muslims though not in a majority. There are Khwai in Xinjiang too.

Dogs are practically non-existent in China. We did not see a single dog during our stay in that country and only half a dozen flies. However we were told that dogs are allowed to be kept in the rural areas and in some parts of China their meat is eaten. A possible foreign exchange earner for Pakistan.

Thursday, 24 Aug 1978, Abbottabad
Ziaul Haq swore in a new cabinet of 22 ministers yesterday. Five are from Muslim League, three from the Jamaat-i-Islami, three from the Jamiat-ul-Ulema-i-Islam and two from the PDP. The remaining nine are other civilians. An interesting appointment is that of Mir Ali Ahmed Talpur as defence minister. It makes no difference to the people. The musical chairs will continue for some time and these people will be discarded when it suits Ziaul Haq. No generals have been taken in the cabinet and Ziaul Haq was anxious to give the impression that the civilian cabinet will take all decisions including those pertaining to policies when elections will be held, which he 'hoped' would be by October 1979. He has, therefore, not committed himself on the elections and has put all the onus for their delay on the UDF. It will also be the UDF that is likely to take the responsibility for the decision on Bhutto's fate—whose case is likely to be decided or rather come up for a decision by the end of September or October.

Omar was busy getting things sorted out before his departure for London tomorrow night. It has been nice having him here. He has developed a great deal of maturity and understanding. He works very hard on his subject and is very interested in it. He will be spending a year more in the UK (at Essex University) for his Masters and we shall look forward to his return after completing his studies later next year.

Ali is staying here a little longer and is planning to stay in Karachi on his way to London. He is also doing very well there. It is very nice having him back here for his summer vacations. He will be much longer in the UK and it is very convenient that Shirin is in the UK too.

Omar reminded me that I had to send a postcard and a small gift to the family we had visited in Shen-yang and gave me their address.

Saturday, 26 Aug 1978, Rawalpindi

Addressed a press conference. Spoke about the worsening economic situation and the inability of the government to cope with it.

Had dinner with the Chinese ambassador at Islamabad. Khudai Noor, Nuruddin Jatoi, Munir Shah, Mushir, Razvi, Wazir Ali, Rafi Butt, Colonel Tassaddaq, and Akbar Khan Bugti were also present. After dinner, we decided that the national working committee meeting should be in Quetta on 21 and 22 September.

Wednesday, 30 Aug 1978, Abbottabad

Spoke to Wazir Ali. I told him that he should ensure that Nawaz Sharif and Amin Butt (the chartered accountant) attend the 9 September board meeting of the party paper at Rawalpindi. It is becoming impossible to finance the paper any longer and we will probably have to close it down. The response of the party has been poor—only Munir Shah has increased his investment by another Rs25,000 to Rs50,000.

Monday, 4 Sept 1978, Abbottabad

Khuda Dad Khan called. He said that martial law authorities were telling prospective candidates to join the Muslim League and he named George Sikandar Zaman, Hanif Khan, Iqbal Khan Jadoon and Nawabzada Azmat Ali Khan of Kohat in this context. He said that Lieutenant General Fazle Haq is particularly active in the matter. This tallies with my own information.

Gavin Young of the *Sunday Observer*, who had met me last year, telephoned asking to see me. Asked him to lunch on Thursday, 7th.

There is complete confusion about Eid. It was announced at midnight that the moon had been sighted in Dera Ismail Khan and Peshawar and the martial law administrator had decided that Eid will be celebrated today. People here took out a procession in protest and our driver Khushaal joined in. They shouted slogans against the government and said that Eid could not be celebrated after 28 fasts. At *sehri* time 03:00 again the government announcement was repeated on loudspeakers. Then at 07:00 came another announcement that it was not Eid and today would be another fast. In Peshawar and all of NWFP, except Hazara division, Eid was celebrated today. This evening we looked hard into a clear sky for the moon but none of us—Amina, Ali and Shirin on the roof—could see the moon. Nevertheless the TV announced at 19:00 that the moon had been sighted and Eid will be celebrated tomorrow. A sad commentary on the state of affairs at the end of the twentieth century and quite understandable for a thoroughly incompetent priest-ridden government.

Incidentally the new government is talking of celebrating the Pakistan Day on 27 Ramzan (14 August 1947 was on 27 Ramzan) instead of the traditional 14 August. It will lead to further confusion and will mean that people will be celebrating this on different days.

Saturday, 9 Sept 1978, Rawalpindi
BBC reported 53 people killed in Tehran riots yesterday and 68 today. Shah's position is precarious and I do not think that he can last very long.

Ziaul Haq went to Tehran today via Kabul where he stopped for a few hours and met President Taraki of Afghanistan.

Monday, 11 Sept 1978, Abbottabad
Ali left with Mushir Pesh Imam for Rawalpindi on his way to Karachi from where he will leave for London in a week's time. Ali has relaxed here and spent most of his time meeting friends and listening to music. He is, however, very interested in his subject and will do well in his profession—*Inshallah.*

Wednesday, 13 Sept 1978, Abbottabad
Akbar Khan Bugti has been disqualified by a martial law tribunal from standing for elections for seven years. Surprising, since he had not been served with a notice and had not been heard.

Thursday, 14 Sept 1978, Abbottabad
Heard the news that Ziaul Haq has proclaimed himself the president of Pakistan from 16 September when Fazal Elahi Chaudhry retires. Fazal Elahi's five years in office were to be completed on 14 August 1978 and he had tendered his resignation.

Friday, 15 Sept 1978, Abbottabad, Rawalpindi, Lahore
Arrived in Karachi at 18:30 to a tumultuous welcome. A large crowd with drums and pipes, cars and scooters welcomed me at the airport. My trouser hip pocket was picked and I lost my purse and my driving license. The second such experience. I had lost my purse ten years earlier in 1968 when I had addressed a PPP meeting in Lahore (when Bhutto was in jail). I managed to save my watch. It has been so long since public activity has been banned that I had become careless.

Saturday, 16 Sept 1978, Karachi
Ziaul Haq took the oath of office as president of Pakistan. Spent the day at Mushir's and Micas (Humayun Gauhar's) office meeting people. Approved the draft instructions for the party election prepared by Raja Afzal of Jhelum. Was shown the map and the cover prepared for my book *The First Round.*

Monday, 18 Sept 1978, Karachi
Addressed a press conference and expressed dissatisfaction with the accountability process (particularly the way Akbar Khan Bugti had been disqualified without a hearing) and the lack of publicity for Tehrik-i-Istiqlal news on TV and radio.

Spoke to Lieutenant General Abbasi, the martial law administrator, Sindh, and protested at the arrest of Chhapra. (He was arrested today afternoon for last night's meeting). Abbasi was very officious and rather pompous on the telephone. I told him that his action was not justified in view of the fact that ministers (Prof. Ghafoor Ahmed) have been having similar meetings in violation of martial law. I also told him that it appeared that the government had picked on the Tehrik-i-Istiqlal for victimisation and if this was so, I would not take the situation quietly. The conversation ended abruptly and it appears that we will be forced into confrontation with the government which I do not want — at least at this stage.

General Ziaul Haq telephoned a little before midnight about the Asghar Chowk incident. I told him that we did not want confrontation but were ready if he pushed us into it. I repeated my demand that our workers be released. He asked that I should wait for another two months before resuming full political activity by when Bhutto's case would be decided. I am not satisfied with this conversation and I feel that the line adopted by Ziaul Haq will lead the country into difficulties. He offered me the use of the radio and TV instead of holding public meetings — an offer he has made twice since January. I do not think he is serious about it, since it has not been followed up by his government. He also said that he would apply these restrictions equally on his ministers who so far have been flouting martial law orders on the use of loudspeakers and holding of public meetings.

Wrote letters of thanks to Wang Ping-nan (president Chinese People's Friendship Association) and a few others for their hospitality during our visit to China.

Wednesday, 20 Sept 1978, Quetta
Addressed the Quetta District Bar Association. Called on Sardar Khair Bux Marri and exchanged views on the national scene.

Dinner with Akbar Khan Bugti. Heard that his son Saleem Bugti had also been disqualified for seven years from taking part in elections. He was required to appear before the tribunal on 24 September and this decision has been taken without giving him an opportunity to do so.

Khair Bux Marri was very cynical about the role of the army and felt that we in Pakistan were going through a neo-colonial era in which the military and the bureaucracy had replaced the British colonists. They would not, he felt, let go their hold easily. Since they were from Punjab, he felt that this power junta had acceptability there and the reaction against it was naturally greater in the other provinces — which he resents being termed 'smaller provinces'. He asked whether Balochistan was smaller than any other province in size or in resources? Altogether a very useful meeting. This Baloch attitude on national affairs is understandable and we will have to remove these irritants before a genuine federation can emerge.

Thursday, 21 Sept 1978, Quetta

Meetings of national working committee at Anwar Khan Durrani's house from 10:00-16:30. Discussed the general political situation, possibility of a death sentence for Bhutto and its possible consequences, particularly of martial law, consequences of the UDF forming governments in the provinces, party elections and progress of party work. Discussion was useful, the level high and members were critical of the role of our second level leadership.

Friday, 22 Sept 1978, Quetta

Decided to call for applications for party tickets first for National Assembly constituencies and then for provincial assemblies constituencies. This process is to be set in motion after the party elections are completed. It was also decided that candidates selected for National Assembly constituencies are to be consulted when awarding tickets for the provincial assemblies. The award of tickets would be provisional and will be confirmed, if the candidates' work in their constituencies is found to be satisfactory.

Party symbol was discussed and it was decided that we should ask the chief election commissioner for the 'sickle' as the symbol of our party. Mushir will try to arrange a meeting with the chief election commissioner, Maulvi Mushtaq Hussain, on 2 October. Party line on provincial autonomy was discussed and it was agreed that the present party line as enunciated in my recent statements and the party manifesto was adequate. It was decided to hold the next meeting of the national working committee at Peshawar on 16 and 17 November 1978.

Addressed a press conference at Anwar Durrani's in which the press was given three strongly worded resolutions against victimisation of Tehrik-i-Istiqlal by the government, discriminatory treatment in the matter of accountability, time on radio and TV and arrest of party workers.

Said my Friday prayers at a city mosque where the *khatib* spoke a lot of nonsense. It is a pity that most of our *maulvis* who lead Friday prayers have neither the education nor the intelligence to make full use of the opportunity for the betterment of society. This particular *maulvi* spent his time relating irrelevant and ridiculous tales which had nothing to do with religion.

Tuesday, 26 Sept 1978, Abbottabad, Havelian, Lora, Murree

Left at 08:30 for a tour of my National Assembly constituency NA-13 Abbottabad-II. Addressed gatherings at Havelian, Karakki, Jabri, Banda, Kohala, Ropar, Ghanbir, and Lora. Arrived at Murree at 19:45 in pouring rain. We were met at Ghora Gali by Haji Akram, our provincial candidate for the Galiat constituency, and Malik Mansoor and a large number of party workers. Discussed the problems of the Lora area and decided to: (a) Start a development trust for the area. (b) With the funds so raised: (i) Lay a two mile pipe for drinking water from Dunna Nural to Dabran for a population of four to five thousand of Pattay Mundrian, Dakhan, Lassan and Danna. (ii) Start a college at Lora. (iii) Run at least three dispensaries in the constituency. (iv) If funds permit, construct a rope bridge near Banda (Jabri) for the people of Dakkan Paysar.

For this purpose decided to meet the commissioner on 29 September and asked Aleem to enquire from the provincial government whether it could handle any of these projects.

The points to be taken up with the commissioner Hazara are: (a) Increase the present ratio of wheat of four seers per head per month to eight seers because of the failure of the crop this year. (b) Hospital at Lora. (c) Water pipe project. (d) Rope bridge at Jabri (Banda).

Wednesday, 27 Sept 1978, Murree, Swar Gali, Nathiagali, Abbottabad

Met a number of delegations in the early morning including one of horse renting union who complained that horses are not allowed on roads in Murree, causing them loss of livelihood and another, of Kashmiris who suggested that visas should be allowed to Indian held Kashmir so that they could meet their relatives.

Addressed a sizeable gathering of workers on the lawn of the house where I was staying. Another meeting at Sawar Gali. Maulana Noorani was addressing a gathering in a mosque at Barian a mile away so I called on him and we talked on national issues for about half an hour.

Later stopped at Khaira Gali and Tauhidabad and addressed a gathering in Ahle Hadis mosque. The *khatib* in his well prepared address of welcome asked me questions on why the Tehrik-i-Istiqlal had left the PNA—the usual line adopted by the UDF parties. I think that he thought that he had me cornered. I spoke for about 45 minutes and enjoyed it thoroughly. By the time I finished, the audience was visibly impressed by my logic and the justification of our exit.

Visited the party office at Kalabagh. Discussed local problems and promised Rs15,000 for a water pipe line near Khaira Gali. The local population is putting up an equal amount.

Thursday, 5 Oct 1978, Lahore, Sheikhupura

Addressed the Sheikhupura District Bar Association in the morning and the workers of Sheikhupura district in the afternoon. Arrived at Lahore at 18:30. It is apparent that there is not much life left in the PPP movement launched a few days ago. One person who tried self-immolation died of burns yesterday. Benazir Bhutto and Farooq Leghari were taken into custody yesterday and so were many other workers at different places. I said at the Gujranwala district bar yesterday that no movement can succeed if the leaders do not lead. I do not think that the PPP is capable of launching any movement effective enough to get Bhutto out of jail.

Had dinner with Khurshid Kasuri. His father, Omar Kasuri, Omar's wife and Bakhtiar were there. Took opinions on Bhutto's fate. Mian Sahib, Khurshid and Bakhtiar thought that he would be hanged.

Sunday, 8 Oct 1978, Lahore, Rawalpindi

Called on Chief Justice and Begum Anwar ul Haq at their Harley Street residence. Anwarul Haq and I had attended a course at the Imperial Defence College in UK together in 1955. He said that the Supreme Court had not as yet made up its mind about the Bhutto case and I got the impression that the verdict may go either way.

Monday, 9 Oct 1978, Rawalpindi, Abbottabad

Major Nadir Parvez of Attock conspiracy fame called in the morning and signed the membership form of the party. He has considerable influence in Faisalabad and is a prospective candidate for the National Assembly.

Received a letter from Shirin and another from Omar, who has joined Cambridge for post graduate studies in M.Phil. He likes Cambridge. Ali is living on the campus at the Thames Polyclinic.

Saturday, 21 Oct 1978, Rawalpindi, Abbottabad

Last day of manifesto committee's deliberations. Agreed on all points except policy regarding industry. Wazir Ali, supported mildly by Akbar Khan Bugti, was in favour of: (a) Private industry with up to ten employees. (b) Cooperatives with ten employees per shareholder. (c) State industry confined to steel, energy, communications, shipping, oil, petro chemicals.

Wajid Razvi and Mushir were in favour of retaining present private sector industries in the private sector. Otherwise they agreed with the suggestions made by Wazir Ali. Decided to put up both proposals before the national working committee. Mushir will bring the draft manifesto for discussion to Rawalpindi and we will meet on 30 October.

Today's papers reported Ziaul Haq as having said that he was willing to hand over power to PNA if they merged into one party. The trouble is that he knows that they will not do so and they know that if they did so, there was no guarantee that he would abdicate power.

Monday, 30 Oct 1978, Islamabad, Abbottabad

Mushir and I called on Justice Maulvi Mushtaq Hussain to ask for the 'sickle' as the party's election symbol. He said that the election order will have to be amended as the 'sickle' was not in the present list of symbols. He hoped that there would be no difficulty but said that it was possible that someone may raise an objection—possibly the government—as it was similar to the communist symbol. He said he would let us know in a couple of weeks.

Maulvi Mushtaq said that elections could not be held before 15 June 1979 as voters' lists and other work would not be completed before that date. He said that 60 days were required for the electoral process to be completed, so at least two months clear notice would have to be given. He said that 15 October was the likely date and said that if this date was not adhered to he would resign his office as chief election commissioner. He felt that Ziaul Haq wants to hold elections in October 1979. Maulvi Mushtaq Hussain thought that A.K. Brohi was an evil influence on Ziaul Haq and he was doing his best to obstruct the electoral process.

Thursday, 2 Nov 1978, Chinjah, Massa Gojran, Jabri, Abbottabad

Started a tour of my constituency on foot. Half an hour's climb took us on top of a hill overlooking Massa Gojran. Another half an hour took us to the village where we were received by the locals and school children. Maulana Shafi welcomed us and I spoke briefly. Asked them to repair their primary school for which I promised some financial assistance. Resumed our walk at 10:30 along the bridal path and for a while on the recently constructed road to Jabri. Arrived at Jabri village and were met by the local population led by Malik Abdul Rehman and his cousin Naib Subedar Abdul Rehman. They are our staunch supporters though Malik Abdul Rehman opposed me in the March 1977 election. He is a Dhoondh or Abbasi and was a supporter of Inayat ur Rehman.

Altogether a very useful and successful visit. No government official had visited the area since 1947, when Tollington, a British settlement commissioner, had been to this part of Hazara, so ill served with communications.

Friday, 17 Nov 1978, Peshawar

A stormy session of national working committee. The committee which was appointed yesterday to look into the affairs of Tehrik-i-Istiqlal Sindh and Karachi (Wazir Ali, Syed Munir Shah, Moinuddin Shah, Zahur Butt, A.B. Awan and Khudai Noor) recommended unanimously that: (a) Jamil Ahmed Tambakoowala's membership should be terminated as decided by provincial working committee Sindh. (b) N.K. Jatoi and Obaid-ur-Rehman should be stripped of their party offices of chairman Sindh and joint secretary centre but may contest elections for offices in the forthcoming party elections.

The working committee considered these recommendation and decided that: (a) Jamil Ahmed Tambakoowala's membership should be terminated as recommended. (b) N.K. Jatoi and Obaid-ur-Rehman should not be stripped of party offices but should be debarred from taking part in the forthcoming party elections.

Obaid-ur-Rehman accepted this decision but N.K. Jatoi resigned his party office as a protest and walked out followed by Akbar Khan Bugti, who we thought had gone to persuade him to stay but learnt later that he also disagreed with the decision. Asaf Vardag went with him but came later and told us that both (Jatoi and Akbar Khan Bugti) had resigned from the party but he had asked them to withhold the announcement of their resignation for three days to give him time to sort the matter out. Jatoi and Bugti left for Karachi in the evening. Everybody else was in agreement with the decision taken. Ahmed Mian Soomro was appointed chairman Sindh.

Jatoi has not done a stroke of work in the four years that he has been chairman Sindh except sack people from the party at regular intervals. He has not toured the province at all and he never even acknowledged any letter addressed to him. His exit—though it will cause some ripples in the party—will be good for the Tehrik-i-Istiqlal.

Akbar Khan Bugti is likely to leave the party in a day or two and his exit will have both positive and negative repercussions. Those who joined with him and who are his supporters in a tribal environment will leave but his exit will also be hailed by many who did not favour his joining the party. In Balochistan, the party will be weakened and it will have to re-orientate its strategy and thinking more on ideological rather than on tribal lines.

The national working committee considered the party manifesto and agreed on the agricultural policy, retaining the limit of 25 acres per head and the formation of cooperatives.

Saturday, 18 Nov 1978, Peshawar
Third day of national working committee meeting. Asaf Vardag raised the question of Nur Uddin Jatoi's resignation and suggested that he should be allowed to take part in party elections and if this was done he could possibly be persuaded to stay in the party. Also this might stop Akbar Khan Bugti from resigning from the party. The working committee discussed this and did not agree to change its decision.

Thursday, 21 Dec 1978, Multan, Lahore
Zulfikar Ali Bhutto concluded his three-day appearance before the Supreme Court in the Nawab Ahmed Khan murder case. He wept on the first day and cracked jokes on the second. There is some sympathy

for him although no one doubts the correctness of the death sentence awarded by the Lahore High Court. In his concluding address today, he warned of the grave consequences of his being hanged. The judgment of the Supreme Court is anyone's guess but knowledgeable opinion (Mian Mahmud Ali Kasuri amongst them) is that the court will uphold the Lahore High Court verdict. What Ziaul Haq will do is not so certain. He has said many times that he will not change the verdict of the Supreme Court (meaning that he will hang Bhutto if the court so decides) but he is not known for doing what he says he will do.

I expect that the Supreme Court will take its decision by 16 January (it will probably be in recess from 22 December to 9 January).

Friday, 22 Dec 1978, Lahore
Amina and I dined with Sylvi Sher Ali. (Her husband Major General Nawabzada Sher Ali Khan Pataudi was away in Islamabad). Moinuddin (Sylvi's father) was there. Moin had an interesting theory about Bhutto. He said that if he (or his wife on his behalf) had pleaded insanity, he could have been acquitted in this case. I am inclined to agree with him. However, it is too late now. The arguments are over and only the sentence remains to be heard.

Saturday, 23 Dec 1978, Lahore
Zulfikar Ali Bhutto's case ended in the Supreme Court. The judgment has been 'reserved' and is expected to be announced in the second half of January. His appearance—at his request—in the Supreme Court has I feel not been helpful to him. He has stressed full confidence in the Supreme Court and has acknowledged that he has been given a patient and a fair hearing. Justice Anwar ul Haq has conducted the case very well and shown tolerance and patience in dealing with the case.

Diary 1979

Friday, 16 Jan 1979, Karachi

J.A. Rahim called. He is willing to join the Tehrik-i-Istiqlal but wants to address a press conference to express his views on the *mullahs*. He said that it was only fair that we should decide whether we still wanted him after his press conference.

Sunday, 21 Jan 1979, Lahore

Fourth national council elections of Tehrik-i-Istiqlal were held in the central office, Ghazi road, today in a relatively calm atmosphere. I was elected unopposed as president and Mushir was elected as secretary general after an interesting contest. Mushir (82), Wajid Razvi (62), and Asaf Vardag (43) contested the elections. I had maintained my neutrality and the result was what I had expected. Wajid Razvi and Asaf Vardag conducted themselves very well and congratulated Mushir in suitable terms after the result was announced. There was a taxi strike today and partly because of this, the total number of councillors who attended the session today was somewhat thin, the total number of central councillors being around 230.

Monday, 22 Jan 1979, Lahore

Second day of party's central elections. Addressed the council and told the members that I would step down from party office after general elections in the country and the restoration of democracy.

It was also decided that the next meeting of national council will be held in Quetta on Thursday, 19 and Friday, 20 July in which I will ask for an amendment to the party's constitution to the effect that no person will hold the office of party president or secretary general for more than two consecutive terms.

Mian Mahmud Ali Kasuri, Dr I.H. Qureshi, Begum Sabiha Shakil and Baz Mohammad Khan Mehtar Zai were elected vice presidents, Nafis Siddiqui as publicity secretary, Nisar Ahmed Khuhro, Syed Mukhtiar Ahmed Bacha, Manzoor Ahmed Wattoo and Azher Hussin Zaidi as joint secretaries general and Mian Khurshid Mahmud Kasuri as treasurer. Elections were conducted in a very good atmosphere quite unlike the Punjab elections.

Addressed the press after the party elections and confirmed the adoption of the 'sickle' as the party's election symbol.

Tuesday, 23 Jan 1979, Lahore
Dinner with Mian Mahmud Ali Kasuri. Mian Sahib was advocating (1) presidential system of government in Pakistan; (2) proportional representation in the elections and party list; and (3) smaller provinces—about sixteen instead of the present four (in order to reduce the power of Punjab and thereby establish a workable federation). He intends raising these issues in the party's national working committee. He also intends visiting Quetta during the next few days to meet some Baloch leaders in order to try to get them to join the Tehrik-i-Istiqlal.

Saturday, 3 Feb 1979, Karachi
Ayatollah Khomeini, who arrived in Tehran three days ago from Paris after 17 years in exile, was to address a press conference today.

Had a talk with J.A. Rahim who decided to join the Tehrik-i-Istiqlal. He will be announcing his decision on 6 February. Iqbal Burney was also agreeable but somewhat shy of making a formal announcement. He is a highly respected person in the journalist community and should be an asset to the party.

Monday, 5 Feb 1979, Karachi
J.A. Rahim (former minister in Bhutto's government and secretary general of PPP) issued a statement joining Tehrik-i-Istiqlal. He is a man of character and highly intelligent. Has a reputation of being a socialist of the extreme variety but in my discussions with him I have not found him unreasonable.

Tuesday, 6 Feb 1979, Karachi
In the Nawab Ahmed Khan murder case the Supreme Court upheld the verdict of the High Court Lahore (four to three) sentencing Zulfikar Ali Bhutto to death by a majority. This brings to an end the first phase of this case. Bhutto has been allowed one week to put in a review appeal. The verdict is not unexpected.

No further restrictions have been placed on political activity, other than those which already exist but schools and colleges have been closed. I do not expect any spontaneous reaction against the Supreme Court decision but some sporadic trouble will probably take place in the interior of Sindh.

Tuesday, 13 Feb 1979, Lahore, Sargodha (Lallian-Chillanwali)
Left for Sargodha at 09:15 along with Mushir Pesh Imam and Nisar Khuhro. A lunch meeting at Mehar Ghulam Abbas Lalli's at Lallian. Later stopped briefly to call on a local 'Peerni' [a female pir] who gave us tea. I do not believe in Pirs or Peernis but she has a following in the area.

Today's programme at the Peerni's place at Lallian and at Silanwali was characterised by dancing horses, bands and dancing men and probably boys dressed as women—an odd start for the Islamic era launched by Ziaul Haq.

Wednesday, 14 Feb 1979, Sargodha, Phulaswan, Bhalwal, Alipur Noon
Heard that the Supreme Court heard Bhutto's appeal for a review of the court's decision in his case and decided to give more time to the defence to prepare the case. 24 February was fixed as the date for the hearing and it is expected that the appeal will be rejected on that day. In the meantime Nusrat Bhutto has filed a writ in the Sindh Shariat Bench (these benches have been recently created) to ask that the evidence of 'approver' Masud Mahmud in Bhutto's case should be declared invalid as an approver's evidence is not—according to her—applicable under Islamic law. Earlier, yesterday Malik Ghulam Jilani's application of writ in the Lahore High Court asking for a stay of Bhutto's execution and offering to pay blood money or *qisas* was rejected by the High Court.

Thursday, 15 Feb 1979, Alipur Noon, Jaharabad, Naushera, Sargodha
The Sindh High Court Shariat Bench has rejected Mrs Nusrat Bhutto's writ application about the invalidity of an approver's evidence in the Bhutto case. The decks have now been cleared for the drop scene and I expect that the Supreme Court will give its decision on 24 February. After that it will be Ziaul Haq's decision in the mercy appeals that will decide Bhutto's fate. Ziaul Haq's decision is anyone's guess. I

think that circumstances suggest that Ziaul Haq will reject the mercy appeal.

Fazal Elahi Chaudhri, the former president of Pakistan, joined many others seeking clemency in Bhutto's case.

Friday, 23 Feb 1979, Abbottabad
Mr Nasiri called. Nasiri is a US citizen—originally an Afghan and is married to General Abdul Razzak Khan's daughter. Razzak was the Afghan air force chief between 1954 and 1970 and was later imprisoned by the late President Daud. He is still in jail serving a life sentence. I gathered from Nasiri's conversation that the Pakistan government is backing the refugees from Afghanistan to start guerrilla operations in Afghanistan against the Taraki government. Nasiri said that he was off to Abu Dhabi to seek financial support from the Sheikh of Abu Dhabi. I gathered that the US government was likely to back such a move and possibly funnel support to Pakistan through Saudi Arabia or the Gulf Sheikhs. Rather risky on the part of the Pakistan government to get involved in such planning but with Jamaat-i-Islami in the seat of power this is just what they will try to do. Nasiri was talking about a Wazir Malik (who claimed to have the following of 400,000 armed men from Balochistan to Chitral), having pledged his support to a holy war in Afghanistan. I told him that it was most unlikely that any Malik could muster more than 1,000 rifles and if the rest of their planning was based on such bogus information, they were wasting their time.

I feel that Pakistan must stay clear of the Afghan problem and should not convert Pakistan into a base for operations against Afghanistan. In any case I doubt that any world power is ready at present to stick its neck out to mount such an operation. The risks are too great and Pakistan's own survival and security would be placed in jeopardy.

Thursday, 1 March 1979, Abbottabad
Ziaul Haq spoke at a press conference at Lahore indicating: (a) He would abide by the Supreme Court verdict in Bhutto's case hinting that he would hang Bhutto if the Supreme Court did not change its verdict. (b) He would announce the date of election 'well before' 14 August 1979. (c) Only two months campaigning would be allowed.

(d) The civilian government would not be asked to resign and would stay in office before and during the elections. (e) The army would have a constitutional role in certain specified circumstances.

Monday, 5 March 1979, Peshawar, Bannu
Brigadier Zafar, military secretary to Ziaul Haq, telephoned to say that Ziaul Haq wished to see me. Told him that I would be available on 14 or 15 March. He said that I should give him an earlier date, so I said that I could also come on the 12th. He said he would call back.

Tuesday, 6 March 1979, Bannu, Dera Ismail Khan
The response in Bannu is very good. Today was like an election campaign. People are enthusiastic and receptive. Whilst I was addressing the meeting at Serai Haji Zar Ali Shah, Brigadier Zafar telephoned again asking me to see General Ziaul Haq on 12 March in Rawalpindi.

Met Ijlal Hyder Zaidi, the chief secretary NWFP. He is an old acquaintance—deputy commissioner, Sukkur in 1968.

Monday, 12 March 1979, Abbottabad, Rawalpindi
Met General Ziaul Haq for about an hour. My first meeting since 13 June 1978. Talked generally about elections and other related matters. He talked of completing the electoral process by August and suggested holding local bodies elections first with which I could not agree. He also suggested some enhanced powers for the president which I said we could look at and could give our views only after we had seen the proposal. I made it clear that any changes in the constitution should be made only by an elected assembly.

Friday, 23 March 1979, Karachi
Pakistan Day. Ziaul Haq announced that general elections would be held on 17 November 1979.

Saturday, 24 March 1979, Karachi
Supreme Court unanimously rejected the review petition against their judgment in Bhutto's case. The legal battle to save his life has therefore ended and it is now upto Ziaul Haq to save his life, if he wishes to do so. The announcement of an election date yesterday was

obviously to distract public attention from Bhutto's fate. Zia's other pronouncement indicate that Bhutto will be hanged. But Ziaul Haq is very unpredictable and we will have to wait for a few days more to see the finale.

Tuesday, 27 March 1979, Sukkur, Karachi, Lahore

Newspapers say that Bhutto has been served with a 'death warrant' which means that he could be hanged in a few days if Ziaul Haq does not accept his appeal, which has not been submitted as yet. Five more days remain for the appeal to be submitted. Whether he will be hanged is, however, anyone's guess.

Monday, 2 April 1979, Serai Alamgir, Rawalpindi

BBC broadcast tonight said that Benazir Bhutto (Zulfikar Ali Bhutto's daughter) had been told by the jail superintendent that she and her mother could see her father tomorrow and that this could be her last meeting with him. BBC thought that Bhutto could be hanged on Wednesday, 4 April.

Wednesday, 4 April 1979, Thana, Mingore

Zulfikar Ali Bhutto was hanged at 02:00 in Rawalpindi district jail this morning. His body was later flown to Larkana where he was buried in the presence of his relatives at 10:30.

Thursday, 5 April 1979, Mingora, Tallah (Dir), Thana

Called on the Wali of Swat. Invited him to allow his son Amirzeb to join the Tehrik-i-Istiqlal. He is inclined to agree but asked me to allow him a couple of months to allow the dust to settle after Bhutto's hanging and to consult his supporters. The Wali is also anxious to keep on the right side of the government but I think that he will ultimately join us. His political position is good and he can influence three National Assembly and nine Provincial Assembly seats.

The commissioner Malakand called to convey a request from Lieutenant General Fazle Haq, governor NWFP, to see him on my way back. Agreed to do so tomorrow afternoon.

Heard of some disturbances in Thana and Batkhela against Bhutto's hanging and heard on BBC of some trouble in Rawalpindi. PPP, leadership is, however, totally ineffective and I do not expect the present disturbances to last for more than a few days. The PPP leadership had misled the party workers to believe that Ziaul Haq could not possibly hang Bhutto—hence the sudden shock. But they will get over it particularly because their remaining leadership is totally incapable of leading any movement on a national scale. Sporadic cases of arson and stoning will however occur.

Friday, 6 April 1979, Thana, Sakhakot, Peshawar, Abbottabad
Had lunch and a long chat with Fazle Haq (the governor). He appeared impressed with the Tehrik-i-Istiqlal's progress and read out a letter written by him in June 1978 to Ziaul Haq in which he had said that the Tehrik-i-Istiqlal is the party to be watched. He appeared quite relaxed although today was a Friday and Bhutto's *qul*—demonstrations were expected. Ziaul Haq telephoned Fazle Haq (whilst I was with him) to ask about the general situation in the province. I learnt from Fazle Haq about Bhutto's last few days. Fazle Haq had known that Bhutto would be hanged three days before his hanging. Nusrat Bhutto tried desperately to see Ziaul Haq the day before he was hanged but was not granted an interview. However, a general called on her instead. She pleaded for mercy and asked that her husband should be allowed to leave the country. She said that he would be ready to promise that he and his family would not indulge in politics ever again.

Thursday, 19 April 1979, Serai Alamgir, Rawalpindi, Abbottabad
Radio announced the *en bloc* exit of Baloch leaders from the NDP. Ghaus Bux Bizenjo, Ataullah Mengal, Gul Khan Nasir and half a dozen other prominent persons addressed a press conference at Karachi and resigned their membership of NDP.

Saturday, 21 April 1979, Rawalpindi
Brigadier Zafar, military secretary to General Ziaul Haq, contacted me whilst I was in Rawalpindi and enquired whether I could see Ziaul Haq today. I told him that I was on my way on a two weeks tour of Balochistan and Sindh and would not be available till 5 May.

Thursday, 26 April 1979, Quetta, Sibbi, Khanpur
The visit to Balochistan has been useful particularly at this time when NDP is in disarray. Mian Mahmud Ali Kasuri (who has been with

some of the Baloch leaders in NAP) has been meeting a number of them during his stay in Quetta, amongst them, Ghaus Bux Bizenjo, Gul Khan Nasir, Mahmud Kurd and Hashim Khan Gilzai. Mian Mahmud Ali is anxious that they should join us but I feel that we should move rather warily. Their joining us without a reasonable identity of views on national issues and the party programme could create serious difficulties later. However, exchange of views would be useful. I have already asked Mushir to arrange a meeting with Ataullah Khan Mengal on 1 May.

Haji Maula Bux Soomro was at Shikarpur and thought that my tour of Sindh was a little too early (after Bhutto's hanging). I explained that this was not a factor with me in arranging the tour and judging from the public response today and the size of the meeting at Khanpur the visit did not appear to be ill-timed.

Tuesday, 1 May 1979, Mirpurkhas, Hyderabad, Karachi

May Day. I complete my current tour of Balochistan and Sindh today which I started from Dera Ghazi Khan on 21 April. It has been a very successful trip and the response has been excellent—particularly in Sindh where I have addressed ten meetings. Five of these were scheduled and and the other five were unscheduled gatherings. If all goes well and there is no unforeseen development, the Tehrik-i-Istiqlal should emerge as a strong force in Sindh. There is a considerable emotional attachment with Bhutto but there is goodwill for Tehrik-i-Istiqlal as well. The PNA parties are particularly unpopular.

On reaching Hyderabad addressed a convention of Sindh Istiqlal Student's Federation in Latifabad.

Ataullah Khan Mengal came to dinner in Karachi and we discussed the possibilities of his group joining us. We agreed that we should not rush into it and that, should they feel so inclined, the common ground between us should be examined in depth. I asked him to let me know if and when they are ready to do this. Ataullah appears a balanced person and has a healthy outlook on national issues. If a lasting arrangement can be worked out with these Baloch leaders, it would be in the overall national interest.

Wednesday, 2 May 1979, Karachi, Lahore

Called on Maulana Shah Ahmed Noorani. We discussed the general situation and agreed that: (1) local bodies elections should be held before general elections; (2) amendments to the 1973 constitution of any kind, especially enhancement of the president's powers and giving the armed forces a role in politics were totally unjustified. We agreed that both our parties would oppose these moves.

Met workers at the Asghar Chowk party office. Khurshid Sohail of Dubai donated some money to the party as also Raja Abdul Rehman. I paid back part of the money to Mushir which he had advanced for the acquisition of the Asghar Chowk party office. Lunched with Altaf Gauhar.

Thursday, 3 May 1979, Lahore

National working committee meeting held in the central office. Discussed election strategy, the political situation, the future of PPP and my forthcoming meeting with Ziaul Haq. It was assumed that Ziaul Haq would discuss: (a) local bodies elections; (b) powers of president; (c) role of the armed forces. It was decided that: (a) local bodies elections should not be held before the national elections; (b) the newly elected National Assembly alone had the right to amend the constitution and enhance the powers of the president; (c) the armed forces had no role in politics.

Saturday, 5 May 1979, Lahore, Rawalpindi

Met Ziaul Haq along with Mian Mahmud Ali Kasuri and Mushir Pesh Imam and stayed with him for one-and-a-half hour. Told them that: (a) local bodies elections should not be held by him. He had no mandate to do so. He could however, we suggested, obtain an assurance from political leaders that they would hold these elections within 90 days of coming to power. (b) he should not amend the 1973 constitution to enhance the powers of the president. This should only be done by an elected assembly. (c) he should not produce a legal framework order. Political parties could reach an agreement amongst themselves and produce ground rules. (d) unrestricted political actively should be allowed so that political parties can reach the people. Only thus can strong political institutions be created and political stability ensured.

Ziaul Haq revealed that the modalities of the electoral process will take 76 days and that he will allow 45 days of full campaigning. He also talked of a referendum to seek the peoples' mandate on the powers of the president. Mian Kasuri ridiculed the idea of a referendum on a constitutional issue of this kind which few will be able to understand. Mahmud Haroon and General Arif were also there. The latter indicated that political parties will be allowed to buy time on radio and TV for political campaigning. Our stand on all these issues was clear and unambiguous.

Sunday, 27 May 1979, Islamabad, London
Amina and I arrived at London airport at 17:00 local time after an hour's stop at Tehran. Were not allowed to leave the aircraft at Tehran.

Monday, 28 May 1979, London
Went over to Zahoor Butt's where some Tehrik-i-Istiqlal workers had come to meet me. Drew up a programme for our stay in UK. They were keen that I should address public meetings which I refused to do because I do not like the idea of speaking on national issues outside Pakistan and because I want a quiet stay so that I can see my children.

Friday, 8 June 1979, London
Redrafted parts of the Tehrik-i-Istiqlal manifesto. Rewrote the introduction and the preamble to the chapter on transportation as well as the operative paragraphs of this chapter.

Wednesday, 20 June 1979, London
Heard Ziaul Haq on BBC in an interview he had given in Rawalpindi the other day. He was not convincing about his resolve to hold the elections on 17 November nor of his not having any political ambitions.

Maulana Abdus Sattar Khan Niazi, Zahur ul Hasan Bhopali and Maulana Noorani's brother, Mr Siddiqui Jilani, called. Maulana Noorani is arriving in London on 1 July—the day I leave for Pakistan. Maulana Abdus Sattar Khan Niazi and I discussed the political situation in Pakistan and confirmed the arrangement already agreed between Maulana Noorani and myself that we should meet immediately after Eidul Fitr to try to agree on candidates for the elections. We also agreed that we should meet in Lahore on 28 August and discuss the provincial and the national lists.

Monday, 25 June 1979, Maidenhead

Altaf Gauhar telephoned to say that Aziz Ahmed had written a lengthy letter which had appeared in the daily *Jang* (and presumably *Dawn*) expressing his views on events mentioned in my book *The First Round*, with particular reference to Bhutto's role. However he appears to have confirmed that a meeting took place between Marshal Chen Yi and Bhutto in Karachi. The other points were mainly a contradiction of Altaf Gauhar's points mentioned in his foreword.

Wednesday, 4 July 1979, Islamabad, Nathiagali, Abbottabad

Met Air Marshal Ayaz Ahmed Khan in Chaklala. Talked about high living in the armed forces. High living and enjoyment is the order of the day amongst most senior officers in the armed forces. Their houses are luxuriously furnished and their cars are getting bigger and more expensive every year. God help Pakistan.

Thursday, 5 July 1979

Two years ago, General Mohammad Ziaul Haq assumed power by ousting Bhutto. He has managed to hang on by postponing the October 1977 election and dodging the naming of a date until recently when he announced that elections will be held on 17 November 1979. The economic situation has deteriorated and prices have gone up. People are fed up—(not well fed) and the military rule is unpopular. Few believe that Zia will hold elections and the general feeling is that either he will be ousted by a person who will not hold elections or that he will create a situation (e.g. trouble on our western border with Afghanistan) and use this to postpone elections.

Sunday, 8 July 1979, Peshawar, Karachi

Miram Jan Khan Malikdin Khel [a distant cousin well informed on tribal affairs] called from Bara. He said that high prices were causing great resentment amongst the people. Price of sugar was Rs16 per kg, *Gur* [jaggery] Rs11, *Atta* [flour] Rs3 per kg.

He also confirmed that the government was sending the Khyber militia to fight along with Afghan volunteers against the Taraki government. These militia who were sent in plain clothes were armed with 'everything except aircraft and tanks'. He said that a number of them had been killed and many of those wounded were in our hospitals. Fort Salop is being used as a base for these operations. According to him the Taraki government is in a strong position and is in control of the situation generally though considerable fighting is taking place in the mountains. He said that according to his information, the poor people in Afghanistan are generally happy. The government is much more efficient than any previous government. Decisions that took days and months previously are being taken in hours. He said that the Afridis were not taking part in the fighting against the Taraki regime. Miram Jan also said that tension existed between the Orakzai and the Afridi tribesmen over a piece of land called Shaldara which lies between the Orakzai and Afridi areas. He thought that the government is instigating the Orakzais to stake their claim over this territory. He also said that the Taraki government had been trying to get the Afridis to create trouble for the Pakistan government by taking the Orakzais on in this area. He thought that the possibilities of Afghan involvement in this area existed. Miram Jan said that most of those people who had fled from Afghanistan—including those *mullahs* who were instigating the tribesmen on our side—were well-to-do people 'with fat bellies'.

Lunched with Lieutenant General Fazle Haq. Exchanged views on the national and international (particularly Afghanistan) situation. He was apprehensive about the position of the PPP—a view that I did not share for I believe that they will be squarely defeated at the polls.

Left by PIA for Karachi where I arrived at 19:00. Was given a big welcome and went in a large procession of cars, Suzukis and trucks to Pesh Imam's where I addressed the workers who had participated.

The PNA (or what is left of it) had made a call for a general strike for today. It was fairly effective in Karachi but not so elsewhere.

Monday, 16 July 1979, Quetta, Rawalpindi

Dinner with General Ziaul Haq. It appeared that he was contemplating holding election partially on 'party list' basis. It is intended to combine two constituencies into one. The person getting the largest number of votes would win and the party getting the highest number of votes would also win. He also intends enhancing the powers of the president but these will be less than those in the 1973 constitution. He is also contemplating banning the PPP. In the meantime political parties are being asked to hold their elections.

I emphasized the need for holding elections on schedule and for the right of the PPP to contest. I said that our party did not recognise his right to alter the constitution and that we would prefer to defeat the PPP at the polls.

Friday, 20 July 1979, Abbottabad
Agha Murtaza Pooya, the owner of the daily *Muslim,* called. He talked about starting the daily *Muslim* from Lahore and Karachi and an Urdu daily *Mussalman* from Rawalpindi. Wanted me to put in a word for him with General Ziaul Haq so that he could get its 'declaration' speedily. I explained that I did not have such an equation with the martial law government as to get his problem solved. However I wished him luck.

Saturday, 28 July 1979, Abbottabad
General Ziaul Haq announced some tax reliefs in a radio and TV broadcast yesterday evening. Dry milk and kerosene oil have been exempt from duty and domestic gas prices have been reduced. Some allowances for salaried personnel drawing less than Rs1500 per month and 'non-development' and 'development' expenditure has been reduced by Rs550 million and Rs800 million respectively, import of cars above 16 cc for the government has been banned and expenditure on establishments frozen. Altogether an inadequate approach to a very unsatisfactory situation. Non-development expenditure has increased from Rs5.75 billion in 1970-71 to Rs29.54 billion in this year's budget. Drastic remedies are necessary and the present government is not capable of dealing with the situation. Nor can any other party except the Tehrik-i-Istiqlal make the drastic cuts necessary to put things right and create the necessary atmosphere for an increase in national production.

Monday, 6 Aug 1979, Islamabad

Met General Ziaul Haq in the evening and stressed on him the serious consequences of postponement of the elections. He assured me that under no circumstances would the elections be postponed. He is set on proportional representation and local bodies polls but said if these should in any way interfere with the holding of elections on 17 November, he would not go ahead with these measures. I told him that a categorical public statement in this matter would help restore public confidence.

Tuesday, 21 Aug 1979, Abbottabad, Islamabad

Left Abbottabad in the morning and attended a meeting of the national working committee to discuss the party's stand on local bodies election. It was felt that the martial law regime had ulterior motives in holding these elections and would use these for a mandate for enhancing the president's powers and the role of the army, the postponement of general elections, etc.

Wednesday, 22 Aug 1979, Islamabad, Karachi

Amina, Ali and I left by PIA for Karachi. At Karachi Amina and I attended an *iftar* reception given by Begum Shahida Jameel at Lakham House in honour of the newly elected office bearers of the Karachi Women's Oganisation. Begum Shahida Jameel is the granddaughter of Huseyn Shaheed Suhrawardy and is one of our active workers. She is the joint secretary of the Karachi divisional organisation.

Thursday, 6 Sept 1979, Lahore

Fourteenth anniversary of the 1965 war. Did not send a message to the armed forces today as I did not feel up to it–their role ever since has not been one that has served the interests of the country.

Sunday, 9 Sept 1979, Lahore

Mian Kasuri did not turn up today for the national working committee meeting as he was probably upset that we should have expressed some reluctance to award Khurshid a NA ticket for Lahore-VI (old IV)— Mozang area. Some of us felt that Nawaz Sharif would be a stronger candidate for that constitutency and Khurshid should contest from the

Gulberg, Model Town, Kot Lakhpat area constitutency, from where he contested in the March 1977 elections.

Tuesday, 11 Sept 1979, Lahore, Rawalpindi, Abbottabad
Called on Maulvi Mushtaq Hussain, chief election commissioner, and stressed upon him the importance of elections being held on 17 November. Told him that a postponement would mean confrontation with the army with inevitable consequences. He was hopeful that election's would be held, though he was not certain. He said that he was planning announcing the election schedule on 15 September. Seven days for nominations and 22 days (from 15th) for withdrawals. Ziaul Haq is likely to take a decision on the 13th.

Wednesday, 12 Sept 1979, Abbottabad
Hectic activity all over the country in connection with local body polls. Political parties are not allowed to take part but members of political parties may take part. No campaigning, no flags, no banners, no posters, no meetings—an odd election. Polling is on 25 September. It is generally believed that Ziaul Haq has a motive in holding these elections other than the one publicly stated. He probably wants to use it to delay the polls or get a body of elected men set up to seek a mandate to acquire extra powers or an extension of his tenure. His credibility and that of his regime is at a very low ebb and I do not think that he can pull it off, at least for very long. Anyway we will know in a few days whether he intends going ahead with the elections. If he does not, his replacement by some other general may follow.

Thursday, 13 Sept 1979, Abbottabad
Aslam Khan Khattak (a former governor of NWFP) called and discussed the political situation. He was not in favour of the elections being held and favoured handing over of power by the army without elections. He, however, agreed to support the Tehrik-i-Istiqlal if elections are held.

The TV news announced that the government had decided to hold the next elections on the basis of proportional representation with the present demarcation of constituencies.

Sunday, 16 Sept 1979, Islamabad

Sardar Sikander Hayat Khan, the secretary general of PNA, called to discuss the registration of political parties and to suggest that Tehrik-i-Istiqlal should not register itself. I told him that we had taken this decision in the larger national interest as we felt that this was the only way to avoid a confrontation with the army. I said that we must explore all possible avenues to move peacefully towards our goal of restoring democracy. I suggested that the PNA should also submit itself to providing the information that the martial law regime has sought. The PNA is considering this matter today.

Friday, 21 Sept 1979, Peshawar

Khurshid Kasuri came from Lahore. He was of the opinion that Lahore-VI would be the most suitable constituency for him. Incidentally he and Nawaz Sharif have applied for a party ticket for this constituency. Khurshid thought that in the event of my contesting from Lahore-VI, Omar Kasuri and Nawaz Sharif would be the most suitable candidates for the two provincial seats and that he would then like to contest from an adjoining NA constituency.

Called on Ayaz and Jeena in the evening. They have recently moved to a new air force house near 66 The Mall. The air force—as indeed the army—are really living it up these days. Mercedes cars, lavish accommodation, luxurious furnishings, servants and staff are improving in quality and quantity at a rapid rate. A sorry spectacle for a country that is near bankruptcy.

Tuesday, 25 Sept 1979, Lahore

Called at the residence of the late Maulana Maudoodi to condole his death. He had died in the United States four days ago. A great scholar of Islam, his death is a great loss to the Jamaat-i-Islami and will be mourned by his followers in different parts of the world.

Local bodies elections will be held in Punjab, Sindh, and NWFP today. Balochistan will be holding theirs on the 27th. These have been held on a non-party basis but the PPP has participated almost on a party basis.

Discussed the formalities in connection with the registration of political parties and the TV and radio programmes in which political parties are being allowed to appear.

Election commission announced the election schedule today. Nomination papers will be accepted from tomorrow until 2 October which is the last day for withdrawals.

Discussed the allocation of NA seat, Lahore-VI, to Nawaz Sharif or Khurshid Kasuri. Resolved the matter by deciding to stand from this constituency myself. Nawaz Sharif to contest NA Lahore-VII and Khurshid will contest a PA seat.

Dinner with Nawaz Sharif at his Model Town house.

Wednesday, 26 Sept 1979, Lahore

Attended *janaza* prayers for Syed Abul Ala'a Maudoodi, the founder of Jamaat-i-Islami, at Qaddafi Stadium. About 100,000 people attended. Amina went to the Maulana's Ichhra residence to condole with her cousin, the Maulana's wife.

Signed forms for candidature from NA-78 Lahore-VI and NA-190 Karachi-VIII and gave these to Khurshid Kasuri and Mushir Pesh Imam for submission on 29 September.

Dinner with Nawaz Sharif. Ziaul Haq said in Quetta today that he would not hold elections if he felt that the integrity and ideology of Pakistan was threatened. He used highly derogatory language about politicians and gave the impression that he would postpone the elections once more.

Thursday, 27 Sept 1979, Lahore, Islamabad

Flew to Islamabad with Khurshid. Addressed a hurriedly called press conference and condemned in strong terms Ziaul Haq's statement of yesterday. Warned him of the serious consequences of the postponement of elections. Reiterated our earlier stand that Ziaul Haq's mandate would end on 17 November 1979.

Khurshid Kasuri submitted the party accounts and application for registration. Secretary election commission found the registration papers in order and said that we were one of the two parties who had maintained their accounts properly. The other being the Jamaat-i-Islami.

Saturday, 29 Sept 1979, Abbottabad

A busy day. A number of people called to obtain party tickets for the elections. Humayun Saifullah Khan and Saleem Saifullah Khan called from Bannu. Saleem will be standing on our ticket from Bannu's National Assembly constituency. Sayed Munir Shah also came.

Spoke to Chandi (Abida Hussain) at Jhang. She wants her group to join us but is thinking of contesting the election to the National Assembly as an independent. Arranged to see her in Lahore on 1 October.

Sunday, 30 Sept 1979, Abbottabad, Islamabad
Quite a rush of people wanting to join Tehrik-i-Istiqlal. Jamali from Nawabshah telephoned. I spoke to Aslam Khan Khattak, who said that his group would like to join (including Sardar Inayatullah Gandapur and Nawabzada Azmat Ali Khan). I filed my nomination papers for NA-13 Abbottabad-II. Osman telephoned to say that Ayub Khan of Elahi came and expressed his desire to join Tehrik-i-Istiqlal. He will be filing his papers for the NA sent from Batagram/Kohistan area.

Monday, 1 Oct 1979, Islamabad, Lahore
My papers were filed from NA-86 Lahore-II yesterday and from NA-190 Karachi-VIII today. Left for Lahore by PIA with Amina. Meeting of the central parliamentary board. Quite a rush of candidates. Decided that Asaf Vardag should contest from NA-86 Lahore-IV. Mushir left for Rawalpindi to appear before the election commission for the symbol and the registration.

Tuesday, 2 Oct 1979, Lahore, Islamabad
Was asked by military secretary to Ziaul Haq to see him in Rawalpindi. Left by PIA by the morning flight and met him in the evening. He wanted my views regarding PNA's stand regarding 'registration' and extension of date of nomination. I suggested that he should accommodate them by relaxing the conditions of registration and should extend the date of nomination provided the date of election is not changed.

Wednesday, 3 Oct 1979, Islamabad, Lahore
Left for Lahore. Went to the central office. Called on Justice Jamil Hussain Razvi and Sheikh Ghiasuddin who had proposed my name for election to constituency NA-86 Lahore VI. Discussed election problems of my constituency with Khurshid and Malik Hamid Sarfaraz. Arif Nizami called. Met at Wazir Ali's after dinner and gave

final shape to the publicity campaign. Arranged that all the material should be distributed by 18 October. Let us keep our fingers crossed and hope that Ziaul Haq does not alter the election schedule. He may well do that. The PNA does not appear keen on the elections and Zia is looking for an excuse.

Thursday, 4 Oct 1979, Lahore

Completed selection of about forty National Assembly candidates from different districts of Punjab. A big rush at the central office.

Called on Majid Nizami in the evening. Discussed campaign arrangements for NA-86 Lahore-VI with Bakhtiar Kasuri. Decided to attach him with Begum Mehnaz Rafi for work amongst the women. Provincial chairmen started work in connection with selection of provincial candidates. They will be arriving here tomorrow evening.

Radio and TV started a campaign to the effect that there is a general demand amongst the public for a postponement of the election. It is indicative of Ziaul Haq's thinking and the possibility of a postponement is now real.

Friday, 5 Oct 1979, Lahore

Continued examination of NA constituencies of Punjab and finished our work except for almost half a dozen seats. Also heard some appeals.

Addressed a press conference on the agricultural policy of Tehrik-i-Istiqlal and also spoke of the possibility of the postponement of elections. Advocated strongly that elections should not be postponed. Dinner with Nawaz Sharif.

Saturday, 6 Oct 1979, Lahore

Completed allocation of NA tickets in all provinces. Some appeals remain to be heard. Amina addressed a women's meeting.

Sent Osman to Peshawar to be present tomorrow at the hearing of an appeal filed by Gohar Ayub in the Peshawar High Court to the effect that I am not a member of the Tehrik-i-Istiqlal!

Sunday, 7 Oct 1979, Lahore

Completed the award of party tickets to NA candidates and the hearing of appeals of provincial candidates. However did not formally announce the decisions.

Government announced that registration rules have been relaxed and those parties that had not registered, but submitted their accounts (PNA), will be allowed to file their papers until 13 October. Heard later from Mushir at Islamabad that elections are being postponed till 7 December.

Had a meeting at 4 Fane Road to discuss organisational matters for NA-86 constituency. Appointed Mazhar Hussain (formerly of the PAF) as my election agent.

Monday, 8 Oct 1979, Lahore
Spent the morning at the central office putting finishing touches to the candidates' lists for national and provincial assemblies. Heard Mushir about his visit to the election commission yesterday. Fresh orders have been issued by the government and there is complete confusion.

Addressed a press conference and warned the government of the consequences if the election date is postponed. Saw the election office of Nawaz Sharif in NA-87. Also saw Nawaz Sharif's old house on Railway road as a suitable site for my central office which had started functioning today at 4 Fane Road.

Tuesday, 9 Oct 1979, Lahore
Today was the last day for withdrawal of nomination papers by candidates. However in view of the confusion prevailing—as a result of changes in the electoral procedure—I decided to instruct our candidates not to withdraw their nomination papers as yet. Spoke to the chief election commissioner, Justice Maulvi Mushtaq Hussain, who confirmed that there was no need for our candidates (who had not been given our party tickets) to withdraw their forms. He said that our members too would be allowed to file their nomination papers again until 13 October. Decided to fill those constituencies that had been left vacant and meet again in Lahore on 15 October.

Dropped in at Khurshid Kasuri's. Naseer A. Shaikh was also there. He was hinting that he would join the party and help us financially if he was given a Senate seat. I told Khurshid that we should not accept his donation at this price. He is one of the so called '22 families'.

Wednesday, 10 Oct 1979, Lahore, Karachi

Confusion prevails about the elections. Spoke to the chief election commissioner to enquire whether the candidates' list had to be sent to the provincial election commissioners or not. He confirmed that it need not be sent. He said that we would be given the same facilities as are being extended to the newly registered parties. However returning officers at many places were demanding certificates from our candidates to show that they were our approved candidates. I spoke to the chief election commissioner an arrival at Karachi and he again confirmed this.

At Lahore I addressed the ISF students at 4 Fane Road. Met some candidates there. Ghulam Haider Bharwana of Jhang joined the Tehrik-i-Istiqlal.

Thursday, 11 Oct 1979, Karachi

Met the provincial candidates from my national constituency NA-190 (Karachi xvi, xvii, xviii, xix) Ahmed Mian Soomro called. Discussed allocation of seats in Karachi.

Rahim Bux Soomro came. Heard about Nazir Ahmed's condition. He is in an advance state of cancer and not likely to live more than a few days. I was very upset to hear of Nazir's condition. He is a very nice man and a good friend.

Instructed the provincial chairman to hand over the list of candidates to the provincial election commissioners. Discussed progress of the publicity campaign with Humayun Gauhar.

Friday, 12 Oct 1979, Karachi

Signed party ticket certificates (650) and arranged distribution to provinces. Met workers and candidates. Attended briefly a meeting chaired by Humayun Gauhar to organise the work in my *halqa*. The women had another meeting in the evening.

Called on Afroze. Did not see Nazir Ahmed as he was sleeping. I was told that he was in very poor condition. Poor Afroze was naturally very upset. Her two sons Tariqi and Shuddo were there.

Saturday, 13 Oct 1979, Karachi, Lahore

Chief election commissioner telephoned to inform me about the altered election schedule. The new polling date has not been mentioned but the withdrawal date has been extended to 20 October.

Lunched with Maulana Shah Ahmed Noorani. The press joined us and we said that if political activity was not allowed we would have to reconsider whether it was any use taking part in the elections.

Left for Lahore by PIA. Kamal, the actor and producer, was with me and offered to work for us in the elections.

Sunday, 14 Oct 1979, Lahore

Made some changes in the party lists for different provinces for submitting to election commission. This will be the final list for the election, which does not appear to be taking place.

Decided to call the meeting of the national working committee on 18 October followed by a meeting of all National Assembly candidates and Provincial Assembly candidates from Punjab.

Monday, 15 Oct 1979, Lahore

Newspapers carried reports of indefinite postponement of elections. All signs point in this direction. Discussed the various possibilities with Mian Mahmud Ali Kasuri and Wazir Ali.

A number of pressmen dropped in to discuss the general political situation in the country. Decided to hold the meeting of national working committee at Rawalpindi instead of Lahore on the 18th and to postpone the meeting of National and Provincial Assembly candidates.

Tuesday, 16 Oct 1979, Lahore

Discussed possibilities of cooperation among various political parties in the event of indefinite postponement of elections, which appears imminent. Arif Nizami of *Nawa-i-Waqt* came to lunch. Wazir Ali was also there. Discussed the action that General Ziaul Haq was likely to announce.

Later heard Ziaul Haq's broadcast. A shocking affair. Banning of all political activity. Disbandment—whatever it means—of political parties, sealing of offices of political parties, freezing of their funds. No political statement. No statement to the press. No meeting with foreign pressmen. Censorship of newspapers and banning of some newspapers. Powers of search.

Ziaul Haq also announced that martial law would henceforth be 'real'. So we have had a bogus martial law so far. And then, the biggest joke of the year: he expressed the hope that the people would cooperate with him in the future as they have done in the past. Had dinner at Mian Mahmud Ali Kasuri's. Maulana Abdus Sattar Niazi dropped in after dinner.

As I was going to bed after listening to the 23:00 BBC news, the police arrived to serve a detention order on me for a period of two months.

Wednesday, 17 Oct 1979, Lahore, Tarbela rest house (Mardan district)

Left Lahore with Amina under police escort at midnight. Drove all night and were met by NWFP police at Hassan Abdal at 06:00. I was told that I would be going to the Tarbela rest house on the right bank of the Indus in Mardan district. Reached the rest house, a shabby though picturesque place about three quarters of an hour's drive from Hassan Abdal. Amina helped to settle down. The assistant commissioner Swabi called a short while later.

Sub Martial Law Administrator Mardan, DC Mardan (Anwar Saifullah Khan) and the SP Mardan called in the evening. I learnt from them that some fifteen of our prominent workers, including Syed Munir Shah, Mukhtiar Bacha, Sher Bahadur, Aleem and Farooq Adam, had been arrested. The only other people to be arrested in the NWFP were PPP workers and a few Mazdoor Kissan Party people. Mufti Mahmud had not been arrested nor had Maulana Noorani been taken into custody. I understand that in other provinces too Tehrik and PPP workers had been arrested.

Went out for a walk in the evening. The hut where I am staying is situated on a rock overlooking and on the edge of the Indus River some two miles below the dam site. Its approaches are secluded and there is no habitation of any kind within a mile of it on either side. Ideal for walks.

Anwar Saifullah Khan brought today's newspapers, which because of the censorship, made dull reading.

Thursday, 18 Oct 1979, Tarbela rest house (Mardan)

Ziae and Tassaddaq came at about 10:00 along with Samad. Afzal followed a short while later. Amina left with them for Abbottabad. She has not recovered fully after her jaundice earlier this year. I asked her to get herself X-rayed by Dr Alam (at Lahore) who is I believe an experienced radiologist in detecting stone in the gall bladder. A doctor in the UK had suggested that her jaundice could probably have been caused by a stone in the gall bladder. She will have herself checked by Dr Azmi at Karachi and also have her tooth attended to. She has been so busy helping me that her health has been neglected.

Today's papers confirmed that Mian Tufail, Mufti Mahmud and Nasrullah Khan had not been taken into custody. However, I was told by Tassaddaq that Maulana Noorani had also been arrested.

Lieutenant General Fazle Haq, governor NWFP, called. He was apologetic that this was done against his advice and better judgment. I told him that they would soon regret their decision. Learnt from him that Munir Shah and Fakhruzzaman Khan are in Haripur jail. Aleem is probably in Peshawar jail. Farooq Adam could not be located and Nasirullah Khan Babar of PPP had also gone underground. Fazle Haq indicated that some new civilian ministers would be taken in. Some possible names that he mentioned were. Mir Afzal Khan, Gohar Ayub, Hanif Khan, Noor Hayat Noon, Hamid Raza Gilani, Ghulam Mustafa Jatoi and Hanif Ramay. It would be a very good thing because those who joined Ziaul Haq would be fully exposed.

Fazle Haq also said that I would be shifted to Abbottabad in the next few days. Learnt from Fazle Haq that the name of this place is Payhur. Payhur is a canal that takes off from here into Mardan district. The rest house was built in the late 1930s by the canal department.

Friday, 19 Oct 1979, Payhur rest house (Mardan district)

'A sceptre once put into the hand, the grip is instinctive, and he who is firmly seated in authority soon learns to think that security and not progress is the highest lesson of statecraft' — (J.R. Lowell).

Today's *Jang* carried the news of Fazle Haq's visit to me. Obviously given by him to give the impression of a dialogue between us to discredit me. *Jang* also reported Ziaul Haq as having told newsmen yesterday that Tehrik-i-Istiqlal was the only party that had done its home work and was ready for elections.

Tariq and Osman came with my clothes and some books. Osman is going back to Essex University, UK, on Sunday, 28th.

Saturday, 20 Oct 1979, Payhur rest house (Mardan), Abbottabad
Left Payhur rest house for Abbottabad at 17:30. The house is guarded by the police and entry to it only by the inmates is allowed. This includes Ziae who was away at Rawalpindi and returned late in the evening. Adey [my mother] is also here. Osman is away at Rawalpindi.

Sunday, 21 Oct 1979, Abbottabad
Osman returned from Rawalpindi. Brigadier Zahir Qureshi, the martial law administrator at Abbottabad, called. The local Additional SP also called.

Nawaz Sharif telephoned from Lahore to enquire about our welfare. He had mounted an effective campaign in NA-87, Lahore. Appears a likable and dedicated worker. Wazir Ali also telephoned.

Aleem is wanted by the police, being on the list of people to be detained. They have not been able to locate him as yet.

Osman and Ziae are to go to Sawar Gali to leave some tin sheets there. I had donated these for a school a couple of months ago.

Monday, 22 Oct 1979, Abbottabad
Osman and Ziae left for Sawar Gali, Nagri Totial, Lora, Jabri, etc. to leave some tin sheets for the mosque at Seer and some water pipes for the Batangi area.

Newspapers carried a report of a writ in the Supreme Court filed by Malik Hamid Sarfaraz against my illegal detention. The writ has been admitted by Justice Riaz Hussain who has forwarded it to the chief justice for consideration by a bench of the Supreme Court.

Wednesday, 24 Oct 1979, Abbottabad
Have put on weight so started a planned programme of light exercise and diet. It should be easy in my situation to shed some weight. There is always a brighter side to any situation.

The *Hurriyat* reported that Mushir was coming to Rawalpindi to consult 'my lawyers'. I do not know who the lawyers are with whom Mushir is coming to consult and for what.

Thursday, 25 Oct 1979, Abbottabad
Whipping and raids by martial law authorities are in full swing. Ziaul Haq believes that the economic problems can be solved by terrorising the people. Such action against hoarders is only scratching the surface. The real problem is low production and a regime of this kind cannot make any significant change in the situation.

Friday, 26 Oct 1979, Abbottabad
Mian Mahmud Ali Kasuri, Mushir, Ahmed Mian Soomro and Zafar Ali Shah came to discuss the desirability of taking legal steps. Decided to put in a writ on my behalf questioning the right of Ziaul Haq to take the steps that he had taken on 16 October. The petition will be filed on my behalf by Mian Mahmud Ali Kasuri.

Monday, 29 Oct 1979, Abbottabad
The SSP called to serve a 'memorandum' from the deputy martial law administrator NWFP explaining the grounds for my detention until 23 December. He has quoted two of my utterances in which I had criticised the martial law government. He is of the view that if not detained, I will be a threat to peace and lawful conditions. The SSP asked me to sign as having read the notice which I declined to do.

Wednesday, 31 Oct 1979, Abbottabad
Mian Mahmud Ali Kasuri telephoned to say that he would be coming for consultations on 2 November. He said that he had been allowed to bring one other advocate with him and asked who that person should be as there were a number of lawyers helping him with the case. I suggested that he bring Mushir with him.

Flogging for social crimes such as kidnapping, high prices, smuggling and hoarding is in full swing. The prices of vegetables have come down by 50 per cent. Prices of other commodities have not dropped significantly. However, vegetables are beginning to become scarce. Roads, after a cleaner appearance for a few days, are coming back to their dirty self. The initial effect of the 'real martial law' of Ziaul Haq is predictably beginning to wear out.

Thursday, 1 Nov 1979, Abbottabad

Eidul Azha. Omar has passed his M.Phil. We were very glad to hear this as Omar had worked very hard for it. He is expected here about the middle of this month. Amina tried to telephone Omar at Cambridge but was told by the exchange that we were not allowed to use the telephone for calls outside the country.

Sunday, 4 Nov 1979, Abbottabad

Malik Hamid Sarfaraz's writ petition was heard by a bench of the Supreme Court in Lahore. Chief Justice Sheikh Anwar ul Haq, Justices Shafiur Rehman, Zullah, Nasim Hassan Shah and Chauhan, comprised the bench. Mian Mahmud Ali Kasuri and Aitzaz Ahsan appeared for the plaintiff. The writ was against my illegal detention. Mian Sahib asked that the full court should hear the writ. This was rejected by the court. He then objected to Sharifuddin Pirzada appearing as the attorney general as he was also a minister. This plea was also rejected. Mian Sahib then withdrew the petition and informed the court that writs on my behalf are being moved in all the four High Courts for a ruling on the action taken by Ziaul Haq; against his banning of political parties, detention of political workers and postponement of elections.

Monday, 5 Nov 1979

Omar's convocation at Cambridge today. Received a letter from Ali.

Wednesday, 7 Nov 1979, Abbottabad

Except for the BBC news, a normal day in captivity. BBC in its Urdu news bulletin and in 'Sairbeen' gave the gist of a press statement issued on my behalf by Zahuruddin Butt in London today. It criticised martial law and forecast banning of political activity. It was written on 16 October before Ziaul Haq's announcement. It called for a general strike in Pakistan on 17 November. Zahur Butt also announced the formation of an 'action committee' that will act as the voice of the Tehrik-i-Istiqlal and will function so long as restrictions on political activities continue in Pakistan.

Friday, 9 Nov 1979, Abbottabad

Newspapers reported the filing of writs by Tehrik-i-Istiqlal leaders at Karachi. Peshawar and Quetta. Mian Sahib will be doing the same at Lahore, presumably tomorrow.

Hugh Catchpole was given the Sitara-i-Imtiaz at an investiture ceremony at the Abbottabad Public School yesterday by Fazle Haq, one of his former pupils.

Monday, 12 Nov 1979, Abbottabad

Hamida spoke to Omar this morning and told him that he should return here by 1 December if he wanted the lecturer's job in the Punjab University. The registrar of Punjab University has written to say that Omar's application on the proper form should reach him by 7 December. Omar would rather stay on abroad as he can get a good job in UK but we would like him to come back.

Whilst speaking to newspaper editors in Karachi yesterday, Ziaul Haq said that total imports of the government alone amounted to Rs30.55 billion.

Ziaul Haq said that censorship of news would continue and changes of governors or in his cabinet were not planned for the time being. He said that he was satisfied with the public response to the measures that he had taken which he described as 'positive'.

Thursday, 15 Nov 1979, Abbottabad

Karim Aga Khan and his wife are visiting Pakistan these days and Ziaul Haq is giving them the 'head of state' treatment and as usual is over-doing it. He behaves more like a clown than as the president of a country.

Friday, 16 Nov 1979, Abbottabad

Mian Sahib arrived and discussed my writ petition before the Lahore High Court. Agreed to change the 'prayer' on the lines suggested by me that is to challenge the justification for martial law. He asked me to write to him to say that I wished to make a statement before the court in support of my petition and wished to be present in the court when the hearing takes place.

Saturday, 17 Nov 1979, Abbottabad

Today elections were to take place and the day for which I had made a strike call in my letter of 16 October.

In Abbottabad there was no response to the strike call and I assume that there was no response at any other place either. With complete censorship of newspapers and flogging and imprisonment for lesser offences, this was not unexpected. However the call—symbolic that it was—served the purpose of registering a protest against the unjustified action taken by Ziaul Haq.

Incidentally today was also the day, when 11 years ago (1968), I had addressed a press conference criticising Ayub Khan's repressive regime in Lahore and thus entered active politics. In retrospect, Ayub Khan's regime was better than what we have experienced under Bhutto and Ziaul Haq.

BBC in its evening Urdu broadcast said that a group of Pakistanis demonstrated outside the Pakistani High Commission in London today. It also said that my daughter, Shirin was amongst the demonstrators. Omar, Osman and Ali must also have been there.

Pakistan TV news showed Ziaul Haq riding a bicycle to office today.

Monday, 19 Nov 1979, Abbottabad

Ziaul Haq inaugurated the beginning of the fifteenth century Hijra with a radio and TV broadcast for which he cycled to the TV station. He advised the nation in his broadcast that in future people should greet each other by saying *Assalam-o-Alaikum* and *Walaikum Assalam-o-Alaikum Rehmatullah-o-Barkat-o-hoo*. There is certainly a lot of novelty about him.

Tuesday, 20 Nov 1979, Abbottabad

TV and radio news and other TV and radio programmes have deteriorated sharply. Today's TV news devoted eleven minutes to the fifteenth century Hijra celebrations, three minutes to sighting of the Moharram moon, two minutes to General Sawar Khan, three minutes to General Fazle Haq, one minute to General Rahimuddin and one minute to General Abbasi—governors of Punjab, NWFP, Balochistan and Sindh respectively. The remaining time of some four or five minutes was given to news of the much heralded progress being made under the present regime.

Wednesday, 21 Nov 1979, Abbottabad
BBC news, early this morning, announced that some people, reported by various sources to be between 60 and 600, had taken over Haram Sharif in Makkah. There had been some firing and some people, including an important religious figure, had been killed. Saudi Arabia has been cut off from the rest of the world since yesterday but news received early today from Riyadh said that troops had been sent to Makkah. In Pakistan a strike was observed everywhere as soon as news reached the people. Not a very good beginning for the start of the celebrations to usher in fifteenth century Hijra. These celebrations start today on 1 Moharram.

Ziaul Haq toured Rawalpindi city on a cycle and addressed people at different places. He said that this tour was not political. This statement (an obvious lie) was characteristic of him because that is exactly what it was. He is campaigning for a referendum or a presidential election. It is a convenient way to campaign when the opposition is locked up.

Probably as the result of a misleading news item about the incident in Makkah, mobs attacked the US embassy in Islamabad, the US consulate in Lahore, the US information centre and the British information centre in Rawalpindi and set fire to these buildings. A US guard was shot in Islamabad and considerable damage was done. People went in large numbers in buses and vans from Rawalpindi to Islamabad and chaos and hooliganism prevailed for a long time.

Thursday, 22 Nov 1979, Abbottabad
Second day of processions and strikes all over the country. It is understood that the band of armed people who have occupied Haram Sharif are claiming that one of them is the Mahdi or Messiah that Muslims believe is yet to come. Saudi government announced that the situation is now fully under control though a few of the 'renegades' are still in occupation of a part of the Haram Sharif. It is expected that they will have been rounded up or killed within the next 24 hours.

The United States has decided to evacuate families of their embassy staff to the States after yesterday's violence. A number of convents and American banks were also attacked. In the embassy incident in Islamabad, two Americans and two Pakistanis were killed.

Friday, 23 Nov 1979, Abbottabad
BBC announced in its morning news bulletin that the total number of deaths in the US embassy incident in Islamabad was six (and more bodies had been found in the debris of the embassy building yesterday).

Saturday, 24 Nov 1979, Abbottabad
Amina complained to the sub martial law administrator, Abbottabad, that our telephone had been cut off since 22 November. He later called on me and had the telephone restored. It was an unnecessary measure prompted by the somewhat disturbed situation in the country. Unnecessary because the telephone is tapped and all conversation is listened to by military intelligence. It would appear to be more beneficial for them to listen to our conversation, rather than deny themselves the opportunity.

Sunday, 25 Nov 1979, Abbottabad
Omar arrived in Islamabad by PIA early this morning. He has completed his studies in Cambridge and has got his M.Phil. degree. He intends applying for a lecturer's post in economics in the Punjab University. It is good to have him back.

The Saudi government announced today that Haram Sharif had been finally cleared of armed renegades who had been in occupation there for the last ten day. A number of people on both sides have been killed.

Monday, 3 Dec 1979, Abbottabad
The 'renegades' in Haram Sharif are still holding out, though newspapers say that prayers in the Haram Sharif have been resumed. It is now obvious that this was an attempted coup and that it was not localised to Haram Sharif. Attempts for a take-over were probably also made at Madina and Riyadh. The Saudi government has said that

it will give full details when Haram Sharif has been completely cleared.

Shah of Iran has been shifted to a hospital in Texas. The occupation of the US embassy in Tehran continues. The US embassy in Tripoli was burnt yesterday.

Wednesday, 5 Dec 1979, Abbottabad

The Saudi government announced that Haram Sharif had eventually been cleared of all those who had been hiding in the underground. The Saudis had suffered 50 casualties. The renegades (who were mostly Saudis and also included some Yemenis, Egyptian, Kuwaitis and Pakistanis) had lost 75 men. The remaining 150 had been captured. The person who had claimed to be the 'Mahdi' has either been killed or was amongst the injured.

Friday, 7 Dec 1979, Abbottabad

Mian Mahmud Ali Kasuri came. We discussed the statement that I am to make in the Lahore High Court on 15 December. Agreed that I will draft the statement and discuss it with him on 14 December in Lahore. He wanted a 50-page statement but I feel that it is not the length but the content that matters. Finalised the first draft of my statement.

Saturday, 8 Dec 1979, Abbottabad

Added some more pages to the draft finalised yesterday and telephoned Mian Mahmud Ali Kasuri to say that I will send this draft to him tomorrow. Asked him to look at the draft along with Aitzaz Ahsan, Khalid Ranjah and Wazir Ali. Also telephoned Mushir and suggested that he might also go to Lahore tomorrow and look at the draft.

A nephew of Shah of Iran—second son of Princess Ashraf—was shot and killed on a Paris street yesterday. The Shah is now in a USAF hospital in Texas.

Monday, 10 Dec 1979, Abbottabad

Finalised the second draft of my statement incorporating a few more pages and decided to send it to Lahore.

Saturday, 15 Dec 1979, Abbottabad

Spoke with Mian Mahmud Ali Kasuri and told him that the detention order passed by the martial law administrator Punjab had been withdrawn (I was told this by Brigadier Zahir Qureshi, sub martial law administrator in Abbottabad today) and I was now being detained under the order issued by the MLA NWFP which expires on 23 December.

Mushir telephoned later to say that the court presided over by Maulvi Mushtaq adjourned after an hour's session. Maulvi Mushtaq and Zakiuddin Pal indicated that they had submitted their resignation from chairmanship and membership respectively of the election commission. The matter would be decided in a couple of days when the court would take up my case. They would then decide about the question of my not having been allowed to attend the court by the government of NWFP. Mushir suggested that if the prayer is changed to ask the federation to hold elections instead of changing the election commission. In that case it would be possible for Maulvi Mushtaq and Zakiuddin Pal to stay on the bench.

Sunday, 16 Dec 1979, Abbottabad

Amina's birthday. Telephoned her at Lahore and wished her a very happy birthday. Told Omar to buy a birthday cake for her.

Wednesday, 19 Dec 1979, Abbottabad

Asaf Vardag told Ziae that he had reason to believe that the draft that I had sent to Lahore had reached the government. This is surprising since I had sent five copies by hand (of Ziae) to Mian Mahmud Ali Kasuri and he was going to discuss the draft with Malik Wazir Ali, Aitzaz Ahsan, Dr Khalid Ranjha and Asaf Vardag. Ziae said that according to Asaf Vardag a copy could have been given to some other person too. Security is not a strong point with our people and Asaf Vardag's conjecture may well be true. However, no harm is done because the government will in any case get it when I give it to the court and moreover the final statement is substantially different from the first draft. Such a risk is well worth taking and mutual consultation in such matters is far more important than the risk of disclosure. Too much security at the cost of consultation produces mediocrity and often leads to major errors.

This principle also applies to defence matters where an obsession with security has sometimes brought disaster. The launching of our armour in the Khem Karan sector in the 1965 India-Pakistan war in a cloak of security was so ill-conceived and severe that even important commanders were kept in the dark and maps of the area were not made available. This had its inevitable consequences. A fine balance in such matters is, therefore, vital. Too much security can be harmful just as too little can spell disaster.

Spoke to Mian Mahmud Ali Kasuri. He said that the Lahore High Court continued with my petition today. Maulvi Mushtaq Hussain and Zakiuddin Pal decided to continue on the bench and ruled that the election commission was not to be a party. The next hearing will be on Saturday, 22 December which will be the last hearing before the winter recess. Mian Mahmud Ali Kasuri said that it will probably be known on 22 December whether I will be produced in court. The court ruled that its proceedings will not be censored. This was done as a result of a contempt of court petition filed on my behalf as a result of heavy censorship of all newspaper reports of the proceedings of the court on 15 December when my petition came up for hearing.

Thursday, 20 Dec 1979, Abbottabad
BBC broadcast that Lahore High Court had ruled that court proceedings could not be censored. It did this in response to my complaint that the government had been guilty of contempt by censoring proceedings of the court.

Friday, 21 Dec 1979, Abbottabad
Indian elections are drawing close (in January) and all indications show that Indira Gandhi is doing well. She is drawing large crowds, has substantial Harijan support and a good standing among the Muslim voters. She has made a bid for the Muslim vote and Imam of Jamia Mosque of Delhi, Imam Abdullah Bokhari (Amina's cousin), has, after changing his position a couple of times, lined up with her. She has also concluded an electoral alliance with Sheikh Abdullah's Jammu and Kashmir National Conference. Today the High Court cleared her of a contempt of court case which has further strengthened her position. Her son Sanjay Gandhi also appears to have rehabilitated his position considerably.

Saturday, 22 Dec 1979, Abbottabad

The additional SP Abbottabad called and, as expected, delivered an order from the martial law headquarters Peshawar confining me for a further period of two months. The earlier period of confinement of two months was to expire tomorrow (23 December).

Mian Mahmud Ali Kasuri telephoned to say that he had started his arguments in my case in the Lahore High Court. The court will now take up the case on 15 January. They are obviously in no hurry.

Sunday, 23 Dec 1979, Abbottabad

A number of PPP leaders, amongst them Farooq Leghari and Sheikh Rafique, were released yesterday. I understand that Tikka Khan has also been released.

Conditions in Afghanistan continue to be disturbed and the flow of refugees into Pakistan continues. Their number now is estimated at close to 400,000 with approximately 5,000 entering Pakistan daily. The Pakistan government gives them an allowance of Rs4 per head per day. For 400,000 people this would be close to Rs50,000,000 per month. The administrative costs would be in addition. Assuming that these are of the same order the cost would be Rs100,000,000 a month and if the figure of refugees remains at 400,000 the annual cost would be approximately Rs1,200,000,000. This flow of refugees is partly due to Ziaul Haq and his Jamaat-i-Islami colleagues having encouraged the refugees to come to Pakistan—arranged press conferences, processions, meetings, etc. However the United Nations and Saudi Arabia are at present helping Pakistan in meeting the expenditure but the situation could well go out of control.

The Soviet Union is increasing its commitment to Afghanistan. There are some 5000 Russian troops there, most of whom are military advisers. An airfield north of Kabul is being used by them for landing supplies and most of their force is based there. Their helicopters and aircraft are being used by the Afghans but some of these are operated by Russian crews.

Our diplomatic relations with Afghanistan have not been cordial since Daud's death. There seemed to be a thaw towards the end of Taraki's rule but with his elimination by Amin, relations again became strained. Border incidents have been taking place and meeting between foreign ministers has had to be postponed three times for various reasons. Agha Shahi, Ziaul Haq's foreign affairs adviser, is to go to Kabul on 30 December in an effort to repair the fences. Afghanistan is only one of the examples of our 'lame duck' foreign policy being run by Ziaul Haq and his bureaucratic advisers.

Professor Salam who won the Nobel prize for physics (along with two other Americans) is here these days and is being given the red carpet treatment by the government. Much is being said of Islam and its contribution to the sciences and of Dr Salam being the second distinguished Muslim (after Iqbal) to have made such a contribution in the field of education and knowledge. It is being conveniently forgotten that according to the constitutional amendment that was made, Dr Salam who is a Qadiani, is not a Muslim. Professor Salam, however, fully deserves the acclaim and is perhaps the only person who has in the last few years succeeded in giving a civilised air to the stinking reputation that Pakistan has acquired internationally.

Monday, 24 Dec 1979, Abbottabad
Newspapers confirmed today that Tikka Khan has been released. Mrs Nusrat Bhutto and her daughter are, however, still detained at Larkana.

Nawaz Sharif telephoned yesterday to say that he would be coming to see me tomorrow. Telephoned the SMLA and got permission for him to see me and to stay for lunch.

Tuesday, 25 Dec 1979, Abbottabad
Birthday of Jesus Christ and Mohammad Ali Jinnah. Christmas day. Also Nawaz Sharif's birthday.

Nawaz Sharif, his wife and children came and stayed for lunch. Nawaz Sharif mentioned that Yusuf Haroon, who is on a visit to Pakistan these days met him the other day and said that he was here on Ziaul Haq's invitation. Ziaul Haq had sought his advice on the situation and he had had a number of meetings with him. Yusaf Haroon said that Ziaul Haq was thinking of forming his own political party of 'Good People'. He said that Ziaul Haq thought highly of Wali Khan, Sherbaz Mazari and myself and would welcome our cooperation in his venture. I told him that Ziaul Haq must be in a really bad situation to have to rely on Yusuf Haroon's advice—who had been out of Pakistan for the last ten years. I also thought that Wali Khan was already cooperating with him and had advised him some time ago not to hold elections. However Wali Khan would not openly collaborate with Ziaul Haq. As for myself and the Tehrik-i-Istiqlal, I could not possibly contemplate such an idea. I said that I did not give any credence to Yusuf Haroon's suggestion but I was of the views that Ziaul Haq was not as yet ready for a dialogue with political elements or myself. He may, however soon be in this position. Time was against him and he would be in trouble before long. In the meantime I will bide my time. My detention would not necessarily help Ziaul Haq. We had always stood by certain principles and would not give up what we had fought for so long.

Friday, 28 Dec 1979, Abbottabad
Hafeezullah Amin's government was overthrown in a coup yesterday evening and he was executed after a summary trial by the 'Revolutionary Council'. Babrak Karmal, vice premier in the government of late President Taraki, has assumed control.

Saturday, 29 Dec 1979, Abbottabad
I feel that Russia is now too deeply involved in the affairs of Afghanistan to be able to extricate itself. The effect of its actions in Afghanistan on the Muslim population of the Soviet Union (about 50 million) is a factor that it will have to bear in mind and could cause it embarrassment. On the other hand the nature of the country, tribal and social structure of the society and the United States and Saudi interests in events there, are likely to create difficulties for the Soviet Union. It would be surprising if Babrak Karmal could prove successful in controlling the insurgency and in normalising the situation with Soviet assistance.

Sunday, 30 Dec 1979, Abbottabad
BBC said that the United States was considering giving military assistance to Pakistan. The situation in Kabul is normal but some fighting was reported in Jalalabad yesterday.

The Security Council is taking up discussion of the United States proposals of economic sanctions against Iran.

Omar received a telegram from the Punjab University requiring him to appear for his interview on 1 January. He had applied for the post of a lecturer in economics.

Monday, 31 Dec 1979, Abbottabad
1979 has been a year of turmoil and crises. The 1970s saw the establishment of democracy in South Asia which rapidly ended in its degeneration and the establishment of autocratic governments in Bangladesh, Sri Lanka, and Pakistan. Only in India where Indira Gandhi, had, like Bhutto, moved towards an autocratic government, has democracy survived. She was defeated in the elections of 1977 and replaced by an elected government. It has been proved that the roots of democracy are well established in India.

Diary 1980

Tuesday, 1 Jan 1980, Abbottabad
Spoke to Omar in Lahore. He has had his interview. He said that the interviewers—some of them judges—did not show much interest in the proceedings and appeared to have made up their mind beforehand. The Russians appear to be consolidating their hold over Afghanistan. Russian troops have reached Herat and Jalalabad and are reported to be moving into other provincial towns. Nearly 35-40,000 Russian troops are now reported to be in Afghanistan and about the same number on Afghanistan's borders in the Soviet Union.

Demonstrations took place in Tehran and Mashhad against the Soviet Union. The Russian flag over the Soviet embassy in Tehran was burnt and an anti-Soviet demonstration took place outside the Afghan embassy in Mashhad.

The United States has taken a strong stand against the Soviet action and Carter has indicated that the United States will do more than merely make statements. He has also said that the United States will stand by Pakistan if its security is threatened in any way.

It is now clear that the Soviet action in Afghanistan has given a new dimension to the international situation and is likely to have repercussions worldwide.

Wednesday, 2 Jan 1980, Abbottabad
Kurt Waldheim (secretary general of the United Nations) has arrived in Tehran before the Security Council assembles again on 7 January to discuss the United States's proposal to apply sanctions against Iran. Khomeini has said that he would not meet him and the students who are holding the Americans hostage have said that Waldheim will not be allowed to meet the hostages either. Pakistan has sought clarification of the United States's statement that it will supply military aid to Pakistan.

Thursday, 3 Jan 1980, Abbottabad
The chief of staff of the armed services in Turkey has given an ultimatum to the prime minister, Suleyman Demirel, and the politicians that unless they improve the law and order situation and take effective measures to improve the economy, he will step in. He has asked the political parties to make the democratic parliamentary system work more effectively. Suleyman Demirel's government has only been in office for a month and cannot be blamed for the unsatisfactory situation. His and Bulend Ecevit's party cannot (or will not) function as a coalition. There have been over 1000 deaths in violent incidents in the last twelve months. Under the circumstances a military take-over in Turkey appears to be imminent.

India went to the polls today. There is general lack of interest in the elections in India and the polling was low—partly because of the cold. Tomorrow is the last day of polling. Results will be known on Sunday. The contest appears to be between Indira Gandhi's Congress and Jag Jivan Ram's Janata Party though indications are that neither will be able to secure a clear majority. There has been a relatively large number of incidents of violence.

Friday, 4 Jan 1980, Abbottabad
Kurt Waldheim returned to New York from Tehran evidently without achieving anything.

Soviet troops—now reported to be around 50,000 in Afghanistan— have thinned out of Kabul and have moved into the countryside to quell the revolt of tribesmen. Sporadic resistance of Afghan troops and some casualties are reported.

Saturday, 5 Jan 1980, Abbottabad

President Carter has announced the cancellation of wheat supplies (17 million tons) to the Soviet Union. Also announced the stoppage of technological aid to the Soviet Union and the sending of military assistance to Pakistan. The Security Council is meeting to discuss the Soviet intervention in Afghanistan.

Things in Pakistan are quiet. The martial law regime does not appear to be in any immediate trouble and is in effective control. Political activity is down to zero and the press is effectively gagged. The Russian take-over of Afghanistan has however added a new dimension to the national scene and some new developments are expected.

Sunday, 6 Jan 1980, Abbottabad

Qaddafi has broken off relations with Yasser Arafat and the PLO on the grounds that the organisation is no longer performing aggressively against Israel and is seeking a settlement.

Ayatollah Shariat Madari has announced the dissolution of his political party following clashes between his supporters and those of Khomeini. He has also declared his unqualified support for Ayatollah Khomeini and the Islamic revolution in Iran. Clashes have taken place in different parts of Iran between Shias and Sunnis in which 35 people have been killed. A demonstration in support of Khomeini took place in Iran in which a million people took part.

The American defence secretary has gone to China for consultations on the Afghan situation and to forge a common line of action. In Afghanistan people of Showla-i-Javaid (a pro Communist organisation) have clashed with government forces. Afghanistan has allowed foreign journalists into the country.

Wednesday, 9 Jan 1980, Abbottabad

Saudi Arabia hanged 63 people who had occupied Haram Sharif. Indira Gandhi has won 351 seats out of a total of 554.

Saturday, 12 Jan 1980, Abbottabad

Ziaul Haq made a speech at Mingora (Swat) in which he made the government's first policy statement on the Russian military intervention in Afghanistan. It was a denunciation of Russia's action and to that extent indicates that the martial law regime has taken an anti-Soviet line and moved closer to the United States.

In a statement yesterday, Indira Gandhi has expressed sympathy with the Russian position. This statement is indicative of India's foreign policy in the new year.

Omar's article on 'Basic needs concept' was published in the weekly *Viewpoint*.

Sunday, 13 Jan 1980, Abbottabad
Ziaul Haq is on a tour of the NWFP, talking of unity in the face of the 'Russian' move in Afghanistan and as usual suggesting that this unity is best achieved under his guidance and leadership. 'Islam in danger' is the slogan—which has been flogged so often before. God help Pakistan.

Monday, 14 Jan 1980, Abbottabad
Nusrat and Benazir Bhutto appeared in a writ of habeas petition in the Sindh High Court yesterday and were told that the government had extended their detention by another three months.

Tuesday, 15 Jan 1980, Abbottabad
Since the Soviet Union had vetoed the US resolution for economic sanctions against Iran in the Security Council the matter has been taken up in the General Assembly. Another resolution calling for the withdrawal of Russian troops from Afghanistan was approved by the General Assembly by 108 nations voting in favour, 18 nations voting against and 18 abstaining.

President Tito is seriously ill with a clot in his leg. An operation has proved unsuccessful. He is 87. President Carter has approved a $400 million aid package for Pakistan (subject to Congressional approval). It is understood that this figure will be increased to one billion dollars.

Ziaul Haq addressed a press conference and answered questions from foreign correspondents who are accompanying Lord Carrington, the British foreign secretary, who is currently on a visit to Pakistan. A poor performance. He started by trying to maintain a neutral and non-committal kind of stance and finished with a clear condemnation of the USSR's action.

Wednesday, 16 Jan 1980, Abbottabad
Ziaul Haq completes three months of his second and 'real' martial law. Suppression is almost complete and there has been no let up in the repressive measures adopted by the regime. There has been no noticeable improvement in the economic situation which has come under severe strain as a result of the increase in fuel prices and the influx of Afghan refugees whose figure now exceeds 400,000. (Ziaul Haq gave the figure as 430,000 in his press conference yesterday). There is no political activity of any kind and the Afghan situation has further confused the people. The developments in Afghanistan and Indira Gandhi's election in India are likely to strengthen Ziaul Haq's position in Punjab but will also speed up and activate those elements— particularly in Balochistan, Sindh and NWFP—who have contacts outside the country. American aid, if properly used, will undoubtedly improve, at least temporarily, the economic situation and provide relief to the people. The question is whether the international developments around Pakistan will give Ziaul Haq time to strengthen his position and whether the political climate in the country will permit him to continue for long in the seat of power. The next few months will provide the answer to many of these questions.

Saturday, 19 Jan 1980, Abbottabad
Spoke to Mian Mahmud Ali Kasuri and Wazir Ali. They said that the High Court was not likely to send for me. In any case they had asked the NWFP advocate general, who appeared before them today, to explain in writing why I should not be called.

President Tito's leg was amputated today. His second operation to treat a blood clot and gangrene.

Received a letter from Kirsten Basse from Denmark on behalf of Amnesty International asking about my welfare and conditions of detention.

Sunday, 20 Jan 1980, Abbottabad
Mufti Mahmud, Nawabzada Nasrullah Khan and some others addressed a gathering at Masjid-i-Shuhada' at Lahore on Friday announcing the formation of Majlis-i-Jehad and asked Ziaul Haq to:
(a) Actively help the Afghan refugees in operating against the Afghan

government. (b) Boycott the Moscow Olympics. (c) Allow political leaders to mobilise public opinion against the Soviet Union.

They are meeting next Friday in Peshawar.

Got permission for Mian Mahmud Ali Kasuri and Wazir Ali to visit me on Thursday.

Wednesday, 23 Jan 1980, Abbottabad

Jimmy Carter has done well in the Iowa state primary and is ahead of his rival Edward Kennedy. US presidential elections are due towards the end of this year. His Republican opponent is likely to be George Bush who is also ahead of his rival Ronald Reagan in the first primary. The Iran and Afghanistan crises in which Carter has taken a popular stand has built up his position and has weakened that of Kennedy. Edward Kennedy's election plank is based on domestic issues which have, for the present at any rate, gone into the background.

The United States has decided to boycott the Moscow Olympics if Russian troops do not leave Afghanistan within one month. There is very little likelihood of their doing so. The Russians appear to be adopting a tougher stand in their internal affairs too. Nobel Prize winner (for peace) Andrei Sakharov was arrested yesterday and externed to a town, (Gorki), within the Soviet Union. He played a prominent part in the production of the hydrogen bomb for the Soviet Union and was also an ardent supporter of human rights and the reduction of tension between the West and the Soviet Union.

Thursday, 24 Jan 1980, Abbottabad

Mian Mahmud Ali Kasuri and Wazir Ali came and stayed here for about six hours. We discussed my statement to be made before the Lahore High Court. Mian Mahmud Ali Kasuri was certain that I would not be called to appear before the court and so decided that he himself should read it out (or hand it over) to the court when the next hearing takes place on 2 February. Also discussed the Afghan situation and agreed that the alternatives for Pakistan either way were grim.

Saturday, 26 Jan 1980, Abbottabad

Bani Sadr, the Iranian finance minister, is reported to be leading in the Iranian presidential election. People in Kurdistan have not voted as the Kurd candidate was disqualified, because he had not voted during the referendum on the new Iranian constitution.

Ayatollah Khomeini has been in a Tehran hospital because of a heart condition. He is 79 and his general condition is reported to be satisfactory.

Israel has returned a part of the Sinai to Egypt under the Camp David agreement and the two countries are to sign a treaty and establish diplomatic relations today. As a demonstration of its displeasure at this happening, the Islamic Foreign Ministers' Conference which was to start in Islamabad today has been postponed for tomorrow.

Sunday, 27 Jan 1980, Abbottabad

Abol Hassan Bani Sadr, the finance minister (and former foreign minister) has been elected as the president of Iran with an overwhelming majority. His nearest rival was Admiral Madani (the former chief of staff of the Iranian navy). Bani Sadr had resigned from the post of foreign minister when he was accused by the students and religious elements of being too soft with the United States. He has said on his election that he will try to resolve the hostage crisis and take steps to stabilize the economy of the country.

The Islamic Foreign Ministers' Conference opened in Islamabad today.

Mahnaz Rafi telephoned to say that Omar had been selected for the lecturer's post in the Punjab University. Omar is very pleased about it and is looking forward to a teaching career in the Punjab University.

Tuesday, 29 Jan 1980, Abbottabad

The Islamic Foreign Ministers' Conference ended in Islamabad today. Thirty-six countries participated. Syria, South Yemen, Upper Volta and Uganda did not attend. Afghanistan also did not attend. Its membership has been suspended as was done for Egypt some time earlier. Burhanuddin Rabbani of Jamaat-i-Islami of Afghanistan who is head of the alliance of six parties representing the Afghan refugees also addressed the conference. The alliance was formed two days ago and it is to be seen whether it lasts.

Sunday, 3 Feb 1980, Abbottabad

Omar spoke to Dr Rashid Amjad of Punjab University who told him that he (Omar) had scored the highest marks in the interview held on 1 January at Lahore for the lecturer's post in economics. However the government had imposed a ban on his employment and his being taken was in some doubt—on political grounds.

Dr Zbigniew Brzezinski, President Carter's adviser on National Security, is on a visit to Pakistan and held talks with Ziaul Haq about the Afghan situation and Pakistan's needs. It appears that the United States will increase the aid figure considerably beyond the $400 million initially announced. My own guess is that it will be of the order of two billion dollars, both for economic and military aid.

Ziaul Haq told Air Marshal Rahim Khan that the Afghan situation was a blessing in disguise for him. Pakistan may not be able to survive more blessings of this nature.

Wednesday, 6 Feb 1980, Abbottabad

Ahmed Mian Soomro telephoned from Karachi. He had met Chaudhry Zahur Elahi and Nasrullah Khan in Lahore. The former felt that the hands of Ziaul Haq's government should be strengthened by joining it but the latter was of the opinion that a movement should be launched against the regime.

Sunday, 10 Feb 1980, Abbottabad

BBC and VOA broadcast the gist of my statement handed over to the Lahore High Court on 9 February. They said that it was the first open criticism of Ziaul Haq since the Russian invasion of Afghanistan.

Monday, 11 Feb 1980, Abbottabad

The daily *Guardian* in its issue of today published my application to the Lahore High Court.

American hostages completed their 100th day in captivity in the US Embassy in Tehran. It now looks as though the newly elected Iranian president, Abol Hassan Bani Sadr, will move towards a settlement of the issue with the United States. Imam Khomeini, who was reported to have a heart condition, made a fighting statement on the first anniversary of the Iranian revolution—or rather his assumption of power after the Shah's departure last year.

President Tito's condition (he had had his left leg amputated about a month ago) is reported to have deteriorated. The Yugoslav leader is 87.

Wednesday, 13 Feb 1980, Abbottabad
In an editorial, *Pravda* strongly attacked Pakistan's policy towards Afghanistan and said that the Pakistan Air Force had been violating Afghan air space and Pakistan Army formations had taken up positions on the Afghan border. It accused Pakistan of playing an anti-Soviet role. Foreign Minister Andrei Gromyko who is on a visit to India also warned Pakistan of working for US interests in the area and said that Pakistan's policy could prove harmful for it (Pakistan). Indira Gandhi has been trying to persuade the Russians to withdraw from Afghanistan as otherwise Pakistan would be armed and converted into a 'US base' in the area.

The US is reputed to have succeeded in making arrangements with Jordan for transit and base facilities for its bases in the event of hostilities in the Middle East caused by Russian moves in the region.

Thursday, 21 Feb 1980, Abbottabad
The SSP Hazara, called to see me with a communication to extend my detention uptil 21 April 1980. The letter said that because of my statement of 16 October (which was a letter released at a press conference in London) I was likely, if allowed to move about, to create a law and order problem. Not unexpected.

Wednesday, 27 Feb 1980, Abbottabad
Today's newspapers reported Ziaul Haq as having said yesterday that the people should liquidate those elements within the country who are likely to damage it. He was addressing the army garrison at Kharian Cantt. He did not explain who would determine whether a person was likely to damage the solidarity or integrity of the state. A highly irresponsible statement which could promote anarchy and lawlessness but mercifully Ziaul Haq's reputation as something of a joker is so well established and his credibility so low, that not many people take any notice of his utterances.

Thursday, 28 Feb 1980, Abbottabad

Newspapers reported Mufti Mahmud as having said in an interview to *Keyhan International* in Tehran that Ziaul Haq had saved Pakistan from disintegration. I feel that it is inevitable that a polarisation of political forces will take place in Pakistan with the reactionary elements lining up behind Ziaul Haq. It would help Ziaul Haq initially but will not be a bad thing in the long run for the country, when these elements are exposed.

Monday, 2 March 1980, Abbottabad

The bench of the Lahore High Court hearing my complaint asked the government lawyer to let them know in three days time when Ziaul Haq intends to hold elections. The court also expressed its displeasure at my statement having been published in the British press.

Thursday, 6 March 1980, Abbottabad

Mian Mahmud Ali Kasuri called and stayed for lunch. Mian Sahib had been invited to attend the 'convention' being held by some political leaders in Rawalpindi today and tomorrow. Most of these people had been in Ziaul Haq's government in the past, had advised postponement of the election and represented the extreme right that was fully committed to a strong anti-Soviet line. I, therefore, advised that we should not get involved with them. We discussed various alternatives and I expressed the view that a few political parties who had not been associated with Ziaul Haq and had maintained an anti-Zia (or at least a neutral) posture—calling for a government comprising people who had been elected in the March 1977 elections—would help to break the political deadlock. These parties should be the PPP, TI, NDP, JUP and some Baloch elements. This government should have complete powers and Ziaul Haq could perhaps continue as a constitutional president until elections are held. This interim government should fix a date for the elections and run the affairs of the country. It was my view that people elected in March 1977 still had a representative character. However I did not favour calling the assembly elected in the March 1977 election. Many of the members then elected had been disqualified by Ziaul Haq and convening this assembly would be confirming Ziaul Haq's action which the PPP at least would find embarrassing. I also did not favour a suggestion which is being mooted these days of calling the Senate because the Senate was born out of the 1970 elections which had lost its representative character. However I told Mian Sahib that I had no illusions about the suggestion that I was making would be accepted by Ziaul Haq at present. He was certain to disagree with any proposal which would have the effect of reducing his powers but it would have the merit of showing an 'alternative' to the people which at present is not visible. It would raise hopes and increase the level of opposition to the martial law regime.

Saturday, 8 March 1980, Abbottabad
The students in control of the US Embassy and the hostages in Tehran have decided to hand over the hostages to the revolutionary council. The foreign minister, Qotbzadeh, is to take over the hostages today. The Tehran Radio said that he will also take over the embassy but the students have said that they will hand over the hostages but not the embassy. The United Nations mission that is investigating the excesses committed by the Shah has completed its work and will leave Tehran after meeting the hostages.

Thursday, 13 March 1980, Abbottabad
Syed Zafar Ali Shah came and told me of the farce that Ziaul Haq enacted by calling the district council chairmen's convention at Islamabad (in the National Assembly building) on 5 and 6 March. Zafar Ali Shah struck the only discordant note in the entire proceedings. He thought that in spite of—or rather because of—the servile and laudatory speeches of the delegates, the convention was a complete failure. It was so obviously rigged that it did not impress any one. The speeches of the delegates had to be cleared by the government and in most cases were written by people in the ministry of 'local bodies and self government'.

Tuesday, 18 March 1980, Abbottabad
Six major generals were promoted to lieutenant generals yesterday. Governors and ministers will remain on the active army list.

Ziaul Haq spoke yesterday about a 'conspiracy' to carry out a coup. Major General Tajammul Hussain was arrested a few days ago and although Ziaul Haq did not mention him by name, he indicated that he was the main person involved. Obviously there are others involved too, many of whom have also been arrested and will be tried. Ziaul Haq also said that there is a foreign hand in this conspiracy—but this is a common allegation often made for most anti-government actions in Pakistan.

Tajammul Hussain is a distinguished soldier who is known for the battle of 'Hilli' in East Pakistan in 1971. He is a very religious person and very intense in his beliefs. He believes in a pure Islamic state. Was in the Tehrik-i-Istiqlal for about a year until a few days before the banning of political parties in October 1979 when he left the Tehrik-i-Istiqlal to form his own political party. I do not think that any attempt that he would make to oust Ziaul Haq would have been aimed at establishing a democratic order, nor could he be working for a foreign power.

Wednesday, 19 March 1980, Abbottabad
Rafi Butt came to say that a Colonel Tirmizi, assistant director of the Intelligence Bureau at Islamabad, had called on him to ask what the Tehrik-i-Istiqlal felt about Ziaul Haq after his recent action of retiring some generals. Tirmizi had informed him that these generals had opposed the elections. Tirmizi wished to know whether Tehrik-i-Istiqlal was now willing to 'accommodate' Ziaul Haq. I told Rafi Butt to tell Tirmizi that his job was spying and not political negotiations and that he should confine himself to his job.

Omar arrived from Lahore for a couple of days' stay. The Punjab University has still not given him his appointment letter although he was selected in the interview on 1 January.

Wednesday, 2 April 1980, Abbottabad
Mrs Nusrat Bhutto and her daughter have not been allowed to visit Zulfikar Ali Bhutto's grave on his death anniversary. The government opposed this and said that a law and order situation was likely to arise. These two ladies and I are the only persons under preventive detention at present.

Tuesday, 8 April 1980, Abbottabad
BBC in its news bulletin this morning gave prominence to the resolution of the Tehrik-i-Istiqlal working committee at Lahore on 6

March asking for lifting of the martial law, release of political prisoners and holding of elections.

Wednesday, 9 April 1980, Abbottabad
Mrs Nusrat Bhutto and her daughter, Benazir, were released yesterday. I am probably the only person under political detention at present—and likely to remain so.

Wednesday, 16 April 1980, Abbottabad
Fazle Haq, the governor of NWFP, is on a tour of Hazara and we have had to suffer electricity breakdowns for long periods. General Iqbal was here a few days earlier and we went through the same experience. Every time a VIP arrives in this town, all electric supply is rearranged for the extra lights required and the regular consumers have to make do with candles and have to forego the use of electric appliances.

Thursday, 17 April 1980, Abbottabad
Major General Abid Bilgrami telephoned from Abbottabad to say that he and his wife will be coming to see me tomorrow. Also said that he had been told by Lieutenant General Fazle Haq—who is also in Abbottabad—that the police on guard at my house was being withdrawn tomorrow morning and that I was being released. Difficult to believe—let us see.

Friday, 18 April 1980, Abbottabad
Abid Bilgrami, his wife, Akbar Bilgrami, and Major General Rafi called. The local superintendent of police also called to inform me that my detention had ended and I was now free—as free as one can be in Ziaul Haq's Pakistan.

Decided to call a meeting of provincial chairmen and general secretaries along with Mian Mahmud Ali Kasuri and Mushir on Wednesday, 23 April to discuss future line of action.

Sunday, 20 April 1980, Abbottabad
Peter Nieswand of London's *Guardian* came for an interview. A large number of people called. Edward Mortimer of *The Times* of London telephoned from Peshawar to say that he will be coming to see me tomorrow.

Monday, 21 April 1980, Abbottabad
Edward Mortimer of *The Times* and Ian Jack of *Sunday Times* called. BBC broadcast my statement given to Peter Nieswand in its evening bulletin.

Wednesday, 23 April 1980, Abbottabad
Held a meeting to discuss our future course of action. Mian Mahmud Ali Kasuri, Pesh Imam, Ahmed Mian Soomro (Sindh), Khudai Noor (Balochistan), Munir Shah (NWFP), Malik Haider Osman, Rafi Butt, Mumtaz Tarar, Zafar Ali Shah, Qulbi Raza Fauladi (Balochistan), Nafis Siddiqui (information secretary) attended. Decided to disregard martial law order restricting political activity and to revive the party and ask TI members nominated to provincial advisory councils to resign. Also decided to make our decisions public at a press conference at Islamabad on 24 April. Appointed Zafar Ali Shah chairman Punjab in place of Malik Wazir Ali who is abroad.

Thursday, 24 April 1980, Abbottabad, Islamabad
Instructed provincial chairmen (those of Balochistan, Punjab and NWFP were present) to openly defy martial law in the event of my arrest by addressing meetings in public.

Tuesday, 29 April 1980, Karachi
Met Ghaus Bux Bizenjo and Abdul Hamid Khan Jatoi in the evening. They agreed that their party, the National Progressive Party, will make common cause with us for the restoration of democracy. Bizenjo and Abdul Hamid Khan were very bitter about the treatment of the smaller provinces and the suffering of their people under the military regime. Agreed that I should approach other political parties.

Wednesday, 30 April 1980, Karachi
Met Ghulam Mustafa Jatoi at lunch. My first meeting with a PPP leader in about eight years. He said that his party was ready for cooperation though Mrs Nusrat Bhutto was still very bitter about my role in the ouster of her husband. Agreed that I should prepare a draft declaration.

Met the press in the afternoon. Attended a reception at Ahmed Mian's place. Ghaus Bux Bizenjo, Abdul Hamid Khan Jatoi, Prof.

Shah Faridul Haq, Zahur ul Hassan Bhopali and Mairaj Mohammad Khan were also present. Discussed the mode of cooperation with Bizenjo, Jatoi and the JUP leaders. Agreed that all parties should be approached and the movement should include all political elements. They asked me to take the initiative. Maulana Noorani is abroad and is likely to return by the middle of May.

Thursday, 1 May 1980, Karachi
Lunched with Zahur ul Hassan Bhopali and the top leadership of JUP in Karachi. Discussed the desirability of cooperation with other political parties on a one-point programme—the holding of elections under the 1973 constitution.

Mushir gave the draft declaration that I had drawn up to Ghulam Mustafa Jatoi and Ahmed Mian handed it over to Bizenjo. Also gave a copy to Shah Faridul Haq. PPP said that they will give their reaction by about 6 May. JUP is contacting Maulana Abdus Sattar Khan Niazi.

Friday, 2 May 1980, Karachi, Quetta
Left by PIA for Quetta. Received a message from home secretary Balochistan on behalf of the governor, Lieutenant General Rahimuddin Khan, to have dinner with him or to meet him. Declined the invitation. Condolence call at Ziae's house on the death of his father.

Monday, 5 May, 1980, Abbottabad
Marshal Tito, president of Yugoslavia and co-founder of the Non-Aligned Movement, died yesterday after a protracted illness. His left leg had been amputated 3½ months ago.

Thursday, 8 May 1980, Abbottabad, Lahore
Left for Rawalpindi. Met Salamat Ali who had returned from Karachi after meeting Benazir Bhutto. He has the impression that the two ladies have no intention of taking an active part in the campaign against the present regime. Arrived at Lahore in the late afternoon. Met Maulana Abdus Sattar Niazi, Pir Barkat Shah and Akbar Saqi at Omar Kasuri's. Mian Mahmud Ali Kasuri and Ahmed Mian Soomro were also present. Maulana Niazi was not happy about any kind of cooperation with PPP and was even averse to putting his signature on

a joint declaration demanding elections. Pir Barkat Shah however was more reasonable. Agreed that we should wait for Maulana Noorani's return. He is coming back to Pakistan, in a few days time, after a four-month stay abroad.

Saturday, 10 May 1980, Lahore

Went to the Lahore High Court to attend the hearing of my petition but the case was postponed (without hearing) to the 12th because of the illness of one of the judges. About 500 workers had come. Called on the lawyers in the bar association.

Attended meeting of national working committee at Anwar Ali Noon's. Discussed the general situation and the party's line of action. The national working committee approved of the action that I had taken since my release on 18 April. It also decided that we should not seek an alliance with other political parties and go it alone. The attendance was good. In all 39 attended, including special invitees. Dr I.H. Qureshi and Raja Afzal of Jhelum have retired from politics. After the meeting discussed programme of my visit to Peshawar and Multan during the next few days.

Thursday, 15 May 1980, Abbottabad

Geoff Harriet of Australian TV interviewed me. Shafqat Rasul head of Istiqlal Students Federation, Punjab, came. Finalised programme of visit to Multan, Nawabshah, Hyderabad and Karachi starting on 25 May.

Geoff Harriet confirmed what Ian Jack of *Sunday Times* had told Mian Mahmud Ali Kasuri that Benazir Bhutto was very bitter about me and Tehrik-i-Istiqlal and ruled out any possibility of cooperation between our two parties in the future. They regard the Tehrik-i-Istiqlal as the real political threat in the future.

Sunday, 18 May 1980, Abbottabad

Islamic Foreign Ministers' Conference started at Islamabad yesterday with a conciliatory note about Afghanistan following the offer by Babrak Karmal for negotiations with Iran and Pakistan and a guarantee by the Soviet Union and the USA that they would not interfere in Afghan affairs. China has condemned this move as an attempt on the part of the Afghan regime to secure recognition and the new US secretary of state has expressed skepticism about it. He is meeting Andre Gromyko, the Soviet foreign minister, in Vienna today. BBC and VOA have talked about a 'serious internal situation' in Afghanistan. Western media report that the Karmal regime has very little control over the situation. Mukhtar Hassan, the *Jasarat* correspondent, who had been arrested in Kabul a few months ago was released three days ago.

Tuesday, 20 May 1980, Abbottabad
Omar came from Lahore in the evening. He has been offered the lecturer's post in the economics department of Punjab University and is starting work on 26 May.

Wednesday, 21 May 1980, Abbottabad
Mushir came in the afternoon and left after a couple of hours. He told me of his talks with Ghulam Mustafa Jatoi. Apparently Mrs Bhutto does not want to do anything for the time being. Jatoi thought that she was not capable of leading the party. This is as I had expected and it is better in the long run to go it alone. We shall pursue the line that we have already adopted.

Thursday, 22 May 1980, Abbottabad
Islamic Foreign Ministers' Conference ended in Islamabad today. They reiterated their demand that Soviet troops should vacate their aggression of Afghanistan. They also appointed a three-men committee to draw up a line of action to achieve this.

Saw an interesting programme on TV about translations of the Quran. The first translation of the Quran was by Azizullah Matiari in 326 Hijri in Sindhi language. It is a measure of the richness of Sindhi language and culture.

Saturday, 24 May 1980, Abbottabad, Peshawar
Omar and Ziae left for Lahore. Amina and I left for Peshawar. We were joined by party workers *en route* and we arrived in a procession of about 70-80 cars and Suzukis. Police was with us but did not interfere with the procession. Addressed the district bar association at Peshawar. Good response.

Sunday, 25 May 1980, Peshawar, Multan

Left for Faisalabad and Multan by PIA via Rawalpindi. Was met at Faisalabad by party workers and was joined there by Zafar Ali Shah who had been touring Sargodha, Jhang, and Faisalabad. Was given a warm welcome at Multan airport and went in a procession of cars which was interrupted by the police at different places in an attempt to disperse it.

Went to late Maulana Hamid Ali Khan's residence to offer condolences. Was stopped by a magistrate and heavy police force a few hundred yards from his house in Chowk Bazaar and was served with an externment order to leave Multan district and not to re-enter for seven days. I refused to comply. The magistrate after consulting higher authorities (on the telephone and on wireless) apologised and withdrew the order.

Monday, 26 May 1980, Multan, Karachi

Addressed the district bar association at Multan. Very good response. Left for Karachi in the afternoon by PIA along with Mehar Rafique. Was met by workers at Karachi. Called on Begum Akhter Suleman in the evening to condole the death of her husband. Also called on J.A. Rahim.

Ziaul Haq announced severe measures to further curb political activity. Bar associations are forbidden from inviting political leaders to address them. If they do, their members are liable to 14 years imprisonment, 25 lashes and confiscation of property. Government may arrest anyone causing disruption and creating a law and order situation. Justice Maulvi Mushtaq Hussain has been moved to the Supreme Court and Shamim Hassan Qadri appointed chief justice of Lahore High Court.

Tuesday, 27 May 1980, Karachi, Nawabshah

Our PIA plane was delayed at Karachi airport for 1½ hours, evidently to give time to the Nawabshah administration to pressurise the local bar association to withdraw their invitation extended to me to address them. When we arrived at Nawabshah I was informed that the district bar association president had withdrawn his invitation. I met party workers at Ghulam Rasul Shah's residence. Left for Moro with Ghulam Mohammad Jamali where we were entertained to a massive dinner for 1,000 people including many political figures of the area. Stayed the night at the residence of our host Khan Mohammad Jamali. Decided to continue my programme of visit to Hyderabad tomorrow and address the district bar if allowed by the members. This would be a violation of martial law.

Wednesday, 28 May 1980, Hyderabad, Karachi

Left for Hyderabad at 07:00 and arrived there 3½ hours later. The district magistrate with a strong police force met us at the courts and warned me that I was not permitted under martial law to address a gathering. I told him that I was well aware of the law and proceeded to address the lawyers who had assembled in the bar room. The DSP at the door warned the lawyers entering the room that they were liable to be arrested. The attendance was very good and the response excellent. Criticised Ziaul Haq and the military junta and warned them that if allowed to continue the country's security would be endangered.

Lahore High Court Bar Association passed a strong resolution against Ziaul Haq's latest measures as also the Karachi bar. The Lahore High Court bar in addition called for a boycott of all courts, observing a strike on Sunday, 1 June.

Thursday, 29 May 1980, Karachi, Peshawar, Abbottabad

Birthday of Hazrat Ali and the day of my third internment by Ziaul Haq (first at Murree, second and third at Abbottabad).

Members of the national working committee in Karachi met late in the morning and two police officers called during our meeting to convey the externment order of the Sindh government to me. They said that government wanted me to leave for Peshawar. A written order signed by the home secretary was given to me and I left by PIA for Peshawar arriving there at 17:00. I was received by the DC Peshawar and some police who served another order signed by martial law administration NWFP, Lieutenant General Fazle Haq, confining me to my house, 23 Kutchery Road at Abbottabad. Arrived there at 20:45. Amina had left for Lahore by car in the morning. She telephoned later in the evening and I told her to stay on in Lahore until 2 June. My telephone was disconnected as we were speaking.

Before leaving Karachi, I handed over to Mushir a list of 26 names of persons who would assume responsibilities of president of the party in turn, in the event of arrest of the person whose name appeared above theirs, in the list. Ziaul Haq is addressing the nation on 3 June.

Friday, 30 May 1980, Abbottabad
BBC in its news bulletin at 20:15 said that Mian Mahmud Ali Kasuri had addressed a press conference at Islamabad criticising the martial law regime and Ziaul Haq's latest amendment to the constitution. He has also said that the Tehrik-i-Istiqlal will continue its defiance of martial law which it regarded as illegal.

Saturday, 31 May 1980, Abbottabad
Superintendent of police called to enquire whether I had any problems and to inform me that only my immediate family, that is, wife, mother and children could see me. An interesting feature of this detention is that four police women, three of them in *burqas* are on duty at the gate. I understand that the intention is to obviate the possibility of my escaping under cover of a *burqa* disguised as a woman. I told the SP that these women were sleeping in a tent adjacent to the policemen and this was hardly the thing to do in an Islamic state. In any case, I assured him that I had no intention of escaping and that the new iron fence around our compound should, in any case, make this difficult.

Received a letter from Admiral Muzaffar Hassan announcing his decision to retire from politics. Dr I.H. Qureshi and Raja Afzal of Jhelum had left earlier. The working committee has now lost three of its members. Dr I.H. Qureshi had been won over by Ziaul Haq and had ceased to be useful to the party and Raja Afzal of Jhelum and Muzaffar Hassan were bureaucratic in their approach to things and, according to their own admission, misfits in politics. That the realisation reached a point of decision in the present circumstances, is a measure of their determination—or the lack of it—to face the challenge. The Tehrik-i-Istiqlal will not be the poorer with their departure.

Sent out a policy directive to the party on how to work in the present circumstances. Also a list of 26 names of people who will perform the duties of acting president in the event of arrests of person whose name appears highest in the list. They are required to address a press conference within three days of assuming their office and violate martial law within the next seven days. Party leaders are to lead and are to protect the workers as far as possible. No one is to enter into any dialogue with the government nor to form any alliance with any other political party.

Sunday, 1 June 1980, Abbottabad
Omar was to start work at the Punjab University, economics department as a lecturer today.

Lawyers all over Pakistan observed a boycott of the courts as a protest against Ziaul Haq's latest measures restricting the powers of the judiciary.

Tuesday, 3 June 1980, Abbottabad
Ziaul Haq spoke on radio and TV. As usual a deplorable affair.

Wednesday, 4 June 1980, Abbottabad
Amina and Omar arrived in the evening. Omar has started work in the university and delivered his first lecture yesterday.

Amina told me that Mian Mahmud Ali Kasuri resented the directive that I had issued on 29 May refraining 'acting presidents' from entering into alliances with other parties. This was in accord with the decision of the national working committee earlier this month at Lahore and essential to prevent chaos. I am surprised that Mian Sahib should not have seen the danger of allowing every 'acting president' (the list has 26 names) to enter into an alliance with some political party.

Thursday, 5 June 1980, Abbottabad
The lawyer community seems to be stirring a bit. A national convention of lawyers has been called at Lahore on 19 June and resolutions have been passed by the Peshawar High Court Bar Association and the Karachi Bar Association demanding withdrawal of restrictions imposed on the civil courts by Ziaul Haq and for the holding of elections in the country. The Peshawar High Court Bar Association has in addition decided to boycott the courts daily for one hour. This reaction of lawyers is largely the result of Ziaul Haq's

speech of 3 June in which he spoke out his mind on the future of the judiciary and partly the result of my address at the bar associations.

Saturday, 7 June 1980, Abbottabad
Mian Mahmud Ali Kasuri is addressing a press conference on 9 June at Islamabad, and Sargodha and Faisalabad Bar Associations on the 12th. He is also likely to lead a lawyers' procession at Lahore on the 19th.

Sunday, 8 June 1980, Abbottabad
Zafar Ali Shah sent me a copy of the statement that Mian Sahib intends to make at the press conference. It is well worded except for a suggestion that Ziaul Haq should hand over to the Supreme Court which should hold elections. Although the suggestion is in the present circumstances reasonable, it will, I fear, have a dampening effect on the movement that we are trying to mobilise and will once again open the door for negotiations. It would also be contrary to the public stand that I had adopted in my address to the bar associations in which I had said that we (that is the political party or political parties that take part in the movement to oust the junta of generals) would hold the elections. However I do not think that I should stop Mian Sahib—the acting president of the party—from airing his views in a manner decided upon by him and our other colleagues. I wrote to Mian Mahmud Ali Kasuri accordingly.

Ziae says that according to Zafar Ali Shah, Mian Mahmud Ali Kasuri wants to get arrested but does not know how to go about it. I feel that there are good chances that with the programme that he has drawn up for the next few days, he will be locked up before very long. I understand that at the meeting held the other day (which Mian Sahib had called) Malik Wazir Ali advocated a strong line but at the same time expressed his inability to come forward and be arrested.

Monday, 9 June 1980, Abbottabad
BBC and Voice of America radio broadcasts reported large scale fighting close to Kabul. Asadullah Amin, a brother of the former Afghan president, Hafizullah Amin, was executed in Kabul yesterday. A number of other associates of the late Hafizullah Amin, were also executed for 'anti-state' activities.

Sunday, 15 June 1980, Abbottabad
Amina returned by lunch time and told me that the police had broken up the meeting that she was to address before her arrival. They had surrounded the hotel early in the afternoon, taken away the banners and told the organisers that the meeting could not be held.

Thursday, 19 June 1980, Abbottabad
General Abdul Qadir a member of the politburo in Afghanistan is reported to have been shot and injured in the foreign ministry premises in Kabul. He has been sent to Moscow for treatment. It is reported that he was fired at by a member of the Khalq Party. Abdul Qadir played an important part in the coup that toppled President Daud in 1978.

Kurt Waldheim, the UN secretary general, gave in a speech some interesting details of the waste of world resources on armament. He said that the nuclear capability or weapons at the disposal of world powers today was enough to kill the entire population of the earth ten times over. Also that $10 million are being spent on armament every minute. He also said that the total amount being spent on health schemes, such as eradication of malaria, etc., is less than one day's expenditure on weapons. A sorry commentary on the state of the world and the total bankruptcy of international statesmanship. It is all the more regrettable when the vast majority of the people all over the world want peace and prosperity.

BBC in its evening broadcast said that about 2,500 lawyers held a convention at Lahore. They passed resolutions demanding restoration of the powers of the High Court and holding elections within three months. Also restoration of freedom of press and a call for a general strike on 5 July. They took out a procession which was stopped near the Anarkali Chowk and dispersed after a mild baton charge. About sixty persons were arrested amongst them Malik Qasim (secretary general) Muslim League and Aitzaz Ahsan (Tehrik-i-Istiqlal). Yesterday's news had said that another 'leader' of Tehrik-i-Istiqlal had been arrested when he was leaving Quetta for Lahore.

Friday, 20 June 1980, Abbottabad
This morning BBC and VOA news said that most of those people who were arrested in Lahore yesterday were released after a short while and that no one is reported to have been injured.

Bashir (my PA) told me yesterday that he had learnt that the government intends confiscating (or resuming) all or part of the land of my house, 23 Kutchery Road. The local military estate officer has received instructions from the quarter master general GHQ to prepare a case for this purpose. They have already issued an order or an ordinance that empowers them to resume any 'old grant' leased land in cantonment areas.

Today's papers gave the government's version of the convention at Lahore and said that 84 persons were arrested but released later. They also gave a statement by Ahmed Saeed Kirmani, the president of the High Court Bar Association, who was thrown out of the convention.

Saturday, 21 June 1980, Abbottabad

Large-scale killing of people of Bengali (East and West Bengal) origin who form a majority in Tripura state in India by the tribal people. Over a thousand have been killed. The tribesman or the old inhabitants of Tripura resent the settling of Bengalis from Bangladesh and West Bengal in their state.

In Iran there is an open rift between President Bani Sadr and the Islamic Republican Party (the party of the clerics). Ayatollah Khomeini has so far maintained a neutral posture. Heads of the three defence services have been replaced again. The Islamic Republican Party has a majority in the assembly.

Sunday, 22 June 1980, Abbottabad

The Russians announced the withdrawal of some of their troops 10,000 from Afghanistan. Wrote to Asaf Vardag, Aitzaz Ahsan and Taj Mohammad Langah congratulating them on their efforts to make the All-Pakistan Lawyers Convention a success.

Monday, 23 June 1980, Abbottabad

Sanjay Gandhi, Mrs Indira Gandhi's son, was killed in an air crash in Delhi this morning. He was piloting a single engine aircraft along with the chief flying instructor of the Delhi Flying Club, Mr Saxena. The plane crashed less than a kilometre from Mrs Indira Gandhi's residence. One report says that his aircraft hit a tree at the bottom of a loop. He was a keen flyer and had taken over this plane (new aircraft) only yesterday. It appears to have been a case of low acrobatics. Government has ordered an inquiry.

Thursday, 26 June 1980, Abbottabad

Ghulam Ishaq Khan made his two hour budget speech on TV and radio. He appeared to be pleased with himself and the state of the economy—a confidence that is misplaced. The defence budget is up by Rs153 million and the price of *atta* and sugar has been raised. Also cigarettes will cost more and the sales duty on cars has been hiked.

The BBC said that Mufti Mahmud and the Shias have criticised the manner in which *zakat* is being enforced. Mufti Mahmud has said that *zakat* cannot be enforced on those assets that are not visible. So he argues that it should not be deducted from savings accounts in banks. The Shias maintain that *zakat* collected from them can only be spent on Shias. They are holding a convention to discuss this issue on the third anniversary of Ziaul Haq's rule. It only now requires Maulana Noorani to come out with another *fatwa* to make the confusion complete.

Sunday, 6 July 1980, Abbottabad

The Shah of Iran's condition is reported to have deteriorated. He is in a Cairo hospital and has had a second operation in four days.

Because of Mian Mahmud Ali Kasuri's illness (slipped disc) the next person on the list of 26—Allama Aqeel Turabi should be taking over as acting president of the party any time now. Mian Sahib has borne the responsibility well but has been handicapped by his indifferent health.

Thursday, 10 July 1980, Abbottabad

Received a letter from Thames Polytechnic to say that Ali had passed in his BSc in Architecture and was exempted from taking Part-I of the examination for ARIBA (Association of Royal Institute of British Architects).

Saturday, 12 July 1980, Abbottabad

The BBC news this morning said that the so called PNA (for it is now JUI and Nasrullah Khan) has said that if Ziaul Haq does not hold elections (or take steps to hold them) by 1 September, they will launch a movement. Mian Tufail Mohammad has released a letter which he has written to Ziaul Haq advising him to hold elections.

Thursday, 17 July 1980, Abbottabad

Ronald Reagan won the Republican nomination for the US presidency at Detroit and chose George Bush as his running mate.

The condition of the ex-Shah of Iran, Raza Shah Pehlavi, is reported to have deteriorated in a Cairo hospital.

Sunday, 20 July 1980, Abbottabad

Mushir Pesh Imam, Allama Aqeel Turabi (the acting party president), Ahmed Mian Soomro, Syed Munir Shah and Syed Zafar Ali Shah came to Abbottabad and sent me a letter seeking my guidance on: (a) Alliance or cooperation with other political parties. (b) Whether my petition in the High Court should be revived.

I sent Amina to meet them and said that whilst I favoured cooperation with all political parties, I was against a formal alliance at this stage. I also said that the Jamaat-i-Islami and the Pagara Muslim League were with Ziaul Haq's regime and would sabotage any movement. Mushir had also written about getting Ziaul Haq to hold elections. I said that no election with Ziaul Haq in control of the country's affairs should be acceptable. We must insist on the army's exit and that the election should be supervised by a political government. Allama Turabi said that if 14 August is not Eid, he could address a meeting on that day at the Quaid-i-Azam's mausoleum and he thought that he and Obaid-ur-Rehman would be arrested on that day. They also decided to hold a party council meeting at Lahore on 22 August.

Tuesday, 22 July 1980, Abbottabad

Ayatollah Khomeini has expressed strong disapproval of the way the government is functioning in Iran. This he has done for the second time during the last few weeks. He wants the pace of the 'Islamic' revolution to be stepped up. No let down and no compromises. Bani Sadr's position and that of the 'revolutionary committee' that he heads has thus been undermined. Turmoil and change is to be expected in Iran.

Wednesday, 23 July 1980, Abbottabad

A quiet day. Spent my time supervising the repairs to the staff quarters (former stables and servants quarters). I am having them renovated to make them livable. Amina and I have spent three years in a section of these, in a 9'x9' room, when the main building was burnt in 1973. It had mud walls and I am having these lined with baked bricks on the outside. The repairs to the quarters will be completed in a few days.

Thursday, 24 July 1980, Abbottabad

Aitzaz Ahsan and his wife called and I spoke to them at the gate.

Sunday, 27 July 1980, Abbottabad

Mohammad Raza Shah Pehlavi, ex-Shah of Iran, died in a Cairo hospital at the age of 61 after a prolonged illness. He had been suffering from cancer. He had ruled for 37 years, until January last year, when he was forced to leave the country.

Tuesday, 29 July 1980, Abbottabad

Mohammad Raza Shah Pehlavi was buried in Cairo. He was given a state funeral. Pakistan was not represented. Ex-King Constantine of Greece attended the state funeral.

The Iranian parliament has not been able to agree on the appointment of President Bani Sadr's nominees as prime minister. Ayatollah Khomeini has refused to resolve the deadlock.

Monday, 4 Aug 1980, Abbottabad

Abdul Latif Khan (DC Abbottabad) and the SSP, called to inform me that I was to be shifted to Dadar Forest rest house on Wednesday, 6 August. Amina was in the same place, when she was placed in detention in May 1977.

Anis telephoned Tariq to say that Mushir and Obaid-ur-Rehman had been taken into police custody last night.

Tuesday, 5 Aug 1980, Abbottabad

The BBC gave details of arrests in Karachi. Maulana Ehtram ul Haq Thanvi was also arrested yesterday. He, Mushir and Obaid-ur-Rehman are in Karachi central jail.

Wednesday, 6 Aug 1980, Abbottabad, Dadar

Left (along with the SP Abbottabad) for Dadar. Arrived there 1½ hours later at 12:15. I am staying in the same one room cottage where Amina was lodged in May 1977 when she had to undergo detention. Dadar's elevation is about the same as Abbottabad (4,000 feet above sea level). The surroundings are pleasant and the compound is fairly large—about an acre and a half—though the broken nature of the ground and the rocks will not permit taking a walk around the place.

An assistant superintendent of Haripur jail and a jail staff has been posted here and the rest house has been converted into a sub-jail. The place has electricity and water but I am told that the voltage drops in the evenings and the electric gadgets do not function satisfactorily. I have brought a small TV set and will see whether it works. I also have a small radio set but was told that I could not bring a tape recorder.

The Mansehra DC received me here. The assistant superintendent jail is staying in another cottage about 25 yards away. My room is just large enough for a double bed. A jail warden is on duty outside my room and will maintain a 24 hour watch. The compound is well guarded by Frontier Constabulary—at least a platoon strength. Probably the same people who were guarding me at Abbottabad. They arrived here a couple of hours after me. The AC Mansehra called in the evening.

Saw a large number of camps of Afghan refugees between Abbottabad and Dadar. Some tents of refugees are pitched outside the jail compound. The SP Abbottabad told me that they were becoming a problem for the administration.

Thursday, 7 Aug 1980, Dadar

An uncomfortable night. Electricity failed at least a dozen times and without a fan, the room was humid and warm. The TV did not work last night. The sound was alright but the picture was missing. Will try it with an outdoor aerial and will ask Amina to bring one with her when she comes on Eid day. There is no fridge, so the storage of food is not organised. It is not possible to preserve food stuff such as butter. No butter at *sehri*. The cook is the same person who cooked for Amina when she was here. He has come from the Mansehra rest house.

The Voice of America in its 06:30 news (Urdu service) broadcast said that I had been shifted to Dadar jail because I had abused the privileges extended to me at Abbottabad. It quoted a source saying that 150 party office bearers had visited Abbottabad since my second detention on 29 May this year. As if to say that one of the conditions of my detention was that the entry of ordinary citizens to Abbottabad was also to be prevented by me. I had of course not met anyone.

The deputy commissioner called and his representative brought the ice box that I had asked Amina to send.

Friday, 8 Aug 1980, Dadar
The electricity behaved better last night and I was able to sleep. The TV did not work again. The jail superintendent tells me that this is the general complaint by a few people who have TV sets here. The supply of food stuff is erratic as these are supplied from Mansehra. A representative of the accounts office comes every day and takes orders for the next day but generally he brings only half the things ordered. I have not been able to get any butter so far and even if he gets it, it melts by the time it arrives here. The clothes are sent to Mansehra for washing because the only *dhobi* works for the TB sanitorium next door and I do not like my clothes mixed up with those of TB patients. I wash my own small clothes such as undergarments. I also clean my own room.

Saturday, 9 Aug 1980, Dadar
The Voice of America broadcast in its morning news bulletin that Asaf Vardag had addressed a press conference yesterday criticising the government and inviting arrest. He is the acting president of the party after Obaid-ur-Rehman's arrest.

Mohammad Ali Rajai has been chosen—against President Bani Sadr's wishes—for the post of prime minister by the majority Islamic Republican Party in Tehran yesterday.

It rained last evening and we were without electricity for the whole night. However it was cool and I did not miss the fan. Wrote to Amina asking for a cardigan and a few other things. The assistant superintendent told me that he had received my letter yesterday and had sent a few things which I will receive tomorrow. I give my letters in an open state to the assistant superintendent who hands them over to the Intelligence man. Since the man cannot read English, the letter is taken to Mansehra, censored and then sent to Abbottabad.

Got some butter today for the first time which had melted during its journey here. It had been purchased in Abbottabad. Have kept it in water to preserve it for *sehri* tomorrow.

General Yahya Khan died in CMH Rawalpindi last night.

Monday, 11 Aug 1980, Dadar
The BBC in its morning Urdu news broadcast said that government circles in Islamabad were concerned with Ayatollah Khomeini's appeal to Muslims everywhere to topple corrupt and anti-people governments. The Ayatollah had specifically mentioned Pakistan along with Turkey, Afghanistan, Egypt and Iraq. The BBC also spoke about the general political situation in Pakistan. In its evening Urdu news broadcast it said that a student from Sindh, Nazir Abbasi, was reported to have died in detention. It is understood that he was tortured in jail. He is reported to have been agitating for the separation of Sindh from Pakistan.

Mohammad Ali Rajai was formally voted prime minster of Iran by the Iranian parliament today. With a bit of luck and the cooperation of the ulema, we should be able to celebrate Eid on the 13th. Tomorrow is the 29th fast.

Tuesday, 12 Aug 1980, Dadar
The Eid moon was sighted today. So tomorrow will be Eidul Fitr.

The BBC in its evening Urdu bulletin announced that Asaf Vardag had been arrested.

Wednesday, 13 Aug 1980, Dadar
Eidul Fitr. Adey [my mother], Amina, Nasreen, Omar, Osman, Rabia and Mohammad came at about 11:45 and stayed until 14:45. They had lunch here. It was good to see them all. Although the time was all too brief. Adey appeared upset and kept asking as to when I would return home. I told her that I was very comfortable and asked her not to worry. Rabia had brought a flower for me. Amina said that she had been told that she could apply to see me after two weeks. Omar's university will re-start after the summer holidays on 1 September. He is leaving for Lahore on the 15th and Amina will accompany him to Rawalpindi.

In the last seven days I have become well adjusted here but I missed the family and the children after they left. However, I shall get used to this.

Thursday, 14 Aug 1980, Dadar
'Independence' day. Hardly so. After 33 years, the country is under a dictatorship worse than during the British days. The people have no say in national affairs and Islam and the people are being exploited mercilessly. Saw in the *Guardian* of 6 August that Dr Aizaz Nazir, the secretary general of Pakistan's underground Communist Party, and ten others were arrested for subversive activities against the state.

My preoccupation here is writing my book on my experiences in Pakistani politics and some systematic reading. As well as watching 'Iqra' on TV—a ten-minute programme of reading from the Quran—every day. I have read two books last week: *Gokhale, Gandhi and Nehrus* by B.R. Nanda and the *Abuse of Power* by James Margach. I am now reading *Islam in History* by Justice Mohammad Munir.

Ayaz was awarded the Hilal-i-Imtiaz in the Independence day honours today. He seems to have impressed Ziaul Haq!

Friday, 15 Aug 1980, Dadar
Gave a letter for posting and sent a telegram to Ayaz congratulating him on his award which I said, I am sure, was well 'earned'.

Refixed the TV aerial and the reception improved greatly. It is now possible to see TV programmes. Amina had told me of the place where Ali had fixed the TV aerial when she was here in 1977. I have fixed it near that place.

President Jimmy Carter has been adopted as the Democratic's candidate for the US November presidential election. It should be a close contest with Ronald Reagan.

One hundred and five persons have been killed in Hindu-Muslim clashes in Uttar Pradesh in India. The trouble started when a pig entered the Eidgah at Muradabad at the end of Eid prayers. Curfew has been imposed in a number of places including Delhi.

Saturday, 16 Aug 1980, Dadar
Started my Pushto chit chat with the assistant superintendent jail, Ashraf Khan, from today. I take an hour's stroll in the morning and

he keeps me company. Also chatted a little in the afternoon with Taza Gul, the prison guard from Charsadda.

Sunday, 17 Aug 1980, Dadar

The BBC broadcast the news of Asaf Vardag's arrest in its Hindi bulletin. The Urdu news bulletin had broadcast this on 12 August.

Since I am effectively sealed off, there is not much else to write about. The newspapers (which I am given) have hardly any news in them except sermons on Islam which Ziaul Haq and his media are giving day in and day out. They do not appear to realise that this policy could be counter-productive.

Monday, 18 Aug 1980, Dadar

The role of the media in United States politics can be gauged from a report of the Voice of America this morning, that there were 10,000 newspaper, TV and radio people covering the Democratic Party convention in New York, in which the number of delegates was 3,000.

The assistant superintendent jail told me this morning that as an 'A' class prisoner I was entitled to send out four letters a week.

Tuesday, 19 Aug 1980, Dadar

Radio Pakistan announced a new martial law order that provided for punishment of a 14 years RI, flogging and fine for anyone organising or attending a press conference, meeting, reception, procession or demonstration within the limits of the federal area of Islamabad.

Wednesday, 20 Aug 1980, Dadar

Wrote a letter to Amina and gave it to the assistant superintendent. There is a post office here and the mail is now posted here after it has been censored. It is sent by the government transport service which is not regular and does not come every day.

Thursday, 21 Aug 1980, Dadar

The government sponsored *maulvis'* conference is starting in Islamabad today to discuss the Islamisation of laws. Mufti Mahmud and Maulana Noorani have refused to attend.

Pakistan is likely to send (according to BBC and VOA) one division of the army to Saudi Arabia in return for $1,000 million.

Sardar Khan Orakzai, the third acting president of Tehrik-i-Istiqlal, has called on Ziaul Haq to resign and hand over power to the judges of the Supreme Court. He has also announced a party council meeting on 24 August in Peshawar.

Friday, 22 Aug 1980, Dadar

Amina, Nasreen, Omar, Rabia and Mohammad came at midday, stayed for lunch and left at 15:00. It was nice to see them again. Omar had come to Abbottabad from Lahore and is returning there this evening. Amina, Nasreen and the kids are leaving for Karachi on the 24th and are returning on 1 September. Rabia (six years old) was very affectionate. She told Nasreen yesterday that she should meet Ziaul Haq and tell him to release me. If he does not agree, Rabia said that she should ask him how would he feel if he was kept locked up.

Lawyers held a convention at Karachi yesterday and took out a procession. Government used Frontier Constabulary to beat up the demonstrators. Tear gas, batons and rifle butts were used. A number of people were injured and nine lawyers and two other people were arrested. They are being tried by a military court. Some people stoned the police and according to BBC some policeman (or Frontier Constabulary) were injured.

Saturday, 23 Aug 1980, Dadar

BBC reported that the lawyers action committee had decided that if the nine lawyers arrested in Karachi were not released forthwith, more lawyers would court arrest. They also decided if these lawyers are tried in a military court they would not offer any defence.

While addressing the *maulvis'* convention Ziaul Haq has said that whenever he holds elections in Pakistan, he will only allow those people to contest who are good Muslims and good Pakistanis. Presumably he will decide who is a good Muslim and a good Pakistani.

The IG prisons, NWFP, and the superintendent Haripur jail called. BBC in its evening news broadcast said that political parties are becoming active and mentioned Tehrik-i-Istiqlal's convention at Peshawar being held tomorrow. It also mentioned that Malik Qasim, the convener of the lawyers action committee, had called for united action by political parties and had asked them to sink their differences. My own assessment and experience is that it was not their differences—for on the issue of restoration of democracy there is no difference of opinion—but the lack of courage and the fear of martial law that has been preventing them from coming forward. The lead that the Tehrik-i-Istiqlal took was designed to create the right atmosphere which would induce others to follow and I am glad that it has had that effect. However I expect Ziaul Haq to react strongly to any action by political parties and the next few weeks will set the pattern for the events to follow.

Sunday, 24 Aug 1980, Dadar

Mrs Nusrat Bhutto and Benazir Bhutto were externed from the Punjab for three months and sent back to Karachi from Lahore where they had come for a wedding.

Monday, 25 Aug 1980, Dadar

Ziae brought a voltage stabiliser for me. I did not see him. The voltage stabiliser improved the TV reception. Between peak hours (19:00 to 21:00) the voltage drops to 120. The voltage stabiliser puts it upto 190 which is not satisfactory but makes the picture sharper.

I understand that if I do not write letters home, I can, according to jail rules be allowed weekly visits. I have therefore stopped writing letters which are in any case read and censored. My last letter to Amina was written on 20 August.

Tuesday, 26 Aug 1980, Dadar

In its Hindi morning service the BBC reported that Tehrik-i-Istiqlal had held a meeting at Peshawar in which it had demanded elections according to the 1973 constitution.

No news of Pakistan for the last few days in the Urdu services of BBC and VOA. Radio Moscow seldom gives any news of Pakistan except about the use of Pakistan as a base for operations in Afghanistan.

The Soviet Union is celebrating the 1000th birth anniversary of Abu Ali Ibne Sina (also known as Avicenna) in his hometown of Afshan, near Bokhara in the Uzbekistan republic. He was a mathematician, philosopher, historian and poet and is also known as the father of surgery. The Soviet Union is also holding a conference of Muslim ulema to celebrate the beginning of the fifteenth century of the Hijra calendar.

Wednesday, 27 Aug 1980, Dadar

Wrote to the DC Mansehra to complain about the unsatisfactory arrangements for washing of clothes. The local *dhobi* works for the TB sanitorium (next door) and the clothes are sent to Mansehra. They are returned to me in a worse condition than when they were sent and have dirt marks that were not there when given for washing. I do my own washing of small items of clothing such as vests, drawers, napkins, socks and small towels but larger items such as bed sheets, towels, pillow cases and shirts have to be sent to Mansehra.

My daily routine here is:

06:10-07:00	BBC and VOA news. (I also listen to the 05:00 BBC world news almost every second day).
07:00-08:00	Making my bed, cleaning of shoes. Washing of clothes, shave and bathe.
08:00-08:30	Breakfast. Arrange flowers.
08:30-10:00	Walk on the lower lawn.
10:00-13:00	Newspapers. Arrange flowers.
13:00-16:00	Reading or writing.
16:00-16:30	Radio Moscow Urdu service news and commentary.
16:30-17:00	Walk.
17:00-18:00	Pushto news on TV from Peshawar and 'Iqra'.
18:00-19:00	Walk.
19:00-21:30	TV.
19:30	Dinner.
21:45 or 22:00	Sleep.

Thursday, 28 Aug 1980, Dadar

BBC said this morning that Karachi lawyers had observed a strike yesterday because the ten lawyers who had been arrested recently had not been released. Giving unemployment figures in UK it said that there were two million unemployed in UK—eight out of one hundred of the population. This is the highest rate of unemployment in UK since the thirties. No wonder that Ali found some difficulty getting a job after his BSc (Honours) in architecture. However I understand from Shirin's last letter that he has since got a job for £4000 a year.

Jang reported that a case had been registered against Syed Munir Shah and thirteen other workers of Tehrik-i-Istiqlal for making inflammatory speeches in Peshawar on 24 August.

Friday, 29 Aug 1980, Dadar

Eighty people have been tried and shot so far in Iran for plotting to overthrow the government and kidnap or kill Ayatollah Khomeini. Mohammad Ali Rajai, who has been prime minister now for nearly three weeks, has not been able to announce a cabinet as yet because of lack of agreement between him and President Bani Sadr. The president's approval is necessary before the prime minister can appoint a minister.

Radio Pakistan announced the unearthing of a conspiracy, which according to the government has been working underground for some time. It implied that it was a communist 'cell'. Some arrests have been made.

Saturday, 30 Aug 1980, Dadar

The 'conspiracy' story was repeated prominently in the BBC and VOA broadcasts this morning.

The strike in the Polish Baltic ports is reported to be approaching a settlement. The hostages in Iran have completed 300 days in custody (I have completed 275 days). President Bani Sadr has 'appealed' for their release. So has Qotbzadeh, the foreign minister.

Sunday, 31 Aug 1980, Dadar

The secretary general of the Karachi Bar Association has been arrested, bringing the total number of lawyers arrested in Karachi in connection with the incident on 21 August to eleven (VOA).

The Jalalabad-Kabul road which was closed to traffic for about four days, because of operations by Mujahideen, has been reopened.

Indira Gandhi has protested to the USA for not abiding by a trade agreement. The USA has banned those items which are subsidised by the Indian government.

Monday, 1 Sept 1980, Dadar
The AC Mansehra visited me and I told him about the various administrative problems.

Mohammad Ali Rajai, the prime minister of Iran, has announced his new cabinet.

Wednesday, 3 Sept 1980, Dadar
The BBC and the VOA said that a meeting had taken place yesterday at Karachi 'hosted' by Mrs Asghar Khan at which besides the Tehrik-i-Istiqlal, others present were the JUP, Muslim League (Malik Qasim group) and National Liberation Front (Mairaj Mohammad Khan). Ghaus Bux Bizenjo had agreed to attend but did not come. It was decided to contact other parties, broaden the front and then demand lifting of martial law, freedom of the press and the formation of a national government for the purpose of holding elections. It was also said that the PPP leaders are holding consultation amongst themselves as also the PNA which had announced earlier to launch a movement if its demand to announce the holding of elections is not met by 1 September 1980. Amina is not expected here today and may come on 5 September.

Thursday, 4 Sept 1980, Dadar
Amina, Anwar and Omar arrived at midday and stayed for lunch. Heard from Amina that Nafis Siddiqui had been arrested in Karachi yesterday. He had done good work before his arrest. Mahfooz Yar Khan has also been arrested. Sardar Khan Orakzai, the acting president of the party, will probably be arrested before long.

Friday, 5 Sept 1980, Dadar
Sent a telegram to Nur Khan whose mother died a couple of days ago.

Yesterday's newspapers mentioned prominently that Radio Tehran had called upon the people of Pakistan and Saudi Arabia to rise in armed revolt against their governments. Today's papers carried editorials criticising the Iranian government for what they termed as its 'anti-Islam' policy. Ayatollah Khomeini had, about a couple of weeks ago, expressed sympathy with the struggle of the people of Afghanistan, Pakistan, Iraq, Turkey and Egypt against their governments. The Iranian charge d'affaires in Islamabad had subsequently said that Ayatollah Khomeini's remarks had been misunderstood. The Radio Tehran broadcast and two or three editorials of the Islamic Republican Party's official newspaper, which carried at least one signed editorial by Moosavi the editor, who has since been appointed foreign minister, confirm the thinking of the Iranian government towards Pakistan. They regard Ziaul Haq and the junta as American stooges. However, our newspapers, in their government inspired editorials, have taken the line that Radio Tehran is controlled by leftist or communist elements inimical to Islamic unity. It is a clumsy line because it is unthinkable that Radio Tehran should not be under the control of the government. Moreover Khomeini himself had spoken in a similar vein. It is also significant that Ayatollah Khomeini has not as yet agreed to meet Ziaul Haq. This major cleavage in Iran-Pakistan relations will add to the worries of Ziaul Haq and will influence the Pakistan Shia community's views about the government in Islamabad. The demands of the Shias about *zakat* are to be agreed to by 15 September. Mufti Jaffar Hussain, who is regarded by Allama Aqeel Turabi as a government stooge, is presenting his draft agreement to Ziaul Haq on 7 September.

The campaign for the United States presidential election due in the first week of November 1980 is moving into full gear. There are a few interesting features of this election. Candidates are paid a fairly large sum for their campaign expenses if they secure a minimum of 5 per cent of the votes cast. The independent candidate, Anderson, is experiencing financial difficulties but after this ruling by the Supreme Court, he will be able to borrow money for his campaign expense. He is certain to get more than 5 per cent votes. Another feature of this election is the importance of the Jewish vote. Jews in the United States number only 3 per cent of the population but control the media—which plays an important role in the election. Their turn-out on election day is also very high. They can also help the campaign with money. For these reasons candidates try to woo the Jewish population. Both Carter and Reagan are trying to assure the Jews of their pro-Israel stand in the Arab-Israel dispute and the Jewish vote appears at present to be divided. Whatever the result, the United States policy cannot go against the interest of the world jewry and of Israel.

Saturday, 6 Sept 1980, Dadar

Armed forces day. The assistant superintendent went home for a night yesterday afternoon. BBC said that Mairaj Mohammad Khan of National Liberation Front has said that the meeting of four party leaders under Begum Asghar Khan's chairmanship in Karachi did not mean that they had formed a 'front'. He said that no meaningful alliance could be formed until the 'progressive forces' joined hands.

The political spectrum in Pakistan presents an interesting picture. The four political parties that assembled in Karachi the other day are in my view the only genuine opposition to the present military regime. Of these the JUP and TI can be regarded as major parties. The Muslim League of Khawaja Khairuddin and Malik Qasim has a small following but is not much smaller than Pagara's Muslim League. Mairaj Mohammad Khan's NLF is a tiny party limited only to Karachi. He is himself a progressive but is still hypnotised by the Bhutto family.

Sherbaz Mazari and the NDP are anti-government. Sherbaz is close to Fazle Haq (MLA NWFP) and Abbasi (MLA Sindh) he was in school with both of them. Moreover Wali Khan and Naseem Wali Khan have a good understanding with Ziaul Haq. When Mian Mahmud Ali Kasuri saw Arbab Sikander Khan Khalil of NDP some months ago to determine whether there was any common ground between our two parties, Arbab Sikander said that Ziaul Haq's government was the best that Pakistan has so far had and he saw no reason to try to oust him.

Similarly Pir Pagara is fully with Ziaul Haq and his Muslim League should be called 'Ziaul Haq Muslim League'. Pagara is politically untrustworthy and is a reactionary.

Nawabzada Nasrullah Khan has no real party but survives politically on alliances and political parleys. He is not with Ziaul Haq but is not politically reliable. Suffers from complexes and is a reactionary. He is not likely to play a constructive role in national politics and cannot leave other reactionary elements whose leadership he manages to secure.

Mufti Mahmud and his JUI do not represent a strong opposition to the military regime. He is flexible in his approach. Will stay with any grouping so long as he is made the leader.

Jamaat-i-Islami is the real 'king's party'. It is fully with Ziaul Haq but will put up a façade of opposition to keep in line with the public mood.

The PPP is a party like a body without a head. It has a following but the ladies are not capable of providing political leadership in the present circumstances. They cannot be removed by the party. Their second level leadership is dominated by opportunists, most of whom had joined this party for personal gains and are staying with it because they feel that the party has an appeal for the masses. The party has been victimised by Ziaul Haq and there are numerous criminal cases against their leaders including one for non-payment of Rs250,000 in income tax against Mrs Bhutto. Moreover after Bhutto's hanging, they, particularly Mrs Bhutto and her daughter, have no stomach for confronting the government. The two ladies cannot forget my role in Bhutto's ouster either. They will wait and try to ride the crest of a public movement when it has fully developed.

Ghaus Bux Bizenjo's National Progressive Party is at present difficult to assess. He and the Baloch leaders have been at the receiving end of things for a long time and will not, I feel, take a strong stand against the government particularly because most of them do not have much faith in Pakistan's capacity to survive in the present circumstances. However, I had a good meeting with Bizenjo, when I was in Karachi three months ago, but then he is a political animal and his talk may not have shown his real mind.

The other parties such as Taj Langah's alliance of leftist parties and C.R. Aslam's Socialist Party have some following. Will be in opposition to the government and will probably be willing to join hands, though their strength is limited.

The Mazdoor Kissan Party of Afzal Bangash has considerable strength in certain parts of NWFP and I believe that Afzal Bangash is in Moscow—probably waiting for developments to take place here that will be favourable for his return. In this situation I have not been in favour of any formal alliance. However, if all the parties get together only to say that martial law should be ended, a civilian national government should be formed and elections held within three months it will have been an achievement. Because of the government's influence over some of these parties, even their getting together for this limited purpose appears unlikely.

In the circumstances, cooperation between the four parties that met at Karachi is a step in the right direction and it will be interesting to see what developments take place in the next few weeks. Tehrik-i-Istiqlal's cooperation with other parties is limited for the purpose of ending martial law and holding of elections and we do not intend having an election alliance with any party. This view is strongly held by the party and has been expressed in meetings of the national working committee and the national council.

Tuesday, 9 Sept 1980, Dadar

Aitzaz Ahsan came. A special branch officer from Abbottabad, Mr Fazal Dad, was also here and his instructions were to sit and listen to our conversation. According to Aitzaz this is not proper since my case is against the government, a representative of the government cannot listen to the client's instructions to his counsel. The assistant superintendent checked up with the superintendent, Haripur jail on the telephone and confirmed that there was nothing in their rules or instructions to permit a private conversation between us. After taking tea and refreshments Aitzaz therefore returned to Lahore. He will be reporting to the Supreme Court and asking to be allowed to see me without a special branch representative. Ziaul Haq is visiting Mansehra district tomorrow.

Wednesday, 10 Sept 1980, Dadar

The Amir of Kuwait has left after a lot of handshakes and kissing—Arab style. Ziaul Haq visited Mansehra today.

Friday, 12 Sept 1980, Dadar

While speaking to press correspondents at Karachi yesterday Ziaul Haq has said that he will be making an announcement within the next fortnight—before going to New York to address the United Nations General Assembly, that would, he hoped, end the present uncertain political situation in the country. He said that he would also speak about the formation of the new cabinet and the federal advisory council. The VOA said that when asked whether he has been in touch with political leaders, he said that he has been and named Pir of Pagara, Chaudhry Zahur Elahi and Ghulam Mustafa Jatoi. The VOA said that the government news agency later withdrew the name of

Ghulam Mustafa Jatoi. The VOA further said that Mrs Bhutto's private secretary, Qazi Ghaus, has been arrested in Karachi and Sheikh Rafique, the president of the Punjab PPP who was arrested in connection with the lawyer's procession on 21 August, has been moved from Lahore to the Karachi central jail.

Saturday, 13 Sept 1980, Dadar
India and Iran have agreed on a bilateral trade agreement. Iran will supply oil to India and India will supply machinery which was banned for export to Iran by western countries. India's exports to Iran are likely to be worth one billion dollars in the next year. This is a significant development which will inevitably affect Pakistan-Iran relations, which have already deteriorated considerably. India is also considering helping Iran in running some of its industries.

Sunday, 14 Sept 1980, Dadar
Wrote to Shirin. Her letter took 20 days to reach me and I told the assistant superintendent that he should tell the Intelligence people that they should not sit on letters for so long. Shirin had criticised the government and the letter must have been sent up to higher authorities for clearance before delivering it to me.

Monday, 15 Sept 1980, Dadar
The government announced its decision not to levy *zakat* on anyone who gives a written statement that compulsory levy of *zakat* is against his religious beliefs. However such applications will be placed before the Zakat Council and if rejected, a fine, equivalent to the amount levied will be charged. Mufti Jaffar Hussain has expressed satisfaction with this decision and must, therefore, have been assured that no Shia's application will be rejected.

This exemption will not, however, be with retrospective effect. On the law providing for the amputation of the hands of a thief the government has not agreed to change it to accommodate the Shias whose law requires that fingers (instead of the hand) of a thief should be cut. Again Mufti Jaffar Hussain must have been assured that no Shia's hands will be cut. This is not really a problem because no one's hand has been cut so far anyway.

Friday, 19 Sept 1980, Dadar

The assistant superintendent of jail returned from Haripur and was complaining that he had been here almost two months and had not been relieved. The cook is also very unhappy here and wants to go back to Mansehra. It appears as if I am the only one who is not complaining.

Monday, 22 Sept 1980, Dadar

A *mashaikh* [religious scholars] conference started today in Islamabad chaired by the leading self-styled shaikh, Ziaul Haq. It is an attempt to mobilise all the reactionary forces in his support.

The daily *Jang* confirmed that Mushir and Obaid-ur-Rehman had been released.

Thursday, 25 Sept 1980, Dadar

Afghan refugees who have pitched their tents around the rest house here are moving back to the Peshawar area.

Friday, 26 Sept 1980, Dadar

The BBC said last night that Ghulam Mustafa Jatoi had been approached to be the prime minister with the assurance that if he accepted, elections would be held. Also that Mrs Bhutto and Benazir in an interview given to Peter Nieswand of the *Guardian* had said that anyone joining the government would be expelled from the PPP and that the situation was now more favourable for cooperation between political parties who do not join Ziaul Haq's government.

Saturday, 27 Sept 1980, Dadar

Six Afghan helicopters attacked one of our border posts in the Bajaur area. Ziaul Haq in a press conference last night said that a major and a havaldar had been killed and a *jawan* of the Frontier Constabulary injured. He said that these were Russian type helicopters and implied that these were flown by Russian pilots. He said that there had been over 200 violations of our air space during this year. Ziaul Haq said that he was leaving for Tehran and Baghdad on the 28th where he would be joined by Habib Shatti, the secretary general of the Islamic conference. They would try to resolve the dispute between Iran and Iraq and stop the war. A short while later Mohammad Ali Rajai, the

Iranian prime minister, said in a radio speech that anyone was welcome to come to Iran to see the war damage but he and his government were not willing to discuss a ceasefire with Ziaul Haq or anyone else.

Ziaul Haq also said in the press conference that he would not be making an announcement about the internal political situation before his departure for the USA as he had said he would do earlier. He would do this immediately after his return. He has been saying this since May and I doubt that he will say or do anything even after his return.

Lieutenant General Fazle Haq, governor NWFP, came and stayed for an hour. He said that the government was willing to release me if I did not criticise the martial law regime like I had when I was released in April. I declined to give any such undertaking. He left in a helicopter for Naran. In his conversation he said the following: (1) Wali Khan had met him four times during his recent visit to the UK and had told him that he would not join the government or support them openly but they could count on his full cooperation. (2) He did not trust Ghulam Mustafa Jatoi and was against making him the prime minister. He felt that he would thus be able to build up the image of the PPP. He had advised Ziaul Haq against any civilianisation of the regime. (3) Ziaul Haq had taken no decision as yet and was not likely to make any changes in a hurry. (4) If a civilian cabinet was to be formed in the NWFP he would like to select George Sikander Zaman as minister and possibly Mahmooda Saleem (who does not appear to be agreeable). (5) The Afghan problem was a 'blessing in disguise'. (6) Lieutenant General Abbasi, the governor of Sindh, had told him that I had said in a speech in Karachi that he (Fazle Haq) and Rahimuddin (the governor of Balochistan) were engaged in smuggling.

I told him that the allegation about my speaking about him and Rahimuddin is untrue and that I had never spoken about them. I said however that I had called Ziaul Haq a liar which he was.

Fazle Haq was unnecessarily courteous and friendly. He said that by keeping me detained they were helping to build up my image. I told him that I did not need their help.

Monday, 29 Sept 1980, Dadar
Ziaul Haq is due in Baghdad today. Fazle Haq completes his tour of Mansehra district today. Kala, the sweeper, told the assistant superintendent that he would not work for Rs30 a month. He is a permanent employee of the TB sanitorium. The assistant superintendent is running around trying to make alternate arrangements.

The major killed on the 25th in the attack on one of our posts in the Bajaur area by an Afghan helicopter was from a place near Dadar. Six army truck loads of troops passed through here to attend the funeral at his village.

Tuesday, 30 Sept 1980, Dadar
Seventeen people, including eleven lawyers, who had been arrested in Karachi recently, were released yesterday.

Kala, the sweeper, was re-employed on assurance of higher wages by the forest department. This reminds me of Major General Haq Nawaz Khan who, when he was chairman of Thal Development Authority, had told me once that his terms and conditions of service were not satisfactory and he could not continue like this. He had asked me how he should go about getting these conditions (pay, allowances, etc.) improved. I had asked him whether he was willing to resign if his request was refused. He had said no and I had then advised him to carry on with the existing terms and conditions of service. Kala, the sweeper, had the right approach.

Wednesday, 1 Oct 1980, Dadar
Ziaul Haq addressed the UN General Assembly today. His speech had a couple of interesting features. The UN delegates did not stand up when Ziaul Haq arrived, as is customary for heads of state and the speech was preceded by *tilawat* on the public address system. The speech lasted one hour and thirty minutes and half of it was quotations from the Quran and on the virtues of Islam. His performance was true to form as he could not help telling a lie even there. After having spoken for half an hour he said that he would not tax their patience much longer and will speak for exactly another 35 minutes. He then proceeded to read out his written speech for another one hour.

Thursday, 2 Oct 1980, Dadar
The Islamic foreign ministers in their meeting in New York have asked Ziaul Haq and Shatti (the secretary general of the OIC) to continue their efforts to bring about a ceasefire between Iran and Iraq.

Friday, 3 Oct 1980, Dadar, Abbottabad
The SP, Abbottabad, came to inform me that I was to be moved to 23 Kutchery Road, Abbottabad and I left at about midday. Nasreen, Rabia, Mohammad and Omar were there. Also Tariq and his children were awaiting my return. Nasreen left for Peshawar later in the afternoon. The conditions of the detention are similar to what these were before, except that the telephone has not been disconnected.

Saturday, 4 Oct 1980, Abbottabad
Omar left for Lahore. Ziaul Haq met Carter in Washington yesterday and expressed the hope that Carter would be re-elected so that he may continue to provide leadership to the world. Carter said that if Palestine is attacked, the US would carry out its obligations according to the 1959 agreement.

BBC said that I had been shifted to my house probably as a result of the meeting between Carter and Ziaul Haq. Actually I was moved before the meeting.

Wednesday, 8 Oct 1980, Abbottabad
Nawabzada Nasrullah Khan is reported to have said in Lahore yesterday that ten political parties, including NDP, PPP and Tehrik-i-Istiqlal, had agreed on an arrangement for elections and the end of martial law. He said that an announcement is expected later this month. I have no information about any such agreement except that we have been trying for some such declaration.

Thursday, 9 Oct 1980, Abbottabad
Ziaul Haq said yesterday that except for Tehrik-i-Istiqlal, all other political parties had asked him to postpone the election in October 1979. He was addressing a gathering of Pakistanis in Vienna yesterday.

Mian Mahmud Ali Kasuri telephoned to say that Nawabzada Nasrullah Khan had been to visit him and had invited the Tehrik-i-Istiqlal to a meeting in Karachi on the 13th.

Saturday, 11 Oct 1980, Abbottabad

Anwar (my younger brother) went to the Iranian embassy the other day and registered himself for fighting against Iraq.

Ziaul Haq returned to Rawalpindi yesterday after a two week tour abroad, amongst scenes of welcome reminiscent of the last days of Z.A. Bhutto—bands, gates, flowers, policemen in plain clothes. An obviously government organised welcome. He said on arrival that press censorship would continue and that Pakistan was ready to re-enter the Commonwealth, if it was invited to do so 'honourably'. 'We do not want to crawl back,' he said. He had also said something like this about two years ago. It appears that the Commonwealth is not anxious to have Ziaul Haq's Pakistan back in a hurry and rightly so, for this is a decision which only a popularly elected government should take or at least a popular government, if not an elected one. Ziaul Haq's government is neither.

BBC relayed a very good statement of Nisar Osmani on his election as president of PFUJ about the lack of press freedom in Pakistan.

Tuesday, 14 Oct 1980, Abbottabad

Mushir and Syed Munir Shah came in the afternoon. Mushir had brought a message from Ghulam Mustafa Jatoi to ask whether Tehrik-i-Istiqlal was prepared to join a government headed by him. Ghulam Mustafa Jatoi has been assured by Ziaul Haq that he will hold elections within six to eight months, end martial law courts and allow political activity. He has also asked him to choose his ministers except two generals whom Ziaul Haq will nominate. I told Mushir that I felt that Ziaul Haq had no intention of giving up power and his past performance does not inspire confidence in his promises. However if a practical proposal is made by him it should be examined. I was of the view that Ziaul Haq was not serious about the formation of a civilian government. I suggested to Mushir that Tehrik-i-Istiqlal's reply should be that we should be told what exactly the proposal is and then be given an opportunity to consult each other. The Tehrik-i-

Istiqlal will only take a decision after mutual consultations and I will not decide unilaterally.

Mufti Mahmud died in Karachi today of a heart attack. He was a good old soul and helped to keep the PNA together longer than it would have stayed otherwise.

Wednesday, 15 Oct 1980, Abbottabad
Amina telephoned Mushir at Karachi to say that he should file a writ against the ban on my entry into Sindh province.

Thursday, 16 Oct 1980, Abbottabad
Liaquat Ali Khan's death anniversary. My one year in detention is completed today. Sent a telegram of condolence to Mufti Mahmud's son, Fazlur Rahman.

Friday, 17 Oct 1980, Abbottabad
Wrote to Mian Mahmud Ali Kasuri asking him to take over responsibility of acting president from 1 November.

Saturday, 18 Oct 1980, Abbottabad
Zafar Ali Shah telephoned to say that he had been to Faisalabad where the person in whose house the convention was being held had been arrested the previous day. Khudai Noor telephoned from Quetta to say that he had been released.

Monday, 20 Oct 1980, Abbottabad
Justice Safdar Ali Shah against whom a case has been started in the judicial national council for improper conduct has resigned from the supreme council. He was one of the two judges who had given a dissenting vote in the Zulfikar Ali Bhutto case in the Supreme Court which resulted in Bhutto's hanging.

Eidul Azha today. My third Eid in detention since 16 October 1979.

Tuesday, 21 Oct 1980, Abbottabad
Mohammad Ayub Khuhro died last night.

Wednesday, 22 Oct 1980, Abbottabad
The Iranian Majlis is likely to debate the hostages issue on Sunday, 26 October. It appears that there is a possibility that the matter may be resolved before the American presidential election on 4 November, which will help Carter. The Iranians may well like to do this as Ronald Reagan's policy in this matter is likely to be tougher. Yasser Arafat is trying to mediate in the Iran-Iraq conflict which is now a month old.

Saturday, 25 Oct 1980, Abbottabad
Ziaul Haq spoke at a reception in Karachi and made it clear that he had no intention of holding elections in the foreseeable future.

Monday, 27 Oct 1980, Abbottabad
Twenty-second anniversary of Ayub Khan's take over of the country in 1958. Colonel Tassaddaq Hussain Khan died in Rawalpindi this morning. He had had a heart attack a month ago. Amina had spoken to him to enquire about his health only about an hour before he died and he had said that he was very well and had recovered. Tassaddaq was a member of the party's national working committee and had worked selflessly for the party. His death is also a personal loss to me as he was a good friend and helpful. A very sincere man. May his soul rest in peace.

Wednesday, 29 Oct 1980, Abbottabad
Mian Mahmud Ali Kasuri came, but an inspector of the special branch (Fazal Dad) insisted on sitting to listen to our conversation. Mian Sahib objected and tried telephoning Fazle Haq (the governor), home secretary and deputy martial law administrator but could not contact anyone. We, therefore, did not discuss anything concerning the writ.

Monday, 3 Nov 1980, Abbottabad
Amnesty International has asked Ziaul Haq to free political prisoners and to stop the hanging and whipping of people. Amnesty has said that the incidence of hanging in Pakistan is the highest in Asia (BBC, VOA). Ziaul Haq attended a reception in his honour to felicitate him on his performance in the UN. The arches, gates, banners and buntings arranged on a big scale (at government expense) at these functions are reminiscent of Ayub Khan's and the Bhutto regime's last days.

Such functions may be justified for a visiting head of state but are totally unnecessary for a head of state in his own country.

Wednesday, 5 Nov 1980, Abbottabad

Ronald Reagan won a sweeping victory in the United States presidential elections. Anderson, the independent candidate, secured only 6 per cent of the votes cast which is 1 per cent more than the minimum for saving one's security deposit. Ronald Reagan at 69 will be the oldest person to assume office of president in US history. He will be the 40th president of the US. Reagan is likely to take a tougher line against the Soviet Union and is committed to scrapping the SALT II agreement which he wishes to negotiate again from a position of strength. He is likely to extend greater support to countries threatened by the Soviet Union and dictators of the right can expect US backing. Reagan and the new US administration should suit Ziaul Haq better though support of rightist dictators is a common factor in US policy—Democrats and Republicans alike.

Friday, 7 Nov 1980, Abbottabad

The BBC said that a spokesman of the Pakistan government in reply to the statement issued by Amnesty International has said in Islamabad that only I and Asaf Vardag are the two political prisoners in Pakistan and that we are not prisoners of 'conscience' but are being held on 'security' grounds.

Saturday, 8 Nov 1980, Abbottabad

Omar in his letter which I received yesterday has written that it was rumoured in Lahore that Ziaul Haq was trying to persuade me to join a civilian government as defence minister. He appeared worried and thought that it would not be wise to do so. Amina told him on the telephone that the rumours were baseless and I had no intention of doing any such thing.

Wazir Ali on the other hand asked me to consider joining a civilian government, as its head if called upon to do so under special circumstances. He feels that the Soviet Union and India are bent on disintegrating Pakistan and a situation could soon develop in which Ziaul Haq and the armed forces will need political support to save the country. He feels that an election is at present out of the question and that the only two political parties that are relevant are the PPP and the Tehrik-i-Istiqlal. He is of the opinion that the PPP, or rather the Bhutto ladies, have an equation with the Soviet Union and India and would want to make Pakistan a Soviet satellite. He felt that the Tehrik-i-Istiqlal alone could play a constructive role or else resign itself to wither away in the fast changing circumstances.

I told him of my conversation with Mushir and said that I did not see what purpose our association with a military regime would serve except discrediting ourselves and going back on the stand that we have consistently taken over the years. He said that he is thinking of an arrangement under which Ziaul Haq and the army would shed power and confine itself to its professional functions. All this was so very hypothetical and I did not think that the proposal was worthy of serious consideration.

Sunday, 9 Nov 1980, Abbottabad

Two bomb explosions took place at Quetta yesterday, one near the police lines and the other near the martial law headquarters. No one was injured. Ziaul Haq cancelled his three day tour of Balochistan which he was to start tomorrow. The government announcement said that he was indisposed.

Sadiq Qotbzadeh, the former foreign minister of Iran, was arrested in Tehran for criticising the Islamic Republican Party and Mohammad Ali Rajai's government for its policies, particularly its handling of the hostages crisis. President Bani Sadr has criticised his arrest. Qotbzadeh is due to marry Ayatollah Khomeini's granddaughter and the BBC said that this should be adequate insurance for his safety.

I wrote a letter to Syed Zafar Ali Shah asking him to hand over responsibility of chairman Punjab to Malik Wazir Ali who wishes to resume this appointment.

Monday, 10 Nov 1980, Abbottabad

The BBC gave details of my detention during the last twelve months quoting the *Guardian* of today.

Sadiq Qotbzadeh was released because of Ayatollah Khomeini's intervention. Ziaul Haq appeared on TV yesterday on the eve of the first day of the fifteenth century Hijra. He appeared quite well and there were no signs of his reported indisposition.

Saturday, 22 Nov 1980, Abbottabad
Justice Safdar Ali Shah, a former judge of the Supreme Court of Pakistan, is reported to have gone to Kabul to seek asylum. He was one of the judges who had given a minority decision against Bhutto's hanging. He was later charged for having given his age incorrectly when he had first sought employment. As a result he had resigned from the Supreme Court. Justice Safdar Ali Shah's exit from Pakistan will be an embarrassment for Ziaul Haq's regime as he is likely to talk about matters connected with Bhutto's trial which will not reflect creditably on Ziaul Haq's already discredited regime.

Monday, 24 Nov 1980, Abbottabad
Maulana Noorani called at Tariq's. He wished to meet Amina so she met him there. Maulana Noorani said that Mahmud Haroon had met him and had enquired about what he felt about re-introducing the 1956 constitution. He wanted to know my reaction. Maulana Noorani has already discussed this with Mian Mahmud Ali Kasuri, Wazir Ali and probably Mushir Pesh Imam. It is clear to me that Ziaul Haq has no intention of parting with power. He has hung on to power for three-and-a-half years by fooling the people and now by talking of things like the 1956 constitution, he would like to keep people guessing for another three years. The 1973 constitution has general acceptability and there is no disagreement between political parties about sticking to it as a starting point. Ziaul Haq wants to create disruption and disagreement among political parties by starting a debate on this constitutional issue.

Thursday, 27 Nov 1980, Abbottabad
Tehrik-i-Istiqlal held a convention and a meeting of its national council at Lahore today. The BBC in its evening Urdu news said that the national council had passed a resolution to say that Ziaul Haq intends to hold a referendum to ask the people whether they wanted an 'Islamic' system. The resolution said that there is no need for a referendum but if it must be held, the question to be asked should be whether the people want a military regime or democracy.

Friday, 5 Dec 1980, Abbottabad
Huseyn Shaheed Suhrawardy's 17th death anniversary. His granddaughter, Shahida Jameel, and her husband Choudhry Jameel, are active workers of our party. Choudhry Jameel is the chairman of the Karachi organisation.

Morarji Desai has said that when he was prime minister of India, the Soviet Union had suggested that India should attack Pakistan.

Sunday, 14 Dec 1980, Abbottabad
Asaf Vardag was released this morning. He had completed a little over four months in prison. According to the government, I am the only political prisoner in Pakistan now. Amjad Hussain, the alleged murderer of Hayat Mohammad Khan Sherpao, was arrested in Peshawar a couple of days ago. He had been arrested some years ago but had succeeded in obtaining release on bail and had absconded to Afghanistan. He is being tried by a military court.

Tuesday, 16 Dec 1980, Abbottabad
Heard from Ziae that according to an employee of the MEO (Military Estate Office) the government will soon serve me a notice to take over my house and land at 23 Kutchery Road.

Diary 1981

Wednesday, 7 Jan 1981, Abbottabad
Ziaul Haq told the press today that he will be forming a 300 member national council by about March, including one person from each National Assembly constituency. He also said that he will be forming a new federal cabinet but he has said this half a dozen times before.

Wednesday, 21 Jan 1981, Abbottabad
The 52 American hostages in Iran were released shortly after Ronald Reagan's swearing in, in Washington today. They were flown to Algiers and later taken from there to Wiesbaden in Germany where they will be received on behalf of the US president by Jimmy Carter. They had been in custody for 444 days, about a month less than me.

Sunday, 25 Jan 1981, Abbottabad

The third Islamic seminar is opening in Makkah today. Libya and Iran have refused to attend. Egypt and Afghanistan are debarred from attending.

Lieutenant General (Joe) Yousaf died in Islamabad today. He had a stroke in London some months ago. A very nice and kindly person. He will be missed by his many friends. Chiang Ching was sentenced to death after a trial in Beijing today. So was one other, a former vice chairman of the Chinese communist party. Both sentences have been deferred for two years.

Monday, 26 Jan 1981, Abbottabad

In his speech at the Islamic conference in Taif, Prince Fahd, the Saudi prime minister (and the king's brother), has said that three billion dollars were required for the Islamic Development Fund of which the Saudi Arabian government would give one billion dollar. It is interesting that the Saudi government has spent two billion dollars for the construction of the Islamic conference building at Taif. A conference building larger than the United Nations building in New York which has the largest conference hall in the world. Forty palaces, one for each head of delegation, a super luxury hotel and a sophisticated communication system are some of the things on which this amount has been spent. Fifty million dollars or an equivalent of Rs250 million have therefore been spent on each head of state by Saudi Arabia. A far cry from the Islam under whose name they have assembled. Two billion dollars could have been better spent on the starving and half naked Muslims of some poor countries and the spirit of Islam would have been better interpreted if the heads of state and their entourage had camped in tents and held their deliberations under canvas. Incidentally every country represented, except perhaps Malaysia, is ruled by a dictator or has an autocratic regime. Ziaul Haq's statement yesterday that Karmal's government is not allowed to represent Afghanistan in the Islamic Conference because it does not represent the people of Afghanistan is meaningless. He himself does not represent the people of Pakistan nor does any other delegation except that of Malaysia at the Islamic summit. The only other Islamic country, which could claim to have a representative government, Iran, is not represented at Taif.

Thursday, 29 Jan 1981, Abbottabad
The *Nawa-i-Waqt* of today carried a story about the Islamic Conference at Taif. It said that the meat was flown from the United States. Five thousand meals are prepared daily for the 38 heads of state and their entourage. A Lebanese head cook has 35 cooks from different countries working under him. The 5000 meals comprise about 70 dishes. Fruit is flown in from France and Lebanon. Twelve thousand litres of apple juice, 12,000 litres of grape fruit juice and 36,000 litres of Vichy water has been flown in from France and Lebanon. (Source: Saudi newspaper *Arab News*)

Friday, 30 Jan 1981, Abbottabad
Mushir arrived in the afternoon. He had brought a draft statement with him, with which he said most parties have agreed, including Mrs Bhutto's PPP. I suggested that the draft, as it is, does not make any impact. It merely asks Ziaul Haq to hold elections within three months. Something that everyone has been saying for the last 15 months. I suggested that it would be better to agree that political parties will themselves form a government with the purpose of holding elections. The point to remember was that Ziaul Haq will not abdicate power merely by political parties making a declaration but such a declaration will help to create a climate in which a movement can at some stage be built up. Who will head the interim government was therefore a matter that need not be gone into at present because it is not relevant. G. Allana called on Amina in Karachi. He said that he had come as Nusrat Bhutto's representative.

Tuesday, 3 Feb 1981, Abbottabad
Received a notice from the MEO, Abbottabad, that government intends resuming 4,588 squares yards of our 23 Kutchery Road land, without compensation, (over nine kanals) under Order Number 179 of the governor-general of India of 12 September 1836. I have been given 30 days to file my objection. King William IV was the king of England in 1836.

Friday, 13 Feb 1981, Abbottabad
Mian Mahmud Ali Kasuri came. We discussed the MEO's notice and decided to file a case in the senior civil judge's court at Abbottabad by 28 February.

Saturday, 14 Feb 1981, Abbottabad

Nawabzada Nasrullah Khan was arrested and taken to his home in Khangarh. Student disturbances have taken place in Lahore, Multan, and Rawalpindi. Some 20 students have been arrested in Rawalpindi. The Punjab University and colleges in Lahore, Multan, and Rawalpindi have been closed. Trouble started when students started burning buses in incidents that appear to have been started by an altercation between a bus conductor and a student in Multan. The BBC reported that in Rawalpindi, the students who were arrested were trying to take out a procession against martial law and Ziaul Haq.

Major General Tajammal Hussain has been sentenced to 14 years RI by a court martial for an alleged attempt to overthrow the government. His son and nephew have been sentenced to ten years RI each and dismissed from service. Both were also army officers. Tajammal Hussain was for some time in the Tehrik-i-Istiqlal. He believes in a Khomeini type change in Pakistan. His views tend to be extremist and he wants to bring in a purely religious state in the country. He regards Ziaul Haq's efforts at Islamisation as attempts at window dressing and without substance.

Sunday, 15 Feb 1981, Abbottabad

The BBC's evening news bulletin spoke of student disturbances in Dargai, Rawalpindi, Lahore, Multan, and Quetta. One student had been injured by firing at Dargai. Some arrests have been made including some of political leaders.

Monday, 16 Feb 1981, Abbottabad

The BBC's morning bulletin reported that Mian Mahmud Ali Kasuri and Fazlur Rahman (Mufti Mahmud's son) had been arrested. Aitzaz Ahsan had also been taken in for interrogation.

Friday, 20 Feb 1981, Abbottabad

The BBC in its evening bulletin said that Jamiat-ul-Ulama-i-Pakistan (JUP) has refused to join the nine parties in signing the declaration that they have made. Maulana Abdul Sattar Khan Niazi has said that the declaration of the nine parties makes no mention of enforcing an Islamic system in the country and that his party could not agree to work with the PPP and other socialist, leftist or communist parties.

Bizenjo's party has also declined and Pir Pagara's Muslim League is well known as the GHQ party. Ziaul Haq is therefore likely to have the open support of Jamaat-i-Islami, JUP and Pagara's Muslim League and the silent support of Bizenjo and his party.

The political line-up is now fairly clear. Bizenjo will have the opportunity to work under the guidance of his old benefactor, Mahmud A. Haroon. Within the alliance, at least one party, the NDP, is also likely to play to Ziaul Haq's tune.

Sunday, 22 Feb 1981, Abbottabad
Mushir came and discussed the party's national working committee meeting held on 20 February in Rawalpindi. The national working committee had asked that it should decide the matter of succession after Mian Mahmud Ali Kasuri. After discussion decided that the order of succession should be: (1) Syed Munir Shah, (2) Asaf Vardag, (3) J.A.Rahim, (4) Khudai Noor, (5) Ahmed Mian Soomro, (6) Fakhruz Zaman Khan, (7) Malik Hamid Sarfraz, (8) Nafis Siddiqui, (9) Azhar Zaidi, (10) Malik Haider Usman, (11) Nisar Ahmed Khuhro.

Also discussed the MEO's notice (regarding acquisition of my land by the government) with Mushir, Younas Tanoli and Tariq.

Student disturbances took place in Peshawar yesterday. About 2,000 students took arms from the university armoury and a clash took place with the police when they took out a procession. Four policemen and some students are reported wounded. Rifles and revolvers were used by the students. The Peshawar University and colleges in Peshawar, Nowshera, Mardan, and Charsadda have been closed.

Mrs Bhutto and her daughter have been banned from entering the NWFP. She wanted to go to Peshawar to sympathise with the students injured in the disturbances yesterday. Mairaj Mohammad Khan, who was in Rawalpindi, has been sent back to Karachi and Sardar Abdul Qayyum Khan has been externed to Azad Kashmir.

Monday, 23 Feb 1981, Abbottabad
General Tikka Khan was placed under house arrest and Major General Nasirullah Khan Babar and Aftab Sherpao were arrested in Peshawar as also Samad Khan, a former minister in the NWFP in the PPP government.

In Multan, Khalilur Rahman of Nasrullah Khan's PDP was sentenced to one year's RI and Rs 200,000 fine by a military court for, according to the BBC, giving a reception for Nasrullah Khan.

The government has also announced that the person who was killed when a bomb that he was carrying exploded a short while before the arrival of Pope Paul at the Karachi Stadium the other day, has been identified as an active worker of the PPP, Aslam Pathan of Khairpur.

Wednesday, 25 Feb 1981, Abbottabad

The BBC said that large scale arrests had taken place in Lahore and other parts of the country including that of Kaswar Gardezi, secretary general of PNP, Malik Qasim and two of Mian Mohammad Ali Kasuri's sons. (Probably Omar and Bakhtiar). Mrs Bhutto and Benazir have been barred from entering Punjab for three months. Khurshid Hassan Mir has also been arrested. His Awami Jamhoori Party and Awami Tehrik (a group of six parties) have applied for joining the alliance of nine parties. There has been trouble amongst students in Karachi where an army major's jeep was burnt. Pakistan Railway Workers Union has announced its opposition to the government and support of the alliance of opposition parties.

Thursday, 26 Feb 1981, Abbottabad

The BBC's evening news bulletin said that the action committee of the nine parties' alliance (which it called MRD or Movement for the Restoration of Democracy) had met in Lahore at an unknown place and it agreed on a programme of strikes, demonstrations, social boycott and civil disobedience. The BBC said that more arrests had been made bringing the total to more than 35. Bakhtiar Kasuri telephoned late in the evening to say that police had entered their house 4 Fane Road, and baton charged them. Omar Kasuri and Khurshid had been arrested earlier yesterday. Lawyers are observing Monday, 2 March as a protest day against the government.

Friday, 27 Feb 1981, Abbottabad

Some twenty doctors were arrested in Rawalpindi after having been invited for discussion of their demands. Doctors all over the country have decided to go on strike until these doctors are released and their demands met. The striking doctors are young government doctors and they have said that they will not even attend to emergency cases. Mian Mahmud Ali Kasuri, Omar Kasuri, Syed Munir Shah, Asaf Vardag and Mahnaz Rafi have been arrested in addition to some 40 others from our party.

Saturday, 28 Feb 1981, Abbottabad
Radio Pakistan said that Fazlur Rahman (Mufti Mahmud's son) who had been arrested four days ago has said that he had signed the declaration in his individual capacity and not as the representative of the JUI. He said that not a single member of the JUI was under detention anywhere in the country and that his party had nothing to do with the declaration.

The BBC has started calling the nine parties the MRD or the Movement for the Restoration of Democracy. Not a bad name which will, I think, stick. Bakhtiar Kasuri telephoned to say that Amina should come to Lahore immediately to keep-up the momentum of the movement. I explained that she is busy in connection with Omar's wedding and that it is not possible for her to come at present. In any case she will be externed from Punjab and thus prevented from doing any political work. Mian Mahmud Ali Kasuri is now in Kot Lakhpat jail, Khurshid and Omar Kasuri are in the camp jail in Lahore.

My complaint in respect of the MEO's notice about my land acquisition was handed over to the registrar of the senior civil judge Abbottabad. The judge will consider my request for an interim injunction tomorrow.

Sunday, 1 March 1981, Abbottabad
From information received so far, the following from Tehrik-i-Istiqlal have been arrested during the last few days: Mian Mahmud Ali Kasuri (VP arrested on 15/2/81), Syed Munir Shah (chairman NWFP. Arrested on 26/2/81), Asaf Fasiuddin Vardag (chairman Punjab), Malik Hamid Sarfaraz (v. chairman Punjab), Begum Mehnaz Rafi (chairman women's wing Punjab), Rafi Butt. (v. chairman Punjab), Mumtaz Ahmed Tarar (v. chairman Punjab), Khurshid Mahmud Kasuri (party treasurer), Aitzaz Ahsan, Omar Kasuri, Abdul Qayyum Pahat (chairman Lahore division), Mian Mushtaq (chairman Lahore city), Sheikh Rashid Ahmed (released after two days), Shah Nawaz

(advocate), Syed Zafar Ali Shah (member national working committee), B.K. Tabish (Faisalabad division).

It appears that arrests are still in progress and the list is likely to rise. Begum Mahnaz Rafi is lodged in Kot Lakhpat jail, as are most of the others.

Monday, 2 March 1981, Abbottabad
Amina arrived late in the evening after some panic because a PIA Boeing on its flight from Karachi to Peshawar had been hijacked and made to land at Kabul and for a short while it was not clear which flight had been hijacked.

Wednesday, 4 March 1981, Abbottabad
The hijacked plane is still at Kabul though the hijackers have released eighteen women and nine children as they had no connection with the PPP. A PIA plane that went to Kabul to fetch the released 27 was not allowed to land at Kabul.

Thursday, 5 March 1981, Abbottabad
Received a letter from the home secretary NWFP that the commissioner Hazara had been authorised to permit lawyers to see me as and when required, in connection with my case against the government. (MEO's notice for land acquisition).

Saturday, 7 March 1981, Abbottabad
Tariq, son of the late Major General Qazi Rahim and a second secretary in the Pakistan embassy in Tehran, was shot and killed by hijackers in Kabul yesterday. It appears from the BBC and Radio Pakistan's version of the hijacking affair that the hijackers are connected with the PPP. They claim to be responsible for the bomb explosion in the meeting of the Pope in Karachi and, according to the Pakistan government, in the explosion in the High Court premises in Lahore and a few other such incidents.

Murtaza Bhutto (Zulfikar Ali Bhutto's son) is reported to have met the hijackers soon after their arrival at Kabul airport and he is said to be the secretary general of their organisation, Al Zulfikar. The Pakistan government has made a strong protest to the Kabul government, which it says is encouraging the hijackers and actively impeding a settlement of the affair.

Babrak Karmal has asked the hijackers not to kill any more hostages. A World Bank official who is one of the hostages has asked Kurt Waldheim, the US secretary general, to intervene. The hijackers were insisting on the release of all political prisoners and have set today as the last date for the acceptance of their demand.

Mushir arrived late at night. The intelligence officer deputed to be present during Mushir's conversation with me was cooperative. He went out with Ziae who had returned from Peshawar at about the same time. Spoke to Omar at Tarbela earlier. He had been to see the place where I was lodged for a couple of days after my arrest in October 1979. He liked the seclusion of the place.

Monday, 9 March 1981, Abbottabad

The hijackers with 100 hostages took the PIA Boeing from Kabul to Damascus last night. Mrs Bhutto, Benazir and another 30 persons were arrested early yesterday. The two ladies are under house arrest in Karachi. Fazal Bhatty, our district chairman Rawalpindi, was also arrested on the night of 7/8 March.

Ziaul Haq announced his long awaited and much talked about cabinet. He has shed Lieutenant General Ghulam Hussain and Major General Shahid Hamid and taken on half a dozen equally uninspiring people. Major General Jamaldar, Lieutenant General Saeed Qadir, Major General Rao Farman Ali of East Pakistan fame and three more soldiers. In addition he has included Ghulam Dastgir Khan (Gujranwala) of Pagara Muslim League, Afifa Mamdot (DGK) Pagara Muslim League, Raja Zafarul Haq (Rawalpindi) Pagara Muslim League, Raja George Sikander Zaman (Haripur) PPP, Zafarullah Jamali (Nasirabad) probably PPP, Dr Nasirudin Jogezi (Loralai, Zhob) and Fakhr Imam (Multan), at one time Tehrik-i-Istiqlal. A total of 20 ministers and a few ministers of state. Ilahi Bux Soomro and Arbab Niaz Ahmed (mayor of Peshawar city) are also two of the ministers. Those belonging to political parties will obviously owe allegiance to Ziaul Haq and not to the party to which they belong. Pagara Muslim League is in any case with the government and the few from the PPP are not men of any conviction or character. Nine of the previous ministers are going to continue to serve.

Tuesday, 10 March 1981, Abbottabad

Ziaul Haq announced the appointment of some more ministers in his cabinet: Arbab Jehangir (Peshawar), Salim Saifullah (Bannu), Mohammad Abdul Baqi (Kohistan), Shujaat Ali Khan, and Abdul Hashim Khan. The first four are well known people and the last relatively unknown. Not a bad selection but will not make any difference to the unpopularity of the regime. Zafar Gondal was arrested in Lahore on 8 March. The hijackers, now in Damascus with 102 hostages, have set 10:00 hrs GMT tomorrow as the deadline for the acceptance of their demands. They have given a list of 55 prisoners (political according to them) whom they want released and flown out of Pakistan before 10:00 GMT tomorrow. An airhostess who was unwell has been released in Damascus and one more hostage was released before their leaving Kabul.

Wednesday, 11 March 1981, Abbottabad

Ahmed Mian Soomro came to speak on behalf of Mahmud Haroon, the interior minister who had asked him (Ahmed Mian) to speak to me on Ziaul Haq's direction. He said that the government wanted to know whether I was prepared to discuss the national situation in view of the critical conditions that have been created and the developments that have taken place. He said that the government was not specific about what condition and development it referred to, but thought that the rising incidences of violence, the hijacking, strikes, etc. have provided the backdrop to their approach. I told him that Ziaul Haq and his regime has no credibility left and that they were bent on hanging on to power at all cost. I thought that things had not deteriorated sufficiently as yet for them to be willing to talk sense and they would climb down only when water has passed over their heads. I was not willing, I said, to meet Ziaul Haq at Rawalpindi but had no objection to meeting him or one of his responsible representatives here at Abbottabad. Ahmed Mian Soomro asked whether I would be prepared to meet Mahmud Haroon at Abbottabad. I told him that Mahmood Haroon has no relevance in this situation and I did not think that he has any influence on Ziaul Haq but I would not object to meeting him if only to listen to what he has to say.

Monday, 16 March 1981, Abbottabad
Rafi Butt and Fazal Bhatty were sent to Gujranwala jail from Rawalpindi.

Tuesday, 17 March 1981, Abbottabad
Mahmud Haroon (minister of interior) called. He was at pains to explain that he was not an emissary of Ziaul Haq, though he had come with his blessings. He wanted my views on the current national situation. I told him that the government held all the cards and I was in no position to express views on the mess Ziaul Haq had got the country into. He then gave me his views, which were critical of the regime. In fact his views on the regime, as expressed to me, were similar to my own. He said he felt that the country is heading for disaster, Ziaul Haq is unreliable and he had no credibility, did not want to part with power and did not intend sharing it with anyone. He spent a couple of hours with me and it appeared that he is on a probing mission. He had no concrete proposals and I made no suggestions either. My view is that Ziaul Haq is looking around but things have to get much worse before he will be willing to negotiate or talk sense. Whether that will be too late, is a question mark.

Thursday, 19 March 1981, Abbottabad
Amina arrived from Lahore after stopping at Gujranwala, Gujrat and Jhelum *en route*. She called on the wives of those of our workers who had been arrested. Ziae also called at the jails in Lahore, Gujranwala, Sahiwal, Jhang and Faisalabad and left some fruit for our workers there. He met Hamid Sarfaraz in Sahiwal jail.

Friday, 20 March, Abbottabad
Ziaul Haq's government started an all out publicity offensive against opposition parties (particularly the PPP) and today's evening TV news spent 15 minutes on this subject. Ghulam Dastgir Khan was shown addressing a public gathering at Gujranwala and *khateebs* [prayer leaders] were shown condemning the opposition to government during the Friday congregations at different places. The hijacking incident is the central point in this propaganda.

Saturday, 21 March 1981, Abbottabad

Mahnaz Rafi's daughter telephoned to say that her mother (in jail) had been told that if she says that the Tehrik-i-Istiqlal has nothing to do with the MRD, she could be released. Amina spoke to her and told her that she should not say any such thing.

Radio Pakistan announced in its evening news bulletin today that Sardar Abdul Qayyum Khan of Azad Kashmir had addressed a press conference at Islamabad and had said that as chairman of MRD for this month, he was directing all MRD parties to suspend their activities. He said that he was convinced that the PPP was involved in the hijacking affair. This party should either be expelled from the MRD or other parties should leave this organisation. He said that he was seeking the government's permission to meet the leaders of MRD parties in detention for consultations. The timing of Sardar Qayyum's announcement is designed to sabotage the 23 March programme of public meetings and it is obvious that he has done this at the government's behest. He is known for this kind of role during the days of the previous regime. Pakistan TV gave seven minutes to this news of the MRD out of the ten minutes of the 17:45 bulletin. The BBC which gave this news, also said that Nafis Siddiqui, acting president of Tehrik-i-Istiqlal, has disassociated the Tehrik-i-Istiqlal from Sardar Abdul Qayyum's statement and has said that his party was in the MRD and that Sardar Abdul Qayyum had no right to issue this statement.

Malik Haider Osman came. Our telephone has been out of order since this morning and the ASI at the gate would not allow the telephone linesman to check it for making it serviceable.

Sunday, 22 March 1981, Abbottabad

Ghulam Mustafa Jatoi, who was to address a meeting at Karachi tomorrow, has been externed from Karachi and Sherbaz Mazari from Sindh.

Over 40 persons have been arrested in Karachi including Kaniz Fatima, a labour leader. Mukhtiar Bacha has been arrested in Mardan.

Monday, 23 March 1981, Abbottabad

Forty-first anniversary of Pakistan Day. Mahfooz Yar Khan was arrested at Quaid-i-Azam's mausoleum in Karachi. Incidents of strikes, stoning of cars and burning of buses and burning of a petrol pump took place in Sindh.

Tuesday, 24 March 1981, Abbottabad

Ziaul Haq announced major changes in the 1973 constitution which included confiscation of assets and banning of those political parties not registered in 1979. New oaths for judges (which in effect require them to owe allegiance to the military regime rather than to Pakistan or its constitution) and the appointment of a vice president. PPP will therefore stand banned as also the National Democratic Party and PNP of Bizenjo. Parties not so far registered, can apply to be registered provided they fulfil certain conditions regarding 'belief in the ideology of Pakistan', etc.

Wednesday, 25 March 1981, Abbottabad

The US administration is considering giving $500 million military and economic aid to Pakistan. India has protested against this move. Chief Justice of the Supreme Court, Anwar ul Haq, three other judges of the Supreme Court and a number of High Court judges have refused to take the new constitutional oath. The new amendment takes away all powers from the Supreme Court and makes a mockery of the judiciary. Judges have in effect been reduced to personal employees of Ziaul Haq.

Thursday, 26 March 1981, Abbottabad

The three judges of the Supreme Court (besides Anwar ul Haq) who refused to take the oath are Dorab Patel, Maulvi Mushtaq and Fakhruddin G. Ebrahim. Two out of the three judges of the Balochistan High Court declined to take the oath as also a number of Lahore High Court judges. All judges of the Peshawar High Court were sworn in, amongst them Karimullah Khan Durrani, now a judge of the Federal Shariat Bench. Justice Abdul Halim was sworn in as the acting chief justice of the Supreme Court. In the eyes of Justice Anwar ul Haq and the other judges, who have not taken the oath, Ziaul Haq's government is therefore not lawful. Anwar ul Haq has agreed, rather belatedly with the position I had taken on 16 October 1979.

Nafis Siddiqui came clandestinely and he discussed the party line in the present situation. He is the acting president of the party for this month and will be handing over to Haider Osman on 31 March. There are warrants for his arrest as also for that of his wife Shahida. Both of them are active workers. Nafis has done very well in projecting the MRD and the party's activities before the media (BBC and foreign press). The MRD parties met at Lahore and issued a statement saying that Ziaul Haq had in effect abrogated the 1973 constitution and was therefore a 'traitor'. The MRD in Balochistan also said in a statement that Ziaul Haq was driving the country towards a civil war.

The MRD meetings in Lahore and Quetta congratulated the judges who had refused to take the oath. The former chief justice Anwar ul Haq speaking with the press criticised the constitutional measures adopted by Ziaul Haq. Heard in the evening that Mahnaz Rafi had been released and Anjum (general secretary ISF) and Mustafa Kamal (president ISF) had been arrested.

Saturday, 28 March 1981, Abbottabad
Nawaz Sharif came to Tariq's and met Amina. He said that he had been asked (or rather his father had been asked) that he should join the Punjab government and had agreed. Amina told him that he would be making a mistake and should decline the offer. He said he did not know how to say 'no' especially as Jilani the governor had been 'so nice to him'. Poor fellow. The BBC said Siddiqui had addressed a press conference in which he had expressed surprise at the western countries supporting the right of Afghan people to select their own government and saying nothing about the right of the people of Pakistan to have a government of their choice. He likened the occupation of Afghanistan by the Russian army to the role of the Pakistan army in Pakistan. Nafis has been making some very timely and appropriate comments lately. This one is particularly timely as Lord Carrington, the British foreign secretary, is in Pakistan praising the role of Ziaul Haq's government.

Sunday, 29 March 1981, Abbottabad
Amina had another session with Nawaz Sharif. He is confused and says he does not know what to do. Another way of saying he will join the government.

Tuesday, 31 March 1981, Abbottabad
Yahya Bakhtiar was sentenced to five years RI by a special tribunal for rigging the result of the election in his National Assembly constituency in the 1977 March election. He is probably the only one sentenced for rigging the election and it is not a coincidence that he was Bhutto's defence counsel in his trial. It is significant that the proceeding was initiated against him after Bhutto's hanging.

Wednesday, 1 April 1981, Abbottabad
Ahmed Mian Soomro telephoned. The so-called rightist parties have been discussing the possibilities of an alliance. The JUP, ML (Pagara) and AJK Muslim Conference are likely to agree on some kind of an agenda. The Jamaat-i-Islami's collaboration with them is not certain. The JUI of the late Mufti Mahmud is split into his son Fazlur Rahman's and Darkhwasti groups.

Thursday, 2 April 1981, Abbottabad
Pagara Muslim League and Jamiatul Ulama-i-Pakistan formed an alliance, which they said, was neither against the government nor the MRD or the Jamaat-i-Islami. They said that their purpose was to persuade Ziaul Haq to restore democracy according to the 1973 constitution and to fight against those elements that were against the ideology of Pakistan and believed in terrorism. Sardar Abdul Qayyum Khan's AJK Muslim Conference has agreed in principle to join them but Sardar Qayyum will try to contact JUI (Darkhwasti Group), Jamaat-i-Islami and Khaksars to join this alliance before he formally announces his own party's decision. Of these three, Jamaat-i-Islami's joining is doubtful but the other two will be very willing to join. The press conference in which this alliance was announced was covered by government controlled TV and radio and this event was also given full coverage by the government controlled press. Zahur ul Hassan Bhopali has been expelled from the JUP. Maulana Noorani is on a visit to South Africa. Ziaul Haq addressed a press conference this evening on his return from Iran and Iraq (as a member of the Islamic peace committee) in which he said that he would soon consider allowing limited political activity. However he has no credibility left and no one believes anything he says. He had said this in reply to a question by Saud Sahir (correspondent of *Badban* newspaper) who

had asked Ziaul Haq when this 'farce' will end. Saud Sahir had said that political parties, whilst being called defunct, are holding press conferences, meetings and he (Ziaul Haq) had even welcomed the grouping of some of them into an alliance (Pagara Muslim League and JUP). He said that the government may as well regularise the situation and end this joke.

Saturday, 4 April 1981, Abbottabad
Second death anniversary of Zulfikar Ali Bhutto. In spite of restrictions imposed by government, a large number of people—a few thousand—gathered at his graveside at Garhi Khuda Bux. Anti-Ziaul Haq slogans were raised. An effigy of Ziaul Haq was burnt and a couple of CID men beaten up. A government building was stoned in Karachi. Sardar Abdul Qayyum in a speech yesterday said that the country is more important than democracy. He is now fully with Ziaul Haq.

Sunday, 5 April 1981, Abbottabad
Amina spoke to Shahida Nafis and learnt that Khudai Noor and Maula Bux Zehri had also been arrested on 3 April. This will be their second spell of detention since Ziaul Haq's 'real martial law'.

Wednesday, 8 April 1981, Abbottabad
The BBC's morning news bulletin said that a PPP lawyer of Peshawar, Kanwar Abbas, had been admitted to hospital, allegedly after having been tortured by the police. The police says that he fell down in the bathroom and the bar association has asked for Kanwar Abbas to be produced within 24 hours, so that they can ascertain the facts.

The BBC also quoted Malik Haider Usman, the acting president of Tehrik-i-Istiqlal, as saying that Ziaul Haq had said that he may carry on for six months or six years. The 1973 constitution (which he says still exists) lays down the tenure of a government as six years. Ziaul Haq has already completed nearly four years. Malik Haider Usman also said that Ziaul Haq's second extension of tenure as chief of staff of the army had also expired. The BBC also quoted Rana Zafarullah, the acting chairman of MRD for the month, as saying that Ziaul Haq was distorting Islam to suit his own ends. Shahida Nafis telephoned. She is shouldering her husband's responsibility of central information secretary. The hearing of my land case was postponed to 12 April.

Thursday, 9 April 1981, Abbottabad

Ziaul Haq is out on a public contact or rather a councillors' contact tour. Speaking in Lahore today he has given an outline of thinking for the future. He intends appointing a committee comprising federal and provincial ministers to prepare a draft of an Islamic constitution. This draft will then be approved by the ulema (religious scholars). The committee will travel extensively and consult every shade of public opinion before it finalises its draft. This draft will then be placed before the nominated National Assembly (or Majlis-i-Shoora). It will then be discussed. If approved it will be put before the public, presumably in a referendum. If approved by the public, it will become the constitution under which the first 'Islamic' election will be held. After the election, power will be transferred to the elected government. It is obvious that each step could take up to a year or more and there is therefore no danger of Ziaul Haq's position being challenged by a tailor-made election. A truly Machiavellian plan designed to ensure that he stays in power indefinitely. Major General Rao Farman Ali Khan of East Pakistan fame is likely to be one of the committee, to be charged with producing the draft constitution.

Saturday, 11 April 1981, Abbottabad

Ziaul Haq is in Abbottabad today in connection with some seminar at the medical college and his usual chat with the 'dignitaries', councillors and the like. Yahya Bakhtiar, former attorney general, now serving a sentence in Quetta jail, was beaten up by the jail staff. Lawyers have protested and have asked for the dismissal of the jail superintendent. MRD had a meeting in Peshawar. Naseem Wali Khan presided.

Wednesday, 15 April 1981, Abbottabad

Some ten PPP workers were sentenced by a military court to imprisonment terms and lashes. A couple of days ago Mumtaz Bhutto and eleven other persons were told to report to the police within 14 days. In the event of their failing to do so they are likely to be given 14 years imprisonment and confiscation of property.

Friday, 17 April 1981, Abbottabad

Omar's *valima* lunch at the Abbottabad club. Omar and the top party leaders received the guests at the Abbottabad club. I am told that the function went off very well. I could not attend due to my continued detention.

Saturday, 18 April 1981, Abbottabad

Received a large number of telegrams congratulating me on Omar's wedding, amongst them one from Ziaul Haq.

Monday, 20 April 1981, Abbottabad

The BBC said that the High Court (probably of Sindh) had issued an injunction restricting Mrs Bhutto and her family from selling or gifting their property. This is probably a prelude to the confiscation of their property in a legal suit.

Thursday, 23 April 1981, Abbottabad

The United States has agreed to extend $2.5 billion in aid to Pakistan over the next five years. Of this $400 million will be military aid and $100 million economic aid. (Incidentally Israel is receiving $2.4 billion US aid annually half of which is military aid).

Saturday, 25 April 1981, Abbottabad

The martial law cabinet of Punjab was sworn in. Amongst them was Nawaz Sharif, another Tehrik-i-Istiqlal casualty. Khudai Noor telephoned to say that he was released yesterday.

Sunday, 3 May 1981, Abbottabad

It was reported that last night's earthquake was quite widespread and shook the northern parts of Pakistan. No loss of life has been reported as yet. Amina went upstairs to get Adey (my mother) from her room and struggled with her to get her moving. Adey was complaining of pain in her legs and would not move. Eventually with great difficulty Amina managed to get her out of the house. The earthquake was of course over by then. If the the house had collapsed, Amina as well as Adey would probably not have been able to get out.

Friday, 8 May 1981, Abbottabad

There is a political lull in the country. Political activity, what little there was of it, is now underground. Most of the second level leadership of the Tehrik-i-Istiqlal is in prison as also most of the top leadership of the PPP. I do not think that anyone from the NDP is in jail. Nor anyone from any of the three Muslim Leagues. Malik Qasim, Nasrullah Khan and a few of their people are in jail. Fatehyab Ali Khan of Mazdoor Kissan and Mairaj Mohammad Khan are also in jail. There are also a number of workers from Khurshid Hassan Mir's and Taj Mohammad Langah's parties (that are not in the MRD).

Thursday, 14 May 1981, Abbottabad

With the onset of summer and most of the political opposition behind bars, the government appears to be comfortably in the saddle. The new Sindh cabinet was sworn in today with some old PPP and JUP members, notable amongst them were Rasul Bux Talpur of the PPP and Yousaf Ahad of JUP. Pir of Pagara is trying to bring the Jamaat-i-Islami and the JUI into his recently formed alliance. Today's *Nawa-i-Waqt* says that Khawaja Khairuddin (the president of the Qasim Muslim League) has been released and is likely to join the Pagara-JUI alliance leaving Malik Qasim in the opposition.

Saturday, 23 May 1981, Abbottabad

Zafar Ali Shah's detention period has been extended by another three months. This has already been done in the case of Mian Mahmud Ali Kasuri.

Tuesday, 26 May 1981, Abbottabad

The daily *Muslim* reported that Maulana Noorani had resigned from the presidency of JUP and intends concentrating on *tabligh*. The *Muslim* quoted Maulana Abdul Sattar Niazi as having said this. There have been differences of opinion within the JUP for some time. Abdul Sattar Niazi is a particularly difficult person to work with—unbending and aggressive, he does not fit in easily in any organisation. He is currently the general secretary of the JUP. Moreover Zahur ul Hassan Bhopali who was reported to have been expelled from the party by Maulana Noorani appears to have the support of Prof. Shah Faridul Haq and Allama Al Azhari.

Thursday, 28 May 1981, Abbottabad
Yahya Bakhtiar, who had been sentenced to five years RI by a military court for rigging his election in his constituency in 1977 and was serving his sentence in the Quetta jail, was released yesterday.

Friday, 29 May 1981, Abbottabad
I have completed one year in detention since 29 May 1980. With the six months that I had served in detention earlier, this brings the total period in detention since 16 October 1979 to one-and-a-half year.

Saturday, 30 May 1981, Abbottabad
President Zia-ur-Rahman of Bangladesh was killed early today in an attempted coup allegedly organised by Major General Manzoor. The vice president, Justice Abdul Sattar, has declared a state of emergency and the service chiefs have reiterated their loyalty to the government in Dhaka. Major General Manzoor is controlling the Chittagong area including the radio station and the airfield. In its evening broadcast, Pakistan TV showed some nervousness and originality in announcing the news. It referred to President Zia-ur-Rahman as 'Rahman' omitting Zia except in the first reference. It also referred to Major General Manzoor as a '*sharpasand*' (miscreant) who, it reported, was leading the gang, which killed President Rahman. Major General Manzoor has said that the ten-year old treaty with India (signed in 1972) has been abrogated and he has claimed the disputed islands in the Bay of Bengal as Bangladesh territory.

Sunday, 31 May 1981, Abbottabad
The situation in Bangladesh is still confused but it appears that Major General Manzoor's position is not strong enough to succeed in his purpose.

Tuesday, 2 June 1981, Abbottabad
The SSP Abbottabad, Mazhar Sher Khan, came to deliver another detention order—same as the one I received a year ago signed by Major General Fazle Haq.

Wednesday, 3 June 1981, Abbottabad
Major General Manzoor who was reported arrested in Bangladesh is now reported to have been shot. It appears that this was done while

he was in military custody. Two of his compatriots are also reported to have been shot with him. A number of others have been arrested and will be tried by court martial.

Wednesday, 10 June 1981, Abbottabad

The BBC said that Israeli aircraft had flown low over Saudi Arabian territory on their way to Baghdad refuelling both on their way out and back. I wonder what the US supplied early warning system was doing at the time. The US insists that it knew nothing about the raid until after it had been carried out. A state department official while condemning Israeli action has said that the US remained committed to the security of Israel. Prime Minister Begin of Israel has said in a press conference that Israel will do this again if necessary. This action of Israel has raised the threshold of preventive air action by countries involved in regional or global disputes and has increased the possibilities of nuclear conflict in sensitive regions. Pakistan, which is reported to be close to producing a nuclear bomb, could be the target of similar action by Israel or India. With aerial refuelling, Pakistan is no longer out of Israeli range. However Ziaul Haq's pro-western policy does not make an Israeli attack likely, at least for the time being.

Thursday, 11 June 1981, Abbottabad

Hamid Baloch, who had been sentenced to death by a military court, was hanged yesterday. The high court had stayed the execution of the sentence but after the new martial law order subordinating the High Court to martial law; the military court sentence was carried out. Hamid Baloch was accused of firing at an Omani colonel who had come to Makran on a recruiting visit. The colonel had not been hit, but it is alleged that another person was killed. However it was found later that this person was in fact alive. He was then charged for killing yet another person and sentenced to death.

Friday, 12 June 1981, Abbottabad

Mian Mahmud Ali Kasuri has been shifted from Kot Lakhpat to Sahiwal jail. Aitzaz Ahsan has been moved to Lahore jail from Multan and Qayyum Pahat from Lahore to Multan.

Sunday, 14 June 1981, Abbottabad

Malik Haider Usman came in the evening. Discussed party matters, MRD and the general political situation. Learnt that Asaf Vardag has been sent to Bahawalpur jail from Faisalabad.

Monday, 15 June 1981, Abbottabad

The US deputy secretary of state is on a visit to Islamabad to discuss the aid programme to Pakistan. The VOA said that it is a five-year programme of $2.5 billion, one-fifth of which is military aid and is likely to include at least fifteen F-16s, and some advanced type helicopters. Jimmy Carter's offer which Ziaul Haq had termed 'peanuts' was a little less than half this amount.

Tuesday, 16 June 1981, Abbottabad

The agreement reached between the US and Pakistan is now reported to amount to $3 billion in aid. Half of it is for economic and half for military assistance over a five-year period.

Wednesday, 17 June 1981, Abbottabad

Received a letter from Syed Moin Shah in Faisalabad jail. He is being kept in a condemned prisoners cell without light or fan and is being asked to sign a bond, which he has refused to do. He suffered a mild heart attack on 14 May, was taken to the district hospital the following day and put back in prison. The Iranian parliament began the impeachment of President Bani Sadr.

Friday, 19 June 1981, Abbottabad

Omar Kasuri and Khurshid Kasuri have been moved to Kot Lakhpat from Camp jail Lahore.

Monday, 22 June 1981, Abbottabad

Amina and Shahida Nafis went to Oghi today and tried to convince Fakhruz Zaman Khan that he would be making a mistake if he joined the nominated federal council. I do not think that they could convince him because he has probably gone adrift and is beyond redemption.

Tuesday, 23 June 1981, Abbottabad

Shahida Nafis left for Rawalpindi and onto Karachi. She was to address a meeting at Haripur on the way. Mushir telephoned from

Rawalpindi. K.H. Khurshid of Azad Kashmir is disqualified for seven years for alleged misappropriation of Rs1500 during his presidency of Azad Kashmir. An amazing decision when others, who are known to have embezzled millions, are going about without any inconvenience. Today's newspapers also said that the Tehrik-i-Istiqlal's registration as a party in Azad Kashmir has been withdrawn. Mushir wanted to know whether he should talk with martial law authorities about it. I told him not to. It did not matter, as any meaningful election under the martial law regime is not possible. Decided that Nisar Khuhro would be the acting president of the party from 1 July in place of Haider Usman who will perform the duties of additional secretary general.

Wednesday, 24 June 1981, Abbottabad
Mian Mahmud Ali Kasuri telephoned from Chaudhri Abdul Rahim's at Sahiwal to say that he was released today. He had been arrested on 6 February 1981. Ziaul Haq spoke on TV and radio. One hour of rubbish and a complete waste of time.

Thursday, 25 June 1981, Abbottabad
The BBC evening news said that in addition to Mian Mahmud Ali Kasuri, Malik Qasim had also been released. Both have been released unconditionally on medical grounds.

Friday, 26 June 1981, Abbottabad
Ghulam Ishaq Khan addressed a press conference on TV on the budget. Spoke in English, which is no better than his Urdu. Could not therefore make much sense. A typical sentence. 'We will *Insha Allah* "tape" the resources to fill the "gape" in the "plain".' What he probably meant to say was tap, gap, and plan.

Saturday, 27 June 1981, Abbottabad
Ziae left to visit our detenues at Kot Lakhpat, Faisalabad, Jhang, Multan, Bahwalpur, and Sahiwal jails. He will also call on their families to see whether they need any assistance and will also check on the arrangements for the families of Abdul Qayyum Pahat and Asaf Vardag to visit them at Multan and Bahawalpur respectively. Ziae should be back by 5 July.

Nawaz Sharif (formerly Tehrik-i-Istiqlal) appeared on TV to announce the Punjab budget.

Wednesday, 1 July 1981, Abbottabad
Mushir came in the morning. I briefed him about my views on Mian Mahmud Ali Kasuri's message which I have received yesterday that I did not favour our detenu signing bonds and did not like Mian Sahib meeting Ziaul Haq's ministers to seek their release. Mushir is going to Lahore tomorrow and will be seeing Mian Sahib.

Thursday, 2 July 1981, Abbottabad
Mushir telephoned from Rawalpindi to say that Khurshid and Omar Kasuri were released today.

Thursday, 16 July 1981, Abbottabad
Mian Mahmud Ali Kasuri telephoned to say that the entire MRD council was arrested last night at Lahore. Learnt later that there were 14 in all. Amongst them, Nisar Khuhro (our acting president), Malik Haider Usman (our additional secretary general), Khawaja Khairuddin, Manzar Masood (Azad Kashmir PPP), Chaudhri Arshad (PDP), Zuberi (NDP). Mian Sahib did not attend the meeting, as he was unwell. Mushir was away in Bombay. Sherbaz Mazari and Ghulam Mustafa Jatoi did not attend the meeting.

Saturday, 18 July 1981, Abbottabad
Mian Mahmud Ali Kasuri came. It was nice to see Mian Sahib after his release three weeks ago. He suggested that we might permit our party members in prison—at present 15—to sign bonds to secure their release. I told him that I had been in contact with almost all of them and knew that the majority of them would not want to sign a bond. I mentioned the names of Syed Munir Shah, Asaf Vardag, Malik Hamid Sarfaraz, Inayat Gill, Aitzaz Ahsan, Raja Mahboob, B.K. Tabish, and Nafis Siddiqui. I also said that it involved an important point of principle. A directive of this kind by the party, would damage the party immeasurably and nullify the good name it had earned over the years by its sacrifices and sufferings. Mian Sahib eventually agreed but asked whether I would object if the MRD issued such an appeal. I told Mian Sahib that I would be against the idea of the MRD issuing

such an appeal. In any case, the MRD has in it Ghulam Mustafa Jatoi, whom the government has not arrested and who is known for his pro-government leanings. Also discussed the question of the party leadership and agreed that Azhar Zaidi shall be the party's acting president and Younas Khan the acting additional secretary general. Azhar Zaidi, in the event of his arrest, should be followed by Mian Manzoor Watto and Inamullah Khan. In the next meeting of MRD on 10 August the party should be represented by Azhar Zaidi only.

Sunday, 19 July 1981, Abbottabad
The BBC in its news bulletin last night said that Pakistan has been told that the F-16 aircrafts will not be available to it for some years as these are required to replace the obsolete aircraft in the US Air Force.

Wednesday, 22 July 1981, Abbottabad
Ashraf Hashmi of daily *Muslim* telephoned to say that Begum Bhutto and Benazir have been released today. The two ladies have gone through a great deal of suffering and I am glad that they have been freed. Nusrat Bhutto was in Karachi jail and Benazir in Sukkur.

Saturday, 25 July 1981, Abbottabad
Lieutenant General Fazle Haq came and stayed for about an hour. He appeared on a probing mission to assess how I feel about things after one year in detention. He last visited me in September last year at Dadar. I reminded him that very few people knew where the governor-general, Ghulam Mohammad lay buried although he was considered very powerful when he was the head of government. The present rulers should not make the mistake of considering themselves immortal. I also told him that I took strong objection to his saying in his detention order that there was danger to the security of Pakistan if I was freed. No one has the monopoly of patriotism and I told him that I did not need a certificate from him or Ziaul Haq about patriotism. He said that what he really meant was that I was a danger to the regime. The trouble is that the interest of the government and of the country are considered the same in Pakistan. Before leaving he hinted that I could be released but I told him that I did not want any favours from him or any one else.

Sunday, 26 July 1981, Abbottabad
Younas Khan telephoned to say that Aitzaz Ahsan and Zafar Gondal had been released and that the 14 who were arrested at the MRD meeting at Lahore on 15 July are also being released.

Monday, 27 July 1981, Abbottabad
Syed Moin Shah was released yesterday. Malik Haider Usman, Nisar Ahmed Khuhro and others arrested on 15 July have also been released. Mushir came today. He said that Benazir Bhutto who apparently had not been released earlier, is being released today and that he understood that others who are under detention are also likely to be released. He said that Habibullah Piracha, who was a friend of the Sindh governor, had told him a few days ago that Fazle Haq will be visiting me shortly which he did an 25 July. Habibullah Piracha also told him that Ziaul Haq would be seeing me in Abbottabad after Eid.

Tuesday, 28 July 1981, Abbottabad
Three more of the fourteen arrested in Lahore on 15 July were released today. The BBC said that others were likely to be released before Eid. Benazir has been brought to Karachi jail from Sukkur and is still in detention.

Thursday, 30 July 1981, Abbottabad
Received a letter from Ziae to say that all except Nafis Siddiqui, Asaf Vardag, Babar Shaheen, Inayat Ali Gill, Malik Hamid Sarfaraz, B.K. Tabish and Naheed Afzal from the Tehrik-i-Istiqlal had been released.

Sunday, 2 Aug 1981, Abbottabad
Eid ul Fitr. My fourth Eid in captivity.

Monday, 3 Aug 1981, Abbottabad
Mian Mahmud Ali Kasuri telephoned to say that Asaf Vardag and B.K. Tabish had been released. Voice of America yesterday said that a group of Pakistanis armed with automatic weapons attacked the Al Zulfikar training camp in Kabul (probably on 26 July) and killed three guards and injured ten persons. It also said that these persons were

not Mujahideen. It appears that a party was sent to Afghanistan by the Pakistan government for this purpose.

Wednesday, 5 Aug 1981, Abbottabad
Ziaul Haq announced that at 09:00 on 14 August every citizen of Pakistan, except those in uniform, will be dressed in the national costume and will stop wherever he is, stand up and sing the national anthem. All traffic will stop. Even in aeroplanes, flying at 09:00 passengers will sing the national anthem. Did not say whether they will keep their seat belts on. Every home will fly the national flag. Railway trains will be decorated and will blow their whistles at 09:00. People will come out in the streets and will be required to look happy at the dawn of another year of freedom under Ziaul Haq. This is indicative of what is in store for Pakistan—a totalitarian state on the fascist model.

Saturday, 8 Aug 1981, Abbottabad
TV and radio propaganda for celebrating 14 August is in full swing and most of the TV time is taken up with this. I suppose that after 14 August another two weeks will be spent on letting the people know how this day was celebrated. By then, 6 September will be due, and we will be subjected to more propaganda about the great achievements of the Pakistan Army in the 1965 India-Pakistan war.

Monday, 10 Aug 1981, Abbottabad
Mian Mahmud Ali Kasuri telephoned to say that Nawabzada Nasrullah Khan had been released and he had met him in Lahore.

Thursday, 13 Aug 1981, Abbottabad
Asaf Vardag and Syed Moin Shah came and stayed for two hours. We discussed the situation in the country. Both were in good spirits and appeared none the worse for their time in jail. I expressed my views as follow:

1. The interest of the superpowers is to deny this area (Pakistan) to each other.
2. The United States is likely to want to develop Pakistan as an Egypt type base in this part of the world, where it will not have

defence personnel but where it would like to have base facilities to operate from, in the event of an emergency.

3. The Soviet army comprising 175 divisions is deployed as follows: (a) 100 divisions along the Chinese border. (b) 50 divisions along NATO's border. (c) 15 divisions opposite Azerbaijan for a move towards the Gulf. (d) 5 divisions in Afghanistan. (e) 5 divisions in reserve.

4. Although the USSR has the capacity to raise more divisions, its present deployment suggests that it has no plans to increase its commitment in Afghanistan or on the Pakistan-Afghan border in the near future.

5. The United States interests are well served by Ziaul Haq but they would like him to obtain a mandate to rule. It is possible that they have therefore delayed the delivery of fifteen F-16s to Pakistan, which is not likely for two or three years.

6. On the other hand, Egypt is being supplied forty F-16s by December this year.

7. The US Congress is likely to discuss aid to Pakistan before October 1982, when India's objections and Ziaul Haq's position in the country will be considered and debated.

8. It is likely then that Ziaul Haq will take a political initiative. This could be in the form of a referendum or an election or both, some time in 1982-83.

9. Whether we take part in this will depend on the party.

10. I am likely to be released if and when such an initiative is taken and unlikely to be released before that.

11. Any change in the army leadership in Pakistan is not likely to be in favour of a change for democracy. A coup within the army is therefore not a matter of comfort for us.

12. The slogan of restoration of democracy has limited appeal restricted to a section of intellectuals and is not of much interest to the general public.

13. In the present circumstances it is important that we should place before the people our views on important national issues so that the image of our party emerges as a progressive revolutionary force.

14. With this in view I have been working on the following subjects: (a) Pakistan foreign policy (Afghanistan). (b) Government's non-

productive expenditure. (c) The aid burden. (d) Corruption in the regime. (e) Industrial and labour policy. (f) Education policy.

15. Some of the information can be made public (though at present it is a difficult task) and some other matters, that is, foreign policy and industrial policy will need party approval before they can be released.

16. When these matters reach the public, and if this can be done effectively, Tehrik-i-Istiqlal's image will emerge in an effective manner enabling it to fill the present political gap.

17. There is a need to organise the students to devote much more time and efforts to their activities. In spite of working for only seven days, we made reasonable showing in the recent Punjab University elections. Munir Shah should concentrate on Peshawar University and Asaf Vardag should look after student affairs particularly in the Punjab University and prepare for participation in elections in at least half a dozen universities in Pakistan.

18. When our industrial and labour policies have been made known we should also work with the workers.

19. We are opposed to a permanent structure for the MRD but should stay in it. The only two parties in it, which matter, are the PPP and Tehrik-i-Istiqlal.

20. The government appears to be negotiating with Mrs Bhutto and is trying to persuade her (and her daughter) to retire from politics or at least to maintain their silence.

21. It would not be in the national interest for me to compromise with the government. So I intend to maintain my stance until I am released unconditionally.

22. Tehrik-i-Istiqlal should: (a) Hold on to our present stand and not bend in the present difficult circumstances. (b) We should not invite trouble but should remain in action and keep the party alive. (c) Let me take the pressure, which I can do by maintaining our present stance until the government finds it in its interest to release me.

We then discussed our attitude if Ziaul Haq wished to meet me. Syed Munir Shah was of the view (strongly expressed) that I should refuse to see him unless he visits me at my home.

Asaf Vardag said that Nasrullah Khan had been critical of TI although he also praised me for the manner in which I was opposing the regime. He is strongly for MRD and is close to Maulana Fazlur Rahman.

Syed Munir Shah suggested that we should establish contacts with the major powers, the army generals and the bureaucracy.

I told him that I was not against keeping in touch with everybody but it would be a mistake to think that we could change the situation with the help of these elements. Nor was it desirable that we should think in these terms. The superpowers will only act in their own interest and we cannot lean on them and become their tools, as this would not be in the national interest. The generals will not wish to restore democracy and the bureaucracy has limited value in such a situation. They are the servants of their masters, whoever they happen to be. We must therefore think of building up our own strength, change the thinking of the people and prepare ourselves for a long and hard struggle. There is no short cut to success, I told them. An interesting meeting though there was not enough time to discuss the many other issues we wished to talk about. They left as they had arrived, covered by blankets in the back of the car.

Friday, 14 Aug 1981, Abbottabad
The thirty-fourth anniversary of Pakistan's independence. It was celebrated on a very big scale, decorations, lights, and all. Singing of national anthem at 09:00.

Saturday, 15 Aug 1981, Abbottabad
The BBC announced the release of a number of political prisoners in Pakistan. Amongst them General Tikka Khan and Farooq Leghari the secretary general of PPP.

Saturday, 22 Aug 1981, Abbottabad
Air Vice Marshal Mohammad Ghulam Tawab, a former chief of air staff of Bangladesh, was arrested today on his return to Dhaka after six years in West Germany. He had come back to Dhaka about a year ago when he was promptly put on to a plane leaving for Bangkok. He has been arrested ostensibly on a four-year-old charge of corruption in the purchase of an aircraft for the Bangladesh airline. It is obvious however that the real reason is that the government regards him as a threat to the present regime. Tawab met me when I was on a visit to

London a couple of years ago. He is intensely interested in politics. On his arrival in Dhaka today, he told the press that he had no future plans and had come home to rest. Elections in Bangladesh are due in October.

Wednesday, 2 Sept 1981, Abbottabad
There is a move by Sardar Shaukat Hayat to call a meeting of leaders of all political parties in Karachi around 11 September (anniversary of Quaid-i-Azam's death). Daulatana is also sponsoring this move. I suggest that we should not attend such a meeting because half of these gentlemen are with the government.

Monday, 7 Sept 1981, Abbottabad
Air Force day. Benazir Bhutto was released from Karachi jail in order to enable her to attend her sister's wedding. Benazir will be sent to jail after the wedding.

Wednesday, 9 Sept 1981, Abbottabad
Fazle Haq, governor of NWFP, has spoken at Mingora (Swat) of Malakand division having become a base for anti-state activities. He said that the Mazdoor Kisaan Party and the Al Zulfikar organisation are indulging in anti-state activities.

Saturday, 12 Sept 1981, Abbottabad
The government banned a meeting called by Sardar Shaukat Hayat Khan to discuss the present situation. Sherbaz Mazari, Khawaja Khairuddin, Pir of Pagara, Mian Daulatana and Ghulam Mustafa Jatoi were due to attend.

A course was started by the government for the training of Qazis (religious scholars). Indira Gandhi has said that Pakistan does not wish to solve the Afghan problem because it suits the present government to keep the problem alive. There is a ring of truth in it. There was a mild earthquake at midday.

Sunday, 20 Sept 1981, Abbottabad
The government announced the termination of PIA flights to Kabul from today as a protest against the Afghan government's refusal to hand over the hijackers of the PIA Boeing hijacked on 2 March to the

Pakistan government. I feel that this is the type of policy that has been pursued by us for the last thirty years. The end of our air link with Kabul is not in our interest and is not likely to worry the Afghans.

Wednesday, 23 Sept 1981, Abbottabad
Twelve persons sentenced to death for the murder of President Zia-ur-Rahman of Bangladesh were hanged this morning. Ninety persons have filed their nomination papers for the presidential election in Bangladesh due on 15 November. Amongst them are General Osmani, Sabur Khan, Dr Aleem Al Razee and Prof. Muzaffar Ahmed.

Friday, 25 Sept 1981, Abbottabad
Chaudhry Zahur Elahi was shot and killed in Lahore today, His driver was also killed. Justice Mushtaq Hussain who was travelling in the same car was injured. M.A. Rehman escaped unhurt.

Saturday, 26 Sept 1981, Abbottabad
Chaudhry Zahur Elahi was buried in Gujrat today. The BBC said that Murtaza Bhutto had telephoned their representative, Mark Tully, in Delhi and said that his organisation, Al Zulfikar, was responsible for the attack on Chaudhry Zahur Elahi and Maulvi Mushtaq Hussain. He had said that a Dr Mussaddaq and a person named Iqbal had carried out the attack. It is usual for terrorist organisations to accept responsibility for such incidents sometimes when they have not been responsible for them but unusual to name the people involved.

Thursday, 1 Oct 1981, Abbottabad
Mian Mahmud Ali Kasuri called. He is in favour of an organisational structure for the MRD. I told him that I did not favour the idea. Mian Sahib was agreeable to assuming responsibility of acting president of the party. I asked him to do so.

Monday, 5 Oct 1981, Abbottabad
Mr Maruf, deputy director of Intelligence, telephoned from Islamabad to say that Khawaja Masroor Hussain, the DIG Intelligence, will call on me on the morning of 8 October 1981. I wonder what this is about.

Tuesday, 6 Oct 1981, Abbottabad

Today's *Jang* published an article by Maulana Kausar Niazi in which he quoted late Chaudhry Zahur Elahi as having told him in a meeting, a few days before his death, that there were only two politicians on the list of Al Zulfikar who were to be killed. One was Chaudhry Zahur Elahi and the other Maulana Kausar Niazi. Zahur Elahi had apparently been told this by the martial law authorities in Karachi.

President Sadat of Egypt was killed while reviewing a parade in Cairo today on the anniversary of the 1973 war against Israel. Vice President Hosni Mubarak escaped and the defence minister, Abu Ghazala, was injured. A large number of people were injured and some more killed. A group of six: one major, one lieutenant and four men, jumped down from a vehicle as it was passing the saluting dais and started firing at the reviewing stand.

Wednesday, 7 Oct 1981, Abbottabad

Ayub Khan and Iskander Mirza overthrew a democrative government 23 years ago on this day. Anwar Sadat is to be buried on Saturday. There is jubilation in Syria and Libya and amongst PLO on his death. It is now known that his assassination was the work of an extreme rightist group of fanatics.

Thursday, 8 Oct 1981, Abbottabad

Khawaja Masroor Hussain, head of the central intelligence bureau, came to call on me yesterday. He said that he had been told by Ziaul Haq to see me, the purpose being to seek my views on the general political situation. Governments establish this kind of contact from time to time with political leaders to keep themselves aware of their thinking. I told him that I had nothing new to say, that my views about the martial law regime and its consequences were unchanged and that I was not in a position to give them any advice.

Thursday, 15 Oct 1981, Abbottabad

The BBC said that the Tehrik-i-Istiqlal working committee had met in Lahore, despite the ban and had condemned the trend towards violence in politics, blaming the government for repressive policies, which force the people to indulge in unlawful activities. It asked for my release as well as that of other political prisoners. Journalists observed protest meetings at different places in the country against censorship and restrictions on the press.

Friday, 23 Oct 1981, Abbottabad
Khan Abdul Qayyum Khan died last night. He was in his late 80s. Radio Pakistan praised his services to Pakistan. It appears that only a dead politician is a good politician for Ziaul Haq. The government controlled press and radio had similarly been effusive in their praise of Mufti Mahmud and Chaudhry Zahur Elahi after their death.

Saturday, 24 Oct 1981, Abbottabad
Ziaul Haq said in Lahore today that *Insha Allah* (God willing) the president's advisory council will be announced next month. It will then be charged with approving a constitutional set up for Pakistan, which is being prepared by the ministry of law and the Islamic advisory council.

Speaking at a function of doctors in Lahore today Ziaul Haq gave the following figures: (1) Five thousand medical graduates are being produced by 16 medical colleges in the country every year. (2) The government is spending Rs150,000 on each graduate whereas the medical fee the student has to pay is Rs16 per month. (3) The number of doctors, nurses and hospital beds has increased as follows:

Year	Doctors	Nurses	Hospital beds
1947	1,360	88	14,000
1981	24,000	9,000	47,000

Sunday, 25 Oct 1981, Abbottabad
Ziaul Haq cancelled his visit to Gilgit scheduled for today because of a minor illness. Some six months ago he had cancelled a visit to Quetta also because of an illness. It transpired that he had done so rather crudely for security reasons. However, he continued to attend functions in Rawalpindi.

Monday, 26 Oct 1981, Abbottabad
The BBC said that the national working committee of the Tehrik-i-Istiqlal had met in Karachi under the chairmanship of Mian Manzoor Ahmed Wattoo. The national working committee had termed Ziaul

Haq's federal advisory council, which he says will be convened in November, a 'fraud'. It said that only elected representatives of the people had the right to change the 1973 constitution.

The International Herald Tribune of 20 October gave some details of the petroleum reserves in the world. Seventy per cent of Japan's requirement of oil is met from the Middle East. The US reserves will begin to deplete in ten years time and those of the USSR four years later.

Friday, 6 Nov 1981, Abbottabad

Justice Anwar ul Haq failed to be elected to the International Court of Justice. He got only one vote in the Security Council. The other six judges elected secured more than eight each. In the General Assembly he got 24 votes whereas the minimum required was 80.

Saturday, 7 Nov 1981, Abbottabad

Justice Sir Abdur Rashid died in Lahore yesterday at the age of 94. He was the first chief justice of Pakistan; and had administrated the oath of office to the Quaid-i-Azam, as governor-general, in Karachi on 14 August 1947.

Sunday, 8 Nov 1981, Abbottabad

A spokesman of Tehrik-i-Istiqlal (Nafis Siddiqui) has condemned the hypocritical role of the Jamaat-i-Islami. According to the BBC, this statement was occasioned by a statement of Professor Ghafoor Ahmed, secretary general of Jamaat-i-Islami, in which while demanding elections, he had criticised those parties that were opposed to Ziaul Haq's regime.

Tuesday, 10 Nov 1981, Abbottabad

Our wedding anniversary. Nasreen telephoned to congratulate us. Mian Tufail Mohammad is reported to have expressed his satisfaction with the Islamisation of society by Ziaul Haq, though he felt that the process could be speeded up.

Thursday, 19 Nov 1981, Abbottabad

The Lahore High Court criticised Ziaul Haq's statement to the press and termed his refusal to restore democracy and freedom of the press as un-Islamic.

Saturday, 21 Nov 1981, Abbottabad

The Pakistan government's press statement issued yesterday says that one of the assassins of Chaudhry Zahur Elahi was killed in a shoot-out in Karachi. It is alleged that when a police party approached a flat where these suspects were residing they were fired upon with automatics; one police officer was also killed. It would have been easier to surround the house and force the suspects to surrender, smoke them out or starve them to surrender. The killing of one of these people who is alleged to be Chaudhry Zahur Elahi's killer is rather fishy and suggests that the government had an interest in removing an important witness.

General Ershad, the chief of staff of the Bangladesh Army, has said that the army should have a constitutional role. He said that the president, Justice Abdul Sattar (who was sworn in yesterday), is appointing a committee to examine the desirability and the extent of the army's role in national affairs.

Sunday, 22 Nov 1981, Abbottabad

The MRD has issued a statement in Karachi condemning Ziaul Haq's statement that Pakistan was not ready for democracy. It has termed the creation of a nominated federal advisory council as undemocratic and un-Islamic. Mian Mahmud Ali Kasuri has returned to Lahore after attending the Karachi MRD meeting.

General Evrin, president of Turkey, arrived on a six-day state visit to Pakistan today as the guest of fellow usurper Ziaul Haq. Both heading unrepresentative governments in their countries have called for the establishment of a representative government in Afghanistan.

Saturday, 28 Nov 1981, Abbottabad

Omar took part in the university staff election for the post of secretary of the association. The pro-government (Jamaat-i-Islami) panel won the election with 165 votes as against Omar's 102. It was a very good effort, considering the atmosphere of repression in the university and open government support for the Jamaat candidate. Those of the teaching staff, who do not toe the line, have been pushed out of the university and the atmosphere generally is unhealthy.

Sunday, 29 Nov 1981, Abbottabad

In a speech in the presence of industrialists yesterday, Ziaul Haq said that the private sector is the third force in Pakistan, the other two being the army and the bureaucracy (Daily *Muslim*). He also told them that there is no question of elections in the country in the near future and they could invest without any fear of a change of government.

Wednesday, 2 Dec 1981, Abbottabad

Two Afghan helicopters strafed a bus and a military post four miles inside Pakistan near Naushki. This was one of the many such incident in the recent past. Today's daily *Jang* (Lahore) said that the government is prosecuting some five men involved in a bomb case, when a bomb was thrown at me at Lahore railway station on 23 March 1975. It is alleged that efforts were also made to assassinate me at my public meeting in Lahore at the instance of the PPP government of that time.

Thursday, 10 Dec 1981, Abbottabad

Today was human rights day all over the world. Typical of the hypocrisy of the military regime in Pakistan that it was celebrated by the government throughout the country.

Wednesday, 23 Dec 1981, Abbottabad

President Reagan announced that the US would stop all economic aid to Poland, including shipment of grain and food supplies, so long as martial law continues and solidarity is banned. He said that the US could not support a regime that was suppressing its people. A remarkable statement considering the US role of supporting dictators all over the world, including Pakistan.

Thursday, 24 Dec 1981, Abbottabad

Ziaul Haq announced the long talked about federal council or the Majlis-i-Shoora. Fakhruz Zaman Khan, Begum Sabiha Shakil, Chaudhri Mumtaz Tarar, Qurban Ali Chauhan, Ayub Khan of Elahi and Chakar Khan Domki are some of the Tehrik-i-Istiqlal people who have joined the council. Also includes Syed Moin-ud-Din Shah at one time of TI. Most of the people named are people who have been known for joining the winning side after the elections.

Friday, 25 Dec 1981, Abbottabad

In addition to the names of TÍ people who have been nominated to the federal advisory council, Obaid-ur-Rehman, Jam of Lasbela and Riaz son of (late) Khuda Dad Khan have also been nominated. The total number of TI members therefore is eleven of whom five were office bearers at various levels. The other six were members only, having joined for a ticket in the 1979 general elections which did not take place.

Thursday, 31 Dec 1981, Abbottabad

Last day of 1981. A particularly bad year. Relations between the Soviet Union and the USA have worsened. Israel has become more aggressive, annexing the Golan Heights. The Iran-Iraq war shows no sign of ending. Fighting in Afghanistan continues. Zia-ur-Rahman of Bangladesh and Anwar Sadat were killed during 1981. Flight Lieutenant Gerry Rawling carried out a coup in Ghana today. Earlier he had handed over power to a civilian government in 1979. Appears to be in control of the situation.

Diary 1982

Thursday, 7 Jan 1982, Abbottabad

Amina, along with Mushir, J.A. Rahim and Nafis Siddiqui were externed from the Punjab for three months following the Tehrik-i-Istiqlal national working committee meeting. Amina returned with Nasreen late in the morning. She will now leave for Karachi via Peshawar, though she will have to cross a part of the Punjab *en route*.

Saturday, 9 Jan 1982, Abbottabad

Osman came and spent a few hours with me. Spoke to him about Wazir Ali's proposal of an alliance with the PPP. Osman is violently opposed to the suggestion. He feels that the Tehrik should stand alone and that its image that has already been built up would grow further. He is of the opinion that joining with PPP and other elements will reduce the TI's appeal for those elements who would otherwise want to support it. J.A. Rahim holds similar views.

Monday, 11 Jan 1982, Abbottabad
The federal council (Majlis-i-Shoora) had its first sitting in Islamabad this morning. Khawaja Safdar was appointed the chairman. Ziaul Haq announced the end of pre-censorship of the press (daily newspapers). He said that the federal council could suggest changes in the martial law orders, amendments to the constitution, new martial law orders and the desirability or otherwise of restrictions on political activities. He said that the two main tasks were Islamisation of society and the ushering in of Islamic democracy in Pakistan.

Tuesday, 12 Jan 1982, Abbottabad
Characteristically, after announcing the lifting of pre-censorship for daily papers, Ziaul Haq only a few minutes later, when speaking to the press, said that they were not permitted to publish any political news. The so-called relaxation therefore has no meaning.

Ziae went to Haripur to see Younas Khan, the office secretary of our party from Peshawar, in jail. He has been in detention for some three months allegedly for distributing pamphlets.

Wednesday, 13 Jan 1982, Abbottabad
The BBC said that Amnesty International had published a detailed report on the denial of human rights in Pakistan. It said that the right of *habeas corpus* allowed in the 1973 constitution has been denied; 6,000 persons were imprisoned during 1981 for demanding civil rights, 10 persons were killed in police custody, a record number of people are being hanged every year. A.K. Brohi said that about 800 people are hanged annually. The military and the police can arrest anyone without warrant, police can search without warrant, civil courts cannot examine or consider any case initiated by martial law, minor violations of martial law orders such as addressing a gathering of more than four persons can result in whipping, 14 years RI and confiscation of property, hands can be cut and detenus cannot obtain any legal advice or assistance, people can be left in detention without trial indefinitely.

Thursday, 14 Jan 1982, Abbottabad
Received Amnesty International's report by mail today. Surprising that it should get through the censors.

Sunday, 17 Jan 1982, Abbottabad
My 61st birthday. Received a large number of telephone calls, cards and telegrams. The best letter was from Chaudhry Safdar Ali, the publicity secretary of the party from Lahore. It congratulated me on my birthday and on the birth of Omar's daughter. He wrote that she could say with pride when she grows up that her grandfather was under detention and grandmother banned from entering Punjab when she was born. Omar telephoned in the evening to say that the police did not allow the birthday function to take place in Lahore and turned away a large number of people who had gathered. They all went to 4 Fane Road. It was a good gathering. So were the ones at Peshawar and Abbottabad. Rawalpindi also had a good meeting.

Saturday, 23 Jan 1982, Abbottabad
Mushir attended the land case in the local court. The next date is 27 February. Discussed the political situation and I suggested to Mushir that: (a) We should not join any greater or other alliance with Jamaat-i-Islami or Pagara League. (b) Should not make statements to the press giving an impression of successful parleys between political parties as these only build up false hopes and confuse the people. (c) Work quietly without inviting restrictive measures by the government. (d) Step up building the ISF.

The government took action against a large number of political workers restricting them to their provinces or districts. This is probably in response to the much advertised meeting of the MRD on 27 January by its current chairman (for this month) Sherbaz Mazari.

Sunday, 24 Jan 1982, Abbottabad
The BBC said last night that amongst others, Amina's entry into Sindh had also been banned for three months. She will therefore be confined to NWFP. Mian Mahmud Ali Kasuri's entry into Sindh is also banned for three months.

Monday, 25 Jan 1982, Abbottabad
The SSP called to serve an order on Amina under martial law order 48, banning her entry into Sindh for the next ninety days (until 21 April 1982). The order said that the government had information that she was going to Sindh shortly with the intention of creating a breach of the peace and to violate martial law orders. It is evident that Ziaul Haq's government is not well informed.

Wednesday, 27 Jan 1982, Abbottabad
Ghaus Bux Bizenjo, who was externed from Sindh last week, was externed from NWFP on arrival in Peshawar and was today also externed from Punjab on arrival at Lahore. He will therefore now be confined to Balochistan. Amina is better off than him, she can move around in NWFP as well as in Balochistan.

Tuesday, 2 Feb 1982, Abbottabad
The federal finance minister, Ghulam Ishaq Khan, in a press conference today said that there have been a 25-fold increase in drug traffic in Pakistan since 1980. Fazle Haq (governor of NWFP) said today that there was only one political detenu in NWFP.

Zain ul Abedin of PDP, the current chairman of MRD for the month, addressed a press conference in Karachi yesterday. Other party heads were present. Nafis Siddiqui represented Tehrik-i-Istiqlal. Zain ul Abedin said that Pir Pagara and Maulana Noorani wished martial law to continue, therefore there was no likelihood of their joining the MRD. It is certainly true of the Pir of Pagara.

Wednesday, 3 Feb 1982, Abbottabad
Sent Fazle Haq the cutting of *Pakistan Times* of today showing him inspecting WAPDA installations at Tarbela dam. Out of the party of about twenty-five, ten were security personnel in uniform. I wrote: 'This heavy security in a restricted area is hardly necessary for a popular regime.'

Monday, 22 Feb 1982, Abbottabad
Josh Malihabadi died in Islamabad this morning. He was the last of the old generation of renowned poets. A revolutionary and an independent thinker, he was often criticised for his unorthodoxy.

Friday, 26 Feb 1982, Abbottabad

A large number of people were arrested in different parts of the country yesterday and today: over 500 in Karachi, about 200 in NWFP and a few hundred in Punjab. The government said that most of these people were involved in anti-state or terrorist activities. This follows the announcement of the government a few days ago that the police had arrested a number of people who had brought a copy of the Quran from Afghanistan to use as a booby trap. A great deal of publicity has been given to this incident. The copy of the Quran was shown on TV and processions and strikes held in different parts of the country.

Saturday, 27 Feb 1982, Abbottabad

Arrests continue all over the country. It is significant that some incident takes place every time the government is about to come down on political workers or parties. The hijacking of a PIA aircraft in March 1981 preceded the clamp down on political activities and the incident of the Quran preceded the rounding up of a large number of people. The government's hand in such incidents cannot be ruled out.

Mushir came in connection with the Abbottabad land case, which was postponed, to Wednesday, 17 March. We discussed the political situation and I advised him to clarify the Tehrik-i-Istiqlal's position about taking in Jamaat-i-Islami and Pagara League in the MRD by saying: (a) Both these parties are with the government and Tehrik is not in favour of associating with them in MRD. (b) Talk of a wider alliance, therefore, causes confusion in the public mind. (c) Talk of a formula being prepared for presentation to Ziaul Haq for handing over power is ridiculous because Ziaul Haq has not indicated that he wishes to do so. It would only have a meaning if Ziaul Haq makes a public announcement to this effect.

Mushir said that this reflects the thinking of the national working committee and that he would make these views known to the press in two or three days.

Monday, 1 March 1982, Abbottabad

Ziaul Haq is reported to have said that he is in touch with me and that I was well and happy.

Wednesday, 3 March 1982, Abbottabad
Pagara, Sherbaz, Ghulam Mustafa Jatoi, Chaudhri Arshad (PDP) and Mushir met at lunch at Maulana Noorani's yesterday and made a statement to the press suggesting that Ziaul Haq should form a national government with himself as the head and that this national government should hold election. This is quite contrary to what I had told Mushir to say to the press. However I will wait to see what Mushir has to say to the press tomorrow before I decide what to do. If Mushir is going to follow a different line, it would be better for him not to visit me. His visits create the impression that he is following my briefings.

Thursday, 4 March 1982, Abbottabad
Mushir addressed the press at Karachi today and said that the Jamaat-i-Islami and the Pagara Muslim League did not want elections and the Jamaat-i-Islami represented the government's point of view. He said that if in spite of this, these parties were allowed to join the MRD, the Tehrik-i-Istiqlal would have to reconsider the desirability of its continuance in this organisation.

Friday, 5 March 1982, Abbottabad
Mushir's press statement was well reported in today's newspapers. His statement has, I feel, adequately clarified the Tehrik-i-Istiqlal's position. J.A. Rahim, who was also present, spoke and expressed similar views.

Sunday, 7 March 1982, Abbottabad
Arbab Sikander Khan Khalil was shot and killed near his home in Tehkal Bala in Peshawar early this morning. He was a decent man and a man of principles. Ahmed Mian Soomro came to visit me and stayed for lunch. He said that the law and order situation in Sindh is chaotic. Holdups and dacoities are common and the police and the administration is often mixed up in these cases.

Thursday, 30 March 1982, Abbottabad
Newspapers in Pakistan appear to be completely subdued. No political news of any kind is published ever since Ziaul Haq spoke harshly to newsmen at Lahore airport the other day.

Thursday, 8 April 1982, Abbottabad

Quoting its correspondent in Islamabad, Alexander Thompson of the BBC gave a rosy picture of Balochistan and spoke of the development being carried out in the province by the present regime. In actual fact most of the projects are in the Hala area near Karachi where non-Baloch are running these projects and benefiting from them.

Wednesday, 14 April 1982, Abbottabad

Ziaul Haq spoke in Faisalabad yesterday and said that he visualises a definite role for the armed forces in the constitution. He said that he intended to amend the 1973 constitution, so that the three services chiefs are made members of a national council with powers to interfere with or take over the government whenever they felt it is necessary. He said that the president would be given more powers with control of the armed forces.

Thursday, 15 April 1982, Abbottabad

In answer to a question in the Majlis-i-Shoora, Yaqub Khan, the foreign minister, said that out of the 64 Pakistan ambassadors abroad, 28 were career diplomats and 24 non-careerists. Out of the 24 non-careerists, 14 were defence service officers. He did not say whether the 14 defence service officers were serving officers (which they probably are). In that event, some of the remaining 10 non-careerists could be retired senior defence service officers. Moreover 28+24 is 52 whereas the total number of ambassadors is 64. Twelve therefore remain unexplained—also probably army officers.

Sunday, 18 April 1982, Abbottabad

Wali Khan returned from Kabul where he had gone to see his father. He was given a warm welcome in Kabul by the Afghan government and met Babrak Karmal with whom he discussed Pakistan-Afghan relations.

Wednesday, 21 April 1982, Abbottabad

Ziaul Haq has said that elections will only be held when the business community felt secure and gave him the green light. A truly capitalist agent.

Friday, 23 April 1982, Abbottabad

Students of Islami Jamiat Tulaba attacked the office of daily *Jang* and *Nawa-i-Waqt* in Lahore yesterday and damaged and burnt property. This was done because these newspapers had published a news item that the *nazim* of the Jamiat in Lahore was caught with a revolver when boarding the PIA plane to Peshawar on 21 April (same plane by which Omar flew to Peshawar) and was arrested (later released on bail). Demonstrators at the offices of the newspapers were armed and fired indiscriminately. They also beat up some newspaper employees and manhandled a lady reporter. Some 30 of these students were arrested on Friday and another 50, when they staged another demonstration today. These arrests were preceded by a baton charge and tear-gassing.

This incident is the result of government patronage, which the Islami Jamiat Tulaba and its parent organisation, the Jamaat-i-Islami, have enjoyed for the last four years.

Saturday, 1 May 1982, Abbottabad

In a statement to the press on 24 April the *nazim* of Islami Jamiat Tulaba Punjab has compared the arrest of the head of IJT on 23 April with the attack on Khana-i-Kaaba by suggesting that both incidents were equally reprehensible and therefore evoked spontaneous reaction from the students.

Saturday, 8 May 1982, Abbottabad

At the workers' meeting in Abbottabad yesterday Syed Munir Shah was authorised to fill vacant appointments. Dost Mohammad Khan Tareen was appointed provincial vice chairman in place of Abdul Haq Shah who has been inactive. Abdul Haye was appointed district general secretary in place of Sardar Ghulam Mustafa. A number of people, including Abdul Rahman Gujjar, Naseem Bangash, Shah Jehan, Lala Mohammad Iqbal and Nawabzada Bakhtiar, all from Mansehra district, were appointed to the provincial working committee. Attendance was very good and every worker of consequence was present, amongst them were Fida Mohammad Khan and Malik Ghulam Rabbani and Jumma Khan. Mukhtiar Bacha, the newly elected provincal general secretary, was also present.

Tuesday, 11 May 1982, Abbottabad

Spoke to Omar and suggested that he should keep on writing for the newspapers.

The Iraqis appear to be on the run and Iranian forces are engaged in fierce fighting to retake Khurramshahr. If they succeed, which they are likely to, Iraq will have vacated Iranian territory. Iran may then possibly enter Iraqi territory and move on towards Baghdad. Iranian successes appear to be uniting the US oriented Arab countries to move in support of the Iraqi regime. Sultan Qaboos of Oman is on a visit to Egypt and Saudi Arabia. Jordan, Iraq and the Gulf kingdoms are wooing Egypt, which was until recently a pariah in Arab politics. Syria and the PLO are not likely to join this move.

Thursday, 13 May 1982, Abbottabad

Pir Pagara has said that Muslim League will take part in an election held on any terms by Ziaul Haq, even if it is on a non-party basis, for a National Assembly with limited or no powers. Mian Tufail Mohammad of Jamaat-i-Islami has expressed similar views in a BBC interview.

Saturday, 15 May 1982, Abbottabad

According to the report of the auditor general of Pakistan, published in the *Star* of Karachi on 15 May, Rs1,272 million were embezzled by different ministers of the central government during the last fiscal year. It says that no ministry had even replied to the auditor general's observations. An inevitable consequence of a system in which the government that is not accountable to public opinion.

Saturday, 29 May 1982, Abbottabad

My two years of continuous detention ended today. A large number of people telephoned to enquire whether I had been released. Spoke to Mian Mahmud Ali Kasuri. He is thinking of filing a writ in the Peshawar High Court although he says that it will not be entertained. I am held under martial law order Number 12, para 3 and MLO 78. According to Mian Sahib, MLO 12 says that a person may not be kept in continuous detention without trial for more than two years. All this is however only of academic interest as there is no law in Pakistan today.

Sunday, 6 June 1982, Abbottabad

Ziaul Haq and his martial law government has advanced yet another reason, the large number of political parties in Pakistan, as an excuse for not holding elections. This is a ridiculous argument as voters in most countries, including Pakistan, usually cast their votes for two or three parties only. This happened in East Pakistan in 1954 when the Muslim League was overwhelmingly defeated. This happened again in 1970 when only the Awami League (in East Pakistan) and PPP (in West Pakistan) emerged with the largest number of seats. About two dozen parties had taken part in the elections. In UK in 1978 there were 78 political parties and since then the SDP (Social Democratic Party) and the National Front have been added bringing the total to 80 political parties.

Thursday, 10 June 1982, Abbottabad

Heard Ziaul Haq on TV in his press conference on his return from Jeddah, after attending the meeting of the Ummah's peace committee. Some of the howlers: 'We are fully behind the injustice in Lebanon;' 'We are looking for a problem of the Afghanistan issue;' 'We want justice for the PUPIL (sic) of Afghanistan'.

Governor Fazle Haq called and stayed for an hour-and-a-half. He was here in connection with the foundation laying of the Ayub Medical Complex and the 'Piffer' week. He said that the government would be prepared to release me if I could give them an assurance that I would be 'moderate' in my criticism of the regime. I told him that I was not prepared to do this. Otherwise an amiable visit.

Sunday, 20 June 1982, Abbottabad

The Shoora had a session on Lebanon yesterday and since most of the members spoke of *jihad* and urged the Pakistan Army to be sent to fight the Israelis, their speeches could not be heard on TV. Only their faces were shown.

Heard of some instances of nepotism of the regime. Air Commodore Saleem (formerly secretary air HQ) has been posted to PIA as general manager 'Americas'. He has no commercial experience of PIA. He belongs to the supply branch of the PAF and his appointment as air secretary was also made by Ziaul Haq. An air commodore has been posted as director stores in PIA. His wife is said to be Begum Ziaul

Haq's school friend from East Africa. Lieutenant General Arif's brother has been given a group eight job in PIA without going through any selection process. Large numbers of such appointments have been made in place of the PIA personnel retrenched recently. Ziaul Haq's family has been given twelve free tickets for overseas travel by PIA by Shakil Express. Ziaul Haq owes PIA Rs90,000 for private travel during last year, which he has not paid. Mr Saleem, the managing director, has taken no action. PIA fares have been raised partly because: (a) defence service personnel travel at 50 per cent; (b) press people travel at 50 per cent; (c) non-Baloch posted in Balochistan travel at 50 per cent.

Monday, 21 June 1982, Abbottabad
Mairaj Mohammad Khan, Zuberi of NDP and Alamdar Haider were put in prison for 30 days. Khairuddin, Maulana Ehtram ul Haq and Maulana Sher Afzal were detained in their houses and police is looking for Nafis Siddiqui who has gone underground. These arrests are meant to forestall a procession that MRD has planned for 23 June, the first of Ramzan, in sympathy with PLO and to demand that the Pakistan Army be sent to Lebanon. The BBC reported that 100 people had been killed in Shia-Sunni clashes in the Parachinar area. The trouble appears to have been started when the Shias tried to build an Imambara (a shia place of worship).

Wednesday, 23 June 1982, Abbottabad
A procession against the martial law government and in support of Palestinians was attempted in Karachi yesterday. A large number of arrests were made and the crowd, said to number a few thousand, was baton charged and tear-gassed. Amongst those arrested were Nafis Siddiqui, Shahida Nafis and Rukhsana Zahoor. The BBC said this morning that the government had said in a press statement, that most of those arrested had been released.

Malik Shahzada Khan Mohmand, a member of the Majlis-i-Shoora, was shot and killed outside the National Assembly building yesterday.

Tuesday, 29 June 1982, Abbottabad
As reported in this morning's papers Mumtaz Tarar made a good speech in the Majlis-i-Shoora yesterday. He was critical of the budget and of the government and called the Shoora a waste of time. Logically he should resign his membership of this body.

Thursday, 22 July 1982, Abbottabad
Eidul Fitr. My sixth Eid in captivity since 16 October 1979.

Monday, 26 July 1982, Abbottabad
Jamhooriat published a speech of Mahmood Azam Farooqi (ex-MNA) in which he has asked as to who is paying for Ziaul Haq's *Umrahs* on which he goes frequently and on which he is accompanied by a large entourage.

Friday, 30 July 1982, Abbottabad
The BBC said that the government has instructed newspapers in Pakistan not to publish the name of any politician or of a political party. They cannot also mention anything about any movement for the restoration of democracy. They may however publish editorial comment on the political situation. This restriction will initially last for two weeks, presumably because the government does not want to foul the atmosphere before the 14 August celebrations that are being arranged by the government.

The BBC also said that on 11 July a large band of armed Afghan refugees attacked a village near Haripur and looted property on a large scale. One girl was killed and when the villagers wanted to take out a procession and march toward Islamabad, they were beaten up, baton charged and tear-gassed by the police. Gulbadin Hikmatyar, a refugee leader, visited the village and promised compensation.

Wednesday, 11 Aug 1982, Abbottabad
The Sri Lankan ambassador died suddenly of a heart attack whilst calling on Ziaul Haq. It appears that Ziaul Haq's lethal qualities are now taking a more apparent form. A press correspondent died in Karachi the other day while asking him questions.

Friday, 13 Aug 1982, Abbottabad
Today was the culmination and climax of the government's media campaign for tomorrow's celebrations. A shameful performance in view of the complete absence of civil liberties in Pakistan and the suffering of the people in Lebanon. The nation has never been brainwashed to the extent that Ziaul Haq and his Goebble (General Mujib-ur-Rahman, secretary ministry of information) have done, during the last few years.

Sunday, 15 Aug 1982, Abbottabad
I completed one thousand days in detention since 16 October 1979 on 12 August. Today is therefore my 1003rd day.

Friday, 20 Aug 1982, Abbottabad
Syed Munir Shah was externed from Punjab for three months after addressing the Gujranwala Bar Association.

Thursday, 9 Sept 1982, Abbottabad
Sheikh Abdullah, the Kashmiri leader, died last night. He was 76. Sardar Ibrahim, Sardar Qayyum and a number of other people were arrested in Azad Kashmir yesterday.

Monday, 13 Sept 1982, Abbottabad
Zahur ul Hassan Bhopali, formerly of the JUP and a member of Ziaul Haq's nominated Majlis-i-Shoora was shot dead today in Karachi.

Wednesday, 15 Sept 1982, Abbottabad
Bashir Gemayel, president-elect of Lebanon, was killed in a bomb explosion in Beirut.

Ziaul Haq has said that he will 'crush' all anti-social elements. In spite of such statements made at regular intervals the acts of terrorism are on the increase and likely to increase further, so long as political repression and the present restrictions on political activity last.

Thursday, 16 Sept 1982, Abbottabad
The Kuwaiti consul general was shot and wounded in Karachi today. The assailant escaped.

So far, over a thousand persons have been arrested in connection with Zahur ul Hassan Bhopali's murder.

Monday, 20 Sept 1982, Abbottabad
Sent an article on the Kashmir problem with Samad to Omar in Lahore, for getting it typed. Also gave him a letter for Mushahid Hussain, editor *Muslim,* about columnist Khalid Hassan's 'Private View' in which he had made fun of Nur Khan. I thought that the article was in very bad taste.

Tuesday, 21 Sept 1982, Abbottabad
Muslim published my letter to the editor about Nur Khan.

Wednesday, 22 Sept 1982, Abbottabad
Rafi Butt's newspaper, *Haider*, was banned from Azad Kashmir allegedly for propagating pro-Israel and pro-Moscow views. A very odd allegation as I think that the *Haider* puts forward no views of any kind. In any case there is very little similarity between Israeli and Soviet views.

Thursday, 23 Sept 1982, Abbottabad
Nur Khan telephoned to thank me for my letter to the *Muslim* of 21 September. He said that he would try to get permission to see me sometime next month.

Saturday, 25 Sept 1982, Abbottabad
A demonstration of about 400,000 people took place in Tel Aviv against Begin, calling for an enquiry into the killings at the two Palestinian camps in Beirut. Begin has refused to hold such an enquiry.

Monday, 27 Sept 1982, Abbottabad
Ziaul Haq passed a new martial law order under which anyone damaging government property or creating insecurity or frightening people can be sentenced to death. The order is with retrospective effect, from 5 July 1977. Another interesting feature of this order is that it cannot be challenged in a court of law and the accused is presumed guilty unless he proves himself to be innocent. The accused

is to be tried by a martial law court, which will deal with the case on the basis of police evidence or opinion. This law is the limit in lawlessness and suppression.

Tuesday, 28 Sept 1982, Abbottabad
Eidul Azha. My seventh Eid in detention.

Sunday, 10 Oct 1982, Abbottabad
The fourth session of the Majlis-i-Shoora opened in Islamabad on 9 October. Ziaul Haq made a lengthy oration. Appeared to be rattled by the deteriorating law and order situation in the country. Threatened to use his new martial law order 53, which gives the government powers to hang people (see 27 Sept) for almost everything including Shia-Sunni trouble in the coming Moharram.

Tuesday, 12 Oct 1982, Abbottabad
Pir Khalid Raza Zakori gave a reception for federal minister, Arbab Niaz. He had given a reception some time ago for another federal minister, Zafarul Haq. He is also the vice president of Pir Deval Sharif's organisation of *mashaik* [religious leaders]. I have therefore removed him from the national council of the party of which he was a nominated member.

Saturday, 16 Oct 1982, Abbottabad
In an interview to the BBC Ziaul Haq said that he believed that God had sent him to lead and serve the people of Pakistan. He would stay as long as God wishes. In Islam, he said, it did not matter how a person assumed office, the important thing was whether he was following the tenets of Islam as laid down by the Quran and Sunnah and if he did so he had a perfect right to rule. He said that Islamisation of a society was a lifetime work and implied that he could stay as long as he lived. He said that it was possible that he might want to leave earlier but only if God willed that he should (*Muslim*, 17 October 1982).

The only redeeming feature of this interview is that he appears to have lost his sense of balance and therefore possibly his end is now nearer. But may be God wants Pakistan to suffer a little longer.

Monday, 18 Oct 1982, Abbottabad

A plot to hijack a PIA aircraft was unearthed in Holland and eighteen persons were arrested in Amsterdam. Sixteen of them were released as no offence had as yet been committed and two were externed.

Tuesday, 19 Oct 1982, Abbottabad

Received a book written by Shabbir Hussain Shah titled *History of the PAF 1947-1982*, which should have been more appropriately called *The Life and Times of Air Chief Marshal Mohammad Anwar Shamim*. It is a crude attempt to build up his image though it is a good reference book, badly edited and poorly printed. It has numerous errors.

Wednesday, 20 Oct 1982, Abbottabad

Ziaul Haq is on a visit to China, kissing and embracing every Chinese he meets. He has a large entourage with wives and hangers on. Appears on the TV daily and seems to be revelling in it. Before he sees Reagan on 7 December, he will have visited China, North Korea, India, Indonesia, Malaysia and Singapore and will therefore be considered knowledgeable on the problems of these countries. Pakistan has been elected a member of the UN Security Council for two years. Will be seeing more of Yaqub on TV.

Thursday, 28 Oct 1982, Abbottabad

Ashura day. Decided to write a note on the future of MRD suggesting a line of action for the future. I feel that perhaps the most important reason for it being unable to mobilise public opinion is its failure to put up a clear alternative to Ziaul Haq's regime. Naming a caretaker government which will run the country for six months and a few principles that will be followed during this period would go a long way towards mobilising public opinion. Elections could be organised and held by a caretaker government after the six-month period. The MRD should stop issuing appeals to Ziaul Haq to hold elections and transfer power for this is an exercise in futility. He has no intention of leaving.

Sunday, 31 Oct 1982, Abbottabad

Nasreen's birthday. Telephoned her. Rabia and Mohammad are very excited about their mother's birthday and have refused to give her the present that Amina had given Rabia for Nasreen. Rabia insists that she will give it to her after she returns from school. She wants to be present to enjoy Nasreen's excitement.

Thursday, 4 Nov 1982, Abbottabad
Ziaul Haq is on his tour of Indonesia along with his entourage of 85 persons comprising wives, friends and lackeys. Abdul Ghaffar Khan who was detained in the Kheshki rest house near Nowshera a couple of days ago has been moved to Lady Reading Hospital in Peshawar for chest pain. He is 93.

Saturday, 13 Nov 1982, Abbottabad
Yuri Vladimorovich Andropov was named the general secretary of the central committee of the Soviet Communist Party. A former head of the KGB, he has held important ambassadorial appointments as well. A head of state has not been named as yet.

The *Muslim* of today carried an unusually forthright editorial criticising the martial law regime. Mrs Nusrat Bhutto has been allowed to travel abroad for medical treatment. A medical board constituted by Ziaul Haq earlier had not found anything wrong with her but has now changed its recommendations and has suggested that she may be allowed to go abroad. I think that both the first and the second recommendation have been made at the government's instance. The second because considerable adverse publicity was being given to Ziaul Haq's refusal to allow her to travel. Sent a telegram to wish her bon voyage.

Sunday, 21 Nov 1982, Abbottabad
Ziaul Haq has said in a press interview on arrival in Karachi that he has no intention of releasing me, Benazir or Nasrullah Khan, as we would spoil the atmosphere if we were released.

Monday, 29 Nov 1982, Abbottabad
Omar came in the evening along with Fatehyab Ali Khan, the chairman of the Mazdoor Kissan Party and of the MRD for the current month. Fatehyab Ali Khan came to suggest that the four detained leaders of MRD, Benazir, Nasrullah Khan Maulana Fazlur Rahman and myself should go on hunger strike. He said that the other three

had agreed, and that if we did, a movement would start and we would be released. I told him that I did not agree with the suggestion because hunger strike is something foreign to the tradition of our people and in such matters like starting a movement, timing is of the essence. This so called 'hunger strike' would fail and the MRD would suffer a blow from which it may not be able to recover, I advised patience and suggested that MRD should wait for a more opportune moment. That moment as far as I could see has not arrived. I also suggested that traditional methods of holding press conferences, issuing press statements and arranging advertised meetings should be given up and work should be carried out quietly. Pamphleteering should be used. I did not meet Fatehyab Ali who had dinner at Tariq's.

Thursday, 9 Dec 1982, Abbottabad
Ziaul Haq is having a very busy time in the USA, kissing and embracing every one he can get close to. Made a very poor speech at Reagan's dinner in his honour yesterday. A typically hypocritical and fawning attitude. Assured Reagan that he will always find Pakistan standing behind him and giving him a helping hand whenever he needed it. Should have been very well received in Washington.

Saturday, 18 Dec 1982, Abbottabad
Javed Khanzada, the deputy commissioner, called in the afternoon. He disclosed during our convention that Gulbadin Hikmatyar, an Afghan leader in Peshawar, has a bank balance of Rs75,000,000 in Pakistani banks. He also said that a large number of terrorists have infiltrated into Pakistan with the mujahideen.

Wednesday, 29 Dec 1982, Abbottabad
Mian Mahmud Ali Kasuri came after a long absence. He talked about the desirability of forming a close 'union' between the parties of the MRD and a resolve to contest elections as one party and stay together for at least five years. I told him that I did not think that this could inspire confidence in the public. I told him that experience of alliances in Pakistan had not been very positive and such an idea, even if it could work, would not mobilise the people. Gave him my paper (on this subject) to read. I had written this as an epilogue for my book but

had decided against sending it to the publishers. Mian Sahib was also very keen on elections within the party.

Friday, 31 Dec 1982, Abbottabad
The last day of 1982. Another year of suffering for the people of many countries—Poland, Pakistan, Iran, Lebanon, Afghanistan. Ziaul Haq has tightened his grip on the country, which has reached new depths of suppression. The Islamic system that he talks about is visible in the form of rituals, sermons and punishments. The structure of the society remains highly exploitative with opportunities for the rich and suffering for the poor. Corruption is rampant and nepotism is rife. Amina and Nasreen returned from Rawalpindi late last night. Amina met Mrs Ziaul Haq at the wedding of Khaqan Abbasi's daughter and received a bear hug from her.

Diary 1983

Tuesday, 18 Jan 1983, Abbottabad
Yesterday was my fourth birthday in captivity. Received a bouquet of narcissi from Abdul Wali Khan who had attended the reception given by Syed Munir Shah yesterday for my birthday.

Friday, 4 Feb 1983, Abbottabad
Nafis Siddiqui was expelled from the party by the Karachi divisional organisation (Chaudhri Jameel) for activities against the party's interests.

Saturday, 12 Feb 1983, Abbottabad
Samina took part in a demonstration in Lahore organised by the Women's Action Forum (chairperson is Begum Mahnaz Rafi). About 200 women took part. They were tear-gassed and baton charged by the police and 30 of them were arrested. Samina was among those arrested. She also received some injuries on her shoulder and back. Amina and I have both been injured by police baton charge at different

times. Samina was released after some time. The incident received wide publicity in the international media and the BBC, the VOA and Radio Deutschland mentioned it in their evening bulletins. Spoke to Omar and Samina who were at Malik Ghulam Jilani's in the evening.

Thursday, 24 Feb 1983, Abbottabad

Amina wrote to Mrs Mabille of Amnesty International. Omar was to come today but could not do so because of trouble in the university. Jamiat boys were beating a student outside Omar's class and Omar intervened to save the boy. At this one of the Jamiat boys took out a revolver. Omar caught hold of the revolver and in the process was hit by one of the Jamiat hooligans.

Omar has filed an FIR. He telephoned to say that he and his like-minded professors were getting together to decide what has to be done about this exhibition of hooliganism on the campus. Omar hopes to come tomorrow.

Friday, 25 Feb 1983, Abbottabad

Omar arrived in the morning. Discussed the programme of mobilising the students in Lahore from the Punjab University and the colleges. Omar is taking a strong stand with the vice chancellor regarding yesterday's incident, which may result in his having to leave the university. He is going to speak once a week in Prof. Tahir-al-Qadri's mosque on economic issues and will also teach eight periods a month in a new institute of higher studies that he and some friends have opened in Lahore.

Tuesday, 1 March 1983, Abbottabad

Mushir came to visit me. Discussed the party line on the appointment of a permanent head of MRD and the issue of a 31-point programme of the MRD. I explained my view that we should maintain our objection to the appointment of a permanent head of MRD, disassociate ourselves from the discussion on this subject but accept the decision when it is taken by the MRD. On the question of a 32-point programme; this in my view amounts to an election manifesto and only made sense if the MRD converted itself into an election alliance. Since we were opposed to an election alliance, as were some other parties, we should not accept this. We joined the MRD on a four-point programme and should not go beyond it. If the MRD insists on going ahead with it we should leave the organisation.

Sunday, 6 March 1983, Abbottabad

The vice chancellor has warned Omar that he would take disciplinary action against him if the boycott of the classes by the economics department teachers (started because of the incident on 24 February) does not end.

Sunday, 20 March 1983, Abbottabad

Shia-Sunni riots continued for the fourth day. Five people have been killed and over a hundred wounded so far. This is the result of the religious bigotry fanned by Ziaul Haq for the last five-and-a-half-years the destruction of the judiciary, suppression of the press and clamping down on every kind of self expression.

Monday, 21 March 1983, Abbottabad

The Voice of America broadcast this morning said that 7 persons have been killed in riots in Karachi so far and 210 wounded. Over 100 arrests have been made. Munir Shah has gone underground and intends surfacing in Lahore on 23 March.

Wednesday, 23 March 1983, Abbottabad

Pakistan day. The people are in bondage and the *chowkidars* (the armed forces) have taken over the country. Tehrik-i-Istiqlal and MRD are staging demonstrations in different parts of the country but there was no mention of this in the evening news bulletin of the BBC. Omar has brought General Musa's book on the 1965 India-Pakistan war. He has been very critical of my book *The First Round* and his book appears to be written to refute some of the statements in my book. His book, *My Version*, is a highly subjective book and I do not think that Musa has managed to whitewash his conduct of the 1965 war. Anyway it is good that he has written on this subject even though belatedly.

Thursday, 24 March 1983, Abbottabad
Munir Shah telephoned today to say that eight persons of the Tehrik-i-Istiqlal had been arrested in Peshawar yesterday including, Mukhtiar Bacha, Haji Hazrat Faqir, Khaliq Dad Khan, Amanullah Khan Mohmand. He said that the MRD in Peshawar did not take part in the proceedings, which resulted in a baton charge and then arrests. He also said that the show in Lahore in which he had taken part was very successful.

Monday, 28 March 1983, Abbottabad
Spoke to Omar who said that a number of people have my book *Generals in Politics* in Lahore. Abdul Qadir Hassan of *Nawa-i-Waqt* has written a column in today's edition entitled 'Asghar Khan in Delhi'. He has criticised me for publishing my book in India which according to him is an 'enemy' country. He writes that it would have been better if I had waited till Ziaul Haq's regime ended and then had got the book published. Strange logic. When Ziaul Haq and his cronies depart, even Abdul Qadir Hassan will be writing, criticising him for his policies and his reign of repression.

Tuesday, 29 March 1983, Abbottabad
Ziaul Haq has eulogised the services of the 22 families to the development of Pakistan (*Muslim,* 29 March 1983) and has said that the derogatory manner in which the term has been used has put the country back at least 15 years.

Friday, 1 April 1983, Abbottabad
Mushir came with Shaikh Rashid (later minister in General Musharraf's government) as his driver. Discussed the general political situation, line to be taken within the MRD and other party matters. Gave him four copies of my book for Ian Hoare of BBC who wanted these for a review of the book.

Saturday, 9 April 1983, Abbottabad
Wrote to J.A. Rahim to tell him that I liked his draft of the manifesto. Suggested a couple of changes, also told him that I thought that his press conferences on prices of oil and on the government's policy on nationalisation were very good. Amina will take the letter with her tomorrow.

Tuesday, 12 April 1983, Abbottabad
Quoting the prime minister of Afghanistan the BBC said that half the hospitals and schools in Afghanistan as well as 17 per cent of the transport system had been destroyed by the insurgents. He said that the country had suffered a loss of $300 million equivalent to the aid received by the country in twenty years.

Sunday, 24 April 1983, Abbottabad
Air Marshal Rahim Khan came to lunch. He is making a statement in reply to General Musa's statement in his book *My Version* that I had spoken to Air Marshal Arjun Singh on the telephone during the Kutch operation in April 1965.

Thursday, 28 April 1983, Abbottabad
Yesterday's *Jasarat* reported Mian Tufail Mohammad as saying that Ziaul Haq had told him that he would be releasing me very soon. If he does so, it will be the first promise that he would have kept.

Sunday, 8 May 1983, Abbottabad
Khurshid Kasuri came today. He is keen that we should try and reach an understanding with Ziaul Haq without giving up our basic stand on major issues. He is of the view that we should take part in any elections that are held even if these are for limited participation in power. Told him that all this was hypothetical and a discussion on this was premature as no one had sought our cooperation and the conditions for an election had not been spelt out. Gave Khurshid a copy of the Urdu translation of *Generals in Politics*.

Wednesday, 11 May 1983, Abbottabad
The MRD approved the 31 points which is in fact a party manifesto for a future election and a step towards an election alliance. The Tehrik-i-Istiqlal has been opposed to an election alliance and therefore to our commitment beyond the four points of the MRD. I believe that the national working committee has decided not to accept any move to enlarge the scope of the four points, which was the basis for the formation of the MRD. This development (the approval of the 31 points by the MRD) will therefore pose a problem for the Tehrik-i-Istiqlal about its continued association with the MRD.

Tuesday, 24 May 1983, Abbottabad

Zahur Butt came to visit me today. Discussed the MRD. I was of the opinion that the MRD was a non-starter. Khawaja Khairuddin was probably hand in glove with the government as were a number of its other leaders. It suited the government to have the MRD going as it is. The movement announced for 14 August would be a flop. Because (1) rains and floods are not a suitable time for a movement; (2) people would be too involved with the local bodies elections; (3) Ziaul Haq's announcement of 14 August or earlier about a future setup would divert public opinion. I also said that accepting the 31 points would be a step towards an election alliance from which it would be difficult to retract. The problem as I saw it was the lack of an alternative to martial law. The people did not accept the MRD as an alternative as they rightly felt that the MRD could not run the country in the event of martial law ending and political power being handed over to it. The Tehrik-i-Istiqlal can be the alternative if we chart our own course, work really hard and get out of this alliance of doubtful utility. The Tehrik-i-Istiqlal national working committee would be considering its future line of action in its meeting in Karachi on 9 and 10 June.

Thursday, 26 May 1983, Abbottabad

Mian Mahmud Ali Kasuri and Omar Kasuri came. We discussed MRD, local bodies elections and party elections. Mian Sahib agreed that the MRD was a dead horse and that we should get out of it. He was however anxious that we should do so in a manner that caused us the least embarrassment. Mian Sahib was in favour of taking part in local bodies elections by declaring that we should ask the people to support candidates who would fight for the people's rights. We should also put our people up for elections. He was keen on party elections without delay. I was in agreement with him on all three points.

Saturday, 28 May 1983, Abbottabad

Air Vice Marshal Akhtar died in hospital on Thursday, 26 May. Amina had called on him in CMH Rawalpindi about a month ago. Akhtar and I had joined the air force together and had served together in different places over a long period. We were in the same squadron in Burma during the Second World War. He had had some kind of glandular trouble for some years. He was a very nice man. A good friend whose death is a very sad event. I am sorry that I was unable to attend his funeral and cannot even go to offer my condolences.

Monday, 4 July 1983, Abbottabad
Sherbaz Mazari was externed from Sindh for 90 days. He will probably be confined to his village Rojhan.

Tuesday, 12 July 1983, Abbottabad
My eighth Eid in captivity.

Saturday, 23 July 1983, Abbottabad
Tehrik-i-Istiqlal's national working committee met in Karachi on 21 and 22 July. Fifteen persons attended. Syed Munir Shah presided. It was decided to remain in the MRD and not to participate in the local bodies elections.

Sunday, 24 July 1983, Abbottabad
Ziaul Haq returned to Islamabad after a five-day state visit to Japan and a shopping spree in Hong Kong. His son, a UBL employee, was given precedence after Ziaul Haq and at par with Prince Akihito, the crown prince of Japan. On arrival in Tokyo, Ziaul Haq was received by the chief of protocol and when he went to call on the emperor, he received the emperor instead of being received by him.

Wednesday, 27 July 1983, Abbottabad
Omar met Syed Munir Shah last night. He said that in the national working committee meeting in Karachi on 21 and 22 July, Rana Arshad, Khurshid Kasuri, Aitzaz Ahsan, Mahnaz Rafi, Azhar Hussain Zaidi, Nisar Khuhro, Allama Turabi and Jamali were in favour of continuing our association with the MRD and our full participation in its deliberations whereas, J.A. Rahim, Mushir Pesh Imam, Munir Shah, Mukhtar Bacha, Shahida Jameel, Imtiaz Phoolpoto, Zahoor Butt and Sahibzada Munir (special invitee) were in favour of getting out of MRD or at least not attending its meetings.

The NWC endorsed J.A. Rahim's definition of the word 'secular' which he said meant *dunyavi* or worldly and not *la deenyat* or anti-religion.

Two SAM 7 missiles are reported to have been discovered from the residence of Aftab Gul, an advocate of Lahore. He and his wife and children are in the UK. His father, a retired army major, has been arrested. SAM can be fired from the shoulder and is effective against low flying aircraft upto four kilometres. About two years ago a SAM was fired on Ziaul Haq's aircraft near Islamabad airfield but did not work.

Saturday, 30 July 1983, Abbottabad

Received a telegram and a letter from J.A. Rahim submitting his resignation because of differences with Mushir. Decided to send Omar to Karachi with letters for Rahim and Mushir.

Sunday, 31 July 1983, Abbottabad

Nawa-i-Waqt published a list of 43 army officers who had been given jobs in grade 19 and above during the last six years. This list does not include names of those given diplomatic jobs—which are numerous.

Newspapers are full of what Ziaul Haq is going to do or say on 14 August. The consensus appears to be that he will announce some changes in the 1973 constitution or at least in the election rules. Some of the conditions he is likely to impose are: (1) prescribe qualification for candidates (2) permit candidates to contest only from the constituency where their names are registered as voters (3) a candidate will not be allowed to canvas for votes or campaign outside his/her constituency (4) elections to provincial assemblies will be held in 1984 and the National Assembly in 1985.

It is said that he is likely to hold a referendum within 90 days of this announcement.

There is little doubt in my mind that anything that he does will be designed solely to keep himself in power and not to hand over power in an election held for this purpose.

Tuesday, 2 Aug 1983, Abbottabad

Reports indicate that my book *Generals in Politics* is in great demand all over the country. It has been available in bookstalls and most of them have run out of stocks.

Monday, 8 Aug 1983, Abbottabad

Newspapers say that Ziaul Haq is to address the Majlis-i-Shoora on Friday, 12 August. Is expected to make his much-trumpeted announcement about the democratisation of his regime. It is certain to be a farce. Amnesty International has asked Ziaul Haq for my release.

Wednesday, 10 Aug 1983, Abbottabad
Omar received a show cause notice from the Punjab University as to why disciplinary action should not be taken against him for allowing Samina to take part in a women's procession ostensibly against the government in February this year. Apparently there is a law that dependents of government servants cannot take part in such activities and university teachers have been classified as government employees although this was not so three years ago when Omar joined the university.

Thursday, 11 Aug 1983, Abbottabad
A large number of arrests of political workers have been made to forestall any agitation by the MRD on 14 August. Syed Munir Shah, Mukhtiar Bacha, Akhtar Mehmood, Nusrat Niaz, Parveen Asghar and Rana Arshad Khan of Tehrik-i-Istiqlal have been arrested.

The BBC announced that Haji Ghulam Ahmed Bilore, the secretary general of NDP and the current chairman of the MRD, has resigned from both the party and the MRD offices. He has done this because Ghaffar Khan had stated that the PPP is in league with the military regime. He has called upon Wali Khan to return home and save the party.

Friday, 12 Aug 1983, Abbottabad
Addressing the Shoora, Ziaul Haq announced the salient features of his framework for the formation of representative government. These are:

1. Elections to the provincial assemblies, Senate and National Assembly to be completed by 23 March 1985.
2. Martial law to remain till then.
3. The 1973 Constitution to be amended to give the president, powers to: (a) Select a prime minister. The person so selected is to obtain a vote of confidence in the National Assembly within 60 days. (b) To appoint governors, chief justice, services chiefs, election

commissioner. (c) Dismiss the prime minister if he feels that he does not enjoy the confidence of the electorate. In this event re-elections will be held within 75 days. (d) Return a bill passed by the National Assembly for re-consideration.

The president will be the supreme commander and chairman of the services chiefs committee. A national security council will be created by the president, which will decide whether a national emergency can be declared. Voting will be on the basis of adult franchise. A person will not be able to canvass for himself as this is un-Islamic. Professional people will be nominated to the assemblies (presumably by the president). These will include ulema, teachers, doctors, lawyers, industrialists, labour, farmers and women. As expected, therefore, Ziaul Haq is holding elections only in order to perpetuate himself in power.

Omar went to Rawalpindi to speak to Mahmud Durrani, Ziaul Haq's military secretary, about clemency for a labour leader (a Baloch) who has been sentenced to death for a murder he did not commit some eight years ago. He also finalised the draft reply to the show cause notice he has received from the university.

Amina received an order of the Punjab government yesterday, forbidding her entry into Punjab for three months from 1 August 1983.

J.A. Rahim issued the draft manifesto of the party at a press conference yesterday.

Saturday, 13 Aug 1983, Abbottabad
Khudai Noor, Haji Mir Tareen and Anwar Durrani of Tehrik-i-Istiqlal are reported to have been arrested in Quetta. Reaction in political circles specially in the MRD to Ziaul Haq's speech of yesterday is unfavourable.

Sunday, 14 Aug 1983, Abbottabad
Khurshid Kasuri was arrested. Demonstrations were reported in Rawalpindi and Sukkur.

Tuesday, 16 Aug 1983, Abbottabad
Disturbances and meetings continued in the country, particularly in Sindh. Rail track was removed near Ghotki, a riot took place in

Nawabshah prison, where one person was killed and six injured. Demonstrations took place in Karachi, Hyderabad, Sukkur, Dadu and Thatta. Ghulam Mustafa Jatoi and Mairaj Mohammad Khan were among those arrested.

Syed Munir Shah telephoned from Bannu to say that he was being shifted to Dera Ismail Khan jail. He did not say from where he was telephoning.

Wednesday, 17 Aug 1983, Abbottabad

Disturbances continued in Sindh. One person was killed by police firing in Dadu. Two prominent MRD leaders were arrested in Karachi (according to the BBC) where 'thousands' of people staged a demonstration. Mrs Wali Khan and a large number of people (probably of NDP) were arrested today.

Thursday, 18 Aug 1983, Abbottabad

Malik Haider Osman telephoned Ziae to say that Mushir Pesh Imam had spoken to him on the telephone and had indicated that the purpose of the national working committee meeting in Karachi tomorrow was to decide to leave the MRD. Told Ziae to telephone Malik Haider Osman, Pesh Imam, Begum Shahida Jameel (for J.A. Rahim) and convey my views, which are: (a) Fourteen members of the national working committee, mainly those in favour of remaining in the MRD, are in jail and one, Ahmed Mian, is abroad. A decision to quit the MRD in their absence would be improper. (b) To quit the MRD at this stage when it has launched a movement and many of its leaders are in jail is morally wrong and politically unsound. (c) Such a decision will be resented by those of our workers who are in jail and will be criticised by the public.

I also suggested that not only the Tehrik-i-Istiqlal should not quit but such a discussion on this subject in the national working committee in the present circumstances, would be wrong. I further suggested that instead of thinking of quitting, the members of the national working committee should take active part in the movement and get arrested.

Begum Wali Khan was arrested yesterday and has been brought to Thai Rest House, near Abbottabad.

Friday, 19 Aug 1983, Abbottabad
More arrests in Rawalpindi and Lahore. Heard that Ghaffar Khan has also been brought to Thai Rest House near Abbottabad. The BBC interviewed Wali Khan in 'Sairbeen' tonight.

Saturday, 20 Aug 1983, Abbottabad
The government banned the publication of the instalments of my book, *Generals in Politics* in the *Haider* from today.

Sunday, 21 Aug 1983, Abbottabad
The MRD movement continues. Situation in Sindh is disturbed. Demonstrations and attacks on government buildings continue. Mushir is reported to have made a statement to the press to the effect that Tehrik-i-Istiqlal workers should not court arrest. If this is correct it is likely to cause confusion and will damage the MRD movement. Zahur Butt visited Abbottabad yesterday and met Omar. I conveyed to him that this was not my thinking. Today's *Nawa-i-Waqt* therefore carried Zahur Butt's statement quoting me as saying that Tehrik-i-Istiqlal workers should take full part in the MRD movement and court arrest.

Monday, 22 Aug 1983, Abbottabad
Omar came from Rawalpindi, very excited about the way the MRD movement was building up against the military regime. He suggested that a clear lead should be given to the party. I decided to write to J.A. Rahim and gave him a letter to be sent to Rahim along with Zahur Butt tomorrow—suggested in the letter that he might appoint Asaf Vardag as secretary general in place of Mushir who is leaving in a few days for the USA for medical treatment.

Tuesday, 23 Aug 1983, Abbottabad
Mian Tufail has said that Jamaat-i-Islami will never take part in any movement against the military regime in Pakistan. (*Muslim,* 23 March 1983).

The BBC reported that a large procession of 50,000-100,000 people led by the Pir of Ranipur was taken out yesterday. Three persons were killed by police firing in Khairpur. A number of government buildings were burnt. Disturbances also took place in Hyderabad, Mirpurkhas,

Jamshoro and Shikarpur resulting in damage to government property. Amina called at the Thai Rest House gate with some fruits for Begum Nasim Wali Khan.

A serious incident took place at Khandkot in Jacobabad district, where a clash occurred between the police and the public. Firing took place from both sides and the railway station, a bank and some government buildings were burnt. Three people are reported killed. Speaking to the press in Karachi shortly after this incident, Ziaul Haq said that the situation in Sindh was to be regretted but was nothing to worry about. Some people were arrested in Karachi and a clash took place there.

Wednesday, 24 Aug 1983, Abbottabad
Gul Akbar Afridi, vice chairman Tehrik-i-Istiqlal, Peshawar, and Mohammad Hussain advocate of Tehrik-i-Istiqlal were arrested in Chowk Yadgar yesterday whilst defying martial law. A jail in Larkana district (Kambhar) was attacked yesterday and a number of prisoners freed. The Lahore-Karachi highway was blocked for some time and arrests were made in Karachi and Lahore.

Thursday, 25 Aug 1983, Abbottabad
Disturbances in Sindh continue. A railway station in Larkana district was attacked and three persons killed including one policeman.

Friday, 26 Aug to Monday, 5 Sept 1983, Abbottabad
Disturbances in Sindh, now in their third week, continue. Nothing much in Punjab, NWFP and Balochistan (except sporadic arrests) as yet.

Khawaja Humayun, general secretary Tehrik-i-Istiqlal Karachi, was arrested yesterday.

Tuesday, 6 Sept 1983, Abbottabad
Newspapers reported that Syed Munir Shah has been moved to Haripur jail from Bannu district jail. Sherbaz Mazari, currently under detention in a forest rest house in Multan district, is reported to have had a heart attack. His wife has asked that he should be shifted to the cardiovascular hospital in Karachi. My book *Generals in Politics* has been banned by the government of Punjab.

Haji Yusaf Lacewala, the president of Khairuddin Muslim League Karachi, died in Karachi jail yesterday. He was 35 and reported to have been in good health. Post mortem did not reveal anything. Prison officials say that death probably occurred because of a heart attack. His brother had however seen him the previous day and found him well.

Thursday, 8 Sept 1983, Abbottabad
Ziaul Haq visited Jacobabad amongst strict security. Daily *Haider* reported that he travelled from the airport to the town by helicopter. Addressed some 150 officers and a few councillors in the city hall. Of the 68 district councillors, only 11 were present and of the 27 city councillors only seven. The district chairman and a number of councillors have resigned. He flew to Lahore for the night.

Friday, 9 Sept 1983, Abbottabad
Ziaul Haq continued his nonsensical tour of Sindh, addressing select gatherings in rooms, flying in and out by helicopter and spending the night at Lahore. His speeches are becoming more and more intolerable. Full of Islam padded with hypocrisy. He said in Shikarpur today that whereas a civilian government could be overthrown by a movement, it was not possible to remove a military government in this manner. Demonstrations and arrests took place in many places in Sindh, Lahore and Peshawar.

Zahir Shah, Khan of Kalash and Dr Rehman Khan of Chakdarra both of Dir district were arrested in Qissa Khwani Bazaar, Peshawar, yesterday.

Saturday, 10 Sept 1983, Abbottabad
Ziaul Haq's car was stoned in Dadu today and a clash took place between the police and the demonstrators. The police fired in the air and used tear gas shells. A DSP died of heart attack and an SP suffered a heart attack. Ziaul Haq's speech on TV to a selected audience in Dadu was totally inappropriate and defensive. He said that he was willing to talk to the opposition leaders if they had any proposals — very different from his position of only two days ago.

Sunday, 11 Sept 1983, Abbottabad
A number of ladies, including Aitzaz Ahsan's mother and wife, were put under house arrest in Lahore. Mahnaz Rafi was moved to Kot Lakhpat jail.

Monday, 12 Sept 1983, Abbottabad
More trouble in Sindh. Ziaul Haq completed his tour of Sindh and expressed 'satisfaction' with the state of affairs there.

Wednesday, 14 Sept 1983, Abbottabad
B.K. Tabish, acting general secretary Punjab, was arrested in Regal Chowk, Lahore yesterday. It is reported that the army (or probably the Frontier Corp) was used to fire on a crowd in Hala yesterday. Complete strike in a number of towns in Sindh.

Saturday, 17 Sept 1983, Abbottabad
Some 72 persons, mostly Tehrik-i-Istiqlal workers, who had been arrested in Punjab, were released today including Aitzaz Ahsan, Khurshid Kasuri, Nusrat Niaz, Mahnaz Rafi and other women workers.

Sunday, 18 Sept 1983, Abbottabad
Eidul Azha. My ninth Eid in captivity. Khalid Mansur, the commissioner Hazara, and the DIG called to say 'Eid Mubarak'. The government announced that 962 persons had been released in Sindh. Do not know whether there are any Tehrik-i-Istiqlal workers amongst them.

Monday, 19 Sept 1983, Abbottabad
Lieutenant General Fazle Haq, governor NWFP, called. He was critical of Lieutenant General Abbasi, governor Sindh, for mishandling the situation and also of Ziaul Haq. Said that Ziaul Haq was thinking of sending him to Sindh or Punjab but he did not want to go. Said that Abbasi was being appointed chief of the joint staff in place of Iqbal and Rahimuddin as vice chief of army staff in place of Sawar Khan. He felt that he had better qualifications to be the VCAS than Rahimuddin.

Asked me whether I would be prepared to meet Ziaul Haq if I was called. I replied that there was nothing to talk about and since it was clear that Ziaul Haq wished to perpetuate himself in power any meeting would be futile. He then asked me what I thought should be done. I suggested the following: (a) release all political prisoners; (b) lift ban on political parties and political activity; (c) hold elections to the national and provincial assemblies in accordance with the 1973 constitution by March 1984; and (d) transfer power immediately afterwards.

Fazle Haq said that he would be seeing me again. Appeared worried. He also said that he would not ban my book in the NWFP. I wonder. Asaf Vardag came in the evening and saw Omar.

Tuesday, 20 Sept 1983, Abbottabad
Some more violations of Pakistan air space took place yesterday by the Afghan air force. On Monday, six Afghan Mig-21 aircraft had bombed a village near Parachinar.

Saturday, 24 Sept 1983, Abbottabad
Women took out a procession in Lahore today. Fourteen of them were arrested, amongst them Asma, Malik Jilani's daughter.

Sunday, 25 Sept 1983, Abbottabad
Spoke to Khurshid at Lahore to enquire about his father, Mian Mahmud Ali Kasuri's health. He said that Mian Sahib was a little better and it was being planned to shift him to Fauji Foundation hospital near Rawalpindi.

Mrs Zahur Butt (who has flown from London) telephoned from Jinnah hospital where Zahur is under treatment after his road accident. She said that his condition was critical. Telephoned Quddus and asked him to contact Dr Sulaiman who is treating him and try to do whatever is possible to help.

Tuesday, 27 Sept 1983, Abbottabad
Spoke to Quddus in the evening to enquire about Zahur Butt's condition which was slightly better. Also spoke to Mrs Butt. The doctor thought that it should be possible to move him to the UK in six weeks time and he should be on his feet in six months time.

Thursday, 29 Sept 1983, Abbottabad

The BBC reported that an armed encounter took place near Qazi Ahmed in Sindh between a civilian crowd and the army. It is reported that people had obstructed the road and when the army tried to clear the obstructions they were fired upon in which one soldier was killed. The army then fired back by which, according to a government announcement, 17 people were killed. However, local newsmen reported that 30 people were killed. During the local bodies elections which were taking place in Karachi and in some of the districts in Sindh some persons were wounded by firing and a police station was burnt. In Sukkur and Jacobabad too, armed conflict took place between the public and the police. In Multan yesterday when local bodies elections took place in Punjab, four persons were killed in a clash with the police. The BBC reported that the turnout in Karachi and other cities of Sindh was about 30 per cent but was even lower in the rural areas. In some places there was no polling at all. Firing by the army could have serious consequences.

Friday, 30 Sept 1983, Abbottabad

Spoke to Omar in the morning. The Punjab government has announced that the Punjab University and the colleges will open tomorrow. Omar says that tension is growing in Lahore.

The BBC said that the army had opened fire with a machine gun when over 30 persons were killed near Qazi Ahmed yesterday. Eight more people are reported to have died in hospital since. Three soldiers were reported killed. Arrests and disturbances continued in the country, particularly in Sindh today. Yesterday in an article by Hamlin on the situation in Sindh *The Times* of London said that Punjab has not stirred as yet but since the road and rail communications between Karachi and the north are interrupted, it is likely to scream for democracy when shops run out of supplies and petrol pumps are without petrol. A very fair assessment.

Saturday, 1 Oct 1983, Abbottabad

Mrs Nisar Khuhro telephoned from Karachi to say that her husband was arrested last night in Larkana and Imdad Chandio in Warah (Larkana district). Casper Weinberger, the US defence secretary, is on a 36-hour visit to Pakistan. Whilst addressing refugees in a camp near

Peshawar he promised increased aid to the mujahideen fighting against the Russian and Afghan forces in Afghanistan.

Spoke to Zahur Butt's mother at Karachi. She said that Zahur is much better now.

Sunday, 2 Oct 1983, Abbottabad
The second phase of local bodies elections took place in Sindh. Elections were held in two phases to redeploy the police and the army. The BBC reported that voter's turnout in the rural areas was 5 per cent. At some stations there was no voting at all. A clash took place with the army at Moro where the road had been blocked. Seven people were reported killed. At 30 other places, government buildings were attacked. Bomb explosions took place in Larkana and Khairpur.

Rahim Bux Soomro appeared on TV. It was a ten minute programme. His speech had been heavily edited and he spoke for only four minutes. Both the start and the finish were very abrupt and had obviously been cut.

Monday, 3 Oct 1983, Abbottabad
Mrs Nisar Khuhro telephoned from Karachi to say that Imdad Chandio had been beaten badly in the Larkana police station and that her husband was probably being released in a day or two.

My book *Generals in Politics* was banned in the NWFP last week. It has already been banned in the other provinces earlier. When he met me on 19 September, Fazle Haq had said that he would not ban my book in the NWFP. Another promise broken.

Omar telephoned Amina to say that Ahmed Raza Khan Kasuri is planning to offer arrest and wants to announce his plan of joining the Tehrik-i-Istiqlal before he courts arrest.

Disturbances continued in Sindh. Four soldiers and seven civilians were reported killed in Moro in an armed clash today.

Tuesday, 4 Oct 1983, Abbottabad
Nisar Khuhro telephoned on being released. Imdad Hussain Chandio is still in police lockup and Nisar confirmed that he had been beaten and tortured by the police. Shams Khan Cholani and his son Haji Khan both of Tehrik-i-Istiqlal were arrested with them and are also in the police lockup.

The BBC reported that ten persons were killed including two soldiers when a clash took place in Larkana district when people were going from Mirpur Bhutto to Ratodero to take part in a public meeting and were stopped from going there.

Friday, 7 Oct 1983, Abbottabad
Omar's article 'Economic implications of political discontent' appeared in the *Muslim* today. He had analysed the economic impact on the country, if the present situation continues in Sindh.

The BBC reported a clash between the police and demonstrations after Eid prayers in Quetta. It is believed that at least one person was killed as a result of police firing.

Monday, 10 Oct 1983, Abbottabad
Ahmed Mian Soomro came today. Asked me whether he should court arrest. Told him that he should, and should also tell Qazi Hafizur Rehman, Khaliq G. Khan and Sahibzada Munir to do likewise. He said that he would court arrest in Jacobabad on 16 October. Heard from him that Rao Yaqub, our chairman Nawabshah district, had been arrested and is in Nawabshah jail. Ahmed Mian is planning that Qazi Hafizur Rehman should court arrest on the day following his arrest and should be followed by others. He said that he would also ask Chaudhri Jameel to court arrest.

Tuesday, 11 Oct 1983, Abbottabad
Maulana Shah Ahmed Noorani and four others of JUP had a meeting with Ziaul Haq yesterday. It appears that nothing was agreed except that further talks may take place. Ziaul Haq has indicated that he will be holding talks with other political leaders within the next four days. The BBC in its evening news said that he intends holding talks with six political parties, three of whom are in the MRD. The BBC further said that these parties were PDP, NDP and Tehrik-i-Istiqlal.

Thursday, 13 Oct 1983, Abbottabad
Maulana Noorani has accused Ziaul Haq of bad faith. He said that contrary to the assurance given to him that his point of view on the talks will be allowed to be published in the newspapers, the government instructed the press to publish only the version given to them by the

government-controlled news agencies. He said that Ziaul Haq does not seem to want to part with power and was holding talks to buy time. Jamiatul Ulema-i-Islam (Darkhwasti group) delegation which was to meet Ziaul Haq today refused to do so at the last minute. Reasons given were that the government had not allowed Maulana Noorani's press statement to be published in the papers and that the leader of the delegation, Maulana Obaidullah Anwer, had suddenly developed heart trouble. The BBC said that this was a setback for the martial law government. Disturbances and arrests continued in Sindh today.

Friday, 14 Oct 1983, Abbottabad
The NWFP working committee of Tehrik-i-Istiqlal held a meeting today. Today's newspapers reported that Ziaul Haq has invited the Jamaat-i-Islami, Pagara Muslim League, Khaksars (Ashraf Khan), Maulana Kausar Niazi's Progressive People's Party and Sardar Qayyum's Muslim Conference to meet him for discussions during the next few days. The BBC reported that some lawyers have been arrested in Lahore to pre-empt the demonstration being arranged by the lawyers on 19 October in Lahore.

Saturday, 15 Oct 1983, Abbottabad
General Arif (Ziaul Haq's chief of staff) telephoned to say that he would like to call on me tomorrow morning. I complete my fourth year of detention tomorrow (I was arrested and placed in detention on 16 October 1979).

Aitzaz Ahsan was arrested today on his way from Lahore to Faisalabad. A Muslim League delegation had talks with Ziaul Haq today.

Sunday, 16 Oct 1983, Abbottabad
Lieutenant General K.M. Arif, chief of staff to Ziaul Haq, came this morning and stayed for three hours. He explained that Ziaul Haq wanted to meet me but Arif had suggested that he (Arif) should see me first. He briefed me about the meeting with JUP and with Pagara Muslim League.

The JUP wanted elections early and had said that they were ready for elections at three months notice. They had suggested that either registered parties only or all parties should be allowed to take part. They were prepared for either alternative. Pir of Pagara wanted at least one year for elections but would prefer if power was transferred to his party so that he could hold the elections under a national government to be formed by him.

Arif said that Ziaul Haq had an open mind. He would be prepared to hold elections on a party basis but would prefer if the first election was held on non-party basis so that these are held without the turmoil and emotion associated with party elections. The 'Supreme Security Council', he explained, was meant only to advise the president on one or two matters. One of these was the need for the imposition of a state of emergency. He said that except for the chairman of the joint chiefs of staff and the three services chiefs, the other dozen or so would be civilians, that is, four or five ministers, the speaker of the National Assembly, the chairman of the Senate, the chief justice of the Supreme Court, one or two other judges and a couple of others. About the date of elections too, he said that Ziaul Haq had an open mind and these could be held earlier than March 1985. This was only the date before which he was committed to hold elections. He said that they were afraid that if they announced the date too early, it will generate 'election fever' which would create problems, as had happened, he said, in Yahya Khan's time who had allowed one year for campaigning.

He said that Ziaul Haq had asked him to elicit my views on these different possibilities. I told him that I had been effectively isolated for full four years—by a strange coincidence it was exactly four years ago today, that I was arrested—and was not in a position to make any commitment on behalf of my party in the present circumstances. Moreover, I said that ours was a democratic party and I could take no step without a mandate from my party. In addition to my party, it was also necessary to consult the other parties in the MRD, with whom we were now associated. Arif asked me to give the names of these persons whom I would like to meet. The government, he said, would be happy to make my meeting with them possible. I explained that it was not a question of meeting a dozen or even twenty or thirty people. I had been isolated for so long that I would have to move around and meet my workers and those of other parties to get a feel of the situation. When asked what I would then suggest I said that the least the government should do was that political activity should be allowed, limited at first if necessary, and all political prisoners should be released. Only then was a fruitful dialogue possible.

On being repeatedly assured about Ziaul Haq's sincerity and determination to restore democracy I said that my own understanding of the situation was that Ziaul Haq and the junta did not intend handing over real power to the elected representatives of the people. I said that any dialogue could only be held if we were persuaded to believe that the general's junta really wanted to shed power. I said that I had an open mind and was willing to change my views but only if given sound reasons and if their professions were backed by meaningful acts. Ziaul Haq's pronouncements, I said, should have convinced any sensible person that he did not want to leave. General Arif said that he had read my book and was aware of my views about them but would like to assure me that they did not want to hang on to power. I told him that the other point I wished to make was that their approach and the slow speed with which they were moving made me feel that events would overtake them before they could go through with their programme and that they may never be able to hold any meaningful elections if they went about things as they were doing now. The same familiar story of too little too late.

General Arif then told me that he had benefited greatly by his talks with me and would suggest that I should meet Ziaul Haq and tell him all this myself. I said that for this Ziaul Haq would have to visit me here as he (Arif) had done. He indicated that this might be possible.

Some other points made by General Arif were: (a) They had seen some messages exchanged between the Soviet Union and India about the situation in Sindh and were concerned with the contents. (b) The PPP or at least a section of it were not interested in participating in elections.

I told Arif when he left that I would be releasing a brief statement to the press about our meeting. He said that he had no objection.

Tuesday, 18 Oct 1983, Abbottabad
Ziaul Haq held talks with Khaksars and Jamiat Ahle Hadis. Allama Ehsan Elahi Zaheer was not in the Ahle Hadis delegation.

Wednesday, 19 Oct 1983, Abbottabad
Today was the lawyers' protest day against the martial law regime. A clash took place with the police in the premises of the Lahore High Court when lawyers tried to take out a procession. Police threw stones

and bricks at the lawyers and baton charged them. A number of lawyers, amongst them Dr Parvez Hassan and Omar Kasuri of Tehrik-i-Istiqlal, were injured. Some lawyers were taken into custody. Lawyers protest meetings and processions took places in other parts of the country. Lawyers clashed with the police in Karachi too, where the president of the High Court Bar Association and some others were arrested.

Lieutenant General Faiz Ali Chishti announced his decision to join the Azad Jammu and Kashmir Muslim Conference of Chaudhri Noor Hussain at a public meeting in Mirpur, Azad Kashmir.

In an attempt to round-up some people, a clash took place near Qazi Ahmed in Sindh. Twelve persons are reported killed, amongst them some men of the Frontier Constabulary.

Thursday, 20 Oct 1983, Abbottabad

An interesting article appeared in the *Jang* yesterday (by Irshad Ahmad Haqqani) about my meeting with General Arif. The meeting appears to have aroused considerable interest. It has been the subject of comment by the BBC daily since 16 October.

Omar telephoned to say that Ahmed Mian Soomro had telephoned him this morning to say that he was courting arrest at 13:00 today in Jacobabad. Amina spoke to Dr Parvez Hassan at Lahore about yesterday's incident in which he had been injured. Heard later that Ahmed Mian Soomro had been taken into custody in the main bazaar in Jacobabad when he defied martial law orders.

Instructed Ziae to telephone Malik Haider Usman, Mehar Rafiq Joota and Azhar Zaidi (all members of the national working committee) to get themselves arrested by 25 October. Will be instructing four or five persons daily for courting arrest—priority being given to national working committee members and prominent office bearers.

Friday, 21 Oct 1983, Abbottabad

A German, Wolfgang Freiherr Von Erffa, walked in to see me. The police could not react in time. However, I explained to him that I was under detention and his coming here might put him in trouble with the authorities. He said that he was connected with the CDU, a German political party and wanted to talk with me about Pakistan. I persuaded him to leave.

Qazi Hafizur Rehman, general secretary Tehrik-i-Istiqlal, Sindh, offered himself for arrest in Shikarpur today and was taken into custody.

Saturday, 22 Oct 1983, Abbottabad
Ziaul Haq addressed the eighth session of the Majlis-i-Shoora. It appears that he has learnt no lessons. He said that there was no room for political parties in Islam and asked his Shoora to reconsider its earlier recommendations.

Monday, 24 Oct 1983, Abbottabad
Lieutenant General Arif is reported to have met Nawabzada Nasrullah Khan at his residence in Khangarh where he is under detention. Nasrullah Khan's reply was, it is reported, similar to mine, that is, release of political prisoners and revival of political parties before any talks could take place. He is reported to have said that these can only be on the holding of elections on the basis of the 1973 constitution.

Tuesday, 25 Oct 1983, Abbottabad
A spokesman of the information ministry told the press yesterday that 4,070 people had been arrested since the MRD movement started in mid-August and 52 had been killed. Of those arrested, he said, 1,783 were still in jail. Of those killed, eight were policemen and one an army man. So far 115 Tehrik-i-Istiqlal workers have been arrested of whom 33 have been released. Chaudhri Jameel offered himself for arrest in Karachi yesterday and was taken into custody. More Tehrik-i-Istiqlal workers were arrested in Gujranwala and Sialkot.

The BBC said that a spokesman of the Pakistan government had denied that any meeting had taken place between Lieutenant General Arif and Nawabzada Nasrullah Khan. This is odd since the reports of this meeting have been appearing prominently in the national press for the last two days.

Wednesday, 26 Oct 1983, Abbottabad
Mehar Rafiq Joota has announced that he will be courting arrest today in the district courts in Multan. A procession of railway and factory workers was taken out in Lahore. The BBC reported that 10,000 people took part. The police did not interfere. Though the procession

was primarily for presenting the workers' demand for increased salaries and allowances, the processionists shouted anti-martial law slogans.

Thursday, 27 Oct 1983, Abbottabad

Today's reports indicate that the railway workers procession yesterday in Lahore was a very different story than that reported by the BBC. Police resorted to baton charge. Bashir Zafar, a Lahore leader, was injured and workers burnt buses, cars and petrol pumps. Trouble started when the police tried to confine them to the railway station premises. They eventually broke out and went to the Lahore streets. An effigy of Ziaul Haq was burnt and it was clearly an anti-martial law demonstration.

Mehar Rafiq tried to court arrest but was not taken into custody. He addressed a fairly large gathering in the district court premises in Multan. Tajammul Iqbal, acting general secretary of Tehrik-i-Istiqlal, Punjab, courted arrest in Faisalabad yesterday.

Friday, 28 Oct 1983, Abbottabad

Ghaus Bux Bizenjo left his village Nal where he had been confined and was re-arrested about 30 miles away. He was brought back and is now detained in a rest house in Khuzdar.

Saturday, 29 Oct 1983, Abbottabad

Mian Tufail Mohammad of the Jamaat-i-Islami was asked to leave Balochistan today. He addressed a meeting in Quetta yesterday and is reported to have been critical of the martial law government. He was in any case due to leave Quetta today and his externment order is meant to confer some respectability on the Jamaat-i-Islami because Mian Tufail and his party are hand in glove with Ziaul Haq.

Sunday, 30 Oct 1983, Abbottabad

Omar telephoned to say that he has been served with a show cause notice by the university authorities to explain why he should not be dismissed from service for his alleged involvement in the labour demonstration in Lahore on 26 October. The notice says that Omar instigated a group of students to damage government and public property. Omar is to appear before a board on 1 November.

Monday, 31 Oct 1983, Abbottabad

Spoke to Omar. He is appearing tomorrow before the university professor appointed to hear his reply to the charges made against him and intends asking for more time (ten days) to prepare a proper reply to the charges levelled against him.

Tuesday, 1 Nov 1983, Abbottabad

Spoke to Omar. He was told today that he could have another 24 hours for his reply. So he will be re-appearing tomorrow before the professor appointed to hear his reply. It is obvious that the authorities have already decided what to do and are going through the necessary formalities. Omar said that he will stay on in Lahore for a few more days, until this matter is settled one way or the other.

Mrs Nisar Khuhro telephoned to say that her husband had been taken away by the police.

Wednesday, 2 Nov 1983, Abbottabad

Mrs Nisar Khuhro telephoned to say that her husband and Zia Ahmed Jalbani, our chairman, Larkana district, have been put in the Larkana district jail.

Omar gave his written reply to the charges against him today. He was told that the authorities' decision will be made known to him possibly by Saturday, 5 November.

Friday, 4 Nov 1983, Abbottabad

Omar telephoned to say that he has been served a notice under martial law 51 asking him to explain within seven days why he should not be dismissed from service. He is preparing his reply.

Saturday, 5 Nov 1983, Abbottabad

Omar arrived last night. Discussed with him the reply that he will be submitting to the martial law administrator Punjab (Zone A) on 10 November.

Shahida Jameel telephoned to say that Aslam Qureshi of Tehrik-i-Istiqlal (Nazimabad) courted arrest in Karachi today.

Sunday, 6 Nov 1983, Abbottabad
Spoke to Mrs Nisar Khuhro. Khuhro and Zia Jalbani have been shifted to Sukkur jail where according to Mrs Khuhro some prisoners are being tortured and where political prisoners were beaten.

Monday, 7 Nov 1983, Abbottabad
The BBC reported this morning that a riot had taken place in Sukkur jail where about a 100 political prisoners are lodged. They were baton charged by the police who also resorted to firing in the air.

Wednesday, 9 Nov 1983, Abbottabad
Spoke to Omar. He has written out his reply to the notice received by him from the martial law administrator Zone A (Lieutenant General Ghulam Jilani Khan) and will be submitting it tomorrow. The university authorities are also proceeding with the case against him and have asked him to produce his witnesses on Saturday, 12 November.

Today's *Muslim* reported that Rais Maula Bux Korai, a prominent member of Tehrik-i-Istiqlal Moro, was shot dead by dacoits yesterday.

Thursday, 10 Nov 1983, Abbottabad
Speaking in the Shoora Mahmud Haroon, said that 61 persons had been killed and 200 injured in the recent disturbances in Sindh. Of these, he said, 25 per cent were people of the security forces. He also disclosed that 4,691 people had been arrested of whom 2,121 had been released. There were 2,570 still in detention. These figures are on the low side. The number killed, according to reliable unofficial sources, is over 250 and the number of those jailed is also greater.

Friday, 11 Nov 1983, Abbottabad
Omar handed in his reply yesterday to the martial law administrator's charges.

Abdul Haye, general secretary, Tehrik-i-Istiqlal, Abbottabad district, telephoned to say that Lala Iqbal had courted arrest in Mansehra today and Mushtaq Hussain Khan (chairman of Mansehra district) and Shah Jehan Khan had been taken into custody by the police.

Saturday, 12 Nov 1983, Abbottabad
A number of demonstrations were held against the martial law regime in Sindh and some other parts of the country today. A large number of arrests, baton charge and clashes took place in Karachi, Dadu, Hyderabad, Mirpurkhas, Sukkur, Khairpur, Lahore and Peshawar. In Peshawar 20 lawyers were reported arrested.

Tuesday, 15 Nov 1983, Abbottabad
Shaikh Sharif, the chairman Jhang city and acting chairman Punjab, courted arrest at Lakhshmi Chowk in Lahore today.

Friday, 18 Nov 1983, Abbottabad
Asaf Vardag, the acting secretary general of the party, was arrested in Rawalpindi on his return from a tour of Kohat, Bannu and D.I. Khan.

Saturday, 19 Nov 1983, Abbottabad
Jamiat-ul-Ulema-i-Pakistan started their anti-government movement yesterday by addressing Friday congregations on the role of martial law and the problems facing the people. The MRD continues to offer arrests but its tempo has slowed down considerably.

Sunday, 20 Nov 1983, Abbottabad
Colonel Hassan Khan of Gilgit, who had joined the Tehrik-i-Istiqlal some six years ago, died yesterday. He and I were at the Indian Military Academy (Dehra Dun) together.

Tuesday, 29 Nov 1983, Abbottabad
Omar telephoned in the afternoon to say that he received his dismissal orders when he returned after lecturing at the Administrative Staff College. This is not unexpected.

Amina, accompanied by Begum Bakhtiar, Nawabzada Bakhtiar and Ziae visited the families of Sadiq Shad and Lala Iqbal at Mansehra. They are in Haripur jail. She has met Mushtaq and his wife in Abbottabad hospital and has spoken to Mrs Shah Jehan at Haripur. Her husband, an advocate, is also in Haripur jail and Mrs Shah Jehan has been there for the last three days trying to see her husband.

Thursday, 1 Dec 1983, Abbottabad
Shahida Jameel telephoned to say that her husband Chaudhri Jamil has been awarded three months RI and Rs50,000 fine. If he fails to pay the fine he will have to undergo another nine months RI. Chaudhri Jameel was arrested or rather courted arrest in Karachi on 24 October.

Friday, 2 Dec 1983, Abbottabad
Amina left for Lahore this morning. She called on Mrs Asaf Vardag, Mrs Gulzar (wife of one of our arrested workers) and Mrs Nadir Parvez. Nadir Parvez was released today.

Nisar Khuhro telephoned from Larkana to say that he and Zia Jalbani had been released from Sukkur central jail. Imdad Chandio had been tried and awarded one year's RI, 15 lashes and Rs50,000 fine. Qazi Hafizur Rehman is also being tried. He is lodged in Sukkur district jail. Imtiaz Phoolpoto is in Karachi central jail.

Thursday, 15 Dec 1983, Abbottabad
While speaking to the press in Lahore yesterday Ziaul Haq indicated that he would not be releasing Nasrullah Khan, Benazir Bhutto and myself as yet. This could however mean that he could be releasing us shortly. His reputation for not doing what he says he will do, is now well established. However it does not mean that he will always do whatever he says he will not do. Rather complicated but that is just how Ziaul Haq is. He loves tying others in knots and in the process ties himself too.

Wednesday, 21 Dec 1983, Abbottabad
Ziaul Haq addressed a public meeting in Multan today with government managed arrangements: arches, buntings, street dancers, cheer leaders and other paraphernalia that surpassed anything that his predecessors— Ayub Khan or Bhutto—had ever done. This meeting must have cost the government a lot of money that could have been better spent (*Dawn* of 22 December reported attendance as 75,000 men).

Thursday, 22 Dec 1983, Abbottabad
The BBC in its evening Urdu service (Sairbeen) said that the *Guardian* had published a letter written by the head of the economics department of Essex University and three other professors, protesting against the

dismissal of Omar by the martial law administrator, Punjab, early this month. The BBC said that Omar had been victimised for his liberal democratic views and for standing upto the pressures and interference in university affairs of a 'fundamentalist religious party'. It praised Omar as an outstanding student from Pakistan who had studied at Essex University.

Sunday, 25 Dec 1983, Abbottabad
Quaid-i-Azam's 107th birthday today was celebrated with the usual hypocrisy and profession of pious intent.

Saturday, 31 Dec 1983, Abbottabad
An earthquake today. It was quite widespread and damage in NWFP, Northern India and Central Asia was reported by the BBC. About eight people are reported killed near Peshawar and one in Chitral. However more damage and deaths are expected as the full effect is known in a couple of days. Incidentally the earthquake which caused major damage and about 5,000 deaths in the Northern Areas in 1974 also occurred on 31 December.

So ended 1983, a turbulent year, during which the people of Pakistan stirred but not sufficiently to make a dent in the military regime of Ziaul Haq. Exploitation in the name of Islam continues and it will be some time before the people shake off the coterie of generals who are riding on the nation's back.

Diary 1984

Wednesday, 4 Jan 1984, Abbottabad
Mushir brought a letter from J.A. Rahim suggesting that I should, if asked, not refuse to negotiate with Ziaul Haq. He is of the view that Ziaul Haq should be told to quit and leave the country.

Thursday, 5 Jan 1984, Abbottabad
Mr Catchpole, my old teacher at the RIMC Dehra Dun and now at the Abbottabad Public School, came to tea and brought three bottles of honey.

Today's *Dawn* reported that the government has withdrawn its orders against landlords, when the movement in Sindh was at its height. Ziaul Haq ordered a review of the implementation of the 1959 and 1972 land reforms with a view to ascertaining whether landlords had circumvented these reforms. This was meant to put pressure on the feudal elements in the PPP who had played a leading role in the MRD movement. This had the desired effect. Ghulam Mustafa Jatoi of PPP and Abid Zuberi of NDP, both now in jail, have come out with statements advocating negotiations with the government. Zuberi has, in a letter to the acting secretary general of the MRD, Malik Qasim, said that a continuance of the movement would endanger the feudal socio-economic order, suggesting that the present social order should be maintained. Zuberi has also said that the US had let the MRD leadership down suggesting that there was some link between some of the MRD leadership and elements in the US administration. Both these statements are amazing. The Tehrik-i-Istiqlal cannot be a party to either. It stands for radical changes in the present socio-economic order and cannot involve itself in any move to solicit outside support or act as an agent of a foreign power. If Zuberi's letter is genuine (a copy was given to me by Mushir Pesh Imam yesterday which was handed over by Zuberi to Mehfooz Yar Khan but is unsigned) and if it is not disowned by the MRD it would be difficult for Tehrik-i-Istiqlal to continue its association with it for very long. Today was late Zulfikar Ali Bhutto's birthday.

Friday, 6 Jan 1984, Abbottabad
Wrote a letter to J.A. Rahim to communicate my views on Abid Zuberi's (central information secretary, NDP) letter written from Hyderabad jail. His letter makes shocking reading.

Wednesday, 11 Jan 1984, Abbottabad
Benazir Bhutto has arrived in Geneva. She issued a statement on her departure from Karachi saying that she will be running the party from abroad in consultation with her mother and Shaikh Rashid, the party's senior vice chairman who is in Bulgaria. A unique situation in which three sick persons will be running a political party from exile. This could only happen in the PPP.

Thursday, 12 Jan 1984, Abbottabad
Omar telephoned Dr Parvez Hassan and asked him to speak to the home secretary so that Amina's programme to visit Faisalabad and Sargodha tomorrow is not interrupted. I advised Amina to come back directly tomorrow if the authorities are adamant in not allowing her to proceed to Faisalabad. However she was determined to go to Faisalabad.

Saturday, 14 Jan 1984, Abbottabad
Amina returned after a six-day tour of Gujrat, Gujranwala, Lahore, Quetta, Multan and Faisalabad. She met workers and their wives at these places and felt that the tour was useful.

Saturday 11 Feb 1984, Abbottabad
Lahore *Jang* reported that the local administration had switched off the microphone during Omar's speech at Tando Kolachi near Jhuddo in Mirpurkhas district, ostensibly because he was speaking against the government.

Thursday, 16 Feb 1984, Abbottabad
Wrote to the 13 electors of the party president (in accordance with the modified procedure) that I did not wish to contest the election and was not a candidate for the post. Ahmed Mian Soomro telephoned complaining about J.A. Rahim. He sounded very excited.

Monday, 27 Feb 1984, Abbottabad
Sent my proposal for the holding of party election from *halqa* level upwards to provincial level. This proposal is better than the earlier one in which elections were proposed from top to bottom. This is more logical, more democratic and can be completed in a shorter time. Omar's article on government policy about students unions, 'Can banning solve the problem', appeared in the daily *Muslim* today.

Thursday, 1 March 1984, Abbottabad
Ayub Awan came. Told me that chief secretary Jamil Ahmed of the Balochistan government had been sacked last year because he had been told by the governor to do everything necessary to make people on the government approved list (to be given to him) win the

forthcoming election. This he had refused to do. Governor Rahimuddin had therefore removed him from his post. Ziaul Haq had sent for Jamil Ahmed later and told him that he was 'arrogant'.

Saturday, 3 March 1984, Abbottabad

Received a letter from J.A. Rahim saying that whilst he believes in democracy in the country, he does not believe in democracy within the party. He wrote that he will resign from the party if it disagrees with him or criticises him for the actions that he has taken during his tenure as acting president. With this attitude it will indeed be difficult for him to continue in the party.

Lieutenant General Rahimuddin and K.M. Arif are being appointed chairman joint chief of staff and vice chief of army staff respectively on 22 March 1984. The first is largely a ceremonial post and the second a sensitive appointment at the seat of power, the GHQ. Rahimuddin was governor of Balochistan and K.M. Arif was chief of staff to Ziaul Haq. Generals Iqbal and Sawar Khan, the present incumbents of these two posts, are being retired but no doubt they will be suitably accommodated.

Monday, 5 March 1984, Abbottabad

Sent the list of nominations to the national working committee to Mushir, J.A. Rahim and Khurshid. Also replied to J.A. Rahim's letter of 28 February about 'democracy' in the Tehrik-i-Istiqlal.

Ziaul Haq dismissed Abbasi (Nawab of Bahawalpur), Rao Farman Ali and Naseeruddin Jogezai from his cabinet yesterday after showering praises on them, in his usual hypocritical manner, for the 'great services' rendered by them to Pakistan.

Saturday, 10 March 1984, Abbottabad

Tariq (my brother) was told by the AC Nowshera (who is a friend of his) that each *tehsil* in the NWFP has been allotted a quota of 10,000 men to be brought to Peshawar for Ziaul Haq's so-called public meeting due on 12 March. Abbottabad district has been allotted 100 buses to transport people for the meeting. The army will provide 20,000 men in civilian clothes and the police 10,000. Buses and trucks are required to make themselves available for transporting people and anyone who does not do this will have his registration of the vehicle impounded.

Monday, 12 March 1984, Abbottabad

Ziaul Haq addressed a meeting in Peshawar stadium today. The BBC reported that 40-50,000 people were present. Slogans were raised against Ziaul Haq and crowd was baton charged. Some students were arrested and beaten by the police.

Sunday, 18 March 1984, Abbottabad

A military court in Peshawar sentenced some students of the Islami Jamiat Tulaba to up to one-year's imprisonment, lashes and fine (in one case of Rs100,000). This should bring the Jamaat-i-Islami to its senses though I do not think that even this will end their long flirtation with Ziaul Haq. The students are accused of rowdyism in the university, attacking the vice chancellor's office, stoning of government and police vehicles and creating disturbances in Ziaul Haq's public meeting on 12 March.

In its issue of 15 March 1984, *The Financial Times* of London has commented on my struggle for democracy, and Ziaul Haq's plans for strangulation of democracy in Pakistan.

Friday, 23 March 1984, Abbottabad

Pakistan Day. More generals and air marshals promoted. A lot of people in jail. Did not listen to Ziaul Haq's harangue on TV. Amina telephoned (from Lahore) to enquire whether I had been released. Someone had told her this would be done on 23 March; obviously this person did not say which year.

Worked out the percentage votes cast in the local bodies polls in August 1983 in Abbottabad district. From figures supplied by the local government office dealing with this subject, the figure was 22.26 per cent for the district of Abbottabad. Out of 30 seats 29 were contested and 2,06,905 persons voted. Total voters in the 29 constituencies were 929,306. Abbottabad district is fairly typical of NWFP except that I think that the percentage of votes cast in the trans-Indus districts would have been less. People have a personal interest in local bodies elections, as in most areas they know the candidates personally. In national and provincial elections that relationship is not there and if a full campaign, i.e. processions and public meetings are not allowed, the enthusiasm is not likely to be aroused sufficiently and the percentage of votes cast will be much lower.

Saturday, 31 March 1984, Abbottabad

Party elections were held on the second day of the national working committee meeting in Peshawar today. All members except those in prison (Khan Mohammad Jamali, Phoolpota, Khudai Noor) and Zahur Butt who is in the (UK) and of course myself, attended. Mian Mahmud Ali Kasuri was elected acting party president.

Amina arrived late in the evening with Nisar Khuhro and Imdad Hussain Chandio. They told me that J.A. Rahim was very upset at not being elected vice president. Those elected were:

Vice Presidents	Mian Mahmud Ali Kasuri, Mushir Pesh Imam, Mir Haji Tareen
Secretary General	Asaf Vardag
Information Secretary	Khurshid Kasuri
Joint Secretaries	Qazi Hafizur Rahman, Rana Mohammad Arshad Khan, Qalbi-i-Raza Fouladi, Shaukat Nawaz
Treasurer	Dr Parvez Hassan

Sunday, 1 April 1984, Abbottabad

Wazir Ali and Parvez Hassan came today. Had useful discussion with them about forming of planning teams, which the national working committee has asked me to do. Finalised the list except for a few names. Wazir Ali wants to come again to discuss the desirability of taking part in a Ziaul Haq election. He thinks that we should take part in any circumstances. He will be coming again to discuss this.

Monday, 2 April 1984, Abbottabad

Spoke to Omar. He said that *Jang* (Lahore) had quoted J.A. Rahim as saying that the Tehrik-i-Istiqlal elections held in Peshawar on 31 March were rigged, in which money played a part and as a result *waderas* (feudal lords) had been given offices. He is reported to have said that he would decide in a few days whether he should stay in the party or leave. The accusation about rigging and money having been used is totally baseless and about *waderas* equally untrue. It appears that this was Rahim's first experience of a party election and that he is still suffering from a PPP hangover. If he had won the election he would have found it fair. A sad reflection on a man who apart from his cranky nature could, because of his undoubted intellect, have contributed something to the party's thinking.

Tuesday, 10 April, Abbottabad

Khurshid Kasuri and Rana Arshad of Sahiwal came. Discussed the advisability of Tehrik-i-Istiqlal taking part in future elections, MRD and other related matters. Khurshid was keen that we should take part in any kind of election that Ziaul Haq would hold. If we were given a long period of campaigning we should stand alone and if the period of campaigning was short (as he thought that it was likely to be) we should enter into an alliance with MRD parties. I explained my point of view that: (1) I was not in favour of taking part in any election which was not for real transfer of power. (2) Ziaul Haq would not part with power so there is no point in taking part in his future election. (3) If we took part in an election which was not for transfer of power we would prolong martial law and the Tehrik-i-Istiqlal's image would be irreparably damaged. (4) Ziaul Haq would give very little time for campaigning and the turnout, if we boycotted the election, would be low. I also told Khurshid that unless I was persuaded to believe that was wrong, I would oppose any decision of the national working committee to the contrary and would not myself associate with any farcical electoral process.

Thursday, 12 April 1984, Abbottabad

Telephoned Syed Munir Shah to say that I liked his letter to Altaf Hassan Qureshi of *Urdu Digest* declining his invitation to attend his conference in which Ziaul Haq was to be the main speaker. Munir Shah had written that he could not attend a conference on national unity to which Ziaul Haq, who is the symbol of national confusion and disunity, had been invited.

Sunday, 15 April 1984, Abbottabad

Received a letter from J.A. Rahim informing me that he is leaving the party. He does not believe in running the party democratically and could not accept his defeat in the party elections (on 31 March) in which he was a candidate for the post of vice president—which he lost by two votes.

Monday, 23 April 1984, Abbottabad

Dr Ahmad Hassan Kamal came to see me today. Omar is planning to start an Urdu weekly with Kamal's help on socio-economic problems of Pakistan. Dr Ahmad Hassan was running a magazine *Naqeeb-i-Islam* for Jamiatul Ulama-i-Islam for some years, between 1962–72. An experienced political worker with progressive views. He is a political writer and has been doing very useful work for the Tehrik-i-Istiqlal during the last few months.

Monday, 30 April 1984, Abbottabad

Omar's writ against his dismissal by Punjab University was heard by the Lahore High Court and the advocate general was asked to explain some points. Another hearing has been fixed for a later date.

Sunday, 6 May 1984, Abbottabad

Omar's article 'Jamaat-i-Islami in historical perspective' appeared in the *Muslim* today. It is a very good analysis of the Jamaat's philosophy and aims, and is a part of the chapter that Omar is writing for the book, *Islam, Politics and the State*, that I am editing. Sent Omar two chapters, 'The lighter side of the power game' for publication in a newspaper. They will serve as an introduction to this book.

Thursday, 8 May 1984, Abbottabad

The MRD's central committee met in Lahore yesterday and decided to admit the NAP (Pakhtunkhwa), the eleventh member party, into the alliance. It was also decided to appoint Nasrullah Khan as the convener for the next three-month period.

The second instalment of Omar's article, 'Jamaat-i-Islami in historical prospective' appeared in the *Muslim* yesterday.

Thursday, 10 May 1984, Abbottabad
Ziaul Haq has clamped down on the press and has forbidden the publication of any opposition news. This is a reaction to the release of some political leaders and their criticism of the martial law regime. The newspapers today carried no news of a political nature. Ghulam Mustafa Jamali has been released. Mohammad Khan Jamali was released a few days earlier.

Saturday, 12 May 1984, Abbottabad
Completed my four years in captivity since 16 October 1979. These 1,460 days do not include the five-week period in April and May 1980 when I was out of detention.

Wednesday, 16 May 1984, Abbottabad
George Bush, the US vice-president, is on a visit to Pakistan and is being treated royally by Ziaul Haq. Dancing eunuchs, waving school children and flower showering 'crowd' not to mention gifts and bowing by obsequious officials, are greeting him everywhere. As expected, he is very pleased with Pakistan's international role and 'glad to learn' of Ziaul Haq's programme of a 'gradual move' towards democracy.

Sunday, 3 June 1984, Abbottabad
The BBC reported that Pir Pagara's followers (Hurs) are being armed to fight 'anti-state' elements and generally to help the police and the armed forces.

Monday, 11 June 1984, Abbottabad
The BBC reports casualities in the Golden Temple, Amritsar, which the Indian Army stormed a week ago. It said 1,000 were killed, including 200 army men. Official figures place the casualties at 300 with 50 servicemen. Jarnail Singh Bhindranwale, the 37-year-old leader of the Sikhs, who had occupied the Golden Temple, fought to the last. His body was found riddled with 72 bullet holes. A retired army major general was also killed fighting against the Indian Army.

This action of the Indian government has evoked strong reaction in the Sikh community. There have been at least two mutinies by Sikh troops, one in Rajasthan by 400 Sikh soldiers and another in Bihar by 200 Sikh soldiers. An army brigadier was shot dead and six officers wounded. A Sikh member of the Lok Sabha of Congress (I) has resigned and Khushwant Singh, a liberal newspaperman and a renowned writer, as well as an independent member of parliament has renounced his Padma Bhushan, the highest Indian civil award. There have been skirmishes and protests all over India and a protest meeting of 25,000 Sikhs in London yesterday.

Indira Gandhi's action in the Golden Temple could prove to be a serious miscalculation by the Indian government and is likely to lead to greater problems for India in the future. It will be remembered as comparable with or worse than General Dyer's action in Jallianwala Bagh in the same city of Amritsar in 1919.

Tuesday, 12 June 1984, Abbottabad
More mutinies by Sikh troops have taken place in India, in Kashmir and in Pune. The BBC evening bulletin said that Sikh troops in eight places had mutinied totalling over 1,000 men. Some had been killed and many taken prisoners.

Saturday, 16 June 1984, Abbottabad
The budget for the year 1984-85 was announced by Ghulam Ishaq Khan two days ago. Non-productive government expenditure is up by Rs5.5 billion. Defence budget is up by 9 per cent. Taxes have therefore been levied to the tune of Rs5.5 billion to meet the increased expenditure. Taxes on gas and diesel have gone up.

Thursday, 21 June 1984, Abbottabad
My 1500th day of captivity since 16 October 1979. This does not include the days spent in detention in July and August 1977 when Ziaul Haq took over and locked up PNA and PPP leaders.

Saturday, 30 June 1984, Abbottabad
Eidul Fitr. My tenth Eid in captivity.

Tuesday, 3 July 1984, Abbottabad
Omar's 31st birthday. Celebrated it with a birthday dinner and a cake that Amina had baked.

Monday, 9 July 1984, Abbottabad
Completed the final draft of my chapter 'Pakistan's geopolitical imperatives' which I will now send to Islamabad for typing in its final form. This will probably be the last chapter of my book, which Omar and I feel, should be called: *Islam, Politics and the State: The Pakistan Experience*.

Tuesday, 10 July 1984, Abbottabad
Dr Zia-ul-Haq, an Islamic scholar and an economist, sent his article, 'Islamisation of economy and society in Pakistan' for inclusion in my forthcoming book. It is a very good analysis of the exploitation of religion for the perpetuation of a suppressive regime.

Thursday, 26 July 1984, Abbottabad
Asaf Vardag came in the evening. Told him that I thought that the discussion by the national working committee of the desirability of taking part in Ziaul Haq's elections was unnecessary and unfortunate. All the more so because I had warned, Mian Sahib, Khurshid Kasuri and Asaf Vardag that they will not be able to arrive at a decision but will succeed in conveying their thinking to Ziaul Haq. This is exactly what has happened. Most of the members have expressed themselves in favour of taking part in any kind of election and have thus strengthened Ziaul Haq's hands in holding a meaningless election. They have also conveyed the clear impression that the Tehrik-i-Istiqlal is ready to take part in elections without waiting for my release, thus making it unnecessary for Ziaul Haq to release me. I told him that the national working committee—barring Malik Hamid Sarfaraz who had expressed the view that the subject should not be discussed—had shown a lamentable lack of political sense. Also discussed the progress of party elections and expressed my unhappiness with the unnecessary degree of polarisation within the party. I pointed out that the national working committee, in spite of discussing the problem of participation in elections for over eight hours, had concluded that a decision on this issue was premature and therefore did not take one. However the details of their discussion featured in the daily *Nawa-i-Waqt* and the *Jang* the next morning and the national working committee's views are now known to the government (including those of individual members).

Friday, 27 July 1984, Abbottabad

The BBC announced this morning that the Majlis-i-Shoora has passed a bill making a Muslim woman's and that of a member of a minority community's evidence equal to half that of a Muslim male. Also compensation to be paid for the murder of a Muslim woman and of a member of the minority community will be half that for the murder of a male Muslim. A shameful decision.

Monday, 30 July 1984, Abbottabad

Pakistan government has asked the Afghan Mujahideen organisations to remove themselves from Peshawar by the end of August. This is a sequel to the bomb explosions in which some people were killed. It is believed that this bombing was the work of Afghan government agents. The Mujahideen will now build their offices outside Peshawar.

Thursday, 2 Aug 1984, Abbottabad

Khurshid Kasuri came and we discussed Tehrik-i-Istiqlal's stand in the forthcoming MRD meeting on 7 August regarding MRD structure and election alliance. He thought that if we do not agree to go along with them — the others appear to be agreeable — we might be expelled from the MRD. I told him that the national working committee had decided against the 'structure' and against an election alliance so we had to abide by the national working committee decision. I do not think that the MRD would be so stupid as to expel the TI on that account, but if they did, it won't matter.

Monday, 6 Aug 1984, Abbottabad

Abu Saeed Envar died in Lahore yesterday. He was an experienced and an old member of the Tehrik-i-Istiqlal.

Friday, 17 Aug 1984, Abbottabad

Adey (my mother) wanted me to sleep in her room in the afternoon, which I did. She cannot walk properly, and with Amina away, I have to watch her and help her with things. Her memory too has almost faded and she does not know where she is, but she recognises her children when she sees them. Does not remember the grandchildren. She is 86.

Saturday, 18 Aug 1984, Abbottabad
Syed Munir Shah and Mukhtiar Bacha have been elected chairman
and general secretary respectively of the Tehrik-i-Istiqlal, NWFP.
Wrote to congratulate them both.

Thursday, 30 Aug 1984, Abbottabad
Mian Mahmud Ali Kasuri and Omar Kasuri came in the evening. I
was sorry to see Mian Sahib so weak. He is hardly able to walk, is
losing weight and looked unwell. He was very keen that we should
take part in the elections regardless of what they were being held for
and what the terms were. Told him that I did not see any point in
participating in a contest, which had no purpose.

Tuesday, 4 Sept 1984, Abbottabad
Afzal (my brother) told me that Ziaul Haq had sent for him a couple
of months ago and he had therefore met him. The meeting had been
arranged through a common acquaintance. Afzal said that Ziaul Haq
had told him that he should try and persuade me to participate in the
elections. During their meeting, which lasted 45 minutes. Ziaul Haq
made the following points: (a) He held me in high esteem. (b) He
wanted to pull the army out of politics but this must be done slowly
as otherwise there would be another martial law. (c) Army officers
were becoming corrupt so it was important to pull the army out of
politics. (d) He was thinking of allowing only three parties to
participate in the elections. (He did not say which three).

Friday, 7 Sept 1984, Abbottabad
Eidul Azha. My eleventh Eid in captivity.

Friday, 14 Sept 1984, Abbottabad
According to the BBC, after a three-day secret meeting in Lahore the
MRD leaders have decided: (1) To boycott any elections which are
not free, fair and in accordance with the 1973 constitution. (2) To form
an electoral alliance in any future elections in which the MRD takes
part, and after the election to stay together in the government.

Eleven parties took part in these discussions, all agreed to sign the
declaration except the Tehrik-i-Istiqlal which will refer it to its
national working committee for ratifying it. The BBC also broadcast

Benazir Bhutto's interview in which she expressed agreement with the first point but said that she did not know anything about an electoral alliance.

Two Afghan aircraft bombed a place four miles from Spinwam (in North Waziristan).

Friday, 21 Sept 1984, Abbottabad
Andre Gromyko has met Yaqub Khan (Pakistan's foreign minister) in New York and warned him of continued support for the Mujahideen in Afghanistan. Babrak Karmal has also spoken of the right of 'hot pursuit' into Pakistan if Pakistan continues in its present policy *vis-à-vis* Afghanistan. In a recent programme the ABC network in the US has said that the Senate was briefed by the US intelligence that there was a possibility of a preemptive strike against Pakistan's nuclear installation near Kahuta by India.

Monday, 1 Oct 1984, Abbottabad
Razvi, formerly of *Jang* Peshawar and now editor of a local newspaper *Jiddat,* telephoned at about 22:30 to say that the NWFP government had informed the press that I had been released. A large number of calls from the press followed from different places. It appears that the news this time is authentic.

Tuesday, 2 Oct 1984, Abbottabad
The police was withdrawn at 09:00 and thus my continuous detention of 1,603 days under Ziaul Haq appears to be over. I was flooded by the press and workers and well-wishers from Hazara, Rawalpindi, Lahore, Murree and other places. Panels of *Jang* and *Nawa-i-Waqt* and representative of *Dawn, Amn* and other papers came from Rawalpindi and Islamabad.

Associated Press of France (AFP), Press Trust of India (PTI), Associated Press and the BBC (Alex Brodie) interviewed me on the telephone. The BBC had given an inaccurate description of my past political career in its morning international and Urdu services but corrected itself in its evening broadcast. It gave a commentary on me in 'Sairbeen' in the 20:30 service.

Wednesday, 3 Oct 1984, Abbottabad

A large number of people called including contingents from Faisalabad, Peshawar, Mardan, Attock and Swat. About 100 people had lunch here.

Thursday, 4 Oct 1984, Abbottabad

Another day of a flood of callers. Zahur Butt telephoned from London. The daily *Jang* Lahore had published a totally baseless statement attributed to me criticising the PPP in its yesterday's edition, which Khurshid Kasuri had contradicted. This contradiction was published in most newspapers today.

Friday, 5 Oct 1984, Abbottabad

A large number of people called from different places, in Sindh, Punjab, NWFP and Balochistan.

Sunday, 7 Oct 1984, Abbottabad

More people came today. A large delegation from Gujrat (about 40) came at lunchtime. Managed to give them all food. Shaukat Nawaz Khan brought about 80 people from Khanpur. There were also people from Kohistan, Swat, Rawalpindi, Abbottabad and Mansehra. Anwar Ali Noon and Begum Mahmud Shah from Rawalpindi also came.

Monday, 8 Oct 1984, Abbottabad

Former Justice Fakhruddin G. Ebrahim (of Supreme Court) called. Telephoned our house in Islamabad, which has been illegally occupied by a retired army colonel, and spoke to the wife of Colonel Mahmud, the occupants of our house. She appeared to have no intention of moving out. The Ziaul Haq variety. We had given the house to Haroon who had allowed them to live there. They are not our tenants.

Wednesday, 10 Oct 1984, Abbottabad

Malik Qasim (Muslim League), Majeed Nizami and Mujeeb Shami (*Nawa-i-Waqt*) came. A large number of workers from Mansehra, Haripur Abbottabad, Lahore, Rawalpindi, Swat, Kahuta and Ferozwala came.

Thursday, 11 Oct 1984, Abbottabad

Fifty-eighth meeting of the national working committee was held. Discussed the desirability or otherwise of taking part in non-party elections. The national working committee decided that the party should not take part in non-party elections. It also decided that even 'party elections' would not serve any purpose unless: (a) These were for transfer of power. (b) Press is free. (c) Political parties were allowed to campaign. (d) Political prisoners were freed. (e) The national working committee decided to authorize the party president to nominate 50 members to the national council instead of the 30 at present (only for the forthcoming election).

Drew up a programme of my tour of Sindh starting from 20 October. Agreed on calling a press conference in Abbottabad tomorrow at 11:30.

Friday, 12 Oct 1984, Abbottabad

Second day of national working committee meeting. Was served a notice by the police early in the morning signed by the home secretary, government of Sindh, banning my entry into Sindh for 30 days. Had finalised my programme of tour of Sindh starting on 20 November but that will not be possible now. Addressed a press conference. The BBC (Alex Brodie) Reuters, AFP and most national newspapers were represented. Told them that the national working committee had decided that the Tehrik-i-Istiqlal will take part in elections only if these are held on a 'party basis'.

Sunday, 14 Oct 1984, Abbottabad

Asaf Ali came in the evening. He had called on Ziaul Haq earlier today. Ziaul Haq had told him: (1) Elections would be on non-party basis. (2) He could ask a person from amongst those elected, to form the government and give him 30 days to do so. (3) He will amend the 1973 constitution.

Friday, 19 Oct 1984, Abbottabad

Iqbal Khan Jadoon, a prominent political leader of Hazara, died in London today.

Sunday, 21 Oct 1984, Abbottabad, Peshawar
Arrived in Peshawar at 15:15 and addressed a workers' meeting at Munir Shah's residence. Called on Nasirullah Khan Babar. His father-in-law had died last week.

Monday, 22 Oct 1984, Peshawar, Jhagra, Mardan
Addressed a well attended meeting at Jhagra arranged by Javed Khan (the district information secretary), and the nephew of the late Hashim Khan of Jhagra, an old Muslim League leader of the NWFP.

Wednesday, 24 Oct 1984, Mingora, Chakdara, Wari, Thana
Left Mingora at 09:00 and called on the Wali of Swat before leaving. I had sent him a letter to say that I had come to Swat the previous evening and had not called on him because in the present circumstances, I had considered it advisable for him, for me not to do so. He had sent word that he wanted to see me, even if it was for a few minutes. He has aged (is about 75) but looked well enough. Was very pleased to see me.

Thursday, 25 Oct 1984, Thana, Shergarh, Mardan
There is a complete blackout of my news in all newspapers. However Rafi Butt's *Haider* is defying the press advice. His newspaper may well be closed.

Friday, 26 Oct 1984, Abbottabad
Zaheer Abbasi came from Islamabad to discuss the notice that he is giving to Colonel Mahmud and his wife, who have illegally occupied our house in Islamabad.

Tuesday, 30 Oct 1984, Abbottabad
Mushahid Hussain telephoned to say that he and Kuldip Nayar would like to see me. Told them to come tomorrow at 10:00. Syed Munir Shah telephoned to say that the other MRD leaders had arrived in Peshawar and suggested that I should also come there. Explained that in view of Maulana Noorani's and Kuldip Nayar's visit this was not possible and that I shall look forward to meeting some of them in Lahore.

Wednesday, 31 Oct 1984, Abbottabad

Indira Gandhi, the Indian prime minister was shot and killed, reportedly by her Sikh security guards early this morning.

Kuldip Nayar and Mushahid Hussain came to interview me today. Kuldip Nayar's questions were aimed at finding out what I would do if I was prime minister for instance: (a) Policy towards India. (b) Attitude towards Ziaul Haq. Whether I would agree to become prime minister if Ziaul Haq was president. (c) Whether I would order a tribunal to try generals for corruption.

Told him that these questions were so hypothetical that they did not merit a reply. In any case, I said, I saw no danger of my assuming this responsibility in the near future. However, I said that: (a) We wanted friendly relations with India. (b) We had nothing personal against Ziaul Haq. It was the army as an institution that should be taken out of politics. (c) The appointment of a tribunal was a matter that would have to be gone into at the appropriate time.

He further asked whether I was in favour of Pakistan acquiring the capability to manufacture a nuclear bomb. Told him that I was not.

Maulana Noorani, Pir Barkat Shah, Akbar Saqi and about half a dozen others of JUP came a little later. Discussed the general political situation with Maulana Noorani. Mushir Pesh Imam also joined us a little before lunch. Found ourselves (Maulana Noorani and I) in general agreement on our assessment of the situation.

Issued a joint press release to say that we both agreed not to take part in non-party polls and to consult each other from time to time.

Saturday, 3 Nov 1984, Lahore

Addressed the Lahore High Court Bar Association (president Khalid Ahmad). A very well attended meeting. Response was very good. Spoke about: (a) Sindh. (b) Foreign policy, particularly Afghan policy, and US interests in this area. (c) Rights of Qadianis to live as equal citizens.

Indira Gandhi was cremated in New Delhi today.

Sunday, 4 Nov 1984, Lahore, Rawalpindi, Abbottabad

Was woken up early today to be shown an externment order requiring me to leave the Punjab and stay away for three months. The magistrate said that the government wanted me to leave by the 07:00 plane. Since it was 06:00 and the time was rather short, I said that I would leave by the next (10:25) flight.

Asked Aitzaz Ahsan over and told him to file a writ on my behalf. Khurshid Kasuri came later and I left at 11:00 by PIA. Was met at the Islamabad airport by ASP Rana Altaf and was brought to Abbottabad. The ASP was an interesting and educated person. Talked intelligently about national affairs. Asked for a copy of my book, *Generals in Politics* which I gave him.

Monday, 5 Nov 1984, Abbottabad
Went over to Gohar Ayub's in the morning to check on the jeep track between Khanpur and Islamabad without having to go through Punjab (since my entry is banned in Punjab but not in the federal territory of Islamabad).

Wednesday, 7 Nov 1984, Abbottabad
Malik Wazir Ali came to stay. Discussed the question of taking part in Ziaul Haq brand of elections. He was of the view that we should take part no matter what the terms.

Amina, Omar and Samina attended a reception given by the Soviet ambassador in Islamabad. Amina was given VIP treatment and the Soviet ambassador told her that he would be seeking permission to see me in Abbottabad.

Saturday, 10 Nov 1984, Abbottabad
I was informed (in writing) by the commissioner Hazara that the government of Balochistan had banned my entry into the province. Therefore cancelled my programme of visit to Quetta on 11 November and decided to go to Karachi instead on the 14th. Spoke to the home secretary NWFP earlier to inform him that I was planning to go abroad and this would necessitate boarding the plane in Rawalpindi. He said that he would find out and let me know whether I could go abroad and if I could board the plane in Rawalpindi.

Sunday, 11 Nov 1984, Abbottabad
Mushir filed a writ petition in the Balochistan High Court against the ban on my entry into Balochistan province. The writ was admitted for hearing on 25 November. I released the names of 45 persons whom I

have nominated as members of the party's national council, in accordance with the party constitution.

Monday, 12 Nov 1984, Abbottabad
The superintendent of police came to deliver the government of Balochistan's letter banning my entry into the province for three months.

Tuesday, 13 Nov 1984, Abbottabad
The US counsul in Peshawar called and wanted clarification of Tehrik-i-Istiqlal's policy and thinking on national affairs, foreign policy, Afghanistan, US-Pakistan relations, etc.

Ahmed Mian Soomro has been told by the home ministry Sindh that the provincial government had sent me a letter banning my entry into the province. Told him that since I had received no such information, I would be leaving as planned at midday tomorrow.

Wednesday, 14 Nov 1984, Peshawar, Mardan, Sakhakot, Abbottabad
The DC Peshawar called this morning to say that my entry into Sindh was banned. He said that a letter from the government of Sindh was on its way. The home secretary NWFP, Jamshed Burki, also telephoned to confirm this and to say that there was no objection to my proceeding abroad, as my name was not on the exit control list. I could board the plane at Islamabad (although my entry into Punjab is banned).

Thursday, 22 Nov 1984, Abbottabad
The home secretary NWFP (Jamshed Burki) telephoned to say that the government of Punjab would not permit me to pass through Punjab on my way to Islamabad where my entry has not been banned. However as a special case they would permit me to do so on my way to the airport to catch the plane on my way to London.

Friday, 23 Nov 1984, Abbottabad, Peshawar
Attended the meeting of the national council. A great deal of heat was generated in the election of the central office bearers.

Wednesday, 28 Nov 1984, Abbottabad
Spoke to Jamshed Burki, the home secretary NWFP, to inform him about my programme of going to Islamabad on 1 December and then flying to London the following day. The road journey of some eight miles from Afzal's house in Islamabad to the airport involves having to pass through half a mile of Punjab territory (the airport is in the Punjab although it is called 'Islamabad' airport). Also the drive from Abbottabad to Islamabad involves passing through some six miles of Punjab. I therefore wanted to ensure that I would not be prevented from driving through these few miles of Punjab on my way to Islamabad on 1 December and the airport on 2 December. He confirmed that I would not be stopped.

Saturday, 1 Dec 1984, Abbottabad
Ziaul Haq spoke on TV and radio and announced that he would be holding a referendum on 19 December in which people would be asked whether: (a) They approve of the Islamisation process that Ziaul Haq's government has been carrying out in accordance with the commandments of God Almighty as enunciated in the Quran, the Sunnah and the teachings of the Prophet. (b) Whether they wanted a return to democracy. (c) Whether they believed in the solidarity of Pakistan.

If the answer to these questions was in the affirmative, it would be assumed that the people would be voting for Ziaul Haq to stay on as president for another five years.

My first reaction was that people should participate in the referendum and vote a 'No' but on reflection felt that a boycott would be wiser. If the MRD took a clear line for a boycott the number of people turning up would be small.

Monday, 3 Dec 1984, London
Went over to call on Ghaus Bux Bizenjo who is in London. He supported the call of the MRD to boycott Ziaul Haq's referendum and was in favour of boycotting any election that Ziaul Haq may have later, though he thought that he was not now likely to hold one.

Tuesday, 4 Dec 1984, London
Called at Amnesty International to thank them for their efforts for my release.

Thursday, 6 Dec 1984, London

Maliha Lodhi came to see me in the afternoon. She teaches at the London School of Economics and writes for some newspapers and magazines including the Islamabad daily *Muslim*. She asked me to address the Pakistan Council at the LSE which I agreed to do on Tuesday, 11 December.

Friday, 7 Dec 1984, London

Malik Ghulam Mustafa Khar came to discuss the political situation in Pakistan. Mir Ghaus Bux Bizenjo came in the afternoon. Discussed the situation in Pakistan and the consequences of the referendum Ziaul Haq is holding on 19 December.

Thursday, 11 Dec 1984, London

Addressed the Pakistan Council at the London School of Economics. Good attendance. Spoke on Pakistan's foreign relations and answered a number of questions.

Wednesday, 12 Dec 1984, London

Omar and I had lunch at the 'Les Ambassador' club hosted by Mumtaz Bhutto. Hafeez Pirzada was also there. They were of the view that the MRD would be redundant after the referendum (on 19 December) in which they estimated that Punjab would vote for Ziaul Haq whereas Sindh would poll a lower vote, thus weakening the national parties. Regional parties, they thought, would gain strength and the focus of politics would shift to the provinces. Mumtaz Bhutto has been a supporter of a confederation.

Thursday, 13 Dec 1984, London

Omar and I went to Zed Books and I gave them two more manuscripts of my book *Islam, Politics and the State*. They will start work on it on 1 January and hope to have the book out by 1 July. Called on the secretary general of the Amnesty International.

Sir Julian Ridsdale invited me to address members of parliament in the House of Commons. I accepted the invitation and asked Humayun Gauhar to arrange it for early July when the book *Islam, Politics and the State*, should be out and could also be launched in

London. Humayun Gauhar said that he could also arrange a talk at the United Nations in New York. The editor of *South* was also present.

Friday, 14 Dec 1984, London
Ali's wedding. Nikah took place at Zahur Butt's. A simple ceremony. Mrs Butt had taken a lot of trouble over the arrangements. Held a reception at 116 Pall Mall. About 90 guests attended of whom about 25 were Ali's and Manya's (his wife) friends.

Sunday, 16 Dec 1984, London
Left Heathrow airport in the evening by a PIA flight. Dr Maleeha Lodhi interviewed me for the monthly *South* as well as a syndicate (of some magazines) for whom she writes.

Monday, 17 Dec 1984, Islamabad, Abbottabad
Arrived at Islamabad airport where we were received by ASP Rana Altaf of Punjab police as well as two well fed police officers of NWFP police who showed me an order of the NWFP government detaining me at my residence for one week. Was taken to the 'Frontier House' in Islamabad and kept there for some time and then left with a police escort for Abbottabad.

Our luggage was in the meantime examined by the customs (and of course Intelligence) and all books, Amina's and my diaries and a cordless telephone that Omar had purchased on his way out, detained. Learnt on arrival in Abbottabad that Ziaul Haq had addressed a public meeting there this afternoon. Oddly enough, there was no police on duty at our gate or around the premises.

Wednesday, 19 Dec 1984, Abbottabad
Referendum today. Very poor turnout. Ten per cent in towns generally throughout the country. In the rural areas it varied but impartial observers placed it at:

Sindh	0-5 per cent
NWFP	5-25 per cent
Punjab	35-40 per cent
Balochistan	10-15 per cent

It appears to have been Ziaul Haq's second big mistake. The first was to assume power on 5 July 1977.

Visited five polling stations in Abbottabad. All these presented a deserted look. Ziaul Haq expressed satisfaction with the result of the referendum.

Friday, 21 Dec 1984, Abbottabad, Islamabad, Abbottabad
Left for Islamabad by a narrow jeep track via Baghpur Dheri and Makhnial (to avoid going through the Punjab where my entry is banned). Arrived there four hours later. The road from Khanpur turning to Makhnial is jeepable and in reasonable condition. Asked Alex Brodie of BBC and Michael of AFP to come over to Afzal's house to give them my views on the referendum.

Thursday, 27 Dec 1984, Abbottabad
Fifty-ninth meeting of the national working committee. Decided that all members of the party who are members of district or other councils, shoud be asked to explain why they should not be expelled from the party for working for Ziaul Haq in the referendum. It was agreed that changes in the central office bearers should be made along with the announcement of the new working committee after about a month. General opinion was against taking part in any kind of election held by Ziaul Haq. Discussed the suitability of various persons for central offices and decided upon the following:

Vice Presidents	Mian Mahmud Ali Kasuri Malik Hamid Sarfaraz Khudai Noor Khan Ahmed Mian Soomro
Secretary General	Asaf Vardag
Information Secretary	Khurshid Kasuri
Joint Secretary General	Syed Azhar Hussain Zaidi Inamullah Khan Nisar Ahmed Khuhro Rana Mohammad Arshad Khan Rana Mohammad Arshad Khan
Treasurer	Dr Parvez Hassan

Diary 1985

Thursday, 3 Jan 1985, Abbottabad, Mansehra, Abbottabad
Maliha Lodhi telephoned from London to ask whether I wished to say anything about what Ziaul Haq had said in his interview to her about me the other day. Omar spoke to her and told her that since whatever I might say will not be published here, there is no point in saying anything.

Monday, 7 Jan 1985, Abbottabad
Tom Heneghan (Reuters), his wife Elisabeth Auvillain (Radio France), Michel Martin-Roland and his wife and Don Larimore (VOA) came for lunch. Spoke to Khan Mohammad Jamali who confirmed what Tom Heneghan had told me earlier today that Ghulam Mustafa Jatoi had met Ziaul Haq a few days ago. Jatoi has contradicted this news.

Thursday, 10 Jan 1985, Abbottabad
Was told that there had been a large number of arrests of MRD workers in Lahore presumably as a preventive measure for the demonstration being planned for 12 January. The daily *Jasarat* of today said that Ziaul Haq was likely to meet me.

Friday, 11 Jan 1985, Abbottabad
Rafi Butt telephoned to say that he had met Zafar Ali Shah and Shaikh Rashid and had told them if they did not publicly announce the suspension of their election campaign, they could have to leave the party. He said that Shaikh Rashid was repentant but Zafar Ali Shah wished to meet me to explain his position. However he felt that he had gone too far to withdraw from the contest at this stage. Told Rafi Butt that in that case, there was no point in Zafar Ali Shah undertaking a trip to Abbottabad to explain things.

Saturday, 12 Jan 1985, Abbottabad
Ziaul Haq announced his election programme. Non-party election will be held for the National Assembly on 25 February and for the provincial assemblies on 28 February. Since the national working

committee had decided not to meet in the event of non-party polls, I am not calling a meeting of the national working committee. The whole exercise is a bigger fraud than the 19 December referendum and will help to mobilise the opposition against the regime.

A demonstration was staged in Lahore outside Neela Gumbad mosque. Khurshid Kasuri, Hamid Sarfaraz and Aitzaz Ahsan were arrested. Khudai Noor and Malik Haider Usman telephoned. They agreed with me that Ziaul Haq's conditions for participation in elections were unacceptable. However Asaf Vardag was of the view that we should participate on Ziaul Haq's terms. Khurshid telephoned late at night to say that he and the others had been released. Also spoke to Malik Qasim. A number of newspaper correspondents telephoned to ask for my reactions to Ziaul Haq's speech.

Friday, 18 Jan & Saturday, 19 Jan 1985, Abbottabad
Two day meeting of MRD central council. All leaders attended except Rasul Bux Palejo and Mairaj Mohammad Khan. It was decided not to take part in the elections being held by Ziaul Haq and to ask that we will consider participating only if: (a) Martial law is lifted. (b) The press is free. (c) Political prisoners are released. (d) Elections are held strictly in accordance with the 1973 constitution (and the rules as these existed on 4 July 1977) on a party basis.

Also decided that if these conditions are not met, we will not accept any election under martial law and will consider any one taking part in these elections as guilty of subverting the constitution. It was also decided that anyone who files his nomination papers will be expelled from the party. It was decided that two subcommitees will assemble in Lahore to (1) study the organisational structure of the MRD and (2) the provincial autonomy issue. The next meeting of the MRD will be held on 22 January in Lahore.

A useful meeting. My first in the MRD. Attendance was good and decisions more or less unanimous.

Benazir Bhutto telephoned from London (or France) to enquire about the decisions taken at the MRD meeting. Our first conversation.

Sunday, 20 Jan 1985, Abbottabad
K.H. Khurshid (a former president of Azad Kashmir) came. Shaukat brought a message from J.A. Rahim to say that he wanted to rejoin the Tehrik-i-Istiqlal. Told him that J.A. Rahim was free to do so.

Monday, 21 Jan 1985, Abbottabad
Left for Lahore by car, along with Omar, to attend the meeting of the MRD, in spite of the ban on my entry into Punjab. We were stopped by the police at Tarnol, short of Rawalpindi and told that I could not proceed further. Returned to Abbottabad. Similarly Wali Khan was also turned back at Gujar Khan. Learnt later that there had been a number of externments from Punjab and some more arrests notably, Mairaj Khalid, Nawabzada Nasrullah Khan, Malik Qasim from Lahore and Mahmudul Haq Usmani in Karachi.

Tuesday, 22 Jan 1985, Abbottabad
Altaf Hasan Qureshi of *Urdu Digest* came. Discussed the political situation and expressed grave concern at Ziaul Haq's move.

My statement regarding Dr Henry Kissinger's utterances about the 'heroic role of Pakistan in the defence of the free world' and about the referendum, appeared in full in *Dawn* and some other papers today.

The BBC news said that Iqbal Haider and Ghulam Rasool Soomro (PPP) have also been arrested. Ghaus Bux Bizenjo has been externed from Sindh.

Friday, 1 Feb 1985, Abbottabad, Peshawar
A police officer came later, at night to inform me that I would not be permitted to go to Mardan tomorrow. I am scheduled to go there to address the district bar association. Told him that I would proceed as planned unless served with written orders or stopped by the police.

Saturday, 2 Feb 1985, Peshawar
The written order banning my entry into Mardan district for 30 days was served on me early today. Met the press in the afternoon but learnt later that the government had imposed a ban on publication of statement of all opposition leaders, Statements of only those taking part in the 'election' may be published.

Friday, 8 Feb 1985, Islamabad, Abbottabad
Wali Khan, his wife, Syed Munir Shah, Syed Mukhtiar Bacha, Inayatullah Khan (of Nowshera) and about a hundred workers of the MRD were arrested in Peshawar and Mardan last night.

Sunday, 10 Feb 1985, Abbottabad
An ASI brought orders of the district magistrate of Dera Ismail Khan banning my entry into the district for 30 days.

Wednesday, 13 Feb 1985, Abbottabad
A London jury acquitted Clive Ponting, a civil servant, of charges of supplying a Labour MP information about the sinking of the Argentinian ship Belgrano. The jury ruled that loyalty to the country and loyalty to the state are not synonymous. That the civil servant acted correctly in informing the Parliament of an action taken by the government which in his opinion was against national interest. The Belgrano was sunk when it was sailing away from the proscribed zone and not entering it as the world was told.

Thursday, 14 Feb 1985, Abbottabad
Malik Hamid Sarfaraz came about midday from Karachi. Told him to avoid arrest and to see Wali Khan (if possible—who is under detention at his home near Charsadda) and Syed Kaswar Gardezi of PNP in Lahore and discuss the organisational structure of the MRD.

Monday, 18 Feb 1985, Abbottabad, Peshawar, Karachi
Left with Omar for Peshawar and then by PIA for Karachi. Left Abbottabad for Peshawar. Dodged the CID motorcyclist but must have been noticed and reported to Karachi because we were met by a police contingent on arrival at Karachi. The aircraft was parked on arrival at some distance from the terminal building. I was told that I could not leave the airport and would have to leave Karachi (and Sindh). I demanded a written order before I complied with his request. He said he did not have a written order and insisted that I should accompany him. After some altercation, accompanied him to the VIP lounge. After a couple of hours I was served with an externment order for 30 days.

Tuesday, 19 Feb 1985, Karachi, Peshawar, Abbottabad

The BBC in its early morning broadcast reported my arrest. Miss Weaver of *Sunday Times* came and sent two questions which I replied through Omar. Left by the 15:00 flight for Peshawar and arrived at Abbottabad at 21:00.

Mushir Pesh Imam was arrested and put in Karachi prison early morning today.

Friday, 22 Feb 1985, Abbottabad, Mansehra

A busy day. Miss Weaver (*Sunday Times* and *Christian Science Monitor*) came to interview me. She was followed by Mohammad Aftab and Richard Bile of Associated Press. Ayaz, my brother-in-law, said that Fauzia (his daughter) was very upset that I would not come to her wedding reception. I explained that since Ziaul Haq was attending, I would not like to attend. However I agreed to come for the *mehndi* on 3 March and *nikah* on the 4th morning, provided I am not detained or restrained from doing so.

Saturday, 23 Feb 1985, Abbottabad

Gave a statement to the press as well as the BBC, Reuters and Associated Press of America contradicting Ziaul Haq's figures about the 1970 and 1977 polls in Pakistan. He had said that the turnout had been between 40 and 55 per cent of the registered voters. In fact the turnout had been 66 per cent in 1970 and 63.3 per cent in 1977. He had also said that a turnout of 40 per cent would mean normal participation in the polls. This suggests that he will resort to rigging and will ensure a turnout of above 40 per cent. My own guess is that he will ensure a result a little over 50 per cent, could be about 52 per cent.

Monday, 25 Feb 1985, Abbottabad

Ziaul Haq's elections for the National Assembly were held today. Omar visited polling stations in Haripur and Havelian area and I visited about five polling stations in Abbottabad. Polling was low in comparison with our experience with previous elections. Reports from all other places such as Karachi, Lahore, Rawalpindi, Peshawar, Mardan, Quetta, Sahiwal, Faisalabad, Vehari and Multan indicated a similar situation. Polling in Sargodha city was however reported to be about 30 per cent. The BBC's evening news reported that polling was fairly high in rural constituencies was therefore something of a surprise.

Asaf Vardag, Malik Haider Usman, Khurshid Kasuri and Rao Khurshid (of Sahiwal) were arrested in Lahore during a demonstration today.

Tuesday, 26 Feb 1985, Abbottabad
Heard election results today. Considering the reports of low poll, results of voting which the government claims to be collectively 50-55 per cent appears unbelievable.

Wednesday, 27 Feb 1985, Abbottabad
The election commission announced that 52.9 per cent votes had been cast in the National Assembly polls.

Saturday, 2 March 1985, Abbottabad
Ziaul Haq announced his amendments to the 1973 constitution, making it virtually impossible for him to be removed. He has assumed powers to dissolve the National Assembly and for appointing the governors, the prime minister and federal ministers. The governors will likewise exercise the powers of the president in their respective provinces.

Sunday, 10 March 1985, Abbottabad, Sajjikot, Abbottabad
Ziaul Haq announced the revival of the 1973 constitution minus 27 articles relating to human rights, and press freedom and issued other ordinances, which effectively alter the shape of the 1973 constitution. Article 6, which relates to the death penalty for anyone overthrowing a civilian government, similarly remains suspended.

Monday, 11 March 1985, Abbottabad
Ahmed Mian Soomro resigned membership of the party. He is probably aspiring to be a senator.

Monday, 18 March 1985, Abbottabad
Ziaul Haq has decided not to call for the election expense accounts of candidates for the recent elections. This was a statutory requirement

which Ziaul Haq has decided to waive because he said that much more money had been spent than stipulated and he does not want to do the *bismillah* of the National Assembly meeting with a lie. The expenditure limit for the NA election is Rs40,000 whereas people have spent as much as Rs4,000,000 or even more. The permitted amount therefore was only one hundredth of what was spent in many cases.

Wednesday, 20 March 1985, Abbottabad
Ziaul Haq announced the appointment of Mohammad Khan Junejo as prime minister, Khawaja Safdar as speaker of the National Assembly and Ghulam Ishaq Khan, the chairman of the Senate.

Saturday, 23 March 1985, Abbottabad
Pakistan Day. The new National Assembly met today and was addressed by Ziaul Haq with the usual clichés and sermons. He named Mohammad Khan Junejo as the new prime minister and then called an MNA to say *Dua*. This was an odd affair, for the *dua* did not seem to end. He went on asking the almighty to put everything right and people must have heaved a sigh of relief when he ended his wailing. He appeared to be weeping and was trying his best to make everyone else cry too.

Friday, 29 March 1985, Lahore
Attended the award ceremony of the Human Rights Society at Falettis. Was given a gold medal for my contribution to human rights in Pakistan. Very good attendance. Spent a very busy day meeting delegations and pressmen all day.

Sunday, 31 March 1985, Lahore
Mohammad Khan Junejo spoke on TV and radio. Appears a colourless personality. Ziaul Haq seems to have made a good selection. Junejo should serve him well.

Wednesday, 17 April 1985, Karachi
Home secretary, government of Sindh, conveyed a message to me through Pesh Imam and Chaudhri Jameel requesting me to cancel my programme of visit to Hyderabad and Mirpurkhas tomorrow. I refused to do so.

Thursday, 18 April 1985, Karachi, Mirpurkhas, Hyderabad, Karachi
Left for Hyderabad along with Omar and about a dozen party workers including Khan Mohammad Jamali, Chaudhri Jameel, Nisar Khuhro and Imdad Chandio. Was given a rousing reception on arrival and proceeded to lead a procession. Was given a very good reception at Mirpurkhas where I addressed workers (including the police). A very good tour.

Tuesday, 30 April 1985, Faisalabad, Gujranwala, Lahore
Addressed a very well attended meeting of district bar association Faisalabad before leaving for Nankana Sahib where I addressed a meeting of Tehrik-i-Istiqlal and MRD workers. Left for Gujranwala after lunch and led a procession to address a large meeting.

Wednesday, 1 May 1985, Lahore
Addressed a very well attended meeting in Lakshmi Mansion area. Enthusiastic and a very responsive crowd.

Friday, 3 May 1985, Lahore, Sahiwal
A very noisy procession with some 150 motorcyclists leading. Addressed a good meeting.

Saturday, 4 May 1985, Sahiwal, Pakpattan, Burewala
Went on to Mandi Burewala where I addressed a good meeting. After lunch went to Multan and led a procession to the city where I addressed a large meeting. Talked of trying Ziaul Haq for treason for violating the constitution, and of enquiring into the wealth amassed by people in high government offices and their relatives since 5 July 1977, and of trying them. Very good response.

Wednesday, 8 May 1985, DIK, Tank, Abdul Khel, Bannu
Was received a little short of Serai Naurang by a massive procession of trucks and cars and of course people. Addressed an enthusiastic crowd on arrival at Serai Naurang and again some six miles short of Bannu. Addressed a large and enthusiastic gathering in intermittent rain in Bannu. Stayed at Mahmash Khel with Syed Munir Shah.

Thursday, 23 May 1985, Abbottabad
Dr Mahbub ul Haq announced the 1985-86 budget in the assembly. Some improvements in the taxation structure but no change in the main budget concept. The 13.13 per cent inflation factor has been applied to the defence bill; increase on defence is therefore the largest increase so far, 10 per cent tax on petroleum products, WAPDA and rail fares. Another feature is that the annual development budget has been combined with the revenue budget thus showing defence as 24 per cent of the budget instead of the 47 per cent of the revenue budget that it was last year. A crude attempt to hoodwink the people.

Tuesday, 4 June 1985, Abbottabad
Rao Rashid of PPP gave an interview some time ago to the editor of *Atishfishan* which accused me of being in league with the US, and the Tehrik-i-Istiqlal and me in believing in coming to power through intrigue and the army's help. An amazing accusation, which could only be done at the government's instance. Will have to review our relationship with the PPP and MRD. Telephoned Khawaja Khairuddin to say that in view of Rao Rashid's interview, which has been published in the form of a book, the MRD meeting scheduled for 11 and 12 July in Quetta will not be held.

Saturday, 6 July 1985, Quetta, Karachi
Shias (mostly Hazara) took out a procession to agitate for the enforcement of the Fiqh-i-Jafria and were stopped and tear-gassed by the police. Firing took place from both sides in which 12 persons were reported to have been killed.

Tuesday, 9 July 1985, Karachi
The national working committee meeting concluded in Jamali House today. Decided not to increase the level of the Tehrik-i-Istiqlal's involvement with the MRD. I explained that only the party council could do this as any thing more than the present involvement would be a step towards an electoral alliance and the formation of one party; and that this would be an infringement of the independent character of our party. This I said was not within the power of the national working committee to approve. Discussed a number of other organisational matters.

Saturday, 13 July 1985, Moro, Nawabshah, Punnal Khan Chandio, Khairpur, Nathan Shah, Larkana

Left Moro early today for Nawabshah where I addressed the district bar association. Then called at Punnal Khan Chandio, 16 people from which village had been killed by military action near Sakrand on the main highway during the 1983 disturbances. Another 54 had been wounded. Drove in a procession of more than 300 cars and was given a tumultuous reception, all the way and in Larkana town. Addressed a packed meeting at Nisar Khuhro's residence. The procession and the meeting were reminiscent of the scenes of the anti-Ayub movement but were considerably more impressive. The response is excellent and it appears that the rejection of Ziaul Haq's regime is complete.

Sunday, 14 July 1985, Larkana, Naudero, Shikarpur, Sukkur

Addressed the Larkana District Bar Association. Very good response.

Saturday, 20 July 1985, Abbottabad

Shahnawaz Bhutto, son of late Zulfikar Ali Bhutto, was found dead in his flat in Cannes (in south of France) yesterday. Foul play was not suspected but French authorities are making enquiries.

Monday, 22 July 1985, Abbottabad

Received a letter from the head of Intelligence in the district informing me that my entry into Sindh had been banned. This has probably been done as a precautionary measure for the funeral of Zulfikar Ali Bhutto's son in Garhi Khuda Bux (Larkana). Similar orders have been served on a number of people including Bizenjo, who has not been externed from Sindh but has been detained for 30 days in Karachi.

Friday, 26 July 1985, Abbottabad

A police officer called today to deliver a Sindh government order banning my entry into the province for 90 days under the maintenance of public order. The order is based on a 'source' report saying that I am likely to visit Sindh to incite the people against the government.

Wednesday, 14 Aug 1985, Abbottabad-Sialkot
Arrived in Wazirabad at 16:00 and led a large procession to Sialkot.
Covered the 25-mile journey in three-and-a-half hours. An impassive
though chaotic journey to Sabzi Mandi where I addressed a large
public meeting, which was marred slightly by our people over-reacting
to some fairly harmless pro-MRD and pro-PPP slogans.

Thursday, 15 Aug 1985, Sialkot-Gujrat
Addressed the Sialkot District Bar Association. Also addressed the
local press club members. Left for Gujrat and led a large procession
from the Chenab bridge. Very good response from the public *en route*
and in Gujrat city. Addressed a large meeting.

Wednesday, 11 September 1985, London
Attended the launching of my book *Islam, Politics and the State* at
the School of Oriental and African Studies in London University.
Nearly 200 people attended, including five persons from the BBC.

Friday, 13 Sept 1985, London
Called on Dennis Healey of the Labour party in his office in the House
of Parliament. He suggested that I should meet Ronald Spiers, a
former US ambassador to Pakistan and now in the state department.
He also suggested that I should try to arrange a visit to and a talk at
Brookings Institute in Washington.

Spoke to Amjad in Washington and asked him to arrange a meeting
with Ronald Spiers and a talk at Brookings Institute.

Dinner at Naeemul Haq's. Met a large number of people, including
Imran Khan, the cricketer who, I was told, is thinking of joining the
Tehrik-i-Istiqlal, when he retires from active cricket in a year or
two.

Saturday, 14 Sept 1985, London
Visited the Muslim College, 20/22 Creffield Road, London W5 3RP,
and met its principal Zaki Badawi. He appeared an enlightened person
and had a healthy approach to the teachings of Islam. The college is
a remarkable venture run on modern lines for the teaching of *imams*
and *muftis* as well as people in Islamic journalism. Badawi, a scholar
of considerable fame, is an Egyptian who I understand is running this

institute with Libya's financial support. Presented a copy of my book, *Islam, Politics and the State* for the library.

Tuesday, 24 Sept 1985, Washington
Spoke at the Carnegie Endowment, at 11 Dupont Circle NW, Washington DC. About 50 people attended amongst them were Selig S. Harrison; former ambassadors to Pakistan, Spires, Van Hollen, Sobers, Robert Peck, deputy assistant secretary for South Asia in the state department and a number of other state department and defence department officials, university professors and Afghanistan and Pakistan specialists.

Tuesday, 26 Sept 1985, Washington DC
Had lunch at Shezan with Peter Galbraith (on the staff of foreign relations committee), Mrs Van Hollen, Mrs Schumacher (Pakistan desk in the state department), Peter Snow (human rights, state department). Discussed US policies in regard to Pakistan and Afghanistan.

Dinner with Shahid Hussain of the World Bank. Moeen Qureshi, the senior vice president of the World Bank and his German wife and M.M. Ahmad were also there. Shahid Javed Burki and his wife joined us after dinner. Had an interesting conversation.

Moeen Qureshi was of the view that the National Assembly experiment was not likely to succeed, that Junejo would probably go and if that happened the hard-line general's lobby would have the upper hand. He thought that Ziaul Haq should be helped to succeed with his move towards 'democracy'. The alternative, he thought, was much bleaker.

Wednesday, 9 Oct 1985, Abbottabad
Someone telephoned form London to say that John Caoo and Dick Melton will be arriving in Islamabad on 17 October and would call on me on 18 October in connection with the sale of aircraft. I told him that he had probably got the wrong air marshal. The person calling said that they had been given my number by 'the group captain' in the Pakistan embassy. Very odd.

Thursday, 10 Oct 1985, Abbottabad
Aitzaz Ahsan has been giving odd statements to the press. It appears that he is preparing to leave the party. Decided to ask him (and the other members of the national working committee) in Lahore to issue a statement to the press denying reports appearing in the *Nawa-i-Waqt* of a rift in the party. Told Khurshid Kasuri to get this statement signed and issued. He contacted Aitzaz Ahsan who was not ready to sign it. Gave him a revised statement on the telephone. Khurshid Kasuri will contact him again and ring back tomorrow.

Friday, 11 Oct 1985, Abbottabad
Khurshid telephoned to say that Aitzaz Ahsan has gone to Gujrat and was not available.

Saturday, 12 Oct 1985, Abbottabad, Hassan Abdal, Pindi Gheb, Mianwali
Left for Hassan Abdal at 07:30 with Omar. Arrived at the rest house at Hassan Abdal at 09:00 where I was to meet Maulana Noorani. Was told that the administration (DC and SP) had given instructions that we were not to be allowed to meet at the rest house. We therefore moved to a roadside restaurant where we discussed the political situation in the country.

Friday, 18 Oct 1985, Rawalpindi, Lahore
Were met on arrival at Lahore, by Mumtaz Joya, AC Lahore city, who informed me that the government had banned the youth meeting on Hall Road, Lakshmi Mansion area. Chairs, banners, etc. had been removed, the ground flooded and some of our people arrested. Also .that I would not be allowed to go there. Drove to Khurshid Kasuri's where I discussed the strategy with Asaf Vardag, Haider Usman, Begum Mahnaz Rafi and a few others. Decided that Asaf Vardag should address a press conference that evening which he did. Omar who had also been arrested was released at about 20:00.

Saturday, 19 Oct 1985, Lahore
Met central office bearers and the provincial chairman at Khurshid Kasuri's. Decided: (a) To take a strong stand on the 1973 constitution issue in the MRD meeting in Karachi on 24 and 25 October (short of

leaving the MRD) (b) To make some changes in the party's election procedure.

Later addressed the Pakistan Society at Malik Amjad Hussain's place.

Decided to constitute a disciplinary action committee to go into the attitude of Aitzaz Ahsan towards the party. Appointed Begum Shahida Jameel and Dr Ahmed Hussain Kamal to undertake this task.

Thursday, 24 Oct 1985, Abbottabad
Received the order of the home secretary Sindh banning my entry into the province for 90 days.

Friday, 25 Oct 1985, Abbottabad
Fatehyab Ali Khan has been put in prison and Iqbal Haider has gone underground. An odd beginning of so called 'return to democracy'.

Sunday, 27 Oct 1985, Abbottabad
Reagan was reported in the *Muslim* of yesterday to have told Rajiv Gandhi (as given to the press by the Indian prime minister) to stop Pakistan from developing a nuclear weapon. Whatever that might mean. This could also mean a preventive strike. My statement on this appeared in today's newspapers.

Thursday, 5 Nov 1985, Abbottabad
Amina, Omar and I attended the 68th anniversary reception of the October Revolution in the Soviet Embassy in Islamabad. The Soviet Ambassador was very friendly and wanted to meet me to discuss various matters.

Monday, 11 & Tuesday, 12 Nov 1985, Abbottabad
Asaf Vardag came for lunch. Discussed party matters and role of National Assembly and the Senate. Agreed that the only opposition of any kind during the eighth amendment bill in the National Assembly came from three members, Mumtaz Tarar, Nur Khan and Shahid Zafar of Rawalpindi.

Thursday, 14 Nov 1985, Abbottabad
Received a copy of Aitzaz Ahsan's reply to the disciplinary action committee's communication requiring his explanation. The committee has suggested that his membership of the national working committee and the national council (to which he has been nominated) should be terminated. I agreed with their recommendation. His reply is not only inadequate but also displays a lack of a sense of responsibility.

Saturday, 16 Nov 1985, Abbottabad
Mushahid Hussain, editor, *Muslim*, telephoned to say that he had fixed Friday, 29 November for the panel discussion on problems of Pakistan's security at the Holiday Inn in Islamabad. I agreed to participate. The others asked are Agha Shahi, Dr Eqbal Ahmad (from New York) and Mian Mohammad Tufail.

Sunday, 17 Nov 1985, Abbottabad
Mr Catchpole came to see Omar to get a letter published in the *Muslim* about the effects of giving up English as a medium of English in Pakistani schools. Matriculation examination will be in Urdu in all subjects (except English) from 1988 and this he thought, will create serious problems in comprehension particularly in science subjects. He is an experienced and dedicated educationist.

Friday, 22 Nov 1985, Abbottabad
Shahida Jameel issued a statement explaining the reasons for disciplinary action against Aitzaz Ahsan.

Monday, 25 Nov 1985, Abbottabad
Aitzaz Ahsan's membership of the national working committee and the national council was terminated.

Friday, 29 Nov 1985, Abbottabad
Came back to Rawalpindi and attended a seminar on perspective on Pakistan's security, organised by the *Muslim*. Agha Shahi, Mian Tufail Mohammad of Jamaat-i-Islami, Dr Mubashir, Dr Eqbal Ahmed from New York and myself comprised the panel. Dr Eqbal Ahmad was very good and gave everyone a lot to think about. The audience was very

receptive and comprised the intellectuals of Islamabad as well as diplomats, and government functionaries.

Thursday, 19 Dec 1985, Abbottabad
The Punjab Tehrik-i-Istiqlal removed Chaudhry Aitzaz Ahsan from party membership on 14 December for continued violation of party discipline.

Sunday, 22 Dec 1985, Abbottabad
Khurshid Kasuri telephoned to say that over 25 MRD leaders and workers including Malik Hamid Sarfaraz had been arrested in Lahore presumably to prevent them from holding a meeting on 25 December.

Monday, 23 & Tuesday, 24 Dec 1985, Abbottabad
Nasrullah Khan and some thirty workers of the MRD were arrested in Lahore to prevent the MRD meeting in Mochi Gate on 25 December Hamid Sarfaraz and Manzoor Gilani of Tehrik-i-Istiqlal were among those arrested.

28–31 Dec 1985, Lahore
Heard Ziaul Haq's speech on TV on 30 December when he announced the lifting of martial law and the state of emergency. Civil rights have been restored but it was not clear how these and other freedoms would be affected by the presidential orders about which nothing has been said and which have not been withdrawn. The martial law orders and regulations which have been given constitutional status are not such as to affect civil liberties. Since the political parties act rules have not been spelt out it is not known in what manner the political parties will be regulated and the degree to which their freedom will be curtailed. The eighth amendment in any case gives Ziaul Haq tremendous powers. In spite of all this what has been done is a step forward, albeit belated, towards democracy.

All governors except Lieutentant General Jehandad Khan of Sindh have been changed.

General Musa is the new governor of Balochistan, Ghafoor Hoti of NWFP and Nawab Sajjad Qureshi of Punjab.

Diary 1986

22–24 Jan 1986, Abbottabad

The national working committee decided that the party should register in accordance with the government's declaration of 30 December. Decided to hold public meetings in Lahore on 7 March, Sukkur 23 March, Peshawar in first fortnight of April, Quetta on 25 April and Karachi sometimes in May or June. Also decided to participate in the MRD meeting in Lahore on 29 January and the party's central council meeting on 30 and 31 January.

26 Jan to 4 Feb 1986, Lahore, Quetta, Multan, Sukkur

The MRD public meeting at Mochi Gate in Lahore on 29 January. PPP created trouble when I rose to speak. Clashes between their workers and ours.

The MRD central council meeting on 30th and 31st. NDP announced their rejection of 1973 constitution. Matter could not be resolved so decided to meet again in Karachi on 29 March. Because of the behaviour of the PPP workers at Mochi Gate on 29 March decided that the Tehrik-i-Istiqlal will in future hold separate meetings.

Tuesday, 25 Feb 1986, Bahawalpur, Qaimpur, Chishtian Hasalpur, Bahawalnagar, Lalika

Addressed the district bar association at Bahawalpur. A very good session. In answer to questions from PPP members I spoke out against the anti-people's policies of Bhutto's government. My speech and answers were very well received. Moved on to Bahawalnagar and Minchinabad and addressed gatherings at Qaimpur (small), Chishtian, Hasalpur (a good meeting with about 5,000 people).

Bahawalnagar and Lalika (a very good gathering). Shafqat Lalika, who is the vice chairman of our Bahawalpur legislative organisation and lives in Lahore, arranged an excellent meeting of about 3,000 peasants in a rural setting. Altogether a useful visit to Bahawalpur district. The response in rural areas appears to be good, but a great deal of work still needs to be done.

Wednesday, 26 Feb 1986, Lahore

Addressed the Minchinabad (*tehsil*) Bar Association. Went on to Mazharabad near Dipalpur where Rao Kaiser, our chairman Okara district, had arranged a good meeting.

Thursday, 27 Feb 1986, Lahore

Called on Arif Nizami in the Services Hospital. He had been injured in a car accident in which his two year-old son was killed and wife injured. Also called on Nisar Osmani, bureau chief of *Dawn* who had also been injured in a car accident recently.

Friday, 28 Feb 1986, Lahore

Went to see the central office which had been sealed by the martial law authorities on 16 October 1979 and opened up a couple of months ago. It was in a shocking state of disrepair.

Friday, 7 March 1986, Sukkur, Lahore

Addressed a very successful public meeting at Jinnah Park, Larkana. About 30,000 attended. *Nawa-i-Waqt* and *Jang* Lahore reported the crowd at 50,000 and *Dawn* Karachi reported the figures as 15,000. Morale of our workers is very high after this very successful meeting in a town generally regarded as a stronghold of the PPP. Moreover the PPP had held daily corner meetings to dissuade the public from attending our meeting and had torn our posters (for the meeting) in Larkana. All provincial chairmen, Khudai Noor and Allama Turabi, addressed the meeting. Our workers came from many places to attend the meeting. A very good show and a good start for our public contact programme in Sindh.

Saturday, 8 March 1986, Larkana, Karachi

Some people called in the morning at Nisar Khuhro's to congratulate me on the very successful meeting yesterday. It was confirmed that PPP had arranged to disturb the meeting by firing.

Sunday, 23 March 1986, Lahore, Abbottabad

Attended a meeting in connection with the 28 March public meeting. Earlier met Major General Tajammal Hussain's son who wanted me to help to try to get his father's remaining sentence commuted.

Tajammal is serving a ten-year sentence for a conspiracy to overthrow the government. He denies having been involved in such a conspiracy.

Friday, 28 March 1986, Lahore
Public meeting at Mochi Gate. Good participation by party workers from all over the province. A satisfactory meeting. About 50,000 people. About 16 speakers which rather spoilt the effect. Each speaker spoke for about five minutes and I spoke for 20.

Saturday, 29 March 1986, Lahore
Nawa-i-Waqt reported yesterday's meeting as 'very large' which was an exaggeration. Other papers—*Muslim, Dawn*—reported it as a well-attended meeting. Generally the event was very well reported.

Thursday, 3 April 1986, Abbottabad
Asaf Vardag came and briefed me on the MRD meeting in Karachi on 29 and 30 March. Vardag told me that he would be contesting the party election for the secretary general's post. Khurshid Kasuri is also contesting for secretary general. Membership will start on 15 April and will continue until 1 July when elections at the lower tiers should start.

Friday, 11 April 1986, Peshawar
Addressed a well attended meeting at Jinnah Park (formerly Cunningham Park). Our workers from all over NWFP and also from Attock, Rawalpindi, Gujrat and Lahore had also come. A very spirited meeting with good response.

Tuesday, 15 April 1986, Abbottabad
The US bombed targets in Libya including Tripoli and Benghazi. The Voice of America reported 70 people killed and about 100, including women and children, injured. I issued a statement to the press condemning US action against Libya and suggested that Pakistan should condemn it.

Thursday, 24 April 1986, Lahore
Meeting of the national working committee in the central office, Jaura
Pul. Mian Khalid Rashid had done an excellent job in renovating the
place and making it usable once again. Discussed various issues.
Decided not to withdraw the registration of the party—as suggested
by the MRD. Also decided not to have joint public meetings with the
MRD.

The national working committee decided (I was not present) that
Omar should assume responsibilities of chairman Youth League.

Thursday, 1 May 1986, Abbottabad
Khaqan Abbasi, a minister in the federal government and at one time
a Pakistan Air Force colleague, came. He wanted me to meet Junejo
which I saw no point in doing.

Wednesday, 7 May 1986, Abbottabad (Haripur)
Addressed a very big public meeting in Haripur. Probably the largest
ever held there. Certainly much larger than the PNA election meeting
in 1977.

Friday, 20 June 1986, Abbottabad
The MRD agreed on the issue of provincial autonomy—only four
subjects with the centre. It also agreed to meet in Karachi on 23 and
24 July.

Saturday, 21 June 1986, Abbottabad
Khawaja Khairuddin, Major Ijaz Ahmed and Chaudhri Arshad came
in the evening. Khairuddin said that he thought that the MRD will
break up at the next meeting in Karachi on 23 and 24 July. Other
points he made were: (1) NDP is not likely to budge from its stand
disowning the 1973 constitution and will therefore have to leave the
MRD. (2) Chaudhri Arshad of PDP said that if the 1973 constitution
is not accepted by the MRD and all parties do not reiterate their
support for it, his party (PDP) will have nothing to do with the MRD.
(3) The alliance of so-called four leftist parties is not likely to
materialise. (4) Bizenjo's PNP and other parties, that is all the MRD
parties minus PPP and NDP, were in favour of forming a meaningful
alliance along with JUP, in the event of the MRD breaking up.

A representative of Piyar Ali Allana of PPP came to see Omar today to try to persuade the Tehrik to reach an understanding with the PPP. Piyar Ali Allana, also spoke to Omar on the telephone (from Karachi).

Thursday, 17 July 1986, Abbottabad
Malik Qasim came to discuss the MRD. He is hoping to be the next secretary general of the MRD. Khawaja Khairuddin has resigned.

Friday, 18 July 1986, Abbottabad
Khurshid Kasuri came. He has had meetings with former PPP members in the UK and said that some of them were interested in the Tehrik-i-Istiqlal. Briefed him on the line to be adopted at the next MRD meeting in Karachi on 23 and 24 July which he wants to attend along with Asaf Vardag.

Saturday, 19 July 1986, Abbottabad
Omar telephoned from Mukhtiar Bacha's in Mardan. He had had a very good visit to Tangi and a good meeting in Mardan. He is leaving for Batkhela and Thana tomorrow and will stop briefly in Shergarh on the way.

Friday, 25 July 1986, Islamabad, Abbottabad
Addressed a large public meeting at Panjgran in Islamabad federal area today. Raja Bashir Ahmed joined the party having organised it with Syed Zafar Ali Shah's cooperation. I was met at Margala Pass and led a procession.

Wednesday, 13 Aug 1986, Multan, Karachi
Large number of arrests all over the country. Section 144 has been imposed in Punjab and Sindh. Benazir was prevented from boarding a plane at Karachi airport and Nasrullah Khan was arrested on arrival in Multan.

Thursday, 14 Aug 1986, Karachi
Independence Day—independence from the British but not from our generals.

Some disturbances in Lahore and Karachi, where the MRD tried to defy the restrictions. Four persons were reported shot and killed by the police in Lahore, lawyers were baton charged and a number of people arrested. In Karachi, Benazir and Bizenjo were arrested when they tried to address a meeting. Some political workers were also arrested.

Sunday, 31 Aug 1986, Abbottabad
Ghulam Mustafa Jatoi formed a new party to be known as National People's Party in Lahore yesterday.

Saturday, 6 Sept 1986, Abbottabad
Armed Forces day. A Pan Am B-747 with 390 passengers was hijacked by four Palestinians at Karachi at 21:00 last night. A shoot-out took place, a Pakistani commando force attacked the hijackers in the plane. Seventeen persons were killed and over fifty were injured. Two hijackers were killed and two were captured. The largest hijacking operation with the largest number of casualties so far, anywhere.

Tuesday, 9 Sept 1986, Abbottabad
All the MRD detainees in Sindh, including Ghaus Bux Bizenjo, Khawaja Khairuddin, Mairaj Mohammad Khan and Benazir Bhutto were released last night. Those arrested and detained in Punjab are also likely to be released soon.

Saturday, 11 Oct 1986, Abbottabad, Islamabad
The BBC estimated the gathering in the MRD public meeting in Abbottabad to be 40,000. *Frontier Post* improved on that by reporting it as being over 150,000. Tariq said that the DC had told him that he estimated the gathering as 20,000 and said that they had noted that 851 vehicles (of all kinds) came from outside Abbottabad for the meeting. At an average of 20 persons per vehicle the number of persons who came or were brought from outside was 15-16,000. Therefore about 5,000 locals attended. The most notable thing was the complete lack of discipline in the meeting which was a picture of chaos and confusion. The MRD met today and decided not to reply to my letter of 12 August addressed to Malik Qasim. In accordance with our decision we are now left with no option but to leave the MRD which I propose to announce tomorrow.

Sunday, 12 Oct 1986, Islamabad, Abbottabad
Issued a press release to announce our decision to leave the MRD.

Friday, 28 Nov 1986, Lahore
Punjab party elections in the central office at Jaura Pul started after midday and ended at 03:30 (29 November). Haider Usman was elected chairman by a margin of some 40 votes against Rafi Butt. The elections were held in a very congenial atmosphere and were well contested. Some 250 councillors participated.

Tuesday, 16 Dec 1986, Abbottabad
Pushtoon-Mohajir riots continue in Karachi. Over 120 deaths and hundreds of people have been reported injured during the last three days.

Thursday, 25 Dec 1986, Karachi
Toured Orangi and saw the terrible effects of rioting. It appeared that there was no government in Karachi and that people had gone berserk. Spoke to people at a couple of places and heard their woes. Returned before re-imposition of curfew at 17:00.

Diary 1987

Sunday, 1 Feb 1987, Karachi
Called on Maulana Noorani along with Dr Rahim ul Haq, Chaudhri Jameel and Zia Ispahani and had dinner with him. Agreed with him to try for a common approach among political parties followed by an all parties conference to put pressure on Ziaul Haq for the holding of an early election.

Thursday, 5 Feb 1987, Usta Mohammad, Rojhan Jamali
Addressed the district bar association Jacobabad. A number of persons including the general secretary of the district bar association joined the party. Was given a very good reception on arrival in Shikarpur where I addressed the workers.

Sunday, 22 Feb 1987, (Amangarh) Peshawar
Tehrik-i-Istiqlal held a public meeting in Chowk Yadgar and took out a big procession from Chowk Yadgar to Soekarno Square. Meeting was well attended.

Tuesday, 24 March 1987, Lahore
Allama Ehsan Elahi Zaheer was injured in a bomb blast at Qila Lakshman Singh, where he addressed a public meeting last night. Some eight people were killed and many injured. Called on him in Mayo Hospital.

Friday, 27 March 1987, Lahore
Dinner at Shahnaz Javed's. She and her husband Javed Rafi showed dedication to the party, and made pledges of substantial monthly financial support to the party funds.

Monday, 13 April 1987, Abbottabad, Lahore
Omar Kasuri telephoned to say that his father, Mian Mahmud Ali Kasuri died this morning. This is sad news. Mian Sahib was a veteran fighter for human rights. We shall miss him. Decided to leave for Lahore this evening. The *janaza* prayers are tomorrow morning.

Tuesday, 14 April 1987, Lahore, Abbottabad
Attended Mian Mahmud Ali Kasuri's *janaza* at Khurshid's Gulberg residence. The body was taken to Kasur for burial. A large number of people attended. Later called at the residence of the late Allama Ehsan Elahi Zaheer to offer condolences at his demise.

Saturday, 20 June 1987, Quetta
Called on the sons of Nawab Ghaus Bux Raisani who was killed recently.

Tuesday, 30 June 1987, Abbottabad
Omar Hayat Qureshi, our chairman Jhang, telephoned to say that the administration did not want us to hold our public meeting in the bazaar and threatened action if we did. Told him that we will go ahead as planned.

Tuesday, 2 July 1987, Sargodha, Faisalabad, Jhang, Faisalabad
Reached Jhang at about 22:00 and addressed a big public meeting in
Rail Bazaar.

Sunday, 5 July 1987, Abbottabad
Ziaul Haq completed his tenth year in power.

Wednesday, 19 Aug 1987, Abbottabad
Pir Syed Ahmed Gillani head of Ittehad-i-Milli, an Afghan resistance
organisation called. It was an interesting meeting, which helped me
understand their point of view better.

Friday, 28 Aug 1987, Abbottabad, Peshawar
Called on Wali Khan in Lady Reading Hospital to enquire about Khan
Abdul Ghaffar Khan (96) who has been in a coma for the last month
or so. Had dinner with Afghan Consul General who had came to
Peshawar to see us off to Kabul at the invitation of the Afghan
government.

Saturday, 29 Aug 1987, Peshawar, Torkham, Jalalabad, Kabul
Left for Torkham in a motorcade of about 40 cars. My delegation
comprised: Khurshid Mahmud Kasuri (secretary general), Inamullah
Khan (chairman NWFP), Walid Ahmed Khan (general secretary
NWFP), Khudai Noor (chairman Balochistan), Mian Kamal Khan
Badini (chairman Chagi district), Dr Rahim ul Haq (chairman Sindh),
Rana Mohammad Arshad Khan (acting chairman Punjab), Mohammad
Rafi Butt (chairman Rawalpindi city) and Omar (Istiqlal youth).

Were met at Torkham by the Afghan minister of higher education,
Burhan Ghiasi, the governor of Ninghar province, and officials of the
foreign office. Was given a warm reception and taken to Jalalabad.
Visited an olive factory and left for Kabul by a military plane after
lunch.

The aeroplane had to gain a height of 8,000 metres over the
airfield before setting course for Kabul and carried out a sharp descent
on arrival at Kabul (security precautions). *En route*, when passing
over high ground, the aircraft fired decoy rockets as a safety measure
against possible stinger missile attacks. A stinger missile is heat and
noise seeking and has a time limit of 13 seconds, which is enough to

take it to a distance of 8,000 metres. Decoy rockets were also fired when we were in the circuit over Kabul.

We were received on arrival by Mr Abdul Rahim Hatif, the president of the National Front and the chairman of the National Reconciliation Council.

Stayed at the state guest house, which was originally constructed as the residence of King Zahir Shah's son.

Sunday, 30 Aug 1987, Kabul

Called on Abdul Rahim Hatif, the president of the National Reconciliation Council at his headquarters. He gave us a detailed analysis of the situation and the working of his organisation. Later called on the foreign minister, Abdul Vakil. It was an interesting meeting. Abdul Vakil attached great importance to our visit and called it historic.

Monday, 31 Aug 1987, Kabul, Mazar Sharif, Kabul

Flew (in a military air craft) to Mazar Sharif following the same procedure of safety precautions. Was received by the party general secretary and the governor of Balkh province. Offered *fateha* at the tomb of Hazrat Ali (who is believed by some people to be buried here). Then drove to the historic city of Balkh, 24 kilometres away. Saw the historic mosque of Balkh as also the grave of Rabia Balkhi. She was killed about 1,000 years ago by her brothers when it was discovered that she was in love with a slave of her father, the king of Balkh. She was tortured and before dying wrote some verses of poetry on the walls of her prison cell with her blood. She was a renowned poetess. Visited a large fertilizer plant. Returned to Kabul in the evening. Saw the proceeding on TV of 'Pashtoonistan' day observed in Kabul today. We had been asked whether we wished to attend the function but had decided not to do so. Earlier in Mazar Sharif we met Najmuddin Kaviani, secretary of the international committee of the ruling party.

Tuesday, 1 Sept 1987, Kabul

Called on the president of the Democratic Republic of Afghanistan, Haji Mohammad Chamkanni and later Suleman Laik (the minister of tribal affairs). Offered (*zohar*) prayers at a mosque in Kabul. The mosque was jampacked and although it was a large mosque, people were praying on the pavement outside. There must have been 5-10,000 people. A much larger gathering than could be seen for *zohar* prayers on a normal day in Pakistan in a large city like Lahore, Peshawar or Karachi.

Saw Babar Bagh on the outskirts of Kabul and earlier lunched at Kargah Lake with Sarfaraz Mohammad, deputy minister of foreign affairs, Ajmal Khattak and Afrasayab Khattak were also there. Ajmal Khattak later called on me at the state guest house where we all are staying and gave us his assessment of the Afghan situation. He told us that the Afghans (the government and the people) attached great importance to our visit.

Had dinner at the party headquarter hosted by Suleman Laik, the minister of tribal affairs. Saw a cultural (music and songs) show after dinner.

Wednesday, 2 Sept 1987, Kabul

Visited the military museum and saw weapons said to be captured from the hostiles. Amongst them a 'blue pipe missile'. Called on Dr Najibullah, the secretary general of the People's Democratic Party. Talked with him for two hours about Pakistan-Afghanistan relations. He said that his party attached great importance to Tehrik-i-Istiqlal and myself and wanted our help to solve the Afghan problem. Dr Najib later accompanied me to the state guest house where we were staying and condoled with Khurshid Kasuri (on his father's death) and also met the other members of our delegation.

Addressed a press conference. Attended a dinner hosted by Abdul Rahim Hatif at the former Inter Continental Hotel. A music session accompanied the dinner, which is the usual practice in Afghanistan. Heard today that Pakistan newspapers had published a story yesterday that our aircraft on its flight from Jalalabad to Kabul had been attacked by the mujahideen and that a reception camp at Dakka, between Torkham and Jalalabad, had been destroyed by hostile fire!

Thursday, 3 Sept 1987, Kabul, Jalalabad, Peshawar, Abbottabad

Left Kabul by a military aircraft for Jalalabad and then for Torkham we were seen off by the general secretary of the PDPA Nanahar Province, the governor and the area army commander at Torkham and were received by a large number of party workers. Met the press on crossing the border.

Monday, 19 Oct 1987, Abbottabad
Met Khurshid Kasuri at our Islamabad house. Khurshid wanted me to come to Lahore on 21 October to meet Hamid Sarfaraz who he said wishes to come back to the Tehrik-i-Istiqlal. Agreed to do so.

Wednesday, 21 Oct 1987, Abbottabad, Lahore
Went to Lahore. Met Malik Hamid Sarfaraz at Khurshid's and agreed to his return to the Tehrik-i-Istiqlal.

Thursday, 22 Oct 1987, Lahore, Islamabad
Omar organised a demonstration in Rawalpindi against US action against Iran in the Gulf.

Saturday, 31 Oct 1987, Bhanot, Karachi, Islamabad
Ziauddin Ziae died yesterday of a heart attack in Quetta. A great personal loss to me and to the party. Ziae was a dedicated worker and gave all his time to the party. Ali flew to Quetta to attend the funeral.

Monday, 2 Nov 1987, Islamabad, Quetta
Left for Quetta with Amina and Omar. Went to Ziae's and condoled with his family. It was his *qul* today. A large number of people were there.

Monday, 9 Nov 1987, Abbottabad
Allama Iqbal's birthday. Ayub Bokhari (Zahid Bokhari's brother) along with a delegation of some Shias came to explain the role of the government in fanning anti-Shia feelings in Attock. Shia-Sunni riots had taken place there during Muharram.

Wednesday, 11 Nov 1987, Karachi
Naeemul Haq called to say that he had been in touch with General Wali Khan, son-in-law of late King Zahir Shah, who had confirmed that Zahir Shah, would be pleased to meet me if I came to Rome. Dr Rahim ul Haq also called.

Thursday, 12 Nov 1987, Karachi
Chaudhri Jameel and Shahida Jameel had a long session with Wazir Ali and have apparently decided to leave the Tehrik-i-Istiqlal.

Friday, 20 Nov 1987, Lahore
Wazir Ali, Khurshid, Mahnaz, Ruknuddin and Rafi Butt had a long meeting to discuss party strategy. They decided to: (1) collect funds from amongst themselves (and myself) to enable the party to carry out effective political work for six months; (2) suggested that I should call a meeting of elected office bearers every month, to informally discuss party strategy. (I had been doing this already except for the last six months).

Tuesday, 1 Dec 1987, Abbottabad
Sixteen people are reported to have been killed in local bodies polls held yesterday.

Friday, 11 Dec 1987, Abbottabad
President Reagan of the US and Gorbachev (the Soviet leader) reached an agreement on the banning and destruction of all medium range nuclear weapons and also agreed to examine the reduction of long range missiles by 50 per cent. Both regarded the Washington summit to be very successful and agreed to meet again towards the middle of next year. They discussed the evacuation of Soviet troops from Afghanistan but could not agree on the modalities of withdrawal. I feel that the Afghan issue will be resolved before long, probably during 1988.

Saturday, 26 Dec 1987, Abbottabad
Three explosions took place in Islamabad market today. One person was killed and about thirty wounded. The first incident of this kind in Islamabad.

Diary 1988

Wednesday, 6 Jan 1988, Islamabad, Peshawar, Islamabad
Lunched with Fazle Haq (former governor of NWFP) and invited him to join the Tehrik-i-Istiqlal. He was inclined but said that he will consult his friends and let me know in a fortnight's time.

Sunday, 10 Jan 1988, Islamabad
Khurshid met Fazle Haq and discussed the possibility of his joining the Tehri-i-Istiqlal.

Tuesday, 14 Jan 1988, Islamabad
Muslim League has appointed Syed Munir Shah as chief organiser of the party for NWFP.

Sunday, 17 Jan 1988, Islamabad, Abbottabad
My 67th birthday. Shirin telephoned from Miami, Ali from Karachi and Omar from Peshawar. Samina, Omar and their children gave me a very nice writing table for my birthday and Amina a book on birds.

Thursday, 21 Jan 1988, Abbottabad, Peshawar, Islamabad
Went to Peshawar to attend *Namaz-i-Janaza* of Ghaffar Khan. About 10,000 people in pouring rain attended the *janaza* in Jinnah Park.

Saturday, 6 Feb 1988, Faisalabad, Karachi, Faisalabad, Islamabad
Attended Toba Tek Singh district convention at Kamalia. About 5,000 people were present. A great deal of enthusiasm. Khurshid, Mahnaz, Shahtaj Qizalbash, Omar and Qayyum Pahot came from Lahore. Some workers from Faisalabad, Jhang, Multan, Sahiwal district and Sheikhupura also came.

Monday, 8 Feb 1988, Islamabad
Omar left for Lahore and later left for New Delhi. Should be back on 16 or 17 February after attending a seminar on Asian youth in Kabul.

Tuesday, 9 Feb 1988, Islamabad
Omar should have left Delhi for Kabul early today. Cordivez finished his parleys with Afghanistan and Pakistan today. He announced that agreement had been reached on the settlement of the Afghan issue and that he expects the talks being held on 2 March to be the final meeting. Gorbachev, the Soviet president, has announced that if a final agreement is reached in Geneva by 15 March, withdrawal of Russian forces will commence on 15 May and will be completed within ten months.

Thursday, 26 Feb 1988, Karachi
Dinner with Maulana Noorani. Discussed the invitation of the government to discuss the Afghan situation. He was in favour of attending the meeting.

Sunday, 28 Feb 1988, Karachi
Second day of the national working committee. Qazi Abid, federal minister of information, called to deliver Junejo's letter inviting me to a conference on 5 March to discuss the Afghan issue. NWC discussed the matter and decided that I should attend the meeting to express our point of view.

Saturday, 5 March 1988, Islamabad
Attended the meeting of political leaders with Mohammad Khan Junejo. It appears that there is pressure on the government to sign the Geneva accord by Pakistan's allies that is, the US, Saudi Arabia, Iran and China. The general opinion in the meeting, except for the fundamentalist religious parties, (Jamaat-i-Islami, both JUI and both Ahle-Hadis) was in favour of signing. The Soviets are insisting that the agreement be signed by 15 May so that they can commence their withdrawal by 15 May.

Sunday, 6 March 1988, Islamabad
Second day of the round table conference. Everyone agreed that the Geneva accord should be signed. Six religious parties (not the JUP) wanted the Geneva accord signed only if a government acceptable to the refugees was installed in Kabul. Others (13 parties) including JUP wanted the agreement signed and effort made to ensure that conditions are created for the return of the refugees.

Monday, 14 March 1988, Lahore, Islamabad
Meraj Khalid of the PPP, one time chief minister of Punjab, called. He feels close to us and agrees with the policies of the Tehrik-i-Istiqlal. Might be prepared to join us. Is very unhappy in the PPP.

Tuesday, 15 March 1988, Islamabad
I met Mustafa Khar at the Adiala jail where he is undergoing a four-year sentence for not turning up before a martial law government to answer queries in connection with his wealth (tax) returns. He had asked me to see him.

Sunday, 10 April 1988, Miami (Florida USA)
A big explosion took place at 10:00 at the Fyzabad Ammunition Depot, between Islamabad and Rawalpindi (known as Ojhri camp) and caused havoc in both the cities. First reports put the number of dead at 80 and injured at 800. Missiles, rockets and bombs went off and flew in all directions, hitting schools, houses and shops in both the cities. Missiles hit or fell near the Holiday Inn, the Chinese embassy, the US embassy, at least two schools and some other buildings in Islamabad. Ojhri camp depot was being used to store supplies for Afghan guerrillas and first report said that at that time Afghan trucks were being loaded with missiles. It is thought that a fire broke out by 'accident'. Khaqan Abbasi, MNA, (an ex-PAF officer), who rushed to see what was happening (or was perhaps driving by), was killed by a missile hit and his son seriously injured. It took about an hour for the 'fireworks' to stop.

Telephoned Jeena (my sister) in Islamabad to enquire. A rocket had landed a few yards away from her son, Asad, in his school, but he was not injured. Yasmeen goes to the same school but is away in Lahore with Omar and Samina. Faree's classroom in the Government College Islamabad was hit by a missile but she had taken the children out of the room a couple of minutes earlier. No one was injured. Ziaul Haq is away in Kuwait and is busy trying to solve the problems of the Islamic world.

Sunday, 29 May 1988, Islamabad
Ziaul Haq dissolved the National Assembly and dismissed Junejo's government. He announced that election will be held in accordance

with the 1985 constitution (within three months). Junejo had returned from a far East tour an hour or so before Ziaul Haq's announcement.

Monday, 30 May 1988, Islamabad
Heard Ziaul Haq's speech in the evening, which was a repetition of his speech yesterday. It is clear that unless he backtracks which he has shown previously that he is capable of, elections will be held: (a) within 90 days; (b) on a party basis; (c) registered parties only will be allowed to take part.

Thursday, 9 June 1988, Islamabad, Abbottabad
Ziaul Haq announced an 18-man cabinet of discredited Muslim League courtiers.

Sunday, 12 June 1988, Karachi
Attended the meeting of the Sindh working committee at Rahim ul Haq's. Met Mir Ghous Bux Bizenjo. He asked me to attend the all parties conference, which he and Nasrullah Khan have called for 15th. I declined since the national working committee had decided against it and there was not enough time (two days) to reconsider the decision. Bizenjo thought that Ziaul Haq needed time to reorganise the Muslim League and was therefore likely to postpone the elections until about October or November. He also thought that the election could be on a non-party basis.

Monday, 20 June 1988, Abbottabad, Islamabad, Abbottabad
The US political counselor, Edward Abington, called to discuss the general political situation and the Tehrik-i-Istiqlal's views on foreign relations particularly its attitude towards the US.

Thursday, 23 June 1988, Islamabad
Attended a meeting of the central office bearers of the party at Zafar Ali Shah's. Discussed invitations to join all parties conference. Consensus was against joining APC. The meeting felt that I should contest elections form NA-12 and NA-13 (Abbottabad district).

Saturday, 25 June 1988, Abbottabad, Islamabad, Lahore, Islamabad

Dr Akmal came. Omar had met him earlier. Akmal has decided to join the Tehrik-i-Istiqlal. Addressed a press conference at Khurshid's in the afternoon. Mushahid Hussain, former editor of the daily *Muslim,* announced his decision to join the Tehrik. Decided to hold a meeting in Lahore on 30 June at which Dr Akmal will announce his decision to join the Tehrik.

Thursday, 30 June 1988, Islamabad, Lahore

Omar and I flew to Lahore. Addressed a meeting of about a 100 intellectuals. Dr Akmal Hussain, a renowned economist, and Mahmud Mirza announced their decision to join the Tehrik-i-Istiqlal.

Maulana Akbar Saqi formerly of JUP and now NPP called. He is willing to join the party but wanted some time to consult friends.

Thursday, 7 July 1988, Abbottabad, Islamabad

Chaudhri Mumtaz Tarar came to lunch. He is part of a group of which the other members are Fakhr Imam, his wife Abida Hussain, Javed Hashmi, Arif Sayial and Chaudhri Shafique of Faisalabad, all former MNAs. They are favourably inclined towards the Tehrik-i-Istiqlal and are likely to join it if the next election is held on a party basis. We should know shortly. There is some talk of a referendum before the election in which Ziaul Haq is likely to change the system in favour of a presidential type of government. Omar had dinner with Fakhr Imam and Abida Hussain and discussed various possibilities with them.

Saturday, 9 July 1988, Abbottabad, Haripur

The reception and the procession in Haripur was very good. About a hundred vehicles and about 2,000 people took part. Mumtaz Tarar, ex-MNA, also came to witness the meeting.

Monday, 18 July 1988, Abbottabad, Islamabad

The US ambassador called. It appeared from his talk that elections are likely to be non-party.

Wednesday, 20 July 1988, Abbottabad
Ziaul Haq addressed the Senate today and announced that elections
to both the national and provincial assemblies would be held on 16
November 1988. His reasons for not holding elections within 90 days,
by 27 August were: (1) It would be inconvenient because of rains in
August. (2) August is the month of Moharram. (3) About 100,000
people are away on Haj. (4) Voters' lists and demarcation of
constituencies require some changes. An amazing performance.

Thursday, 21 July 1988, Abbottabad
Ziaul Haq announced that the 16 November elections will be non-
party though political parties will be allowed to propagate their
programme and take part in the campaign. The purpose is obvious that
elected people come into the assemblies as independents and he (Ziaul
Haq) would not be required to call upon the leader of the majority
party (since there will be none) to form a government.

Mushahid Hussain and Akmal came for lunch. Wanted cooperation
with other opposition/political parties and suggested that I should
meet their leaders.

Wednesday, 3 Aug 1988, Karachi
Called on Maulana Noorani. Discussed possibility of cooperation with
JUP and agreed on basic principles. Called on Ghulam Mustafa Jatoi
and had similar talks with him.

Thursday, 4 Aug 1988, Karachi
Called on Benazir Bhutto and discussed the general situation in a
pleasant atmosphere. Khurshid Kasuri, Rahim ul Haq and Zia Ispahani
accompanied me. Decided that Khurshid Kasuri and Farooq Leghari
should explore the possibilities of cooperation. Later called on
Sherbaz Mazari and had similar talks.

Tuesday, 9 Aug 1988, Lahore
Called on Qazi Hussain Ahmad and discussed possibilities of
cooperation with Jamaat-i-Islami. Later called on Nawabzada
Nasrullah Khan.

Wednesday, 17 Aug 1988, Abbottabad, Peshawar
Heard the news of the death of Ziaul Haq and 36 others in an air crash near Bahawalpur. The US ambassador, Arnold Raphel, was also killed in the same accident. Appears to have been a case of sabotage or possibly of a surface-to-air missile having been fired at the aircraft.

Saturday, 20 Aug 1988, Islamabad, Abbottabad
Attended the funeral of Ziaul Haq. A gigantic affair. People from all over came, many on foot for many miles.

Wednesday, 31 Aug 1988, Islamabad
Called on Ghaus Bux Bizenjo at Yousaf Masti Khan's and later he had dinner with me. Discussed possibilities of an alliance or an electoral understanding. Khurshid had also come from Lahore and joined in the discussions. Agreed that we should try to form an alliance of NPP, ANP, PNP, and TI and possibly JUP. Decided that Bizenjo will contact Jatoi and also Nasrullah Khan and I shall contact JUP and Wali Khan.

Thursday, 1 Sept 1988, Islamabad
Bizenjo called. Yousaf Masti Khan was with him. Khurshid Kasuri, Zafar Ali Shah and Rafi Butt were also there. Spoke to the press after our meeting. Fakhr Imam (former speaker of NA), his wife Abida Hussain, Javed Hashmi and Mumtaz Tarar called in the evening.

Sunday, 4 Sept 1988, Islamabad
Military secretary to Ghulam Ishaq Khan telephoned to convey Ishaq Khan's invitation to lunch tomorrow.

Monday, 5 Sept 1988, Islamabad, Abbottabad
Lunched with the acting president, Ghulam Ishaq Khan. There was no one else present. A pleasant affair. Impressed upon him the need to hold party-based elections and the dismissal of 'caretaker' provincial governments. He said that the matter of party-based elections was *sub judice* since it is before the Supreme Court and a decision is expected in the first week of October. He was certain that the decision would be in favour of party-based elections. But did not know whether political parties will be allotted party symbols. He felt that party-based elections could be held without party symbols. I

found this rather illogical. He also appeared reluctant to dismiss the provincial governments. I feel that Ghulam Ishaq Khan is anxious to appear impartial but is in fact biased towards the Muslim League, the chief minister's Muslim League, rather than the Junejo League.

Tuesday, 6 Sept 1988, Abbottabad
Omar left Islamabad for Karachi to meet Benazir Bhutto and had a meeting with her in the afternoon. The purpose was to explore the possibilities of cooperation with the PPP in the event of the emergence of a king's party, which appears a possibility.

Thursday, 8 Sept 1988, Abbottabad
Omar left for Peshawar. In addition to Benazir Bhutto and Maulana Noorani he had also met Fatehyab Ali Khan and Mairaj Mohammad Khan in Karachi and had addressed a meeting at Kala Pul.

Khurshid Kasuri came from Lahore. He told me about his meeting with Maulana Noorani and Abdul Sattar Niazi in Lahore and their aversion to the ANP (Wali Khan) joining the proposed election alliance.

Friday, 9 Sept 1988, Abbottabad
Wazir Ali telephoned from Lahore to say that he had met Wasim Sajjad of Junejo League and felt that they were keen to have an arrangement for election with us. He said that Wasim Sajjad or Junejo will be contacting me in a day or two.

Saturday, 10 Sept 1988, Abbottabad, Akora Khatak, Abbottabad
Mohammad Khan Junejo telephoned and asked me to dinner in Islamabad on 12 September. He appears to be wanting an election alliance.

Monday, 12 Sept 1988, Abbottabad, Islamabad
Held a meeting with Junejo about the desirability of an election alliance. Agreed to meet again in Islamabad on 24 September, along with Maulana Noorani and Bizenjo.

Wednesday, 14 Sept 1988, Islamabad, Lahore
Left for Lahore and met Wazir Ali, Mahnaz Rafi, Rafi Butt, Parvez Hassan and Khurshid. Nawaz Sharif telephoned and asked for time to call. Agreed to meet him on Friday morning.

Thursday, 15 Sept 1988, Lahore
Met Maulana Noorani and five of his central committee members. Discussed possibilities of an election alliance. Maulana Noorani agreed on an election alliance but was very cautious; suspicious of Pagara and of his influence on Junejo. Also about the possibility of the two Muslim Leagues uniting. There is weight in both these possibilities. Maulana Abdul Sattar Niazi was violently opposed to Bizenjo's PNP being accepted in the alliance, because of his stand on four nationalities and about his not being in agreement with him (Niazi) about the nature of the state. It appears that the formation of the alliance is not going to be plain sailing.

Friday, 16 Sept 1988, Lahore, Islamabad
Nawaz Sharif called in the morning at Khurshid's. He suggested that Tehrik-i-Istiqlal should join in an alliance with his Muslim League. Told him that this was not possible, suggested that he and the provincial cabinet should resign from office.

Saturday, 17 Sept 1988, Islamabad
Khurshid and Wazir Ali came and we discussed the party's point of view in the meeting with JUP and the ML (J).

Tuesday, 20 Sept 1988, Lahore, Faisalabad, Lahore
Left for Faisalabad in a procession from 4 Fane Road at 10:30. Arrived at Dhobi Ghat ground at 19:30 at the head of a large procession. About 60,000 people in the public meeting.

Friday, 23 Sept 1988, Islamabad
Meeting of national working committee. Discussed desirability of election alliance and its form. Eighteen members were against any kind of alliance. Sixteen were in favour of an alliance with JUP and Junejo's Muslim League. It was decided that I should be given full powers to take a decision in this regard. Rafi Butt, Qayyum Pahat and

one or two others wanted an alliance with the chief ministers ML, which was violently opposed by most of the members.

Saturday, 24 Sept 1988, Islamabad
Met Wazir Ali and Khurshid and gave them my decision, after much discussion about the terms of the alliance. The terms acceptable to the Tehrik-i-Istiqlal were: Separate party manifestos. Four or five common subjects only to be defined such as the Objectives Resolution, 1973 constitution and in accordance with this a democratic, parliamentary welfare state, rights of individuals, etc. Also agreed to a common flag and election symbol. Also discussed a programme of public meetings for first half of October and to delay meeting of parliamentary board until 6 October.

Thursday, 27 Sept 1988, Abbottabad
Spoke to Maulana Noorani and agreed to meet on 3 October in Islamabad. Will then meet Junejo on 4 October.

Thursday, 29 Sept 1988, Abbottabad, Sherwan, Abbottabad
Mohammad Khan Junejo telephoned to confirm our meeting at Islamabad on 4 and on 5 October. He said that Hamid Nawaz Chattha, speaker of the NA (and member of Junejo's ML) is calling a meeting of the NA on 2 October.

Friday, 30 Sept 1988, Abbottabad
Begum Fakhruz Zaman Khan of Oghi called and joined the Tehrik-i-Istiqlal. She is a candidate for NA-15 and PF-46.

Saturday, 1 Oct 1988, Abbottabad, Islamabad
Over two hundred people have been killed during the last two days in Karachi and Hyderabad when people in cars, opened fire on passers-by. The trouble started in Hyderabad and Latifabad and then in Karachi. Many parts of Karachi are under curfew.

Sunday, 2 Oct 1988, Islamabad
Mohammad Khan Junejo called. Discussed the problems in connection with the proposed election alliance. The ML (J) is not in favour of a common symbol as they wish to retain the ML symbol, the hurricane

lamp. The Supreme Court decided that the election will be on a party basis and that political parties will be given their own symbols. Decided to visit Karachi tomorrow for a day in connection with the disturbances and the killings there.

Monday, 3 Oct 1988, Islamabad, Karachi
Left for Karachi. Visited the Jinnah Postgraduate Medical Centre, where about 200 people injured in the riots were hospitalised. A terrible sight. Rahim Bux Soomro's son was the doctor there and showed us around. Then called on Maulana Noorani and discussed the proposed alliance.

Wednesday, 5 Oct 1988, Islamabad, Gujrat, Islamabad
Addressed a good meeting at Gujrat about 12-15,000 people. A spirited procession from the outskirts of the city to Wattianwala Talab, the place of the meeting. The meeting with Junejo scheduled for 4 and 5 October did not take place.

Saturday, 8 Oct 1988, Islamabad
Meeting of JUP, ML and Tehrik at Mohammad Khan Junejo's residence. Agreed to form an alliance to be called the Pakistan Awami Alliance with a supreme council of party heads. A secretary general for three months, Major General Ansari of JUP, and a treasurer, Brigadier Asghar of ML for one year.

Thursday, 13 Oct 1988, Karachi, Islamabad, Abbottabad
Filed my nomination papers for NA-191 Karachi South-III Met party office bearers at Zia Ispahani's. Left for Islamabad by the afternoon flight. Called on Syed Sajid Ali Naqvi and discussed possibilities of cooperation with Tehrik-i-Nifaz-i-Fiqh Jafria. He was keen on joining the alliance that we have formed. Told him that we will put forward this proposal at the next summit meeting of the alliance on 16 October and let him know.

Saturday, 15 Oct 1988, Islamabad
Junejo telephoned to say that Fida League of Fida Mohammad Khan had merged with his and he would brief us on the various aspects of this, when we meet.

Sunday, 30 Oct 1988, Karachi
Addressed a meeting in Orangi for Naeemul Haq and another in Azam Basti where Sarwar Awan and his workers made an unsuccessful attempt to create trouble. A very good meeting.

Monday, 31 Oct 1988, Karachi
Addressed a good meeting at Dawood Chowrangi in Landhi for Umar Farooq, an NA candidate. Left for Lahore at 22:00.

Tuesday, 1 Nov 1988, Karachi, Lahore
Arrived at Lahore from Karachi a little after midnight. Travelled to Chichawatni and addressed a very good meeting for Shahnaz Javed.

Wednesday, 2 Nov 1988, Islamabad
Addressed a public meeting in Islamabad along with Maulana Noorani organised by Zafar Ali Shah and later another in Trunk Bazaar, Rawalpindi.

Thursday, 3 Nov 1988, Serai Alamgir, Gujrat, Gujranwala, Lahore
Addressed meetings at Serai Alamgir and Gujrat before addressing a public meeting in Gujranwala.

Friday, 4 Nov 1988, Lahore
Spent the day at Lahore and addressed five meetings in Khurshid's constituency.

Saturday, 5 Nov 1988, Lahore, Sialkot, Lahore
Addressed a meeting in Sialkot. Returned to Lahore for the night. Junejo withdrew without any warning from the alliance, in very suspicious circumstances. I am sure that Military Intelligence has played a role in this. This last minute withdrawal by the Junejo Muslim League will cause confusion and damage us considerably.

Wednesday, 16 Nov 1988, Abbottabad
Elections to the National Assembly. I lost on all seats as also Maulana Noorani, Ghaus Bux Bizenjo, Prof. Ghafoor Ahmed, Ghulam Mustafa

Jatoi, Sherbaz Mazari, Prof. Shah Farid ul Haq. PPP was in the lead till midnight.

Thursday, 17 Nov 1988, Abbottabad
PPP has got 92 Natioal Assembly seats by the evening with the Islami Jamhoori Ittehad bagging 54. Pakistan Awami Ittehad have got three seats (Maulana Abdul Sattar Niazi, Dr Sher Afgan and Major General Ansari). Independents about 40 and ANP, JUI, Mustafa Khar and Nasrullah Khan about nine.

Sunday, 20 Nov 1988, Abbottabad
PPP has won almost all NA and PA seats in Sindh except for independents who have won about one-fifth of the seats. Of these, the MQM has won almost all the seats in Karachi and Hyderabad. Neither the PPP nor the Islami Jamhoori Ittehad are in a position to form a government in the country without the help of the independents who are about 40 and smaller parties, about 10.

Thursday, 1 Dec 1988, Abbottabad (Phoollan Di Bandi)
Ghulam Ishaq Khan asked Benazir Bhutto to form a government at the centre. Her party, PPP, has the largest number of seats in the National Assembly—97.

Friday, 2 Dec 1988, Abbottabad, Islamabad, Abbottabad
Attended the oath taking ceremony of Benazir at the President House, Islamabad. Khurshid had also come from Lahore.

Thursday, 22 Dec 1988, Islamabad
Meeting of the national working committee at Zafar Ali Shah's to consider my resignation from office of party president and the causes of failure of the party in the recent elections. The national working committee with a vote of 24:1 rejected my resignation and asked me to continue. Rafi Butt wanted the resignation to be placed before the national council and an acting president appointed for the interim period. It was evident that the party would not agree to any other person for the post of party president and a large number of persons may leave the party if I quit the office at this time. So, reluctantly, I agreed to stay and sought the national working committee's mandate

to make changes in the party organisation where I considered necessary. Decided to address a press conference on 24 December.

Friday, 30 Dec 1988, Abbottabad, Islamabad
Bizenjo had telephoned last night to say that he had come to Islamabad and wanted to meet me. Discussed the merger of progressive parties. He had spoken to Ghulam Mustafa Jatoi, Abdul Hamid Khan Jatoi and Mustafa Khar who wanted to join such a party. In addition, he felt that Nawabzada Nasrullah Khan (Chaudhri Arshad had met Bizenjo and expressed his willingness to join), Mumtaz Bhutto, Abida Hussain, Abid Hassan Minto would also agree. He had not contacted Wali Khan as yet. Agreed to discuss the matter further in Karachi when I go there on 11 January and in the meantime he should contact the remaining people. Feroz Ahmad, the writer, living in Washington DC, called.

Diary 1989

Monday, 30 January 1989, Lahore
Khurshid, Wazir Ali and Mahnaz (who was away in Tehran) are anxious to join some other party. Khurshid and Wazir Ali are in favour of the PPP and Mahnaz in favour of the IJI or merge with other parties. This mindset has done a great deal of harm and has been responsible for our failure.

Tuesday, 31 Jan 1989, Lahore
Meeting of district chairmen of Punjab and some other special invitees. About 30 people attended. The morale of the workers was good and they were generally in favour of going it alone.

Thursday, 9 Feb 1989, Abbottabad, Rehana
Amina and I went to Rehana to condole with Gohar Ayub on the death of his mother, Begum Ayub Khan. Lieutenant General Habibullah Khan was also there.

Sunday, 12 Feb 1989, Islamabad, Abbottabad
A demonstration was organised in Islamabad led by Nasrullah Khan, Kausar Niazi and Maulana Fazlur Rehman. Six persons were killed and over 80 wounded. Omar and Syed Zafar Ali Shah also participated. One boy was shot and killed whilst trying to pull down the US flag over the American Centre. An ugly affair. The demonstration was in protest against the publication of a book *The Satanic Verses* by Salman Rushdie.

Saturday, 18 March 1989, Lahore
Called on Ghaus Bux Bizenjo and told him that we were not thinking of a party merger which did not appear to be a practical proposition.

Wednesday, 29 March 1989, Abbottabad
Samina telephoned to say that a letter had been received for me from Naeemul Haq, Ashraf Liaquat Ali Khan and Zia Ispahani resigning their memberships of the party. They are obviously looking for greener pastures and are likely to join the PPP.

Saturday, 1 April 1989, Karachi
Earlier Zia Ispahani and Ashraf Liaquat called. They along with Naeemul Haq have resigned their membership of the party which I have accepted.

Monday, 3 April 1989, Karachi
Ashraf Liaquat came to say that he does not wish to leave the party and that he had been misled by Zia Ispahani.

Tuesday, 2 May 1989, Lahore
Addressed a very good gathering at an *iftar* party given by Mahnaz Rafi. Earlier Mahnaz and Khurshid called.

Saturday, 3 June 1989, Miami
Martial law had been declared in Beijing some two weeks ago and the army took action today against the students in Tiananmen Square. Over a thousand are reported killed. Ayatollah Khomeini died, aged 89.

Friday, 3 Nov 1989, Peshawar
Attended the NWFP party council meeting and elections. Inamullah Khan was elected chairman and I was one of the 25 to be elected national councillors from the NWFP.

Saturday, 4 Nov 1989, Peshawar, Abbottabad
Mahnaz Rafi was elected chairperson Punjab in Lahore yesterday.

Monday, 20 Nov 1989, Islamabad, Abbottabad
Khurshid called from Lahore to say that all of those who had been invited to attend the 23 November meeting on the merger of various parties had agreed to attend except the PNP. He had not been able to contact JUI (Maulana Fazlur Rahman).

Thursday, 23 Nov 1989, Abbottabad
Twenty-seven representatives of some eight or more political parties and also some independents met at Khurshid Kasuri's house in Lahore to examine the possibility of a merger or alliance of like-minded parties. The PNP did not attend and Sherbaz's NDP—although it was represented—is likely to join the PPP. Sherbaz spoke at Benazir's public meeting in Kashmor today. Most of those present favoured an alliance and not a merger. Not a very encouraging response. Tahirul Qadri's Awami Tehrik is only interested in an alliance. Mairaj Mohammad Khan of QMA and Nawabzada Nasrullah Khan of PDP are in favour of a merger.

Monday, 11 Dec 1989, Islamabad, Lahore
Met Tahirul Qadri at Khurshid's and discussed proposal to form an alliance. Agreed in principle and asked that half a dozen people should discuss the details. Zafar Ali Shah, Khurshid Kasuri and Mahnaz Rafi will represent us.

Saturday, 16 Dec 1989, Lahore
Met Tahirul Qadri and discussed the draft declaration of the alliance to be called Pakistani Awami Mahaz.

Thursday, 21 Dec 1989, Abbottabad

Spoke to Khurshid in Karachi. He had met Mairaj Mohammad Khan yesterday who will be going to Lahore tomorrow to meet Tahirul Qadri. Could possibly join the alliance but had some reservations.

Sunday, 24 Dec 1989

Asaf Vardag came. Told me that Dr Rahim ul Haq is thinking of leaving the party to join the IJI. He has been behaving peculiarly for some time and is not likely to stay with us for long. His wife is keener than he to jump onto the IJI bandwagon.

Tuesday, 26 Dec 1989, Abbottabad, Islamabad

Left for Islamabad. Khurshid Kasuri came and discussed the proposed alliance. Later Mairaj Mohammad Khan called for the same purpose. He had some objections to the proposed draft declaration.

Sunday, 31 Dec 1989, Lahore

Had a meeting with Tahirul Qadri at Khurshid's. Mairaj Mohammad Khan arrived later from Karachi and decided that he should see Tahirul Qadri later at night to clear up the doubts and objections he had to the organisation of the alliance.

Diary 1990

Tuesday, 2 Jan 1990, Lahore

Prof. Tahirul Qadri telephoned from Jhang and I told him that the proposed supreme council must have all powers and this must be clear in the declaration. Told him that I preferred if a convenor of the supreme council was appointed by rotation for three months.

Tuesday, 9 Jan 1990, Lahore

Met TNFJ delegation led by Agha Sajid Naqvi and Dr Tahirul Qadri of PAT at Khurshid's. Decided not to form an alliance but agreed to enter into an 'ishtrak-i-amal' (cooperation) which would involve joint public meetings but no combined name, organisation or flag. A lot of time was spent on petty matters such as: (1) Who should read out the announcement on the delegation to the press. (2) In what order should the names of the three leaders be released to the press for the press conference tomorrow. Tahirul Qadri was keen that he should take precedence and his associates manoeuvred to get this done. The meeting which started at 10:00 ended at 18:00. PAT's representatives, minus Qadri, came to see Khurshid again later and complained about his (Khurshid's) attitude accusing him of lowering Qadri's importance. They suggested that Qadri should sit in the centre when reading the declaration to the press tomorrow. I have never experienced such pettiness in politics before.

Wednesday, 10 Jan 1990, Lahore, Karachi
Addressed a joint press conference with Tahirul Qadri and Allama Sajid Naqvi and announced 'Ishtrak-e-Amal' between our three parties.

Thursday, 11 Jan 1990, Karachi
National working committee meeting. Discussed our participation in the joint public meeting at Minar-i-Pakistan on Friday, 2 March.

Sunday, 21 Jan 1990, Karachi
Dr Rahim ul Haq called (I had asked him to see me) and I told him that I had been receiving reports that he had decided to leave the party to join the Muslim League. He denied this but was not convincing. It is a matter of time before he leaves.

Monday, 22 Jan 1990, Karachi, Lahore
Left Karachi for Lahore. Discussed progress of alliance with PAT, and TNFJ. Khurshid described his battle with representatives of PAT, particularly Maulana Ahmad Ali Kasuri.

Thursday, 1 Feb 1990, Peshawar, Karachi, Islamabad
Left Peshawar for Karachi and attended a press conference addressed by Khalil Ahmad Nainitalwala, vice president of the National People's Party, who announced his decision to join Tehrik-i-Istiqlal.

Sunday, 4 March 1990, Islamabad, Abbottabad
Omar telephoned to say that Aitzaz Ahsan wants to call on me on 8 March to deliver an invitation from Benazir for a meeting on 11 March on Kashmir.

Thursday, 8 March 1990, Abbottabad, Islamabad
Aitzaz Ahsan the federal interior minister called to deliver Benazir Bhutto's invitation to a meeting on Kashmir on 11 March, which I accepted.

Sunday, 11 March 1990, Islamabad
Attended an all parties conference at the prime minister's secretariat called by Benazir Bhutto for a briefing and discussion on the Kashmir issue. Parties outside the National Assembly also participated.

Wednesday, 4 April 1990, Abbottabad, Islamabad
Came to Islamabad and met Abida Hussain (MNA) at her request. She is active in trying to organise a 'third force' of political parties other than PPP and IJI and asked whether I would be willing to attend their preliminary meeting to be held in the third week of this month in Clifdon (Murree). I said that I would. She has some interesting names of people who she said she has contacted and who are willing to associate with her. Amongst them, Akbar Khan Bugti, Khaliquzzaman of Hala, Hamida Khuhro and Arbab Jehangir.

Monday, 23 April 1990, Abbottabad, Islamabad
Omar and I went to Syeda Abida Hussain's for dinner. Her husband Fakhr Imam, Akbar Khan Bugti, Agha Shahi, Iqbal Hyder Zaidi and some others were also there. She is trying to hammer out an alliance of political forces other than PPP, IJI and the *maulvis*, although her leanings and more particularly of her husband's appear to be towards the IJI or Muslim League. She is rabidly anti-PPP.

Tuesday, 24 April 1990, Islamabad, Abbottabad
Syeda Abida Hussain and Fakhr Imam called.

Friday, 4 May 1990, Islamabad
Dinner with Syeda Abida Hussain. Some 20 persons, including Akbar Khan Bugti, were present. Amongst those who attended were Abdul

Hamid Khan Jatoi, Makhdoom Khaliquzzaman, Hamida Khuhro and
Balakh Sher Mazari.

Tuesday, 17 July 1990, Abbottabad
Syeda Abida Hussain telephoned to say that she wishes to discuss the
proposal to create a third political platform. Decided to meet during
the next few days.

Wednesday, 18 July 1990, Abbottabad, Islamabad, Abbottabad
Saw Syeda Abida Hussain in the afternoon and discussed the formation
of a new political platform. She and the others, Bugti, Jatoi and
Nasrullah Khan, prefer a party whereas I am in favour of an alliance,
at least initially. Most of the others want a single head whereas I
favour a presidium of three or four with a secretary general and there
may be a single head after proper elections are held. She wants to
convene a meeting of Nasrullah Khan, Bugti, Ghulam Mustafa Jatoi
and myself either in Karachi or Islamabad on 23 or 24 July.

Monday, 6 Aug 1990, Abbottabad, Islamabad, Karachi
Samina telephoned at 17:00 from Islamabad, to say that tanks and
vehicles were moving towards the assembly chamber and that
probably the National Assembly and the government was being
dismissed. This proved correct when President Ghulam Ishaq Khan
addressed a press conference on TV a little later. Not at all unexpected
as Benazir's government had proved totally incompetent and
corrupt.

Tuesday, 7 Aug 1990, Karachi, Islamabad
Decided to cancel my tour of Sindh and returned to Islamabad. Saw
Syeda Abida Hussain and discussed her idea of a third political force
which does not appear to be materialising. Decided to call a meeting
of the national working committee on 12 August in Islamabad.

Sunday, 12 Aug 1990, Islamabad
Held a meeting of the national working committee to discuss the
Tehrik's line of action. Agreed to enter into an alliance with one of
the two major political forces, the PPP and the IJI or other opposition

parties. I did not favour going into the interim government though some of the members were keen to do so.

Thursday, 14 Aug 1990, Islamabad
Khurshid came early today to say that he had been sounded by Kamal Azfar (special assistant to Prime Minister Jatoi) whether I could accept a federal ministership in the interim government.

Wednesday, 15 Aug 1990, Islamabad
Prime Minister Ghulam Mustafa Jatoi called in the morning to 'pay his respects' and seek my cooperation. Khurshid Kasuri was with me and we talked briefly about the general situation. Apparently accountability is being carried out under PPO 16 and PPO 17, under laws enacted in 1977 by Ziaul Haq and not repealed later, which allow legal proceedings against all holders of public offices (which term includes MNAs and MPAs) by a judge of the High Court. Hearing is to be on a day-to-day basis. Penalty can be up to seven years imprisonment and disqualification from seeking public office for five years. Roedad Khan thought that there would be about 50 people against whom they will proceed and it should not take very long to deal with this problem. People who had received loans from banks and land would be included.

Saturday, 18 Aug 1990, Abbottabad, Islamabad
Malik Hakmin Khan of PPP called. He said that he had been sent by Benazir to try and negotiate an understanding of cooperation between PPP and TI. Heard his views. The PPP appears to be very keen for such an arrangement.

Sunday, 19 Aug 1990, Islamabad
Malik Hakmin Khan and Farooq Leghari of PPP called and continued the discussions.

Tuesday, 21 Aug 1990, Islamabad
Saw President Ghulam Ishaq Khan. He said that seat allocations will take time and advised us to field our candidates and make adjustments later.

Sunday, 26 Aug 1990, Abbottabad, Islamabad

Went to Islamabad and met Roedad Khan to enquire about the method of accountability. Expressed my objections to the one-sided accountability being carried out. Malik Hakmin Khan of PPP called. He wishes to arrange a meeting with Benazir and said that PPP was more than willing to enter into an electoral alliance with us. The IJI appears to be in a state of disarray and will not, I think, be able to arrive at a decision on seats until quite late.

Monday, 27 Aug 1990, Islamabad, Abbottabad

Zafar Ali Shah accompanied me to meet Ghulam Mustafa Jatoi, the prime minister. Asked him to expedite decision on seats. He said that he would let me know in a couple of days. Asked Zafar Ali Shah to go to Lahore to brief Khurshid about the situation and the advantages to the party in an alliance with the PPP.

Wednesday, 29 Aug 1990, Abbottabad, Islamabad

Syed Zafar Ali Shah called and Khurshid arrived from Lahore in the afternoon. Discussed the pros and cons of an alliance with PPP and agreed to receive Benazir Bhutto tomorrow, 30 August, to discuss the possibilities.

Thursday, 30 Aug 1990, Islamabad

Allama Sajid Naqvi with a delegation of TNFJ called. He wanted an alliance with us. Agreed to examine the possibility.

Benazir along with her husband, Asif Zardari, Sardar Farooq Leghari, Naseerullah Khan Babar, Kazmi and Malik Hakmin Khan called. Discussed the forthcoming elections and agreed on an alliance for the elections and 'thereafter'. Benazir was very keen on the 'thereafter'. She was keen that I should contest against Nawaz Sharif in Lahore. Agreed on a common symbol for the alliance, which could be the arrow. Set up a committee comprising Khurshid Kasuri, Sardar Farooq Leghari, Zafar Ali Shah and Malik Hakmin Khan to discuss the modalities and to finish its work within a week.

Friday, 31 Aug 1990, Islamabad

A delegation of TNFJ called again this morning. They were desirous of joining our newly formed alliance with PPP.

Saturday, 1 Sept 1990, Islamabad

Stayed on in Islamabad as Khurshid was to discuss allocation of seats with Farooq Leghari and he wanted me to be readily available for consultations. Khurshid's talk with Leghari was satisfactory. He said that they were willing to accommodate us on reasonable terms. He promised that Mahnaz Rafi would be number 1 on the list of women to be brought into the NA on the women's quota.

Malik Hamid Sarfaraz (one time TI and now president of NPP, Punjab) announced his decision to rejoin Tehrik-i-Istiqlal.

Sunday, 2 Sept 1990, Islamabad, Abbottabad

Colonel Iqbal Jan, the army station commander, telephoned to say that he had received a letter from GHQ regarding the acquisition of a part of my residence, 1 Kutchery Road (court case) and would call at 10:00 tomorrow.

Monday, 3 Sept 1990, Abbottabad

Colonel Iqbal Jan called to see the compound and report to the GHQ in connection with the case of land acquisition.

Tuesday, 4 Sept 1990, Abbottabad

Inayatur Rahman Abbasi called and asked for support as an independent candidate for NA-12 (Abbottabad). He is a Muslim Leaguer and is not likely to get the IJI ticket. Gohar Ayub Khan called and sought support in NA-13 (Haripur). He is likely to be the IJI candidate.

Wednesday, 5 Sept 1990, Abbottabad

Aftab Sherpao telephoned and we agreed to meet in Islamabad on 8 September. About 150 office bearers of the PPP called in the afternoon. Discussed matters of common interest in the forthcoming elections and allocation of seats. Decided to meet workers of PPP in Haripur on 8 September.

Thursday, 6 Sept 1990, Abbottabad

Syed Sultan Shah, president PPP Hazara, called and suggested that I should try to bring the alliance and ANP together. Spoke with Nasim Wali Khan and Haji Ghulam Mohammad Bilore as well as Benazir.

Then spoke to Sherpao. It appears that the gulf between them is too wide to be bridged, at least at present.

Monday, 10 Sept 1990, Karachi
Met Maulana Noorani and discussed prospects of understanding between our two parties. Later had a four-hour meeting with Benazir Bhutto at Bilawal House to discuss the name of our alliance and its symbol. Also discussed matters pertaining to its organisation and seats. Agreed to call it the Peoples' Democratic Alliance, with the 'arrow' as its symbol. The organisation at the central level would be a central committee with the four party heads and two each of their nominees and provincial heads as members. A secretary general (Khurshid Kasuri), an information secretary (Iqbal Hyder), a treasurer (Kabir Ali Wasti, ML), a coordination secretary (Malik Hakmin) and an additional secretary general (TFNJ). The organisation is to be reflected at provincial and district levels. Later had a press conference. Benazir wanted me to contest on NA-95 where Nawaz Sharif had won in the 1988 elections. Shahid Nabi Malik candidate from PP-122 (under NA-95) called later in the evening to discuss my candidature from NA-95.

Tuesday, 11 Sept 1990, Karachi, Islamabad
Decided to contest from NA-95 Lahore. Informed Khurshid Kasuri who informed Benazir Bhutto in Larkana. I will not be contesting from Abbottabad.

Khurshid telephoned from Lahore later in the evening to say that Benazir had telephoned to ask whether I would mind her contesting from Lahore (she is already contesting from two Nawabshah constituencies, one Larkana and NA-1 Peshawar). Told him to tell her that this was not desirable, as it would divide our effort and reduce the chances of my success. She agreed not to contest from Lahore.

Wednesday, 12 Sept 1990, Islamabad, Lahore, Abbottabad
Left for Lahore. Decided that I should contest only from NA-95. So did not file my nomination papers from NA-93 and returned to Islamabad and then to Abbottabad.

Sunday, 16 Sept 1990, Abbottabad, Islamabad

Spent the day winding up at Abbottabad to proceed to Lahore for the elections. The Islami Jamhoori Ittehad is in a state of confusion with the Muslim League (which has two groups) up in arms for not getting a fair deal in the allocation of seats. The ML is putting up its own candidates with a separate symbol. In NA-13 (Haripur) Gohar Ayub is being opposed by Seth Nasim of ML. In NA-95 (Lahore) Nawaz Sharif and I are being opposed by Humayun Akhtar (son of late Lieutenant General Akhtar Abdur Rahman) as well as candidates from JUI (Darkhwasti) and PDP of Nasrullah Khan.

Thursday, 20 Sept 1990, Lahore

Had a meeting with the two provincial candidates for PP-122 and 123. Decided a number of issues and agreed to meet at 11:00 every morning.

Friday, 21 Sept 1990, Lahore

Met a large number of people, mostly PPP workers. Addressed a meeting at Mozang. Earlier Jehangir Badar called and we finalised the programme of my meetings in Lahore. Decided that I should arrive at the Lahore railway station on 28 September and proceed in a procession to Gawalmandi where I will address a public meeting.

Saturday, 22 Sept 1990, Lahore

Visited Khurshid and discussed problems of finalising the election programme. Addressed a large gathering in Gawalmandi and opened about six PPP offices in that area. Led a procession in the area. A tiring experience. It was very hot and humid and the pushing and pulling crowds made things very difficult. However, the enthusiasm of the crowds compensated for the discomfort.

Sunday, 23 Sept 1990, Lahore, Karachi

Learnt from Mahnaz that PPP was not willing to concede more than one provincial seat to TI in Punjab. Decided to go to Karachi to discuss this with Benazir. Khurshid and I left for Karachi and saw Benazir at Bilawal House. Had dinner there. She agreed to concede seven provincial assembly seats as follows:

1. Azam Bhatty   Rawalpindi
2. Shaikh Islam   Shikarpur
3. Qazi Amir Abdullah   Mianwali
4. Mian Mushtaq   Lahore
5. Syed Manzoor Gilani   Pakpattan
6. Idrees Bajwa   Sialkot
7. PP-41:TI can adopt any one from Bhakkar.

Monday, 24 Sept 1990, Karachi, Lahore

Got the authority letter from information secretary of the alliance, Iqbal Haider, for the seven provincial candidates on which agreement was reached as well as for myself, and Sajjad Dar NA-85 Sialkot. Spoke to Ahmad Dara, chairman TI Karachi. He was hopeful of getting three provincial seats from PPP for Karachi. Opened some offices in Guru Mandir and Mozang areas of Lahore late at night, after arrival and addressed a gathering.

Tuesday, 25 Sept 1990, Lahore

Called on Aslam Gill, president of PPP Lahore, and discussed programme of my reception in Lahore. Decided that it should be on 1 May and not on 28 Sept as 28th is a Friday. Selected the house of late Justice Jameel Hussain Rizvi as my election office, where I was given a rousing reception.

Thursday, 27 Sept 1990, Islamabad, Sargodha

Left for Sargodha by a Fokker as the guest of the PAF for the 25th reunion of the 1965 war. About 1,500 retired officers of the PAF had come from all over the country by C-130s. A very interesting day. Met a lot of old faces. Amongst the former C-in-C/CAS were Nur Khan and Zafar Chaudhri. Returned to Islamabad in the afternoon and attended a dinner in the PAF officers mess in Chaklala.

Friday, 28 Sept 1990, Islamabad, Lahore

Air Commander Sajjad Haider called. He is going to work for me in the election in NA-95. Opened a few offices on Fleming road and earlier attended a meeting organised by the Lahore PPP to give finishing touches to the programme of my procession from the railway station to Gawalmandi. Opening of offices on Fleming road developed into a sizeable procession. Very enthusiastic participants.

Monday, 1 Oct 1990, Lahore
Led a large procession from the railway station to Gawalmandi Chowk where I addressed a public meeting. It was a large gathering of a very enthusiastic crowd. Omar came from Haripur and also spoke.

Wednesday, 3 Oct 1990, Lahore
Met Benazir Bhutto at Gulzar's. She had returned last night from a visit to Sialkot where she said, she had a poor reception of only about 10,000 people. She said that the local organisation had made no arrangements. She left later for Gujranwala. I led an Eid-i-Milad procession in Jehangir Badar's constituency NA-96 from Delhi Gate to Bhatti Gate.

Friday, 5 Oct 1990, Lahore
Spent a very busy day. Met PPP and office bearers of NA-95 and also PIA union members brought by G.M. Shah. Met Gulzar at Khurshid's and also Agha Syed Sajid Naqvi. Later went on a tour of Gawalmandi, Kisban Nagar, Basti Saidu Shah, Janabi Devi and Beadon Road to open offices. Spoke to Omar who was feeling fairly confident about NA-13, Haripur, but thought that the contest will be close.

Sunday, 7 Oct 1990, Lahore
Addressed the Lahore High Court Bar Association. A very good gathering which was very responsive. Addressed a very big public meeting in Mozang. The crowd was nearly as large as that at Gawalmandi on 1 October. Held a meeting with PPP representatives on organisational matters.

Tuesday, 9 Oct 1990, Lahore
Accompanied Benazir to the Lahore High Court for the hearing of her case before the tribunal. Also attended the hearing of a petition against the dissolution of the assemblies. Later addressed a good meeting at old Anarkali. Addressed a press conference of foreign journalists along with Benazir.

Sunday, 14 Oct 1990, Lahore
Addressed a public meeting for Malik Mairaj Khalid in NA-100. Another public meeting at Garhi Shahu at the point where NA-95 and

NA-94 meet. Addressed another meeting at Mozang Adda. Both were large meetings.

Monday, 15 Oct 1990, Lahore
Addressed three public meetings at Shahdara. NA-92 for Sheikh Rafique Ahmad and Mian Mushtaq, Lunda Bazar NA-95 for Zafar Ali Malik and PP-123 and Mochi Gate NA-96 for Jehangir Badar.

Tuesday, 16 Oct 1990, Lahore, Kasur, Lahore
Went to Kasur and addressed two public meetings in support of Lieutenant General K.M. Azhar of JUP. Maulana Noorani was also there. Sajjad Haider left for Islamabad to attend the hearing of my complaint regarding pre-poll rigging by Nawaz Sharif. About 14,000 bogus votes have been registered and about 40,000 duplicate identity cards have been issued.

Wednesday, 17 Oct 1990, Lahore
Addressed a meeting in Sanda. Earlier gave instructions for finalising plans for 24 October. Malik Saeed Hassan and Sajjad Haider met the chief election commissioner in Islamabad about our complaint regarding pre-poll rigging. Mahnaz Rafi and Zia Rizvi met the returning officer of NA-95 in Lahore about the situation in the *halqa*. He agreed to take some steps to obviate the chances of rigging. Spoke to Mumtaz Rathore, the prime minister of Azad Kashmir, and asked him to accompany me to Haripur for Omar's public meeting on 20 October.

Thursday, 18 Oct 1990, Lahore
Addressed a meeting in Sheikhupura near Kamoke at the request of Muneer Hussain Gilani of TNFJ and another meeting in NA-95 in Saadi Park. Both were good meetings.

Saturday, 20 Oct 1990, Lahore, Islamabad, Haripur, Islamabad
Left for Islamabad. Assembled at Kashmir House and left from there for Haripur at 13:15 along with Ishaque Zafar, speaker of Azad Jammu and Kashmir Assembly, and Sahibzada Akram Shah, deputy secretary general of JUP. Omar met us with a large procession of about 200 vehicles short of Khanpur and we reached Haripur at 17:00 drove

through the city and to the meeting ground. It was a very large meeting. People were very responsive and the roads were also full of people. The crowd must have been about 40,000. Omar was very pleased but I telephoned Samina later from Lahore to say that Omar should not think that he had won the election as yet. There was no room for complacency as a large meeting does not necessarily mean a victory at the polls.

Major General Asad Durrani, head of ISI, called at 23:00. He told me that (1) Mrs Nusrat Bhutto had divulged some state secrets to the US government (she has been in the USA since early August) about our nuclear capability. (2) About sixty members of Al-Zulfikar organisation had been arrested who had confessed their Indian connection. He said that the total strength of Al-Zulfikar was over 4,500. All were Sindhis.

Monday, 22 Oct 1990, Lahore

Was informed by two men who said that they were on phone-tapping duty at the behest of the Military Intelligence. They had heard a conversation of someone with AC Saddat that the truck carrying ballot papers had entered the Ittefaq foundary premises. Decided to write and inform the election commission.

Benazir arrived in Lahore from Faisalabad. Her arrival was delayed and so was therefore the procession, which took about six hours to move from Shahdara to Chauburji. It was a very large procession and the people were very enthusiastic. It had to be ended at midnight, as this was the deadline for ending the campaigning.

Wednesday, 24 Oct 1990, Lahore

Polling day. Massive rigging took place in the afternoon. Haji Mohammad Sharif, a provincial candidate of IJI from PP-122, Haji Tahir and Chaudhri Abid who had been released on bail two days ago attacked polling stations at Madressah Kuliatul Binat near University Ground Ward 70, Government. Community High School, Kot Abdullah Shah, Mozang and at Arabistan-i-Sufia Ward 71 at the point of a gun, filled ballot boxes with IJI ballot papers. Additional bogus voters list, which we did not have, were produced in the afternoon and bogus voters allowed to poll these votes. Bogus identity cards were used and people allowed to poll at more than one place. Nawaz Sharif who had not been able to have successful meetings in Lahore and who appeared to have lost the support of the public in NA-95, had made sure that he wins this seat. PDA fared badly throughout. Benazir lost in Peshawar, as did Wali Khan, Nasrullah Khan, Abida Hussain and Fazlur Rahman. Omar also lost by about 10,000 votes.

Thursday, 25 Oct 1990, Lahore
A large number of workers called at the 11 Fane Road office. Almost all wanted the PDA to boycott the 27 October provincial assembly polls. Benazir is not in favour of a boycott. She is unable to come to Lahore and Fakhruz Zaman of PPP addressed a press conference this evening to say that the PDA will participate in the provincial assembly polls on 27 October.

Visited a PPP worker of Gawalmandi who had been shot in the leg yesterday by the mayor of Lahore and his cronies at polling stations. Also visited Bukhari, the campaign manager of Zafar Ali Malik, the PDA candidate of PP-123, who had been beaten up at a polling station at Gawalmandi yesterday by IJI workers.

Decided to keep my office for NA-95 at Zia Rizvi's office at 11 Fane Road open. Nadeem and Ashraf will work there on a voluntary basis. Murshid will also help.

Friday, 26 Oct 1990, Lahore
Wound up matters at 11 Fane Road. Asked Mohsin Musa, (son of Wing Commander Musa), to look after my office at 11 Fane Road. Nadeem will cooperate.

Saturday, 27 Oct 1990, Lahore
Provincial elections, a continuation of the farce we witnessed on 24 October. Very few people lined up to vote and some of the polling stations were not manned.

Held a meeting with Benazir and Allama Sajid Naqvi of TNFJ. Decided to issue a press release on the poll rigging and to issue a White Paper on the rigging. Also decided to meet on 30 October in Islamabad to review the situation.

Sunday, 28 Oct 1990, Lahore

Provincial assembly elections showed IJI had made a clean sweep almost everywhere. The performance of 24 October was repeated yesterday. It is now clear that the election has been rigged in a big way, by a centrally controlled operation organised by the Inter Services Intelligence (ISI). The method applied appears to be: (1) Blank ballot papers having been used to increase the votes of IJI candidates. (Approximately 20,000 additional votes having been cast in selected constituencies.) (2) Sacks containing ballot papers were taken after polling to selected places where ballot papers were put in before being taken to the returning officers. (3) Intervention by armed people at selected polling stations.

Khurshid Kasuri telephoned to say that the meeting of NA candidates would be in Islamabad on 3 November and not 30 October.

Tuesday, 30 Oct 1990, Islamabad, Abbottabad

Left Islamabad for Abbottabad with Amina and Omar. Escaped a serious car accident, when I dozed off while driving. Omar, on the front seat, took control of the steering.

Thursday, 2 Nov 1990, Abbottabad, Islamabad

Left for Islamabad with Amina and Omar. Attended a meeting of PDA National Assembly ticket holders. Reviewed the rigging in the elections of 24 and 27 October. PDA also decided that its MNAs will attend the National Assembly session being held tomorrow. It was also decided to observe a protest procession on 6 November against the demolition of the Babri Masjid in India.

Sunday, 5 Nov 1990, Abbottabad

Received an invitation from the president house to the swearing in ceremony of Nawaz Sharif tomorrow and by Nawaz Sharif to a dinner tomorrow in Islamabad.

Monday, 6 Nov 1990, Abbottabad, Islamabad

Nawaz Sharif was declared elected as prime minister this morning. Benazir made a very good speech as leader of the opposition.

Thursday, 8 Nov 1990, Islamabad, Lahore

Khudai Noor telephoned to say that Akbar Khan Bugti had been to see him to seek our support for forming a government in Balochistan. Later Akbar Khan Bugti telephoned. I telephoned Benazir and suggested that we might do this against Taj Mohammad Jamali of the IJI. She asked me to speak to Fateh Mohammad Hasnie. Could not contact Hasnie, so asked Khurshid to contact him.

Left Islamabad for Lahore with Amina. Arrived at 16:00. Visited the seven wards of PP-122 in Halqa-95. Met workers of the PPP. They were in reasonably good spirits considering the experience of the elections.

Friday, 9 Nov 1990, Lahore

Went to 11 Fane Road and met workers and discussed accounts of election as well as rigging detail with Mohsin Musa. Ladies had a meeting with Amina. Went to wards of PP-123 to thank workers. They were pleasantly surprised that I should have come to thank them for their work. They said that no one had done this before.

Saturday, 10 Nov 1990, Lahore, Islamabad

Met ward office bearers (of 15 wards) of Halqa NA-95 of PPP and advised them how to look in the future to prepare for putting voters' lists right and to participate fully in the national consensus due in March 1991.

Sunday, 11 Nov 1990, Islamabad

Addressed the press. Spoke about pre-poll rigging and the rigging on 24 October. Gave proofs of bogus entries in voters' lists.

Tuesday, 11 Dec 1990, Islamabad

Second meeting of the PDA constitutional committee. Discussed by-elections on 10 January (21-NA and PF seats) and decided to take part.

Agreed to ask for fresh elections. PDA's, central coordination committee will meet in Karachi on 31 January. Benazir, Allama Sajid Naqvi, Malik Qasim and twenty-two others will attend.

Wednesday, 26 Dec 1990, Karachi

Called on Maulana Noorani. Discussed the possibility of his JUP joining the PDA. Professor Shah Farid ul Haq said that if the JUI could be persuaded to join, they (the JUP) would find it easier to follow. He thought that in that event the chances of their joining would be 90 per cent.

Diary 1991

Friday, 11 Jan 1991, Lahore

Addressed a meeting of the central coordination committee of the PDA at Khurshid's. Benazir, Malik Qasim, Sajid Ali Naqvi and others attended. Omar and Charles Amjad Ali addressed the meeting on the work they had done so far on the White Paper.

Thursday, 17 Jan 1991, Abbottabad

The US invaded Iraq early today. The US have about 500,000 troops in Saudi Arabia and an armada of ships and some 1,400 combat aircraft. It is an uneven contest and Iraq will suffer grevious damage.

Tuesday, 20 Jan 1991, Islamabad, Abbottabad

Addressed a press conference on the Gulf issue. Asked for withdrawal of Pakistan troops (about 10,000) from Saudi Arabia and an end to the bombing of Iraq.

Wednesday, 23 Jan 1991, Abbottabad, Rawalpindi, Abbottabad

Addressed a public meeting at Fawara Chowk, Raja Bazaar, Rawalpindi, in support of ending the bombing of Iraq by US and allied aircraft.

Thursday, 24 Jan 1991, Abbottabad

Went to the court of senior civil judge Abbottabad to record my evidence in the land case (23 Kutchery Road). The case has been going on since 1981. The army wants to acquire my property.

Saturday, 26 Jan 1991, Abbottabad, Islamabad
Maulana Abdul Sattar Khan Niazi, federal minister for local bodies and some thing else, and Sardar Yaqub Nasir, minister for environment, called to discuss the Gulf situation and explain the government's point of view. Told them that the Pakistan Army contingent in Saudi Arabia should be withdrawn immediately and the US should stop its bombing of Iraq in which over 300,000 people are reported to have been killed in the last ten days. Maulana Niazi's views on this issue are the same as mine.

Monday, 28 Jan 1991, Lahore
Met Khurshid and Mahnaz and discussed the Gulf situation. They were both of the view, strongly held, that I should not ask for the removal of our forces from Saudi Arabia.

Nawabzada Nasrullah Khan called to invite me to an all parties conference that he is calling on 2 February. Suggested that Khurshid should contact other PDA parties. I said that I was not averse to the idea. Decided that Malik Hamid Sarfaraz should represent TI. Then took out a procession from Nasir Bagh to Regal Chowk against US bombing of Iraq and addressed the crowd at Regal Chowk.

Friday, 1 Feb 1991, Chechawatni, Toba Tek Singh, Faisalabad, Lahore
Left for Toba Tek Singh and addressed the public in the City Chowk and PDA workers at Mian Tanveer Alam's residence. Addressed workers in Faisalabad and arrived in Lahore late in the evening. Nawaz Sharif wanted me to attend his briefing to the opposition parties, which I declined.

Tuesday, 5 Feb 1991, Karachi
The government had called for a strike on Kashmir today to divert attention from Iraq and all offices were closed and government transport ordered off the roads.

Saturday, 9 Feb 1991, Karachi
Addressed a meeting, along with representatives of parties associated with the recently held all parties conference on the Iraq issue in Empress Market. Maulana Noorani, Mairaj Mohammad Khan,

Fatehyab Ali Khan, Munnawar Hassan of Jamaat-i-Islami and about half a dozen other speakers took part.

Saturday, 16 Feb 1991, Abbottabad
Khurshid telephoned to say that Benazir wanted me to contest the Senate seat from Islamabad. I was not in favour.

Sunday, 17 Feb 1991, Abbottabad
Younas Khan, formerly of Tehrik-i-Istiqlal, called from Peshawar. He is wanting to return to TI and suggested that I should ask Asaf Vardag and others who had left with him, such as Haider Usman, also to return to TI. He thought that they were inclined to do so. Told him that I will consult the party about the desirability of taking them back. Spoke to Khurshid and told him that I was not interested in contesting for the Senate seat.

Tuesday, 19 Feb 1991, Abbottabad
Khurshid telephoned to say that Benazir wanted a meeting of the PDA to discuss the continuous participation or otherwise in Nawabzada Nasrullah Khan's meetings against US bombing of Iraq. Told him that a meeting just for this was not necessary. We had committed ourselves to these meetings and should continue these. Those who can attend should do so. In any case, I said the Iraq issue is likely to be settled in the next few days.

Saturday, 23 Feb 1991, Abbottabad
The US's ultimatum to Iraq to withdraw from Kuwait expired at 17:00 GMT today with Iraqi forces entrenched in Kuwait. Iraq had agreed to the Soviet formula, which was acceptable to the US.

Monday, 25 Feb 1991, Abbottabad, Islamabad
Left for Islamabad. Took part in a seminar arranged by a defence committee, of which Omar is the member, at the Islamabad hotel. Qazi Hussain Ahmad of Jamaat-i-Islami and Ajmal Khattak of ANP also took part. The topic was the 'Gulf situation'.

Sunday, 10 March 1991, Abbottabad
Benazir telephoned to say that the briefing for the rigging should be on the 14th afternoon as she will be in Islamabad on that day.

Sunday, 17 March 1991, Islamabad
Benazir came to call, thinking that the meeting on the White Paper on rigging (to be held on the 14th), was today. Discussed the draft and the state of the country. Decided to launch the White Paper on 1 June.

Wednesday, 20 March 1991, Abbottabad
Khudai Noor telephoned to say that Akbar Khan Bugti wanted PDA to support his nominee for the Senate chairmanship. This made no sense to me as the IJI has a vast majority. Later Saleem Bugti telephoned. Spoke to Benazir and later to Akbar Bugti. PPP is putting up Syed Abdullah Shah, the former speaker of Sindh Assembly, for the Senate chairmanship. PDA has only 5 votes as against about 70 of IJI so the contest will only be symbolic. The IJI is putting up the former speaker Wasim Sajjad.

Wednesday, 27 March 1991, New York (USA)
A Singapore Airline aircraft was hijacked by four Pakistanis who, it is said, were PPP sympathisers and wanted the release of Asif Zardari and other PPP prisoners in Pakistan. The aircraft was stormed at Singapore airport and the hijackers were killed.

Tuesday, 11 June 1991, Islamabad
A meeting of PDA heads, one representative from each party and the secretary general took place at my house. Benazir, Allama Sajid Naqvi, Malik Qasim, Farooq Leghari, Iftikhar Jilani, Zafar Ali Shah, Kabir Wasti, Akhunzada Anwar of TNFJ and Khurshid Kasuri attended. Agreed: (1) In any further election there should be quota of seats for each party. Also agreed that PPP should finalise its views on allocation of seats in the next two months and that PDA meeting should be held on 29 August to finalise the matter. (2) Secretary general should address a press conference at the Assembly cafeteria at 17:00 tomorrow.

Nawabzada Nasrullah Khan called in the evening and wanted to hold an all parties conference to discuss the formation of a caretaker (or a national) govternment as he called it. Agreed to meet. However his enthusiasm was dampened by the appointment of Asif Nawaz Janjua as the next chief of staff of the army. He had thought that the political uncertainty prevailing in the absence of a successor to Mirza Aslam Beg would induce greater pressure on the Nawaz Sharif government by the opposition getting together for the formation of a national government.

Wednesday, 12 June 1991, Islamabad, Abbottabad
Met Benazir and discussed the press conference on the White Paper in the National Assembly cafeteria. Khurshid addressed the press conference and released the findings of the PDA White Paper.

Friday, 14 June 1991, Abbottabad
Khurshid Kasuri telephoned to say that Benazir had asked that I should go to Jacobabad to support Hafeez Pirzada in the by-election. He is the general secretary of the PNP and the PDA is not putting up a candidate against him. However in view of our stand that the 1990 elections were rigged and the assembly is bogus and Hafeez Pirzada is not even a PDA candidate, I regretted that I was not inclined to go. Khurshid said that Benazir insisted that he (Khurshid) should then go instead.

Tuesday, 2 July 1991, Abbottabad
Sahibzada Ishaque Zafar, the speaker of the Azad Kashmir Assembly, called and addressed the press about rigging in the Azad Kashmir elections held on 29 June. Muslim Conference of Sardar Abdul Qayyum won 27 seats out of 29 and PPP only one.

Friday, 26 July 1991, Abbottabad, Islamabad
Omar and I came to Islamabad where I attended the PDA central council meeting. Discussed a number of issues such as the PDA organisation, nuclear policy, Azad Kashmir situation, public contact programme, etc.

Monday, 5 Aug 1991, Islamabad
Lunch at Hakmin Khan's. Kasuri, Benazir, Nasrullah Khan, Hafeez Pirzada of PNP, Mustafa Khan, Malik Qasim, Manzoor Gichki of JWP

and others were there. Benazir was anxious to increase the tempo and she as well as all the others seemed to think that this would topple the government. They wanted to hold an all parties conference before 14 August and thought that this would be enough pressure on Ghulam Ishaq Khan to negotiate with them for the formation of a national government. I was amazed at their naivety and told them so. They obviously thought that if they met before 17 August, the date Mirza Aslam Beg retires, it would make the government panic. Their optimism was, in my opinion, misplaced.

Thursday, 6 Aug 1991, Islamabad, Lahore, Islamabad
Attended a seminar organised by the PPP (Salman Taseer) in Lahore. Malik Meiraj Khalid, Sardar Farooq Leghari, Hanif Ramay and Rashid Qureshi of Nasrullah Khan's PDP also spoke. A very good function, about 1,500 people attended.

Monday, 12 Aug 1991, Islamabad, Lahore
Omar left for Peshawar and I for Lahore. Attended the all parties conference organised by Nawabzada Nasrullah Khan. Agreed to ask for free and fair elections by a neutral caretaker government of national consensus. Also said that if this demand was not met our members would be forced to resign their seats in the NA.

Wednesday, 14 Aug 1991, Lahore
Pakistan day. The government organised a ceremony at Walton (Bab-i-Pakistan) at great cost, said to be Rs30-40 million. Trains and all road vehicles were used by the government for bringing people to Walton.

Saturday, 31 Aug 1991, Abbottabad, Islamabad
Left for Islamabad. Benazir along with Farooq Leghari, Iftikhar Gilani, and Shafqat Mahmud called in the afternoon. Discussed the situation of the PDA's line of action and her tour of northern Punjab on 2 and 3 September.

Wednesday, 11 Sept 1991, Karachi
Khurshid Kasuri, Hamid Sarfaraz, Begum Mahnaz Rafi, Khudai Noor, Omar and I discussed the reply sent to me by Benazir regarding our

demand of quota of seats in the PDA. Decided to seek a solution of the problem.

Attended a PDA meeting at Nishtar Park. It was a good meeting but smaller than I expected. Nusrat Bhutto also spoke in addition to Benazir and about 20 others. Nusrat Bhutto's speech which she read out was very long—over an hour—and would probably have gone on for another hour if Benazir had not asked her, through a written message which she got up to hand over to her, to stop as the people had started to leave.

Tuesday, 12 Sept 1991, Karachi

The newspapers' accounts of the public meetings were very generous. It was pointed out correctly that: (1) The meeting comprised only people from Karachi and no one was brought from the interior of Sindh. (2) All ethnic groups were represented. (3) No firearms were deployed and no firing took place. (4) The meeting was entirely peaceful and it was large. (5) The crowd was very responsive.

The central coordination committee of the PDA met at Bilawal House.

Sunday, 22 Sept 1991, Abbottabad

Saadullah Khan came to discuss the White Paper on the 1990 elections. I had given it to him to read. He an old friend of Ghulam Ishaq Khan and is convinced of Ghulam Ishaq Khan's partiality and of his role in the rigging.

Thursday, 24 Sept 1991, Abbottabad, Islamabad

Attended a reception for Lady Diana, Princess of Wales, at the UK High Commissioner's residence.

Khurshid Kasuri and Omar addressed a press conference on the PDA White Paper, 'How an election was stolen'.

Khurshid Kasuri and Shafqat Mahmud of PPP came to dinner. Shafqat Mahmud, who is one of the two members representing the PPP in the PDA to decide the quota of seats to each component party, indicated that the PPP would agree to thirty NA seats for the Tehrik-i-Istiqlal, five for the TNFJ (Tehrik Nifaq Fiqh Jafria) and five for (Qasim) Muslim League. However he suggested that these should be from those seats that the PPP had lost in the 1988 and 1990 elections.

I told him that whereas I could accept thirty NA seats, I could not agree that these should all be from amongst those that the PPP had lost in these two elections. It was decided that the committee should meet again in Lahore on 28 September and try to finalize their recommendations. They are not likely to discuss the quota from amongst the lost or won seats. This will have to be discussed after Benazir's return from abroad on or about 7 October.

Wednesday, 25 Sept 1991, Islamabad, Abbottabad
Returned to Abbottabad. Nawaz Sharif said that the PDA White Paper on the 1990 elections was full of lies—without reading it, since it was issued only yesterday. The election commission also made a similar statement.

Friday, 4 Oct 1991, Islamabad
Met Fakhruddin G. Ebrahim and discussed with him the statement of the chief election commissioner that he will prosecute PDA leaders for issuing the White Paper and for its contents.

Friday, 11 Oct 1991, Islamabad, Abbottabad
The 'quota' committee held its third meeting in Islamabad today and could not agree on the quota to be allotted to the PDA parties. Decided to meet on 30 October after consulting the heads of parties.

Saturday, 12 Oct 1991, Abbottabad
Called on late Lieutenant General Fazle Haq's sons to condole the death of their father. It appears to have been a highly professional job.

Thursday, 17 Oct 1991, Abbottabad
Mian Aslam Bashir, a cousin of Mian Nawaz Sharif, came to put me in the picture regarding the conduct of his cousin. They have family differences and he accused Nawaz Sharif of misusing his family business, the Ittefaq Industries.

Saturday, 19 Oct 1991, Gujar Khan, Islamabad
Malik Hakmin Khan called to convey Benazir's desire to ask me to speak at the Liaquat Bagh meeting on 24 October, and also try to gauge my stand on the question of quota for TI in the alliance.

Thursday, 24 Oct 1991, Islamabad
A very big public meeting of PDA in Liaquat Bagh today. Meeting started at 17:00 and ended at 23:00. The meeting marked the first anniversary of the rigged election of 1990. About 10 members of TI spoke including Omar.

Sunday, 10 Nov 1991, Islamabad
Khurshid has been telephoning since yesterday trying to persuade me to join Nawabzada Nasrullah Khan's delegation to meet President Ghulam Ishaq Khan. I told him that I will not join this delegation and suggested that no one else from PDA either should go. Benazir wanted Khurshid to represent the PDA with which I did not agree. To simplify matters, Ghulam Ishaq Khan spoke in derogatory terms about Nasrullah Khan's delegation with the press at today's naval parade and the idea of meeting him was given up.

I addressed the press on the futility of the committee appointed by Nawaz Sharif and said that it will serve no purpose.

Monday, 11 Nov 1991, Islamabad, Abbottabad
Spoke to Benazir and arranged provisionally to see her in Karachi to discuss the question of allocation of the number of seats to the TI. The committee of PDA agreed in Lahore to quota as follows for PDA parties: Tehrik-i-Istiqlal 14 per cemt, TNFJ 6 per cent and Qasim Muslim League 5 per cent of all NA, PA and Senate seats. However these are the total number of seats to be allotted and the PPP wants these to be the ones PPP had lost in the 1988 and the 1990 elections. Our point of view is that some of these (preferably ten NA seats for Tehrik-i-Istiqlal) should be the seats that the PPP had won either in 1988 or 1990. I think it would be desirable to discuss this with Benazir before the PDA meeting in Peshawar on 26 November.

Wednesday, 13 Nov 1991, Abbottabad
Spoke to Benazir and agreed to meet her on 24 November.

Tuesday, 26 Nov 1991, Peshawar, Islamabad
Attended a meeting of the central coordination committee of PDA at Aftab Sherpao's. Discussed quota of seats between parties. Benazir was not willing to concede any seats that the PPP had won in 1988 and 1990 elections to the other four parties.

Thursday, 28 Nov 1991, Karachi, Dhaka (Bangladesh)
Left by PIA for Dhaka via Kathmandu with Amina at the invitation of the Bangladesh government. Were received by Zahiruddin Khan, minister of planning, government of Bangladesh, Pakistan deputy high commissioner, protocol officers of the Bangladesh foreign office, Mukhles uz Zaman Khan, B.D. Habibullah, Dewan Shafi ul Alam, A.U. Ahmad. Some press people came to interview me. Received a large number of telephone calls from well wishers. We were received very warmly by everyone. Everybody was very kind and appeared pleased to see us.

Friday, 29 Nov 1991, Dhaka
Spent a very busy day meeting people who came to call. Omar met some of his contacts, and also made contacts for 'Sebcon'. Dinner with General Wasiuddin and his wife at the Kurmitola Golf Club.

Saturday, 30 Nov 1991, Dhaka
A large number of people called. Amongst them Moinul Hussain, son of Manek Mian, the editor of *Ittefaq*. Air Marshals Khondkar and Mumtaz, ex-chiefs of air staff of the Bangladesh Air Force, also called. Earlier offered *fateha* at the graves of A.K. Fazlul Haq, Khawaja Nazimuddin and Huseyn Shaheed Suhrawardy. Dinner with Mukhles uz Zaman Khan.

Sunday, 1 Dec 1991, Dhaka
Called on the Pakistan high commissioner, Anwar Khan, a career diplomat. Three PAF retired officers, Shamsul Haq (an ex airman) and now a very successful industrialist, Wahid un Nabi (a former PAF footballer), and Syed Ahmad, a B-57 pilot, called. Addressed a large gathering of pressmen at the Dhaka Press Club. Had tea with Moinul Hussain, editor of *Ittefaq*. Dinner with some prominent and enthusiastic pro-Pakistan lawyers, amongst them Shafiqur Rahman, a senior advocate of the Supreme Court. They were forming a national united force which they hoped will provide a third force in Bangladesh politics, designed to counter Indian hegemonic designs against Bangladesh.

Monday, 2 Dec 1991, Dhaka

A large number of press representatives called for interviews for their newspapers and magazines including the weekly *Friday*. Lunch with Mr Aziz Mohammad Bhoy in Gulshan. Tea with Air Marshal Khondkar, the first chief of air staff of the Bangladesh Air Force. Later called on Zahiruddin Khan, son of late A.K. Khan. Zahiruddin is minister of planning. Some more retired PAF officers called. Dinner with General Khawaja Wasiuddin.

Tuesday, 3 Dec 1991, Dhaka

Left Dhaka for Karachi. A memorable visit. Everyone who met us was very kind and affectionate.

Friday, 6 Dec 1991, Lahore

Attended the national working committee meeting at Khurshid's. Discussed PDA affairs and the all parties conference. Most members thought that the APC was an attempt to replace the PDA and opposed taking part in its meetings. They thought that the PDA should be represented in its deliberations by the secretary general.

Thursday, 19 Dec 1991, CMH, Islamabad

Ghulam Ishaq Khan addressed the Parliament today. After his arrival-scene, the PTV began to play music. Obviously because there was disturbance in the House. The TV came on again after five minutes with noisy scenes and many interruptions Ghulam Ishaq Khan had to stop his speech many times. A sorry scene. After about half an hour of effective disturbances, which made Ghulam Ishaq Khan cut a sorry figure, the opposition staged a walk out and Ghulam Ishaq Khan was allowed to continue his speech uninterrupted.

Diary 1992

Friday, 7 Feb 1992, Abbottabad
Spoke to Zawar Shah in Multan. He was not very complimentary about the APC public meeting in Multan yesterday evening in which most of the PDA leaders were not able to speak.

Friday, 17 April 1992, Islamabad
Asked Zafar Ali Shah to see me. He was very upset at the attitude of Benazir Bhutto who is not willing to concede any of the seats the PPP had won in 1988 or 1990. She is also not willing to concede the Islamabad seat which the PPP had won in 1988 and where Zafar Ali Shah has a good position.

Decided to call a meeting of the national working committee on Thursday, 30 April in Islamabad to discuss the issues and whether it was worthwhile continuing with the PPP when Benazir does not appear to be willing to facilitate our entry into the National Assembly.

Saturday, 18 April 1992, Islamabad, Abbottabad
I briefed Khurshid Kasuri last night about my conversation with Zafar Ali Shah and told him that I wished the national working committee to meet on 30 April.

Thursday, 30 April 1992, Islamabad
Meeting of the national working committee. About 30 members attended. Discussed PDA's and PPP's attitude towards the quota issue. Various views were expressed but generally there was consensus on the desirability of staying in the PDA and exerting pressure on the PPP to get a greater share of the quota of seats.

Wednesday, 6 May 1992, Abbottabad
Had spoken to Omar in Islamabad last evening. Aftab Sherpao had been to see him to seek my opinion on the invitation extended by Nawaz Sharif to Benazir for talks. Told him that I was not against purposeful talks with a proper agenda such as holding of fresh elections under a neutral caretaker government.

Thursday, 14 May 1992, Karachi, Lahore
The annual budget was announced by Sartaj Aziz. More taxes. The non-development expenditure is up—Rs219 billion—an increase of Rs20 billion over last year.

Monday, 18 May 1992, Islamabad
I called on Benazir Bhutto and tried to persuade her to surrender the Islamabad seat to TI. She said that she would think it over. Also agreed that provincial heads of PPP and TI should also consider the division of other seats.

Friday, 29 May 1992, Abbottabad
Suleman Saddal came with Sajjad Dar from Sialkot and Tariq Anis from Shakargarh (Narowal district). Tariq Anis is a good candidate for NA-91 (Shakargarh) and will be joining Tehrik-i-Istiqlal on 6 June in Sialkot.

Wednesday, 3 June 1992, Abbottabad
Amina and I went to Risalpur for the graduation parade and stayed the night in the Pakistan Army's engineers officer mess. A new palatial building and disgustingly comfortable.

Saturday, 6 June 1992, Abbottabad
Sajjad Dar telephoned to say that Khurshid Kasuri and Mahnaz had attended a press conference in Sialkot in which Tariq Anis had announced his joining the TI. He is a likely candidate from Shakargarh NA constituency.

Thursday, 9 July 1992, Abbottabad
Makhdoomzada Syed Ali Askari called. He appears a peculiar character. Wants to join the Tehrik-i-Istiqlal and wants an important office on joining. Says he is being paid by the government grade 21, and yet is not a government servant. Thinks he could be appointed adviser to the prime minister and in that event wants to continue in the Tehrik-i-Istiqlal. Said he will call on me again tomorrow.

Friday, 10 July 1992, Abbottabad, Nathiagali
Syed Ali Askari called. I advised him that he may join the party if he was willing to start as an ordinary worker and that we could not give

him a position. This I said had to be earned and given with the workers' consent.

Thursday, 16 July 1992, Islamabad

Meeting of central executive committee of the PDA at Malik Hakmeen Khan's. Decided: (1) PDA will resign its seats in the national and provincial assemblies. (2) PDA will not join the APC. (3) PDA will launch a public contact programme with a protest meeting in Karachi on 30 July.

Thursday, 30 July 1992, Islamabad

A protest day was held by PDA all over Pakistan except in Karachi and Peshawar. Omar took part in the demonstration in Islamabad at Aabpara and was arrested by the police along with some 100 workers of PDA including about 25 women. He and the others were released after about four hours.

Tuesday, 15 Sept 1992, Coral Gables, Miami, USA

The BBC gave a ghastly account of the floods in Pakistan where 500,000 people have been evacuated and most of the Punjab has been submerged. However the main cities, such as Multan, have been saved by breaching the bunds and inundating the countryside with its valuable agricultural and cotton lands. In the north, roads and bridges are reported to have been washed away. About 2,000 people are reported killed. About 100,000 troops and almost all the army helicopter force is deployed. The BBC quoting Ahmed Rashid said that the government was slow in reacting. The financial effect of the floods could be crippling for the economy.

Thursday, 24 Sept 1992, Islamabad

Malik Hakmin called. He along with Khurshid were deputed to negotiate with Nawabzada Nasrullah Khan to arrange a joint working arrangement between the PDA and his newly formed National Democratic Alliance.

Wednesday, 14 Oct 1992, Islamabad

Meeting of the PDA was held at our house. All heads of parties participated. Following decisions were taken and an action committee with me as convenor was formed to: (1) Draw out a reconstruction programme for the country highlighting the misdeeds of the present government and their remedies. (2) Draw out a public contact programme for the next few months. (3) PDA to function on its own. (4) PDA will accept like-minded political parties but no discredited politicians. (5) Since he has formed his own alliance, Nawabzada Nasrullah Khan will not be asked to future PDA meetings.

Tuesday, 20 Oct 1992, Peshawar, Mardan, Swabi, Tarbela, Islamabad

At Tarbela, Benazir discussed the need to overthrow the government by public pressure by mid-November. Told her that the public was not ready for it and such an attempt would fail. Naveed Malik, who appears to be very close to her, and Agha Murtaza Pooya were vehemently opposed to my views and thought that the public was ready to do anything at her call.

Tuesday, 27 Oct 1992, Islamabad, Lahore, Okara, Lahore

Went by the morning flight to Lahore and then by road along with Benazir to Okara. A big procession. Very good response. Stopped briefly at three places. We left Lahore at 11:30 and arrived for the public meeting at 19:30. Large crowd—about 15,000 people which is a very big meeting for Okara. Left after dinner at Rao Sikandar Iqbal's place, an ex minister in the PPP government of Benazir Bhutto.

Thursday, 5 Nov 1992, Islamabad

The action committee of the PDA met at Karachi. Discussed the progress of the movement launched a couple of weeks ago. Drew out a programme of meetings in eleven places in Punjab, two in NWFP and one in Balochistan. Also discussed with the PPP (Sherpao and Shafqat Mahmud) the question of allocation of seats in the event of an election. Agreed to discuss the question of allocation of specific seats with the PPP's provincial president and try to agree on the maximum number of seats.

Monday, 9 Nov 1992, Islamabad

A busy day receiving telephone calls from Khurshid about the 'Long March' to Islamabad. It has been decided to hold the PDA meeting at

Malik Hakmin's. Benazir appears set to announce a date. I have told them that, in my opinion, the public is not ready for such a venture and the effort is likely to fail unless there are some other factors that I am not aware of. Kabir Ali Wasti, Zafar Ali Shah and Afzal Khan of PQP who called today, hold the same views.

Malik Hakmin called in the evening. He had been sent by Benazir to get me to agree to call a few other persons, not in the PDA, to the gathering tomorrow. I said that I had no objection, provided they did not attend the PDA meeting. Advice without responsibility, I maintained, is a dangerous thing. The decision should be taken by the PDA heads and the others should be told about it and asked to cooperate with us.

Tuesday, 10 Nov 1992, Islamabad

A meeting of PDA heads, Khurshid Kasuri (secretary general) and Farooq Leghari was held at Malik Hakmin Khan's. It was decided to announce a 'Long March' to the presidency in Islamabad on 18 November. I opposed the move as in my opinion we would not be able to muster enough public support. Malik Qasim of the Muslim League agreed with me that the move lacked adequate public support but agreed with Benazir that the 'Long March' should nevertheless be made. Syed Sajid Ali Naqvi of the TNFJ had the same views as Malik Qasim. Benazir was adamant that it was a matter of 'do or die'. Since the PPP would be making the major effort and was determined to go ahead, we acquiesced. Benazir announced this to a press conference. I feel that it is a wrong decision, ill-timed and is not likely to yield any result. It appears that some one, possibly the army, has encouraged her to go ahead. I feel that some people close to her have led her up the garden path.

The plan for the 18th is equally stupid; a public meeting at Liaquat Bagh, Rawalpindi at 15:00, followed by a procession to Islamabad after the meeting. Dusk is at 17:00 and the procession, if it ever reaches Islamabad, will not get there before nightfall. In any case the chances are that the buses that the PPP plans to bring to Islamabad from various cities of Punjab and the NWFP will be stopped at source or *en route* and will not get there.

Monday, 16 Nov 1992, Abbottabad, Islamabad

A large number of arrests have been made all over the country Khudai Noor telephoned to say that Fateh Mohammad Hasni was arrested some thirty miles from Quetta. He was leading a fairly large procession of vehicles to Islamabad, when they were stopped by the militia who fired in the air, baton charged them and fired tear gas shells. Some twenty workers were injured. Khudai Noor had left via Loralai and returned to Quetta from Muslim Bagh when he got the news.

Tuesday, 17 Nov 1992, Islamabad

Khurshid Kasuri came to lunch. Heads of PDA parties and some NDA leaders met at our house at 15:00 to discuss the assembly point and the strategy for tomorrow. Decided to meet at Benazir's house at 14:00 and to proceed to Liaquat Bagh from there. Maulana Kausar Niazi said he had information that we would be arrested tonight or tomorrow morning.

Benazir addressed a press conference of about 150 press reporters.

Omar left for Haripur to lead a procession, or rather to get arrested tomorrow.

Wednesday, 18 Nov 1992, Islamabad

The day of the much heralded 'Long March'. Went to Benazir's house. We got into a Pajero driven by Lal Khan of the NPP with Benazir, Jatoi, Iftikhar Jilani, Khurshid and myself. Drove at great speed by different roads towards Rawalpindi. Lal Khan drove over a barbed wire concertina fence. The barbed wire got entangled at the bottom of the vehicle and punctured it. Changed into Murtaza Pooya's car, which was following. Drove through by lanes led by a couple of boys on a motorcycle and entered Rawalpindi. Drove around Rawalpindi in the Raja a area for a couple of hours and were tear-gassed repeatedly as a large crowd gathered and accompanied us in the procession. Reached Liaquat Bagh, the starting point of the 'Long March' and were arrested shortly afterwards. The DIG police, took over our vehicle and after driving us around under a police escort, brought us to the state guest house at Rawalpindi. After being detained there, we were taken to the Islamabad airport where Benazir was put on to the 23:15 PIA flight to Karachi, which was delayed to leave at 02:30. We were then allowed to proceed to our houses in Islamabad.

Thursday, 19 Nov 1992, Islamabad

PDA action committee met at midday and we decided to continue with the 'Long March' organised by the PDA and already announced by Allama Sajid Ali Naqvi of the NFJ for today afternoon. In spite of heavy rain the procession was held. Also decided to hold another march on 22 November from Liaquat Bagh to Islamabad. Spoke to Benazir in Karachi. Her externment orders have been withdrawn. She will fly to Peshawar tomorrow. Addressed a press conference. Agha Murtaza Pooya and all his members (total of 2) of the Hizb-i-Jihad were arrested as they left the house. As also Malik Qasim and Kabir Ali Wasti. Khurshid Kasuri and Omar Kasuri were also arrested earlier.

Amina, Samina and Rabia visited Asma Jehangir in the local police station in the evening and gave her a pillow and a blanket.

Friday, 20 Nov 1992, Islamabad

PDA action committee met at our residence and we decided that the 'Long March' will start from Liaquat Bagh tomorrow and the leadership will try to get there. Malik Qasim who has gone to Lahore will return for this march tomorrow.

A PDA meeting of party heads will be held in Karachi at Ghulam Mustafa Jatoi's house at 16:00 on 22 November.

A long march journey will be undertaken by PDA leaders by train from Karachi to Rawalpindi on 23 November.

Addressed a very well attended press conference on our programme of the 'Long March' and the decisions taken.

Saturday, 21 Nov 1992, Islamabad

Malik Qasim led the 'Long March' from Liaquat Bagh and was arrested along with Agha Murtaza Pooya. A number of pressmen called. Farooq Leghari told me that Senator Dole, member of the US Senate foreign relations committee, wrote to Nawaz Sharif on 19 November about the suppression of civil liberties in Pakistan, suggesting in fairly strong language that the government should put an end to it.

Sunday, 22 Nov 1992, Islamabad, Karachi

Left for Karachi. Attended a meeting of PDA and other 'Long March' leaders at Ghulam Mustafa Jatoi's. Finalised details of the train journey to Islamabad. Tickets have been bought but no reservations of berths have been made. Decided to spend 24th night in Lahore after arrival there (by Khyber Mail) and leave for Rawalpindi on the morning of the 26th.

Monday, 23 Nov 1992, Karachi, Lahore

Left Karachi along with Benazir, Mustafa Jatoi, Allama Sajid Ali Naqvi, Malik Qasim, Hafeez Pirzada, Kausar Niazi, Murtaza Pooya, Afzal Khan of PQP and about another 100 workers. Train left Karachi at 22:00. large number of PDA workers and the public greeted us *en route* and the train arrived at Lahore at 22:30, three hours late. A large crowd at Lahore railway station greeted us.

Thursday, 26 Nov 1992, Lahore, Rawalpindi, Islamabad

Left by Tezgam at 12:30. Stopped at Gujranwala, Wazirabad, Gujrat, Lala Musa and Jhelum *en route*. Benazir got off the train at Lala Musa as her entry to Rawalpindi was banned. Very heavy police arrangements *en route* especially at Rawalpindi. No one had been allowed at the railway station which was full of police. Islamabad was full of armed police. Islamabad was also heavily barricaded and the government has inadvertently helped to boost the movement by its stupid reaction. It is over-reacting to every thing. Islamabad again gave the look of a besieged city with police and barbed wire at many places.

Friday, 27 Nov 1992, Islamabad

The PDA and the NDA leaders (those who are cooperating with us) met at Agha Murtaza Pooya's. Decided for the third phase of the 'Long March' to start from Multan on 3 December and conclude on 5 December via Vehari, Mandi Burawala, Arifwala, Pakpattan, Kasur and Lahore. Nusrat Bhutto presided and I addressed the press conference. I told Khurshid to inform Benazir (who is in Lahore) that I could not continue to tour in the 'Long March' with discredited elements.

Saturday, 28 Nov 1992, Islamabad, Abbottabad
Omar was released from Haripur jail along with some 400 other political workers.

Saturday, 5 Dec 1992, Dipalpur, Kasur-Lahore
Addressed large gatherings *en route*. Very good public response. Entered Lahore at about 17:00 in a massive procession. Addressed a big gathering at Faisal Chowk.

Sunday, 6 Dec 1992, Lahore, Islamabad
Babri Mosque in Ayodhya, UP India, was demolished today by fanatical Hindus. Telephoned Benazir in Karachi and Khurshid in Lahore and suggested a meeting to discuss this development.

Tuesday, 8 Dec 1992, Abbottabad, Islamabad, Karachi
Left for Karachi. Attended a meeting to discuss the implications of the burning of the Babri Mosque. Military secretary to the prime minister telephoned Benazir and spoke to her secretary (Naheed) to convey Nawaz Sharif's invitation to meet him on 10 December at 15:00. He later telephoned to convey the invitation to me. I said that this would receive my attention in consultation with the PDA allies. The PDA meeting decided to hold an all parties meeting of opposition parties in Lahore on 10 December.

Thursday, 10 Dec 1992, Karachi, Lahore
The PDA heads met at Gulzar's [Benazir Bhutto's] house at 16:00 to discuss their response to Nawaz Sharif's invitation to meet him today. Khurshid and I were in favour of accepting this invitation but the majority was against it.

Went to attend the APC called jointly by the PDA, the NDA and the IJM (Islami Jamhoori Mahaz) at the house of one of Nasrullah Khan's workers. About 100 people attended. Learnt during the meeting that Nawaz Sharif's meeting had been attended by Wali Khan, Ajmal Khattak, Hamida Khuhro and Mumtaz Bhutto and some other unknown organisation besides government leaders. They had decided that a meeting of the organisation of Islamic countries should be called.

Delegation should be sent abroad to publicise the Babri Mosque affair.

All cases of victimisation of Hindus in Pakistan should be severely dealt with.

There was a general agreement that the governments of India and of Pakistan had both been equally guilty of gross neglect and incompetence in dealing with the situation.

Friday, 11 Dec 1992, Lahore, Islamabad
Attending the second day of the APC at Gulzar's house. Finalised the draft press release.

Sunday, 20 Dec 1992, Islamabad
Spoke to Benazir in Karachi about the public meeting in Liaquat Bagh tomorrow. The administration has flooded the ground and will not allow loudspeakers to be installed.

Monday, 21 Dec 1992, Islamabad
The PDA heads met at our house. Benazir did not come, as she was unwell. Decided to hold a rally in Rawalpindi (which had been forbidden by the administration). Left for Rawalpindi at 15:30 drove through Raja Bazaar. Had a very responsive procession. Ended at Liaquat Bagh where we addressed a fairly reasonable crowd. Meeting ended at 19:30.

Diary 1993

Friday, 8 Jan 1993, Abbottabad
General Asif Nawaz, the chief of the army staff, died suddenly this morning in Rawalpindi, of a heart attack.

Wednesday, 20 Jan 1993, Islamabad, Lahore, Islamabad
Left for Lahore and attended the *qul* of Malik Wazir Ali who died on 18 January

Saturday, 6 Feb 1993, Lahore

Attended the all parties Kashmir conference organised by Jamaat-i-Islami. Almost all political parties, except ANP of Wali Khan and Pakhtunkhwa party of Mahmud Khan Achakzai, attended. The governments was represented by Nisar Ali Khan, Chaudhry Shujaat and Ijazul Haq. The conference was well organised and issued an agreed press statement condemning Indian activities in occupied Kashmir and expressed support for the freedom fighters.

Sunday, 7 Feb 1993, Lahore, Shakargarh, Sialkot

Left Lahore for Shakargarh. Mahnaz Rafi accompanied. Was given a big welcome on arrival at Shakargarh and addressed a very good gathering. About 4,000 people at Tariq Anis's residence.

Tuesday, 9 Feb 1993, Lahore, Gujranwala, Lahore, Islamabad

Addressed the Gujranwala District Bar Association. Later attended a brief ceremony organised by Syed Ashfaq Ali Shah who rejoined the Tehrik-i-Istiqlal. He had been one of our early members and had been inactive for some time.

On our return to Lahore stopped at Khurshid's and discussed General Aslam Beg's statement, Benazir's possible rapprochement with the government and the presidential election.

Thursday, 18 Feb 1993, Islamabad

Sardar Farooq Leghari came. He explained the reasons for Benazir accepting the position of chairperson of the foreign relations committee.

Wednesday, 24 Feb 1993, Karachi

Called on Amin Fahim the Makhdoom of Hala. He is a PPP member but on the fringe. A pleasant person. Discussed the general political situation and condoled with him on the death of his father the late Makhdoom Talib ul Maula.

Thursday, 25 Feb 1993, Karachi

Called on Nisar Khuhro to condole the death of his father-in-law. In the afternoon launched Major General Akbar Khan's book *Raiders in Kashmir*.

Monday, 1 March 1993, Islamabad
Finalised the draft for the press conference on 3 March calling for Ghulam Ishaq Khan's impeachment.

Dr Charles Amjad Ali came with very good material on the ordinances issued by GIK (82 in all), in two years, on the constitution and on the eighth amendment. Decided to address another press conference about the middle of March.

Wednesday, 3 March 1993, Islamabad
Addressed a press conference and read out a statement calling for Ghulam Ishaq Khan's impeachment for misconduct.

Thursday, 4 March 1993, Islamabad, Abbottabad
Yesterday's press conference, which was an outright rejection of Ghulam Ishaq Khan and asked for his impeachment, received cautious reporting in the papers.

Saturday, 6 March 1993, Abbottabad, Islamabad
Received a message from Sajjad Dar in Sialkot that Suleman Saddal has been killed. He was shot by three assailants. Decided to go to Sialkot tomorrow to attend his funeral.

Sunday, 7 March 1993, Islamabad, Kotli Loharan (Sialkot), Islamabad
Left for Sialkot with Zafar Ali Shah to attend Suleman Saddal's funeral. Suleman Saddal a prominent worker of Tehrik-i-Istiqlal had been shot yesterday by six assailants on motorcycles. They had fired as he was standing outside a shop near the police station.

Thursday, 11 March 1993, Islamabad
Addressed a press conference on the 82 ordinances passed by President Ghulam Ishaq Khan in the last two years. Agha Murtaza Pooya and Ahmed Raza Kasuri called. They were certain that Ghulam Ishaq Khan would sack the Nawaz Sharif government and dissolve the assemblies.

Wednesday, 17 March 1993, Islamabad, Lahore

Addressed a gathering of youth. Some 300 students of various youth organisations announced joining the Tehrik-i-Istiqlal, a very successful gathering.

Tuesday, 23 March 1993, Abbottabad

Rained all day. A very wet parade (23 March parade) in Islamabad. These parades are a waste of effort. All they succeed in doing is showing off equipment and weapons — almost all obsolete — manufactured by the US or Japan. The parade was followed by dancing *mirasis* or eunuchs, on floats. Hardly a show to accompany a parade of the fighting services. I am glad that I retired long before all this started.

Thursday, 1 April 1993, Islamabad

The city is rife with rumours that the government is being dismissed by Ghulam Ishaq Khan and the assemblies are being dissolved. By-election to about thirty-five NA and PA constituencies are nevertheless being held in Sindh on the seats vacated by the MQM.

Sunday, 4 April 1993, Peshawar

Drove to Wali Bagh and called on Wali Khan. He had suffered a heart attack some three weeks ago but is better now. Heard on the 21:00 news that Nawaz Sharif had nominated Ghulam Ishaq Khan to contest the presidential election as a Muslim League candidate.

Monday, 5 April 1993, Peshawar, Nowshera, Islamabad

Left for Islamabad at midday and attended a wedding at the Islamabad club of Ashraf Hashmi's daughter. A large gathering of politicians of different hues. The place was full of rumours. The general opinion was that anything could happen at any time and Ghulam Ishaq Khan would sack Nawaz Sharif sooner or later.

Tuesday, 6 April 1993, Islamabad

Sajjad Dar and Luqman Saddal (brother of late Suleman Saddal) came from Sialkot. Luqman Saddal wishes to join the party. Ghulam Mustafa Jatoi called to discuss the political situation. He is a supporter of Ghulam Ishaq Khan and is working hard to get rid of Nawaz Sharif's government.

Saturday, 17 April 1993, Karachi

Listened to Nawaz Sharif's speech on TV which was clearly an indictment of Ghulam Ishaq Khan and largely justified.

Sunday, 18 April 1993, Karachi

Addressed a press conference at Niamat Khan's. Criticised Ghulam Ishaq Khan and supported Nawaz Sharif's allegations against him.

Ghulam Ishaq Khan dismissed the central government and dissolved the National Assembly. Balakh Sher Mazari was sworn in as the prime minister with Hamid Nasir Chattha and Farooq Ahmed Leghari of the PPP as ministers.

Tuesday, 20 April 1993, Karachi, Islamabad

Left for Islamabad. Attended the PDA heads meeting at our house. Told Benazir that we had not been kept informed of talks with Ghulam Ishaq Khan and Nawaz Sharif and that I felt that it was wrong of her to have decided to back Ghulam Ishaq Khan on his wanting to dismiss Nawaz Sharif's government without his agreeing to our other terms, that is, the head of government not taking part in elections, appointment of a new election commissioner and dissolution of provincial assemblies.

Wednesday, 21 April 1993, Islamabad

Malik Hakmin Khan called and I told him to arrange a meeting with Asif Zardari to discuss the PPP's policy in the present situation.

The central office bearers of the TI met to discuss the situation— 15 participated. All, except Zafar Ali Shah, Qazi Amir Abdullah and Shafique (Ziae's brother), were keen to join the caretaker government as a part of PDA.

Thursday, 22 April 1993, Islamabad

Mumtaz Tarar, Hamid Sarfaraz, Hanif Goraya, Barrister Sultan Mehmood and a number of others—all struck by the political fever of uncertainty prevailing in the country—came. Syed Zafar Ali Shah, was very agitated with the attitude of Benazir, also called. Heard later in the evening that over a dozen people had been sworn in as ministers, including Asif Zardari, Aftab Sherpao, Aitzaz Ahsan, Fateh Mohammad Hasnie of the PPP and Ghulam Mustafa Jatoi's son, Maulana Kausar Niazi and some other disreputable characters.

Friday, 23 April 1993, Islamabad
Benazir telephoned in the evening to say that she wanted Omar to be made a minister of state as well as Mahnaz Rafi. She had offered the same to Khurshid which he had declined. I spoke to Amina in Karachi and to Samina and they both did not like the idea. Samina also spoke with Omar and he also did not approve. Mahnaz came from Lahore accompanied by Khurshid and his wife. Discussed the desirability of Khurshid accepting Benazir's offer. After a prolonged discussion and in view of the fact that party workers and prospective candidates wanted the TI to accept the offer, I agreed. Spoke to Sherpao and told him that Khurshid should be made a full-fledged minister. He has to speak to Benazir and will let me know.

Sunday, 25 April 1993, Islamabad, Abbottabad
Afzal Khan and Latif Afridi of PQP, Khurshid and Mahnaz met at my house to discuss the offer made by the government (through Benazir) to us to allow Mahnaz to join the government. Mahnaz was very keen and Khurshid was supportive.

Tuesday, 27 April 1993, Islamabad
Attended a stormy meeting of TNFJ, PQP (Afzal Khan) and TI (Khurshid Kasuri and myself) and decided to call a meeting of PDA heads urgently. TNFJ was represented by Muneer Hussain Gilani and Hasnie of Multan.

Wednesday, 28 April 1993, Islamabad
PQP, TFJ and TI heads met this morning. TNFJ was represented by Gilani and Hasnie from Multan. Decided to confront Benzair with our strong dissatisfaction with her attitude towards the other parties of the PDA and to call for the immediate allocation of seats between component parties.

Thursday, 29 April 1993, Islamabad
PDA heads met and there was strong criticism of Benazir and her high-handed handling of the situation. After a lot of argument it was decided that Malik Qasim, Khurshid Kasuri and Afzal Khan of PQP should be full ministers and Munir Gilani of TFJ should be a minister of state. Khurshid called later to thank me for my support for his

appointment and to convince the family that Omar—now in the USA—should contest NA elections.

Friday, 30 April 1993, Islamabad
APC held their meeting. I did not attend. Decided that a delegation of NDA and PDA under chairmanship of Nawabzada Nasrullah Khan should meet Ghulam Ishaq Khan to place demands of APC, namely, (1) dissolution of assemblies (2) appointment of neutral election commission (3) elections on due date, 14 July.

Khurshid Kasuri called to seek my permission to accompany Nasrullah Khan to meet Ghulam Ishaq Khan. I agreed.

Saturday, 1 May 1993, Islamabad
Syed Zafar Ali Shah called. He has lost the Supreme Court bar general secretary's election and was very angry at Khurshid accepting to be a minister in the government. He was almost incoherent with anger and thought that we had damaged the interests of the party irreparably. I did not agree with him that Khurshid was sold out to the PPP.

Monday, 3 May 1993, Islamabad, Abbottabad
Khurshid Kasuri telephoned to say that he has been given the ministry of parliamentary affairs.

Tuesday, 4 May 1993, Abbottabad
Met the press of Abbottabad and spoke against the use of the army to supervise the elections on 14 July. With 200 polling stations in each constituency and 207 NA seats (207 x 200) about 40,000 polling station will require to be monitored and with about four polling booths in each polling station, about 160,000 polling booths will have to be supervised. It will be impossible to provide so many officers and JCO's for the job and in any case they will be able to do little or nothing (except enforce law and order) to stop bogus identity cards and bogus voters' lists. I suggested change of the chief election commissioner and the appointment of an impartial election commission with vast powers to make administrative changes where necessary.

Newspaper reported that Syed Zafar Ali Shah had resigned from the PDA.

Wednesday, 5 May 1993, Abbottabad
By-election to the provincial assembly seats was held in Sindh. Very poor turnout. MQM (Altaf Hussain group) boycotted the elections. Turnout was as low as 3 per cent in some constituencies.

Friday, 7 May 1993, Islamabad
Meeting of the party's central parliamentary board. Decided on some two dozen candidates for the 14 per cent NA seats that we can claim from the PDA. We should be able to get about 12 that we can contest. Omar arrived from the USA early today.

Monday, 10 May 1993, Islamabad
Malik Hakmin Khan called and complained bitterly of the treatment meted out to him by Benazir. He accused her of nepotism in selecting PPP ministers.

Addressed a press conference against placing the election (of July 1993) under army supervision. Instead I suggested that the chief election commissioner should be changed and the election commission reconstituted.

Tuesday, 11 May 1993, Islamabad
Fahd Hussain of the *Muslim* interviewed me. Malik Hakmin and Shafqat Mahmud of the PPP called to convey Benazir's concern at my statement against the use of the army for elections. I reaffirmed my position on the issue.

Wednesday, 12 May 1993, Islamabad
Shahbaz Sharif called and suggested that the Tehrik-i-Istiqlal should leave the PDA and form an alliance with the Muslim League. Asked Mahnaz Rafi to come to discuss possibilities of closer contacts with Nawaz Sharif. She came in the evening and I suggested that she should make it clear that we would not leave the PDA but would be willing to cooperate on matters of national interest, such as the repeal of the eighth amendment.

Wednesday, 19 May 1993, Islamabad
Met the press. Talked about the eighth amendment, the election commission, accountability, the parliament's dubious role, the

ineffectiveness of the caretaker government and other related matters.

Thursday, 20 May 1993, Islamabad
Khurshid telephoned to say that Benazir had held a meeting in Lahore with PDA ministers and had asked them to give her their resignations.

Friday, 21 May 1993, Islamabad
Called on Altaf Gauhar in the evening. He had written a powerful editorial in the *Muslim* today about Benazir's politics. Spoke to Khurshid and suggested that he should resign from the federal cabinet. He was very much against the idea. Said that he would come to see me tomorrow.

Saturday, 22 May 1993, Islamabad
Khurshid Kasuri called in the evening. Discussed the possibility of the restoration of the National Assembly by the Supreme Court.

Sunday, 23 May 1993, Islamabad
Manzoor Ahmed Wattoo, chief minister of Punjab, called to seek my cooperation to keep Nawaz Sharif out of government if the National Assembly is restored.

Tuesday, 25 May 1993, Abbottabad
Mir Balakh Sher Mazari, the caretaker prime minister, telephoned to say that he would like to call on me. Told him that he could do so when I came to Islamabad in a few days. Earlier his private secretary had telephoned to ask me to dinner in Islamabad—for political leaders—which I had declined.

Wednesday, 26 May 1993, Abbottabad
The Supreme Court announced their decision in the constitutional petition of Nawaz Sharif restoring the National Assembly and Nawaz Sharif's government. Ghulam Ishaq Khan accepted the Supreme Court decision. It is probably the first time ever, that a dismissed government or assembly has been restored by a court order.

Saturday, 29 May 1993, Abbottabad, Islamabad
Khurshid Kasuri called. Discussed PDA. Akhundzada Anwar Ali of
Tehrik-i-Jafria called later to discuss PDA affairs and PPP's lack of
interest in it.

Monday, 31 May 1993, Abbottabad
Nawaz Sharif, the restored prime minister, made an offer of a dialogue
with the opposition, which was accepted by the PDA.

Monday, 7 June 1993, Islamabad
Khurshid Kasuri, Mahnaz, Hamid Sarfaraz and Khudai Noor came in
the morning and Omar and I accompanied them to Malik Hakmin's
for the PDA central coordinating committee meeting. Nusrat Bhutto
accompanied Benazir to the meeting. Decided to form a political
committee to negotiate with the government comprising Khurshid
(chairman), Malik Hamid Sarfaraz, (TI), Senator Iqbal Haider (PPP),
Naqvi (TFJ), Kabir Ali Wasti (ML). Also agreed to form parliamentary
boards for NWFP and Punjab when High Court decisions are known
regarding the writs about the dissolution of the provincial
assemblies.

Wednesday, 9 June 1993, Islamabad, Abbottabad
Mahnaz telephoned to say that Manzoor Gilani, the general secretary
of Punjab, had called a meeting of the Punjab council of the party for
a vote of no-confidence against her. As it did not meet the constitutional
requirements (I had not been informed) I asked Khurshid, the secretary
general, to replace Manzoor Gilani with Tassaddaq Baloch as general
secretary Punjab TI.

Saturday, 12 June 1993, Abbottabad
Syed Tasneem Nawaz Gardezi, federal health minister, Rana Nazir
Ahmed, federal minister for population welfare, and Chaudhri Sarwar
called on behalf of the government to discuss the political situation.
We agreed on the need to repeal the eighth amendment.

Sunday, 13 June 1993, Abbottabad
Khurshid telephoned to say that the PDA and the Muslim League had
held their meetings. He said that the meetings were satisfactory.

Wednesday, 16 June 1993, Islamabad, Abbottabad
Lunch with Prime Minister Nawaz Sharif. Khurshid Kasuri, Zafar Ali Shah, Malik Hamid Sarfaraz, Ikram Nagra, Khudai Noor, Mahnaz Rafi, Inamullah Khan, Omar and Sajjad Dar accompanied me. Had about 2½ hour talks. A good meeting.

Thursday, 17 June 1993, Abbottabad
Khurshid telephoned to say that Benazir and the PPP were very disturbed by our line of action. I explained that we could not be lackeys of the PPP and that she should get used to treating us as equals if she wanted the PDA to last. A very difficult thing for her to do.

Sunday, 20 June 1993, Abbottabad
Issued a statement to say that the Tehrik-i-Istiqlal will not be attending the APC meeting called by Nasrullah Khan in Islamabad on 23 June.

Saturday, 26 June 1993, Islamabad
Major General Mohammad Hayat of Azad Kashmir (former president) called and gave a briefing on the corruption of the Sardar Qayyum government.

Sunday, 27 June 1993, Islamabad
The APC held yesterday called for the dissolution of the assembly and the holding of fresh elections. It appears that Ghulam Ishaq Khan may either do this or hold a referendum on this issue.

Monday, 28 June 1993, Islamabad
Told Mohammad Afzal Khan MNA of PQP that it appeared difficult for us to continue with the PPP. Later called on Allama Sajid Ali Naqvi and discussed our continued association with the PPP. Agreed to ask the secretary general to convene a meeting of the heads of the PDA.

Tuesday, 29 June 1993, Islamabad
The two houses of parliaments passed by a comfortable majority of 148 to 7 a bill to impose president's rule in Punjab.

Wednesday, 30 June 1993, Islamabad, Abbottabad
There is confusion as a result of the passing of the bill by combined houses of parliament yesterday. The government said that president's rule has been imposed in Punjab and the president's staff confirmed that the president had given his assent. Wattoo the Punjab chief minister has dug his heels in and is refusing to leave.

Thursday, 1 July 1993, Abbottabad
Nawaz Sharif decided to refer the controversy with the president, as also the interpretation of the constitution regarding control of Punjab, to the Supreme Court.

Monday, 5 July 1993, Islamabad, Karachi
Earlier Mian Shahbaz Sharif called. He talked about Benazir's attitude and appeared to agree to the holding of elections under a neutral government provided the eighth amendment was removed first.

Khurshid called later and I briefed him about my talks with Shahbaz Sharif who had said that they are willing to accommodate the TI by giving seats to our important people. Agreed that Mahnaz and he should discuss the matter on 18 July in Lahore.

Sunday, 11 July 1993, Lahore
Addressed a press conference. Suggested a package deal between the government and the opposition for the repeal of the eighth amendment and elections under a completely neutral caretaker government at the centre as well as in the provinces.

Monday, 12 July 1993, Lahore, Islamabad
Met Maulana Fazlur Rahman. He said that he was trying to arrange a rapprochement between Ghulam Ishaq Khan and Nawaz Sharif. His plan: both stay in their respective places, elections in October and the assemblies elect the president after elections. Punjab to have a neutral government during elections. Other provincial governments stay with the present chief ministers as caretakers and he, Fazlur Rahman, will guarantee their neutrality. How? I did not understand. In Balochistan, the JUI and Bugti will manage the show. A quixotic idea which both Mahnaz and Khurshid thought we should support.

Tuesday, 13 July 1993, Islamabad
Arif Nizami, editor, *The Nation* called. He told me that PPP had been after Wattoo to pay them for the 'Long March' and that he had paid Rs100 million to Senator Gulzar, Benazir's permanent host in Lahore.

Thursday, 15 July 1993, Islamabad
Mian Shahbaz Sharif came. Amongst other things he told me that Nawaz Sharif had proposed to the president my name for the caretaker prime minister, for the election which he is agreeable to holding some time in 1994. He had suggested this for a package deal with the opposition. The army has been entrusted the task of handling the law and order situation in Islamabad tomorrow, the day of the so-called 'Long March'.

The Peshawar High Court upheld the order of the NWFP chief minister to dissolve the assembly. So by-election will be held. The 'Long March' was called off after the chief of the army staff met Benazir and asked her to do so.

Friday, 16 July 1993, Islamabad
Khurshid came in the afternoon. Discussed the proposal of Nawaz Sharif to make me the caretaker prime minister. Decided to decline the offer if it is made.

Saturday, 17 July 1993, Islamabad
The day after the event that was to be—the 'Long March'. My contacts with the PPP and the JUP indicate that they have no clue about what is happening or what is going to happen.

Sunday, 18 July 1993, Islamabad
Khurshid called in the morning. He was very confused. Zafar Ali Shah, Fazal Bhatty and Omar and I discussed the situation with Khurshid and decided to call a meeting of the national working committee on 26 July in Lahore. In the meantime Khurshid would find out whether Benazir wanted to keep the PDA intact.

Learnt that it was decided last night that Ghulam Ishaq Khan and Nawaz Sharif both would go; Wasim Sajjad would take over as president and Moeen Qureshi of the World Bank as caretaker prime minister. Elections would be held by a neutral administration at the centre as well as the provinces. That is what I had demanded. Nawaz Sharif spoke on TV and announced his resignation. Ghulam Ishaq Khan was to speak later.

Monday, 19 July 1993, Islamabad, Abbottabad

Elections were announced for the National Assembly on 6 October and the provincial assemblies on 9 October. Khurshid telephoned to say that he did not see any point in contacting Benzair. The next few days, he said, would show what she intends to do. Malik Qasim had met her yesterday and Mohammad Afzal Khan would be seeing her in a day or two.

Thursday, 22 July 1993, Abbottabad

Khurshid Kasuri, Zafar Ali Shah, Omar and I met to discuss the situation and our continuance in the PDA. We were all agreed that Benazir had no further interest in the continuance of our association in the PDA and it was no use continuing in it. Later Akhundzada Anwar Ali and Wazarat Hussain Naqvi of the TNFJ called. Agreed to meet them after our national working committee meeting in Lahore on 26 July and before the national working committee meeting on 31 July. Arranged to call on the caretaker prime minister, Moeen Qureshi.

Friday, 23 July 1993, Islamabad

Attended the launching of Altaf Gauhar's book *Ayub Khan: Pakistan's First Military Ruler*. It was a very well attended function, over which I presided. Other speakers were Aftab Ahmed Khan, Agha Shahi, S.M. Zafar, General K.M. Arif and Altaf Gauhar. Zahid Malik of the daily *Observer* was the host.

Saturday, 24 July 1993, Islamabad, Lahore

Gave Khurshid the draft of my letter to Benazir about ending our association with the PPP. He thought the draft should be made milder. Will discuss it with him tomorrow.

Sunday, 25 July 1993, Lahore

Discussed the letter to be written to Benazir with Khurshid and Mahnaz. Mahnaz and I called on Abid Hassan Minto and agreed that the Punjab branches of our parties, as well as Ghulam Nabi Kallu's party, should cooperate with each other in future.

Monday, 26 July 1993, Lahore
Meeting of the national working committee to discuss our association with the PDA. About 50 members attended. Every one except two— Fateh Mohammad from Rahimyar Khan and Khan Mohammad Badera from Bahawalpur—felt that we should leave the PDA. Wrote a letter to Benazir to formally disassociate ourselves from the PDA and released it to the press.

Thursday, 29 July 1993, Islamabad
Mushahid telephoned to say that he was trying to arrange a meeting between me and Nawaz Sharif.

Wednesday, 4 Aug 1993, Abbottabad
Syed Iftikhar Gilani, former MNA of PPP and the former law minister, resigned from the PPP for much the same reasons as us, when we disassociated ourselves from the PDA.

Monday, 9 Aug 1993, Islamabad
Khurshid, Mahnaz, Syed Zafar Ali Shah and Khudai Noor held talks with Nawaz Sharif and later with Nawabzada Mohsin Ali Khan for NWFP seats. Muslim League had nothing to offer in NWFP. Meeting for Punjab will be held in Lahore tomorrow. Mairaj Mohammad Khan called again to discuss ways of bringing the MQM into the mainstream of national politics.

Tuesday, 10 Aug 1993, Islamabad
Khurshid Kasuri and our team met the ML team in Lahore today. The talks were inconclusive.

Wednesday, 11 Aug 1993, Islamabad
Called on Altaf Gauhar and, among other things, discussed the split between Nusrat Bhutto and Benazir. According to Altaf Gauhar, Nusrat is keen to get her son back and dislikes Asif Zardari whom Benazir wishes to see as the chief minister Sindh. Met Iftikhar Gilani, former MNA, who had recently resigned from the PPP.

Thursday, 12 Aug 1993, Islamabad, Lahore
Omar left for Peshawar to discuss allocation of seats with Mohsin Ali Khan and to call on the chief minister. Called on Nawaz Sharif with Khurshid and Khudai Noor to discuss allocation of seats.

Friday, 13 Aug 1993, Lahore
Omar was elected chairman of TI NWFP at Peshawar in the meeting of the provincial council of the party.

Monday, 16 Aug 1993, Islamabad
Mohsin (Nawabzada Khattak), the organiser of Muslim League (Nawaz) NWFP, who was to meet Omar did not turn up.

Tuesday, 17 Aug 1993, Islamabad
Death anniversary of Ziaul Haq. Spent the day trying to find out about the seats the Muslim League (Nawaz) would concede to us.

Wednesday, 18 Aug 1993, Islamabad, Abbottabad
Omar left for Peshawar for the day to try to extract some seats for the TI. Mahnaz telephoned to say that Khurshid Kasuri's (Kasur NA) and Zafar Ali Shah's (Rawalpindi city PPI) and Tariq Anis's Shakargarh (Narowal) PP seats had been confirmed. Discussion on other seats is in progress. No decision on Khudai Noor's NA-197 seat yet. Omar telephoned to say that no seat had been conceded to us in the NWFP. I telephoned Shahbaz Sharif and said that PF-38 must be given to TI. Also spoke about NA-197 for Khudai Noor.

Tuesday, 31 Aug 1993, Karachi, Dhaka
Left by PIA for Dhaka with Amina at the invitation of the government of Bangladesh. Were met by BD ministers and Dewan Shafiul Alam. Called on Fakhruz Zaman Khan, former chairman Tehrik-i-Istiqlal, East Pakistan, who was unwell. Later called on Begum Wasiuddin (General Wasiuddin died in November last year). Dinner with the Pakistan high commissioner, Anwar Kamal.

Wednesday, 1 Sept 1993, Dhaka
Laid a wreath at General Ziaur Rahman's tomb. Later went to the council meeting of the Bangladesh National Party. A well organised

affair. Prime Minister Khalida Zia made a long speech. Left after lunch for the tomb of those who had lost their lives in what they call the 'war of independence'. Laid another wreath there and returned to the hotel in the evening. Dinner in the hotel hosted by Mustafizur Rehman, the foreign minister, who was in the PMA in 1952, when Anwar was there as an instructor. Attended a cultural entertainment programme after dinner.

Thursday, 2 Sept 1993, Dhaka, Karachi
Left Dhaka for Karachi and arrived at 18:30.

Friday, 3 Sept 1993, Karachi
Ikram Sehgal called. Discussed election strategy with him as well as the desirability of my taking part in Nawaz Sharif's election campaign. He thought that Moeen Qureshi, the caretaker prime minister, had political ambitions and would be the PPP candidate.

Wednesday, 22 Sept 1993, Abbottabad
Sardar Mehtab Ahmed Khan Abbasi ML(N) candidate for NA-11 called to invite me to Nawaz Sharif's public meeting probably on 27 September in Abbottabad. Do not intend to attend. Nawaz Sharif has been very niggardly in his treatment of our candidates in spite of agreement to adjust people in suitable places even where he had no candidates of his own party, for instance, Khudai Noor in PB-4 and Afzal Soomro PS-31 Sindh. He left the seats open rather than agree to give the common symbol to our men. He also took away Mumtaz Tarar's ticket after persuading him to join the ML and announcing the award of NA ticket to him.

Friday, 24 Sept 1993, Islamabad
Spoke to Khudai Noor (Quetta) and Mrs Khurshid Kasuri (in Kasur). Mrs Kasuri was optimistic about Khurshid's campaign and asked if I could visit Kasur for a public meeting. I agreed.

Wednesday, 29 Sept 1993, Islamabad
Ghulam Hyder Wyne, the former chief minister of Punjab, was shot and killed near Mian Channu.

Friday, 1 Oct 1993, Islamabad, Abbottabad
Saw Benazir in election hour on TV. She read out a well prepared speech in English which Mohammad Jan (our cook) did not understand. Her questions and answers in Urdu were quite good but went largely above the heads of 90 per cent of the listeners. MQM announced its boycott of the elections.

Saturday, 2 Oct 1993, Abbottabad
Sent a message to Moeen Qureshi, the prime minister, to take action to allow the MQM to take part in the elections.

Tuesday, 5 Oct 1993, Abbottabad
Moeen Qureshi, the caretaker prime minister, appeared in a one hour TV programme and it appeared that he was a presidential candidate in the October-November presidential elections.

Wednesday, 6 Oct 1993, Abbottabad
Election day. Cast our votes (Omar, Amina, Samina and I) in the afternoon.

Thursday, 7 Oct 1993, Abbottabad
PPP secured 86 seats in the NA and the PML 74. Khurshid Kasuri lost in the Kasur election. Among those who lost were Maulana Noorani, Maulana Abdus Sattar Niazi, Ghaus Ali Shah, Aitzaz Ahsan, Chaudhry Shujaat and Ajmal Khattak.

Monday, 11 Oct 1993, Abbottabad, Islamabad
Syed Zafar Ali Shah, newly elected MPA from PP-1 called. He is very pleased with himself and rightly so. Got a good number of votes and won from all the 104 polling stations and from every polling booth (about four) in every polling station.

Thursday, 14 Oct 1993, Islamabad, Sargodha, Islamabad
Left for Sargodha to attend the 50th anniversary of No. 9 Squadron formed on 13 October 1943. Amina accompanied me. Some 200 former 9 Squadron officers attended. A busy programme. We left at 1:00 on 15 October by a PAF aircraft and arrived at Islamabad at about 02:00.

Saturday, 16 Oct 1993, Islamabad

Called on Akbar Khan Bugti. Talked about the election of the NA speaker and the prime minister. It appears that horse-trading is in full swing and the outcome is anyone's guess.

Sunday, 17 Oct 1993, Islamabad

Yusuf Raza Gilani of PPP was elected speaker of NA with 106 votes. Gohar Ayub lost with 90 votes. Syed Zafar Ali Shah of PPP won the deputy speaker's election with 115 votes. Nawaz Khokar lost with 81 votes.

Tuesday, 19 Oct 1993, Islamabad, Abbottabad

Benazir was elected prime minister by 121 votes against Nawaz Sharif's 72. The '*lotas*' (Independents), FATA and minorities voted for her when it became clear that she would form the government. The religious parties and Ghulam Mustafa Jatoi did not vote.

Thursday, 21 Oct 1993, Islamabad

Called on General Abdul Wahid Kakar, the COAS, discussed the Mohajir situation in Karachi and suggested that the army should be pulled back from urban centres. Appeared a good professional soldier. We also discussed the role of the Pakistan Army in Somalia.

Saturday, 23 Oct 1993, Islamabad

Went to the chief election commission along with Mrs Khurshid Kasuri to attend the hearing of Khurshid's petition regarding irregularities in NA-106. The date for next hearing was fixed for 10 November.

Monday, 25 Oct 1993, Islamabad

Mumtaz Tarar called. Discussed the presidential election due on 13 November. Met Altaf Gauhar. He had met Benzair Bhutto today and had suggested my name for president. Her response was not hostile. He had also discussed this with Fakhrudin G. Ebrahim, the attorney general designate.

Tuesday, 26 Oct 1993, Islamabad
Altaf Gauhar came and we discussed the latest position regarding the forthcoming presidential polls. Benazir got a vote of confidence in the NA.

Friday, 29 Oct 1993, Islamabad
Khurshid Kasuri came to dinner and stayed till the early hours of the morning. He is suggesting that the TI should merge into the Muslim League (N) as he sees no future for small political parties.

Monday, 1 Nov 1993, Islamabad
Khurshid met Nawaz Sharif today who said that he had no objection if Benazir agreed to have me as a common candidate for the presidency but thought that she was not sincere and would back out. Khurshid later talked to Benazir on the telephone. She wanted Nawaz Sharif to propose my name through 'official channels'. What this meant is anyone's guess.

Tuesday, 2 Nov 1993, Islamabad
Khurshid called from Lahore and later came to Islamabad. He had met Nawaz Sharif earlier today. They discussed the possibility of ML (N) agreeing to my name as a common candidate for presidency. There is a lot of mistrust between Benazir and Nawaz Sharif and they are very suspicious of each other.

Saturday, 6 Nov 1993, Islamabad
The Muslim League announced this evening that Wasim Sajjad would be their candidate for the presidency.

Sunday, 7 Nov 1993, Islamabad
Another day of hectic activity. As the 13th draws near, manoeuvring for the presidential election is becoming very keen.

Monday, 8 Nov 1993, Islamabad
Lieutenant General Azhar and Pir Akram Shah of JUP came in the morning. Khurshid was also here. Azhar had been to see Nawabzada Nasrullah Khan and had got the impression that he would be withdrawing from the presidential contest.

Thursday, 11 Nov 1993, Islamabad
Anwar Khan Durrani, secretary general JWP, came. Benazir asked Omar, Charles Amjad and Kaiser Bengali to meet her. They called on her. She wanted their help and advice and made some suggestions including the possibility of Omar working with Sherpao in NWFP and also of joining the PPP. She said that she was feeling alone and needed advice. She said that she would have agreed to me as president but Nawaz Sharif had not accepted her terms—to do away with the eighth amendment.

Nasrullah Khan and Bugti also announced their withdrawal from the presidential election. They have withdrawn in favour of Leghari. JUI also announced their support for Leghari. It appears that Farooq Leghari's (PPP) position is stronger than that of Wasim Sajjad (ML).

Friday, 12 Nov 1993, Islamabad
Nawaz Sharif tried to persuade Nawabzada Nasrullah Khan to stand as presidential candidate in place of Wasim Sajjad. When he refused—on the plea that it was now too late—he tried to persuade Akbar Khan Bugti. He too declined.

Saturday, 13 Nov 1993, Islamabad
Farooq Leghari won with a majority of 106 votes out of a total of some 440. It appears that Nawaz Sharif mishandled the situation.

Wednesday, 17 Nov 1993, Abbottabad
Addressed a press conference on the need for cooperation between the PPP and the Muslim League for the repeal of the eighth amendment of the 1973 constitution and for the restoration of the women's seats in the assemblies.

Saturday, 27 Nov 1993, Islamabad
Spoke to Mian Khalid Rashid in Lahore. He feels that Mahnaz is spreading quite a lot of despondency by advising everyone that there is no one working for the party. It appears that she is on her way out.

Monday, 6 Dec 1993, Abbottabad
Was interviewed by *Nawa-i-Waqt*. Later had lunch with Majid Nizami. Khurshid and Mahnaz discussed their future course of action. Khurshid said that he (and Mahnaz) would be leaving us soon. He was not yet clear about which party he would join but was of the view that the Tehrik-i-Istiqlal had no future and he had therefore to find new moorings. He will be announcing this shortly. I told him that the parting should be without any bitterness and I wished them well.

Wednesday, 22 Dec 1993, Abbottabad
Called on Prime Minister Benazir Bhutto and asked her to clarify the government's position on: (1) Annulment of the eighth amendment. (2) Proportional representation. (3) Election every four years. (4) Restoration of women's seats. (5) Adult franchise in FATA. She said that they wished to bring about these changes with the cooperation of the opposition but it appeared that the opposition was not in a mood to cooperate. Khurshid called. He had met Farooq Leghari earlier.

Monday, 27 Dec 1993, Abbottabad
Khurshid telephoned to say that he and Mahnaz will be announcing their leaving the TI in the next couple of days. She will go to the Nawaz Muslim League and Khurshid does not appear to have decided about himself as yet.

Wednesday, 29 Dec 1993, Abbottabad
Khurshid and Mahnaz Rafi announced their exit from the Tehrik-i-Istiqlal in Lahore today. I appointed Tassaddaq Hussain Baloch as secretary general in place of Khurshid and Malik Hamid Sarfaraz as chairman Punjab in place of Mahnaz Rafi.

Friday, 31 Dec 1993, Abbottabad
Sherdil Awan, Sher Bahadur (Mardan) Inayatullah Khan (Nowshera) and Pirzada Jamil Shah came and discussed the requirements of someone to replace Omar as chairman NWFP. Omar has told them that he is too busy with Sungi to devote as much time to his party responsibilities as he would like to. They all felt that Omar should be persuaded to stay if possible. Niamat telephoned from Karachi to say that Mushir Pesh Imam is ready to rejoin the TI.

Diary 1994

Monday, 3 Jan 1994, Abbottabad, Islamabad

Manzoor Qadir, TI information secretary Punjab, telephoned from Lahore to say that Chaudhri Riasat, formerly secretary general of Awami Tehrik, and his associates had decided to join the TI.

Friday, 7 Jan 1994, Lahore

Addressed a press conference criticising both PPP and ML as representing a similar political culture. Rana Maqbool Hussain and Hanif Goraya announced the merger of their party ANP, (Jamhoori) with the TI at all levels in the Punjab.

Saturday, 8 Jan 1994, Lahore

Visited Chaudhri Ramzan's office on Turner Road and met members of the Tehrik's lawyers' circle in Lahore. Then went to Kissan Hall where Rana Maqbool Hussain and Hanif Goraya had given a reception for former ANP (Jamhoori) who had joined the TI yesterday. Rana Maqbool also offered Kissan Hall for use as an office. Chaudhri Riasat is announcing joining TI on 21 January.

Saturday, 5 Feb 1994, Karachi

A national strike in support of Kashmir. A stupid idea. My first article appearing in the *Nawa-i-Waqt* and the *Jang* will be on this subject and so will be my press conference tomorrow.

Sunday, 6 February 1994, Karachi

Addressed a press conference and criticised the ordering of strikes in support of the Kashmiris because it does nothing for the Kashmir cause and damages Pakistan's economy by causing great loss to the country. Suggested that every one should work an extra day in a month and give money for the Kashmir cause. The money should, I suggested, be used for foreign publicity to mould western public opinion against India's policy on Kashmir.

Tuesday, 8 Feb 1994, Islamabad
Major General Qamar Ali Mirza, president ex-serviceman's association and Colonel Akhtar, general secretary, called to ask me to attend their rallies and to make me a member.

Thursday, 10 Feb 1994, Islamabad
Khair Mohammad Badera, chairman, Tehrik-i-Istiqlal, Bahawalpur district, was shot in the stomach outside the Bahawalpur session court but survived.

Monday, 7 March 1994, Islamabad
Went to Omar's office and sent a letter to Manzoor Ahmed Wattoo, the Punjab chief minister, asking him to investigate the shooting of Khair Mohammad Badera in Bahawalpur the other day.

Sunday, 27 March 1994, Islamabad, Abbottabad
Khurshid Kasuri was made a central vice president of Nawaz Sharif's Muslim League.

Sunday, 17 April 1994, Islamabad
Omar is not able to devote any time for party work. He is very busy with social work for SUNGI. So appointed Sher Dil Awan as chairman NWFP.

Wednesday, 27 April 1994, Islamabad, Abbottabad
Lieutenant General Azhar of JUP (formerly Yahya Khan's governor of NWFP) telephoned to ask me to an all parties conference sponsored by the JUP in Karachi on 7 May to discuss the law and order situation in Sindh, the nuclear issue and Kashmir. Accepted.

Saturday, 7 May 1994, Karachi
Attended the all parties conference called by Maulana Noorani of JUP. Numerous small and all major parties attended except MQM and AWP. ANP/ML alliance won both seats in by-elections in Kohat and Nowshera.

Sunday, 8 May 1994, Karachi
Asked for General Mirza Aslam Beg to be court martialled for financial misconduct, distributing money to politicians and for his involvement in the Mehran Bank scandal.

Wednesday, 8 June 1994, Abbottabad
General Abdul Waheed, COAS, called. We discussed the Sindh situation (use of army in aid of civil power), General Aslam Beg's conduct and the problem of our house in Abbottabad, which the army wants to acquire. He appears to be a professional soldier. Keen to keep the army out of politics.

Tuesday, 28 June 1994, Paris
Wrote my statement resigning from the presidentship of the party. I feel that someone else should now shoulder the responsibility. I will continue to work for the party. I intend circulating my letter to the national councillors of the party and call their meeting in late October.

Thursday, 4 Aug 1994, Islamabad
Central office bearers of the party and provincial chairmen met, chalked out a programme of my tours for second half of August and September. I told them that I wanted to resign from presidentship of the party in November and suggested collective leadership. They would not hear of it and most of them said that they would leave the party if I did this. I was very disappointed with their approach. Only Omar supported me.

Wednesday, 17 Aug 1994, Abbottabad
Sixth death anniversary of Ziaul Haq. Government blocked all roads to Islamabad. An unnecessary step.

Wednesday, 24 Aug 1994, Abbottabad
In a speech in Azad Kashmir yesterday, Nawaz Sharif declared that Pakistan has the atomic bomb.

Monday, 29 Aug 1994, Kamalia, Lahore
Left Kamalia at 08:15 and arrived in Lahore at 13:45. Attended a very good gathering of businessmen organised by Mian Mohammad Afzal

and Mian Suleman. Dinner with Khurshid Kasuri where he had invited prominent column writers of Lahore such as Irshad Haqqani, Mujeeb Shami, Abdul Qadir Hassan, Hussain Naqi, Abdullah Malik and a few others.

Tuesday, 20 Sept 1994, Abbottabad
ML (N) ordered a strike in the country, which was fairly successful but pointless.

Wednesday, 21 Sept 1994, Abbottabad
Wrote to Syed Zafar Ali Shah terminating his vice presidentship of the party. He has been violating party discipline and openly supporting the Muslim League (N) in its so-called 'Long March' and strike of yesterday.

Sunday, 25 Sept 1994, Abbottabad
Gave a statement to the press defending Air Marshal Nur Khan. He is under attack in the press for his candid but undiplomatic remarks about our military weaknesses.

Saturday, 1 Oct 1994, Islamabad
Attended a reception at the Chinese embassy. Met Air Chief Marshal Zulfiqar there who confirmed the price of one Mirage-2000 to be $50 million as compared with about $17 million of SU-27, a comparable Chinese aircraft. Apparently the PAF is going in for the Mirage-2000, which Zulfiqar feels strongly is very fishy. Someone, he feels, is making a lot of money.

Tuesday, 11 Oct 1994, Peshawar, Abbottabad
A strike ordered by Nawaz Sharif and the ML (N) today. He is trying to step up pressure to oust Benazir. It is very unlikely that he will succeed in replacing her, at least not yet. Benazir sent me a letter complaining about a statement I had made in Peshawar on the 9th that by giving information on 150 Sikh separatist leaders to Rajiv Gandhi, she had helped India end the Sikh insurgency and move the Indian Army from Indian Punjab to Kashmir and thus affect the struggle of the Kashmiris. She wrote that all this was untrue. I am sending her a reply tomorrow.

Wednesday, 12 Oct 1994, Abbottabad, Islamabad

Received a telephone call at midnight that Laji (my elder brother popularly known as Colonel Pasha) had died in a private hospital at 23:10 in Lahore.

Friday, 14 Oct 1994, Islamabad, Skardu

Took off for Skardu for the burial of my brother. The captain of the aircraft persuaded 'operations control' at Islamabad to allow the aircraft to go to Skardu when the weather was not fit for the flight. At Skardu the pilot should have returned to Islamabad but he decided to try a landing, brought the aircraft down through a hole in the clouds and landed safely. I thought that if I were the head of PIA, I would have sacked the captain for gross indiscipline. He had no business to attempt a landing in that weather. We were about 50 on board from the funeral party. Army provided a guard of honour for the burial.

Saturday, 15 Oct 1994, Skardu

Laji was buried near his wife's grave on the hill overlooking Skardu and Shangrila. It is very appropriate that he is buried here, the area that he had conquered from the Indians in 1947/48, the beautiful place he had built and which meant so much to him. Group Captain Shah Khan (ex-PAF) had also come from Gilgit for the funeral.

Monday, 31 Oct 1994, Islamabad

Went to Air Chief Marshal Zulfiqar's. Air Chief Marshal Jamal and Air Vice Marshal Sadruddin were there. Discussed the Mirage-2000 and the 2000-5. We all agreed that these aircraft were not suitable for the PAF. They cost $75 million per aircraft and $1.5 million per air missile.

Thursday, 3 Nov 1994, Lahore (Bhatti Gate)

Addressed a modest but very responsive meeting at Bhatti Gate. Called for a revolution to rid the country of the politics of corruption and to give capital punishment to the criminals responsible of robbing the nation.

Sunday, 13 Nov 1994, Islamabad, Abbottabad
Mian Mohammad Sharif, father of Mian Nawaz Sharif, was arrested today for cheating and forgery.

Monday, 14 Nov 1994, Abbottabad
President Farooq Ahmad Leghari addressed a joint session of parliament. It was reported to have been a stormy and noisy affair, in keeping with the rowdyism common in the National Assembly.

Monday, 5 Dec 1994, Abbottabad
Salahuddin, editor of the weekly *Takbir*, was assassinated in Karachi yesterday evening. He was a respected journalist.

Tuesday, 6 Dec 1994, Abbottabad
A bomb was thrown in a mosque of the Sipah Sahaba in Karachi and about eight people were killed.

Friday, 9 Dec 1994, Abbottabad
Maulana Abdul Sattar Edhi, the renowned social worker, left the country as he feared assassination.

Sunday, 11 Dec 1994, Abbottabad
Russia invaded Chechnya, a former Soviet state, which had declared its independence.

Friday, 23 Dec 1994, Islamabad
Nasreen telephoned to say that General Habibullah Khan had died in Karachi and that his burial will take place in Peshawar tomorrow.

Monday, 26 Dec 1994, Islamabad, Abbottabad
Received a message that Maulvi Mohammad Hussain had died in Fatehjang. He was the district chairman of TI in Attock district. A fine man, steadfast and untiring in his work for the party. I shall miss him. Alas, there are not many like him.

Tuesday, 27 Decembe 1994, Abbottabad, Fatehjang, Abbottabad
Attended Maulvi Mohammad Hussain's funeral. He died of injuries when a log of wood (he was a timber merchant) fell on him. About three thousand people attended the *janaza* prayers in pouring rain.

Diary 1995

Tuesday, 14 Feb 1995, Abbottabad
The Taliban, a youth organization, has taken control of seven of the Afghan provinces and is poised to take control of Kabul. Hikmatyar, who controlled the Pushtoon areas, is in retreat.

Saturday, 11 March 1995, Islamabad
More sectarian killings in Karachi.

Sunday, 12 March 1995, Islamabad
Pir of Pagara's house in Karachi was hit by a rocket. More killings. Benazir has just completed her 24th visit abroad in the last 15 months.

Friday, 2 June 1995, Islamabad, Lahore
Nawaz Sharif discussed with me the need for a conference of parties to discuss the Karachi situation.

Sunday, 4 June 1995, Islamabad
Abdul Haye Baloch called. Discussed with him the possibility of the BNM attending the meeting of parties in Lahore on 7 July to support the five point programme. He was agreeable and said that he would let me know.

Monday, 12 June 1995, Abbottabad
Spoke to Abid Hassan Minto, Yusuf Masti Khan and Latif Afridi and arranged for us to meet on Thursday, 22 June.

Tuesday, 13 June 1995, Abbottabad
Spoke to Ghulam Nabi Kallu and asked him to the meeting in Rawalpindi on 22 June.

Tuesday, 20 June 1995, Abbottabad
Nawaz Sharif, Khurshid, Gohar Ayub and Chaudhri Nisar came to lunch. Nawaz Sharif met the press afterwards. He came to invite me

to a conference in Karachi. I agreed to a moot in the first week of July preferably in Islamabad.

Thursday, 22 June 1995, Islamabad
Met Yusuf Masti Khan, Hasil Bizenjo, Abid Minto, Ghulam Nabi Kallu and Dr Yasin of BNM at Shalimar hotel and agreed to cooperate with each other. Our next meeting is in Lahore on 21 July.

Saturday, 24 June 1995, Abbottabad
Meeting of the central office bearers of the party. Fourteen attended. Briefed them on the talks with Nawaz Sharif and on the meeting with six party heads in Rawalpindi on 22 June.

Monday, 26 June 1995, Abbottabad
Spoke to Azhar Jamil in Karachi who confirmed that Mairaj Mohammad Khan would attend our meeting in Lahore on 21 July.

Tuesday, 27 June 1995, Abbottabad
Addressed the press conference on the new emerging alliance of our seven political parties but spoke mainly about Karachi, where the situation is now very tense.

Wednesday, 19 July 1995, Abbottabad
MQM and government talks are continuing without any let-up in the killings in Karachi. The total this month is 183 killed.

Friday, 21 July 1995, Islamabad, Lahore
Attended a meeting of seven parties at Abid Minto's house in Model Town. Besides his Awami Jamhoori Party, the following attended: Yusuf Masti Khan (PNP), Senator Abdul Haye (BNM), Chaudhri Ghulam Nabi Kallu (Mazdoor Kisaan), Chaudhri Aslam (Socialist Party), Saleem (Qaumi Mahaz Azadi). Agreed on: (1) Peaceful solution of Karachi problem. (2) Election under a neutral government. (3) Abolition of separate electorate. (4) To meet frequently.

Tuesday, 1 Aug 1995
The MQM-government dialogue appears to have broken down, at least for the time being.

Sunday, 20 Aug 1995,
Killings in Karachi continue. Twelve more people killed yesterday. Ajmal Khattak is on a self appointed peace mission to London where Wali Khan is on a visit and Altaf Hussain of MQM lives.

Friday, 1 Sept 1995, Abbottabad
Beant Singh, chief minister of Indian Punjab, was assassinated yesterday.

Thursday, 7 Sept 1995, Islamabad
Manzoor Wattoo's government in Punjab was dismissed by a presidential decree. Horsetrading will follow.

Friday, 8 Sept 1995, Islamabad
Wattoo joined the Nawaz Muslim League because of the tremendous power of a government to ingratiate the people. I think that the PPP and Chhatha will be able to form a government in Punjab without Wattoo.

Saturday, 16 Sept 1995, Islamabad, Quetta
Left for Quetta to address a conference called by Akbar Khan Bugti. Nawaz Sharif and others wanted to create an alliance against the government. I said that a change of government without a change of the system did not interest the people. We had taken part in these movements in the past, had succeeded in changing the government and then the same kind of corrupt feudal politicians had performed no better.

Saturday, 30 Sept 1995, Islamabad
Meeting of central officer bearers. Discussed progress of divisional conventions and party elections. Provincial elections will be held in early November and a national convention and council meeting later that month in Lahore.

Saturday, 4 Nov 1995, Islamabad
Omar has been told by Samia Rauf that the timber mafia in Hazara (Qasim Shah and Muzammal Shah) have planned to eliminate him by the end of this year as he is a thorn in their flesh. She has been told this by a friend in the DIB (Directorate of Intelligence Bureau). I am

going to talk with Samina to find out more about it. In the meantime, I suggested to Omar that he should take some safety measures.

Sunday, 5 Nov 1995, Islamabad
Discussed the threat to Omar with Aleem. He suggested that I speak to Muzzammal Shah or one of the others of his clan and tell him that we have learnt this and they better watch out. This, he thought, would deter them from trying to do any such thing. I plan to do this.

Tuesday, 14 Nov 1995, Abbottabad-Islamabad
Aftab Mirani, the defence minister, gave the details in the Senate of the planned coup in which a number of army officers were involved.

Wednesday, 22 Nov 1995, Islamabad
Spoke to Omar. His friend Major Sami arranged for him to see the Director of Intelligence (who knows Omar) about the threat to Omar by the timber mafia. Omar is coming to Islamabad tomorrow for this purpose on his way to Bakot.

Thursday, 23 Nov 1995, Islamabad
Omar came at about midday to see the director general, Intelligence Bureau, Mr Masud, regarding the threats he has been receiving. Masud said that Gandapur, DIG Intelligence NWFP, will be going into this matter and will see him about it.

Friday, 24 Nov 1995, Islamabad
Party elections for chairmanship of Punjab and Sindh were held today. Malik Hamid Sarfaraz was elected in Punjab. Rehmat Khan Vardag was elected in Sindh.

Sunday, 26 Nov 1995, Islamabad
Zawar Shah of Multan called. He will be announcing rejoining the party at the central council meeting on 29 December. Agha Shahi called.

Thursday, 7 Dec 1995, Abbottabad
Moeen Qureshi, Dr Mahbub ul Haq and Shahid Javed Burki of the World Bank are in Pakistan these days giving their solution to the

worsening economic situation. The problem is well known and the real solution to which they have not referred is the thoroughly corrupt governments that we have had.

Friday, 8 Dec 1995, Abbottabad
Heard from Tariq last night that one of the engines of the PIA aircraft in which Hassan was coming from New York caught fire half an hour after take off and the aircraft had to land back at New York. President Farooq Leghari had a similar experience after take off from Darwin (Australia) a few days ago. The managing director PIA has no time left to run the airline after sucking up to Asif Zardari and Benazir. I believe that the airline is full of incompetent people and the majority of senior staff are political appointees.

Monday, 18 Dec 1995, Islamabad
The government announced the appointment of Lieutenant General Jehangir Karamat as the new chief of army staff in place of General Waheed Kakar.

Diary 1996

Wednesday, 10 Jan 1996, Islamabad
An attempt was made on the life of Nawaz Sharif near Hala yesterday. Sultan Rahi, a well known actor was shot and killed near Gujranwala and an income tax senior officer shot and killed in Lahore. The law and order situation in the country is pretty bad.

Thursday, 11 Jan 1996, Islamabad
Attended the funeral of Khurshid Hassan Mir of the PPP who died last night.

Thursday, 1 Feb 1996, Abbottabad, Islamabad
Wrote a letter to Benazir Bhutto, the prime minister, about IG police Punjab's revelation in a press conference a few days ago to the effect that over 25,000 criminals had been recruited in the Punjab police force during the last ten years.

Thursday, 29 Feb 1996, Islamabad
Benazir announced some changes in the electoral system including joint electorate (double vote for minorities), abolition of ID card for voting, ban on hoardings, wall chalking, etc.

Thursday, 21 March 1996, Islamabad
The Supreme Court took an important decision yesterday that judges could not be appointed without the agreement of chief justice of the Supreme or High Courts. Shaikh Rashid was released two days ago after two years imprisonment for keeping a rifle without license. Interestingly the law was passed during Nawaz Sharif's tenure as prime minister.

Friday, 26 April 1996, Islamabad
The Chechnian leader Dzhokhar Dudayev (whom our Urdu press calls Jaffer Dawood), a former Soviet air force general, was reported killed a couple of days ago in aerial bombardment by Russian aircraft.

Friday, 17 May 1996, Abbottabad
Bhartiya Janata Dal (BJP) formed a government in Delhi with Atal Bihari Vajpayee. With 210 seats in a house of 545, it is likely to face difficulties and it will be difficult for it to survive for very long.

Friday, 31 May 1996, Lahore
Imran Khan came to call along with his brother-in-law and Mowahid Hussain. He sought information on various issues, notably, party elections, rights of women, selection of party leadership. Appeared a nice person with potential of a successful leader.

Saturday, 1 June 1996, Lahore
Visited the Kissan Hall. Mowahid and Hafeezullah Khan, Imran's brother-in-law, came after dinner. Discussed possibilities of cooperation in the future. As a first step I suggested that he should publicly agree with the Tehrik-i-Istiqlal's 1979 manifesto as a guide for him in his future programme. Mowahid and Hafeezullah felt that this should not be a problem as Imran had read it and thought very highly of it.

Wednesday, 12 June 1996, Abbottabad

Ahmad Ali Syed of PTV Islamabad came to interview me for 5 July programme and asked two questions: (1) Did I invite Ziaul Haq's martial law? (2) Who do I think is to blame for the almost 20 years of military rule in Pakistan. I answered that all I had said in my letter to the armed forces was to obey only lawful commands. And that to kill innocent civilians was not a lawful command. I referred to what was done in the Nuremberg trial, and said that my letter was for all time. As regards the 20 years of military rule, I held the public, the politicians and the armed forces responsible but held the public more to blame.

Friday, 14 June 1996, Lahore

Attended national working committee meeting at Mian Mohammad Afzal's house in Gulberg. Imran called in the evening and wanted me to head his manifesto committee. Mowahid and Ashiq Qureshi were with him and they drafted a press statement to be issued tomorrow.

Saturday, 15 June 1996, Lahore

Imran, Mowahid, and Ashiq Qureshi came in the evening. Discussed some more points and areas of agreements.

Monday, 17 June 1996, Abbottabad

Drafted a paper on the basis of merger between Imran Khan's Tehrik-i-Insaf and Tehrik-i-Istiqlal. Saw picture of people attending Maulana Noorani's conference on the budget in Islamabad and was glad that I was not there.

Wednesday, 19 June 1996, Abbottabad

Had a press conference in which I gave copies of my letters to the Chief Justice Syed Sajjad Ali Shah asking for legal action against General Mirza Aslam Beg and Lieutenant General Asad Durrani former DG, ISI, for distributing money which Aslam Beg drew from the Mehran Bank. He distributed it among politicians.

Sunday, 23 June 1996, Islamabad, Abbottabad

Ashiq Qureshi, who is Omar's friend and also of Imran Khan, called to discuss possibilities of a merger between our two parties. He will continue his dialogues with Omar (who was also present) early next month. Their approach is different from ours and they appear to want me with them somehow without having much to do with the party.

Tuesday, 25 June 1996, Abbottabad
Jamaat-i-Islami staged a demonstration in Rawalpindi yesterday, which turned violent. Some people were killed by police firing. Another demonstration is planned for 3 July, which will be joined by Nawaz Sharif's Muslim League and other opposition parties.

Saturday, 21 Sept 1996, Abbottabad
Murtaza Bhutto, Zulfikar Ali Bhutto's son and Benazir Bhutto's brother, was killed last night in an encounter with the police, outside his residence, 70 Clifton in Karachi. Police version is that after Murtaza Bhutto's raid on the CIA headquarter two nights ago to free one of his associates, the government had decided to disarm him and his armed workers, which they resisted and fired at the police. He was killed in the encounter.

Friday, 27 Sept 1996, Abbottabad
Taliban captured Kabul today and hanged Dr Najibullah and his brother.

Saturday, 28 Sept 1996, Abbottabad
Farooq Leghari and Benazir's differences have surfaced and the two had a six-hour meeting yesterday to try to iron them out. The chances are that she will be sacked like two of her predecessors have been before (Junejo and Nawaz Sharif and Benazir herself). An unexpected step from one who has been loyal to her and the PPP. Sharing of power is a difficult thing. It has been said that 'you can sleep in the same bed but you do not have the same dreams'. The ASI (Haq Nawaz Siyal), involved with Murtaza's murder, was found shot in his room last night.

Tuesday, 1 Oct 1996, Islamabad
Called on Ghulam Mustafa Jatoi, whose brother-in-law, Ashiq Jatoi, was killed along with Murtaza Bhutto the other day.

Friday, 18 Oct 1996, Islamabad
General Gul Hamid called. He is trying to build up a pressure group to change the system of government in the country. Wanted me to associate with his efforts.

Friday, 25 Oct 1996, Abbottabad
The political situation in the country is deteriorating and it appears that things are coming to a standstill. Things cannot go on this way for very long. The Jamaat-i-Islami is getting ready for a showdown with the government on 27 October. Large numbers of their workers have been arrested.

Sunday, 27 Oct 1996, Abbottabad
The Afghan civil war shows no sign of ending. Qazi Hussain Ahmad launched his bid to encircle the National Assembly in his effort to oust the government.

Tuesday, 5 Nov 1996, Abbottabad
Omar woke me up at 04:30 to tell me that Farooq Leghari had dissolved the National Assembly and dismissed Benazir's government. Not unexpected and an understandable consequence of her policies. Leghari has the power to do this under the constitution, though I do not think that the elections will take place within three months on 3 February as announced. The six-page indictment is mostly about corruption (according to BBC) and this cannot be put right by 3 February.

Wednesday, 6 Nov 1996, Abbottabad
Sahibzada Yakub Khan, Sadiq Awan, Syeda Abida Hussain, Irshad Ahmad Haqqani, Javed Jabbar, and Shahid Hamid (a lawyer) are some of the new federal ministers. Today's papers say that Fakhruddin G. Ebrahim is likely to be sworn in too. Benazir is not under any restrictions. She addressed a press conference this evening. Her husband is under arrest.

Thursday, 7 Nov 1996, Abbottabad
Fakhruddin G. Ebrahim, Khalid Anwar, (late Chaudhri Mohammad Ali's son) and Memon were sworn in as ministers today. Governors of NWFP and Punjab, Major General Khurshid and Major General Saroop have resigned.

Friday, 8 Nov 1996, Abbottabad

Mumtaz Bhutto was made the chief minister of Sindh. Kamal Azfar remains the governor. The Balochistan Assembly and the provincial government were dismissed. No decision as yet on the Punjab and NWFP.

Sunday, 10 Nov 1996, Islamabad

Malik Meraj Khalid, the interim prime minister, telephoned to say that he will be calling to see me in a day or two.

Tuesday, 12 Nov 1996, Islamabad

Was called by the Supreme Court for the hearing of my letter regarding General Mirza Aslam Beg, former COAS, for distributing Rs140 million amongst politicians through Lieutenant General Asad Durrani ex-DG of ISI (1990). They have fixed 24 November for the next hearing.

Malik Meraj Khalid, the interim prime minister, called. He wants to meet me again in a few days for a more detailed discussion. Wanted my cooperation. Said that I had credibility and people believed me. Told him that I would always talk well of good deeds but could not favour or agree with anything evil or wrong.

Wednesday, 20 Nov 1996, Abbottabad

The Supreme Court did not accept Benazir's writ filed by Aitzaz Ahsan for improper language. It admitted Yousuf Raza Gilani's writ for regular hearing on 30 November.

There is a lot of criticism of the appointment of some people in the caretaker government and the exemption of the president and the governors from accountability.

Friday, 22 Nov 1996, Abbottabad, Islamabad

The interim government and Farooq Leghari are the subject of widespread criticism for appointing incompetent or corrupt people to important posts. The appointment of Mumtaz Bhutto as chief minister Sindh, George Sikandar Zaman as chief minister NWFP, Tariq Rahim as chief minister Punjab, Justice Mujaddad Mirza as the chief of accountability commission who is regarded as totally ineffective, are the subject of criticism. It appears that Farooq Leghari is trying to forge a king's party. Benazir's writ has been returned twice by the registrar of the Supreme Court for containing objectionable language (Aitzaz Ahsan is the lawyer).

Saturday, 23 Nov 1996, Islamabad
Meeting of the national working committee. Forty-two people attended. Opinion was divided about taking part in the elections on 3 February but members were generally in favour. So it was decided to announce at a press conference, that we will take part. Everyone wanted me to take part, which I declined to do.

Sunday, 24 Nov 1996, Islamabad
Went to the Supreme Court for my case against General Mirza Aslam Beg and Lieutenant General Asad Durrani for distribution of money amongst politicians and newspapers for the 1990 elections. Another date will be fixed for hearing.

Monday, 9 Dec 1996, Islamabad
Called on President Farooq Leghari. Told him that his accountability appeared one-sided and Nawaz Sharif's ML had not been dealt with. He explained that this was being done.

Sunday, 22 Dec 1996, Islamabad
Filing of papers for national and provincial assembly seats was completed today. With Farooq Leghari being partisan, Nawaz Sharif's success in the elections appears to be certain. It appears that Leghari has struck a deal with him. Nawaz Sharif met Ghinwa Bhutto (late Murtaza Bhutto's wife) and is likely to make an arrangement with her for jointly opposing Benazir's PPP.

Tuesday, 24 Dec 1996, Islamabad
The Nation and the *Jang* came out with the news that I was being given a very important responsibility to sort out the mess, the country is in; so I was innundated with telephone calls all day from the press and well wishers. Had a tough time telling them that this was all humbug.

Saturday, 28 Dec 1996, Islamabad
Attended the party council meeting. Ikram Nagra was elected as the party president for 1997. Working committee met after the council meeting and decided to form a committee, which will meet on 6 January at Islamabad to decide whether we will boycott the elections. The council was of the view that there is virtually no accountability and corrupt people are therefore likely to be elected.

Diary 1997

Wednesday, 15 Jan 1997, Islamabad
Brigadier Mukhtar Karim and I went to Shifa International Hospital to see Catchpole who, it appeared, was on his death bed. It was a sad sight to see one who had done so much for education in India and Pakistan in such a state.

Agha Murtaza Pooya called in the afternoon. An ally of Benazir, he was very critical of President Farooq Leghari.

Saturday, 18 Jan 1997, Islamabad
A bomb exploded in the sessions court in Lahore. The head of the Sipah-i-Sahaba, an extremist Sunni organisation, and 20 people were killed and the deputy head of Sipah-i-Sahaba, Azam Tariq, MNA wounded.

Saturday, 25 Jan 1997, Islamabad
Appeared in the Supreme Court in the General Mirza Aslam Beg case. The court decided to issue summons to Aslam Beg and fixed 1 February as the next date of hearing.

Wednesday, 29 Jan 1997, Lahore
The action taken by President Farooq Leghari to dismiss Benazir's government was upheld by the Supreme Court. There appears to be no doubt now about the election taking place on 3 February.

Saturday, 1 Feb 1997, Islamabad

Attended the Supreme Court where my case against General Mirza Aslam Beg came up for hearing. He denied having distributed any money to politicians for the 1990 elections. He was asked to submit a written statement and the next hearing was fixed for 24 February.

Brigadier Mukhtar Karim telephoned to say that Catchpole had died in the CMH, Rawalpindi, today after a long illness. He was 90. He had been at the RIMC during my stay there and later founded the Hassan Abdal Cadet College and was principal of the Sargodha PAF Public School for the last fifteen years or so. He had been an English teacher at the Abbottabad Public School. He served in India and Pakistan for 70 years and was a much liked and respected teacher.

Monday, 3 Feb 1997, Islamabad

Pakistan's fifth elections in ten years, Farooq Leghari is carrying out an engineered accountability. His two sons-in-law and a cousin are contesting from Dera Ghazi Khan district. The sons of the chief minister of Sindh, Mumtaz Bhutto, and George Sikandar Zaman, chief minister of NWFP, are also contesting with their fathers' full support.

Tuesday, 4 Feb 1997, Islamabad

Attended Catchpole's funeral service in the church in Rawalpindi. Many of his old students of RIMC, Hassan Abdal and Abbottabad were there. Later flew in the helicopter with Air Chief Marshal Abbas Khattak to Cadet College Hassan Abdal for his burial.

Nawaz Sharif's ML has won a landslide election victory with a clear majority in the NA and the Punjab and near majority in the NWFP. Many of the top leaders have been defeated. Imran Khan's Tehrik-i-Insaf won no seats and fared badly. He had stood from nine NA seats and lost badly on all.

Wednesday, 5 Feb 1997, Islamabad

Some significant things have emerged from the elections of 3 February. Such as: (1) Farooq Leghari made a statement, being interviewed on TV, that the turnout was 25 to 26 per cent. This he said at about 20:00. But the result of the voters, turnout given by the election commission next day was 38 per cent. (2) The first result was announced by the election commission at midnight, eight hours after the close of polling at 16:00. (3) Some results from Sindh were announced 24 hours after the close of polling. (4) Everybody testified to the very poor turnout at the polls.

Assuming that the turnout was 25 per cent, ML (N)'s share would be about 15 per cent or a dismally small percentage of the voters of Pakistan. Imran Khan lost his deposit in six out of seven NA constituencies. Malcolm Fraser, a former prime minister of Australia and head of the Commonwealth monitoring team, said that the general apathy of the voters was a warning to the politicians of Pakistan to mend their ways and indicative of a lack of confidence in the system of government.

Monday, 24 Feb 1997, Islamabad
General Aslam Beg case in the Supreme Court was heard today. He submitted his reply and denied any role in the case. Court ordered that the National Assembly proceeding of 11 June should be obtained to ascertain the contents of Asad Durrani's affidavit. 26 March was fixed for the next day of the hearing.

Friday, 7 March 1997, Islamabad
Dr Abdul Haye Baloch came after dinner and discussed the idea of forming an alliance or a merger of like-minded opposition parties. He favoured the idea. Agreed to finalise this during April.

Friday, 14 March 1997, Dehra Dun, Delhi
After spending two days at Dehra Dun—where I had gone to attend the reunion of my old school, the RIMC—left by car along with Amrik Singh and M.G. Rajwade for Delhi. Stopped at Chetul restaurant near Meerut for lunch. Called on Kirtar Nath Dubey, an old Rimcollian, from Jammu, (my senior in 1933 and 1934). Spoke on the telephone with Arjun Singh and O.P. Mehra, former chiefs of the Indian air force who had been my contemporaries. Arranged to meet them at Delhi Golf Club tomorrow.

Saturday, 15 March 1997, Delhi, Lahore
Gave an interview to *India Today*. Earlier, Pushpinder Singh, a co-editor of the book *Fizaya,* on the 1965 war and PAF's performance, came to give me the book.

Sunday, 16 March 1997, Lahore

Naeemul Haq (one time Tehrik-i-Istiqlal and now with Imran Khan) called. He says that Imran wants to 'get-together' with us and will be calling on me when I return to Islamabad from Karachi.

Sunday, 23 March 1997, Karachi

Pakistan's fiftieth anniversary celebrated today. Some two dozen heads of Islamic states and another two dozen representatives of Islamic countries were invited. The Convention Hall in Islamabad, built at a cost of over Rs2 billion is a disgrace, considering the economic state of the country. A pointless exercise at great cost with great fanfare.

Wednesday, 26 March 1997, Islamabad

Supreme Court hearing of my case against General Aslam Beg and Lieutenant General Asad Durrani has been fixed for 5 July.

Tuesday, 1 April 1997, Islamabad

Malik Hakmin Khan of PPP called. Said that Benazir wishes to ask me to dinner. Told him that in view of our past experience I would consult my political associates and let him know whether I should come.

The NA and the Senate voted unanimously to remove Article 52-8B (power of the president to dismiss the government) from the constitution.

Wednesday, 2 April 1997, Islamabad

A general sense of euphoria after agreement on the removal of Article 52-8B of the constitution empowering the president to dismiss the government and the assemblies. Unless the term of the NA is reduced from five to three years or so, instability will prevail. People will not wait for five years for a change of government.

Sunday, 13 April 1997, Islamabad, Risalpur, Islamabad

Amina and I went in a PAF aircraft along with ACM and Mrs Zulfikar and VCAS Air Marshal Mehdi to review a parade at Risalpur to commemorate the Quaid-i-Azam's visit to Risalpur on 13 April 1948. A nostalgic occasion.

Tuesday, 22 April 1997, Islamabad
Imran Khan of Tehrik-i-Insaf came. He wants to merge with Tehrik-i-Istiqlal but wants to retain the name of his party. Told him to come to the meeting of the dozen or so parties meeting here on 27 April.

Sunday, 27 April 1997, Islamabad
Meeting of 12 political parties. Mahmud Khan Achakzai and Latif Afreedi did not attend. Hafiz Khan represented Imran Khan of Tehrik-i-Insaf as observer. Agreed to form an alliance though some parties were agreeable on a merger. Next meeting of the alliance is being held in Karachi at Rahim Bux Soomro's house on 1 June. Briefed the press after the meeting.

Monday, 5 May 1997, Islamabad
Hearing of my complaint about General Mirza Aslam Beg in the Supreme Court today. Lieutenant General Asad Durrani did not come from Bonn and the court also decided to hear Major General Naseerullah Babar. I decided to ask Wahabul Khairi to assist me in this case. The next date for hearing was fixed for Monday, 16 June.

Monday, 16 June 1997, Islamabad
My case against General Mirza Aslam Beg in the Supreme Court today. His statement was recorded. Lieutenant General Asad Durrani and Naseerullah Khan Babar were also there but they could not be heard. Next date was fixed for Thursday, 26 June.

Thursday, 26 June 1997, Islamabad
Attended my case against General Mirza Aslam Beg in the Supreme Court. Nothing much transpired. Next date of hearing is 8 October.

Saturday, 28 June 1997, Islamabad
Prime Minister Nawaz Sharif asked me to lunch. Khurshid Kasuri was also there. Discussed the talks with India about Kashmir. I suggested that Pakistan should try for a defence pact with China. I explained the difficulties and the advantages of this proposal. Nawaz Sharif was very responsive. He explained the policy towards Afghanistan and agreed that the recognition of the Taliban regime was a hasty step.

Wednesday, 10 Sept 1997, Abbottabad

Taj Mohammad Jamali (former chief minister Balochistan) and Sarbaland Khan Hoti came. Also addressed a press conference. Omar spent a busy day in a conference on the preservation of forests.

Saturday, 18 Oct 1997, Islamabad

Mushahid Hussain called to ask that I should withdraw the case against General Mirza Aslam Beg for drawing money from the Mehran Bank and distributing it amongst politicians, amongst them Mian Nawaz Sharif (Rs3.5 million) in the 1990 elections. The next hearing is on 2 October and the chief justice, Syed Sajjad Ali Shah, is heading the bench for hearing the case. Mushahid felt that because of tension between the prime minister and the chief justice, he may use it against the prime minister. Told him that I could not withdraw the case as that would have serious implications.

Monday, 20 Oct 1997, Islamabad-Abbottabad

Khurshid Kasuri telephoned from Lahore to say that I should not say or do anything in the Mirza Aslam Beg case in the Supreme Court that destabilises the Nawaz Sharif government (the same line that Mushahid Hussain had expounded on 18 October). I told him that my purpose in raising this issue was to stop the armed forces from interfering in politics and to stop the use of public money in politics.

Wednesday, 22 Oct 1997, Abbottabad, Islamabad, Abbottabad

Left early for Islamabad to attend the Supreme Court hearing of the case against General Mirza Aslam Beg and Lieutenant General Asad Durrani. One of the three judges on the bench was absent so the case was adjourned.

Friday, 31 Oct 1997, Islamabad

Nawaz Sharif agreed to the chief justice's demand for five more judges for the Supreme Court.

Thursday, 6 Nov 1997, Islamabad

Hearing of Supreme Court case against General Mirza Aslam Beg and Lieutenant General Asad Durrani for distributing money through the

ISI to politicians in the 1990 elections. The chief justice decided to hear the case in camera on 19 November.

Wednesday, 12 Nov 1997, Abbottabad
Four Americans of Union Texas Petroleum were shot and killed in Karachi today. Also case of Yousuf Ramzi who had exploded a bomb in New York was decided today. He was given 200 years imprisonment. Aimal Kansi's case was also decided. He was given 78 years imprisonment which may be increased to death sentence in a day or two for killing three CIA men in Washington DC, a year or so ago.

Wednesday, 19 Nov 1997, Islamabad
Appeared in the General Mirza Aslam Beg's case in the Supreme Court. Session in camera. Naseerullah Khan Babar recorded his statement. According to him (for which he had copies of cheques) Nawaz Sharif was given Rs20 million by Mehran Bank.

Air Chief Marshal Zulfiqar's committee report on the role of ISI in 1989 showed that their charter included 'to provide, financial and technical support to political parties'.

Supreme Court framed contempt of court charges against Nawaz Sharif during the hearing of another case.

Thursday, 20 Nov 1997, Islamabad
Attended the hearing of my case (Mirza Aslam Beg) in the Supreme Court in which Naseerullah Babar gave some additional evidence. Prior to this, the Supreme Court heard Iftikhar Jilani (advocate for Naveed Malik) and forbade the president from ratifying the bill passed in the National Assembly and the Senate yesterday preventing the Supreme Court from taking contempt action against the prime minister.

The crisis is building up. General Jahangir Karamat has been recalled from a visit abroad. It appears that nothing can happen without the COAS's clearance.

Friday, 21 Nov 1997, Islamabad
Nawaz Sharif decided late last night not to impeach the president. The crisis however is not likely to be resolved. The COAS holds the key to the crisis. This kind of situation is not likely to last.

Saturday, 22 Nov 1997, Islamabad, Sheikhupura
Newspapers reported that Nawaz Sharif had given up the idea of impeaching the president.

Sunday, 23 Nov 1997, Lahore, Islamabad
Continued turmoil with rising tension between the president, the chief justice, and the prime minister. The ceasefire is not likely to hold and unfortunately the judiciary is also taking sides.

Thursday, 27 Nov 1997, Abbottabad, Islamabad
Papers today reported that the bench of the Supreme Court in Quetta removed the chief justice of the Supreme Court, Sajjad Ali Shah, from his post. He in turn declared the action null and void.

Sunday, 30 Nov 1997, Karachi
The crisis in Islamabad between the president, prime minister and the chief justice persists with more serious developments.

Tuesday, 2 Dec 1997, Islamabad
President Farooq Leghari, decided to resign as also the chief justice. Ajmal Mian was sworn in as the chief justice and Wasim Sajjad will be the president until he or a new president is sworn in. The chief justice did not resign but was put on 'restraint'. A new term. It is in fact a 'judicial coup' engineered by the government.

Thursday, 4 Dec 1997, Islamabad
Things appear to have settled down with Farooq Leghari's resignation and the induction of Ajmal Mian as chief justice. However the euphoria, which Nawaz Sharif and his government appear to be enjoying, is not likely to last. The economic conditions are likely to deteriorate and they do not appear to have the capacity to tackle it.

Diary 1998

Thursday, 1 Jan 1998, Islamabad

Justice Mohammad Rafiq Tarar was sworn in as president. A former member of Majlis-i-Shoora. As a member of the election commission in 1984, in Ziaul Haq's famous referendum, he had declared a 55 per cent turn-out (actual was 5 per cent). Had made a trip to Quetta to persuade judges against Chief Justice Sajjad Ali Shah. He has been an employee of 'Ittefaq', Nawaz Sharif's family firm. Not a very good choice.

Sunday, 4 Jan 1998, Islamabad

Amina and I went to call on Zulfiqar (ACM) and his wife. Met his brother Nisar Ali Khan working as legal adviser to the chief election commissioner, who said he felt guilty for drawing his pay with no work. Three inspectors general of police are with him, equally unemployed.

Tuesday, 6 Jan 1998, Islamabad, Abbottabad

Called on Dr Mahbub ul Haq, former minister in Ayub Khan's government and discussed national affairs. He feels that a movement based on the 'society of citizen's rights' launched by me recently could succeed to change the system and that nothing could be expected from the government or from political parties who inevitably compromise on principles. He agreed to cooperate.

Thursday, 22 Jan 1998, Islamabad

Addressed a press conference at the Rawalpindi press club on the causes of sectarianism and our deviation from the Quaid-i-Azam's concept of Pakistan, as enunciated in his speech of 11 August 1947.

Thursday, 5 Feb 1998, Islamabad

A holiday for Kashmir. A pointless exercise. Processions, strikes, and *dharnas* ('sit in' strikes) outside the Indian High Commission.

Sunday, 8 Feb 1998, Islamabad, Abbottabad
Agha Murtaza Pooya called to convey Benazir's message asking me to join her in ousting the government by organising a movement. He said that Nasrullah Khan, Tahirul Qadri, Aslam Beg and Hamid Gul have assured her of their cooperation. I am surprised that she should have had the gall to send me this message. In politics, there are no limits.

Wednesday, 8 April 1998, Islamabad
Telephoned Maulana Noorani to wish him Eid Mubarak and to condemn the trouble against his leading prayers the other day in Karachi.

Tuesday, 14 April 1998, Islamabad
Ghinwa Bhutto, Dr Mubashir, Dr Ghulam Husain and Farrukh Govindi called. They are not keen to hold public meetings, particularly Mubashir Hassan. He thinks that forming of study teams to bring about changes in the system is enough. I was keen to hold public meetings and to start soon.

Thursday, 23 April 1998, Islamabad
Went to the Supreme Court to hear the case of the storming of the Supreme Court by Muslim League workers last month. Ardeshir Cowasjee appeared to give evidence.

Tuesday, 5 May 1998, Islamabad
Air Chief Marshal Zulfiqar asked me to a discussion in which Farooq Leghari, A.B. Awan, Air Chief Marshal Jamal, Abdus Sattar (former foreign secretary), Tanveer Ahmed Khan (former foreign secretary) and a couple of other retired bureaucrats were present. Farooq Leghari talked non-stop for about two hours on the deteriorating economic and law and order situation and on his role as president. He is launching his party in August.

Wednesday, 6 May 1998, Islamabad
Sardar Farooq Ahmed Leghari called to discuss the political situation. A one-sided conversation like yesterday. Imran Khan came later.

Tuesday, 12 May 1998, Islamabad
Air Chief Marshal Zulfiqar wanted me to add my signature to a letter to Nawaz Sharif to explode an atomic bomb in reply to India's tests of three bombs on 10 May. I declined to do so.

Wednesday, 13 May 1998, Islamabad
Late Sardar Abdur Rehman Khan Effendi's son Colonel Yahya Effendi and Siraj, former director general civil aviation Afghanistan in 1966, called. Siraj told me that General Gul Bahar who was president Aryana Airline in 1966, when I visited Afghanistan, is now living as a refugee in Peshawar. I wanted to meet him but did not know his address.

Thursday, 14 May 1998, Islamabad
Saw Air Chief Marshal Zulfiqar and discussed the nuclear explosion. Omar came and suggested a conference on India's nuclear explosion and Pakistan's response. Agreed to hold the conference on 31 May in Islamabad.

Friday, 15 May 1998, Islamabad
Mushahid Hussain, minister of information, called and conveyed Nawaz Sharif's message for cooperation in the present situation, following the nuclear explosion by India. Advised that we should not respond by carrying out an explosion.

Saturday, 16 May 1998, Islamabad
Attended a conference (discussion) on the Kalabagh dam and its alternatives. Technical experts were invited. Had a good discussion. The general opinion was against the construction of large dams (Kalabagh included).

Thursday, 21 May 1998, Abbottabad
Suharto of Indonesia resigned after ruling the country for 32 years.

Wednesday, 27 May 1998, Abbottabad, Islamabad, Abbottabad
Left for Islamabad early today to attend the Supreme Court hearing of my case against General Mirza Aslam Beg and Asad Durrani.

Proceedings did not take place as the attorney general and both the respondents did not come. 17 June was fixed for the next hearing.

Thursday, 28 May 1998, Abbottabad, Islamabad
Pakistan exploded five nuclear devices near Chagai in Balochistan in reply to India's five in Rajistan on 11 May.

Friday, 29 May 1998, Islamabad
A national emergency was imposed at midnight last night and all political activity was banned.

Sunday, 31 May 1998, Islamabad
Daily *News* held a seminar on the nuclear explosion and its after effects. Munir Ahmad Khan (former chairman, Pakistan Atomic Energy Commission), Lieutenant General Kamal Matinuddin, Dr Eqbal Ahmed, Kaniz Fatima, Tanvir Ahmed Khan (former foreign secretary), Dr Hamid Nayyar, Shahrukh Rafi and Ashfaq Saleem Mirza attended. Quite interesting. General opinion was against what Pakistan had done and against India's policies.

Sunday, 14 June 1998, Abbottabad
Meeting of Tehrik-i-Istiqlal's national working committee. Discussed the general situation and the budget. Also discussed Nawaz Sharif's announcement to construct the Kalabagh dam. Every one was in favour of the construction of the dam. I was the only one who felt that efforts should have been made to reach a national consensus before taking the decision. No effort had been made to do this. I feel that this dam will not be built and the announcement has been made merely to get public support in Punjab similar to the atomic explosion.

Thursday, 20 Aug 1998, Abbottabad, Islamabad
Americans bombed Khost with cruise missiles. Also a hospital in Sudan (they said it was producing chemical weapons). Attack on Khost in which a missile landed in Pakistan territory was an attack on Osama bin Laden who the Americans said was responsible for the destruction of the US embassies in Nairobi and Dar-es-Salam. Osama was not hurt.

Friday, 16 Oct 1998, Islamabad
Hamid Khan of Tehrik-i-Insaf came for lunch and discussed possibilities of cooperation between Insaf and Tehrik-i-Istiqlal, possibly a merger. Agreed to discuss the matter on Imran Khan's return from abroad. Air Chief Marshal Zulfiqar came in the evening and briefed me on Jehangir Karamat's retirement.

Sunday, 15 Nov 1998, Islamabad
Imran Khan and his team, Nawabzada Mohsin Ali Khan, Hafeez Khan, and Humayun Gauhar called to discuss merger of Tehrik-i-Insaf and Tehrik-i-Istiqlal. Tassaddaq Baloch, Rehmat Khan, Asaf Vardag, and Fazal Bhatty represented TI. Imran agreed to naming the new party Justice Party. Our two team will meet tomorrow to discuss the agenda for a final meeting of the two teams on 19 November.

Saturday, 21 Nov 1998, Islamabad, Abbottabad, Islamabad
Talks today with Imran Khan's team. Hamid Khan, Mairaj Mohammad Khan, Azhar Jamil, and Dr Naqvi accompanied Imran. They wanted me to be a figurehead, keep the name of Insaf and give us 33 per cent share in the working committee.

Saturday, 28 Nov 1998, Islamabad, Rawalpindi
Meeting of the Tehrik-i-Istiqlal central council. I was elected president. No one else wanted to accept the responsibility. A tough year ahead.

Friday, 25 Dec 1998, Islamabad
Rabia (my granddaughter) has been selected for a UNDP job. She was selected out of 32 persons and very pleased with herself. Rabia is a competent girl and will do well in whatever she does.

Diary 1999

Saturday, 20 Feb 1999, Islamabad
Indian Prime Minister Vajpayee arrived in Lahore by bus on the opening of the bus service between India and Pakistan. There is a slight thaw visible in the relations between the two countries.

Sunday, 14 March 1999, Islamabad
Major General Mujib-ur-Rahman, formerly Ziaul Haq's minister for information and now with Imran Khan, called to discuss a merger of our two parties.

Wednesday, 14 April 1999, Islamabad
Pakistan fired its long-range ballistic missile (or missiles) in reply to India's Agni missile last week. The BBC interviewed me and Shireen Mazari on this development.

Saturday, 24 April 1999, Islamabad
Newspapers published a list of 49 parliamentarians who were WAPDA defaulters and had either not paid the WAPDA bills or had tampered with their electricity meters. Mostly Muslim Leaguers and quite a few ministers including Chaudhry Shajaat, the interior minister. Syed Abida Hussain has already resigned.

Wednesday, 28 April 1999, Islamabad
Went to the Supreme Court for my case about the involvement of the ISI in internal politics and the distribution of money in the 1990 elections. Hearing was postponed to 5 May.

Wednesday, 5 May 1999, Islamabad
The ISI case came up at the Supreme Court today but was postponed again. This time to 19 May.

Wednesday, 12 May 1999, Islamabad
Dr Eqbal Ahmad's funeral today. A great loss to Pakistan. It is a pity that his greatness was not realised by those in power and use was not made of him in the development of education in Pakistan.

Monday, 17 May 1999, Karachi, Lahore
Addressed the Karachi Bar Association. Spoke about the new Supreme Court decision of 14 May regarding contempt in which everyone (mainly Muslim League's MNAs) were let off.

Wednesday, 19 May 1999, Islamabad
The ISI case ended today. Decision will be announced later.

Thursday, 20 May 1999, Islamabad
Asif Zardari is reported to have tried to commit suicide in police custody. His neck had a scar and tongue had to have five stitches. Very odd. Benazir has decided not to return to Pakistan. She has appealed to President Clinton for intervention.

Thursday, 8 July 1999, Abbottabad
Nawaz Sharif returned from Washington after getting 'dictation' from Clinton to withdraw from positions occupied across the Line of Control in the Kargil area.

Monday, 11 Oct 1999, Islamabad
Went to the Supreme Court for the ISI case. Naseerullah Babar had asked for Farooq Leghari to be called to give evidence about the money he had been given by the Mehran Bank. The decision of the court was deferred and I was asked to give my views on the subject. I sent Naseerullah Babar's application to Abid Minto for dealing with it.

Tuesday, 12 Oct 1999, Islamabad
Nawaz Sharif removed General Pervez Musharraf, chief of army staff, and appointed the head of ISI, Lieutenant General Ziauddin in his place. General Musharraf who had gone to Sri Lanka arrived a few hours later and carried out a coup. He dismissed Nawaz Sharif and after some confusion, the situation appeared to be under control. Some arrests but no skirmishes or shooting.

Sunday, 17 Oct 1999, Lahore
General Musharraf spoke in the evening. Announced that he will form a national security council of the three chiefs of defence services and one expert each on law, economics and foreign affairs. This council will have a team of advisers and a cabinet of about ten to run the country. Provinces will have governors with a small cabinet. Announced the start of accountability.

Monday, 25 Oct 1999, Islamabad
The Supreme Court heard Ardeshir Cowasjee's contempt case. The full bench was of 12 judges including two who were also to hear the

government's appeal against my Abbottabad land/house case, which had been decided by the High Court in my favour. Cowasjee's case did not finish today, so my land case was adjourned to a later date.

Tuesday, 26 Oct 1999, Islamabad
Ardeshir Cowasjee telephoned. He has been charged for contempt and his case will reopen on 8 November.

Monday, 1 Nov 1999, Islamabad
Omar has been approached by GHQ to accept ministership or the membership of a 'think tank', in Musharraf's government. He is not inclined to accept, as he does not want to dissociate himself from the social work he is doing in SUNGI. Omar is not inclined to become a part of the military government and discussed the pros and corns with me. He felt that the 'seven points' of General Musharraf, if implemented, are the need of the hour. His association with the government would help to do all that is required to solve the problems of the poor which one can only do by being in the government. After a lengthy discussion, we decided that he may consider joining the government of General Musharraf and stay in it so long as it sincerely works for the amelioration of the conditions of the poor and implement the political and development programme that we have been working for. He could always leave the government if General Musharraf deviates from this declared programme. Omar left for Abbottabad.

Tuesday, 2 Nov 1999, Islamabad
Omar returned from Abbottabad. He has a meeting with a group of generals in GHQ tomorrow to tell them whether he wishes to join and if so, in what capacity.

Wednesday, 3 Nov 1999, Islamabad
Omar went to the GHQ and saw the CGS (Lieutenant General Aziz) and the director of Military Intelligence (Major General Ehsan) at their request. They conveyed General Musharraf's desire that Omar accept the oil and gas portfolio in the federal cabinet. Omar declined, saying that he would only accept the local bodies and local development ministry, which was in line with the social work he had been doing.

Thursday, 4 Nov 1999, Islamabad, Abbottabad
Heard on TV that Omar had been made federal minister for local bodies and rural development and environment. Quite a surprise as he had turned down their offer for oil and gas and thought that was the end of the matter. Omar has left for Islamabad.

Friday, 5 Nov 1999, Abbottabad, Islamabad
Dropped in at Omar's. His oath taking is tomorrow afternoon. Stream of telephone calls and visitors. It appears that being in power is the only thing that works in Pakistan.

Saturday, 6 Nov 1999, Islamabad
Omar was sworn in as federal minister for local bodies and rural development.

Saturday, 13 Nov 1999, Islamabad
Spoke to Majid Nizami in Karachi about 'Sar-i-Rah' yesterday, in which it had been said that a Qadiani *maulvi* had conducted Omar's *nikah*. Since the *nikah* had been solemnized by Qazi Nawaz of Ilyasi mosque, a renowned '*aalim*' of JUI, Qazi Nawaz, or rather his son, intends to sue Maulana Chinioti who had made this statement on the basis of which *Nawa-i-Waqt* had published it.

Tuesday, 30 Nov 1999, Islamabad
Supreme Court heard the court appeal against High Court judgment in my favour for the Abbottabad land case. They dismissed the government's appeal and decided in my favour.

Thursday, 16 Dec 1999, Islamabad
Mixed reaction to Musharraf's speech. The measures that he has announced are reasonable in the circumstances but he could have been more drastic. People's expectations are high and the pace of reforms and accountability slow.

Diary 2000

Wednesday, 5 Jan 2000, Islamabad
Aitzaz Ahsan and Makhdoom Fahim telephoned that Benazir had decided that they should not attend my *iftar* party tomorrow because government ministers may be present and the PPP had not yet decided what their line would be.

Thursday, 6 Jan 2000, Islamabad
Abdul Sattar (foreign minister), Javed Jabbar and Attiya Inayatullah (member security council), Khurshid Kasuri, Sartaj Aziz came for *iftar*. Omar also came.

Sunday, 9 Jan 2000, Islamabad
Eid ul Fitr. Malik Kansi, the federal health minister, called.

Friday, 11 Feb 2000, Karachi
Called on Fakhruddin G. Ebrahim. He was very unhappy about the government not asking some honest judges to take the oath (Mushtaq Memon Karachi) and asking some highly corrupt judges to take the oath. Wanted me to take up this matter with General Musharraf. Explained that I had never met him and had no contact with the authorities.

Friday, 24 March 2000, Islamabad
Musharraf addressed a press conference on the devolution of power and district elections, starting in December this year and ending in July next year. A very long programme.

Saw Lieutenant General Tanvir Naqvi on TV explaining the devolution plan. He and the National Reconstruction Bureau has obviously done a great deal of work on it.

Saturday, 25 March 2000, Islamabad
Bill Clinton, the US president, flew into Islamabad today for five hours after a five-day visit to India. He held talks with General Musharraf and addressed the people on TV.

Wednesday, 29 March 2000, Abbottabad
A representative of Pir Syed Ahmad Shah Gilani called to say that Ahmad Shah Gilani wanted to meet me. He is recognised as being very close to King Zahir Shah of Afghanistan.

Thursday, 6 April 2000, Islamabad
Nawaz Sharif was sentenced to 25 years imprisonment and five others were acquitted in the aircraft hijacking case in which General Musharraf was returning to Pakistan from Colombo on 12 October 1999.

Thursday, 27 April 2000, Islamabad
General Chibber of the Indian army and Mrs Chibber called. He is here to try and find a solution to the Kashmir problem.

Thursday, 4 May 2000, Islamabad
Major General Akram, ISI director, came for what he said was a courtesy call.

Friday, 19 May 2000, Islamabad
Gave a press statement on the rising inter-communal killings. Maulana Ludhianvi was killed in Karachi yesterday.

Saturday, 20 May 2000, Islamabad
Drafted a press statement on the performance of the military government over the last seven months, to be given at a press conference on 22 May. Spoke to Maulana Noorani in Karachi and asked him to give a statement against propaganda being done by some *mullahs* in Hazara against Omar which he agreed to do.

Wednesday, 24 May 2000, Abbottabad
Ajmal Khattak came and stayed for lunch. He is keen to join the government as a member of the security council. He addressed a press conference in the afternoon.

Wednesday, 9 Aug 2000, Abbottabad
Sent out a press release against the government's reported decision not to carry out accountability of religious leaders, retired judges and retired generals.

Sunday, 13 Aug 2000, Abbottabad, Rawalpindi, Abbottabad
Went to a lunch hosted by General Musharraf for about 400 senior defence service officers.

Tuesday, 15 Aug 2000, Abbottabad
General Pervez Musharraf called. New governor NWFP also came along with him. Stayed for about half an hour. Omar was also with him. General Musharraf in his speech on TV last night spelt out his devolution plan and the new set-up at district level.

Hamoodur Rahman Commission's report was published in *Dawn*. It had been released on the Internet in India.

Tuesday, 5 Sept 2000, Abbottabad
Omar came for the night. Discussed his future plans. He intends leaving the government towards the end of the year.

Thursday, 14 Sept 2000, Abbottabad
Wrote to governor NWFP, General Iftikhar Hussain Shah, and General Musharraf about intemperate statement by rabid *mullahs* of Batagram (of Fazlur Rahman's JUI) against women in NGOs. In a meeting a couple of days ago they had exhorted the people to carry away women workers of NGOs, which they could legitimise by performing *nikah* with them.

Wednesday, 20 Sept 2000, Abbottabad
Wrote to Musharraf for: 1. ending the role of ISI, 2. publishing a monthly supplement giving the names of people against whom action has been taken for corruption.

I had written earlier about controlling the *mullahs* who were issuing stupid *fatwas* against women.

Saturday, 4 Nov 2000, Islamabad
Omar came at lunchtime. He is unhappy with the way Musharraf is handling some matters.

Saturday, 2 Dec 2000, Islamabad
Imran Khan and Mohsin Ali Khan called. Agreed to seek an agreement between his and Ajmal Khattak's parties joining an alliance. Also

agreed that we (TI) will examine the possibility of a merger with his party (Insaf) and Ajmal Khattak's NAP.

Thursday, 7 Dec 2000, Islamabad, Abbottabad

Omar leaves for a tour of Dera Ismail Khan, Bhakkar, Layyah, Muzaffargarh, Dera Ghazi Khan and Faisalabad tomorrow. He is the only minister in Musharraf cabinet with a political background and has to do everyone's political work (touring) for them.

Sunday, 10 Dec 2000, Abbottabad, Islamabad

Nawaz Sharif was allowed to leave the country for Saudi Arabia after paying Rs500 million as fine, giving a paper mill (that was running at a loss) to the government and surrendering some property including the Four Seasons Hotel in the UK.

Tuesday, 12 Dec 2000, Islamabad

Minto came from Lahore. Discussed the political situation with him and then attended a meeting at Imran Khan's along with Minto and Ghulam Hussain. Ajmal Khattak, Mumtaz Bhutto, Parvez Ali Shah, ex-MPA of Sindh, Iqbal Ahmed Khan of Chhatha League, Mairaj Mohammad Khan and some others were also there. Discussed need to project our point of view. Agreed that we should be allowed to use the electronic media.

Friday, 15 Dec 2000, Islamabad

Nawaz Sharif's release and dispatch to Saudi Arabia has created quite a commotion and reduced the credibility of the Musharraf government. All kind of speculation is rife.

Saturday, 16 Dec 2000, Islamabad

Anniversary of the surrender in Dhaka in 1971. Held a seminar on whether the armed forces should have a role in politics in Pakistan. Moinuddin Haider, minister in Musharraf's government, also attended. Unanimous view was that the armed forces should have no role in politics.

Tuesday, 19 Dec 2000, Islamabad
Spoke to Imran and suggested that we meet to continue our dialogue for close cooperation.

Wednesday, 20 Dec 2000, Islamabad
General Musharraf spoke on TV to explain the reasons for the release and exile of Nawaz Sharif. Not very convincing.

Saturday, 23 Dec 2000, Islamabad
Called on General Pervez Musharraf. He was receptive to my suggestions to: (1) Give every one equal opportunities to contest the elections. The government appeared to be biased in favour of the pro-government part of the Muslim League. (2) Give everyone an opportunity to express his views on the electronic media. He agreed. (3) Joint electorates. He agreed to examine it. (4) No role for the armed forces in politics. He favoured the presence of the service chiefs in the national security council.

Diary 2001

Monday, 5 Feb 2001, Islamabad
Called on Imran Khan in the afternoon. He appears to be willing to merge his party with Tehrik-i-Istiqlal and call it Justice Party. Is calling a meeting of his central committee to discuss the proposal.

Thursday, 15 March 2001, Islamabad
Imran Khan telephoned. He wants a get-together with me, Ajmal Khattak and Minto. Agreed to meet on Tuesday, 27 March.

Wednesday, 28 March 2001, Islamabad
Meeting with Imran Khan, Ajmal Khattak and Abid Minto. Discussed possibilities of merger of our parties or of working closer together. Agreed that we will keep in touch with each other and take part in meetings together. Imran Khan and Khattak were not in favour of a merger but thought that by holding meetings together our workers will

come closer together and could later move towards a merger of our parties.

Later at night I read in the *News* that Ajmal Khattak had called on General Mirza Aslam Beg and had agreed to form an alliance with Tahirul Qadri and Chhatha (Muslim League). It is an odd kind of behaviour and typical of Pakistani politicians.

Thursday, 29 March 2001, Islamabad

Telephoned Akbar Babar (Imran's media adviser) and told him that I did not approve of Ajmal Khattak's odd behaviour and unless he publicly contradicted the newspaper report in clear terms, the Tehrik-i-Istiqlal could not associate with him politically.

Thursday, 7 June 2001, Islamabad

Asked Omar to see me. I advised him that the suspension of the PIA union was not a big enough issue to resign. PIA is in a mess and the public will support every effort to put it right.

Friday, 8 June 2001, Islamabad, Abbottabad

Omar is leaving for the UK tomorrow. He has decided to stay on in the government till early September.

Wednesday, 20 June 2001, Abbottabad

General Musharraf became President in addition to being the chief executive and chief of army staff. President Tarar was sent home.

Friday, 22 June 2001, Abbottabad

Chief of the protocol telephoned to ask me on behalf of General Musharraf to a meeting of the political leaders on the 27th and lunch.

Wednesday, 27 June 2001, Islamabad

Meeting of political leaders with General Musharraf. Besides myself, Farooq Leghari, Wasim Sajjad, Ilahi Bux Soomro, Nasir Chhatha, Asfandyar Wali, Maulana Fazlur Rahman, Ajmal Khattak, Qazi Hussain Ahmad, Maulana Ehsan ul Haq, Mian Azhar, Maulana Noorani, Allama Sajid Naqvi, Imran Khan, Fatehyab Ali Khan and

Aftab Sheikh of MQM attended. It was regarding Musharraf's visit to India on 14 July. Meeting lasted from 10:00 to 17:00.

Sunday, 8 July 2001, Nathiagali
Omar came in the morning. Discussed his plans. He has met General Musharraf and explained that he wishes to leave the government. Musharraf advised that he should not do so before 14 August.

Diary 2002

Omar's death on 25 June 2002
I was told on 25 June 2002, that Omar had been found dead in his brother-in-law's house in Karachi, early this morning. The police carried out an investigation and were of the view that it was a case of suicide. He was buried in Abbottabad the next day.

My family is, however, convinced that his death was not a case of suicide. This is how his many friends, who had spent the last evening of his life with him in Karachi also feel. He had also spoken with his wife on the night of 24 June and had said that he would be buying some books for the children the next morning before leaving Karachi for Islamabad in the afternoon.

The principal secretary to the chief executive, Mr Tariq Aziz, wrote to me on 9 October 2002 to inform me that the government of Sindh had instituted a judicial inquiry into Omar's death. I replied to Mr Tariq Aziz's letter and requested that a judge of the High Court of Sindh should head the inquiry commission. I was informed by the home secretary Sindh in March 2003 that Mr Justice Roshan Essani of the High Court of Sindh had been appointed to hold the inquiry. Mr Justice Essani had informed my legal counsel, Mr Azizullah Sheikh, that he would start the inquiry after the summer break. In spite of repeated reminders this was not done. Later in January 2004 I was informed by the chief secretary Sindh that Justice Sarmad Jalal Usmani had been appointed to conduct the inquiry in place of Justice Essani who had been retired.

On 23 November 2004 my legal counsel, Mr Azizullah Sheikh, informed me that Mr Justice Usmani was still undecided about holding the inquiry. I informed the home secretary government of Sindh in June 2005 that the High Court judge appointed to conduct the inquiry had not started it as yet and asked him to kindly expedite the matter. In a letter in October 2005 I was informed that the chairman of the tribunal had been posted to Sukkur and the case would be put up to him on his return.

Nothing was done during 2006 and my family and I felt that it was futile to keep on asking the government to expedite the matter. There were, we felt, thousands of such families in the country whose pleas for justice remain unattended and it was pointless to keep waiting for justice to be done. We therefore gave up further efforts to try to expedite the matter. Omar's fifth death anniversary was in June 2007.

The inquiry of Mr Gohar Zaman, a distinguished retired inspector general of police into Omar's death has been included in this book.

25 June 2007

Omar's daughter, Yasmeen, on her father's fifth death anniversary:

When I close my eyes I can still see his face, a face that illuminates with every smile. A faint scar lies on his chin; his eyes are small but always alive and warm. I can hear his footsteps in the corridor; they are always fast as if he had somewhere to go. These are some of the memories I can't let go. They are imprinted in my mind. They keep him alive for me. Today five years from the day I last saw Abba (Father), I know that I am a different person, but I would like to keep his memories and many others with me.

I have tried many things in these five years to stop the pain that started when he died. I have tried to forget, tried to ignore and tried to believe that it has not affected me, but the truth is that I am the person I am today, because of the experiences I have had, the good, the bad and even the worst. What I have learned is that remembering and knowing my father is the only way that the intense pain in my heart turns into love and admiration. That is why I want to remember him and cherish every memory I have of him, but sadly memories don't last forever. Writing them down will be the only way of ensuring that they will stay with me, since the written word is the only thing that lasts forever.

For all the people in my life who did not know my father or who knew him but are now forgetting him I would like to keep these memories alive so that they know how we (my mother, my brothers, I and others who were affected five years ago) are the people we are today. For all the children who have been born in the past five years or are going to be born in the future, I want to preserve these memories.

As the years have passed, people have grown, people have changed, most of us are in accomplished positions (Mashallah), some have left us and many have entered our lives. We are all in different places today than where we were five years ago. Ammi (Mother) who was heading the crafts section in SUNGI then, is heading the organisation today, Abdullah who was in first year of A Levels is now in his third year Architecture, Mustafa who was in eighth grade then has just finished his A Levels and is (Inshallah) going to Cambridge in a few months. I was in my first year BA and am now working in a news channel. Writing all this is easer than living through it. I know how difficult it was then and still is at times to go on with life and strive to achieve our goals. We all have found these five years to be very long and painstaking or at least I have, but there are a few things that kept us going. The first is the support of our family. I don't know how people survive without families—from both my sets of grandparents, my khalas ([maternal aunts] who are like second mothers), phoopos (paternal aunts), other aunts, uncles and cousins. They have all been there for us at any time we needed them. From emotional, financial and residential support they have all stepped up for us not to mention the intense love they have shown us. Today I value my family independently more than I have ever done. I know that without them I would never have been able to do all that I have today, and I deeply pride myself in being part of this family.

The other thing that has kept me going is the legacy my father left us. He didn't leave us a lot of money or cars or houses, but what he did leave will stay with us forever. Today when I am working I experience the impact of his legacy when I meet people who come to know that I am Omar Asghar Khan's daughter. A colleague who has accompanied me for interviews told me that people's expressions change when they discover whose daughter I am. Mustafa had a similar experience when doing relief work after the earthquake in Batagram when a mob of Pathans were attacking the Sungi office in desperation looking for rations. The Sungi staff was trying to stop them. They were going to get violent and then some one pointed to Mustafa and told them that this is Omar's son and the mob calmed down. This realization, I think, also changed his life.

I feel that leaving a good legacy is the best gift any parent can leave a child. Thankfully I have realised this after five years have passed since his death. Now I would like to keep this legacy alive and help everyone to remember Omar Asghar Khan, my father.

Statement of Mr Gohar Zaman Khan, former Inspector General of Police about an Investigation into the Death of Omar Asghar Khan in Karachi on 25 June 2002

Omar Asghar Khan aged 48 son of Air Marshal (Retd) Mohammad Asghar Khan died at Karachi some time after midnight on 25/6/02 in mysterious circumstances in house #28 B-II, Gizri Boulevard, D.H.S., Karachi. The police declared it a case of suicide in a press conference without going through the legal, medical, and investigative procedures. The chemical examiner's report forms the basis of the legal formality, as the post mortem report becomes an integral part of the findings. The police pronounced it as suicide prior to the receipt of both these documents. Furthermore, the investigative side should have examined any chance of foul play and eliminated that possibility through a study of previous conduct of the deceased. Interviews of those he came in contact with during the past day and week, his phone record and its analysis, mail received and other correspondence, his personal computer scanning, opinion of his personal doctor and the physical and medical health picture should have been taken into consideration during investigation. Furthermore, feedback from friends and relatives about his behaviour or previous history was ignored. This process of psychological autopsy goes a long way towards establishing the findings. The subsequent doubts expressed by the media should have counted as public opinion and investigated for possible homicide. The police could not find any finger prints, not even on the water glass lying on the bed side table, or the door bolt which is made of metal, or the fan blades, or the glass window, and not even the all important pen. The pillow case was not tested for stains, hair, etc. and the computer chair with a stain was not tested either.

Reference the report by Dr Zahid Hussein, the chemical examiner to the Government of Sindh at Karachi dated *8/7/2002 # 4706/07* and post mortem examination by Dr Abdul Haque *# 195/02* dated 25/6/02 and the supplementary medico legal report dated *9/7/02*. The chemical examination report is good and almost a complete one eliminating all other options of suicide except one. Results show the deceased to be a normal healthy person. If the police had taken an air sample the chemical examiner would have commented on that. Was there any urine? In such cases there always is. But the police never traced it. There was bleeding from the nose and ears. Is that normal in suicide cases? Of course there is a mention of semen stain. In all such cases semen is found not as a result of excitement but as part of the dying process through choking.

The post mortem which reads like a textbook report says that tip of the tongue is bitten and contused. Hemorrhagic spots are seen on the lower lip. Could this be the result of use of force or pressure? Is it normal to develop such spots in the event of suicide by hanging? Furthermore, under surface of the ligature is dry and glistening, the muscles above and below the ligature mark are echymosed. Is this observation common to suicide by hanging with a bed sheet? The base of the tongue surface shows fine petechial hemorrhages. Is that a normal occurrence? There were marks on the wrists according to eyewitnesses but these are not shown in the medical report. However, the report says there are white marks on the forearms 12cm above the wrists and the right forearm has signs of wrapping. Were the arms tied by cloth, hence the wrapping? There was a mark on the throat, oblique in direction, measuring 29cm in length, 3cm wide in the front and 1.5cm at the ends. Could a 3cm mark be formed by a bed sheet? Would a man first suffocated to death and then suspended or hanged also develop an oblique mark? The condition of the lungs and size show the result of pressure which is caused by strangulation when an extraordinary effort is made to breathe. The cause is given as asphyxia but the tongue is not out as is the case in hanging. The eyes were also nearly closed. Is that normal in such cases? The crucial question of the ligature is tied to the substance used as ligature which was not produced with the dead body by the police, according to the doctor.

Since the circumstances do not point to suicide, it has therefore become necessary to prepare a case against the police findings. The suicide note is always a major factor. In this case the note was written on the back of an envelope. Why would the deceased do that when there was a pad lying on the bedside table? This envelope was sent to the handwriting expert along with a sample of the writing of the deceased by the police for comparison. However, an independent expert opinion is called for.

A dying man struggles hard before breathing his last. But in this case there seems to be no struggle, otherwise the chair with wheels, which his foot was resting upon, should have moved (especially when there was no carpet under the chair) from under the fan position. The lights were off, that is important to note.

The oblique marks on the front and side of the neck (not back) is indicative of suicide by hanging while a horizontal mark is not. But what if a person is suffocated to death and then suspended? Furthermore, the size of the mark is more akin to a rope ligature rather than a bed sheet. Was the bed sheet turned into a rope around the neck? The two bed sheets were also wrapped around the body. How is that possible when, the sheet is also tied around the neck plus thrown across the fan blade? In what sequence was it done?

How did the white marks of variable width 12cm above and wrist occur? The doctor clearly states that there are 'no pressure signs of (wrapping) on Rt. Forearm'. But what about the left forearm? The doctor does not say anything about the pressure signs of wrapping for the left forearm. Is it a wilful omission? Why does the doctor talk about wrapping and not tying when he admits he was not given the substance used for the crime? Let me here explain. The left arm was loosely tied and became nearly free during the last struggle for life but had tie or wrapping marks. The right arm was so tightly tied that it also produced signs of wrapping which were ignored by the medical examiner. The eyewitnesses state that the right arm was so hard to undo that they considered cutting the bed sheet. Also that there were tie marks on both wrists. How does a right handed man tie his right hand behind his back with the left hand with so many knots? Above all no one has ever heard of anyone committing suicide by hanging with both hands tied behind the back. The palms of the hands were pointing outward. There is more than one witness to testify to this.

It is quite obvious that the man was first strangled to death and then suspended from the fan blade. This was not done by the use of force. There are no signs of struggle in the bed or bruises on the body. He was first made unconscious and then the deed was done. The instrument of strangulation was not a bed sheet but a rope. At least two persons committed the act. I am of the opinion that it is a case of homicide. A motive has to be found by the investigators. What I have not been able to establish is the entry of the criminals. How the bedroom door was bolted from the inside is quite possible through the sliding ventilator type window which had no bolt. But the fact that a suicide note was found still remains a question mark. Is it genuine? A reconstruction of the crime can throw light on the case.

ANNEXURE 3.1

Air Marshal M. Asghar Khan's Message to the Officers of the Defence Services of Pakistan

I am addressing this message to the Chiefs of Staff and the 'Officers of the Defence Services of Pakistan.

It is your duty to defend the territorial integrity of Pakistan and to obey all lawful commands of superior officers placed over you. To differentiate between a 'lawful' and an 'unlawful' command is the duty of every officer. Every one of you must ask yourself whether what the army is doing today is 'lawful' activity and if your conscience tells you that it is not and you still carry it out, you would appear to lack moral fiber and would be guilty of a grave crime against your country and your people.

You should by now have realized that military action in East Pakistan was a conspiracy in which the present Prime Minister played a Machiavellian role. You know the circumstances in which military action in Balochistan was engineered and how completely unnecessary this action has been. You are also probably aware of the utterly unnecessary military action taken lat year in DIR in the North West Frontier Province. If you have any interest in national affairs, you must also be aware that during the election campaign the nation expressed its powerful disapproval of the present regime. Following the people's rejection of the Government, you should have been surprised at the election results in which the 'Pakistan National Alliance' which could muster such overwhelming popular support, could only get 8 out of 116 seats in the Punjab. You must surely know that many people were not even allowed to file their nomination papers. Was it not too much of a co-incidence that no paper could be filed against the Prime Minister and all the Chief Ministers of the four provinces? That those who dared to try, ended up in spending a few nights in Police custody? One of them has still not been traced.

Those of you who were even remotely connected with duties in connection with 7th March election would also know of the blatant manner in which rigging took place; Of the hundreds of thousands of ballot papers of PNA candidates that had been taken out of ballot boxes and were found in the streets and fields of Pakistan following the election on 7th March. You would also have seen the deserted polling stations on 10th March, the day of the Provincial polls, following the call for boycott of Provincial elections by the PNA. Nevertheless, Government media announced that an unprecedented number of votes had also been polled at the provincial election and the percentage was said to be more than sixty. Then surely you must have followed the movement which called for Bhutto's resignation and re-elections in the country.

The coming out of women in thousands on the streets in every city and town with babies in their arms was a scene that no one will forget. These were the women who Bhutto claimed had voted for him. The movement proved within a few days that he and his government had been completely rejected by the people. The death of hundreds of our youth and the beating of our mothers and sisters was a scene that may well have stirred you to shame and sorrow. Have you ever thought why the people put themselves to so much trouble? Why must mothers come out to face bullets with babies in their arms? Why do parents allow their children to face police *lathis* and bullets? Surely it is only because they feel that they have been wronged — that they have been cheated. That their basic right of 'HIRE and FIRE' their rulers has been denied them. They understood, when we told them the truth that the Constitution which you as officers of the Defence Services are sworn to defend had been violated. Article 218(3) of the Constitution of the 'Islamic Republic of Pakistan' says: 'It shall be the duty of the Election Commission constituted in relation to an election to organize and conduct the election and to make such arrangements as are necessary to ensure that the election is conducted honestly, justly, fairly and in accordance with law, and that corrupt practices are guarded against.' This, my friend, was not a just and fair election. Bhutto has violated the Constitution and is guilty of a grave crime against the people. It is not your duty to support his illegal regime nor can you be called upon to kill your own people so that he can continue a little longer in office. Let it not be said that the Pakistan armed forces are a degenerate Police Force fit only for killing unarmed civilians. How else can you explain the shooting of a spirited lad whose only fault was to show the 'V' sign to the army in Lahore the other day. The spirit of adventure; of defiance rather than servility needs to be encouraged in our youth and this unfortunate incident is a blot on the name of the army which would be difficult to wipe out. Similarly, shooting by the army in Karachi on an unarmed crowd is unpardonable. Didn't you realize that the poor and hungry people of Pakistan, throughout the 30 troubled years of our history had shown only love and affection for our armed forces. That they wept when you laid down arms in East Pakistan; that they have always prayed for your glory and have literally starved themselves and their children so that you are well fed and our Generals and Senior Officers can live a life that even their British and American counterparts would not dream of. It pains me to say that, that love is now gone. Pray do not let it turn to hate. For should that happen, a tragedy would have occurred in the history of this nation which we in our lifetime may not be able to undo.

As men of honour it is your responsibility to do your duty and the call of duty in these trying circumstances is not the blind obedience of unlawful commands. There comes a time in the lives of nations when each man has to ask himself whether he is doing the right thing. For you that time has come. Answer this call honestly and save Pakistan. God be with you.

ANNEXURE 3.2
Statement of President of Tehrik-i-Istiqlal, M. Asghar Khan, Rawalpindi Thursday, 23 November 1978

The following extract from the new Party Manifesto of Tehrik-i-Istiqlal approved by the Party's National Working Committee at Peshawar on 18th Nov. 1978 is released to the Press:

PREAMBLE

The administrative system prevailing in Pakistan was designed by colonial rulers to serve their purpose of keeping the people in bondage and at the mercy of the officials appointed by those rulers. The system and the imperial mentality inherited by Government Officials have sabotaged every effort of the people of Pakistan to exercise control over their affairs to which they are entitled as a free nation. The institutions of National and Provincial Assemblies and local self government introduced since independence have failed to free the people from the tyranny and corruption of that system and its officials. In fact tyranny and corruption of government officials have attained unprecedented proportions. No progress can be made towards giving our people a life of prosperity as long as this system and the mentality of its officials is allowed to continue. The Tehrik has accordingly decided to root out the present system and the colonial mentality of its officials as the first essential step for the implementation of its revolutionary programme of giving political power and prosperity to the people.

LOCAL GOVERNMENT AND PUBLIC ADMINISTRATION

Division of Responsibilities

(a) Each province shall be administratively divided into 'village', 'Halqa' and District. The boundaries of a Halqa will be those of a Provincial Assembly constituency. There shall be an elected 'Punchayat'/'Jirga' at the village level, a Halqa Assembly at the Halqa level and a 'Council' comprising MNAs and MPAs of the District at the District level. All functions relating to police, education, health, roads, agriculture, land records, land revenue etc—i.e. all the subjects that fall within the powers of the provincial government shall be the responsibility of the Halqa Assembly acting through its executive committee.

(b) The Punchayat shall act as a conciliation committee and a court competent to try petty offences. It will establish and look after primary schools and dispensaries, act as a liaison between the Halqa administration and the village. It shall keep record of births and deaths and endorse mutation in land records. Copies of FIRs relating to the village shall be supplied immediately by the Police to the Punchayat.

(c) The Council of MNAs and MPAs at the District level will co-ordinate the work of the Halqa whenever necessary by calling joint meetings of the Halqa Committee. Without interfering in the daily conduct of work they will provide technical advice and act as a liaison between the Halqa and the Provincial administration.

(d) The Provincial Headquarter organisation working under the Provincial Assembly will deal with legislation, policy-making, planning and budget-making. It will provide technical field services to the Halqas in the spheres of engineering, health, agriculture, education, etc. and provincial level hospitals, Universities, Special Investigating Police, etc.

Allocation of Resources

The provinces shall have complete control over the recruitment and posting etc. of their employees. The allocation of resources, internal and external to the provinces for development shall be done by a Commission having equal representation of each province and the Centre. Cases of disagreement shall be decided by a council consisting of the Chief Justice of the Supreme Court and the Chief Justices of High Courts. The resources available to the Federation after meeting the requirements of its subjects shall be allocated on the basis of the need to bring a Province or any of its parts to the same level of prosperity as the rest of the country.

Responsibilities

Halqa and District Administrations shall have control of their own staff and of operations within their sphere, as approved in the budget and the provincial development plan.

The Centre, Provinces and groups of districts shall have public Service Commissions which shall enjoy the same constitutional protection as given to High Court Judges. These Commissions shall recruit and be the appellate authorities for disciplinary action in the case of officials of executive' rank. The clerical services and those below shall be recruited and finally dealt with by the relevant administrative bodies.

In the Central, provincial and Halqa Assembly there shall be constitutional provision for standing committees for different subjects including Standing Committee on the conduct of Public representatives.

Services

The posts of Provincial Chief Secretaries shall be abolished. The staffs in the Secretariat shall be drastically reduced to a few officers in each department.

Divisions, Commissioners, Deputy Commissioners, Assistant Commissioners, Tehsildars and Magistrates, as they are functioning today, shall be abolished.

The present wide disparities between emoluments shall be eliminated. Perquisites which are an unnecessary burden on the state exchequer shall be abolished. Head of State, Ministers, Governors and all Government Officials will be required to live frugally.

Judiciary

Executive control over the administrative side of judicial organs has undermined public confidence in the independence of the judiciary. The present judicial system and its laws and rules were imposed by a colonial government and have caused incalculable damage to the economy and social integrity of our people. Tehrik will bring fundamental changes in both the organisation of law courts and the procedural codes.

Independence

The Judiciary shall be independent of the executive and the appointment of judges will be free of executive control.

Judicial System

A system of elected jury for the courts shall be adopted up to the sessions Court level. The law of procedure and evidence shall be drastically simplified.

The judicial system shall be reviewed and brought in line with the needs of a progressive society ensuring expeditious disposal of cases.

a. If a criminal case is not decided within six months by the Court from the first presentation of the challan before the Court, the accused will be released on bail and the case shall be decided within six months thereafter.

b. Civil cases shall be decided within one year.

c. Separate family courts shall be established.

Court Fees

Court fees shall be abolished.

ANNEXURE 3.3
Part III of Tehrik-i-Istiqlal's manifesto a statement by Mr Mohammad Asghar Khan (President, Tehirk-i-Istiqlal), at a Press Conference in Karachi on 1 February 1979

CONSTITUTIONAL STRUCTURE

The Federal structure of Pakistan, wherein one Province has out numbered the collective parliamentary strength of all the other provinces has not changed with the separation of East Pakistan. Just as East Pakistan had a larger population than the other four Provinces of West Pakistan put together, Punjab today outnumbers the combined strength of the remaining three provinces. Unfortunately, narrow parochial considerations, political exploitation and decades of dictatorial rule and palace intrigues have further increased the mistrust and misunderstandings between provinces.

In the circumstances in which one Province has a greater population than that of all the other components of the Federation, it is vital that the smaller provinces should be provided safeguards ensuring that their vital interests would not be jeopardized. Only thus can a repetition of the events of the first 24 years of Pakistan be avoided and a lasting basis provided for a united and stable Pakistan in which people of all the provinces can live in equality and brotherhood.

Accordingly:

1. The Federal Government shall be entrusted with responsibility for foreign affairs, defence, currency, International and Inter-Provincial trade and communications.
2. The Federal Government shall have the power to levy and collect taxes for the purposes of the Federation.
3. The Provinces may entrust to the Centre, such additional responsibilities as they may decide.
4. Inter-provincial and inter-district restrictions on the movement of goods or inter-provincial taxes of any kind shall be forbidden and unnecessary road barriers shall be removed.
5. Powers of the Senate will be enhanced.
6. The voting age will be reduced to 18 years.
7. Voting in the Tribal Areas will be on the basis of Adult Franchise

ANNEXURE 3.4

Karachi Feb 5: The following Press statement has been issued by Mr J.A. Rahim, former Federal Minister and Secretary General of the Pakistan Peoples Party:- 'The time has come, I think, that I should now state publicly what my attitude is in the present political situation. This itself will give the reason for my decision to join a major political party, the Tehrik-i-Istiqlal.

Since I first entered the arena of active politics I have held the belief and consistently acted on it, that the major problem for Pakistan was how it could rapidly adapt itself to the modern world. Put even so generally, the concept of modernization is an unmistakable dividing line; those who accept it are clearly distinguished from those who shout slogans demanding the introduction of fanciful institutions and laws that have no relevance to the life of our present age. I shall have to take up the issues arising from the regressive philosophy of the obscurantist at another time, but very soon, and demonstrate by analyzing their premises and arguments the falsity of their claims. For the present it is sufficient to say that we may allow them their claims to speak for their own views but must repudiate their claim to interpret Islam for all Muslims.

Industrialization is in my view the foundation stone of modern society—which is an industrial society. Pakistan cannot be prosperous unless it develops its industrial capacity to a high level. Nature has not, contrary to a belief foisted by landed interests, blessed our desert country with a rich agricultural potential.

I believe also that the State must play the leading role in the process of industrialization and so must actively participate in it.

I have joined the Tehrik-i-Istiqlal because I consider it to be the party best equipped to guide the country under the leadership of Mr Asghar Khan, to a better future. I add an appeal to the progressive minded people who are not already members of this party to join it now.'

(J.A. RAHIM)
Karachi, 5 February 1979.

ANNEXURE 3.5

Press Statement by Mohammad Asghar Khan, 29 March 1979, Rights of Women

While Islam strives to give women dignity and independence and to safeguard them from exploitation, the social customs and the economic and political structure prevailing in the country has effectively subordinated their status and role in society resulting in exploitation, suppression and denial of their rights. Forced marriages, denial of rights to property and other unjust practices have been used to reduce women to a sub-human status, alien to the spirit of Islam.

The constraints that an unjust society places upon women, make it difficult for them to play an effective part in national life. In spite of these handicaps the women of Pakistan have always been in the forefront of every struggle for the rights of the citizens of this country. Their sacrifices in 1947 made Pakistan possible and their courage and determination in 1977 crowned a great people's movement with success. To frustrate the capabilities of half the nation by continuing to deny women their rightful role in moulding the destiny of this nation would not only be an injustice but also a monumental folly. We, therefore, resolve to:

1. Take all appropriate measures to abolish customs and practices which are discriminatory against women and provide adequate legal protection for their rights.
2. Women shall be given the opportunity to fill 10% of assembly seats by direct votes of men and women.
3. Appoint not less than 50% women judges in family courts.
4. Make provision by law for all cases of divorce filed by women to be decided by Family Courts within six months, including the questions of custody of children, maintenance allowance and 'Haq Mehar'.
5. All cases relating to property arising out of divorce shall be entrusted to Family Courts and will be settled within one year.
6. Make changes in the family law to provide greater protection to women against exploitation and social injustice in such matters as divorce, maintenance after divorce and the maintenance and custody of children.
7. Adopt special measure to protect the rights of widows and minor children in matters of inheritance.
8. Take effective steps to protect the interests of widows and minor children in such matters as possession of urban property and agricultural land and ensure that they get their proper share in agricultural yield.
9. Open all Government posts to women. No women shall be considered unfit for such post merely on the ground of being a woman.
10. Provide facilities for education in all branches of knowledge to women.
11. Establish nurseries especially for children of working women.

ANNEXURE 3.6

Details of Arrests—Tehrik-i-Istiqlal
Since 16 Oct 1979

Sl. No.	Name	Date Arrest	Jail	Date Release	
1.	M. Asghar Khan	16.10.79	Abbottabad residence.	18.4.80	
		29.05.80	Dadar & Abbottabad Res.		
2.	Syed Munir Shah	16.10.79	Haripur.	28.10.79	
		26.02.81	Faisalabad.	26.07.81	
3.	Fakhruz Zaman Khan	16.10.79	Haripur.	26.10.79	
4.	Syed Mukhtiar Ahmad Bacha	16.10.79	Haripur.	28.10.79	
		22.03.81	Haripur.	27.05.81	
5.	Aslam Khan Khattak	16.10.79	Haripur.	28.10.79	
6.	Farooq Adam Khan	16.10.79	Haripur.	28.10.79	
7.	Saeed Hameed-ud-Din	16.10.79	Bannu.	28.10.79	
8.	Malik Baz Muhammad Khan Mehtarzai	03.05.80	Quetta.	May '80	
9.	Muhammad Raza Khan	03.05.80	Quetta.	25.05.80	
10.	Amanullah Khan	03.05.80	Quetta.	Dec '80	
11.	Muhammad Ramzan	03.05.80	Quetta.	Dec '80	
12.	Maula Bakhsh Lehri	04.05.80	Quetta.	Dec '80	
		03.04.81	Mach.	16.04.81	
13.	Rafiq Bugti	04.05.80	Quetta. Mach.	Dec '80	
14.	Muhammad Ayub	11.05.80	Lahore	21.05.80	
15.	Mian Maqsood Ahmad	11.05.80	Lahore	21.05.80	
16.	Khuda-i-Noor Khan	18.05.80	Quetta.	18.10.80	
		03.04.81	Quetta.	24.04.81	
17.	Haji Hayat Muhammad Khan Jamaldini	4.7.80	Quetta.	18.10.80	
18.	Musheer A. Pesh Imam	4.8.80	Karachi.	20.9.80	
19.	Obaidur Rehman	4.8.80	Karachi.	20.9.80	
20.	Asif Vardag	8.8.80	Rawalpindi.	14.12.80	

Sl. No.	Name	Date Arrest	Jail	Date Release	
		24.2.81	Faisalabad. Bahawalpur (11.6.81) Lahore (23.7.81)	2.8.81	
21.	Mahfooz Yar Khan	27.8.80	Karachi.	Oct '80	
		23.3.81	Karachi.	4.6.81	
		(9 months R.I).			
22.	Nafees Ahmad Sidiqui	3.9.80	Karachi.	Oct '80	
		3.4.81	Karachi.	24 Sep '80	
23.	Mian Mahmood Ali Kasuri	8.2.81	Kot Lakhpat, Sahiwal (8.6.81)	24.6.81	
24.	Rafi Butt	24.2.81	Gujranwala	11.6.81	
25.	Mumtaz Ahmad Tarar	24.2.81 Jhelum	Gujrat	May '81	
26.	Abdul Qayyum Pahat	24.2.81.	Kot Lakhpat Multan	16 July '81	
27.	Babar Shaheen	24.2.81.	Bahawalpur	14 Aug '81	
28.	Zafar Gondal	24.2.81.	Kot Lakhpat	24.7.81	
29.	Sheikh Nazar Hussain	24.2.81.	Muzzafargarh	May '81	
30.	Muhammad Sharif Gondal	24.2.81.	Wazirabad.	26.3.81	
31.	Azim Mirza	24.2.81.	Gujranwala	8.6.81	
32.	Idrees Bajwa	24.2.81.	Sialkot	8.6.81	
33.	Sheikh Asghar	24.2.81	Jhelum	28.3.81	
34.	Raja M. Salim	24.2.81.	Jhelum	28.3.81	
35.	Mian Mushtaq Ahmad	24.2.81	Kot Lakhpat	26.7.81	
36.	Khurshid Mahmud Kasuri	25.2.81. 15.6.81.	Camp Jail, Lhr Kot Lakhpat	2.7.81	
37.	Omar Kasuri	25.2.81. 15.6.81.	Camp Jail, Lahore Kot Lakhpat	2.7.81	
38.	Zafar Ali Shah	26.2.81.	Jhang	16.7.81	
39.	Begum Mahnaz Rafi	26.2.81.	Kot Lakhpat	26.3.81	

Sl. No.	Name	Date Arrest	Jail	Date Release	
40.	Fazil Bhatti	26.2.81	Gujranwala	4.5.81	
41.	Malik Hamid Sarfaraz	26.2.81.	Sahiwal	23.8.81	
42.	Dr Aitzaz Ahsan	26.2.81.	Multan Lahore (8.6.81)	24.7.81	
43.	B.K. Tabish (Faisalabad)	26.2.81	Jhang	2.8.81	
44.	Shah Nawaz Adv. (Lhr)	26.2.81.	Kot Lakhpat	1.3.81	On Bond.
45.	Javed Bashir (Lhr)	26.2.81.	Gujranwala	26.6.81	
46.	Abdul Qadeer (Lhr)	26.2.81	Jhang	24.6.81	Released on Bond by father
47.	Raja Mehboob (Faisalabad)	26.2.81	Mianwali	26.7.81	
48.	Qazi Khalid Mehmood	Mar '81 ?	Attock	Mar '81	
49.	Dr Sharif Adil	Mar '81	Faisalabad	May '81	On bond by Ch: Akram Hinjra.
50.	Ghulam Nabi Butt	Mar '81	Rawalpindi	8.6.81	
51.	Mustafa Kamal (ISF, Pb. Uni)	26.3.81	Camp Jail, Lhr	20.5.81	
52.	Inayat Gill	28.3.81	Faisalabad	25.7.81	
53.	Imran Alam (ISF, Pb. Uni)	23.3.81	Camp Jail, Lahore	14.5.81	
54.	Akhtar Khattak (ISF, Pb. Uni)	22.3.81	Peshawar	Released	
55.	Abdul Hamid Bhatti	22.3.81	Bahawalpur	15.8.81	
56.	Abdur Rehman Abbasi	29.4.81	Haripur	1.5.81	
57.	Nisar Ahmad Khuro	15.7.81	Camp Jail, Lahore	26.7.81	
58.	Malik Haider Osman	15.7.81	Camp Jail, Lahore	27.7.81	
59.	Nahid Afzaal	23.7.81.	Karachi Police Lock-up Karachi Jail 2.8.81		
60.	Sheikh Muhammad Sharif	16.9.81	Jhang	30.9.81	

ANNEXURE 3.7

PDA White Paper on Election 1990 "How an Election was Stolen"

EXECUTIVE SUMMARY

The rigging of the 1990 elections was not an isolated phenomenon. Rigging was not done by some to simply remain in power and by others to come into power, although this was also among its several purpose. It was part of a larger design to give a certain direction to the politics of Pakistan—to bring back into power the forces that have pre-empted the entry of the masses into politics and prevented them, through the imposition of martial laws and consolidation of an exclusive and elite-based power structure, from assuming charge of their destiny. It was a bid to restore the position prevailing before the elections of 1988 and to destroy the political organizations which sought political mobilization of the common people.

'Rigging' in any election, and particularly in the October 1990 elections in Pakistan, includes much more than just the stuffing of ballot boxes and use of coercive techniques on the day of polling itself. While such traditional methods of rigging did take place on a large scale on October 24 and October 27, 1990, the manipulation of the electoral process began much earlier than on polling day itself, and rigging also took place after the polls closed.

THE ROLE OF THE PRESIDENT

The rigging of elections 1990 involved the whole state apparatus. In the forefront of that apparatus stands the president. The White Paper identifies nine main ways in which the president was involved in the election rigging process.

1. The first step in the attempted demolition of the PPP—and thus the demise of participatory government—was the dissolution of the assemblies. The White Paper documents that this dissolution, ordered by the president on August 6, 1990, was in the nature of a constitutional coup and was done with malafide intent. This malafide intent is shown by the intimidatory manner of the dissolution of the National Assembly and also by the discriminatory way in which the dissolution was carried out at the provincial level with regard to PPP and non-PPP governments and the different way those governors with PPP sympathies were treated.

2. Following the dissolution of the assemblies the president appointed caretakers whose only qualifications seemed to be their antipathy to the PPP and their potential for hurting the PPP. Whereas the dissolution of the National Assembly and the assemblies in Sindh and the NWFP was marked by the complete discontinuity between the PPP governments and the caretaker regimes, the changes in Balochistan and the Punjab (which were governed by the 111 or its allies) were little more than cosmetic.

3. The president's intentions were further revealed in his speeches and statements—particularly his unprecedented speech on the eve of the elections. In these speeches the president attacked the PPP and its leadership, repeated the election propaganda of the IJI campaign and encouraged voters to vote against the PDA

4. In violation of normal procedures, an 'election cell' was set up in the presidency (Aiwan-e-Sadar) and there are strong indications that this cell was used on election night to alter certain results before they were officially announced. The cell was also used to disseminate anti-PPP propaganda in the press. The members of this cell included General (Retd) Rafaqat (former chief of staff of General Ziaul Haq) who was recalled to Pakistan just after the dissolution of the assemblies. General Rafaqat had masterminded the infamous referendum of General Ziaul Haq in December 1984.

5. The president made significant use of his power to appoint and confirm acting judges to the superior courts in such a way as to lead to the suspicion that he wished to influence the proceedings of the superior courts when they were hearing various petitions against the dissolution of the assemblies.

6. The president also employed his power of appointment with respect to the Election Commission so that at its higher levels that commission was staffed with people of known anti-PPP bias, or people who were vulnerable to outside pressure due to outstanding corruption charges against them. In particular, the president appointed Chaudhry Shaukat Ali as secretary of the Election Commission, and gave an out of turn promotion to Mr Humayun Khan to the post of additional secretary.

7. An independent investigation of the accountability process made on behalf of the Canadian government concluded that 'President Ghulam Ishaq Khan, acting on the advice of the caretaker prime minister Jatoi, acted capriciously, vexatiously and for political purposes in preparing and filing seventeen references against the members of the government dismissed by the President...My review of these references...cause me to believe that the seventeen references were made in order to influence the outcome of the general election.'

8. The president and other powerful state agencies went beyond their normal role in a democratic system in providing help to keep the shaky IJI alliance intact and thus make possible the 'one-to-one' election strategy.

THE ROLE OF THE CARETAKER GOVERNMENTS

While the proper role of a caretaker administration is to look after the day-to-day administration of the country and hold fair and free elections, it was quite clear from the moment the names of the caretakers were announced that the purpose of their selection by the president was to destroy the PPP by fair means or foul. As the White Paper documents, the caretakers in fact made no secret of their aim to defeat the PDA. The White Paper discusses ten main ways in which this agenda was pursued.

1. Election cells were set up by the caretaker prime minister and in at least one province—Balochistan. The purpose of these cells was to enable the outcome of the elections to be manipulated for particular constituencies, before the results were announced.

2. The caretakers blatantly misused the electronic media, particularly PTV, to influence the electorate. PTV newscasts were used to broadcast unproven charges of corruption against the PPP and its leadership and to repeat anti-PPP propaganda.

Its current affairs programmes were overtly slanted against the PDA, and the alliance was allowed very little time to put across its own position.

3. The administration was made a tool in the hands of the caretakers and the 111 to ensure the defeat of PDA candidates. To achieve this result large scale transfers of administrative officials was made at various levels in all the four provinces. While not every transfer or posting need be politically motivated, the fact that the caretaker governments, who were in power for less than three months, engaged in a wholesale reshuffling of the provincial administrative machinery, gives rise to very serious questions. The process was most marked in Sindh where, at a conservative estimate, more than 90 officers were transferred and 60 had their services terminated. Pressure was also put on the low-level administration to support the HI campaign. For example at a lambadars conference held in Lahore, Mr Ghulam Haider Wyne, the caretaker chief minister, announced a package of unprecedented benefits for lambadars—with the clearly stated understanding that the lambardars would help to defeat the PDA candidates in their local areas.

4. The caretakers at the federal and provincial level showed no respect for democratic norms, election laws, and the specific instructions of the Election Commission and used powers at their disposal to provide public funds, facilities and employment to get votes from the people. **Among the pre-poll rigging methods used by the caretakers and the IJI, this method proved to be one of the most effective and decisive factors in securing the IJI 'victory'.** In the Punjab alone, close to Rs2.5 billion was made available for development projects recommended by the IJI candidates. The Punjab government is still trying to recover from the results of this reckless expenditure. Mr. Ghulam Haider Wyne, chief minister of the Punjab, in a letter to the federal finance minister, Mr Sartaj Aziz, dated April 2, 1991. requested funds to be transferred to the Punjab government in order to complete schemes started in August-October, 1990. In his letter, Mr Ghulam Haider Wyne, explicitly mentions that 'we have an outstanding liability of Rs80 crore for completion of the schemes initiated during the period August-October, 1990. A large number of these scheme were started on the request of members of the National Assembly.' It is clear from the letter that these schemes were initiated not on the request of the members of the National Assembly but on the request of IJI candidates for the National Assembly, since the assemblies had been dissolved on August 6, 1990, and there was no National Assembly.

5. Besides misusing public funds, the caretaker administration also misused government facilities in support of IJI candidates, particularly the use of government transport for electioneering.

6. The caretaker governments also put a number of administrative hurdles in the way of the PDA. These included the discriminatory attitude of the administration in refusing to issue national identity cards to people who did not have the blessings of IJl candidates or their principle supporters. This amounted to disenfranchising a large number of candidates who were PDA voters. New districts were created and constituency boundaries shifted. The most outrageous display of gerrymandering was the restructuring of the Naushero Feroze district. This administrative delimitation affected three constituencies NA-158, NA-159 and NA-160. Mr Ghulam Mustafa Jatoi was a candidate from NA-158 Naushero Feroze-l, his son Ghulam Mujtaba Khan Jatoi was a candidate from NA-159,

Naushero Feroze-II, and his other son Ghulam Murtaza Khan Jatoi was a candidate from NA-160 Nawabshah-l. The administration also tried to disturb PDA public meetings. On the occasion of at least two major rallies the electricity supply was cut off, and the PDA was prevented from holding its concluding public meeting of the campaign in Lahore as permission to hold a public meeting was not granted.

7. In Sindh, the caretaker government headed by Jam Sadiq Ali, engaged in widespread persecution of PPP leaders, workers and supporters. By the beginning of October 1990, it was estimated that as many as 39 supporters 0 the PPP in Sindh were victimized, arrested and intimidated by the police and other government functionaries. This process accelerated around the election period, with a veritable reign of terror let loose in certain constituencies—particularly those contested by the Jatoi and Jam families. This use of official violence against political opponents is still continuing in Sindh.

8. The caretakers also used bribes and pressure to try and induce certain PDA candidates to withdraw from the elections or to leave the party.

POLL-DA Y RIGGING

As far as rigging during the polls is concerned, the following rigging methods were employed against the PDA, examples of these rigging methods are fully documented in the White Paper:

1. Irregularities in voter registration
2. Provision of supplementary lists to IJI polling agents only and not to PDA polling agents.
3. Shifting polling stations and creating 'ghost' polling stations.
4. Bogus voting with fake identity cards
5. Looting ballot papers and stuffing ballot boxes.
6. Misuse of postal ballots.
7. Preventing PDA voters from entering the polling stations.
8. Arresting, kidnapping, forcibly evicting and threatening PDA polling agents.
9. Refusing to give PDA polling agents the official result sheets.
10. Changing election results during their transfer from presiding officer to returning officer.
11. Changing election results after their declaration.
12. Presence of unauthorized police at polling stations.
13. Lack of action by police on complaints of PDA candidates and agents.
14. Inducing, pressurizing, forcing, and bribing candidates to withdraw.

Despite a large number of complaints filed by PDA candidates and central leaders, before, during and after the polls, the Election Commission failed to take effective measures to prevent widespread rigging from **taking place or to redress the situation**.

Prior to the elections most predictions made by independent news media and other expected the PDA to emerge with a majority of seats as a result of the elections. The actual results came as a great shock to almost all observers, although prior to the polls a number of political leaders, both from the PDA and from other parties, had expressed serious apprehensions about the prejudicial attitude of the state and the likelihood of rigging both before and during the polls. Following the elections, even non-PDA political leaders, including IJI leaders such as Taj Jamali, chief minister of Balochistan and Ghulam Mustafa Jatoi, caretaker Prime Minister, admitted that rigging had taken place during the elections of 1990.

STATISTICAL ANALYSIS
The official results of the National Assembly elections of 1990 awarded the IJI an absolute majority of 105 out of 207 seats. Even before the election results had barely started coming in, the establishment's media managers had begun to attribute the IJI's landslide victory to the strategy of 'one-to-one' contests and to the shift of voter loyalties towards the IJI and its allies. The statistical analysis demonstrators, however, that both the 'one-to-one' strategy and the 'voter shift' theory are fallacious.

Overall, out of the 105 seats won by the IJI, only about 30 seats can be attributed to 'one-to-one' contests. The results in the remaining 75 seats cannot be explained by the strategy of 'one-ta-one' contests. Hard data also does not support the voter shift hypothesis. The PPP/PDA polled in the vicinity of 7.75 million votes in 1988, which actually increased by about half a million to the vicinity of 8.25 million votes in 1990. It is, therefore, clear that there has been no shift of voters from PDA to IJI. The PDA vote bank has remained constant. There has, however, been an increase in the IJI votes. These new votes are reflected in the higher voter turnouts, particularly in constituencies where the IJI has won.

In constituencies where voter turnout increased by 10 per cent or above, the IJI and its allies have won about 60 per cent of the seats and the PDA has won about 17 per cent; with about 23 per cent of seats obtained by other parties and independents. In constituencies where voter turnout decreased, i.e., there was a negative change, the share of IJI and its allies was reduced to about 50 per cent and that of the PDA enhanced two and a half times to over 40 per cent. In general, therefore, it is apparent that the IJI and its allies have been more successful in constituencies where voter turnout increased significantly over that in 1988; while the PDA has been more successful in constituencies where voter turnout increased only marginally or even decreased over that in 1988.

Since the general conclusion of all observers, including international monitoring teams, the press, and even the chief election commissioner, was that the actual turnout on polling day was low—perhaps even lower than in 1988, the high voting figures must give rise to suspicion. This suspicion is increased by the remarkable rise in voter registration and in issuance of national identity cards in certain constituencies only.

Analysis of Results
About 65 constituencies are established as rigged on the basis of the criteria developed in the chapter on statistical analysis. Another 5 constituencies are established as rigged on the basis of hard factual data available with the PDA. Thus the total number of constituencies where a very high probability of rigging is indicated stands at 70.

The key to rigging of the 1990 elections can be found in the mysterious new voters who came out for the first time in the electoral history of Pakistan to vote for the IJI and its allies. The change in the IJI votes in 1990 over 1988 are most interesting.

The minimum number of rigged constituencies in NWFP stands at 6. These have been 'won' by ANP stalwarts like Mr Bilour, Mr Arbab Jehangir and Mr Ajmal Khattak.

The minimum number of rigged constituencies in the Punjab stands at 52. These have been 'won' by IJI stalwarts like Mr Nawaz Sharif, Mr Ejaz-ul-Haq, Ch. Nisar Ali Khan, Lt. Gen. Majid Malik, Mian Zahid Sarfraz, Mr Hamid Nasir Chattha, Mr Humayun Akhtar Khan, Mr Shahbaz Sharif, Mr Liaqat Baloch, Mian Yaseen Wattoo, Mr Javed Hashmi, Mr Fakhr Imam, Mr Ghulam Haider Wyne and others.

It appears that the establishment experts had identified the constituencies in the Punjab and NWFP where there was a close one-to-one contest in 1988. An attempt was made to ensure that the contest remained direct in 1990 as well. In all such constituencies in Punjab and NWFP, the ballot-stuffing exercise was carried out rather subtly. The modus operandi emerges as follows.

There are between 150 to 250 polling stations in each constituency, with an average of 1000 to 1500 registered voters per polling station. While polling was conducted in an apparently orderly fashion in all the polling stations, thousands of bogus votes were also added to the HI tally in an insidious, but subtle, manner.

The minimum number of rigged constituencies stand at 9 in Sindh and 3 in Balochistan. The methodology of rigging in Sindh was completely different from that in NWFP and Punjab. The sophistication and subtlety applied in the two northern provinces was conspicuous by its absence. Instead, brute force was used to achieve the objectives.

The use of force was rendered necessary on account of the following reasons. While Punjab is the only province where the IJI has some independent political following, Sindh is the only province where the IJI has no following whatsoever. The exception, of course, being Karachi and a couple of constituencies in Hyderabad, where the IJI entered into an alliance with the MQM. (In NWFP and Balochistan, the IJI tried to secure a foothold by means of similar alliances with regional parties like the ANP and the JWP).

The fact that the IJI president and now prime minister is shown to have won both the seats, NA-48 and NA-95, through fraudulent means speaks volumes of the credibility of the entire electoral process and the legitimacy of the IJI government. Further, the fact that a major part of the IJI leadership, who have won their seats in the National Assembly through fraudulent means, were also the leading collaborators of the military dictatorship reflects their lack of respect for the will and sovereignty of the people, for the sanctity of the electoral exercise and for democratic institutions.

ANNEXURE 3.8

The defensive strength of Pakistan has been gradually weakening and Pakistan is not in a position today to meet effectively, a threat to its security from the most likely direction. With no capacity to build heavy armaments, tanks or combat aircraft, it is almost totally dependant for defence purchases from abroad, for which it neither has the money nor a reliable source of supply. As against this, India has the capacity to build its own heavy armaments including aircraft and is capable of waging a prolonged war.

A country's defence is an extension of its foreign policy. Our foreign policy has been lacking vision and by ill-timed initiatives we have lost trusted friends. The latest example was the hurried recognition of the Taliban Government in Afghanistan whereas wisdom would have required us to consult Iran on this issue and try to evolve a common policy towards Afghanistan. Our relation with China also appear to have lost their previous warmth and appear today to be devoid of any meaningful cooperation.

In these circumstances, the recent statement of Dr Abdul Qadeer Khan, that we have the capacity to destroy all India's cities within 15 minutes, might have brought satisfaction and a sense of security to the majority of our gullible public but was one which could have been made by an irresponsible politician but not by a scientist who knows better our limitations and capabilities. IT is this kind of chauvinism that has contributed to bringing the country to its present state of shaky existence.

Placed as we are, and with our economic and military limitations, we must consider the options available to us in a realistic manner. The first and probably the least attractive is to give up any hope of securing freedom for the people of Kashmir and mend our fences with India. Having reduced ourselves to a subservient role, we could then reduce our defence spendings and seek close economic and political relations with India. Much as this may appeal to some intellectuals, this course of action would not be acceptable to the people of Pakistan.

The second alternative is to seek the protection of the United States and a defence guarantee from her. Our experience with the United States over the last four decades precludes such a possibility. During our membership of CENTO and SEATO, the United States was committed only to assisting us in the event of aggression by the Soviet Union or China. It specifically excluded India from such a guarantee. Our government knew this all along, but the people only realized this when India launched an offensive in the Punjab in September 1965. Today, close economic and political relations with India are a comer-stone of US foreign policy and it could not agree to get itself involved in any conflict in the sub-continent. Moreover it sees India as a counter to the growing economic and military power of China in South Asia over the next two to three decades.

Iran has been our friend and ally since the creation of Pakistan but we have drifted away from it and do not have a common approach today in the field of foreign relations. Its developing economic ties with India and our inability to evolve a common policy towards Afghanistan have increased the gulf that separates our two countries and makes a meaningful defence arrangement difficult. Moreover our dependence on and leaning towards the United States and its antagonism towards Iran make such an arrangement un-realistic.

The fourth alternative is a mutual defence arrangement with China. Pakistan had a long history of good relations with China and these have till recently, developed to the mutual advantage of both our countries. In the next two to three decades, China's main rival as an economic and military power on the Asian mainland will be India and it is in her interest that Pakistan, situated as it is, survives to help it to maintain a balance with India's growing economic power and military ambitions in Asia. Needless to say, the United States will look upon India's strength as a counter to China with favour, and will assist it to attain that capability. A Pakistan, allied to China and located as it is to the West of India, would confer advantages on China in such a situation. Moreover a defence pact with Pakistan could be seen by China as an advantage in its relations with the Muslim population of Xinkiang and other regions of China with sizeable Muslim populations.

If China can be assured that Pakistan is not seeking a Defence arrangement for gaining an advantage to strengthen her military position in Kashmir and Kashmir is specifically excluded from any such arrangement, an understanding could be reached. Pakistan must satisfy China that it will not interfere on the other side of the cease fire line and the mutual defence agreement should be limited to assisting each other in the event of aggression by a third power. This mutual defence agreement would be in the interest of both countries and would confer tremendous advantages on Pakistan. It would enable her to cut her defence expenditure, pay back her rising debt and usher in an era of progress and economic stability. A clear mutual defence pact with China, located on India's northern borders, would create an atmosphere of security and peace for Pakistan which would make progress possible.

I expressed these views to the Prime Minister in our luncheon meeting of 28th June 1997 and explained that I saw this to be the only practical way of solving our military and economic problems. I hope that he will explore this possibility which if it succeeds, could be a turning point in our struggle for national survival. The alternative is a back-breaking burden of defence expenditure which would serve little purpose because it would still be inadequate.

The struggle in Kashmir has to be fought from within and those who are advocating Jehad from without to liberate the state, are either simpletons or hypocrites. The struggle of the Kashmiris will inevitably bring results and it will have the moral support of all Pakistanis and the sympathies of the free would. A defence arrangement with China to the exclusion of Kashmir, in no way affects the outcome of that struggle which is ultimately bound to succeed.

SECTION FOUR

Reflections

My three and half decades of political struggle was made possible by my belief in certain values that are the foundation of a just society. I have never regarded the attainment of political office as a legitimate goal unless that enables one to make changes in society that one considers essential. If the struggle of the Tehrik-i-Istiqlal over these years inspires some to work for a change in our society so that the life of the suffering people is made a little better, I would feel that we have been successful in our mission. Those who associated with me in this struggle believed in certain values which have been outlined briefly in the following pages.

Character

If the values that the founder of Pakistan had given us were to be summed up in one word, it would be 'honesty'. This is something that is woefully lacking in our dealings and is found to be rare in our day-to-day lives. After I had left the airline, when travelling by PIA once, I found my suitcase damaged by mishandling at the airport. I wrote to the airline and asked for the suitcase to be replaced. I received no reply; so I had it repaired. After about six months, the airline sent me a cheque for the full cost of the suitcase. I returned the cheque explaining that I had had the suitcase repaired and did not now require it to be replaced. My letter must have been read by some of the PIA staff, who talked about it and this incident therefore found a mention in the Karachi newspapers. Some years later when I had to address an ex-servicemen's gathering in Rawalpindi, the stage secretary, when introducing me, spoke of this incident about which he had read as a rare example of integrity. This was met with loud applause. What a pity, I thought, that normal behaviour of straightforwardness should be considered rare and applauded by the audience. Honesty however is not limited to financial dealings. One knows what is right and what is wrong and should do the right thing. When I refused to machine-gun the camel caravan of the Hurs in 1942 from the air, it was because my conscience told me that the killing of unarmed civilians was not my job and was not a lawful command. In 1958 when martial law was imposed in Pakistan, I was the C-in-C of the Pakistan Air Force and knew about it only after it had been imposed on the night of 7 October. Two days later, I learnt from the press that the C-in-C of the Pakistan Navy and I, the C-in-C of the Pakistan Air Force, had been appointed deputy chief martial law administrators. Throughout this period, I performed no martial law duties, attended no martial law meetings and confined myself strictly to my professional functions. It is important that those in authority should set an example to others of integrity and correctness of conduct in all their dealings.

The Pakistan Air Force (PAF) was once asked to advise and assist the Royal Saudi Air Force in the purchase of aircraft from the United States. I was instructed by the government to send a team of officers to accompany a Saudi prince and his team to the United States. This was done and a team of PAF officers was sent to assist in this task. After a few days I received a message from the leader of the PAF team in the USA, that the head of the Saudi team, had asked the aircraft manufacturers what his personal commission would be and that this was being negotiated. I signalled our team to return to Pakistan which they did, leaving the Saudi prince and his Saudi advisers in the United States. The Saudi government complained to President Ayub Khan and I was asked to explain. I told the president that I could not have PAF officers associate with this kind of behaviour and I think that this was the only thing to do.

Soon after I took over PIA I found that my deputy, who was a very competent person, was also the agent for Boeing Aircraft Company and received a commission on any aircraft or equipment that the airline purchased from Boeings. I thought it improper that a senior airline executive should also represent an aircraft company that supplied it with aircraft and told him that he should choose between the airline and the Boeing company. I told him that if he wished to retain the agency for the Boeing aircraft company he should resign from the airline. He explained that he could not leave his link with

Boeings and therefore resigned from the PIA. It was I thought unethical, that a person should hold an important office in the airlines and at the same time represent an aircraft manufacturing company. This gentleman came back some years later as the chief executive of the airline.

My brother Afzal was in the dairy business and had a contract with the PIA for the supply of dairy products. On taking over the airline, one of the first things I did was to terminate his contract. This arrangement with the PIA was the source of more than 50 per cent of his income. Although I had nothing to do with this arrangement and I had no share in his business, I thought that it was not proper that he should do business with the airline as long as I was its chief executive.

Leadership

Leadership is that quality which inspires others to follow. A leader of men is one towards whom others turn in difficulty and from whom they expect guidance and direction. This quality is important for a nation in peace as well as in war, but whereas its absence in peace may cause inefficiency and social or economic decay, its absence in war will almost certainly spell disaster. It is a quality that may be either inherited or acquired. It is influenced by environment and upbringing, by the social and economic structure of a society, by the faith and belief of a people and above all by example.

Leaders of men are to be found in every walk of life. Amongst thieves and robbers, priests and administrators, generals and privates, business executives and workers. Each in his own group stands out as a person whom others acknowledge as their superior. Whether such a person is in a position of authority or not is not really relevant. A true leader will stand out regardless of official recognition. His influence on his fellow men is generally greater if his actions are backed by formal authority but this need not always be so. Whatever his occupation, there are certain traits of character that will generally stand out as common denominators in a wide cross section of society. There are other qualities that are of secondary importance but which do nevertheless assist in the acceptability of a person as a leader of men.

Knowledge and Courage

Perhaps the most important requirement in a leader is knowledge. He must know his profession to command respect. No one will willingly follow a person if he does not know his job, and only if he knows it well, will he evoke respect and attention. This applies with even greater force when safety and security are involved. If there is danger, people will follow a person only if they feel that he knows what he is doing.

Courage is another quality that is admired by all human beings in varying degrees. Courage can be moral or physical, and both have a relationship with integrity. It is only a man of integrity who will show moral courage, and even physical courage is usually to be found among people who cherish certain principles of behaviour born of a sense of integrity. But physical courage is not the preserve of the virtuous; for greed, ambition and an inferiority complex have often led to acts of valour by otherwise ordinary people who could by no means be considered men of integrity. Moral courage is, therefore, the higher of the two virtues. One who has moral courage will usually, though not always, show physical courage, but a person who has physical courage alone may well be devoid of intellectual honesty and reliability. Those who possess both are admired by others and have one of the important qualities that people look for in those whom they would be prepared to accept as their leaders.

Power of Decision

Since a leader must lead there is nothing as frustrating, to those who expect to be led, as indecisiveness. The greater the sphere of influence or authority, the greater the need for this important quality. The more complex an organisation and the more diverse the responsibilities, the more necessary it is for the leader to provide that guidance and direction which is the sole justification for his presence. Too often is this quality lacking in people holding top executive appointments, leading to frustration and inefficiency which is as widespread as their sphere of responsibility.

Social Qualities

Social conduct is another quality which has an important bearing on the acceptability of a leader. Social conduct, like integrity, means different things to different people, but there is always a generally accepted standard in every society and a leader must not deviate too far from the standards regarded as normal by those he expects to lead. The higher the standard of a man's personal social conduct, the greater generally will be his acceptability.

Of these qualities which are not so essential, but which are desirable and have an important influence on a man's acceptability as a leader, perhaps the most important is compassion. The ability to feel genuinely for the well-being of one's fellowmen, and particularly for those less fortunate than oneself, is a quality which is universally appreciated by all human beings. It creates an atmosphere of respect and affection which facilitates control and direction. The feeling of compassion must, however, be genuine, for it is surprising how quickly people will see through any spurious attitude of concern for the welfare of others.

Some of these qualities will be seen, while others have to be conveyed or transmitted. It is, therefore, necessary that a person should be able to communicate his views, thoughts and wishes to others in an effective manner. The ability to speak intelligently, logically and concisely is, therefore, an important attribute of leadership. If speech helps to impress people, so does appearance. The impression that a person conveys by his appearance will undoubtedly have some effect on people, especially on those who do not have the opportunity of seeing a leader from close quarters and thus of forming opinions about his strength and weaknesses.

Importance of Selection
These, then, are some of the qualities that leadership demands. Their relative importance will vary according to the values that society sets on these things from time to time, but it will be rare that a 'leader' emerges in a healthy society if he is devoid of the important attributes which have for centuries influenced man's relations with other human beings. There are, however, times in the lives of nations when moral values are at such a low ebb that the mantle of leadership falls on people who do not measure up to the standards normally associated with the high personal qualities that civilised people expect from persons they would like to follow. Those are, however, temporary conditions which do not alter the accepted standards of human

judgment and social relationship. There will always be times when the 'appointed' leaders prove unworthy of the responsibilities that they are required to shoulder. That is often a question of selection rather than of human values. The ability to choose subordinates, though fundamental to the success of a leader, has not always been essential to his emergence.

Ability to Choose

Of all the qualities of a leader, perhaps the most important for success is the ability to choose. It is certainly the hardest to acquire and, when acquired, the hardest to keep. It is generally not something that is inherited. It is a quality that is developed largely by an intelligent study of human nature and of human conduct, by acquiring a correct sense of values, by observing a high standard of moral and intellectual discipline, and by maintaining the same standard of integrity in one's own dealings as one looks for in others. Only people who possess these virtues can value them in others, and it is rare that people who have not taken the trouble to develop these qualities can appreciate these in other men.

Birds of a Feather

The normal rules of human conduct usually ensure that a talented person, a man of virtue and a man of ability and knowledge, will generally choose as his subordinates people who possess in some degree, the qualities that he himself values; whereas an incompetent person, or one devoid of integrity will generally surround himself with people who are equally incompetent or dishonest. The reasons are not far to seek. An efficient person will only remain so by setting himself a high standard and by not accepting the second best in his work. He can be a man of integrity only if he has striven to remain straight in his dealings with others and has remained true to his conscience. He will not generally tolerate people who are incompetent or dishonest and will rid himself of them at the earliest opportunity. The incompetent person, on the other hand, will not see things the same way. His standard of judgment will be influenced by his own level of integrity and competence. If he does not possess these qualities himself, he will generally not expect these in others. Often, he will be aware of his shortcomings and will invite flattery and enjoy servility. If he happens to have competent subordinates, he will feel uncomfortable in their company. If they are honest and he does not possess this virtue, he will find this an added embarrassment. An intelligent person, if he has a conscience, will find it difficult to hide his contempt for an incompetent superior, and this feeling will become apparent sooner or later. His presence will therefore be an embarrassment, and he will be removed on some pretext or the other. If his ability and integrity are well known, there will be other reasons given. 'Disloyal', 'arrogant', 'temperamental' are some of the labels that are usually hung for such purposes, and it is only when he surrounds himself with equally incompetent persons, that the incompetent superior begins to feel comfortable. He is then the acknowledged 'leader' in the group, the fountain of all knowledge, the one to whom others look with apparent respect and admiration. So it appears to him. This is the price of incompetence; the handicaps of intellectual dishonesty.

People, who do not have a tradition of free speech and who do not possess genuinely democratic institutions, are more likely to indulge in flattery and suppression of the truth than those who have enjoyed these blessings and have valued these sufficiently to have preserved them. Of all the social ills, this is perhaps the worst and one that more quickly than any other robs a people of their self respect and their moral integrity. This also affects the leader and is the hardest to resist. It requires considerable moral integrity to resist the flattery and spurn the servility that surrounds people in authority in such situations. It affects a person's sense of judgment and impairs his ability to choose. Those, who can retain their sense of balance in the face of this persistent disease, are half way to success.

Fairness in Selection

In selection, there is also the question of supersession. The most able are not necessarily the most senior and their advancement over the heads of their seniors is always a somewhat unpleasant affair. It upsets people, requires explaining and is not always easy to carry out especially when the approval of superiors is required. The decision should not only be fair but should also appear to be so. If it is done with meticulous fairness, without other extraneous factors affecting the decision, it is generally well received. It should not be done just occasionally but should always be the rule. There will inevitably be people ready to sympathise with the person who has been passed over, but that person will know that the decision was fair and so will the sympathisers. It will not affect morale adversely; in fact, it will have a healthy influence. If, however, such a decision is based on any other consideration but competence, the effect on morale will be disastrous.

Although the ability to choose is important for 'leaders' in all walks of life, it is particularly so in the fighting services. It is undoubtedly the most important single quality in a service commander. Select a handful of competent subordinates and half the problem is solved. They will in turn ensure that their subordinates are also competent people. This process will be repeated many times, and although mistakes will be made, by and large a healthy and efficient force will emerge. If, however, the top person is incompetent, he will soon surround himself with subordinates who are equally inefficient, and the whole structure will reflect his personality and sense of judgment. The key to the whole matter is the ability of the top man to choose and, easy as it may sound, this is the hardest test of a leader. It is the most difficult quality to acquire, the most difficult to keep and the most difficult to implement. When sound judgment of human nature, moral integrity, courage and conviction are found in a leader, the ability to choose is inevitably present.

Integrity

A real 'leader' is a man of integrity. Integrity has many connotations but, taken in its widest sense, it means reliability. People in different walks of life have their own standard of conduct and code of ethics. If a person disregards these, he is likely to lose the respect and confidence of his fellow men. These standards of conduct are not constant and will vary in different circumstances. A leader, however, will be expected to conform to those standards which are generally accepted as normal in a given society.

Although human values are constant, an individual's approach to them tends to change with the times and environmental influences. Certain human qualities have, however, always been at a premium and one of these is integrity. It is appreciated in friend and foe alike, and of all the qualities that people admire in others—courage, determination, courtesy, kindness and intelligence—this has always been the one that has evoked the greatest respect and admiration. But this quality, though admired in others, does not always inspire people sufficiently to strive to develop it in themselves. A sense of integrity stems generally from moral, religious or spiritual beliefs. These are usually based on the social influences of early years, and sometimes on emotional experiences which often leave a lasting effect on the personality and outlook of an individual. A sense of integrity can also be developed by the educational influences of childhood and by a study of the lives of men who have possessed this virtue. It is, however, developed more easily when living examples of leadership with high standards of integrity are present at the higher levels of national life. When such leadership is available, it cannot fail to influence the standards of integrity and the moral tone of a nation.

Poverty and Character

It is often assumed that economic factors influence the morals of a people and that people who cannot feed and clothe themselves adequately can hardly be expected to remain honest. It is true that economic factors play an important part in conditioning the attitude of an individual towards his fellowmen, but this is by no means the only factor which affects the morals of an individual, nor indeed is it the most important. If this were so, integrity and honesty would be found in proportion to the economic strength of a society and the financial condition of individuals. This, however, is not so; in fact, the opposite is truer of our society today. It is among the relatively well-to-do people that corruption is more prevalent, where morality is at a low ebb, and where integrity is generally lacking. It is also amongst the poorer sections of our society, that a greater sense of honesty and integrity is to be found.

Some Historical Factors

A closer examination of the malaise would show that in Pakistan a number of factors have conditioned our approach towards this problem. The first, and perhaps the most important, is the traditional attitude towards authority that has prevailed on the subcontinent. There are few other parts of the world where invasions have taken place with such frequency as in the territories of the Indus and the

Ganges, and few that have seen such racial variety as the Indo-Pakistan subcontinent. Frequent invasions and the resultant insecurity engendered an attitude towards authority that was a peculiar combination of servility and defiance, of distrust and cooperation. This apathetic approach of the Muslims towards the government was lessened, but not removed with the advent of Muslim rule in India. With the spread of Islam in the subcontinent, the clearly defined rules of this religion, provided for the first time to the inhabitants of this area, a simple and easily understandable code of ethics. Authority, however, remained remote and the approach towards the state was mercenary.

British rule accentuated this trend and the little sense of participation that had existed between the ruler and the ruled disappeared. The attitude towards authority remained one of distrust, often bordering on hostility. This feeling was more marked amongst Muslims, who regarded themselves as the legitimate rulers of the subcontinent. This attitude encouraged the type of non-cooperation with authority that has lingered on to this day. The government was considered alien and cheating it was not considered an immoral act. The well-to-do members of society were, with some justification, considered the creation of the same authority, and the distinction between the government and these elements became blurred. In such a situation, anything could be regarded as fair and a climate was created in which only stronger compensatory influences could keep people on the straight path. The strongest such influence was religion, which arrested what could otherwise have been a steep descent into moral degeneration.

Greed and Morality

The industrialisation of the country, the increased urbanisation of village society, the faster tempo of life and the consequent lack of parental guidance, have all contributed towards an erosion of the standards of morality in our growing generations. The phenomenal increase in consumer and luxury goods has also placed a greater strain on the quality of abstinence and Islamic society has lost much of the puritan outlook which characterised the early and spectacular period of its growth. Greed is today perhaps the most dominant characteristic in the more sophisticated elements of our society. When greed crosses reasonable limits, integrity goes by the board, and since the two are basically incompatible, integrity will inevitably suffer if greed is allowed to develop unchecked.

There is, however, more to integrity than the financial and material aspects. A man of integrity is a man of character and character has a much wider application than purely financial dealings. A man of integrity is one who can be trusted; one who does the right thing without thought of compensation and reward; one to whom the satisfaction of doing the right thing is a greater reward than any material benefits which may attract lesser men. A man of integrity will also express his views fearlessly and honestly, and not be influenced by the temptation to adopt the line of least resistance.

Road to Happiness

The fact is, however, that the easier course is not usually the one which leads to success. If the definition of success in life is happiness, a person cannot—if he has a conscience—be happy unless he respects himself; unless he can truthfully say, when the day's work is done, that he has been honest in his dealings, in his speech and in his actions. Unless, in fact, he is at peace with his own conscience. Those who consider that happiness results from power, authority or position, would do well to remember that no person can command respect and achieve a place in the hearts and minds of his fellow men unless they respect him for his integrity and character. A reputation can only last if it has been cemented by some lasting qualities and no quality counts more than character. Without it, position and wealth have a transitory value, which brings little or no satisfaction to its possessor.

The vast majority of the poorer members of our society are still blessed with certain qualities that the more affluent should try to emulate—a life of simplicity, a code of conduct strongly anchored in religion and in the general acceptability of their fellowmen. Absence of greed and a lack of sophistication keeps them nearer the truth. Degeneration in our society can, however, only be arrested if integrity and character do not remain the preserve of the poor for it will then be only a matter of time before they also lose the urge to conduct themselves with honesty and integrity. It is important that those charged with authority over others, in all spheres of national life, conduct themselves in a manner that does not necessarily bring them material and financial benefits, but which will—when they begin to see things in their correct perspective—bring them true happiness and lasting respect.

Soldiers and Politics

It was 14 August 1947 and the governor general, Quaid-i-Azam Mohammad Ali Jinnah, was the host at a large reception on the lawns of the Governor House in Karachi. As the Quaid moved freely amongst his thousand or more guests, groups of men and women collected around him. Always an impressive and somewhat aloof personality, he appeared to be in a thoughtful mood. News had begun to come in of the killings in East Punjab and this had dampened considerably the spirits of those who had assembled to celebrate this great occasion. It had not, however, lessened the significance of the event in the minds of those who had the good fortune to be present on this historic occasion.

The Quaid had hardly moved towards a group of officers in military uniform when he was surrounded by a young and attentive audience. It was perhaps his first experience of conversing informally with a group of military officers and he appeared to show more than ordinary interest in those around him. If this was his first such experience, it was also the first time that such a large group of service officers had been able to meet so distinguished a national figure. It was their first opportunity to hear his thoughts on some of the problems which were uppermost in their minds. The Quaid had been too absorbed in the political struggle for the creation of Pakistan to have given as much thought to the armed forces as to some of his other more pressing problems. It had also not been desirable that he should seek out military men and discuss matters of policy with them until the new State had been created. He talked briefly and in short sentences about general topics, and as the conversation began to flag, he appeared to be about to move on to talk to some of his other guests.

Just then one of the more senior of the group sought his permission to express his views on certain matters of national importance. The Quaid, who had been doing most of the talking, was probably glad to have someone else make the conversation. He nodded assent and the officer, who had apparently been waiting for this opportunity, said his piece: 'This is a great day for us,' he said, 'in which, we the armed forces, take as much pride as the civilians who have struggled under your leadership to make this day possible. Pakistan, however, has been created in response to an urge and in order to fulfil the aspirations of its people.' The Quaid, for the first time since he joined the group, was beginning to show an interest in the conversation. His eyes became more intent and his expression one of expectancy. He appeared to be listening with interest to what this young officer had to say. 'One of the important purposes in the creation of this state,' he continued, 'Was to provide us an opportunity to shape the country in accordance with our own special requirements, our own beliefs and our own talents. Our people have an inherent genius which should be allowed to flower.'

The Quaid's interest appeared by now to have been aroused and he was listening attentively. The officer, who spoke well, held the Quaid's attention. He continued: 'We find, however, that instead of giving us the opportunity to serve our country in positions where our natural talents and native genius could be used to the greatest advantage, important posts are being entrusted, as has been done in the past, to foreigners. British officers have been appointed to head the three fighting services and are in key senior appointments. This was not our understanding of how Pakistan was to be run.'

The Quaid replied in deliberate and clear tones. Raising his finger, he said: 'Do not forget that you in the armed forces are the servants of the people. You do not make policy. It is we, the civilians, who decide these issues and it is your duty to carry out those tasks with which you are entrusted. The history of Islam teaches us that Muslims have risen to great heights or fallen to great depths. It has been rare that they have followed a middle course. We are a people of extremes. We are either right up or right down. If Pakistan is to be a great nation, it is moderation that we must cultivate. Moderation in thought and moderation in action. Moderation in our dealings with each other and in our international relations.' He left this group with a smile and moved on to talk to some of his other guests.

I have often pondered over the Quaid's remarks, and as one of the group who heard him speak, I have often wondered to what extent Islam, or geographical and racial factors, condition our attitude towards such affairs. Whatever the reasons for our response, all Pakistanis would do well to remember his advice.

The armed forces are trained to value precision, speed, efficiency, integrity and all those other qualities which should be as necessary for success in civilian as in military life. When these qualities appear to be lacking to a marked degree in the social make-up of a nation, the armed forces are inclined to take an active interest in civilian affairs. In such circumstances, it would be well to consider that the remedy for such ills does not lie in a military solution to what is basically a social or economic problem. Political problems require political solutions, and a country's interests are best served if the armed forces concentrate on their main role in life—which is the safety and security of the country—and that also under political direction.

Hope and Disappointment

Of all the problems with which Pakistan is faced today—Kashmir, defence, food, production, export—'unity' is the most important. It is also the most pressing. The two decades since independence have seen a weakening of the bonds that united the people of different parts of the country. The spirit that forged a new nation in the face of heavy odds is in danger of disappearing. If this trend is to be arrested, it is important that the causes of the weakening of the unity be clearly understood. Only then can an intelligent effort be made to recreate the climate which fostered so close a bond between the people who constitute this nation.

Lessons of History

There are few other examples in history where a people, having declared their intention to live as an independent sovereign nation, have achieved their objective within the short span of seven to eight years, and this too against the declared views of the rulers and in the teeth of the bitterest opposition from a powerful, wealthy and highly organised majority community. This could only have been possible by a genuine consciousness of separate nationhood and by the high quality of leadership that made people so intensely conscious of their separate identity as to make their demand irresistible. High quality leadership was, therefore, the first requisite. A common bond on which this unity could be built was the second. The urge for a separate nationhood was provided by religion, a common historical experience and economic and social aspirations.

Leadership, however, cannot be sustained in a vacuum, nor can it survive unless the hopes and aspirations of those who are led are adequately fulfilled. The economic and social ideals of the new state had not been clearly defined before its emergence, nor have successive governments felt it desirable to do so since then. Party manifestoes and programmes which have, with monotonous repetitiveness, emphasised a desire to create an 'Islamic state,' remain unfulfilled. This has been partly due to the limitations imposed by lack of resources and a combination of other circumstances. But it has also been largely due to a lack of purpose and the absence of any real intention to fulfil the hopes and aspirations on which the state was formed. The vested interests which the hierarchy of the ruling political parties represented, should have made it obvious that they would be unlikely to implement a programme which would weaken them economically and politically. The sacrifice of their own interests for the good of the nation was too unselfish a step for most of them to contemplate. Refuge was, therefore, taken in rationalising their actions and in misleading the public by creating an impression of achievement which had little relationship with reality.

An Islamic State

In the religious field, emphasis was laid on form rather than substance, because this did not touch the root of the problem. This encouragement of the ritualistic aspects of religion created the impression of a Muslim state and satisfied the religious urge of the more gullible members of our society. Scant regard, however, was paid to that aspect of Islam which is its most important feature, that is, social justice and human dignity. Those conditions which should be the corner-stone of a Muslim society remained unrealised and the gap between the rich and the poor was allowed to widen. Little or no attempt was made to check the accumulation of wealth and property by those who were in a more fortunate position than others. The image of a state that most Pakistanis had before them, therefore, remained unrealised. This has been the largest single factor which has contributed to the general air of dissatisfaction that has prevailed in the country to this day. This frustration has also lowered public confidence in the sincerity of successive governments and in their inability to live up to their promises.

Prosperity for Some

If, under these conditions, prosperity had been shared by the people of different regions, less dissatisfaction would have resulted. It was, however, inevitable that in the circumstances prevailing, political power, business capacity and social influence should assume considerable importance. Those factors, therefore, usually dictated the degree of support that the government was willing to lend for business and industrial projects in certain areas. Within West Pakistan, particularly after the formation of one unit, reduced emphasis was placed on the development of certain areas, that in the changed political circumstances, in the opinion of the rulers, assumed lesser importance. The fact that these areas were less urbanised also reduced somewhat their influence among the more vocal sections of our society.

In East Pakistan, the lack of indigenous capital and the scarcity of higher educational institutions seriously limited the participation of East Pakistanis in the development of the province. Capital and talent from West Pakistan filled the void, and a process of multiplication provided increased business strength to this powerful community. As this predominantly West Pakistan-owned business expanded, so did the disparity in wealth amongst different sections of society. In East Pakistan wealth, therefore, began to be associated with West Pakistan and the apparent disparity of social and economic standards, therefore, became more apparent, which eventually led to their separation.

Loss of Faith

At the centre, frequent changes of government reduced the effectiveness of the political machinery, and power began to shift more and more into the hands of the civil bureaucracy. From 1951 until 1958 the office of head of state was filled by two senior civil servants, which further hastened this trend. The civil service of Pakistan was manned predominantly by West Pakistanis and inter-wing harmony and understanding, therefore, suffered a further setback.

In 1958 a new factor was introduced into a rather unsatisfactory situation. The abrogation of the constitution and the declaration of martial law made it clear that real power lay with the armed forces. The armed forces, like the civil bureaucracy, were predominantly from West Pakistan and as the new regime became more firmly entrenched, so did the truth of Mao Zedong's famous dictum that all power flows from the barrel of a gun.

The Pakistan resolution, passed in Lahore in 1940, declaring the Muslims of the subcontinent a separate nation, started a controversy about the definition of nationhood which was settled only when the new state came into being. It was ultimately proved that a nation is one when it feels itself to be so. Pakistan can survive only so long as the different people who constitute this nation feel that certain common bonds unite them together. Such bonds are generally based not only on the memories of the past but also on hopes for the future. What then were the memories that proved powerful enough to create a nation in the face of almost insuperable odds; and what were the hopes that united a people who were racially and linguistically as diverse as the Bengali and the Pathan?

Islamic Society

Of all the common bonds that unite the people of Pakistan, Islam is the strongest. It was Islam that forged the people of different races and languages into one nation, and it is this that can help to keep that unity alive. But unity was not born only out of a spiritual or an emotional urge. It was the outcome of centuries of contact with Hindu culture and civilisation and a yearning for a way of life that was deeply ingrained in our thinking. Pakistan held out the hope of economic and social opportunities that the Muslims of the subcontinent had not known for centuries. It also held out the promise of a state built on Islamic values, the most important of which are human dignity, social justice and individual freedom. It is, therefore, not surprising that if these hopes and aspirations remain unfulfilled even after decades of independence, dissatisfaction and disappointment should grow among the people of the country. It is true that some people had in their minds the picture of a utopia that was not possible to achieve, but even the hopes and aspirations of the moderate elements of our society have not been realised. If equality of opportunity, social justice and human dignity typify Islam, then our society today is farther from being Islamic than it was six decades ago. This failure to create a social order that millions had hoped to achieve has caused widespread disappointment. Nowhere was this more strongly felt than amongst the people of the present Bangladesh and the smaller provinces of West Pakistan.

Steps Towards Unity

This unsatisfactory situation can be altered only if the people of Pakistan realise the seriousness of the situation and exert their influence and power to remedy it; and if they so organise themselves that the values for which Pakistan was created are once again held before the nation, not as propaganda slogans but as deliberate steps in the essential process of national stability. The most important step needed to create a climate in which such conditions can flourish, is to shift the focus of power to the people.

Only when this happens can the people of Pakistan exercise the influence in our national affairs that is their right and only when this is achieved will national integration take place. Only then will they experience the power and influence in our affairs and develop the sense of responsibility and concern for the collective security and stability of the country. No amount of industrial development and no measures of public welfare can replace this sense of power and responsibility that only a truly democratic system can confer.

The image of social inequality is now so deeply ingrained in the minds of the vast majority of our people that no half-hearted measures are likely to succeed. No steps, however well intentioned, that do not touch the root of the matter, are likely to solve the problem. It is not good enough to be able to say that the system of election allows the electorate to vote a government into power that adequately represents their hopes and aspirations. It is necessary that the system should in fact do so.

The Alternative

The alternative is a period of growing instability, until a point is reached when bitterness and distrust between the rulers and the ruled further weakens the foundations, on which Pakistan was created. This would be a further setback to the process that symbolised the unification of the different people of this country into one state. The patience and wisdom with which we exercise our influence to create the conditions necessary for an evolution of our society on healthy and sound lines will affect the happiness and welfare of our people for many generations to come. Our ability to transfer power in a peaceful and constitutional manner from a small elite society to a popular base in a way that allows the different people of the country to enjoy equal opportunities and equal power, will determine whether Pakistan survives as an independent state. Unity can exist only with faith—in our common heritage, faith in our common ideals and aspirations, faith in the patriotism and good sense of our people, and faith in our will to survive as an independent and prosperous country.

Problems of our Youth and Education

Few activities in a developing nation deserve so much attention as education, and none has been neglected more in this country. The long term solution of the major problems facing Pakistan, whether social or economic, depends largely on the quality of education provided to our youth. But education, like the administrative services, commerce, industry, banking or any other national activity, is affected by the general tone of the society. It is also influenced by the moral standards prevailing in a society.

There are four main influences that affect the level of learning and the standard of character and integrity imparted to the youth of a country. The first, and perhaps the most important, is the political system prevailing in a country which determines the official guidance and direction that a government provides to the educational institutions. The second is the social system which is the product of both, the political philosophy and the cultural heritage of a nation. The third is the influence of the teaching fraternity, and the fourth is the influence of the parents on the attitude and behaviour of the youth of a nation.

Government Direction

It has been seen that the direction that a government is able or willing to impart to the educational system of a country is generally influenced by two main considerations—financial resources and political expediency. The long term interests of national development, which should be an important consideration, are often overlooked. Since political expediency and long term national interests are generally in conflict, the former assumes greater importance and, therefore, influences the steps that are taken in this sphere. These measures will naturally vary in different countries. In Pakistan, political considerations have undoubtedly been a factor in the direction that education has taken in the country. The most noticeable has been the emphasis on the opening of new institutions rather than the running of existing ones. Sometimes under public pressure, but more often to demonstrate a milestone in achievement, new institutions have been launched without regard to the inadequacies of the existing institutions or the requirement of graduates in the various spheres of national life. Again, either under pressure from local authorities or in deference to individual demands, the number of students admitted to each class has exceeded all reasonable bounds. This has inevitably resulted in a general lowering of the standard of education imparted in our educational institutions.

This kind of negative control has led to a large annual output of half-educated graduates, who can neither find suitable employment nor make any useful contribution to the development of the country. Our limited financial allocations in the field of education have, therefore, been wasted in producing large number of unwanted 'graduates' and in lowering the general standard of those who are later absorbed in the various spheres of our national life.

Society and Education

Any system of education which aspires to make a contribution towards the social and spiritual well-being of a nation must take into consideration those social, historical and religious forces that provide the primary influences in a society. One such influence is that of language. Knowledge and a power of expression can obviously best be acquired through a language with which the people are most familiar. Any departure from this natural law will only impede the progress of education in a society. There is no example in history where a nation has made real progress in the arts or the sciences in a foreign language. No country using an imported or foreign language has as yet emerged as a front rank power. It is significant that although

English has been widely used in India and Pakistan for over a hundred years, few if any have reached a very high level of creative expression in this language. It is true that in a fast-moving technological world, the knowledge of a western language confers certain advantages that should not be lightly discarded. But the emphasis on a foreign language at the cost of a country's own languages not only robs a people of their creative abilities but seriously limits their understanding of problems that can be better explained in a language that they understand and with which they are most familiar.

If language is an important factor in determining the educational progress of a nation, so is the moral and ideological philosophy which influences people's thoughts and actions. Education is essentially a process of moral and intellectual development and it can only flourish in an environment that values moral and ethical standards. Only if these standards are based on values that derive their inspiration from the spiritual roots of a nation, can people develop into useful members of a society.

In an atmosphere riddled with corruption and in a society devoid of social justice, it is unlikely that any, except the baser instincts of man, will flourish. Education, which represents the finer aspects of human endeavour, will therefore, generally be the first to suffer.

Teachers and the Taught
It is inevitable that the general tone of a society, of which the teachers are a part, will affect their thinking and attitude. The inadequacy of budgetary allocations for education, one of the lowest in the world, and the inefficient use of these relatively meagre resources necessarily limits the salary of most teachers to a level only a little above that of domestic servants in the country. In spite of this, the talent that is attracted to this profession is of a standard far above the level that we have a right to expect. The unsatisfactory working conditions, the scale of salaries, the low level of social ethics, and the almost complete absence of official example have all contributed towards reducing the effectiveness and influence of the teaching fraternity on the student population of the country.

Parents' Contribution

Parents, even more than the teachers, exercise a vital influence on their wards. They are also conditioned by the same social influences and the same political and economic forces. If corruption and other social malpractices are commonplace in a society they cannot fail to influence the atmosphere in our homes. Our youth cannot therefore remain immune from the unhealthy influences that they have to live with from a very early age. The contradiction between high moral principles and the low level of moral integrity prevalent in our society creates a conflict in their minds which can only have the most undesirable consequences. In these circumstances, learning loses much of it meaning, and as the years roll by, great damage is done to the future of generations yet unborn. It is, therefore, evident that education cannot flourish in isolation. It is part of a system and will either grow or wither with the climate which that particular system creates. No amount of expense and no amount of effort that does not remedy the basic causes can alter the situation. In these circumstances, commissions and committees appointed to study the problem of education can only raise hopes that have little or no prospects of being fulfilled. Whether Pakistan can emerge as a progressive nation, depends largely on the manner in which its youth is educated. This, in turn, depends on the moral and social climate that exists in our country. Our ability to create the right atmosphere will undoubtedly affect the way in which our youth are brought up. Their upbringing and attitude will in turn determine the future of this nation.

Youth and the Future

The unrest and uncertainty sweeping the youth of the country have certain understandable causes which, when analysed, make an interesting study. These have much in common with the problems of youth in other countries and to that extent this unrest could be regarded as a part of a worldwide phenomenon. But every country has its special conditions, its own cultural and religious foundations, its peculiar geographical factors and historical experiences that influence the actions of its youth. Although many of the factors are common, their relative importance varies in different conditions. It will be seen that the same basic causes usually have different manifestations in different cultural settings. One of the more common of these is the attitude of defiance towards authority.

The urge to revolt against authority is a natural phenomenon amongst youth and manifests itself in various ways. Whether it takes the shape of wearing unconventional clothes or whether it takes some harmful forms, it springs basically from the same urge. A desire to be unorthodox and to be noticed are deeply ingrained in human nature. The more rigid a society and the more severe and unimaginative its control, the more is this tendency likely to manifest itself and the more violent its manifestation.

Idealism and Reality

This revolt against authority breeds an attitude of mind that tends to discard tradition and adopt a new, if not always realistic, approach to life. In this search for the unconventional, idealism plays a big part. The mind of youth is naturally lacking in practical experience and to that extent is relatively unaffected or uninhabited by those considerations which weigh with their elders. Lack of worldly responsibilities and considerations of financial security have not as yet begun to influence their actions. Their approach to life therefore tends to be idealistic. It is well that this should be so, for idealism is as necessary to our life as a purely orthodox approach to our daily problems. The one without the other provides an unbalanced existence and a blending of both in the correct proportions leads nations to great heights.

It follows that the further a social order is from being an ideal society, the greater will be the disillusionment amongst the youth. Since education stresses human values, their absence in our daily lives will, inevitably, create an unfavourable reaction. The quality of the teachers and the leadership that they provide has a great influence on the youth of a country. But the teachers, too, are influenced by society. Their teaching and guidance can carry force only if the social structure reflects some of those human qualities on which they are required to lay stress. The greater the contradiction between basic human values and the norms of a society, the less will be the credibility of those principles that educational institutions are expected to implant in their youth.

One of the forces that should exercise a stabilising effect on society is religion. Every faith is founded on certain principles that in their essence are regulatory in nature and provide the framework within which a society should function. The simpler these principles, the greater their effectiveness, but simplicity alone has seldom inspired people to high ethical or moral standards. The ability of a faith to demonstrate the practical application of its teaching has always been the test of its strength. The greater the gap between theory and practice, the less the influence of religion. The inquisitive mind of youth demands that not only the teachings of religion be understandable but that these should be reflected in their daily experience. Its absence from their lives raises doubts in their minds about the practicability of applying religion in daily life.

The Human Mind

There are few things as active as the human mind and this is much more true of the mind of youth. The process of thinking does not end after school or college hours. In fact, the hours spent outside school are perhaps the most productive from a mental standpoint. It is when the mind is removed from the straitjacket of a school routine that it begins to work in new and interesting channels. It is desirable that during these hours it should be channelled in healthy pursuits, the achievement of which not only provides satisfaction but a sense of challenge and fulfilment. It is in this important field that virtually nothing appears to have been done to provide that essential opportunity without which only undesirable consequences can follow.

Sports and Character

The simplest and perhaps the most effective manner in which the competitive urge in youth can be satisfied is by encouraging their participation in sports. It encourages team-work, which breeds a sense of responsibility. It also introduces them, in a practical and pleasant manner, to the common human experiences of success and failure, of perseverance and lethargy; of courage and cowardice; of magnanimity and narrow-mindedness. It is a tragedy that in a country where land is in plenty, the vast majority of the schools and colleges are almost devoid of playing fields and other recreational facilities.

Neither the cost of playing fields nor the provision of other recreational facilities is beyond our financial capacity. Its importance has, however, apparently escaped the notice of our leaders, whose approach to the problems of our youth has, to say the least, been superficial.

Creative and Aesthetic Values

Just as sports is a factor in developing the outlook of our youth so is the encouragement of those other activities that satisfy their creative urge. Dramas, music and the arts encourage those latent qualities in every human being that require self-expression. Their fulfilment provides satisfaction, which does a great deal to soothe those desires, which, if unfulfilled, inevitably seek other avenues of expression.

Museums and libraries, though representing a different sphere of interest, essentially satisfy an intellectual yearning and meet those aesthetic human needs which require fulfilment. Again, this sphere of our life has been sadly neglected. The lack of awareness of the value of such institutions is, unfortunately, not a rare phenomenon.

To these could be added a long list of other activities that with little or no cost could provide the necessary outlet for our youths' creative urge. But a rarer commodity than mere finances is required — imagination and understanding in the highest echelons of government. Less of servility and more of the ability to advise honestly and with imagination would solve many of our problems. But imagination and honesty are usually uncommon in a system that does not encourage truth, which suppresses human freedom and which does not value human dignity.

The problems of Pakistan's youth, therefore, are essentially the problems of our society and these can be changed only when the people, who run the country, are truly representative of our aspirations and ideals.

EPILOGUE

Judiciary

In any civilised country, the judiciary is the foundation on which the society functions, sets the tone of human conduct and is the guardian of the people's rights. It is tragic that the judiciary in Pakistan has contributed in no small measure to the denial to the people of their rights. It has encouraged their exploitation by people who had no right to control their destinies for the larger part of the country's existence.

When in 1958, the country's constitution was abrogated and martial law declared, General Ayub Khan asked the chief justice of Pakistan in a cabinet meeting in which I was present in my capacity as the commander-in-chief of the Pakistan Air Force, what should he do about framing a new constitution? 'This is no problem,' the chief justice had replied, 'We will draw up a constitution for you and you should, after having it published in the papers, address four public meetings—in Paltan Maidan in Dhaka, Mochi Gate in Lahore, Chowk Yadgar in Peshawar and Nishtar Park in Karachi. In these meetings you should say that they (the people) must have seen the draft constitution published in the newspapers and ask them whether they approved of it.'

'The answer,' the chief justice said, 'would definitely be in the affirmative. "Manzoor Hai", they would say and you will thus have the people's mandate.' Every one present laughed, and Ayub Khan laughed the loudest. 'This is no way of getting a constitution approved,' he said. 'This is a perfectly legitimate way,' the chief justice replied. 'This is how important things were approved in the ancient Greek states—by public acclaim. There is no better way of getting a constitution approved,' he said.

Ayub Khan did not do what the chief justice had said but this was the advice that he had been given in all seriousness by the chief justice of Pakistan. No wonder that the judiciary in Pakistan has been a factor in the shameful slide of the country towards dictatorship.

The majority of the judges, with a few honourable exceptions have thought it fit to support every military dictator by invoking the peculiar Pakistani invention of the 'doctrine of necessity'. It would be unrealistic to expect a change in the attitude of the judiciary until conditions are created in which the people assert their power and this is likely to take some time.

Pakistan's Five Wars with India

In the sixty years of Pakistan's existence it has fought five wars with India. Of these two have been full-scale wars and three limited wars, confined to specific areas in which the air forces or the navies of the two countries were not employed in the conflict. During the last of these conflicts—the Kargil war—both the countries were in possession of nuclear weapons, which mercifully were not used.

Until some time after partition, Pakistan did not clarify its position in regard to the rulers of princely states whereas India had made it clear that they would cease to enjoy the hereditary positions that they had hitherto held. The Maharaja of Jammu and Kashmir, who was a Hindu ruler of a Muslim majority state, had hoped that he might be able to maintain his position in Pakistan and did not therefore accede to India. Pakistan made no move to negotiate with him and in fact rebuffed his efforts for talks. Instead, Pakistani army volunteers and tribesmen were sent with the object of capturing Srinagar, the capital of the state. The Maharaja fled and acceded to India. Fighting continued until the end of 1948, when a cease fire was agreed.

A little over sixteen years later, early in 1965, the armies of India and Pakistan fought again over the Rann of Kutch in Sindh. This area of operation was at the end of the operating range of the PAF's fighter aircraft and we could not therefore provide effective fighter cover to our advancing ground forces. The Indians were dug in and therefore relatively a more difficult target for us to attack. The Indian Air Force was located at relatively shorter distance behind their dug in troops. I therefore felt that the Indian Air Force would be at an advantage and could cause our advancing army serious damage. I knew the Indian Air Force commander-in-chief, Arjun Singh, having served in the Indian Air Force together and telephoned him in Delhi. I told him that if they used the air force in this operation, we would react and the air war would not be limited to the Rann of Kutch area. He said that whether to use the air force was a political decision which his government would take. I told him that I fully understood this but was warning him that the use of the air force in the Rann of Kutch area could well mean an all out war between our two countries. The Indian air force was not used in the Rann of Kutch war and this was I think a big factor in our success in this conflict. General Musa, the army commander-in-chief at the time, has criticised me for telephoning Arjun Singh when the army was fighting a war, as if this was a treacherous act. I feel that this telephone call saved us a lot of casualties and was a big factor leading to our success.

The Pakistan Army's success in this limited encounter led Ayub Khan to over-estimate the strength of the Pakistan Army and Zulfikar Ali Bhutto built up his ego further. In this, Aziz Ahmed, the foreign secretary, also played a part. The president was led to believe that we could, without endangering Pakistan's security, settle the Kashmir dispute and if Pakistan took a military initiative, the Kashmiris would rise against Indian occupation. The foreign office, supported by the military intelligence, assured Ayub Khan that if the Pakistan Army was moved into the Jammu area, the Kashmiris would rise in revolt and India's military position would become untenable in occupied Kashmir. I was the commander-in-chief of the PAF till 23 July 1965 and I had no knowledge of the planning for operation 'Gibraltar', which was launched towards the end of August to move into the Indian occupied Jammu and Kashmir area and to cut off the Indian road link with the Kashmir valley. It was thought that this would be a simple land operation and since surprise was essential, the PAF should not be informed about it, which in Ayub Khan's and General Musa's opinion would unnecessarily increase the risk of leakage of this plan.

At the end of August 1965 I read in the newspapers that Pakistan armour had moved into the Indian held part of Jammu and Kashmir in the Akhnur area. I asked to see President Ayub Khan and met him on the morning of 3 September. I asked the president whether he had decided to go to war. He replied, 'Who has told you so.' 'No one,' I replied. "But, you have moved the armour in the Jammu-Akhnur Area and I am certain that India will react and they are likely to react in Punjab, possibly opposite Lahore. The war,' I said. 'is then not likely to be limited to Kashmir.' 'Oh no,' the president said, 'I have been assured by the foreign office that this will not be so. India is likely to limit the conflict to the Jammu area. He went on to say that Marshal Chen Yi, the Chinese foreign minister, whom Zulfikar Ali Bhutto had met at the Karachi airport two days earlier, when he was on his way to Paris, had also said that he did not think that India would extend the hostilities in Punjab or in other theatres.

I was amazed at the president's assessment of the situation and left his office certain in the belief that we were heading for an all out war. Rather than return to Karachi to my post as the head of the national airlines, I decided to stay on in Rawalpindi. The Pakistan Air Force which I had left a few days earlier had always been on high alert and I visited their operations room in Rawalpindi. I visited them again on 4 and 5 September. I was due to leave for Karachi early on 6 September and decided to visit the PAF operations room on my way to the airport. As I entered the PAF operations room, I immediately realised that war had begun. Everyone was more active than usual. I decided to stay on in Islamabad.

In my book, *The First Round*, published soon after the 1965 war, I have written about these events and there is little need to repeat the whole story here, except to say that so wrongly had Ayub Khan assessed the situation and so badly had he been advised by Zulfikar Ali Bhutto that he was not prepared for a full scale war which he felt had been thrust on him. I was sent to China to ask for Chinese aircraft with specific instructions that these aircraft were not to be flown to Pakistan but sent to Indonesia, then put into crates and shipped to Karachi. Premier Zhou Enlai was aghast when I told him this. He said, 'You are fighting a war, we can fly these aircraft to Peshawar or Sargodha tomorrow from Kashgar, and you want these sent by sea? Ayub Khan had obviously thought that he would annoy the United States, if we sought Chinese help. Pakistan began to seek a ceasefire after the first three or four days of war and hostilities came to an end on 23 September.

The army's next adventure was its attempt to conquer its own country. Much had been written about Yahya Khan's military adventure in East Pakistan. To deny the Awami League of Mujibur Rehman the right to form a government and to rule Pakistan, was a criminal act which has no parallel in contemporary history. Militarily, to launch an operation in East Pakistan separated by a thousand miles of Indian territory and involving a sea journey as long as from Karachi to the South of Europe along the coast of a hostile India, was a Himalayan blunder.

There is also no precedence of a country after having held a widely acknowledged fair election, having denied the majority the right to rule and after having lost half the country not held any meaningful enquiry or punished anyone for this criminal folly. Nations that have been so impervious to such happenings have not survived for very long.

Pakistan's fifth military adventure is a more recent happening. The Kargil episode of 1999 was a natural urge in a soldier for self assertion. A soldier, when placed in authority, will be tempted to try to show his professional competence. A weak political leadership, a military establishment accustomed over half a century to run or manipulate civilian governments, was just the environment in which a newly appointed chief of the army staff could plan a military adventure.

The Kargil heights at an altitude of over 15,000 feet were thinly held by the Indian army where it was militarily at a disadvantage, appeared an ideal theatre to take them on. General Musharraf, the new chief of the army staff, with an ineffective prime minister and minister of defence, decided to repeat what Ayub Khan had tried in 1965. Obviously expecting a localised encounter with the Indian army which was disadvantageously placed, he embarked on an adventure which immediately became an international issue. The United States and the world powers exerted pressure on Pakistan to stop this military adventure and we had to eat humble pie.

It has been well said that 'war is too serious a business to leave to generals alone'. With nuclear weapons on both sides, it is important that generals are placed under tight control. We, in Pakistan, however, have a long way to go. It will be some time before political leadership emerges that has the ability to conduct the country's affairs which will inspire confidence in the minds of the people. Only then will there be a realisation in the officer corp that they are 'the servants of the people', as I had heard the Quaid-i-Azam say to us, a group of armed forces' officers, on 14 August 1947. 'Never forget,' he had said, 'You are the servants of the people and it is your duty to obey the orders of the people's representatives.' The tragedy in Pakistan is that even the people's representatives are chosen in elections that have been rigged by the Inter Services Intelligence Directorate, a branch of the armed forces.

General Musharraf's Seven Years in Power

As General Musharraf completed his seventh year in power it had become clear that he had succumbed to the influences and the temptations which afflict all military dictators. The seven point agenda which he had given to the nation when he had assumed power began to be forgotten. A king's party was soon formed, inevitably with the same people who either themselves or whose ancestors had sided with every ruler since the unconstitutional removal from office of Khawaja Nazimuddin in 1953.

Power, which in Pakistan, had always been centralized, shifted even more to the person of the president. When General Musharraf assumed power, the military which had for almost fifty years influenced policy or had been directly in control through its battalions of serving or retired generals, gradually took over almost every institution in the country. Almost every national activity had, somewhere or the other, a general in control and as power shifted towards the military, graft and cronyism became the order of the day. The desire to have retired generals head civil, industrial or business institutions grew in order to facilitate a 'smooth' relationship with the government, without whose 'blessings' nothing was now able to move.

With many known corrupt politicians as ministers and the National Accountability Bureau having become a farce, cronyism and corruption touched new heights. Since the people had not known anything much better and the country had gradually been sinking into this quagmire of corruption and incompetence, there was no manifestation of their discontent. The devolution of power and the system of elections which was the most important part of General Musharraf's programme was not allowed to function.

A relatively free press which by and large was able to function with greater freedom than it had enjoyed in the days of the political governments of the nineties, acted as a 'safety valve' which helped to increase the tolerance level of the public which would otherwise have reacted in a different manner to changes. Moreover, the powerful United States's support to the military regime of General Musharraf has strengthened his hold over the country to the extent that the international situation in the area is not likely to change significantly in the near future; a military regime in Pakistan is likely to last for some time.

India's reluctance to make any meaningful gesture towards the solution of the Kashmir problem will, oddly enough, further strengthen the military's hold over Pakistan; for it is only when the Kashmir issue is resolved that relations with India can improve, the fear of India from the people's mind can go and, to that extent, the psychological hold of the armed forces over the people's minds weaken.

Unfortunately the political parties that have been associated with running the country over the past few decades have not conducted themselves in a manner that could inspire sufficient confidence in the minds of the people. It would therefore appear that Pakistan is in for a further period of military rule. Unless there is a change in the international scene and in the policies of the United States and until the psychological fear of India is removed, some general or the other is likely to remain in the driving seat. The period of military ascendancy in our political scene can however be reduced if a political leadership emerges in the country strong enough to counter the hold of the armed forces and lessen the fear of our bigger neighbour.

The Future

Bleak as our past has been, there is no need to despair. Nations are not made merely by a colonial power conferring independence on a people. Our part of the world has been visited by conquerors for centuries and rule by aliens has been the norm rather than the exception in what is Pakistan today. It will be some time before we acquire the ingredients that constitute a nation. It is important however that until that happens, we should continue the struggle to differentiate between right and wrong, realise the consequences of giving the corrupt and the incompetent the right to rule our destinies and not accept suffering and injustice.

One of the factors that conditions our thinking and makes the people—particularly in Punjab—look up to the armed forces for protection and leadership is the fear of India. Although it is we, rather than India, that has been the cause of military confrontation, the people are easily led to believe that our larger neighbour is a constant threat from which only the armed forces can save us. The memories of the killings of 1947 on both sides of the border are revived and an ambitious general is always at hand to assume power.

It was tragic that in the short spells, when we did have political leadership as we did in the nineties, this leadership was generally corrupt and incompetent. These political leaders who were voted into power, albeit in largely rigged elections, did not conduct themselves responsibly. The elections were however not always rigged in their favour. The people have therefore largely themselves to blame. If this process is repeated at frequent intervals, as it should be, the people will learn but this process is painfully slow.

One of the factors that affects the people's thinking is Article 52-8 B of the constitution, an amendment brought into the country's 1973 constitution arbitrarily by General Ziaul Haq, which empowers the president to dismiss the government when, in his opinion, it is corrupt or incompetent. This is a factor in leading people to vote irresponsibly, believing that if the government does not conduct itself properly, the president will dismiss it. The voters therefore do not realise the importance of their vote and shift the responsibility which is theirs on to the president. The sooner Article 52-8 B is withdrawn and the 1973 constitution restored in its original form, the better for the country. With all its drawbacks, it is a constitution that was approved by the representatives of all the four provinces of Pakistan, after an election—the only one in the country's history—regarded as 'free and fair'. It is therefore only proper that we should make a fresh start with it.

Pakistan has a future, provided our adventures with India come to an end, we both learn to live as responsible neighbours and people of all the provinces in Pakistan are given equal rights in a truly federal system in which the provincial governments enjoy full powers to run their own affairs.

Our Finest Hour

An earthquake of 7.6 intensity, on the Richter's scale hit the northern part of Pakistan and Azad Kashmir on 8 October 2005. Over 73,000 lives were lost and three million rendered homeless. This was one of the worst earthquakes the world has experienced in the last hundred years. It also affected an area of the highest mountains in the world, an area with sparse communications and altitudes of 4,000–12,000 feet. It also struck at a time of the year when the minimum temperatures were close to freezing and which became colder with every day that passed. The total area affected in this mountainous terrain was about 15,000 square kilometres. Most of the roads in the area were rendered unusable by landslides caused by the earthquake. Thanks to the coverage by the media and particularly by TV and radio, the people of Pakistan and of the world were immediately informed of the disaster and the response of the Pakistani public was magnificent. From the very next day people from all over the country and from places as far away as Karachi which is more than 1,000 kilometres further south, began to bring supplies to this area. On the third day, when the road was reopened to Bagh, a town in Azad Kashmir, the traffic line, bumper to bumper, was 16 miles long with volunteers carrying supplies for the affected. By 11 October all roads to this area had traffic jams, because the system could not cope with the number of vehicles, heading towards the affected area with people bringing supplies for assistance. These vehicles were filled with food, clothing and blankets.

Help for the affected people began to arrive by the third day of the disaster. Because of the weather conditions, the main item required were tents and the need was so great that the requirement was more than the tents available all over the world. Helicopters were also in great demand and some foreign countries, particularly the US, augmented the supply of helicopters to reach the affected remote mountainous areas. In spite of all this it will be many years before the damage can be repaired and those affected can be rehabilitated.

The hopeful thing that has emerged from the disaster is the magnificent response of the Pakistani nation. The manner in which the people responded to this catastrophe shows that the Pakistani nation is alive and has tremendous potential. The Associated Press of France in a dispatch by Deborah Pasmantier of 18 October reported the behaviour of the affected people thus:

Muzaffarabad: There may no longer be any government to speak of but in Kashmir's earthquake-ravaged mountains, villagers are taking order into their own hands, making sure the neediest are fed. A deep solidarity reigns in the hamlets of Azad Kashmir, ensuring survival for far-flung communities where government assistance is yet to come and where aid helicopters have never reached. Villagers who have come to Azad Kashmir's devastated capital Muzaffarabad from the hills some 40 kilometres away say they have lived off donations, often from relatives, that are channelled to those who have nothing. And sometimes, they are willing to go without them to ensure the most vulnerable are taken care of. Dozens of trucks, decorated in gaudy colours in typical South Asian fashion, race in each day to Muzaffarabad, handing out to anyone, anywhere the food, tents and bedding so needed in a region that has 3.3 million homeless after the massive 8 October earthquake. The trucks are often met with mad scrambles, with people taking whatever scraps they can to make it through until their next chance.

But in Monassa village, residents decided that whatever comes their way should be divided up equally. They created a committee to distribute the donations fairly among the 65 surviving families. 'We have the names of the families. When donations come in, we go to them and make deliveries door to door,' said villager Nadim, 25. When a truck from the UN World Food Programme came through with biscuits, the committee was ready to split them up. But the elders said no—they should go to the more distant hamlets. 'It's really hard for people way up in the mountains. They can't be reached by car so let's go and find them,' Nadim remembers the elders saying.

A bit further up in the mountains, the 15 families in Baglota have a similar pact. In the town, bags of donated rice and sugar are stored under a mat amid the rubble. It's also the supply depository for 30 more families living in the mountains and cut off from the world. Hassan Zahoor, an 18-year-old student, is in charge of distribution and he tries to make sure it's done fairly. 'Each family gets 10 kilos of sugar and rice. For the time being there's enough for 15 days. For water, everyone goes to get it from a well that's an hour by foot,' he said. The aid came from relatives in Rawalpindi near Islamabad. Everyone in the village also retrieved whatever plates and dishes they could salvage from the ruins and are sharing them. They pitched in to buy three tents.

In Balakot village, residents firmly refused an offer of aid brought from visiting university students and instructors in Islamabad, redirecting them to a hamlet on the other side of the mountain. 'Three villages refused aid. They said they had enough. They talked about the hamlet of Attayasa that you could only reach by climbing the mountains. It was totally destroyed—10 families completely abandoned,' said teacher Arif Khattar, 30. They asked the survivors of Attayasa to come down to their trucks and the villagers went back with supplies on their backs like Sherpas. 'The big problem is reaching little mountain hamlets that are completely destroyed but still have two or three houses,' said World Food Programme spokeswoman Mia Turner. Even if goods and vehicles seem to be getting through via the village network, what is sorely lacking are tents. Most people are sleeping in the wide open or on makeshift mats despite rains and an approaching winter. - AFP

When the history of the first 60 years of Pakistan is written, it will be said, as it was by Winston Churchill of Britain in 1940, that 'this was their finest hour'. The earthquake of 2005 was a defining event in Pakistan's history. A nation demoralised with the ineptitude and corruption of its rulers, realised its potential and inherent strength and awakened to bring happiness and prosperity to its suffering people. Let us hope that this proves to be true. The 73,000 or so lives would then not have been lost in vain.

INDEX

J